TAKE 22

Judith Crist

TAKE 22

Moviemakers on Moviemaking

New Expanded Edition

Interviews co-edited by Shirley Sealy

A FREDERICK UNGAR BOOK
CONTINUUM • NEW YORK

To those who care enough to share

1991

The Continuum Publishing Company
370 Lexington Avenue, New York, N.Y. 10017

Printed in the United States of America

Library of Congress Cataloging-in-Publication Data

Crist, Judith.
    Take 22 : moviemakers on moviemaking / Judith Crist ; interviews
co-edited by Shirley Sealy.
        p. cm.
    "A Frederick Ungar book."
    Includes index.
    ISBN 0-8264-0537-1 (pbk.)
    1. Motion picture producers and directors—Interviews.   2. Motion
picture actors and actresses—Interviews.   I. Sealy, Shirley.
II. Title. III. Title: Take twenty-two.
PN1998.A2C75   1991
791.43'092'2—dc20   91-20565
                                                                        CIP

Grateful acknowledgment is made for permission to reprint a selection from "Stopping by Woods on a Snowy Evening" from *The Poetry of Robert Frost*, edited by Edward Connery Lathem. Copyright 1923 © 1969 by Holt, Rinehart and Winston. Copyright 1951 by Robert Frost. Reprinted by permission of Henry Holt and Company, Inc.

Contents

Preface to New Expanded Edition

Home at last—in the paperback edition that I had hoped would be the original form of this book.

Writers are, admit it or not, as concerned with form as with content. While preparing this distillation of what I refer to as The Tarrytown Tapes, I wanted it to appear in paperback for purely economic reasons. Beyond its appeal to movie lovers, cineastes, celebrity worshippers, and nostalgics, I wanted it to be as affordable as it would prove valuable to film students. I know too well that they are at the mercy of film educators, let alone us film critics, in learning the nuts-and-bolts, the hows, whys and what-happeneds of moviemaking and, most important, what the moviemaker had in mind. Post facto interpretations have their place, but the horse's— or filmmaker's—mouth is the best source of all. And herein are twenty-two moviemakers involved with seminal and/or neo-classic films, talking with us, telling us about their art and craft and themselves in a relaxed weekend situation.

But writers are, admit it or not, victims of the publishing business. Suffice it that the book came out in a high-priced hardcover, spent its time on store shelves and vanished into the out-of-print limbo. Over the ensuing years I heard from many people around the country who had borrowed the book from a friend or a library and who wanted a copy of their own; we would exchange condolences on its demise. And then along came Michael Leach, of The Continuum Publishing Company, for whom I was writing a foreword for a book on women in film. He too had enjoyed my book and regretted its passing. Could it be brought out in paperback? Home at last.

All we've done is update the post-Tarrytown Film Weekend filmographies of the participants and noted with sorrow the death of our beloved Bette Davis. Otherwise the transcriptions remain—testament to a wonderful series that began in 1970 and petered out with the advancing Eighties. Videotapes did in the appeal of retrospectives; television entertainment shows on network and cable proliferated, presenting moviemakers ballyhooing their latest films in one-to-three minutes and critics (myself among them) dissecting them in two.

Our wonderful audiences have, however, kept the faith as the weekends, now several a year rather than monthly, turned into a potpourri of previews of upcoming films, with filmmaking guests when possible. Movie-theater admission prices have risen 50 percent over these intervening years. The quality of films hasn't—although our previews have included such noteworthy movies as Woody Allen's *Hannah and Her Sisters* and *Alice*; *sex, lies, and videotape*; *My Left Foot, Sweetie, Roger and Me, Driving Miss Daisy, Cinema Paradiso, Mr. & Mrs. Bridge, The Grifters* and *Thelma & Louise*.

The original introduction will introduce you to a time and a place where the movietalk was worthwhile. The book itself will introduce you to moviemakers in their prime telling you how it was—and is—for them. And thanks to those videotapes that did in our retrospectives, you can, in fact, join the conversation after watching on your VCR most of the films that are discussed.

Judith Crist
1991

Introduction

Take 22 moviemakers, sit them down and set them talking about their work, and you may well find out all you wanted to know about moviemaking but never had a chance to ask. This is a book of gleanings, of selections from the Tarrytown Tapes, recordings of sessions with moviemakers—directors, actors and actresses, writers, producers—who have come over the years to the Judith Crist Film Weekends at the Tarrytown Conference Center, in Tarrytown, New York, to re-view and talk about their work.

These are transcripts of conversations held with audiences of 150 to 200 people whom I would describe as Alfred Hitchcock's "sensible" moviegoers, "keenly interested in the craft of cinema without wanting to make a religion of it." What matters most to me about these transcripts is that they are firsthand and authentic, with the creative artist's own explanations and comments—untouched by the egocentric interpretations and subjective interjections of the cinéastes and pedants who have been rewriting and recritiquing film history. These are the filmmakers' reflections and reactions at a certain time and place: perhaps, as Paul Newman said of himself, they no longer agree with themselves, but here they are, the way they were—or are.

Our beginnings have, at best, a slight suspicion of our ends. As journalist and critic, I was an elitist in my youth so that I could be a populist in my middle age. A child of Loew's Paradise, devotee too of the "art" houses of the day, I am of the Agee-an school of criticism, considering it a conversation between moviegoers rather than a laying down of the ultimate truth via the voice of the godlike critic. Above all, it seems to me the joy of criticism is in wanting to share discovered pleasures: you can't kill the trash (and who among us doesn't relish an occasional wallow therein?), but at least you can give the good a push and pass it on.

But one learns early about critical subjectivity, about fallibility, about the baggage one brings to the task. Early on in my career—I was *The New York Herald Tribune*'s critic, Bosley Crowther my opposite at *The New York Times*—there was a lovely illustration thereof, only superficially a matter of semantics. Reviewing a Simone Signoret film, Bosley described the protagonist as a "nymphomaniac," I as a "mature woman," revealing more about our personal morality than about Signoret's performance. On another occasion Bosley confessed himself unable to figure out the "symbolism" of a white horse in Alain Resnais's *Muriel*. I was depressed: I hadn't even thought it was a symbol. A short time later I asked Resnais: the white horse, it turned out, was the only one available at the stable for that day's shooting.

My major critical comeuppance came, however, years later, when George Roy Hill was at Tarrytown and, after a showing of *Butch Cassidy and the Sundance Kid*, was asked by a young admirer why he had resorted to "clichéd" slow motion in the shootout between Butch and Sundance and the bandits. Hill explained at length that he had intended to shoot a stop-motion sequence, that technical matters had gone agley and, much to his regret, he had had to resort to slow motion to save the scene. I listened with sinking heart, for in my review I had eulogized his creativity and sensitivity in using slow motion to reveal Butch's inner reactions to his first killing. When Hill finished his explanation, I could but whip out my review, read my rhapsody aloud and assure one and all that only the critic—like the Shadow—knows.

Our reactions and appraisals and surmises are indeed our own, valid unto us. But one learns the value, as critic as well as journalist, of going to the source for the ultimate fact and intention. We professionals can do it, but what about the "sensible" moviegoer, let alone the student, who learns about movies either from puffery and fan mags or, on the serious side, not only fifth-hand but also from born-yesterday pedants who impose their own judgments along the way? Small chance for the nonprofessional to ask the question and get a truly authoritative answer.

Guest authorities were not on our minds, however, when Robert L. Schwartz, creator of the Tarrytown Conference Center on a turn-of-the-century twenty-six-acre estate overlooking the Hudson River some thirty-five miles from New York City, came my way in the fall of 1971. I was film critic for *New York* magazine, a sister corporation of the center since both were initially financed and owned by the Aeneid Corporation, which was Armand Erpf, known as the Wolf of Wall Street, an art connoisseur, philanthropist, and dedicated supporter of anything of value to New York City. Bob, a journalist turned imaginative entrepreneur, wanted to find a weekend use for the center, whose conferees attended on a Sunday-evening-through-Friday-afternoon basis. He suggested that I conduct a series of lectures on film, but I replied that if there was anything more boring than lecturing on film it was being lectured at about film. Why not *show* movies, "neglected" films (i.e., movies I liked and not many others did) or the kind of semioldie the revival houses hadn't yet approached—and then talk about them as co-equals?

I had found, in my own home, that eating, drinking, and watching movie after movie was the ultimate weekend relaxation. And so we agreed on what we saw as monthly weekend food-and-film orgies, starting with cocktails and dinner on Friday, seeing a movie, talking afterward, seeing a late movie, going on to four films on Saturday, again with postmortems, and, after a leisurely brunch, winding up the weekend around noon on Sunday, with final talk and sharing.

That first October weekend was memorable. My list of films included *The Women,* which I had not seen in years but felt was worth revisiting in the age of feminism. I mentioned to Bob that I'd read that Clare Boothe Luce lived in Hawaii but occasionally came to the mainland. In no time at all, Bob, a man of mighty contacts, found she would indeed be in New York on the right date and was willing to join us—and both of us realized that our mutual friend and colleague Gloria Steinem would add currency to the conversation. Our weekend got off to a gala start with media coverage and some good talk from feisty ladies.

The second weekend, in November, however, opened a new horizon. One of my favorite "neglected" films of the time was Broadway producer Harold Prince's *Something for Everyone,* a biting black comedy with Angela Lansbury and Michael York, among others. Hal owned the only extant 16mm print and lent it to us, joining us for the showing with Eleanor Perry, the screenwriter, with whom he was working on a project. During the postscreening discussion, a production question came up that I couldn't answer and, noting our good fortune, I asked the producer-director to answer it. Hal went to the lectern and question after question followed for over an hour. When he finished, I apologized for "exploiting" him, but he waved away my apologies. He had had, he said, the best of times: "It wasn't the Yale Film Society and it wasn't a bunch of yahoo fans," he said. "I had the rare pleasure of discussing my work with adults."

And this, I realized, was what we could offer moviemakers, that rare opportunity to talk directly to the men and women who pay the five dollars to see their films and to get a response from civilized, intelligent moviegoers who had serious—or, on occasion, trivial—questions and comments to make. For both sides there was a realization and appreciation of the flesh-and-blood involvements on both sides of the screen: for the filmmaker there was the opportunity to reconsider his past work, test out his latest with a preview, gauge his accomplishment—or failure. For us—laymen, aspiring filmmakers or performers, teachers, housewives, professionals, and business people, drawn from the metropolitan area and with major contingents from the seaboard cities—there has been, in frank talk from the makers, a no-nonsense view of how movies are made; a realization of the commitment and the work, and—admittedly— some stargazing.

During that 1971–72 season, we had William Friedkin up with *The Night They Raided Minsky's*; Robert Shaw and Mary Ure, fortunately starring on Broadway together, to talk about *The Luck of Ginger Coffey*; Milos Forman—accompanied, no less, by Liv Ullmann (whom few recognized at that time) and Jean-Claude Carriere (Luis Buñuel's screenwriter)—for a showing of *The Fireman's Ball*; and finally, for what was to become our standard "auteur" weekend, Robert Altman, accompanied by René Auberjonois and John Williams, to take us through *M*A*S*H*, *Brewster McCloud*, *McCabe and Mrs. Miller*, and *Images*. With from four to six of a filmmaker's movies on hand, both artist and audience, offered a retrospective, could appreciate the creator's hallmark as well as his growth and varieties.

Altman, incidentally, came back a year later with *The Long Goodbye* and taught us both a lesson about audience conditioning. We had agreed that since his was the sixth Raymond Chandler screen adaptation, we'd show the five earlier ones—*Murder My Sweet*, with Dick Powell as Marlowe; *The Big Sleep*, with Humphrey Bogart; *The Lady in the Lake*, with Robert Montgomery; *The Brasher Doubloon*, with George Montgomery; and *Marlowe*, with James Garner—to demonstrate the romantic mythology that

Chandler himself, and Altman in his film, saw for sham and fairy tale. But, unwittingly, we so hooked the audience into that mythology that when Altman's movie, replete with Elliott Gould's antihero and Altman's cynicism, was shown, the audience hated not only it but Altman and me. We very simply—and innocently—cut our own throats.

Far from incidentally, we learned a lot about our audience, not only in its perceptions of the guests but also in its reactions to our programs and, perhaps of greatest interest to the moviemakers, to the previews. Later audiences in moviehouses confirmed, for example, their enthusiasm for George Roy Hill's *The Sting,* and Peter Bogdanovich's *Paper Moon,* John Badham's *WarGames,* Woody Allen's *Annie Hall* and *Manhattan*—and their coolth for Francis Coppola's *One from the Heart,* Michael Ritchie's *The Island,* Stanley Donen's *The Little Prince,* Mike Nichols's *The Fortune,* Arthur Penn's *Night Moves.* I remember Nichols's assuring the audience that once they read the critics' views they'd change their minds about his film (co-starring Warren Beatty and Jack Nicholson): *The New York Times*'s Vincent Canby and I turned out to be about the only two critics who liked it. And I remember a woman's eulogizing Penn's work on stage and screen and asking why he made "garbage" like *Night Moves.* I sat speechless with embarrassment; Arthur simply replied, "Because I don't happen to think it's garbage. Next question?" There have been similar incidents over the years but the professionals have proved able to take care of themselves—even when overpraised.

Our second season started out with Peter O'Toole and *The Ruling Class* (with O'Toole afterward taking on all comers at Ping-Pong until dawn). On another weekend, Sydney Pollack and Robert Redford dropped by during the shooting of *The Way We Were* to talk about *Jeremiah Johnson* with us. Alan Bates came for *King of Hearts, Georgy Girl,* and *A Severed Head*; Richard Attenborough for *Oh! What a Lovely War* and *Young Winston.* We had Paddy Chayefsky meditating more on the state of the 1972 world than on his five films, and Woody Allen, on the first of several visits, began, we realized later, gathering his impressions for those film seminars in his *Stardust Memories.* Woody brought an outtake from *Everything You Ever Wanted to Know About Sex* and discussed his choice with us; William Friedkin came back with rushes from *The Exorcist* to give us a foretaste of ghoulish movie magic. Anent the latter and our disillusionments, I've appreciated—as one who wanted but really didn't want Mervyn Le Roy to tell me that the tornado in *The Wizard of Oz* was a black silk stocking twirled before the camera—the discretion of filmmakers about their art: Sydney Pollack educated and fascinated us all with his explanation of how Jane Fonda had her brains blown out in *They Shoot Horses, Don't They?*—but Steven Spielberg said, when asked about the bike riders in the sky in *E.T.*, that he simply waited until the sun was in the right position and told the bikers to take off.

Over the years the stars have shown the humanity and the professionalism beneath the glitter, among them Kirk Douglas, Myrna Loy, Faye Dunaway, Shelley Winters, Raquel Welch, Peter Cook and Dudley Moore, Renee Taylor and Joe Bologna, Rachel Roberts, Jack Lemmon (who brought along Maureen Stapleton and Jack Gilford for auld lang syne), Alan Arkin, Ellen Burstyn, Sylvester Stallone, Kate Reid, Lee Marvin, James Coco, Joan Hackett—and, of course, those whom you'll meet in these pages. Some brought mates and friends, others—rewardingly—their children, as did the filmmakers.

The audience and I had the dream-fulfillment moments of movie-lovers, talking about *All About Eve* with Joseph L. Mankiewicz; *High Noon* with Fred Zinnemann; *Harold and Maude* with Hal Ashby; *The Big Knife* with Robert Aldrich; *Downhill Racer* with Michael Ritchie; *Midnight Cowboy* with John Schlesinger; *The Manchurian Candidate* with John Frankenheimer; *All the President's Men* with Alan Pakula, along with, of course, their later work. Joseph E. Levine with *The Graduate*, Sam Spiegel with *Betrayal*, and David Brown with *The Verdict* were among the producers who offered insights on their part in moviemaking.

There have been some one hundred weekends in the course of our first thirteen years. How to select a sampler for what may well be just the first installment? At this point I must confess that we began taping the sessions casually, primarily to protect our guests from being misquoted afterward. The tapes—reel-to-reel, endless reels, and later stacks of cassettes—were shoved into a cupboard. It was not until four or five years ago, when guests began asking if they could have transcripts, that we began to realize how worthwhile the sessions were. Alas, many of the early tapes were mislaid; all the Woody Allen sessions have disappeared; a number of tapes were mishandled and are incoherent.

But a treasure trove of tapes exists and one could spend a lifetime transcribing them. To fit the confines of a book, we made ruthless decisions, even flipped coins, to provide a broad sampling. What we are after is not the glitz and glamour but the information and the insight, the exchange of experience from a variety of artists—writers, directors, producers, actors and actresses. Above all, beyond the fun of a good read, I've sought to provide a textbook-level source of authoritative information and explanation. The men and women in this first selection are giving of themselves in a serious consideration of the art, the industry, the profession of making movies.

Importantly, they are doing so in a unique situation that allows them to confront both their past and their public. Just as a writer doesn't exist without a reader, so the filmmaker exists, I believe, only with a filmwatcher. Here the two meet, in symbiosis. The interaction is there, from dawn to dusk to midnight, in a gracious estate atmosphere where the relationship goes beyond the screening room. These are not self-conscious press agent–sponsored interviews. It's movie talk. Without false modesty, I have eliminated most of my own comments during the sessions since it is the moviemakers who are at stage center here, and my function is simply that of moderator—more learner, I've found, than leader.

The thanks are many, starting, of course, with those to Bob Schwartz, whose entrepreneurship started the weekends and helped them grow, courtesy of his imagination and enthusiasm and proprietorship of a charming establishment staffed, from top to bottom, by nice people who are very good at what they do. My thanks to Ruth Leibmann for suggesting the book; above all, to Shirley Sealy, friend and fellow critic and good right hand in transcribing and editing and checking, and to Edwin Kennebeck, of Viking, who has put up with my deadline hoggery.

Inherent in all of this is my deep gratitude to the film community, to the moviemakers and their cohorts, from company presidents to clerks, who have made the weekends and their sharing possible.

Peter Bogdanovich

▀▀▀

Peter Bogdanovich was in his teens when he began acting on the stage—in the American Shakespeare Festival at Stratford, Connecticut—and only twenty when he decided to direct his first Off-Broadway play, Clifford Odets's The Big Knife, *in 1959. A few years later he became a film feature writer and critic, with articles appearing in* Esquire, Vogue, The New York Times, Cahiers du Cinéma, *and* New York *magazine, among others. He has also produced a number of books on the cinema artistry of such directors as Orson Welles, Howard Hawks, Alfred Hitchcock, John Ford, and Fritz Lang.*

In 1968 Bogdanovich got a chance to direct a movie of his own, the low-budget Targets. *In his next film,* The Last Picture Show *(1971), Bogdanovich directed and was co-writer on the screenplay, which won both a New York Film Critics' Award and a British Academy Award. He then added the title of producer to that of director and writer for his next few films:* Directed by John Ford *(1971),* What's Up, Doc? *(1972), and* Paper Moon *(1973)—all of which Bogdanovich screened for Tarrytown guests, April 13–15, 1973.*

[After *Targets*]

CRIST: I first saw this film five years ago when I knew Peter Bogdanovich only as someone who wrote soft-cover books about film directors for the Museum of Modern Art. It blew my mind. Alfred Hitchcock pointed out that the essence of horror is not in the heavily made-up ghoul; the true horror exists in bright sunlight. I use the term the "ghouls next door," the ordinary all-American boy and girl who are the monsters who walk among us. The old horror pictures with Boris Karloff and Bela Lugosi were terrifying, but, of course, all those monsters were *manufactured*. Here, the monster is *not* manufactured. The key line in *Targets* is Boris Karloff saying: "Is *this* what I was afraid of?" The monsters are young and handsome and they drive white Mustangs and keep an arsenal in the trunk. Society is creating the monsters. You don't need a makeup department anymore.

I would have given an Oscar to the set designer. I have never seen so absolutely cold and vapid and somehow typical a middle-class home as that one—from the primitive family portrait to that great big bubble of a pink glass ashtray, every aspect of that house was perfect. Further, the film gave a very fine actor, Mr. Karloff, a chance to do some real acting. Finally, we all do have very personal reactions to movies: two years before I saw this one the first time, I had been in Texas giving a lecture at the University in Austin. The day after I left, one of those "very nice boys" we're always reading about climbed a tower at the University of Texas and proceeded to shoot fifteen people. So *Targets* was, for me, a vivid example of life imitating art—and vice versa. It was all of these things that made me think this was a most unusual film—it was elliptic, it was visual, it moved, it held me, it had interesting people. Then, I discovered it was the first work of a young director—*that* Peter Bogdanovich, who'd written all those cinéaste tracts as well as articles for *Esquire*. Peter and I then met, and I discovered how the film was really made. Now Peter can tell you about it.

BOGDANOVICH: Roger [Corman] called me and asked if I would like to make a picture. He said, "I'll let you make anything you want, the only thing is, Boris Karloff owes me two days' work. So here's what I want you to do. I want you to shoot for two days with Karloff. You can shoot about twenty minutes in two days—*I've* shot whole pictures in two days!" He *has*, too. I remember one called *The Little Shop of Horrors*. Anyway, Corman went on: "So now you've got twenty minutes of Karloff, see. Now I made a picture a few years ago," he said, "called *The Terror* with Boris, and I want you to take twenty minutes of Boris out of that film. Now you've got forty minutes of Karloff. Then you can get another bunch of actors and shoot for about ten days for about another forty minutes and you've got an eighty-minute Karloff picture I can release."

What you saw of *The Terror* in *Targets* is much different from what that picture is really like. That opening sentence under our titles—which is Roger's footage—is totally recut. The actual flood sequence in *The Terror* lasted, oh, fifteen minutes, and we cut it down to two and a half for the credits. *The Terror* was not to be believed—here was poor Boris playing the heavy, and Jack Nicholson with his voice in the highest register. I kidded Jack that if they rereleased this picture now, it would destroy his career. Well, I looked at this thing and couldn't see how I could take more than five minutes out of it, if that. But I had all kinds of ideas.

The first idea that came to me was a joke. I thought, We'll begin the picture with the flood sequence cut down, then the lights will come up in the projection room—and there will be Boris sitting next to Roger Corman. And Boris will turn to Roger and say: "It really is a bloody awful movie, isn't it?" Then I got to thinking it wasn't such a bad idea—to establish Boris as an actor, then I wouldn't have to do a period piece, with him in the makeup and all those Victorian clothes and such. Okay, he's an actor: *The Terror* is the movie he's making. Fine, that solved that problem, but I still didn't have a plot. So I tried to think of all the things Boris could be. He could be an actor who secretly wishes he is Cary Grant, so he goes into his dressing room and puts on a handsome-mask; and in this mask he goes to supermarkets where he strangles people behind the frozen-food counters. That didn't work out, thank Heaven.

I realized finally that it was ludicrous for Boris—who was close to eighty at the time—to play a heavy. I hadn't met him yet, but I assumed he was a nice old gentleman. Then I got the idea of taking someone who would be a representative of modern horror—as Judy says, modern horror is the ghoul-next-door. We decided to tell two stories and have them cut back and forth between each other. We had Boris for only two days originally, though I finally talked Roger into paying a bit of extra money and we got Karloff for five days.

CRIST: Did he turn out to be "a nice old gentleman"?

BOGDANOVICH: Yes, and much more: he was really a lovely man. I met him for the first time two days before we started shooting. He said to me [imitating Karloff]: "You have written the *truest* line I've ever read in a script." I was amazed: "Really?" I said, "What did I write?" He said, "You wrote about Los Angeles: 'What an ugly town this has become.' " And he talked for a half hour about how awful L.A. had become. Then he said: "Peter, since I am playing a character who's not far away from what I really am—couldn't we tone down some of those awful things I say about myself?" I said, "No, let's not. The audience will like it if you put yourself down." He said okay, and he did say all those nasty lines about himself that I had written.

So we shot it—and it was rough—because Boris had a terrible case of emphysema—it was the disease that killed him. It was very difficult for Karloff to do any activities like walking and talking at the same time. Most things had to be done with him sitting, which is why those scenes are a bit static. All the stuff he did outside—the drive-in, the scene with me in the car—all that was shot in one day.

On the first day of shooting, here was my own movie, my first, and I knew I had to work fast. In fact, before we started shooting, Corman said to me, "You know about directors, right? You know that Hitchcock plans everything—he writes down every scene that will be shot, and how he's going to shoot it and so on." I said, "Yeah, right." And Corman said, "Howard Hawks doesn't plan anything—he goes out and rewrites and then shoots." I said, "Right." Corman told me that on this picture I should be like Hitchcock—plan everything, because it would save time: "If you stop to think, the whole crew will stop and relax and go read the papers, or whatever." He was right, of course. And it was a piece of advice I still follow. I don't plan *everything* now, but I still try never to stop and say, "What am I going to do now?" Because it's true, everybody goes to sleep, and the momentum is lost.

The first day of shooting was to be outside, in front of the producer's office, where Boris and I talk. We were scheduled to finish everything that had to be shot *outside* with Boris in one day. Well, I got up early, though we weren't going to start shooting until noon because we would be going late into the night to do the drive-in sequences—actually, we ended up at four in the morning.

But I got up early to check out another location, a rifle range—and I got lost in the San Fernando Valley. *Completely* lost, and I became terrified—I couldn't find my way back and I was late when I got to the location; everybody was waiting. Not good on a director's first film and his first day. We were supposed to do a shot with a limousine but the limousine hadn't arrived and wouldn't be there for another hour. I was really getting panicky. We had to shoot something, and the only other thing we could film was a shot with me, coming out the door: my first picture, and the first shot has got to be *me*. Then while I was changing into my costume, I broke this antique watch I had. I'm a little superstitious, and I thought, "Oh, boy, this is going to be a helluva day!"

From that minute on, though, we didn't stop. I don't remember ever stopping to think. It was just go-go-go. Finally, it was midnight, and we had not yet finished the drive-in sequence. It was late, it was cold, Boris was wheezing. I went to him and asked if he could possibly stay with us a little while longer. He said [imitating Karloff]: "I will do it for *you*—but not for *Roger*." He stayed until four a.m., when we finally wrapped and went home. I got in my car and suddenly I was alone, driving home, and I could think for the first time. I realized I had been acting and writing and directing and hurrying—and *I had never had so much fun in my entire life.*

FROM AUDIENCE: Could we arrange to show this film to Congress?

BOGDANOVICH: It's ironic that you should say that because the picture was made without a release. It cost $130,000, which Roger Corman shelled out. $22,000 went to Boris—so the rest of the picture was made for $108,000. Every single studio turned the picture down for release. Finally, through a bit of chutzpah on my part, it was bought by Paramount for $150,000. So Roger got his money back with a little profit, and we had a distributor. Almost immediately after it was bought, in early 1968, Martin Luther King was assassinated. Then, shortly afterward, Bobby Kennedy.

Well, half the people at Paramount said, "Let's release the film right away and cash in on all the violence." The other half said, "Let's just shelve it—we never want to release it." They finally compromised—which is always a bad idea—and the picture came out with an ad campaign—"Why Gun Control?" The studio even added a written prologue to the picture that said: "Why gun control?" It seemed like a political tract or something—and, of course, nobody went to see the picture—they thought it was a documentary about gun control. Then the reviews came out and they were generally pretty good—particularly Judy's. But nobody went to see it, really; and it wasn't released with any degree of passion. A studio can kill a picture faster than the public or the critics. That's one thing I learned from this experience: if a studio doesn't like your picture and get behind it, you haven't got a chance. There *was* some talk of showing it to Congress, and I still think it's a good idea—because you certainly still can buy all that artillery, just as easily as ever. In fact, the gun shops we shot in were worried about what sort of movie we were making. I told them it was about a father and son who went to hunt bears together; it was all about paternal love, being a man, and so on. They liked that.

CRIST: Okay. Your first movie did not exactly set the world on fire, so how did this lead to your second film?

BOGDANOVICH: Well, I was hired shortly afterward by the American Film Institute. They asked if I would make a documentary about a director. I said, yes, if it's John Ford. They said okay, and I started to make a picture which I believe you'll see tomorrow, called *Directed by John Ford*. It took three years to make, mainly because it took the American Film Institute three years to get clearances on the Ford film-clips. In fact they never got the proper clearances on those clips, so the film cannot be shown anywhere—except in private screenings that are free. I finished the picture in 1971.

I also went to work on a picture for CBS—or Cinema Center as it was then called—a film based on a book called *The Looters*, which I never got to make. Don Siegel later made it as a movie called *Charley Varick,* with Walter Matthau. Siegel didn't use my script.

During this period I saw a paperback in a drugstore called *The Last Picture Show*. I said, "Boy, I should make a picture with that title—with my background, that sounds like my kind of title." But I didn't buy the book, and finally someone gave me a copy. It was Sal Mineo. He said, "You'd like this book. I think you ought to make it into a movie." I thought it was really good, though I wasn't sure I could make it as a film. Still, it kept going around in my head. Then I found that somebody else owned the rights. I met the guy, who had a screenplay he'd developed—the *worst* screenplay I had ever read. I said there was only one thing to do with the script—use it for scrap paper. The producer was not too enchanted with me for that remark.

I kept thinking about this picture. Finally, I called **Bert** Schneider, who had produced *Easy Rider* and who had told me he liked *Targets*. I said I had read a book called *The Last Picture Show* and thought it would make a helluva movie. He said, "Send me a copy." I said, "*Buy* a copy." That was very arrogant, but I wanted to see if he was serious. Bert called me four days later and said he'd bought a copy of the book and read it. "It's very good," he said, "let's make it." I said okay, but we have a problem: someone else owns the rights, and a deal had to be made with him. Steve Friedman owned it and Bert made the deal: Friedman got 15 percent of the picture, plus the $35,000 he had paid for the book, plus $20,000 as a fee. I believe he's going to make about a million dollars or more.

While Bert was negotiating this deal, I had agreed to do another picture—with Sergio Leone. Leone had made *A Fistful of Dollars* and several other "spaghetti Westerns." I hadn't made a picture for a year and a half, and this script was submitted; Leone and United Artists wanted me to direct. It was a Mexican revolutionary-war Western, which was called, believe it or not, *Duck, You Sucker!* I called up UA and said, "The script is pretty terrible, but *Duck, You Sucker!*, you're not going to call a movie that!?" They agreed to change the title.

I went to Rome and spent almost three months there, most of the time with a very charming writer named Luciano Vincenzoni—whom you know, Judy. He was the intermediary. Sergio was to be the producer.

How can I describe Sergio? The funny thing was that he had found a cinematic trick: BIG closeups. He would say to me [with Italian accent]: "You begin *CLOSEUP*! Two beeg green eyes!" Of course that's how Clint Eastwood became a star. I ran his spaghetti Westerns and thought they were a big joke. Luciano had written those movies as comedies, but Sergio filmed them as though they were deep tragedies. This tension between the writer's and director's intentions somehow produced pictures that were quite interesting. We would have meetings at which Sergio always arrived about six hours late; then he would begin to act out the scenes for us—at some length. He spoke no English, and I spoke no Italian. Well, he had a little bit of English. [With heavy accent]: "Dot's a good title, *Dockayu Socker*. You say dot in America all ze time—dockayu Socker!" I said, "*I've* never heard it." He said, "*Wot* you say?" "Well," I said, " 'Hit the dirt!' 'Take the high ground'—I don't know."

Sergio came in one day and told us the entire story was about Jesus Christ. If you see the picture he finally made you'll see vague elements of that—James Coburn plays Jesus Christ. If you know that going in, it helps. At one point I suggested that we call the Mexican character Juan, and the Irish character Sean. That way they both were named "John"—and they could call each other Johnny. I suggested we title the picture *Johnny and Johnny*. Sergio said, "Eezz very good, *Johnny and Johnny*. And you beegin with two *beeg* eyes . . . !" I said, "Sergio, look, let *me* direct the picture. I don't *like* closeups." "You don't *like* the closeup!?" Well, that was about the end of it.

Luciano and I were driving through the Rome traffic and he said, "You want to direct this picture?" I said, "Not particularly." He said, "I don't think so! This man make his whole career on the closeup—and you say you don't like the closeup! You are crazy!"

Just before Christmas, I left—by mutual agreement. What Leone really wanted was a surrogate director—somebody to push the buttons. He eventually hired an Italian director and then fired him. Then Rod Steiger said: "Unless you direct it, Sergio, I don't make the picture." So Sergio had to direct. It came out as *Duck, You Sucker!* and made a lot of money—someplace, but not over here.

CRIST: I'm ashamed to say I thought it was fun.

BOGDANOVICH: So did I. Anyway, I came back to the States and went right to work on *The Last Picture Show*—this was in early 1970. We worked for nine months researching and casting it, and shot it in ten weeks. It was released a year later, and established my career.

[After *Directed by John Ford* and *The Last Picture Show*]

FROM AUDIENCE: Mr. Bogdanovich, is telling a good story important to you when you make a picture?

BOGDANOVICH: Yes—if you can really involve your audience in a story, then I think you can get away with an awful lot of other things.

SAME MAN: Like what?

BOGDANOVICH: That's for you to say.

FROM AUDIENCE: I'm very interested in the fact that in your films you keep bringing in clips of old movies or TV shows. For *The Last Picture Show,* did you specifically go out to get that episode of *Strike It Rich*—or was that accidental?

BOGDANOVICH: No, but I must say that several of the best things in *The Last Picture Show* were accidental—like the sun going in and out during the scene at the tank-dam with Ben Johnson. However, I picked that TV show because it was one of the most popular of the period; it wasn't the one I wanted, but *Strike It Rich* was one of the few for which any film was left. What I really had wanted was *Stop the Music* with Bert Parks. In fact, the other TV show we used— *Your Show of Shows* with Sid Caesar and Imogene Coca—I hadn't wanted either. What I originally had in there was a Lucky Strike commercial—with a dancing cigarette box [singing]: "Be happy, go Lucky, be happy, go Lucky Strike" from *Your Hit Parade.* But Lucky Strike said no.

I've used movie clips only in *Targets* and *The Last Picture Show.* There was no clip in *Paper Moon,* and you have to look very hard to see the one clip in *What's Up, Doc?*—it's on TV, and not dwelt upon. Though it *also* was Howard Hawks, I haven't been doing any purposeful homage. I don't like them. Critics have accused me of constantly doing homages, and of imitating other directors and all that—it has become sort of "*the* thing" to write about me.

The sequence you saw in *Targets* from *The Criminal Code* happens to be a Hawks film, it's true, though not the Karloff movie I originally wanted to show. Then, for *The Last Picture Show,* the movie they watched at the end *had* to be *Red River,* simply because I wanted a picture about Texas—with a capital T and there aren't many good ones. So that was that. Even in *What's Up, Doc?* the only reason there's a clip from *Air Force,* which is a Hawks picture, is that I needed some good war footage on television to make a lot of noise, and there happened to be excellent war sequences in *Air Force.* One of the reasons I think *Targets* is a bit self-conscious at times is that it's the only picture for which I consciously did certain shots that were inspired by other directors.

The thing many critics forget—present company excluded, of course—is that every director, except Griffith, has been inspired or influenced by, or has simply stolen from, other directors. And Griffith certainly was influenced and inspired by other pictorial art as well as theatrical production of the period. The use of "originality" per se as a criterion is kind of a twentieth-century phenomenon. The question is whether or not it's a good movie, whether or not it's well made and has something to say. And whether or not there is, in fact, some strong and interesting *individual* personality behind the work. Of course, that's usually up to time to decide. But being inspired by what's gone before is a major part of the evolution of art and civilization.

FROM AUDIENCE: How much control do you have over your pictures, and how much are you involved in editing them?

BOGDANOVICH: I can't imagine what it means to be a director without cutting the picture. To me, they are not separate functions, and never were. In fact, a director always used to physically cut his own pictures, until De Mille got too busy and hired what was called a "cutter." When De Mille said: "Put these two pieces of film together," the cutter would splice them together. The term "editor" is a relatively new word in pictures, like "director of photography," who used to be known as a cameraman. They won't even let you use the word "cutter" today: I tried to use the credit for Verna Fields on *Paper Moon*—Verna liked the word too—but the Film Editors' Union said no; she had to be "editor" or, preferably, "film editor."

CRIST: I think what's behind the question is that we hear so many directors say, "I hate that picture because *they* cut it"—meaning the studio.

BOGDANOVICH: That has not happened to me yet. My contracts give me final cut. It doesn't really happen that often. A more important point is that a lot of directors shoot a *great deal* of film. A movie like *The Last Picture Show,* for instance, which is a longish picture, runs about 10,000 or 12,000 feet of film. In order to achieve 12,000 feet of finished movie, we exposed about 120,000 feet. That's close to average: in other words, about ten to one. Average in terms of the old days.

Today, I could name ten or twelve younger directors who don't shoot that way. On *Easy Rider,* for example, they exposed 600,000 feet, and ended up at 9,000 feet. It's not so much the expense of the film stock, it's the time taken. I try to shoot only what I am going to use in the film. Of course, I may require ten or fifteen or even forty takes on that single camera position before I get what I like, but I never "cover" a scene from many different angles. If I had a scene between Judy and me sitting here, and I knew that in the final film this scene would be shown with just a two-shot of Judy and me—I would not cover the scene. In other words: I would not get a closeup of Judy and a closeup of me, and an over-the-shoulder on Judy and an over-the-shoulder on me, et cetera—which is the way most films are shot. I'd just shoot the two of us sitting here, and that would be it. Knowing this is the sort of thing that saves time and enables you to come in under budget and under schedule—which makes you a hero at the studio. It also saves a great deal of time and effort in the cutting room. My cutter has nothing to do but assemble the pieces of film in the order in which they were made to be put together. Occasionally there is a problem—there always is. If you have a good cutter—and I do: Verna has worked on three pictures with me now—she'll have an idea and contribute something important on every picture. But otherwise, it's a technical job. On *Targets* and *The Last Picture Show* I physically cut the films myself.

FROM AUDIENCE: How involved were you in the casting of *The Last Picture Show*?

BOGDANOVICH: I'm involved in *everything* on my movies—it's difficult for me to walk into somebody else's office and not get involved in *their* problems. I can't get involved in things without starting to direct them. There isn't anybody in *The Last Picture Show* whom I didn't either find or carefully approve. It was the same with the writing of the script, and the locations. That's what I consider "making a movie." I don't think that's arrogant or egotistical—I think it's part of the job.

FROM AUDIENCE: What is the role of the producer?

BOGDANOVICH: Well, there have been a few good and creative producers. Selznick was certainly a creative producer. Goldwyn certainly was a force. Thalberg, they say, was a creative producer. But I don't think you can make a movie sitting in an office. You have to go out on the set and tell them where to put the camera, tell the actors what to do—*that's* making a movie. Bert Schneider, Bob Rafelson, and Steve Blauner on *The Last Picture Show* were a tremendous help—and this is where producers can be very useful—as an encouragement to a director. They don't necessarily contribute that much, but they can encourage the director to go ahead and do the very best he can.

On *The Last Picture Show,* for example, I'd been pressured into an eight-week shooting schedule—against my better judgment. After a week and a half we were behind schedule. I called Bert and said, "Look, Bert, I'm sorry—and I can stop shooting right now—we just won't do the picture. Because I cannot do it in eight weeks." He said, "How long do you need?" I said "Ten weeks." He said, "That would cost an extra $300,000." I said, "Well, it's going to cost an extra $300,000—or I can stop right now. Whatever you want." He said, "The footage looks great, just keep shooting." Well, *that's* a good producer. We did take ten weeks, the picture cost $1.3 million—but, as I said, it has grossed nearly $20 million, so he's not unhappy.

FROM AUDIENCE: Why did you decide to do a comedy like *What's Up, Doc?*

BOGDANOVICH: Well, I like to hear people laughing—that's really it. I get nervous when there is no response at all—often there are scenes that don't call for a response, but I wish people were laughing. My favorite parts of *The Last Picture Show* were the comedy parts. The biggest kick I ever had was going to Radio City Music Hall and hearing 6,500 people laughing with *What's Up, Doc?*

FROM AUDIENCE: In *Last Picture Show,* isn't it true that the only background music is that which comes from radios playing?

BOGDANOVICH: Also in *Paper Moon,* and in *What's Up, Doc?* I think scores are really overused now; too often a score is used to make a point the director can't seem to make visually. I'll never forget a movie I saw called *Hang 'Em High,* with Clint Eastwood, which was quite well directed. Tom Gries directed it. But the producer has put in this incredibly awful score—the picture didn't need one at all. There was, for example, a very effective closeup of a gun—and the music went wild with all kinds of explosive sounds. In bad movies, the sound is very often used to create suspense or tension—when the director hasn't done it visually. In *Targets* I put no music in the suspense scenes because I felt that would be cheating. I believe you have to make your point visually, or you're not good enough.

FROM AUDIENCE: You've directed Barbra Streisand and, according to what we read in the press, she's almost impossible to work with. Is this true?

BOGDANOVICH: Actually, I love Barbra very much. I think she's extremely talented, and a terribly funny person—in *life*. However, she thought that *What's Up, Doc?* was about the worst thing she'd ever had to do. She hated the script from the first draft through the last; she complained about everything. I just kept laughing. Which *threw* her. She'd say, "This is *terrible*, goddamit!" I'd laugh and say, "Oh, Barbra, c'mon, it's fine. It'll be *fun!*" She had really wanted to do a *drama* with me. I said, "I don't want to do a drama with you, I want to do a comedy." She said, "I've just done a comedy." I said, "I've just done a drama." And I hadn't done a comedy picture yet.

Barbra really didn't want to do the picture at all, but she signed a contract which, miraculously, gave her no script approval. The reason she signed that contract was because *her* agent was also *my* agent. And Ryan O'Neal's agent. All through the picture Barbra kept telling Ryan: "Ryan, we're in a piece of shit! I mean, we're *really* in trouble. . . . *I* know what's funny, and *this isn't funny!* What's funny about it?!" Now Ryan, who likes me but who also likes Barbra, and had never done a comedy, either, kept saying: "Well, I kinda—sorta—think it's funny." This was the way the whole sixteen weeks of shooting went. When Barbra had something to do, she did it well, and she would do what I told her to do—if she didn't I'd get angry. So we had this very funny relationship. She'd say, "What do I do?" And I'd tell her. Then she'd say, "Do you think that's *funny?*" The only thing she actually enjoyed doing in the whole picture was the chase—because she didn't have anything to say and she could ride in a fast-moving car.

When the picture was released, I took her to see it at Grauman's Chinese. And the people were *screaming* with laughter—it was bedlam. She said, "Geez, they're *laughing*." I said, "Well, it's *funny*." "Geez," she says, "they think it's *funny*." When the reviews came out saying she was better in *Doc* than she'd ever been, more charming, likeable, et cetera, she called me and said: "What did I do? What's this 'charming'? What did I *do?*" I said: "You were charming because you were just being yourself—you didn't have to wear a lot of makeup or funny clothes. You were more comfortably like yourself than you've ever been in a picture—the reviews are a great compliment to you." Anyway, after that she made *Up the Sandbox*, which was her *drama* and didn't make money. On *Doc* she had told John Calley, the head of the studio: "I'll bet you ten grand it doesn't gross $5 million." Calley said he didn't take the bet only because he knew Barbra wouldn't pay him. The picture will gross $35 million [it eventually grossed closer to $50 million], and Barbra sold her piece of the picture back to the studio for $2.5 million. And that's the picture she didn't want to make. To answer your question, she was *great* to work with!

[After *What's Up, Doc?*]

CRIST: Can you tell us a little bit about the casting of this picture?

BOGDANOVICH: Well, Barbra, Ryan, and I, as I mentioned earlier, had the same agent. She and Barbra asked if I would consider Ryan for this part, and I said: "Under no circumstances—he was that guy in *Love Story*. He was also in *Peyton Place*." The agent said: "Did you ever see him?" I said: "No!" She said: "Would you do me a favor and go see *Love Story*?" I said no, but they kept badgering me, so finally Cybill [Shepherd] and I went to see it one Saturday afternoon. Despite what I thought of the movie, I must say I was impressed by Ryan; he was touching. So I said all right, let's meet him. We had breakfast together one day and he was the most charming fellow in the world, and witty, bitchy, snide, and one of the funniest storytellers I've ever heard. At the time he was into very long hair, and wore leather and all that. Perversely, I was amused at the idea of cutting all his hair off and putting him into seersucker and horn-rims for the role in *What's Up, Doc?*—and he loved it. He immediately started having ideas about what he could do. We got along famously and I think he's just wonderful in the picture—and even better in *Paper Moon*—although that picture as written belongs to the little girl—Tatum—there's no way around it.

FROM AUDIENCE: Can you deny that *What's Up, Doc?* is an homage to the 1930s type of screwball comedy?

BOGDANOVICH: It's not an homage to those comedies. The picture was advertised with a line I suggested: "A screwball comedy. Remember them?" The point is: if I make a Western, would that be considered an homage to *the* Western? Westerns, gangster pictures, musicals—those are *genres*. And screwball comedy used to be a genre—but it's gone out of fashion; nobody seems to have made one since the 1940s. I like this *kind* of movie, so I made one. It isn't just a screwball comedy, of course, it has about every other kind of comedy you can possibly do—except high comedy. It's fairly low. I made this picture to have some fun, and for the challenge—those were the main reasons.

FROM AUDIENCE: I remember that this film had a very funny trailer. Did you make that?

BOGDANOVICH: Yes, I worked on it. We had had a camera crew shooting the making of the picture—for one of those TV featurettes. So when we came to make the trailer, I said: "Look, if we make a normal trailer, we'll be giving away all the gags. So let's make a trailer about making the picture—and make it look like fun." Now when we were shooting the picture—this is one of those happy coincidences—we were doing a scene on the roof in which Barbra sings "As Time Goes By." It was a complicated shot for the camera, involving a turnaround of 180 degrees. Barbra was upstairs yelling at her agent for getting her into this, or something like that, and Laszlo [Kovacs], our cameraman, said we had better rehearse this shot a couple of times. I said: "Fine, I'll do Barbra, and Ryan, you do you." I got on the piano and we played the whole scene. I sang, "You must remember this . . . , " and the rest of it. At the end, as a joke, I leaned over to kiss Ryan—and he fell off the stool, and there was a big laugh from the crew. What they didn't tell us was that they had turned on the camera and filmed the entire rehearsal. The next day, when the rushes came on, suddenly, after a couple of shots of Barbra—there's Ryan and me! And it was pretty funny because both Ryan and I played it fairly straight. I remember Calley called and kidded me: "Gee, you have a pretty voice." Anyway, we decided to use this scene in the trailer to show how I direct, so to speak. Actually, we crosscut between Barbra singing one line of the song, and me singing the next. It was an effective trailer.

FROM AUDIENCE: Can you tell us a little bit about your own background?

BOGDANOVICH: Well, my father was from Yugoslavia. He was Serbian. My mother was Austrian, born in Vienna. They came over here in 1939 because my mother's family was Jewish and they were escaping from Hitler. She was pregnant with me on the boat, but I was born in New York. And I went to Collegiate School, which is a private school. I went there for thirteen years, but didn't graduate. I was a terrible student, and I flunked algebra in my final year, but they didn't want to embarrass me at graduation by not calling my name. So, dressed in my black robe, I went up and they handed me a white envelope with a gray piece of cardboard in it. Anyway, before I graduated, or rather, before I *didn't* graduate, I was already studying acting with Stella Adler. I spent three years with her while I was also going to high school, and another year after. I also did four seasons of summer stock—as an actor—including Joe Papp's New York Shakespeare Festival, and the one in Stratford, Connecticut.

In 1959 I decided to do a play Off Broadway—I wanted to direct *The Big Knife* by Clifford Odets. This is one of the strangest things that ever happened to me. I was nineteen. I wrote a long letter to Odets, who had never allowed any of his plays to be revived Off Broadway. And ten days later my mother comes into my room and says: "You have a letter here from Clifford Odets." It was handwritten. I read it: "You have herein my permission to do *The Big Knife*." I couldn't believe it. It was a very kind letter; he even gave me a couple of tips about how to do the play. Well, here I was at nineteen, with the rights to do this play and, of course, no money at all. It took nine months to raise $15,000. I directed it, co-produced it for the 1959–60 season. We got quite good reviews, but it didn't do too well, and closed after two months. It's the production, however, that *started* Carroll O'Connor. I didn't see Carroll again until a couple of years ago when he was very kind to me while accepting a Golden Globe Award. He said I was an arrogant son-of-a-bitch, but that I had given him his start. He was very funny about it.

After that play, I didn't work in the theatre for a while. I got into writing for *Esquire* and for the Museum of Modern Art. And, finally, in 1964, after directing a season of summer stock, I did another play in New York: *Once in a Lifetime,* which was again about Hollywood. But this was a comedy, and a disastrous flop. After twelve previews, it ran one night. Soon after, I moved to California, where I met Roger Corman. And so on.

CRIST: Peter, what is your feeling about film schools—and majoring in filmmaking?

BOGDANOVICH: I don't think it's such a good idea, really. I don't know what you can learn except by learning about life, and looking at movies. There's not that much, technically, that you have to know about making a movie. There are a few tricks on the way a movie goes together, but that's not the hard part. Gregg Toland, one of the great cameramen, said to Orson Welles: "You can learn how to run a camera in one weekend; I can teach you that." Orson told me that Toland did it in one weekend. The craft of making a movie is very important, but more important is expressing yourself, and having something interesting to express. Maybe it's helpful to go to film school in order to get a job. I don't know. Francis Coppola did, as did several other directors who are now coming up. It worries me a little, the whole idea of going from academia into pictures. I don't really like it—the tradition of movies is against that. All the great directors learned on the job, not in school, and they had an experience of life that gave their work individuality and passion, two things schools tend to knock out of a person.

FROM AUDIENCE: I question what you have to say about academic training in films—in light of your own background. You must admit you learned a lot about directing by being an actor.

BOGDANOVICH: Yes, I think every good director has been, or somewhere inside him is, an actor. For me, however, school wasn't the way, although I learned a lot about theater acting from Stella Adler, and to have been an actor helps in dealing with actors, because you know their problems.

I was once talking with Jack Benny, asking him about Ernst Lubitsch, who had directed him in *To Be or Not To Be*. Lubitsch is among my four or five favorite directors. I asked Benny how Lubitsch directed, and he said [doing Jack Benny]: "Well—he used to act out *every* part! He'd get up, with his cigar, and he'd just *play* the part for you. Maybe it was a little exaggerated but you got the *idea* of what he wanted." I tend to work that way. I don't know how to direct an actor by sitting back and saying, "Why don't you go open the door, et cetera." I usually get up and go over and open the door, and work out the scene by playing it out. Which drove Barbra crazy at first. But my way of directing is to work the physical activities through myself so that I can get an idea of what feels natural and of where the problems are. Then I can discuss them with the players—and help them become comfortable with the challenges. I try never to ask an actor to do something I couldn't do myself.

[After *Paper Moon*]

CRIST: Peter, would you rather people tell you what they think, or do you want to tell us how you feel about *Paper Moon* now?

BOGDANOVICH: I like the picture—I hope you did. [Audience applauds.] I'm very glad, because you're among the first civilians to see it.

CRIST: I think it's a sweet film, and that's a difficult word to use. It's a picaresque film; the humor was generic and I appreciated that. And, as I think you said earlier today, only a father would agree to co-star with a little girl like *that*—because boy, does she steal that film!

BOGDANOVICH: Well, in fact, the picture was stolen for her in the script and in the direction. To a degree, Ryan himself is responsible for her performance—he had to be very patient—because we did several of those things forty or fifty times to get it right, but she is terrific in it.

CRIST: Did you find the script first, and then by happy coincidence get Ryan and Tatum?

BOGDANOVICH: No. I had wanted to do a Western, which Larry McMurtry and I worked out, and he wrote a first draft. It was to star John Wayne, James Stewart, and Henry Fonda, and Ben Johnson, and the Clancy Brothers, Ellen Burstyn, and Cybill Shepherd. Everybody agreed to do it except John Wayne. He said he didn't like the script, and then it all fell apart—that was last summer. I didn't have a picture to make. I was suddenly available, and my agent sent me another copy of a script called *Addie Pray*—which I had read four months earlier but turned down because we were going to do the Western. This time, the agent wrote: "Paramount wants Paul Newman to do this, do you?" I read the second draft, which was a little better than the first. There were only two scenes in it that I really liked—but to have two scenes you like in a script that's been submitted to you is very rare. On most scripts, you can't get past the first page. I thought: Oh, God, finding a little girl—and dealing with stage fathers and mothers and all that. In the script she was twelve, but I thought it would be funnier and more interesting if she were younger.

I had briefly met Tatum on a movie set, so when Polly Platt suggested Tatum might be good for the part, I remembered her. She had quite a husky voice for a kid. Discussing Tatum, of course, Ryan's name came up and I thought he might be good for this, too. The combination also seemed intriguing, so I called Ryan and asked him to read the script. He thought it was terrific and wanted to know who would play the little girl. I said, "Tatum." He said, "Hmm," and then he agreed to do it. Paramount at the time didn't want Ryan and said: "Why don't you use Dustin Hoffman?" I said no. "Warren Beatty?" No. I said if you want me, you have to use Ryan and Tatum.

FROM AUDIENCE: How did you get Tatum to smoke?

BOGDANOVICH: It wasn't easy—because she had to inhale. We got cigarettes made out of lettuce which were made in Texas. They were pretty mild. But about halfway through the picture, she was smoking all the time! She would say, "I need a cigarette—quick." She has now *stopped* smoking, and put on five pounds. The funniest bit to me was when she lit the match with her thumb.

There was an interesting story about the black girl, P.J. [Johnson]. She had never acted before, but she had the part the minute she walked through the door. She came in and looked at me and said, "Oo-ee, you good-lookin'!" I said, "You got the part, kid." When we started shooting she was absolutely terrified, and one of the first scenes we did, stupidly on my part, was the one in the back seat of the car when Tatum's saying: "Does she put out?" And P.J. says: "Just like a gum machine." We did the scene twenty-two times, and P.J. was pretty terrible. I knew it wasn't going to get better so I printed two takes. That was the only time anybody at Paramount called me. They said, "The black girl is not too good." I had to agree, and I decided to go back and cover the scene—which, as I told you, is something I seldom do. We set it up again, and I tried it once more the way we had done it before. I went into the trailer with P.J. and Tatum and rehearsed them for a long time. I told P.J. a story about Howard Hawks. Now, she was only fifteen, and Tatum was not quite nine, but I think when you're directing children, you have to treat them as if they're forty. So I told the two girls about how Howard Hawks had cast Carole Lombard in a picture called *Twentieth Century*, with John Barrymore.

I'm going to lapse into my Howard Hawks imitation here [speaking slowly]: "When Carole Lombard did her first scene with Barrymore, she was terrible—she was just *acting* up all over the place. And Barrymore would look at me and frown. I said, 'I know it.' So I called lunch, and I said to Carole, 'Let's take a walk.' I said, 'How much are you making on the picture?' She told me, and I said, 'Look what would you do if I told you you had earned all your money this morning—and you didn't have to *act* anymore?'

'You're kidding.' I said no. 'Now, what would you do if somebody called you a no-good son-of-a-bitch?' She said, 'I'd kick him in the balls.' I said, 'Barrymore's been calling you that—why don't you kick him?' She said, 'You kidding?' I said, 'No, go ahead and kick him.' So we got back in the scene—and she started kicking him. She was marvelous. I yelled, 'Cut, print.' And Barrymore looked at her and said, 'My God, you were great! What happened to you?' Well, she burst into tears and ran off the set. But from that day on, Carole was great. And she never began a picture after that without sending me a wire that said: 'I'm going to start kicking him.' "

Well, I told that story to P.J., and said the point was that she didn't have to *act* anymore. Just forget about acting, I said. She went into the scene again—and we got it on the second take. She was absolutely wonderful. The same fellow at Paramount who'd called me before called again, said wasn't it too bad that I had to recast the part. I said, nope, it's the same girl.

FROM AUDIENCE: How did you teach Tatum to act?

BOGDANOVICH: We didn't—we just whipped her! No—we all just worked our heads off. Most of the time, it meant feeding her every line, saying it the way I wanted her to say it, and she would repeat it. I remember near the end of shooting, when she comes out of the hotel, she turned and did this little skip. I said, "Cut." And she said, "Did you like the *skip?*" I said *perfect*. She's a wonderful kid, really, but it was a horrible job; it wasn't fun for her—there were a lot of late hours. She was extremely resilient, though. Some of those scenes we shot up to forty times. But I think it was worth it.

CRIST: How did you pick the title *Paper Moon?*

BOGDANOVICH: The book was called *Addie Pray*, which is not a very good title, and I thought perhaps I could get a better one from some appropriate song. So I went through the titles in every song that was at all popular from about 1890 to 1936—looking for a title. I came up with three or four, including *Paper Moon* from the song "It's Only a Paper Moon," which also had some lyrics in common with the theme of the picture. We added the scene where they sit in the paper moon, and the business with the photo, to fully justify the title.

FROM AUDIENCE: Were you interested in showing how the Depression could corrupt people?

BOGDANOVICH: Well, a lot of things can be read into it. But I myself was particularly interested in the story of a weak man and a strong little girl. He didn't have much guts. The only time he really gets into trouble in the picture is when she's not around. Although certainly it's often *funny*, to me it is basically a sad story, because she's stronger and smarter than he is. She has one weakness, however, that he doesn't have—she loves him much more than he cares for her.

FROM AUDIENCE: During the course of the weekend you've made some disparaging remarks about scripts and finding good ones to work with. Do you feel constrained working within the confines of a script that you have to accept from someone else?

BOGDANOVICH: Well, there has been no script that I just accepted— that wasn't completely rewritten, or written from scratch by the writers and me. Credit on a movie is dictated by Writers' Guild rules, not necessarily by what you do. The Writers' Guild rule is that a director is not allowed to have credit on the screenplay of a movie he directed unless he has physically written 50 percent of the script. Few writers write 50 percent of a script—much less directors, because a lot of writing for scripts is done sitting in a room and saying, "Hey, what about if she does this?" and so on.

The carnival scene in *Paper Moon*, for example. We said, "Let's have a carnival scene," and the writer wrote some of the dialogue, I wrote some of it, then he typed it all up. But writing for movies is often a question of conception. When I'm on the set, I have no compunction about changing something. If I like the writer, if he's been as good as Alvin Sargent was, and he's a very, very good writer—if I want to make a major change, I'll call and ask his opinion. If it's a minor thing I'll just put it in. The director often directs the writing of the script as much as he directs everything else in a movie.

Alvin Sargent wrote the two best scenes in the picture—neither of which was in the book. But at our first meeting, we went through the whole script and when it was over Alvin said to me, "You know, at the beginning of this meeting you made the classic director's remark—you said, 'It's a terrific script, Alvin, it just needs a complete rewrite.' "

FROM AUDIENCE: Do you have any regard for the reaction of your audience—I mean, in a picture like *Paper Moon*, which might seem to be a put-down of the middle-class morality of most audiences in the country?

BOGDANOVICH: I've rarely, if ever, so far, thought about the audience. I will make a picture only if I like it. I don't put anything in the picture unless I think it's funny, or interesting, or sad. Luckily, on the last two pictures, what I've liked the majority of the audiences have liked. That's just luck. I don't say: "This will get 'em."

[*Sunday morning*]

CRIST: We were just talking about the difference between having directors as guests and actors as guests. And I've always felt that actors only very rarely have the overall view—unless they're an actor-producer or actor-director.

BOGDANOVICH: They can't, because actors are very much into doing their job. But part of the director's job is to make the actor feel that he's a part of the whole picture. Actors often feel that the director doesn't really care, that the actors are just there to come in, do their stuff, and get off. I think it's better if everyone on a picture is involved in every part of it. On *Paper Moon,* for instance, Ryan was involved from the beginning, and so was Madeline [Kahn]. I'd discuss script changes with them, discuss the ad campaign, let Ryan approve his own stills; let them look at the rushes, et cetera. We cut the picture while shooting it, and ran cut footage for the crew every few days, so that everyone could see how the picture was slowly coming together. It makes everyone feel a part of something evolving, rather than just working ten weeks.

I learned that, indirectly, from a story Don Siegel told me about Howard Hawks. He said that at Warner Brothers, while Siegel was a montage director, Humphrey Bogart was rather intractable, difficult to work with. Yet Siegel came on the set of Hawks's *To Have and Have Not* and saw that Bogart was behaving like a lamb. He was having this wonderful relationship with Hawks. Siegel watched for a while and saw that Hawks made Bogart a part of the whole thing. They would talk together, change the dialogue together. It's important—and it shows in the movies. Even though Barbra, for instance, would argue with me about dialogue, I didn't say, "Oh, shut up." She wasn't always wrong. An actor on my pictures tends to know more about what's going on than he does on other pictures. We rehearse, too, which isn't always done on movies. Even on *Targets*, we rehearsed for two weeks before shooting began just so that everybody got to know everyone else.

FROM AUDIENCE: If you were asked to direct Laurence Olivier or someone of that caliber, would you go through the business of acting out scenes for him?

BOGDANOVICH: Probably. But I don't *always* show the actor how to play a scene—it depends on the actor. In *The Last Picture Show* I don't think I showed Ben Johnson anything. He just came in and did it. I think there were maybe two lines I told him how to read, but that was all. In *What's Up, Doc?* Madeline Kahn just came in and did it. On *Paper Moon*, however, Madeline needed a little more help. Ryan, first of all, had never done anything at all like what we asked him to do on *What's Up, Doc?* and he needed a lot of help. As the picture progressed, he needed less and less. The same happened on *Paper Moon*, which also was quite different from anything Ryan had done.

FROM AUDIENCE: What about working with Cloris Leachman?

BOGDANOVICH: Cloris was interesting—her part was the last one we cast for *Last Picture Show*. She came in and did a nice reading and I said, "Okay, you've got the part, and I want to tell you something—you're going to win the Oscar." She said, "*What?* How do you know that?" I said—and here is the arrogance of youth—"Because anybody who plays the part will win an Oscar." I also told Ben Johnson, who had refused to do the picture, that he would win the Oscar, and he did. Of course, I told Madeline she'd be nominated for *What's Up, Doc?* and she wasn't. But I knew that if *The Last Picture Show* were a successful film that those two parts were Academy Award *kind* of roles.

Now because I had made that remark, all during the shooting Cloris would play a scene and then turn to me and say: "Okay? An Oscar?" Cloris, in life, is completely one thousand percent opposite from the character she played in *Picture Show*. She's very effervescent, often loud, always bubbly, she talks all the time—she's quite aggressive. When she would do a scene there would be this complete switch and she would become that mousy little Ruth. Then we'd cut, and she was Cloris Leachman again. At the end of the day I thought maybe I wasn't getting the performance, because all I could remember was Cloris Leachman, not Ruth. But she was remarkably professional and, to tell you the truth, she had a terrible time because Tim Bottoms was quite rude to her. Other than that, the cast got along very well.

Cloris and Ellen Burstyn became fast friends, which is one reason why Ellen didn't attend the Academy Awards. She didn't want to be competing with Cloris, and of course maybe she sensed that Cloris would win. And you've never met two actresses more diametrically opposed; they both got along wonderfully too with Eileen Brennan. Jeff Bridges, of course, is the most delightful actor to work with.

FROM AUDIENCE: In *Paper Moon*, did Tatum O'Neal know exactly what kind of girl she was playing?

BOGDANOVICH: I don't think so. I asked her to read the script, and I think she got to page twenty. It's very confusing, even if you've worked on a lot of movies, to know exactly where you are each day in a picture, so of course I explained to her, so-and-so already has happened, but this is yet to happen—and so forth. There was a good example on a picture Orson Welles directed called *Touch of Evil*. It was a night sequence being shot in Venice, California. But the night was over, the sun was coming up, and Welles was desperate to get one more shot. His star, Charlton Heston, was on one side of the bridge and Welles, with the camera, was on the other. He yelled across, "Chuck! Quick—run across the bridge." And Heston says, "Orson, I will but—ah, could you tell me *why* I am running across the bridge?" And Orson said, "I'll tell you when you get here!" A lot of the work with Tatum was done that way: "I'll tell you after it's over—just *do* it." Actually, however, she became a real professional as we got into it.

FROM AUDIENCE: Has Tatum seen the movie?

BOGDANOVICH: Yes, but not until it was finished. I didn't let her see the rushes. She loved it—she came running over to me afterward and kissed me.

FROM AUDIENCE: Why didn't you let her see the rushes?

BOGDANOVICH: It's dangerous to let an actor who has never before been in a picture see dailies. I didn't let anyone on *Picture Show* see the dailies simply because it might affect them. Why take a chance? They might like themselves too much or they might dislike themselves too much.

CRIST: Peter, several people expressed the opinion that *Paper Moon* was an homage—if you'll pardon the expression—to Coogan in *The Kid*. I got quite a different feeling; I didn't see Jackie Coogan in this, unless the depiction of every poor waif in the thirties harks back to *The Kid*. Were you conscious of any of this while you were making the picture?

BOGDANOVICH: No, but when I finished it I thought, well, some of the critics called *Picture Show* my *Ambersons* film, and they said *What's Up, Doc?* was *Bringing Up Baby*. So this one is going to be called *The Kid*. It's so predictable. There's no comparison really except that both films are about a child and an older man. So maybe this is *The Champ*, with Wallace Beery and Jackie Cooper. Any picture you make with a kid and an older man will be compared to those two. I haven't seen *The Kid* since I was a child—except for one long sequence, which I used in the Chaplin montage we cut together for the Academy Awards the year Chaplin won a special Oscar. But other than that I don't remember *The Kid*, and I don't remember *The Champ* except that Jackie Cooper cried a lot. That was the one thing I decided Tatum would never do in the picture—cry.

FROM AUDIENCE: You don't allow tears in your movies?

BOGDANOVICH: No, there're no rules. At the end of *Picture Show* Cloris cries, and it's a very moving scene, but, generally speaking, when a character cries in a movie, the audience doesn't. To hold back tears is more affecting than to let it all out.

FROM AUDIENCE: After you got such raves for *Last Picture Show* did that affect the choice of your next picture?

BOGDANOVICH: The luckiest thing that ever happened to me was that I was deep into shooting *What's Up, Doc?* when *Picture Show* opened and got all those reviews. If I had not been in the middle of making a movie and, happily, a pretty frivolous one, God knows what would have happened to me. Because I probably would have started worrying: "How am I going to top myself? Will the new film be better or more important?" Which is really a dead end. *Picture Show* is now just one of the five films I've made—and not necessarily my favorite. I think I've improved as a craftsman since I did it. After Orson Welles made *Kane*, everyone said, "What can he do next?" And Billy Rose, a friend of Orson's, said to him: "Quit, kid—you'll never top it." Well, you can't quit, you know.

FROM AUDIENCE: Which is your favorite picture?

BOGDANOVICH: Well, my favorite answer to that question is John Ford's. When asked his favorite picture, he said: "The next one." At the moment, having seen bits of all of them, I'd say the best directed one in terms of the camera, the most assured, is *Paper Moon*.

FROM AUDIENCE: What would you change in *Last Picture Show* if you could?

BOGDANOVICH: Mainly the way it's shot. The performances are all still good, and that's the crucial thing in a movie, the acting. If the audience is watching the camera, it's either a strange audience or you've made a bad picture. I think the only thing audiences really care about is the actors, and how convincing they are.

Peter Bogdanovich returned to Tarrytown twice—to present Daisy Miller *(1974) and* Saint Jack *(1979). In the intervening years he also made* At Long Last Love *(1975) and* Nickelodeon *(1976). His romantic comedy* They All Laughed *(1981) co-starred the late Dorothy Stratten, a "Playmate of the Year," who was murdered and became the subject of Bob Fosse's 1983 film* Star 80; *Bogdanovich published a memoir of Ms. Stratten titled* The Killing of the Unicorn *in 1984.*

In 1985 he directed the well-received Mask, *starring Cher, followed by* Illegally Yours *(1988). His most recent film is 1990's* Texasville, *a sequel to* The Last Picture Show.

Bette Davis

▀▀▀

The term "movie star" is synonymous with Bette Davis. In her remarkable film career—which began in 1931 with Bad Sister—*she made almost 100 Hollywood films. As a testament to her unique place in cinematic history, in 1977 the American Film Institute gave her its Lifetime Achievement Award.*

Davis was nominated for an Academy Award ten times, but, incredibly, she won only twice—for Dangerous *(1935) and* Jezebel *(1938). She will always be associated with the Oscar, however, for it was she who gave the Academy statuette that nickname. Davis made a more substantial bit of Hollywood history in the mid-1930s when she was the first performer to defy the studio contract system and win the right to choose her own roles. It was after that that she gave some of her most memorable screen performances—in* Jezebel, Dark Victory *(1939),* Juarez *(1939),* The Private Lives of Elizabeth and Essex *(1939),* The Letter *(1940),* The Great Lie *(1941),* The Little Foxes *(1941),* The Man Who Came To Dinner *(1941),* Now Voyager *(1942),* Mister Skeffington *(1943),* The Corn Is Green *(1945), and, most memorable of all,* All About Eve *(1950).*

During the 1960s, Bette Davis was seen in several popular movies in the horror genre—notably Whatever Happened to Baby

Jane? (1962) and Hush, Hush, Sweet Charlotte *(1964). By her first visit to Tarrytown, January 11–13, 1974, she had begun to move more and more into television features.*

[After *Jezebel, Dark Victory,* and *All About Eve*]

CRIST: The first question that comes to my mind, Bette, is how you see the quality of acting in films today—in contrast to what we've been looking at. Do you think it's true that there's no more great acting?

DAVIS: It's not a question of no more great acting—it's a question of totally different kinds of scripts. I don't think the modern scripts have some of the really fascinating parts I was given by my bosses to play. In other words, from a world of *stars* with *leading roles,* you now have maybe five or six important characters. There very seldom anymore comes along what we call a real starring role. I think that's the great difference. There are many roles for men today that are great acting parts. We women sort of had the industry tied up many years ago—it was basically all women stars—and today it's basically men. That has a lot to do with what has happened in the world. There are so many big problems in the world today, maybe women's problems have gone by the board—although they still have them, plenty of them.

FROM AUDIENCE: I assume this has been asked many times, but here it is again—who were your favorite leading men?

DAVIS: I've had the privilege, of course, of working with some fabulous people. But in all those years I worked at Warner's, we really didn't have *big* star leading men. For instance, I considered it a great privilege to work with [Charles] Boyer. Certainly a great privilege when I worked with Mr. [Leslie] Howard. Certainly when I worked with Mr. [George] Arliss as a kid. Certainly when I worked with Claude Rains—I considered myself a privileged actress. But I've never had, per se, one leading man. And as regards the men I've enjoyed working with in films—it depends on which picture it is and what part they played. Of course there was Spencer Tracy—I only did one film with him very early in my career, a very small part, and never worked with him again. I *worshiped* James Cagney, he's one of our great people, but I never had the privilege of working with him as a *team.* Those are basically the men I worked with that I admire the most.

FROM AUDIENCE: What directors do you admire most?

DAVIS: I had *one* top director—and that's Mr. William Wyler. I think he's the greatest man on the screen—and have always thought so. He actually was so helpful to my career at the time we did *Jezebel*. He was the first great director I'd ever worked with and he really let me have it—but to my own good.

FROM AUDIENCE: Did you see Lauren Bacall in *Applause* on Broadway—and what did you think?

DAVIS: Yes, I did see it—and I enjoyed seeing her very much. It was very different from *All About Eve*, because it was a musical, naturally—and I thought that she was marvelous in it. And if I didn't, I wouldn't say so. Interestingly enough, regarding *Applause*, in the film I stood backstage watching Anne Baxter play Eve, and then, twenty years later, I stood backstage in real life watching Anne play Margo. That was an *incredible* experience and she was *absolutely marvelous*, truly marvelous. There was a difference between the way the two actresses played her; Lauren didn't worry about the biggest problem Margo has—which was her age. Anne played it with all of the frights of getting older—which is, of course, what Margo is all about. But it was a weird experience seeing Anne in the role; I felt very, *very old* that day. *Ohhh, boy!*

FROM AUDIENCE: I'd love to know a little bit about your childhood, where you grew up and how you got into films.

DAVIS: I was born in Lowell, Massachusetts, and I lived there two months of my life. I have to be very disloyal and say, thank God my family took me out of there. Then we lived in the suburbs of Boston all during my school years—until I went to New York to study for the theater. The first realization that this would be the life for me was when I was about sixteen years old and I saw the play *The Wild Duck* in Boston. I suddenly thought, someday I'm going to play Hedwig. And I did end up playing that part one day. That's basically it. I'm just a damn Yankee, that's what I am.

FROM AUDIENCE: Miss Davis, most of us get sort of a funny feeling just looking at snapshots of ourselves as youngsters. How does it feel to see these movies of yourself so young?

DAVIS: You should be so glad you *don't know!* [Loud laugh] You know, it really is an unbelievable thing. Who could have imagined that we'd be *stuck* up there. Not that we *have* to look at ourselves.

If I had come out here tonight immediately after you saw *Jezebel,* I would have been thinking, Oh, this poor audience . . . what a change they're going to see. It *is* an incredible experience—it's worse than the snapshots, because in snapshots you can say, well, who can tell how I *really* looked then. But on that screen, you *know* how you looked once.

CRIST: As a writer, I look back and think, Gee, I could really write then. And I wonder if you look back at certain roles and say, for instance, I really *had it* in *Jezebel.*

DAVIS: There are not that many performances you feel that way about; I've certainly felt it about *Jezebel.* There are some parts—for instance in *The Corn Is Green*—that I'd like to redo. I was very young when I played Miss Moffat. I feel I could do it much, much better today. Who knows? Maybe not, maybe it would be worse today, but it would be fun to try. I'm trying to think of what else. . . . Well, I'd still like to do Queen Liz again someday. The first time I played her I was thirty and she was *sixty*—and I really had a great deal of nerve to try it. The second time I played her she was younger and I was older. [Deep laugh] And now that I'm sixty-five years old I'd *love* to redo Elizabeth with Essex one more time. I probably won't; it would be kind of . . . gilding the lily. But now I would feel more comfortable as the older queen. Since I *am* an older . . . queen. [Loud laugh] Oh, I didn't mean that, really. I got stuck on that one and didn't know how to finish.

FROM AUDIENCE: You did *All About Eve* at 20th Century–Fox— were you no longer under contract to Warner's at the time?

DAVIS: That's right.

SAME AUDIENCE: Did you pick the part yourself?

DAVIS: No, I was a replacement—a *desperate* replacement. Claudette Colbert was meant to do it but she hurt her back. And I've *thanked her* all my life. They were desperate because they had location shooting in the Curran Theatre in San Francisco for only two weeks, and *only* those two weeks. So they had to start shooting the following week, and Mr. [Darryl] Zanuck, in *desperation,* said, "Will you help us out? I'm sending you a script." When I started reading it . . . well, I thought I must be the luckiest person in the world.

FROM AUDIENCE: We saw you a few years ago on Broadway doing a musical revue. Did you enjoy that?

DAVIS: *Two's Company* ... yes, though I was very ill at the time. The idea of it was fun. The idea was that after twenty-three years of Hollywood I came back to sort of make fun of myself before I really tried theater, you know? And had I been my peppy self I would have really enjoyed it and we would have been there a long time. It wasn't the best show in the world. It was a bigger show than I wanted; I wanted it to be a really *little* English revue, but it got out of hand.

FROM AUDIENCE: What do you think the film people of today are missing now that the studio era is gone from Hollywood? Do you have any favorite anecdote from your time at Warner's?

DAVIS: Ohhh. No ... I'll tell you, this thing about anecdotes, it's very hard to remember them off the cuff. But we did have more *fun* then. We had *time* for more fun. If we wanted to play a joke on the director we'd lose maybe fifteen or twenty minutes and the world wouldn't come to an end. Today, believe me, there is no room for any offscreen tomfoolery at all. This is one big thing that's completely different. It is such rough work—and it was good that we could do some of those pranks. For instance—I got myself all dressed up for the opening scene of the first film Irving Rapper ever did. I was on the set the whole day—playing an extra—and he never recognized me. Now, you know, you just have to forget it today—they'd have a *fit*. The *fun* is the big thing that's gone. We all miss that.

CRIST: You were mentioning before that you also regret the fact that movies have turned so to location shooting. It is truly remarkable now to think that a movie like *Jezebel* was made entirely indoors—and of course it's my theory that if you traveled the whole world over, you'd never find a great plantation homestead like Halcyon.

DAVIS: Oh yes you would. Yes, we went to Louisiana for *Hush, Hush, Sweet Charlotte,* and worked on one of these plantations. The one in *Jezebel* was copied from real life.

CRIST: Really? It seemed bigger than life, somehow. But, Bette, you were talking earlier about how outdoor locations can really work against the actor.

DAVIS: Well, it isn't like *acting*. They could hire a stunt woman or something. It's so uncomfortable; you stand around waiting for the weather to be right, for the clouds to go, or the snow to stop. It was just lucky that I didn't start in the movies now, because I find this way of shooting totally unpleasant—it's just agony. You can't open your eyes in the sun; it's just terrible. And you have no time to rehearse a scene. They'll just stick you in a car, for instance, and say, "You're going to do these five pages of script and we're going up this mountain and the camera's going to be beside you . . . zip, zip." It has nothing to do with *any kind of professionalism* whatsoever, it's just catch-as-catch-can. If you're lucky and know your lines and the camera crew gets it—then it's printed. I find it tragic.

FROM AUDIENCE: It's true that directing styles have changed along with acting styles. I'd like to know what kind of directors you like to work with—now as well as in the past.

DAVIS: First of all, a great director like Mr. Wyler will let his cast maybe run through the script three or four times. Right? The actors would do it how they felt it, how they saw it. He would then start correcting this or correcting that. That's the performance part of the directing—this was prior to the director's trying *anything* with the camera. You see, the camera should *follow* the actor. Today, the actors are following the camera. In other words, today the directors are making these marvelous crazy setups, and you have to fit your performance into *where the camera is going*. Well, this is absolutely, *totally* wrong. The first method is that of the great director. After seeing what his cast is going to do, giving them suggestions of how it could be better, he then will come to the cameraman and say "Now, we'll photograph *what* they're doing, the *way* they're doing it." That's the ideal way to direct a scene—that's how a man like Wyler or Ford or Capra or any of the other great directors did it. The rehearsal period was very important. Nowadays, there's practically no rehearsal of any kind. It's just, "If you get the lines—beautiful." That's tragic.

FROM AUDIENCE: Of the many roles you've played, which do you think you did the best in, and which is your favorite?

DAVIS: To have a favorite film you have to consider not only what you had to do in it, how great a part it was, how well or not well you did it. There's also the story, how it was edited and how it was put together. Many times you're very disappointed as to how you dreamed it—and how it actually came out. I think *three*—no, *four*—films came out the way I prayed they would. Certainly *Dark Victory*, certainly *Jezebel*, certainly *Now Voyager*, and certainly *All About Eve*. All of those came out with every expectation fulfilled. Many of the others had things I like, but there were disappointments in how the director did it, how it was put together, what was cut out, et cetera.

FROM AUDIENCE: Are there any new directors you admire—as a moviegoer, or as an actress?

DAVIS: Well, I haven't been invited to play with any of these marvelous new directors, so I haven't any opinion of them. I wish they would invite me—because there are many fine young directors, no question. I'm ashamed to say I don't always know their work—I'm extremely lazy about going to films. Every New Year's Eve I resolve: this is the year I will catch up. Maybe I will next year.

FROM AUDIENCE: On another weekend we heard from Joseph Mankiewicz* that other directors warned him about what it was like to work with you.

DAVIS: Oh, yes. They said to him, "You poor thing, you'll go mad, she's a horrible creature." Mr. [Edmund] Goulding is a genius moviemaker, but in my opinion, he was also an extraordinarily difficult man. He was always drifting away from the story. I did about three things with him†—and I *was* a meddler when it came to what I thought a character should be. Goulding also loved to act, so he would act out your part for you. And the way he acted out a role many times did not suit the way I thought the character should be. He *did* find me difficult, because I was very stubborn about the woman I was playing—and I didn't think he could play her as well as I did.

But this is interesting; Mankiewicz didn't tell me all this until we'd been working about three weeks. He said, "You just can't believe the telephone calls I've got." All of them warning him about me. But then he said he'd gotten *one* call from *one* man who said, "You're going to have the most fun you've ever had directing somebody." And I said, "Who said that?" He said, "William Wyler." I said, "I'll settle for that."

*Writer-director of *All About Eve*.
†*That Certain Woman*, *Dark Victory*, *The Old Maid*.

FROM AUDIENCE: Was there any single role you cherish more than others?

DAVIS: Certainly Judith Traherne was one. And I guess as a woman I admire—and have read more about and am crazier about than any other woman in history—I certainly *adored* doing Elizabeth, I *adored* doing her. And, as I said before, I'd like to do her again. Margo Channing is, of course, perfectly beautiful, but a much easier part to play than any of the others. It was pure heaven to play Margo. And Mankiewicz did it so beautifully, wrote it so beautifully, that I don't take great credit for Margo—she was marvelous in the script. I guess those were my favorite people. Oh, and one more was a favorite—in a completely ignored film called *The Catered Affair*. I absolutely adored playing Aggie Hurley because I never thought I could play a woman from the Bronx. I was proud of that because I believe I did it well. Maybe when I'm dead they'll put it on television and you'll all see it.

FROM AUDIENCE: It's been on television already.

DAVIS: Not too often, and it wasn't in any theaters, I'll tell you. [Throaty laugh]

CRIST: Well, I must admit that Miss Davis did suggest that we show *Catered Affair*—but I asked if we could switch to *Payment on Demand*, purely out of my own preference.

DAVIS: It's an interesting thing about *Payment on Demand*. It was really one of the best scripts, and had one of the best directors, and I think we all did a good job on it. It was originally called *The Story of a Divorce*. It is very often the situation in America, particularly, with the kind of driving women that we are, that the woman takes over a marriage. It is the story of a typical American divorce. Dear Mr. Howard Hughes decided that *The Story of a Divorce* wasn't a very exciting title, so he called it *Payment on Demand*, which I thought was so cheap. It broke my heart. And we also ended it in a completely different way from what you'll see tonight. We ended it where the husband comes back. As you'll see, she's been very lonely, and she goes right back to being the same woman. So he just gets up and walks away. This ending would have made it a far more dignified picture to me. But I think it's a nice picture—and Judith loves it, and that thrills me to death, because I am proud of that picture. It also made it to very few theaters.

CRIST: It was about twenty years ahead of its time.

DAVIS: I think probably it was.

FROM AUDIENCE: One of the most outstanding things about *Dark Victory* was how well paced your performances were—you and George Brent—leading up to the crescendo of the final scenes. But I know that this and most movies are shot out of sequence—so how do you learn to pace your acting to follow the drama?

DAVIS: You just have to learn to do it. That is the most difficult thing about going from theater to motion pictures, this lack of sequence.

FROM AUDIENCE: How much does the director help you?

DAVIS: Enormously. But really—Arliss said to me once when I worked with him, when I was very young, "Never do any scene where you don't remember what has come before and what is to follow." If you remember the sequence, basically, emotionally, it will all tie up. Now, if you have a director like Wyler, he will catch it if you're not following continuity. If you have a mediocre director, he wouldn't know the difference. So you really have to be aware of it yourself. But you're right, this is the most difficult thing about working for the screen.

FROM AUDIENCE: When you were under contract to Warner's, did you have any choice at all regarding directors?

DAVIS: Eventually, but not really. I begged to do *Dark Victory*, I begged to do *Jezebel*, and it took me about a year to get each one. They hired Wyler for me. Sometimes you'd get your way, sometimes you wouldn't. But you didn't *really* have any say, which is why there were so many suspensions of actors—you had to fight for *quality*. They were in business, and we were in the artistic end—and there's a vast difference.

CRIST: Do you personally regret the end of the studio system?

DAVIS: I think it's very sad for the actor, yes, because there's no continuity to careers today. You see, *we kept right on working.* It's the public that *finds* you—no studio can make you without the public finding you. Even if some of the things we did were not very good, you were constantly working so people got to know you. But there is no continuity today for the young actors. They have to look for the scripts now and they may not find them. With all the trials of the contract system—and there were *many* trials—this was the glorious part of it. Plus those publicity departments with ninety men in them. They kept your name before the public. This is gone. If you find *one man* in publicity at a studio today, it's a miracle. You know that, Judith. You've been in this business quite a while, too, my dear.

CRIST: Okay, so I did know Jeanne Eagles ...

DAVIS: No, no ... I didn't mean *that*. I meant that there must be such a difference for journalists today. In the old days, interviews were all set up—it was good for you and good for me. This doesn't happen anymore. Plus the young players today don't know the value of a good interview. We were *educated* for public relations, just as we were educated for anything else—but actors aren't educated in that way anymore. They don't care if they get an interview or not; or they don't cooperate and then don't get a good interview. It takes two—the interviewer and the player.

CRIST: You also had something to talk about besides your sex lives, right?

DAVIS: Well, yes ...

CRIST: Which I think is the major change today.

DAVIS: But don't you find an actor's sex life interesting?

CRIST: As we say, I don't care what they do, but do it in private, please.

DAVIS: We *did* it—but we did do it in *private*.

FROM AUDIENCE: Did you enjoy your interviews with Dick Cavett as much as the audience did?

DAVIS: Oh—*I have a ball* with him. I think he's smashing. And, you know, I started doing these talk shows long before most of my confreres did—because I felt it was one of the great new mediums. I've made few *movies* that people remember more than that famous Dick Cavett interview. He does his homework, and he goes back and forth with you; *I love him*. It's a *crime* he's not on every night. I don't understand it. Neither does he.

FROM AUDIENCE: You have managed to lead a more private life than most other film stars, but I wonder how private your life really is. I mean, do you have the freedom to walk down the street and go to a movie, say, without having people come up to you to want to touch you or talk to you?

DAVIS: Well, with all the pleasures in this work, with the pride you can have when people respect your work—there's quite another side to it, too. As regards people speaking to me or coming up to me—this is part of your training. I went to California forty-five years ago. You learn that having contact with the public is part of the work. And if you don't have this attention from the public, you get off the screen. I don't mind it—only once in a while, if you're very tired or something. Basically, I find people quite respectful. I really do. It all depends on how you react. You know, it's very easy to get into a white mink coat with four orchids pinned to it and collect a mob. If they don't recognize you, they're going to *find out* who that is, aren't they? It's very simple to get a crowd, but if you just behave like a human being like everybody else, which you certainly are, people bother you very, very little. Unless it's a professional appearance. Then if they *didn't*, how awful. What if you came out that stage door and nobody was there—ohh, *death!*

FROM AUDIENCE: In *Payment on Demand*, were there any particular problems associated with the making of it, or on the other hand something special you want to remember?

DAVIS: My oldest daughter has a bit part in it—at three years old, a token performance. Generally, we had a very pleasant time making this film—it was a script we all liked; Mr. [Barry] Sullivan is marvelous in it, I think. Basically, it was a very good cast. My private life at the time was in a complete uproar, but *that* I'll not go into. *That* was offscreen. Actually, this was one of the very pleasant experiences. No fights, nobody left the set. It was after we had finished shooting, of course, that Mr. Hughes sent for us to say he'd changed the title and was changing the ending. You know, we've had so many endings changed over the years . . . it breaks our heart. There's only *one* ending for every story—one ending that is *right*, I believe. You wonder why they make the film. They read the script, they buy it, they say "Yes, I want to make this film—marvelous, love it, great, go ahead, here's the money." Then, the minute it's finished they get scared to death. Because this script is honest, you see. Like those costume pictures, the ads would always have a naked body and an actress's head. The first ads for Queen Elizabeth *weren't* of Elizabeth. They used to take your face and stick it on somebody else's body, which had been painted with a black satin dress cut down to *here*. *This* was Queen Elizabeth?? Come on! They'd think they could fool the public. It would fool them long enough to buy the ticket and sit down to watch the movie start. This kind of deception used to make audiences very angry.

FROM AUDIENCE: In the thirties and forties, as you've mentioned, the actor didn't have that much control over the material he was given. But today you have actors controlling their own production companies. What do you think of the movies coming from this kind of control that some artists have today?

DAVIS: I think many actors today are making an enormous mistake saying they can direct, they can edit, they can act, they can write scripts—they can do the whole thing. This is impossible. These are all special talents. I wouldn't think of directing for anything on earth. Of course I've done some *illegitimate* directing during my years on the set—I wasn't supposed to, but that was for self-preservation and the good of the film. Or so I felt. I think this actor-in-production trend is bad, it's seriously bad if the actor has all the control. I think it has been proven so. Don't you?

FROM AUDIENCE: Yes, quite often, I think so. I feel some of the really great work comes out of people meeting head-on and clashing. . . .

DAVIS: Oh, yes . . . well, this is lacking today, *totally*. The movie business today is like the ice cream business—we must all love each other. Of course, we *must* clash in our efforts to make something the best it can be. While I hate to keep quoting him—but he's such a smashing man—William Wyler said to the cast while we were doing *The Letter*, "I don't care how much trouble we have here, I don't care how we hate each other, I don't care how you disagree or I disagree. The only thing that matters is this film that will go into theaters for audiences to see." That kind of attitude is completely lost today, and it's pathetic, it really is. You don't think the executives of Ford Motor Company sit in their meetings and kiss each other, do you? You must have conflict—especially in an artistic venture.

CRIST: I know that the more "happiness" stories you get out of a location—I as a critic become more critical, as a result.

DAVIS: Well, it is possible. *Eve* was the only picture, the only one, where everybody working on it was in seventh heaven, and it all came out right. I've made many films where everybody had so much fun—but the results were so terrible, so terrible. We're not meant to have fun, *this is work.* Everybody thinks that Hollywood is just a gay, mad-mad-mad place. No, it's *work* making a film, it's *murder* work—and it must be, to be good.

FROM AUDIENCE: When you were working on *All About Eve,* were you aware that this was going to be a milestone? A seminal kind of movie?

DAVIS: I think we all believed it. Oh, another *death* thing that can happen on a set is when everybody sits down to see the rushes and you start saying, oh, isn't this *marvelous?* That's *death.* You can't tell what's going to happen till it's all put together. But in *Eve* there was just a smell about it—you just *knew* it had to be great and that it would be great for all of us. But that was a very rare, rare picture in this way—I don't know of another.

FROM AUDIENCE: I'm sure there are a lot of young actresses today who would love to be like Bette Davis. Is there any actress you hold in awe, or ever wanted to be like?

DAVIS: Oh, I've *always* wanted to be Katharine Hepburn. I've wanted to look like her—to have that *marvelous face,* not my round, drawn face. Oh! I *adore* the way she looks. I could *kill* her for the way she looks. [Throaty laugh]

FROM AUDIENCE: There's another neglected film, I think, called *The Star.*

DAVIS: Thank you. I think this was one of the best scripts ever written about Hollywood, about the mediocre star in Hollywood— all he or she cares about are the accoutrements of being a star, and she hasn't any talent. Well, this is what happens—that film was completely ignored. I hope when I'm dead that will be recognized. I thought it was a damned good movie. Sterling Hayden was absolutely marvelous in it, he was perfect. I suggested Sterling for it . . . I wanted him just as he was, of course, the guy who lives in dungarees and the whole thing. So, oh, God, the first day we arrive on the set there's Sterling looking unbelievably gorgeous in a tailored suit. And he was sitting there in absolute misery. I said, "Sterling, what have they done to you?" He said "Look what they've done to me."

Well, it was in moments like this that I gained my reputation. I went in alone with the writers and said, "You let him go home and get those dungarees." Otherwise, the whole point was lost. Sterling was beautiful in that picture.

CRIST: Do many of you in the audience know what *The Star* was about?

DAVIS: It's about a no-talent star who loves the clothes and the lights and all. We won't mention any names. There was no *one* name who inspired this, there were several.

CRIST: Well, if you've read Joe Mankiewicz's *More About All About Eve* you find a very good description of her in the person that Mr. Zanuck had wanted to play Eve. Joe Mankiewicz said that he had worked with her in *Letter to Three Wives,* and he always had the feeling that she was sort of dropping in at the studio, and that she'd put on her interest in acting very much the way she put on her wardrobe for the day's shooting. And he never knew why she actually came into the studio . . .

DAVIS: Because the acting was the least important part of her work.

FROM AUDIENCE: Is there really any film in which you say "Petah, Petah, *Petah* . . . ?"

DAVIS: Noo—I've never said "Petah" in my life. *However,* there was a hero in a film we shall not mention beyond this point, called *In This Our Life—God!* What a movie that was—and Dennis Morgan's name was Peter. It was. A fan found it out and wrote me because I always swore that I never had a leading man named Peter. But she was right. However, I never pronounced it that way, *honestly.*

CRIST: It's exactly the same thing as with Cary Grant saying "Judy, Judy, Judy . . ." Which he never said, but someone impersonating him said it.

DAVIS: Yes, the impersonators do this to us.

FROM AUDIENCE: Miss Davis, who are your closest friends in the business?

DAVIS: The Paul Henreids, all my life they've been my greatest friends. He's a perfectly marvelous man, and I thought he was beautiful in *Voyager,* just beautiful.

FROM AUDIENCE: You've become almost an institution—and there are lines in plays and movies that mention your name or imitate you. Such as *Who's Afraid of Virginia Woolf?*

DAVIS: Yes, the only thing good about that movie was that. The interesting thing is, when I said that line in the movie, I just looked down and said, very quietly, "What a dump." I didn't make anything of the line at all. But Albee had great fun with it.

FROM AUDIENCE: What do you think of the people who impersonate you?

DAVIS: Arthur Blake was the great one. He was the first person to ever impersonate me—and he was absolutely brilliant.

SAME AUDIENCE: Are you flattered by that?

DAVIS: Well, I think if you're not caricatured, you've not *made it*. It means there's nothing that distinctive about you. It took years for anyone to attempt to do me because I played so many different kinds of parts. I used to worry about it, very much. But it finally caught up with me. I don't worry anymore.

FROM AUDIENCE: Miss Davis, did you enjoy making *Baby Jane?*

DAVIS: I enjoyed it very much. It was a marvelous character, you must admit it was a marvelous character. *Hush, Hush, Sweet Charlotte* I didn't like as much. By the time that head came rolling down the stairs I was getting pretty sick of it. It really made me sick just being on the set with it, it was terrible. *Charlotte* went too far. But it was also a very good part. And, you know, between *The Nanny* and *Baby Jane* and *Charlotte*, there I was in this category of tricky-tricky horror films. I'll never make another.*

FROM AUDIENCE: What about *The Anniversary?*

DAVIS: Oh, I *loved* playing her—because there are so many mothers like that. That's another very ignored film, completely ignored.

CRIST: The story was that you really directed that film. Is that true?

DAVIS: I got rid of the first director. He *went*. But Roy Baker, a very fine director in England, and also a man I've known for years, was hired to come in and do it. No, he *definitely* directed it. Oh, I did a little—behind the scenes.

*Miss Davis appeared in *Watcher in the Woods*, 1980, but in a nonhorror role.

FROM AUDIENCE: Have you seen every motion picture you ever did—all the way through?

CRIST: I think I contributed to this question, Bette, because I was relating how when I first met you, you told me you'd never seen *Of Human Bondage* all the way through.

DAVIS: *Bondage*? Yes, I did see it many years later. When it was previewed, I hid under the seat and waited until the entire theater was empty before I left—I hated it so. It's one of the few prints I own. I have seen it all the way through—but I've never enjoyed seeing it. I'm trying to think . . . I didn't see a *darling* little Italian film called *The Empty Canvas*. And quite a few of my television things—I guess I just can't torture myself because I know how horrible they're going to be. You know, we used to make eight or ten a year, in 1932 and '33, and some of those I've never seen, I guess. And thank God some of them have never appeared on television. Most of the ones on television I've seen all the way through.

FROM AUDIENCE: What do you think about the way they've been cut so badly for TV?

DAVIS: Oh! I think the producers who sold their product to the networks should have seen to it that they weren't *allowed* to cut them like this. I mean, eventually, there's not going to be anything left of any of the films. It's the fault of the producers when they originally started selling these films to TV. You know, George Stevens sued the networks because of the cutting of one of his films, but he did not win the case.

FROM AUDIENCE: You haven't mentioned your role in *Mr. Skeffington*.

DAVIS: Yes, I don't often mention Fanny Skeffington. That wasn't one of my favorite films, no, although Ory Kelly's costumes are in that. There's never been a more authentic costume job done, those marvelous early 1900s things he did were just beautiful. Then we had to work very hard to make me pretty. *Also*, I was heartbroken that the film was not done in color. It was one of the few pictures that I think should have been in color. But of course I enjoyed playing that part because of my beautiful Claude Rains.

FROM AUDIENCE: Another movie we're ignoring is *Little Foxes*.

DAVIS: That's right. Actually, I don't think I was very good in *Foxes*. [Groans from audience] This was our third film, Mr. Wyler and I, and it was the one time we were in total disagreement. He did not want me to play it the way Bankhead played it. Well, the way Bankhead played it—and the way Miss Hellman wrote it— there was only one way to play it. It was not a pleasant experience, and it was heartbreaking to me because we were *not* getting on. I couldn't see her played any other way, and Wyler was very rude about the way I played her, *extremely* rude. He *hated* it, as a matter of fact. And, funnily enough, it's one of the roles most people like about my work. Well, I think we're bad judges of ourselves anyway. That's a very serious statement. But I never thought I was any good in it.

FROM AUDIENCE: I'd like to know what films you may have coming up. And, since you come across so well on television, would you consider doing something regularly there?

DAVIS: Well, I have made *eight* pilots. *Eight* pilots. For series. I made my last one last year. It was very amusing, I thought; directed by Peter Hunt. Not *one* of them has ever sold. Obviously, if I've made eight pilots I've thought about television. And I'd be very happy to do a show, if it was a *good* show. Even though I think it's probably the roughest racket of all, from the standpoint of compromising. You can't have perfection on television—there's not time. And that would be tough for me. No, television just doesn't want me in a series—I don't know quite why.

FROM AUDIENCE: Do you think it could be a problem of over-exposure?

DAVIS: Well, it couldn't be over-exposure with me because I find so damn little to do now. [Loud laugh] No scripts are coming along. But there is a great danger of over-exposure in a series; I think this is terribly true. And therefore if you do a series, you shouldn't do a wildly definite character because that could be stamped on you forever. You should play something a little like yourself—and something that's amusing. Either that or murder. Either you do comedy or murder today—there's nothing in between.

CRIST: Was the Peter Hunt pilot the one in which you played a judge?

DAVIS: No, Peter Hunt did *Hello, Mother, Goodbye*. She was a marvelous, marvelous mother.

FROM AUDIENCE: Why don't you and Katharine Hepburn, and Jean Arthur ... and Olivia de Havilland ... get together and write a script?

DAVIS: Can you see the *four of us* in one film? Ha! I mean Aldrich was a genius to be brilliant with Joan and me ... but can you see those four? Oh, no. It would be impossible to get four good female parts, actually. I'm kidding about those four. I just don't know what we could be. *But* ... talk to Miss Hepburn. I'd love to do one with her. I wanted her to do *Iguana* when I did it—you know, Tennessee's [Williams] play. She would have been so marvelous, but she just couldn't get away.

FROM AUDIENCE: When you create a role, what's foremost in your mind? How you sound? How you look? What's going on in the mind of a character?

DAVIS: *All* of it. It all goes together ... what you think, how you look, what your voice would be like. Your wardrobe has to do with it, the sets even have to do with it. Of course, how you think the character is the most important. But, listen, I never knew what to do with Baby Jane until I got into that outfit. I tried every voice for her, I tried *everything* in rehearsal, and I felt I just didn't know what to do with this woman. When I got dressed in *those* clothes with *that* makeup—there she was, it was simple. In that case the externals helped me enormously to know how to be like her.

FROM AUDIENCE: I once heard the story about a famous actor who didn't wear an undershirt in one of his most famous roles—and undershirt manufacturers couldn't give them away after that. Now, an actress of your stature must have some influence on fashion and trends.

DAVIS: You're absolutely right. I've seldom worn hats, and *every* time I'd come to New York *every* hat manufacturer would call me up to say, "Can I bring over a hat?" Because it was influencing women not to buy hats. They'd say, "Bette Davis doesn't wear a hat, why should I?" It does happen. Who was that naked man with no undershirt?

CRIST: Clark Gable.

DAVIS: Oh, yes, of course. Well, men don't need undershirts anyway.

SAME AUDIENCE: Well, I'm wondering if you as an actress feel some responsibility along these lines. I mean, if I think about *Jezebel,* I think gee, if a whole generation of women grew up like this, a headstrong, self-centered woman, it would be a terrible thing.

DAVIS: If we thought that way, there isn't any part in the world we'd play. I wouldn't play Mildred in *Of Human Bondage*. That is, playing someone that you're quite definitely not. But a woman like Julie? Many women, thank God, admired her enormously. I would like to *dare* to be that woman. There's something in all of us that wishes we had guts enough to just—*do it*. But you couldn't play any part in the world if you worried about what influences it would have. You couldn't have any television show that's on today. You'd be worried every time they showed a gun going off. Of course, that's where I think censorship should come in. Violence *is* influencing people. Now there is where your point is well taken . . . but this doesn't have anything to do with the characters being played. You can show an evil person, and that this is *not* the way to be. This is how I've always approached any evil person I've ever played.

SAME AUDIENCE: What if Julie had come out to be a winner in the end?

DAVIS: She *couldn't* have—nobody who behaves that way could be a winner. Mr. [Jack] Warner said to me when I did Judith Traherne, "Who's going to go to the theater to look at a film about a woman who dies?" But she dies so *well* . . . and that could encourage somebody who had to die. Like the woman in *The Anniversary,* you can show women like this, and how perfectly terrible they have been. Take the mother in *Now Voyager*—you *can't imagine* the women who wrote to me after that film saying, "I realize what I did to my children." And the children who wrote me saying they had the same problem with their mother. So, actually, there's not all black and not all white. So, somehow, in a script and in a performance—you must see both sides, and maybe why they became the way they are.

FROM AUDIENCE: I haven't heard you speak of *In This Our Life*.

DAVIS: Well, I was too old to play that part. I thought it was an extremely bad script, and I thought the cast was all wrong. George Brent should never have been in it. It was just an unfortunate film I felt—but a brilliant, brilliant book by Ellen Glasgow. I talked to her about it later. She was horrified by the film.

FROM AUDIENCE: Have we neglected to ask you anything that you're simply dying to talk about?

DAVIS: Ha! . . . No!

FROM AUDIENCE: Did you have as much fun making *The Man Who Came to Dinner* as *All About Eve*?

DAVIS: Oh, no! I was the one who got Warner's to buy *The Man Who Came to Dinner* for John Barrymore and me. But they wouldn't let him play it because he couldn't remember lines. And I said I'll take him just ad libbing. He should have played it, he *should* have. It would have been the last film he ever made. He was dead shortly after that. As it was, I thought it was a very pedantic film, a very dull director, not much imagination. But it was a great property, and I thought it would make a marvelous movie. If it had had a better cast it might have.

FROM AUDIENCE: How do you account for the fact that with the increased level of sophistication today, people still look upon a picture like *Dark Victory* as a really good film?

DAVIS: I think it's a very interesting phenomenon about many of these films of that period. People love them. I don't know why. I'm *glad* they do. I guess they still believe the story, it must be that. I really claim that if a film was good when we made it way back then, it will hold up now. And a film that was bad then will be just as bad now.

FROM AUDIENCE: Your portrayal of blindness in *Dark Victory* was the most authentic I've ever seen. Your eyes seemed to be hooded or something. Was it the lighting?

DAVIS: I really couldn't see. It was mental. I absolutely could not see. That's a hard thing to do, you know.

FROM AUDIENCE: Did you do your own riding?

DAVIS: No, not for Judith Traherne, because of the accident she has. It is very dangerous to do your own riding because a lot of money is at stake with the studio. It's silly to have an accident. The girl who doubled for me was an incredible rider. Much better than I. I've sometimes done riding—but very simple stuff. Not a fall like that.

FROM AUDIENCE: There are actors like John Wayne who adapt every character to their own personality. Then there's someone like Richard Attenborough who sometimes changes himself so much externally and internally that he's hard to recognize. How do you feel about working with either type, and as a member of the audi-ence—how do you like watching them?

DAVIS: Well . . . I certainly would have given anything to have worked with John Wayne. He's the most attractive man who ever walked the earth, I think. And he is basically a *motion picture actor* who plays *himself.* And many of the people who came out from the theater were *actors.* Now, Attenborough I think often disguises himself too much—you don't really get to know him. I think there should be some semblance left of the physical being. . . . Oh, this is a great story: Mr. Warner saw the test of Paul Muni for *Juarez* and Muni was a complete mask, a *complete* mask. He was more Juarez than Juarez. And Warner said, "Why are we paying Muni all this money? I can't *find* him!" [Hearty laugh] So I think there can be too much hiding with makeup. Makeup should *indicate.*

FROM AUDIENCE: I read that Olivier said he couldn't "get" a char-acter until he found the right nose—and he worked with putty making a different nose for his characters. And you mentioned the dress you wore in *Baby Jane* as giving you a feel for the character.

DAVIS: Well, I imagine Olivier gets a feeling for the character out of other things, too, besides whatever nose he decides on. If you're playing a period piece the clothes make you feel of another era, they make you walk differently, act differently. *Jane* was a much more vivid experience than I'd ever had. And if Mr. Olivier—Lord Oliv-ier—wants to change his nose, I say *thank God.* He's heaven on earth.

FROM AUDIENCE: Tell us about Errol Flynn.

DAVIS: A beautiful, beautiful, fascinating man. But not an actor. He admitted that himself.

FROM AUDIENCE: Did it ever occur to you when you were playing opposite him that Ronald Reagan would end up being governor of California?

DAVIS (shouting over the laughter of the audience): It's too *bad* it occurred to anyone—and they got him in. I must tell you—there was a marvelous testimonial for Mr. Warner on one of those big, big sound stages. It was a most emotional and fantastic evening. It was an evening that marked the end of an era. And most all of the Warner's stock players were there, *everybody* was there. And naturally the governor was invited. And instead of very simply taking his place, just sitting down like one of the actors that he once was—we all had to *stand up* for little Ronnie Reagan when he walked into that room. Oh! It was agony.

Bette Davis's last theatrical films were Death on the Nile *(1978),* Watcher in the Woods *(1980), and* The Whales of August *(1987) with Lillian Gish. She starred on television in such network TV films as* Sister Aimee *(1976) with Faye Dunaway;* Strangers *(1979) with Gena Rowlands;* Family Reunion; A Piano for Mrs. Cimino; Little Gloria, Happy at Last; *and HBO's* Right of Way, *co-starring Jimmy Stewart. Beyond her ten Oscar nominations, the most awarded any actress, Miss Davis received countless other honors, including those of the Kennedy Center, in 1987, for lifetime achievements in the performing arts. She died in 1989 at the age of eighty-one.*

Paul Newman and Joanne Woodward

▰▰

Paul Newman and Joanne Woodward met while they were understudies in the Broadway production of Picnic, *and they married a few years later, in 1958, shortly after completing* The Long Hot Summer, *the first of eight films in which they have co-starred.*

During the early days of her career, Georgia-born Woodward was a member of the Neighborhood Playhouse and Actors Studio in New York, and in addition to working on and off Broadway she appeared in over one hundred television shows. An Oscar winner in 1957 for her third film, Three Faces of Eve, *Woodward was also nominated in 1968 for* Rachel, Rachel *and in 1972 for* Summer Wishes, Winter Dreams.

Newman, a graduate of Yale Drama School, has starred in fifty-one films, five of which earned him Academy Award nominations: Cat on a Hot Tin Roof *(1958);* The Hustler *(1961);* Hud *(1963);* Cool Hand Luke *(1967);* The Verdict *(1982). 1986's* The Color of Money, *a sequel to* The Hustler, *won him an Oscar. He was named Best Director by the New York Film Critics for his first effort,* Rachel, Rachel, *starring Woodward. He was both star and director for* Sometimes a Great Notion *(1972), then directed his wife again in* The Effect of Gamma Rays on Man-in-the-Moon Marigolds, *which the Newmans previewed at Tarrytown on the weekend of April 12-14, 1974.*

[After *Count Three and Pray* and *Rachel, Rachel*]

CRIST: Joanne, could you tell us about your affection for *Count Three and Pray,* which was, I believe, your first movie.

WOODWARD: Yes, it was my first movie and also the only movie I really liked—that I really, really enjoyed. I never see it without total enjoyment and thinking, "Oh, God, aren't you darling!"

NEWMAN: A quality she has since lost.

FROM AUDIENCE: But, aside from your sentimental feelings for it, are we supposed to take it seriously?

WOODWARD: I don't think so, but you have to remember that this film was made in 1955, a very different era from 1974. The reason I did it was that I was twenty-four years old back then, I think, and someone gave me the part. I thought, what better part can you have? I get to wear funny clothes, cut my hair, and smoke a cigar. At twenty-four, I didn't think in terms of what was the significance of this film—it was a helluva good part. I worked with a man I adored, Van Heflin; with a director I adored, George Sherman; and a part that I absolutely worshiped. It's not a film I could be objective about. I'm not objective about any of my films, period. They're all like babies I've had. You know, I either like 'em or I hate 'em. In this case, I love that movie—I'm sure it's not great, but I love it.

CRIST: What's your reaction to *Count Three and Pray,* Paul?

NEWMAN: I love it. Joanne did much better her first time out than I did. I did *The Silver Chalice,* if you remember that. There's a reverse snobbery in this, to know that you were in the worst picture made during the entire 1950s. It's pretty much of an honor.

FROM AUDIENCE: I'd like to ask you both, what are your priorities in selecting roles?

WOODWARD: I don't know about Paul, but really I have no priorities. I read a part and it either speaks to my condition or it doesn't. I have no other priorities whatever—except occasionally wanting to go to New Orleans—as we did to do *WUSA,* for example. Paul undoubtedly has a more intellectual reason.

NEWMAN: Well, it really varies. I would hope to do distinguished films, distinguished dramas, distinguished comedies—distinguished anything. Sometimes you settle for something considerably less than that. What I am interested in is emotion in films, the emotions of the actors and how they touch an audience.

CRIST: Could you tell us how *Rachel, Rachel* came your way? Is this something that hits an actor at some time in his life—to be a director?

NEWMAN: Well, I look at the film now and actually wonder what my contribution was. I think it was clumsily photographed, compared to what I know about things now. But the real job in that film is the fact that it was turned down by all seven major distributors. We had no money to start with—we only had a script and Joanne. We took all the funny little furniture out of our apartment and opened up an office there; we signed up a cameraman, a production manager, and a few other people. We had no financing at all. Unbeknownst to us, my agent had been working overtime and finally Warner Brothers called and said they would finance the picture for $700,000 plus 10 percent overcall—if I would sign for two pictures, as an actor, at half my regular salary, and if Joanne would sign another commitment at less than she had been accustomed to making. They really had us over the barrel. We said okay. Then they had this really complicated way of assigning those pictures to myself and Joanne. But I said the deal would be okay only if the guy who was in charge of the studio—whom I trusted—would still be in charge because I didn't want some idiot to be submitting scripts. Suffice it to say that the guy who was in charge of the studio then was not in charge when the picture was over—so we didn't have to go through with those commitments.

So that's the way the picture got on. It cost about $770,000 and grossed about $9 million. And if it were produced today, I don't think it would do half as well. I'm still a sucker for that picture: I borrowed a piece of Kleenex tonight—I knew it was going to happen. But it's so marvelous to remember the details of the picture, how the crew worked. There was a great feeling when we were working on that picture. When people ask what's my favorite, I suppose this is.

CRIST: One of your major triumphs in *Rachel* was that you acquired the television editing rights, is that correct? You were the first director to do so?

NEWMAN: The first director, yes. That's a funny story. Everybody says that agents are parasites and they don't do anything. When you do a picture as an actor sometimes you can be through with it for three months before your contracts come through—because the lawyers have been haggling about whether or not you're going to have a telephone in your dressing room, and all that. So Warner's hadn't signed the contract and the picture had been seen in a fine cut by the Warner Brothers people, who didn't quite know what to make of it. People were coming out of the screenings feeling they'd been hit over the head with a sledgehammer.

So I was hassling with my agent. Now the deal I've always had as an actor is that the picture could not be shown on television—even if it did not make its money back—for five years. If it made its money back, they could not show it for seven years. They were arguing that out, and also I wanted the right to make the television cut. My agent said there was no way he could get that for me. I said, "You're my agent. I pay you. You get it. If I don't sign the contract they can't release the picture." So he came back and said, "We got you five years and seven years, but we can't get you television cut." I said, "David, it's your problem; it's not my problem." He said, "Even if the studio gives us rights to cut, you can't get it from the networks."

The next day after about twelve hours, he came back and said, "You've got television cut." I said, "That's fantastic, how did you do it? I never expected you to get that." He said, "Well, I went into their office and they started giving me the same old hassle, and I said, 'Well, as Paul's agent, I will write you a check for $770,000 and *we* own the picture.' Then there was a furtive discussion among the Warner Brothers people—and they came around." That was the best piece of agentry, I think, that had ever been done.

FROM AUDIENCE: *Sometimes a Great Notion** is a picture that I liked very much and think has been overlooked. I'd like your views about it from the director's point of view.

NEWMAN: I inherited *Sometimes a Great Notion*. We were fifteen days into shooting it before I started to direct. I would never again appear in a film as an actor and direct it too—it's like sticking a gun in your mouth. Your work suffers; if you really work as a director, then your work as an actor is going to suffer and vice versa. But I was ill-prepared for that picture; I hadn't even seen some of the locations. I do think it's a lot better than people give it credit for. They were afraid of it, afraid to open it in New York—so they opened it in Seattle and Portland.

*Also shown as *Never Give an Inch*, 1971.

FROM AUDIENCE: Which do you really enjoy more, directing or acting? And could you give up one for the other?

NEWMAN: It's much more rewarding to direct, there's no question about that. I think it's probably more rewarding to direct even a mediocre film than it is to act in it. The marvelous thing about being a director, since good scripts are increasingly hard to find, is that when you do read a good script like *Rachel* or *Gamma Rays*, you can be connected with it without having to act in it.

FROM AUDIENCE: Miss Woodward, would you like to direct?

WOODWARD: No. Well, not that I wouldn't *like* to direct, because I think that directing, certainly in terms of film, is the most creative thing you can do. I agree with Paul, that an actor in a film, no matter how good, is essentially a noncreative being, or creative only within very small limits. But to direct, I think, takes a breadth of intelligence I don't possess. It truly does—to have the conception, to work with the camera and the actors. And, later, the thing that's most extraordinary to me—and I've watched Paul do it and still don't know how it's done—is to cut a film. I think editing a film is the *most* creative thing; to have the patience to sit there week after week! I'm afraid I'd put together the first rough cut and say, "That's it." I don't have the temperament to direct at all.

FROM AUDIENCE: What first interests you in a character—that idea of getting into a character's mind or finding things you like about a character?

WOODWARD: I'm afraid I work backward—especially for someone trained as I have been. Mine is an odd way to work; I work from the outside in. I always have to know what a character looks like because to me, having studied with Martha Graham, so much that goes on inside is reflected outside; it has to do with the way you move. So I generally start with the way a character moves. I'm not very intellectual, so I can't go to find very specific things until I find them, as Paul would say, viscerally. I took Rachel's movements from my child, Nell. She's very pigeon-toed, so I just took the way Nell looks and grew it up. And somehow, when you move like that—all sorts of things happen to you inside.

FROM AUDIENCE: I'm wondering about *The Effect of Gamma Rays on Man-in-the-Moon Marigolds*—you didn't really like that character, did you?

WOODWARD: I think I didn't like doing the part because it was very unpleasant, but that was the nature of the role—there was no way of dividing it. I didn't enjoy *From the Terrace* for the same reason—except that at least I had all those pretty clothes. In *Marigolds*, I was the essence of ugliness. Of course we carry all that ugliness inside of us—so I was using what was the ugliest part of me both physically and emotionally, and morally and intellectually. I had to live with that ugly part of me—and it was terribly, terribly unpleasant. I wouldn't have *not* gone through it for anything, but I didn't enjoy it, and I don't think my family did either.

NEWMAN: I'd like to say that my wife has played some delightful ladies—sexy, functioning voluptuaries; funny, brittle. And in twenty years she has chosen to bring *one* character home with her . . .

WOODWARD: That's not true. I always bring them home. The others are just so much more palatable.

FROM AUDIENCE: Were you approached as a team for *Man-in-the-Moon Marigolds*? Was it your decision, Miss Woodward?

WOODWARD: Paul decided on it, because he wanted to do it; he liked the play.

NEWMAN: *Uh*-uh!

WOODWARD: No, he didn't *like* the play, but he thought it had great possibilities. He always wanted to do it with me. It was a great stretch for me—but unlike with Paul, audiences don't know what to expect from me; I don't have any burdens placed upon me. They will accept it if it works out. That one, though, I don't know, I've never been quite sure it worked out. But it was one of the stretchiest roles I've ever played. And we used Nell, our daughter.* Paul always wanted to use her and I kept saying no, I don't think so, because I don't think Nell is an actress. But he was right, because although she isn't an actress she's so right for the part.

FROM AUDIENCE: Did you have any other differences of opinion about *Marigolds*?

NEWMAN: We didn't have different visions of how the character should be played. I was convinced the character should come out of the moment—that's not the way Joanne likes to work, and that's

*Listed in the cast of *Marigolds* as Nell Potts.

very uncomfortable for her. There was really no problem about that, though. Basically, the thing that got to Joanne was the permanent wave and the crummy clothes and the claustrophobic set, and the ugliness of that character. And if she felt uncomfortable, I wasn't all that anxious to dismiss that, because it worked very well for the part. There are times when it's better that the actor is off-balance.

FROM AUDIENCE: It's so unusual to see a husband and wife working so well together . . .

NEWMAN: You should see us when we get back to the bedroom . . .

FROM AUDIENCE: I mean, *on* screen.

NEWMAN: We've had very, very good experiences working together.

FROM AUDIENCE: Was there any particular film you worked on together that you disagreed about?

WOODWARD: Yes, Paul didn't want to do that movie, the comedy, *A New Kind of Love* [1963].

NEWMAN: I looked at the script and said, "Geez, this is *yechh!*" And she said, "I think it's rather cute." And I said, "That's because your part is cute. I've just got a bunch of one-liners." She said, "You son-of-a-bitch, I've followed you all over the world, to Israel, France—carrying the family, and you won't . . . ?" I said, "It's marvelous material. When do we start?"

CRIST: I hate to get partisan and tell you who was right.

FROM AUDIENCE: I'd like to ask you, Miss Woodward, how you feel about *Summer Wishes, Winter Dreams* and the character you played.

WOODWARD: I feel very close to the character because it was one of the few times—or maybe the only time—that something was truly written for me, from the very beginning. Also because it was based very much on someone I know. I know that it was slow—I think it is the nature of that film. There is nothing else you can do. If you're going to examine the insides of a woman's mind, it had to be the kind of film it was. Not for one moment did any of us think it was going to be successful, not even Ray Stark [the producer]. We just accepted the fact it was the kind of film it was—and we all cared very much about making it. Sometimes you do that kind of film and say, okay, it's ours—maybe nobody will ever see it, but we love it.

FROM AUDIENCE: After *Summer Wishes,* Miss Woodward, I read an article that said you were tired of playing the same kind of role, like *Rachel, Rachel.* Could you elaborate?

WOODWARD: Actually, I think I was probably quoting a critic—who shall be nameless—who said, "If I have to look at Miss Woodward play one more dreary old maid. . . ." And I thought, Aha! How right you are. After a while there comes a point when you cannot continue to examine the innermost workings of a woman's heart without losing freshness. After *Summer Wishes* and *Rachel* and *Marigolds*—not that I think they're alike in any way—but in a sense these roles are very internal. I'd like to do something that's a little more external, and I'd like to have a pretty dress for a change. It's pure vanity more than anything else.

FROM AUDIENCE: There has been some controversy over public personalities getting involved in politics. Do you think you have more freedom to do so because you are sort of free-lance artists? And do you think the involvement in politics has hurt some actors?

NEWMAN: Yes, it's easier to be involved in politics when you can be more independent—but I must tell you that I haven't made a lot of friends. But my theory is that if you don't have any enemies you probably don't have any character anyway.

[After *WUSA*]

CRIST: I would not have picked *WUSA* among your films to be shown this weekend, but I know that you particularly wanted it shown—that you had a particular affection for it . . .

NEWMAN: Joanne does, but I don't.

WOODWARD: No, I don't. Although I think it's one of the best performances Paul ever gave, and highly underrated. But I don't think the film comes off; I never really liked it—and I only did it because he was in it and we could go to New Orleans. Which is often my reason for doing things.

NEWMAN: Well! I return the compliment. I think it's one of Joanne's best performances. She's very sexy, very vulnerable. We made a lot of mistakes with the picture, but I think the film had much greater potential. Not politically—it should never have been a political picture. But when you're an actor in a picture you sometimes don't see where the whole thing is going. That's my fault. I should have.

FROM AUDIENCE: I think one of the problems with *WUSA*—in regard to box office—was that you were less than what audiences expected you to be—less than the Butch Cassidy kind of personality, something quite different that most people don't want to accept. I wonder if that had anything to do with the failure of the film.

NEWMAN: I think it's a combination of things. When I first started working in films, I think the audience allowed me greater leeway to experiment. For instance, I don't know that they would accept me as Rocky Graziano today.* It's too bad, because there's no sense stretching yourself as an actor to go into a film if you know that by your very presence in that film you will destroy the picture, literally, that the image that audiences have created for you will work against whatever you bring to the film.

CRIST: My own feeling about your role in *WUSA* was that it locked you into a kind of *Hud* character in technicolor and in an urban situation.

NEWMAN: Well, the *Hud* character was something else. That again shows where you sometimes fail in your judgment. I was very excited to play *Hud*, because I thought this is a perfectly amoral, immoral, unethical human being and we will show him for what he is. We didn't reckon with the idea that he was marvelous with the dames, a great drinker and had what I call the external graces. He was funny and bold and tough and great in a fight. And the fact that he had that one single flaw, his immorality, was so overshadowed—and he became a teenage folk hero. So we made a terrible mistake in that direction. The character in *WUSA*, of course, was a dropout—a dropout from his own work, from any kind of social responsibility. So I think there's quite a difference between the two.

FROM AUDIENCE: I'd like to ask you, Paul, about your statement that an actor has to work. You mean artistically? You weren't thinking in terms of economics.

NEWMAN: Both. Oh, sure.

SAME MAN: Which is more important?

NEWMAN: I have a very bad habit of giving away a lot of my money to charity. So I have a foundation that has to be supplied—it's penance for two thousand years of Judeo-Christian guilt for success,

Somebody Up There Likes Me, 1956.

you see. I support that foundation, and at one point I figured out that I supported or was responsible for thirty-two people. That has certain obligations. So you have to work. Then there's the other aspect—you have to work to keep your instrument tuned. It's a double obligation, really.

FROM AUDIENCE: I'm curious about your life-styles. How much time do you have for leisure between films?

WOODWARD: He's been out of work for *months*. [A deep sigh]

NEWMAN: Well, we manage to keep the family pretty much together. When I go on location, they generally come with me—or they did until the last two or three years, when it was really difficult for them to leave school. But Nell learned to walk in Israel; when she started to speak it was in French.

WOODWARD: She lost her first tooth in the elevator of the Ambassador East, between trains. We go back and forth a lot—but it's no odder a way of life than a lot of other people have.

FROM AUDIENCE: Mr. Newman, I recently saw you on a TV talk show in which the host asked you why you have such a successful marriage. And you said, "Well, Joanne and I have absolutely nothing in common." And, aside from Joanne's interest in needlepoint, it seems to me you have a tremendous amount in common. So why did you say that?

NEWMAN: Well, outside of the family and our profession we really don't have anything in common. I mean—a balletomane I'm not. She's a great Anglophile, I'm not. I've always been interested in automobile racing—but it has only been the last year or so that she gets up in the stands and yells a lot.

WOODWARD: I think maybe sometimes it's a good idea, not to have too much in common. A relationship can become too claustrophobic. I happen to be learning a lot about racing, but he's not learning anything about ballet.

FROM AUDIENCE: What do you get out of automobile racing?

NEWMAN: What do I get? A lot of static from my wife.

FROM AUDIENCE: I'm wondering why you'd want to come here and subject yourself to something like this?

NEWMAN: Ahh . . . you get to understand what people are thinking about in motion pictures. The questions they ask in terms of trends and so forth. And, I think Judith will bear this out, the critic lives in a kind of intellectual cloister, and the artists tend to do that too. The only way we can really find out what people who go to movies think about movies is to talk to them directly.

FROM AUDIENCE: I'd like to know who, in addition to each other, you've most enjoyed working with—and why?

NEWMAN: Oh . . . John Huston was a joy to work with. Marty Ritt, George Roy Hill as directors. It's a difficult question. When you have what I call an artistic community, when that functions well—when you go to a director and say, "Why don't we do it this way?" and the director might say, "That's the worst idea I've ever heard—and we're going to do it just the opposite"—that's fine. Without the bad suggestion, the good judgment might never have come into effect. That's all I'm interested in: it's not a matter of pride of authorship, or who gets points for this or that, or a power struggle or anything like that. It's a matter of gathering together all the talent and getting everybody with their engines turning over, so that each one serves as an impetus for the other one. When that works well, that's the best kind of creativity—because it comes out of the floorboards, or from grips or from costume people. It doesn't make any difference where it comes from. If you have that relationship with a director, where you don't have to worry about egos, then you can have a good time. That's why I like to work with George and with Marty, with Huston.

WOODWARD: I don't know that I want to pick any favorites. Obviously I love to work with Paul because he knows me so well; there're no long discussions on the set. I can't stand to *talk,* those endless discussions about how to play the scene. My feeling is that if you discuss a scene that long, it's liable to be out the window. As far as other actors are concerned, I think one of the most fun people I've ever worked with, once I caught on how to work with him, was Orson Welles. I loved him because he was so *there*—everything was just coming at you. George Scott is the same. I was terrified of George Scott but he was enormously exciting because it's like acting with an erupting volcano. I hated working with Marlon Brando—because he was *not* there, he was somewhere else. There was nothing to reach on to. And this is not saying anything behind his back, because it has already been reported that after that picture [*The Fugitive Kind,* 1959], the only way I'd work with Marlon Brando is if he were in rear projection.

FROM AUDIENCE: I wonder if you could comment on the Academy Awards? Are they really that necessary to the industry?

WOODWARD: Oh, I think so. And I'm not any great lover of the Academy Awards—as I've been loudly vocal about. But it does have a kind of importance. I think in terms of deserved honors, it's not legitimate. I think, for instance, the fact that Paul has never gotten an Academy Award is as shocking as the fact that Charlie Chaplin had to wait till he was eighty-seven. But that's neither here nor there. The fact is, the Awards do give interest to the motion picture industry, and create a kind of excitement. And nobody really believes that this is the award for the best performance or the best picture. We know that's not true. But the fact is, it's kind of exciting. I wish they would do it better.

NEWMAN: The Academy Award is an enigma. It doesn't make any difference that *The Sting* is going to get seven Oscars, because *The Sting* is going to do whatever business it's going to do anyway. But for a small picture like *Rachel*, it was terribly important that Joanne was nominated, primarily because you want people to see the film. You make a film so people will go see it, and be touched by it or affected by it. On a picture like Joanne's last one, *Summer Wishes*, it was very important that the film be recognized—however you may look askance at the Academy. Joanne didn't want to go. She knew it would be a real kick in the butt if she didn't win. But she said okay, she would go. And I said, "Have a real good time." Then two of my best friends came up to see me and said, "You know what a schmuck we think you are, don't you? Are you going to let Joanne go by herself?" So I went to the wardrobe department at Universal and got my 1936 tuxedo from *The Sting*—and went. And I did a 360-degree turnaround; I mean, why knock it? The horse may be on its last legs, so why kick it? So I will continue to go to the Academy Awards, even though I'm not a member.

FROM AUDIENCE: I'm interested in the concept of star, and his private personality and his or her public image. Before you came this weekend, we were discussing the disappearing star and the nondisappearing star. The disappearing star is one who disappears into the role, the nondisappearing star is the star who has his or her own stamp on the role, no matter what it is.

WOODWARD: You've got one of each.

SAME AUDIENCE: Right. And you, Mr. Newman, are an actor who puts his stamp on a role—the *Harper* kind of role, the flip *Butch Cassidy,* the machismo-type character. But in seeing you here, I've met a person who is thoughtful, has a sense of humor. Your private person seems to be much more thoughtful and deep than the screen persona. Number one, do you agree? And number two, when you take your screen persona—is there something specific you do to bring out that other you?

NEWMAN: I have no idea. The only thing I do know is that characters have a tendency to wipe off on the actor. For instance, I spit in the street. Now, I never spat in the street until I played Graziano. Graziano spits in the street. I catch myself walking up Fifth Avenue and doing it. That's not Paul Newman of Shaker Heights, Ohio, and Yale University. And there are other things that wipe off on actors. I'm at that point now where I'm not sure what is me and what is the characters that I played ten years ago. I . . .

WOODWARD: You're just an old patchwork quilt.

In recent years, Joanne Woodward has been seen more often on television than in films. She won an Emmy in 1977 for See How She Runs, *and gave memorable performances in* Sybil *and* The Shadow Box, *among other made-for-TV features, and made her debut as a director on a special for the TV series* Family, *created by Jay Presson Allen.*

Newman's post-Tarrytown credits include Buffalo Bill and the Indians *(1976) with Burt Lancaster;* Fort Apache, The Bronx *(1980); and* Absence of Malice *(1982), and, more recently, 1989's* Blaze *and* Fat Man and Little Boy. *He directed TV's* The Shadow Box, *1987's* The Glass Menagerie *(both with Woodward) and 1983's* Harry & Son *(with Woodward and himself). In 1990 they co-starred in* Mr. & Mrs. Bridge, *which won both a New York Film Critics award and an Oscar nomination for Woodward.*

Burt Lancaster

▀▀

New York–born Burt Lancaster was a college basketball star, a circus performer, and an entertainer touring the war zones of Australia, Africa, and Europe before becoming a "legitimate" actor on the Broadway stage in 1945. A year later he was in Hollywood starring in The Killers, *and he has enjoyed uninterrupted superstardom ever since. Lancaster's career spans more than seventy films and includes such a wide range of characters as the swashbuckling hero of* The Crimson Pirate *(1952), the alcoholic husband of* Come Back, Little Sheba *(1953), the vicious columnist of* Sweet Smell of Success *(1957), the Bible-shouting hypocrite of* Elmer Gantry *(1960), the reformed murderer of* Birdman of Alcatraz *(1962), and the fading aristocrat of* The Leopard *(1963).*

Lancaster was one of the first big stars to form a production company, and he produced not only his own films but such independent features as Marty *(1958), a "sleeper" which won four Academy Awards, including Best Picture. Lancaster himself won a Best Actor Oscar for* Elmer Gantry. *At the time of his visit to Tarrytown, October 17–19, 1975, he had just completed filming Robert Altman's* Buffalo Bill and the Indians.

[After *Sweet Smell of Success*]

CRIST: *The Filmgoer's Companion* has an irresistible reference to Mr. Lancaster. He is listed as "athletic American leading man, more recently outstanding performer." It's a marvelous evolutionary reference to an actor who, to me, from *The Killers* on, has always been an outstanding performer. And athletic as well. Mr. Lancaster just completed the filming of a picture with Robert Altman, and I thought we'd start with that one and work backward. Maybe you could give us a preview of *Buffalo Bill*. [*Buffalo Bill and the Indians,* or *Sitting Bull's History Lesson.*]

LANCASTER: You know, in Hollywood we have a saying: we can go to a preview out there and a film is absolutely marvelous; then we put it on the plane to head back east and someplace between Los Angeles and New York the film gets to be terrible. When you ask me what it's like—I've heard that it's sensational. I suppose we need that kind of feedback. But I don't know how the film is going to turn out. I personally feel it will be extraordinary—but that remains to be seen.

CRIST: I think many people might think that you were going to play Buffalo Bill.

LANCASTER: No, Paul Newman plays Buffalo Bill. He's younger, he's better looking, and, nowadays, he's more bankable. That's the simple truth. The character I play is a man called Ned Buntline—the man who first wrote dime novels a hundred years ago about Buffalo Bill. He brought Buffalo Bill to New York and introduced him to theater society. And Bill got smitten, as it were—he went off to write a couple of plays, and then formed his Wild West Show, which was a truly great and wonderful thing.

The story is a very serious one, told with great style and panache, in the atmosphere of a circus. And, underneath, it's a kind of portrait of what a star is. Buffalo Bill was a great star and went through all these things that happen to stars. He had the sycophantic entourage that lived off him and perpetuated his own concept of his legend as a great human being and a great man. Actually, in the film the indication is that he was a first-class shit. He came to believe in the legend out of necessity—out of the necessity to live with himself. He became a terrible drunkard and so forth. And in the movie, the character I play, Buntline, is kind of his conscience. It's very sad, rather poignant, but it's a highly entertaining film, and a meaningful one.

CRIST: You mentioned in passing that Newman is a bankable star . . .

LANCASTER: Aha, I knew you'd want to ask these kinds of questions . . .

CRIST: Well, I know that over the years you've been not only a very bankable star, but also one who did your own banking. At what point in his career does an actor become involved in production? It seems that you were one of the very first to turn in that direction, to say, "All right, I'm tired of this typecasting and from now on I'm going to be in charge of what I do."

LANCASTER: That simply came about through good fortune, in a way. When I was in a play here in New York, I met a small agent, Harold Hecht—small in size but not in brains—who would be representing me in Hollywood. I was going to make a test there. We were having dinner one night and were talking about films in general, and both expressed our dissatisfaction with the current crop of films, how they were made, et cetera. And laughingly, he said, "Well, maybe if you're lucky you'll become a star, and in five years we could be making our own pictures." He wanted to be a producer. Well, a year and a half later we were making our first film, producing it. Things turned out extraordinarily fortunate for me in the sense that I was able to get into a film immediately—*The Killers*—which brought me a lot of attention. So many actors go along for years before they emerge in something and suddenly they're stars.

Many actors just aren't interested in being producers, with all the problems that brings. For one thing, a top actor is extraordinarily well paid, and he usually has a piece of the action and his or her own production company to protect his interests. When you become a director/producer—or just a producer—it's a twenty-four-hour-a-day job. Not many actors want to get involved that deeply, certainly not if they're being paid so well just to go to work and do their schtick and go home at night. Being a producer is a big responsibility and it takes a lot out of you.

CRIST: Of course you also have the double satisfaction of being able to pick your own subject—which not many actors are able to do.

LANCASTER: They can, of course; it depends on your position. If you are a star—I wish we had a different term, but I can't think of one—if you're an important actor, you are offered a great deal of work. And you decide what you want to do. Now, for instance, Bob Altman wants me to do another film for him. And I'm really not terribly interested. I have the right to accept or reject it. Scripts constantly come to your desk—most are rejected out of hand because they're just terrible. They are interested in using you, and you're interested in using them. They want to put your name on a marquee—which is a guarantee of a certain exhibition—except in rare instances, like *Conversation Piece*.

For instance, I'm going to Teheran to do a film* for Carlo Ponti. It's a rather distinguished international cast—Richard Harris, Sophia Loren, possibly Danny Kaye, Michael Sarrazin. And the role I play in the film—and I mention this purely by way of explanation—is that of an Army officer who has the fate of a thousand people on a train in his hands. Well, at one point there was a problem about who was going to play the protagonist or leading part, which would be the Harris part because of its length in the film. I'll be seen in only seven or nine scenes—very much like the role I did recently with Bob Altman. They asked me to play the lead and I said, "No, I'm too old for it—and furthermore, I don't want to work fourteen weeks. I want to do my four weeks and go home." Then came the question of billing—and you must understand that I'm being practical here. I'm considered an important actor in Europe. Europeans like me; my name means a lot on the marquee. And the producers wanted to bill me ahead of Harris and Loren, because they could get more dollars out of it that way. And I said, "No, I'm sorry, you'll have to give me a special billing. My part doesn't warrant having top billing—it's misleading to anyone coming to see the film." I said I'd have to have special billing, but not above the title. They have the right to reject my proposal and not give me the job, but I do have the option of saying let's do it my way or I won't do it.

FROM AUDIENCE: Mr. Lancaster, in *Sweet Smell of Success*—which I assume you put your own money into . . .

LANCASTER: No. Some people have done it, it's true, but generally speaking, no star puts his money into a picture. What you might do, as I have done, is act in a film for virtually no money, but then I have a large piece of the action if it turns out to be successful. Invariably, you know a film like *Sweet Smell of Success* is not going to be successful, and you know it going in.

*The Cassandra Crossing, 1977.

SAME AUDIENCE: That was my question—weren't you taking a real risk in that picture because of antagonizing Walter Winchell and people like that?

LANCASTER: We didn't care a thing about that. What was Walter Winchell going to do, shoot us? That wasn't the disturbing factor. The problem was, we were a young company and we were doing reasonably interesting work, we worked very independently, and this was a labor of love for us. We started out with a $600,000 budget and wound up with a film that cost $2,600,000. We paid Clifford Odets, before he got through with the script, a total of $300,000 that year. The film was a total disaster—it lost $3.5 million. It's one of those things. Yet I can't go anyplace in the world without people talking about how marvelous that picture was. When I tell them it lost money they're stunned, they can't believe it. But we didn't put our own money in it. United Artists put up the money.

CRIST: At the time, *Sweet Smell of Success* was considered an astounding, really daring art film, because of its grittiness.

LANCASTER: It had the special quality of that kind of life. The style of the language Odets used was very "in" New Yorkese, a special-world kind of talk. It's ironic, because we thought the film was going to be, perhaps not a huge success, but certainly a financial success, because Tony Curtis and I had just finished making a film called *Trapeze*—and *Trapeze*, with Gina Lollobrigida, grossed $17 million the first time around. And if that means anything, you would think that the combination can be repeated.

CRIST: Maybe it was the difference between brawn and brains.

LANCASTER: In Hollywood, you go crazy trying to figure out what will make it. There are certain basic things. You know that a best-seller will generally do business. If it's really a best-seller people will go see it, even if they don't like it. They'll be preconditioned for it. It could be a very ordinary film and critically a flop—as most of those films really are. But they seem to strike a basic chord in people—maybe their simplicity, their corniness or whatever. But you can't know in advance if *any* film is going to be a success. It's a crap shoot.

FROM AUDIENCE: You've had other films like *Sweet Smell of Success*. For example, one picture of yours I always wanted to see was *The Swimmer*. It took me years to see it, finally, on television. And

I'm wondering what favorite films you have that never quite made it—maybe because of distribution problems.

LANCASTER: No, it had nothing to do with that. *The Swimmer* is certainly one of my favorites. It's a John Cheever story and there was the very difficult problem of translating a literary work to the screen. Cheever speaks in the short story of how a man is walking through a lane and he smells a fire, it's an autumn fire; he describes it as the smell of autumn in the air. Well, that kind of thing in writing is lovely, especially in Cheever's phrases, but when you try to get this quality onto film, it requires some kind of approach. I'll say that I don't think Frank Perry was able to do this, and I don't know that any other director would have been. But you certainly need someone like a Fellini or a Truffaut, or someone with that kind of imagination to let the camera also tell your story. Film has its own particular life—regardless of what's actually going on in a film. And it needed some kind of strange, weird approach to capture the audience and make them realize that, in a way, they were not looking at anything real. In talking about the script we would say, "I don't know why two men in white coats don't come take this guy away." It should have been obvious that this man was going through something that was not quite real; it was all part of his imagination. But it was played in a realistic sense—so when you come to the end of that film, instead of being sympathetic and heartbroken for the man, you were surprised and shocked.

SAME AUDIENCE: For me the film worked. But I really want to know if the picture didn't make it because of any particular distribution problems.

LANCASTER: No, I don't think so. But it's so hard to tell. For instance, when Dick Brooks and I were working on *The Professionals,* the sales people were brought over to look at the film. Now Brooks is a very definite man about what he wants to do with a film, what he wants people to see. He is the kind of fellow who locks the script in his desk every night and the actors never get their lines until they come on the set in the morning. He's almost paranoiac about it, and Brooks didn't want the studio people to see the film. Mike Frankovich was then head of production and he said, "We've got to show it to them, Dick, because we're going to open in New York soon." The people who say they can look at a film in any form and it won't make any difference—that's simply not true.

A movie is an experience that happens to you for the first time and you react to it. And if a guy shoots a gun and there's no sound, then that scene is going to fall apart for you. Dick understood that it's impossible to get the shape of a picture in its rough form. So he put in a music track and did all these other things so that he had about 90 percent of what the film was going to be. So when the screening was over, all these people jumped up with joy and said, "Oh, boy, that's millions of dollars." Immediately these sales people were enthusiastic, they went out and created their own word-of-mouth. They made tough deals; they had it sold and presold and so on.

But, to get back to a movie like *The Swimmer*, when the studio people see something like that they don't want to get involved. They give in. If they are going out to sell a movie, they've got to have the feeling that they've got something marvelous; they have to have enthusiasm. It's easy to sell the big ones, because everybody gets excited. But the one that's special—assuming that it's also worthwhile—that's very tough.

CRIST: I was very high on *The Swimmer*, too. There is one scene that just devastates me, and it happens to be a scene that was reshot—one that Frank Perry didn't have anything to do with. The word came out shortly after that film was released that there had been a reshooting, and that hint of trouble immediately divided people.

LANCASTER: Well, it had to be reshot, because we had no scene. You see, the actual shooting of the picture was over, finished—but there were scenes missing. I think you're referring to the scene I did with Janice Rule. It was simply not done the first time. Sam Spiegel made the decision—which had to be made—do we or do we not continue to use Frank Perry to do the necessary reshooting? Barbara Loden, who was very unhappy on the film for many reasons, didn't feel a rapport with Frank. She didn't want to do it. So Sydney Pollack came in and we shot the scene with Janice Rule—we were able to do it because it's really the first time you see her character. We had shot some of the scene, but not all of it. The whole film was a disaster. Columbia was down on it. I personally paid $10,000 out of my own pocket for the last day of shooting. I was furious with Sam Spiegel because he was over at Cannes playing gin with Anatole Litvak while he was doing *The Night of the Generals*. Sam had personally promised me, *personally promised me* to be there every single weekend to go over the film, because we had certain basic problems—the casting and so forth. He never showed up one time. I could have killed him, I was so angry with him. And finally Columbia pulled the plug on us. But we needed another day of shooting—so I paid for it. An audience really should just come in and look at a movie and either love it or hate it and go home. But sometimes you want to tell them, "If you only knew what we've been going through!"

FROM AUDIENCE: Would you ever want to direct?

LANCASTER: I have directed a film—many years ago—but no. And I'll tell you why. I find it's impossible to direct a film and play in it, too. I find you cannot serve two masters; it's just too time-consuming. And directing a film—for someone like me, with my temperament—means twenty-four hours a day. I wouldn't know how to do it any other way. It also means virtually a year of work—the preparation, the casting, sweating over the script. For instance, on *Birdman of Alcatraz*, when John Frankenheimer was finished with the film, he had to go very shortly, like within ten days, to begin, I believe, *The Manchurian Candidate*. And he put our film together the best he could under the circumstances. He said, "Burt, I don't know if this is very good, but I have to leave." Well, I took the film and, along with the writer, we spent three months in the cutting room putting it together. We took scenes out, we rewrote a scene, we did a brand new scene with Telly Sevalas—and he was absolutely brilliant in that scene, which turned out to be very important to the film. The work is endless. So you have to say to yourself, do I want to put a year into this? My problem would be that during that year I'd get offered one or two or three things I'd be dying to do—plus the fact they'd give me a ton of money, which I'm very fond of. But the real truth is, of course, that I'm not motivated enough to want to direct.

FROM AUDIENCE: What was your acting experience before *The Killers*?

LANCASTER: I was born in New York City, on 106th Street, and my acting experience started at about age two, in a church, doing the Nativity as one of the little shepherds. I used to go to the settlement house—they'd send us to camp—and they had a community theater. There were some very big people there. There was a man named Bob Parsons, who used to be head of the drama department at Columbia University. In those days there were only three important Off-Broadway theaters. One was the American Laboratory Theater, and the director was Richard Boleslawski, who later directed some of Garbo's films; Eva Le Gallienne's Repertory Theater; and the Group Theater. These were the emerging theaters in the late twenties and early thirties. I used to work in the settlement houses doing plays.

Anyway, Bob Parsons and John Martin, who used to be the dance critic of *The New York Times,* taught at the American Lab; my agent and co-producer, Harold Hecht, was a student there. One of the things they did was go to settlement houses in New York to put on plays just for the experience of it. Parsons thought I was a gifted kid, even though I was only eleven or twelve, and he actually came to my parents' house and asked them how I'd feel about going into drama school. My mother said, "Burton, are you interested?" And I said, "Aw, no, that's sissy stuff. I do that for the settlement house because they send me to camp."

When I was nineteen, I went off and joined the circus, working as an apprentice. That led to vaudeville. Then I went into the Army. I wrote and directed soldier shows. We had a very famous group overseas, in the North African/Italian theater, called *Stars and Gripes;* we got important show people into it, and eventually we had an acting company of about seventy people. So I was building up this backlog of experience, and when I came to New York to be in a play that Harry Brown had written I had had a lot of experience on stage. I just slipped into it quite easily.

FROM AUDIENCE: You mentioned *Trapeze,* and last night we saw *The Crimson Pirate,* and within the last few weeks I took my six-year-old daughter to see *The Flame and the Arrow.* I think you've cheated a whole generation by not making any more films like this—and the question is why?

LANCASTER: Because I'm a cheat! [Laughter] You must understand that those films were a little avant garde because they were not just swashbuckler films, they spoofed the whole idea. They had an undercurrent of something a little bit different. If you remember *The Crimson Pirate,* the character I played said at one point, "Yes, I fell in love—and no self-respecting pirate would fall in love." And when we were doing *The Flame and the Arrow,* we had a scene—written by Waldo Salt, a very fine writer—in which the players' troupe I was in was ready to move into the castle to save the princess or something. And as we go into the castle, I see this fellow and he looks at me as if he knows me and he says, "Robin . . . Hood?" And I say, "Yeah, Sherwood Forest." We were trying to do something a little different—because those Errol Flynn pictures, which were done very lightly, by the way, were presented as being rather serious. Not a lot of people understood what we were doing the first time around. It's ironic that these two films are kind of an insurance policy for me. I happen to own both of them, and every year I rent them out—they go all over Europe—and to this day I get people coming to me and saying, "Please, Burt, do *Son of the Crimson Pirate*." So we sit down and start talking about what we might do. I'd be puffing up the stairs, I'd have a heart attack, the girls would always be leaving me—we've been thinking that kind of thing. But then we think of all the work and expense that goes into it.

FROM AUDIENCE: Mr. Lancaster, how do you feel about Miss Crist's review of *Conversation Piece*?

LANCASTER: I haven't read it. But I know she hated it. I'm perfectly prepared to discuss it.

CRIST: I must admit that I have great difficulty in accepting you in that particular role, as a kind of inert, retired professor of art. And with the suggestion of incest, with just a little more than a suggestion of having an eye for young boys—well, I usually find myself willing to go anywhere you choose to take me, but I could not get into this one.

LANCASTER: For what it's worth, let me just tell you the facts. I don't know if they prove a thing. Understand that I'm asking myself about this, too. This particular picture, quite frankly, has very little for the average American audience. It's a tough film to show; I have no illusions about that. It's fractured in many ways, in terms of what [Luchino] Visconti wanted to say and what he was afraid to say; he didn't want to open up the homosexual angle completely. In a peculiar kind of way this is partly an autobiographical role for him. What he was trying to say, and I don't say he said it well, was that he has never had the capacity to love. He's always maintained an essential kind of loneliness. It's a little like Bob Altman, whom we were discussing earlier—he has around him all these people who adore him. He can do no wrong. He demands of them and they willingly give their fealty and they are trapped, in a certain sense, in his life—as people are sometimes trapped in a power structure. Visconti is a very important man in his country—artistically and politically.

Now, here's a man who loves little boys. It's as simple as that. He is a throwback to the old Roman emperors. He's a very sick man now, but he still looks like a magnificent bull.* He's a highly moral man. He's wonderful to women, very charming. But to him, a woman is a woman, while a young man or boy—his beauty is a compelling factor. The old Roman emperors had their boys, but also had their families and their children. No one looked at it as a demeaning or perverse thing as we know it today; homosexuality had its place, if you will, certainly in the aristocratic society. And everybody knew about it. They were great soldiers, great poets, great men—if we are to believe history. Visconti is that kind of a person. And when Visconti and I were discussing the making of the film we talked about whether he was going to get into the subject of homosexuality. He didn't want to talk about that. Perhaps that was a mistake. This film grossed $5 million in Europe, but I don't think we can get it released here. Now I don't say that we've made a highly artistic film that people here don't understand; I do think there is an audience for it. The reviews in Europe are ecstatic. So you have to shake your head.

We can go back to another film, which Mrs. Crist "hated," which was really one of the most honored films in Europe, all over South America, and in England—called *The Leopard*. Now at first the Italians said, "Why is this American coming here to play this? Why not an Italian?" Well, Visconti tried very hard to get an Italian, but he couldn't find anyone of the physical stature. And now, in Italy, I am thought of as being a great actor—because of that role.

If you know the film *The Leopard*, it's the story of the unification of Italy and the downfall of the ruling class. Now that's the kind of theme that's very meaningful for people even in South America; because they had ties to the Spanish monarchies, they understood it. But here I was sitting in a New York theater once, watching the film, and there was a couple in front of me. And he turns to his girl and says, "When's Lancaster gonna fuck Cardinale?" Now Judy tells me that she can't accept me as a professor— and I see why!

I've always had this problem. After I did *From Here to Eternity,* for instance, I worked for a man called Hal Wallis. He'd never *buy* anything. His ploy would be to wait till nobody wanted a Tennessee Williams play because they didn't think it was viable for the screen, and he'd sneak in and buy it for a song. He did the same

*Visconti died in 1976.

thing with *Come Back, Little Sheba.* I happened to be on a boat fishing with him one day, and we weren't catching any fish. And I looked at him and said I'd like to do that movie. He said it's a woman's play. I said I don't care, I love the male character. I know I don't look like the man, I may be too young—but I like it, I want to play it, it's a challenge for me. Well, the film as you know won an Oscar for Shirley Booth, which it should have. It wasn't a big box-office hit, but it broke $5 million or $6 million, and I was getting paid nothing, he got the play for nothing, but I was quite happy to be in it.

As a matter of fact, it was quite interesting. Despite the fact that I had won the New York Film Critics Award for *From Here to Eternity,* and got an Academy nomination at the same time, I very seldom got good reviews that didn't say, "despite the fact he's too young, he's too athletic—he does seem to have an understanding of the role." I was interested in becoming an *actor;* I was tired of this crap of being a movie star and having them decide what I ought to do because it's popular. And then I meet people who say, Why don't you do another *Crimson Pirate?* I'm sorry, but I'm not going to do that. If they don't like me doing what I want to do, as they say, tough titty.

CRIST: In my own defense, I quickly have to say that in *The Leopard* I thought you were a great prince.

LANCASTER: Well, I read reviews that said, "Obviously Mr. Lancaster doesn't know anything about Italians." That's the one thing I *did* know; I grew up around Italians, lived in their homes, was around them all my life. But it's pretty tough, you know, to be six feet tall, have blue eyes, look like an Irishman, and play an Italian.

FROM AUDIENCE: Of all the different characters you've played, are there any you enjoyed the most?

LANCASTER: From the point of view of challenge, I enjoyed the role in *The Leopard* more than anything I ever did. I got into *The Leopard* in a very peculiar way. A man called Labotta came to Hollywood to ask me to do a kind of swashbuckling Bible picture they do so badly over there. I wasn't interested at all. And he happened to see on my desk a copy of *The Leopard;* he asked if I knew the book and I said yes, I had just bought a dozen copies to give to friends, it's just marvelous. He asked if I'd be interested in playing in it. I said I couldn't play the part. So we forgot about it.

Now, Visconti tried at first to get an actor who had done *Don Quixote* in Russia many years ago, but the man was too old, crowding seventy. Then he made a deal with Olivier. Visconti was not happy about Olivier, but he knew that physically he was right for the part and he knew he could act the role in style. So it was settled that Olivier was to do it. But at just about that point in Olivier's life he was getting a divorce from Vivien Leigh and getting married to Joan Plowright, and he started to do the National Theatre thing. I remember I went to see him in 1963 and he was working and so happy about what he was doing—and getting all of thirty pounds a week. So the dates conflicted and Olivier wasn't available. Labotta proposed me and Visconti said, "*Argh!* Lancaster—he's a *cowboy*, no?" Just at that time *Judgment at Nuremberg* came out and *Birdman of Alcatraz*. Visconti saw them, and he thought, well, *maybe*. And also, it was the old story—they needed an American star to try to sell this in America. In order to get 20th Century–Fox to put up a great deal of the money, they had to get some kind of star. So all of those factors came into it.

Visconti and I became very close associates and friends. People ask if he's a good director. Well, I don't know how good a director is until I've worked with him—but yes, Visconti is good.

FROM AUDIENCE: Have you ever been offered any roles that you refused and later regretted not taking?

LANCASTER: No. I have been offered roles in pictures I knew would make a great deal of money. And I've accepted those roles—for that reason. But also, for other reasons, I've not accepted certain roles. I'll give you two examples—one is *Cleopatra,* the other was *Ben Hur.* William Wyler wanted me to play the Charlton Heston role. And I said to him, "Why do you want to do this piece of crap?" He said, "It's an insurance policy." Sometimes I've turned down pictures because, after five minutes with the director, I knew I wasn't going to get along with him, and I've found some reason to say no. There were other things I wanted to do—one was *The Spy Who Came in from the Cold,* but I happen to think that script was a bad script. And I felt antipathetic toward the director. Whether I was right or not, I never regretted it for a moment.

[After *Elmer Gantry*]

CRIST: I forgot how good *Elmer Gantry* really is—especially if you see it all in one piece, and not broken up by TV commercials. Burt, how did Elmer Gantry come about?

LANCASTER: Back in 1947 I made a film for Mark Hellinger called *Brute Force*. The writer of that film was Richard Brooks, who was not there during the shooting of the film. I met him later and we became fairly close friends for a while. Eventually he went to Columbia and set up his own group—which has now become fashionable—and began to do films of his own choosing. While I was at Paramount doing a film for Hal Wallis, I met Dick one day at a nearby restaurant and he said to me, "Did you ever read *Elmer Gantry*?" And I said, "Oh, yes, Sinclair Lewis was one of my heroes." Dick said, "Well, I think I can get the book—to do a picture. Are you interested in doing Gantry?" I said I thought it would be a very challenging role and all that—but that was the end of it. About a year and a half later I ran into him at a racetrack—I was there with all five of my kids, and losing money. Dick said he was leaving for Europe but that he had the rights to *Elmer Gantry* and was going to prepare a first-draft screenplay while he was away. Well, another year and a half went by and Dick came back, and lo and behold, he sent me the script. It followed almost clinically the pattern of the book. Swifty Lazar was Dick's agent, and I told Swifty after I read the script that I didn't think it was very good; it was overwritten. Swifty transmitted this information to Brooks who was outraged at my audacity for criticizing his work of art. I went to Dick and I said, "Look, do you want me to do this?" And he said, "Yes." I said, "Okay, let's start from the top. You can't show me as a twenty-year-old boy in school, that's out of the question. We have to start in the middle and somehow incorporate some of those early ideas into the script later. Now, if you don't want to go along with me on this, forget it. You go ahead and make the picture the way you want and I'll step out of it." He sort of gritted his teeth and said, "Will you give up golf to come here to the office every day and work with me on this?" I said yes.

So that's what we did: I went to his office and we'd kick this thing around and he'd say, "Okay, go play golf for two days and then come back." So I'd go play golf and come back and he'd have a series of scenes. The next few days we'd talk about them, tearing them apart, deciding what was right and what was wrong and so on. This went on for seven solid months until we got the screenplay you saw on the screen. It was a real collaboration, a labor of love—

and Dick, who is a very difficult man in many ways, became a dear friend, and we made *Elmer Gantry*.

CRIST: I gathered that you didn't end up enemies—because you worked with Brooks on *The Professionals*.

LANCASTER: That's right, and we did much the same thing on *The Professionals*. But the biggest problem we had with *Elmer Gantry* was censorship. In those days we still had a thing called the Legion of Decency, which represented the most powerful censorship group, the one producers were most afraid of. I know that I went to New York and spent three days with a monsignor whose name escapes me, discussing the final line of the picture. It was a different line from what you heard here. It came at the end of the scene where I walk out of the burning church, and down the street. Then Arthur Kennedy yells after me, "See you around, brother." In the present version of the film I just turn around and look back at him and walk away without saying anything. But in the original version, I say, "See you in *hell*, brother." The clerics nearly *died* on that one. But I kept saying, that's what will happen, Gantry is going to hell, he *wants* to go to hell—as all of us are going to go to hell, so to speak. To me it represented the whole reevaluation of what Gantry had gone through and what he was doing, how he was corrupting people. But no dice. The censors thought it was the most vicious thing we could say. They let us use all kinds of damns and hells, but we couldn't have that last line. But, funnily enough we used it in *Buffalo Bill*, at the end of the scene with Newman, who's very angry about what I said to him. I'm getting on my horse to ride away and Buffalo Bill rushes out and very weakly says, "Ned." I turn around and he says, "See you around, Ned." And I say, "See you in *hell*, brother . . ."

CRIST: Despite all that, *Elmer Gantry* was at the time considered a courageous and controversial film. We've come a long way in dealing with religious subjects. By the way, was Jean Simmons married to Dick Brooks at the time?

LANCASTER: No, but their romance started then.

CRIST: She gave a stunning performance in this—was it your casting or Dick's?

LANCASTER: Brooks cast the film. The only one I was accidentally responsible for casting was Shirley Jones. Dick and I looked at a great many Ingmar Bergman films, because we were looking for someone quite different. And although we saw some provocative-looking women, they weren't right, they weren't American enough. Then one night, at home watching television, I saw a Red Skelton movie dealing with the period of the early movies, in which he played a comic who became very famous and then became a terrible person. He married three or four times, always to the wrong women, but he always recalled that there was this girl, a film extra, whom he liked very much, but he never considered her as a wife. She winds up as a drunkard in the drunk tank. Shirley was marvelous in that role, and everybody had thought of Shirley as the girl from *Oklahoma* and that's it. I told Brooks about her and he said, "Oh, no, she can't act, she just sings and dances." I told him to look at that film and he agreed that I was absolutely right. She won an Academy Award for *Gantry*.

FROM AUDIENCE: Why hasn't Arthur Kennedy gotten as far as you and many others? I remember being stunned by him in *Death of a Salesman*.

LANCASTER: I don't know what to say. Certainly Arthur is a very fine actor, very engaging, very attractive. There must be an answer to why someone emerges as a star—some underlying charisma. But maybe that isn't even true. I remember the first time I saw Tyrone Power, and it was clear that this beautiful human being, who was a capable and smooth actor, was going to be a star. He was a beautiful man. There's that aspect of it. Then there's someone like Jimmy Dean, with a unique personality. Brando is perhaps the prime example of someone who combines good looks, animal magnetism, and absolutely superb talent, so it was clear he would be a star. It was understood from the very beginning that Monty Clift was going to be a star. Arthur was a superb actor, but he didn't make it on that level—and I don't know why.

You know, when I went out to Hollywood I went through this numerology bit and they wanted to change my name from Burt Lancaster to Stephen Chase. Then somebody said, "Oh, no, Stephen Chase is an economist." When I went to see [Mark] Hellinger after I decided to do *The Killers,* he asked me, "What's your real name?" I said Burton Lancaster. He said, "What's this talk about Stephen Chase? What's wrong with Burt Lancaster?" So Burt Lancaster was found again, thank God.

FROM AUDIENCE: I've been involved in making a small independent film and we had so many problems, so many personality conflicts, we were just happy to get it all over with. It was not a joyous experience. I'd like to know, based on your long experience, if there are special methods of handling people and situations in the film-making process.

LANCASTER: I would have to know more about the human structure of the particular group with which you worked to make any comment on what went wrong. Filmmaking at its best does become a viable give-and-take kind of thing. When you're working with a man like Bob Altman, for instance, anybody can come in and comment on the rushes, or comment on the script. He's the kind of director who does not hesitate to open it all up. Actually, what he's doing is picking your brains. However, he's an absolute, solid, 100 percent authority figure—and there's no question when he says, "Well, that's a lovely idea, but I don't think we can use that." That's the end of it, period.

I don't know what goes wrong in some instances. In movie-making a certain amount of turmoil is essential, but handling it requires a certain professionalism. There has to be a hierarchical line in which people will have enough respect for those at the top that they will do what they're supposed to do. Making movies is not as though you are working on your own, as an artist or writer. Good painters and good writers—no matter what you hear about them—are all very disciplined people. When we did *The Rose Tattoo* we shot a good deal of it near Tennessee Williams's house in Key West. He would get up every morning at eight o'clock and go into his garage, which was fitted out as an office. And for four hours—*four hours*—he'd write; not a soul would disturb him. After those four hours he'd come out and have his first martini, then about two in the afternoon he'd go swimming. He had to swim under doctor's orders because he had a heart condition. As a matter of fact, he had a cage built for him to swim out in the ocean and protect him from the sharks, which were all over the place. Then in the afternoon he'd take a nap and in the evening he'd start on his drinking—and he'd drink like hell. But no matter what time he went to bed, at one or two in the morning, every morning at eight he'd be in there working. No matter what you do there has to be some structure that everybody adheres to. There can be personality problems and shouting and screaming and all, but when the bell rings, baby, you have to go to work and do it. You have to gear your mind to it. And there comes a point when you also have to say, "We've got to go with this, this is the best we have. We'll worry about how it's received later. We've put our hearts and souls into this, we've broken our backs ... let's make the film." When you go into a film, in my position—or that of any other actor—you can never be sure how it's going to be put together. You've heard the old complaint that "my best performance is on the cutting-room floor." In most cases that's not true—if you have talented, caring people who fit your performance into the slot where it belongs, and who are presenting you at your most cohesive and best. You have to say to yourself, These people are responsible for *this*, and I have to be responsible only for *that*. Working with Bob Altman was something of a turn for me, not through any fault of Bob's—he's a highly creative man and wide open to ideas. But I did something I hadn't done in years. The character I played, Ned Buntline, tells these grandiloquent stories—and you don't know whether they are true or not. I had pages of dialogue, as every scene I was in started out with one of these stories.

Now, I have a twofold problem as an actor—I have to be extraordinarily entertaining, and I run the risk, after telling two or three stories, of being an utter bore. The characters playing around me in *Buffalo Bill* regard me as such after a while—but you, the audience, must never regard me as a bore. So Altman shot it in such a way that the camera moved off me, came back, and moved around to give him the option to cut if my performance began to sag in places. Now if my performance held up, I could stay on longer; if it didn't he'd have the opportunity to cut. We knew this, and we worried about it—I kept trying to cut my speeches down. However, I didn't know for sure how he worked. In a normal give-and-take scene, say I'm having dialogue with you—"*What are you doing home at this hour?*" "What do you mean?" "*You were out with Sam, weren't you, you cunt?*" "Don't you call me a cunt." That kind of scene is simple, you know you're going to be angry and jealous, or whatever. As long as my understanding is solid of what's going on in the scene, I can almost ad lib dialogue. But when you get up and make a speech, or tell a story, nobody is helping you—people are sitting there looking at you, and they may turn away, which is a peculiar feeling. You have to have enormous confidence that you're going to get back your audience. Anyway, I took the script of *Buffalo Bill* and sat with a dialogue coach, an actor friend, for two solid weeks. Every day for three hours a day at my house in Malibu we went over these lines, these stories. It was very dull, very boring work, but very essential.

And thank God I did it, because when I got up to the location I found out that Bob likes to work in this way. He'll set up the scene, we stand there and talk about it, and he says, "You'll move here." And I say, "I'll do this," and he says, "At this point you're not going to be drunk." And I say, "*Right.*" And we talk about it very openly. Now the lights are all set, he brings the other actors in and tells them, "You keep saying your lines and don't listen to this man, talk over him." He says all kinds of things that are totally confusing to an actor. It was like a first-time experience. He'll take three takes and say, "That's it, baby," and you haven't rehearsed at all. Well, I *really* had to be on top of it in this, I had to know what I was talking about. Now I could have come in as a prima donna, walking in and saying, "Wait a minute, I don't know these lines, we've gotta rehearse about ten times." I think if I'd done that, Bob would have had little alternative—he couldn't have fired me then, it was too late in the day. But it would have been upsetting to him. So, this picture really imposed a challenge that I had to rise to. I had to prepare myself for it.

FROM AUDIENCE: Can you give us more of an idea about your own work habits, how you prepare for a role?

LANCASTER: There are some pictures in which, by their very nature, all you have to do is bring your own presence. Here's Burt Lancaster, cowboy. But when you have to reach for something, such as a film I made called *Valdez Is Coming,* well, I talked to a well-known language teacher about what kind of language difficulties a Mexican would have living in the southwest United States during the 1890s, what sort of an accent he might have. Then I went to Los Angeles City College and talked to people in the Mexican-Chicano Studies area. I got a lot of good advice from them. And we had a script boy who was Mexican; I asked him about what it was like being a Mexican living in the United States—even today. He told me a story, that when he was a little boy, having just come to America, he went to school and the teacher would say to him, "Why do you hang your head like that? You're in America now; look at me when you talk to me." Then, he'd go home at night and look up to his father instead of hanging his head, and his father slapped him across the face. My friend said he grew up living in two worlds. In the Mexican scheme of things, you had to have a certain diffidence toward respected figures; it was bad manners to pretend to be equal with them. Well, I used this concept in the early stages of my character, until he went through the experience of literally being crucified. Then he became another person.

So that's one way to prepare for a role. But there are other kinds of roles, say in *Vera Cruz*. That character is Burt Lancaster having a lot of fun—that's all. I did practice shooting the guns until I was an expert at it. That I did. But when I was in *The Flame and the Arrow* or *Crimson Pirate* that was just Burt Lancaster swinging around on bars and trying to be charming. I didn't have to go study a character.

FROM AUDIENCE: Do you ever have any trouble working with other stars? I mean, maybe other stars would not want to be in a film with you because you'd get the attention.

LANCASTER: Oh, I think it's quite the opposite. Most actors are anxious to be in a film with a star. Know what I mean? Well, maybe they may not want to be, but their reasons for not wanting to are because of the kind of fear you talk about.

In *Vera Cruz*, for example, Gary Cooper told me a story after we started working together and became very good friends. Cooper said, "You know, Gable warned me not to do this picture." I'd never met Clark Gable. I said, "What do you mean?" Gable had pointed out the fact that I had just done *From Here to Eternity*, and he said to Cooper, "That young fella will wipe you off the screen, Gary." And I said, "Well, I haven't wiped you off the screen yet, have I?" And that was it. Later I did a film with Gable.

I think that some people who develop a fear of being with other actors, maybe they're losing confidence somehow, beginning to get old and feeling they can't vie with a younger person. Certainly if I worked in a film with, say, Robert De Niro . . . in fact, I just did a film for Bertolucci with De Niro, *1900*, which isn't out yet. But I didn't have scenes with De Niro. I played a grandfather, along with Sterling Hayden, and we did a number of scenes together. We had a great rapport. He's the kind of fellow who, when he sees you, hands you a great big jug of wine and says, "Have a drink." Later, you're sitting there stunned, and stoned, and he says, "It's great fun working with you." Very cute.

But it's always challenging, and there's always a certain amount of fear. In *From Here to Eternity*, in my first scene with

Monty Clift I couldn't stop my knees from shaking. He was so powerful in that scene. It took about three or four rehearsals before I could settle down, but in subsequent scenes I was perfectly at ease with him. You also have to know people. It's important—you cannot work with an actor, a man or woman, without getting to know something about them; you draw from them, they give you something of their personality. If you feel some animosity toward other actors, that can affect your performance and you have to fight like hell to overcome that. Once in a while you run into that situation, working with someone who's unsympathetic—in your terms at least—which causes tension. You have to be totally relaxed when you're acting. Regardless of what big or little talent you have, you can never express it unless you're completely at ease. Of course, there's a kind of tension about performing—but it's a relaxed tension, there's fun in it.

FROM AUDIENCE: Part of the excitement of your performances is that, even when you are subdued, it always looks as if you're about to explode.

LANCASTER: I used to have that. I think it has to do with the way I move. Plus, I am a very intense person, it's true—perhaps that intensity is there and you see it. I used to be quite explosive in the early days. If I thought a director was doing something wrong, I'd be furious. I would argue with him. I remember I had a terrible argument the second film I did, called *Desert Fury*. I can't remember the incident, but the director, an Englishman named Lewis Allen, a sweet man, by the way—he wanted me to do something and I said, "No, that's not right, I'm not going to do it." I turned around and walked to the dressing room and the assistant director came after me whispering, "Burt, you gotta great career, don't do this." I said, "Oh, fuck the career, I'm not going to do it, that's all." And I didn't do it. I had a big argument with Anatole Litvak, in *Sorry, Wrong Number*. But Litvak finally said he could see I was right. If he had wanted me to do something I felt was wrong, I wouldn't have cared what the consequences were, I wouldn't do it.

Well, you know, you mature and you mellow and you realize scenes don't solve anything. So you try other ways. Now, when I run into a situation like that, I'll tell a director how I feel. When I did *A Child Is Waiting*, which was John Cassavetes's first Hollywood picture, I played a character with Judy Garland where I get angry at her. Cassavetes really wanted me to be angry, to rip into it, tear her to pieces, tell her she's a fucking idiot. I said, "John, I can't do that. I'm playing a doctor, a man of enormous responsibility; even if I felt that anger, I'd have to handle it." The character, I felt, would have enough control that he wouldn't succumb to the anger. I told John I thought he was all wet, "But if you want to do it your way, we'll try it." So I played it his way. And I was furious. The next day Stanley Kramer comes in and says, "I just saw the rushes, what were you doing in that scene? You look ridiculous." I looked over at John, and John was very sweet. He said, "Burt didn't want to do it that way, but I asked him to." So we did it over and I told John later, "Johnny, you can't do that . . . you cannot take an actor, even if you're right, when he is so *against* something, and make him do it. You've got to find some other way of doing it that he can live with—and make it right." He said, "Yes, you're right." And we became very good friends after that.

I did this film *Airport* with George Seaton, the director, who's a very lovely man. The film at best is a cockamamie film. But, anyway, Seaton was also the writer, so he had pride of author-ship—and I could sense he was inimical to the idea that I might want to do anything. He had heard about this difficult actor. And so, what I did, very quietly, I went to lunch with him and told him about different things, that I didn't feel right about my character's relationship to his wife, that something felt missing. I imposed the idea on him of "What can I do to help?" And the next thing you know, I got him to rewrite all my scenes. I know how to handle a man like that. You live and you learn, and with luck, you mature.

[After *The Scalphunters*]

CRIST: I'm very fond of this movie, and I sense that you share that feeling, Burt. I was curious about how you met Sydney Pollack, and how this project came about.

LANCASTER: I was making a film in 1960 called *The Young Savages*, and John Frankenheimer directed it. There were three young men in the cast, three actors from the barrios of New York, who had never made a film before—and they turned out to be very refreshing, very good actors—who were coached by Sydney Pollack. Pollack used to teach at Sandy Meisner's school in New York, the Neighborhood Playhouse—he and Mark Rydell were there at the same time, in fact, as instructors. When John Frankenheimer was in New York doing the *Playhouse 90* episodes, he used to go to Sydney's class, and when he came to Hollywood to do this film, he brought Sydney with him to work as a dialogue director. Once in a while you find a dialogue director who is basically a director—and I watched Sydney on the set rehearsing with these three young kids, and I thought to myself, "This fellow is really talented."

At that time, the Music Corporation of America was begining to move over to Universal Studio to begin MCA Productions, and while they were in the process of forming this new production group, they were looking for new young directors to do their new television series and so forth. One day I went up to see Lou Wasserman, who was my agent, and told him I had met a very interesting, very talented young man working on this picture, and I thought MCA would be wise if it would use him as a director. Wasserman said, "Have him come up and see me." Well, Sydney had a call from Wasserman; he went to see him and he started directing television films for MCA. In about a year or so he won an Emmy. It seems there had been a mistake in his contract, allowing him to go out on his own, instead of being tied to a seven-year contract. So Sydney got out on his own and started making films. When we prepared *Scalphunters* I called Sydney to see if he would be interested. Now the writer on this was a man called Bill Norton, and he had no idea of the structure of a film or development of character. He just had a funny, backwoods way of talking and he had posed this exceptionally interesting idea. In the first eighteen pages of the script he had put down the story of a man who meets this runaway slave and takes him with him on the trail, to track down the Indians who stole his furs. But after page eighteen the story just fell apart. So we sat down—my friend Roland Kibbee and Bill Norton and myself—and began to work on the screenplay. Kibbee actually wrote the entire picture, although you won't see his name on it. The agreement was that Kibbee was the producer, Norton was the writer, I was the actor, Sydney was the director. Then we got Shelley Winters. [Laughs nostalgically.]

FROM AUDIENCE: You mentioned that you have five children—are any of them into films?

LANCASTER: I have a son who just wrote a screenplay called *The Bad-News Bears,* which you must go see fifty or sixty times. It stars Walter Matthau and Tatum O'Neal. My son's name is Bill Lancaster . . . he was the boy who played in the *Moses* series with me as young Moses, in the first episode of the six one-hour shows. I think he's very talented—I say with parental pride.

FROM AUDIENCE: I think one of the most underrated films you did was *A Child Is Waiting*. What was it like working with Judy Garland?

LANCASTER: Well, it was difficult at that time, to be honest. I mean, Garland was drinking a great deal, and it was a big effort to get together and get in shape to work. There was no personal problem in working with her, but she was in a period of her life where she just wasn't together. I had to kind of nurse her along with it. And because of her mental condition at the time, she wasn't terribly involved in the part. That picture came about in a strange way. I was asked by Stanley Kramer to look at the television version that Abby Mann had written. We saw it, and I felt that nobody would want to see that picture—except people who have retarded children. But I said, why don't we do it as a kind of public-service thing: we'll all get together and put in maybe $25,000 apiece and do it for $200,000 or so. The picture wound up costing considerably more than that. Ingrid Bergman was supposed to play the female lead, and Jack Clayton was supposed to direct. I came in as a third party.

Suddenly the whole thing blew up. I don't know whether there's any truth to this at all, but I heard that Jack Clayton didn't want to work with me. I said, "Why?" It was evidently because I had fired Alexander MacKendrick. Which was true, we fired him when he did *Devil's Disciple*—but that's another story. MacKendrick is the man who did *Sweet Smell of Success*, and he's a brilliant man. The reasons we fired him had nothing to do with his artistic ability; it had to do with the fact that we had a limited budget.

MacKendrick—when we did *Sweet Smell of Success*—was brilliant, absolutely brilliant, but very indecisive about what he wanted to settle for. Here's the kind of thing he'd do: We had a shot one day near the end of the picture with Susan Harrison, Tony [Curtis], and myself, in which MacKendrick had *forty-five* camera movements on a dolly. We practiced from about nine in the morning to four in the afternoon—just for the camera moves. And at the same time we actors were getting all rehearsal time in so we got very good in this scene. About four in the afternoon, Sandy said let's try a take. Now, mind you, when you see a crab dolly which can move forward, back, sideways, and at the same time the cameraman can zoom in for a closeup or back for a full shot, the work of the dolly has to be perfect. We shot three scenes in a row—and the crew was absolutely perfect. After we got it, Sandy said, "No . . . I don't like it, I don't like it. Let's start all over again." I said, "Whoa, wait a minute, Sandy." I was the producer of the film—that is, my partner and I were—and I said, "You can't do this, we've spent all day on this scene, at $5,000 a day. If you throw this out we've wasted a whole day. I think the scene is marvelous . . . you've got to be more sure of yourself." It *was* marvelous, of course. Well, that picture, which started out with a budget of $600,000, wound up costing something like $2.6 million.

So, when we finally got around to doing *Devil's Disciple*, we said, "Sandy, we've got $1.5 million—if we go over that it's going to come out of our own pockets. Can you do this in a forty-eight-day schedule?" He said, "No question about it, don't worry about a thing." And we said, "Sandy, we're going to have to let you go if you don't stay on schedule—we just can't take it." Well, we shot for one week and we had two days' worth of film—incidentally, the *best* two days of the picture. Then we got a fellow called Guy Hamilton; he did some of the Bond pictures. A very nice man, but not in the same league with MacKendrick. Of course the British press destroyed us for firing our director, and we just had to take our lumps. So, anyway, Jack Clayton had heard about this and he thought I was a terrible fellow and said he didn't want to work with Lancaster. So, with *A Child Is Waiting*, suddenly Ingrid Bergman disappeared—and I didn't know what was happening. There I was with egg on my face.

So instead of getting $25,000 I got $500,000—but I wasn't particularly happy about that. I knew the picture wouldn't make any money—and it didn't. A lot of people, especially people who do have retarded children, were delighted with the picture—they felt it was instructive to them, compassionate to their problems and so on. But it never had a chance.

FROM AUDIENCE: Mr. Lancaster, where do you think the American film industry is today, and what do you think the future of films will be—in social comment, or entertainment, or what?

LANCASTER: Well, from the industry point of view, the American film industry, and the worldwide industry for that matter, is like any other industry—they're interested in making a profit. Their stockholders want to see those profits. But they've come to the conclusion that there is a new, developing audience—young people who have begun to search out films that the industry executives never thought had any entertainment quality. So things have opened up. Censorship has opened up. You can make virtually any kind of film now, say anything you want. There's no question that there's much more freedom. Nevertheless, the industry people proper are not interested in promulgating an art form. They are business people. If you make a film that's artistic and will make money, fine. Let me give you a perfect example. We started out in United Artists in 1953. Two very bright men, Arthur Krim and Bob Benjamin, two young lawyers, came up with an idea that was revolutionary in its time. When you went to the big studios to make a film, there was a studio overhead imposed on you, which was somewhere in the area of 50 percent. It was 65 percent at Metro. As competition increased, in some cases it dropped as low as 35 or 40 percent. When the film went overseas, the film would pay as high as 70 percent because a middleman was involved, and he takes his profit. Krim and Benjamin decided to try to break that pattern. And here's what they did: They came to Harold Hecht and myself and said they wanted to start this idea. "You go rent the stuff you need, stage space and equipment—instead of going to a studio." And they said you'll probably be able to do the film with an overhead of 20 to 25 percent. Which was true. You think of it this way. If you have a film for $1 million, the studio automatically puts it on the books as a million and a half. Now the film has to make a million and a half in rentals before you get a profit area. So we said great; we went out and rented space in sound studios. We rented costumes from someplace else, and there are outlets all over Hollywood for lighting equipment and so on. And we were able to do our pictures for hundreds of thousands of dollars less than if we had gone to a major studio. The first film we did for them, for UA, and they didn't have a dime, was *Apache,* which cost $900,000 and made $6 million. Now the next film we did for them was *Vera Cruz,* with a budget of $1.3 million and it actually went to $1.7 million. Included in that was a salary of $500,000 plus 10 percent of the gross for Gary Cooper. That picture grossed, the first time around, something like $9 million or $10 million. At the same time I was directing a picture called *The Kentuckian* which, interestingly enough, was the most expensive picture we did. It cost $2 million but it grossed $6 million. So again we were ahead of the game.

Then we were preparing a film called *Marty.* The budget on *Marty* was $250,000, and I used to sit at night in Kentucky where we were shooting *The Kentuckian* and I'd say, "Listen, there's this new writer—marvelous, just listen to this." And I read to them from Paddy Chayefsky's script. Right after that I did *Vera Cruz*, and Max Youngstein—who was the third major executive at UA— came down to the set and said to me, "We don't want to do this *Marty*." I said, "What do you mean you don't want to do it?" He said, "Burt, you're gonna pay $250,000 for the picture and you're going to get bombed by the time you pay for prints and adver- tising—it's going to get up to $600,000. And who wants to see a picture with two ugly people?" That's exactly the phrase he used. So I said, "Look, it only costs $250,000. You know you've got an estimated gross on the current picture at about $6 million. You know that this picture with Cooper and me is going to go through the roof. I think you people have a responsibility to underwrite new talent. If you don't want to do it, fine—let's break up our relation- ship and you go your way and we'll go ours." I was a big enough *macher* in those days—I was a *gontser macher*, as Tony Curtis called it—to have them say, "Okay, Burt, don't get excited, we'll do it." They did it. Now *Marty* went out and became the most presti- gious film of its time. It won the Cannes award, it won the Acad- emy Award. Ernie Borgnine won an award. It won the Berlin award, the Moscow award, and, of course, you couldn't count in terms of dollars and cents what that meant to United Artists.

Now all the stars—the Kirk Douglases, the Gregory Pecks, and the Bob Mitchums—they went to United Artists, both because they were saving money and because UA took no artistic control no matter what you did. Once they accepted the script, they turned their backs on it. So you didn't have to worry about the interference of studio heads and that kind of thing. But Youngstein came to me many years later and said, "Let me show you some- thing, Burt, now that it's all over. You *made* us, God knows—but *Marty* has grossed $5.5 million to date in the whole world. *Vera Cruz* has grossed $11 million. That's what we mean, we *want* the $11 million gross—to hell with the Academy Award." Now, they don't quite mean that because, like everyone else, UA yearns for recognition and prestige. But what they said is an elemental truth about the movie business.

So to get back to what you originally asked—the industry is interested in *Jaws*, in *Towering Inferno*. That's all they really care about. Fine, if you want to do something about the ills of the world—if it'll make a buck, they're with you, if it won't, forget it.

That fight will be constant, constant in the industry. But there's still no question about it, you now can do practically anything you want to do—and I see no reason for that to change unless there's a terrible political change, and censorship and fascism come in. So there is that whole look of freedom now, certainly in the artistic field.

FROM AUDIENCE: Is the Hecht-Hill-Lancaster Company still in existence?

LANCASTER: No, it was dissolved, as a matter of fact, in 1958. We were in terrible hot water—about $6 million in the hole. I personally had to do four pictures at a very minimal salary for me, $185,000 a picture, to write off that $6 million.

SAME AUDIENCE: Where did you blow it?

LANCASTER: We blew it by the fact that, you see, we started doing our pictures, taking each picture at a time. Now, Harold and myself and another chap by the name of James Hill—who worked very well with writers—we did one picture at a time. We spent nine months sometimes, not doing anything else but working on that one picture. We'd purchase properties, but we wouldn't get into them. And Harold, who's a businessman, said, "Burt, we can't exist this way." We had seventy people working for us. We had a nut of over $1 million a year just paying secretaries and writers and things of this kind. And it began mounting up. In spite of our successes, we began to hit a period where our films didn't make money. We did *Bachelor Party*, which didn't make money. We did *Separate Tables*, which lost money. A number of other things. Plus all the other properties—several millions of dollars in properties we had bought. We couldn't work any other way. We should have stayed a small company. In fact, they wanted Harold to take over Metro at the time; he didn't want to but I encouraged him because that's what he was good at; he was a man who could keep his hand in a thousand things. But he, too, when it came to our own projects, would worry it to death. Long after we had a script and a cast we thought was fine, he'd say, "Well, I'm not sure about this." Or I'd say, "I'm not sure about this." Or Jim Hill would say, "I think we can improve this." And the next thing you know we're jerking off for six more months on the script and never getting a picture done. So we got to a particular point where we just dissolved the company.

FROM AUDIENCE: What picture has been the most financially rewarding one for you—not necessarily artistically rewarding, but lucrative?

LANCASTER: *Airport*. Well, it turned out that way. The film was a runaway hit, it did $55 million or $60 million—and I had a piece of the gross. So did Dean Martin. Nobody expected it to happen. I felt it would be a popular picture, primarily because it was a bestseller—so people would go to see it whether they hated it or not. But it went way beyond everybody's expectations.

[After *Birdman of Alcatraz*]

CRIST: I understand that you did get to know Robert Stroud while you were preparing *Birdman of Alcatraz*.

LANCASTER: First they allowed me to see Stroud in the warden's office. The next day they let me go visit Stroud in his rooms in the hospital, and be totally alone with him for as long as I liked. The doctor told me that he'd be dead within a year. In the meantime, he had written another book, which involved the law case. The government was trying to maintain that the memoirs he had written while in prison belonged to them, and Stroud's lawyer was trying to let him just publish them as part of his memoirs. The manuscript contained many of Stroud's ideas about the prison system, the rehabilitation process, what was wrong with the system, and so on. He was obviously a very interesting, highly intelligent man. There was then a big law case in Kansas City in 1963, in which the government attempted to obtain possession of his book. Stroud won the case. It was the first time in years that he'd been outside of prison other than when he was transferred from Alcatraz to Springfield. But he died shortly thereafter—as the doctor had predicted. He never was free.

An interesting thing occurred with Stroud at this particular point—his parole automatically came up for review every year. And he insisted on total freedom—no strings. The authorities told me at the time that they were afraid that Stroud had reached the point of total senility, and they were afraid he might get involved in some sexual perversion dealing with little children. That's the way they put it, at least, that he would become a menace to society. He didn't want any nurses, any supervision of any kind. He just wanted to get out.

Stroud was really a fantastic figure. Perhaps he was afraid to leave, I really don't know. He was now a man about 70 and he'd gone to jail when he was 19. He was in prison for something like fifty-two years, with forty-two of that in solitary. There was no one living anymore—except a sister, who was apparently not well. This was another reason the government just could not turn him loose: there had to be someone to care for him.

FROM AUDIENCE: Wasn't it true that he did kill a prison guard . . . and that's something you can't get away with, isn't it?

LANCASTER: Yes, he did kill a prison guard, so that was another reason for lack of leniency in his case. Also, Stroud was a very mean, tough man—he made no bones about it. How much was due to the fact that he really was like this, and how much due to the fact that he was a prisoner for so long . . . we really don't know.

FROM AUDIENCE: How long did it take you to make *Birdman of Alcatraz*?

LANCASTER: The actual shooting was broken up in two parts. We did the entire film, other than the work I had to do with the birds, first. During that period, for about three weeks, I went to do the role in *Judgment at Nuremberg*. After that we started on this film again, and I worked for about two weeks just with the birds. There were some experiences with that. We had about two thousand canaries flown in from Japan. They died like flies. We had a man on the set who worked with the birds. One of the tricks with the birds is that I'd get into a very small cubicle with a sparrow or a canary, and the trainer would take the bird and pull a few feathers from it, which would prevent it from flying. It could only hop around. The feathers grew back, by the way. So I would put my hand near the bird and take some seed, and the bird would hop into my hand. We did this very patiently to get the birds to come to me.

FROM AUDIENCE: Have you ever played a role that has affected your personal life after you finish it?

LANCASTER: One of the problems an actor faces, and it's a very dangerous thing, is to get so involved in a role he loses control of what he's doing. With *Birdman of Alcatraz*—I couldn't stop crying throughout the film. I mean, if there was a line when someone said, "Sorry, Stroud, you can't have your parole," I'd burst into tears. John Frankenheimer would say, "Oh, that's wonderful, wonderful." I said, "Oh no, John, let the audience cry—not me." But I got so emotionally wrapped up in the part. And, as you say, when the film was all over, I felt like I'd lost a child or something: a depressive sort of feeling does carry over. That's true.

FROM AUDIENCE: Was *Birdman* a financial success?

LANCASTER: No. I admitted yesterday that situation in which I had to do four other films to write off some basic losses we had. And this was one of them. Part of the deal I had with United Artists was that with each one of these four pictures they would allocate $1.5 million against the cost, which was, of course, a tax write-off for them. They could pick up their loss. So the picture was budgeted at $2.5 million—and now it became a $4 million picture. At that rate it would have had to gross maybe $10 million before it got into the profit area. The film has grossed $8 million throughout the world—not exactly a loss for them. But no gain for me.

FROM AUDIENCE: Mr. Lancaster, is there any role you haven't done that you hope to do in the future?

LANCASTER: Not really, nothing haunting me. I was asked many years ago to do Hamlet, and later Macbeth. I just don't think I have the confidence in myself to think that I might be able to do something like that. My instincts have been to do something in which I feel more secure—which usually is something that is current, easily identifiable in our world today. Like Stroud. I have strong feelings about our prison system—and I could throw myself into a character like that. It really comes down to the basic fact that I didn't have the guts to do something like Hamlet.

FROM AUDIENCE: Many people in your profession were blacklisted in the 1950s; did you have any involvement?

LANCASTER: I don't want to make this a political discussion, but, in answer to your question, yes. And this relates to problems I've had in making motion pictures. I had my passport taken away. I was reputed to be a card-carrying Communist. I was asked by Jack Warner to sign a loyalty oath—and I refused. In a very small way, certainly not comparable to what others had suffered, I was on blacklists but my position as a star was strong enough, and, of course, there was no evidence whatsoever that I'd had any Communist affiliations. I had some problems, but they didn't amount to much in comparison to some people's.

FROM AUDIENCE: It's often said that film is a director's medium, and the actor is really secondary. But you seem to have brought so much to the movies you've made—is that just because of you and your own personality?

LANCASTER: In the old days you had the star system—and in effect, the director was under orders from studio heads to use the beautiful people in that way and stories were written that showed them off in the most glamorous way. And yet, in spite of that, good directors managed to get good stories and do meaningful work and work out a rapport with the actor. It's true that the tendency now is more toward the director who wants to tell his story—and depending on the quality of the material, actors will submit to the will of the director if that person has enormous talent, and in the long run they will benefit by it, too. So it varies. And of course all good artists, effective artists with personalities of their own, will affect to a great extent what any director wants to do. My experience is that first-class directors have no fear about what would be termed an actor's interference. Good directors are very sure of themselves; like all good creative people, they are open to ideas. They can take them and put them into their focus.

FROM AUDIENCE: You seem to be one superstar who has no hesitation in working with other superstars. You mentioned Gary Cooper, and you've worked a few times with Kirk Douglas, and I wonder how you two get along, since he too is a very powerful actor.

LANCASTER: Kirk Douglas happens to be a very, very close friend of mine. We were both under contract to Hal Wallis and very good friends socially. But I didn't get very close to Kirk until we did *Gunfight at the O.K. Corral.* Hal Wallis wanted me to do it. I didn't want to—but I had two pictures left under my contract with him and I wanted to finish that. Kirk would call me up and say, "Are you going to do Wyatt Earp?" I asked why. And he said, "Well, Wallis wants me to do Doc Halliday—but I don't want to do it. If you do it, I'll do it." I said, "Kirk, I really don't know yet." Finally, I proposed to Mr. Wallis that I would like to do *The Rainmaker*—in which he had planned to use William Holden. Or so he said. I told Wallis I wanted to do these two pictures back to back. And it's true, the Monday after I finished *O.K. Corral* we started *The Rainmaker.* Or was it vice versa? Anyway, I did one of them immediately after the other.

But the particular script that Leon Uris had written on *O.K. Corral* was terribly long and wordy. I asked Mr. Wallis to get another writer at least to do some kind of editing. He didn't want to do it, so I personally got a writer and paid him two thousand dollars a week. I put him in Mr. Wallis's office and I wouldn't let Wallis go out to lunch even; we had to send for sandwiches. We sat in that office for two solid weeks while this man, who was a very good constructionist and understood the dialogue better and was a historian of the West, helped us cut sixty or seventy pages from the script to reduce it to minimal dialogue. Kirk found out about it and he called me and said, "I've read the new script and I think it's wonderful." And he said, "Goddamit, why didn't I do something like that?" He thought it was very admirable—so did I! I said to him, "You know what we've got to do with Wyatt and Doc? We're playing two pre-Freudian fags. We're in love with each other and we don't know how to express ourselves that way—so we just kind of look at each other and grunt and don't say very much, but you know we love each other." I said, "If we can get that idea across we'll have a good film—because there's plenty of action in it."

And in a peculiar kind of way, that's what did come across. Originally he had long speeches by the fire talking about his childhood, and I had long speeches. I said, "We've got to get rid of this junk. This is a Western, and we have to get across the relationship simply by how we relate to each other." And it worked. So, after that, Kirk and I became close friends. When you talk about working with Kirk as a challenge . . . it's always marvelous when you have other big, important people in a film, if the script gives them something to work with and be important too. It always works better.

SAME AUDIENCE: It works, I think, if you have confidence in yourself—which you obviously do.

LANCASTER: Well, in those areas I have confidence. Otherwise, I'm scared to death about most things.

In 1982 Burt Lancaster won his fourth Best Actor Award from the New York Film Critics and an Oscar nomination for his role in Atlantic City. *In 1983 he appeared in* Local Hero. *He co-starred with Kirk Douglas in* Tough Guys *(1986) and with Kevin Costner in* Field of Dreams *(1989).*

Cliff Robertson

▼▼

California-born Cliff Robertson got his first acting job at a summer theater in the Catskill Mountains. Soon he was in New York City appearing in Off-Broadway roles and in 1953 he starred on Broadway in Late Love. The Wisteria Trees, The Lady and the Tiger, *and* Orpheus Descending *are among his other Broadway credits. Throughout the 1950s and early '60s Robertson took leading roles in a number of television dramas—many of them broadcast live—on such prestigious shows as the* Philco-Goodyear Playhouse, Studio One, *and* Playhouse 90. *These included the original productions of* Days of Wine and Roses *and* The Two Worlds of Charly Gordon. *Robertson acquired the film rights to* Charly *and won an Academy Award in 1969 for reprising the role on screen.*

Among the forty-plus movies Robertson has made are Picnic *(1955),* The Naked and the Dead *(1958),* Gidget *(1959),* PT 109 *(in which he played the young John F. Kennedy, 1963),* The Best Man *(1964),* Masquerade *(1965),* The Honey Pot *(1967), and* J.W. Coop. *(1972). Robertson wrote, produced, directed, and starred in* J.W. Coop. *He visited Tarrytown on November 26–28, 1976.*

[After *Charly*]

CRIST: Cliff Robertson and I go way back to when I was a girl reporter and he was a boy astronaut. I was doing a feature about his kiddie television show for the New York *Herald Tribune* and Cliff invited me into his spaceship—and that's all you're going to hear about that!

ROBERTSON: That was *Rod Brown of the Rocket Rangers,* 1953.

CRIST: In those days, Cliff, you were earning a great reputation in the theater: you made your movie debut in *Picnic* in 1955 and went on to a great variety of roles. But with *Charly,* which we've just seen, you did get your Best Actor Oscar. And because in many ways that's a turning point in a career—why don't we start with how you came to *Charly?*

ROBERTSON: In the years before *Charly*—which you can call BC—I had done a number of things on television or on stage that had been rather warmly received by the critics and the public—only to see these properties ultimately bought for some superstar to do in films. I was beginning to get an "always a bridesmaid, never a bride" complex. I had done the original Tennessee Williams play *Orpheus Descending* on Broadway with Maureen Stapleton—only to see it done on film by Marlon Brando, an actor of consummate talent for whom I have great respect. The movie version, as you know, was called *The Fugitive Kind,* and it was disappointing, it just wasn't up to Marlon's usual standards and the movie wasn't that well received. Maureen Stapleton, who had played the lead with me on stage, was given a minor role in the movie, and her leading role was given to Anna Magnani. I had also done a television show that received a lot of attention, which ultimately ended up as a film called *The Hustler.* And, of course, Paul Newman played that role and I again was sitting in the wings. Then, out in California I had done *Career,* only to see Tony Franciosa play my role in the movie. And the final, crowning, inglorious gesture was when I did *Days of Wine and Roses* on *Playhouse 90,* along with Piper Laurie, and in spite of marvelous reviews everywhere, the next thing I knew Jack Lemmon had proceeded to obtain the rights to the property and he was able to put a package together where he played my role in the film—which was directed not by John Frankenheimer but by Blake Edwards—with Lee Remick in Piper's role.

I did not see that particular film, so I really can't comment on it. But I think that probably one of the most flattering things anyone has said to me—and I have to give Jack credit—when he didn't win the Academy Award for that picture he said to me, in a kidding-but-on-the-square way, "You son-of-a-bitch—if you hadn't done that role first, I'd have an Oscar in my hand right now." That was a testimonial to a certain grace on his part, but at the same time, I guess, I had regrets.

This takes us to the beginning of *Charly*, which was originally a short story called "Flowers for Algernon," by Daniel Keyes. The Theatre Guild had it written as a dramatic show for their *U.S. Steel Hour* on TV, and the adaptation was called *The Two Worlds of Charly Gordon*. I was asked to play Charly. We had about six days of rehearsal—it was to be a live show, with all the inherent problems of tripping over cables and racing from scene to scene and hoping your fly was closed. At any rate, in the middle of the week of rehearsal, a very fine actor named Gerald O'Loughlin said to me one day, "Cliff, you're doing a helluva job. With your record, every time you do something well, some movie star ends up doing the movie. Who do you think will be doing this one?" I said, "Knowing Hollywood—maybe Debbie Reynolds."

I guess that conversation reinforced my feeling that somebody was trying to tell me something. I thought, Gee, am I always destined to be doing this? Am I going to be the Marnie Nixon of actors? Marnie Nixon, as you know, is the very fine singer who dubs her voice for movie stars who don't have her vocal qualities. Well, like a vision, something came to me and I said, "Maybe I should go to the mountain." Certainly nobody was going to bring the mountain to one Cliff Robertson, although I was fast gaining a good reputation as an actor. So I called my accountant and said, "I'd like to purchase the rights to this television show." He said, "You're crazy." I said, "Tell me something I really don't know."

After we did the show—which again was so wonderfully received—there were phone calls from the coast. The dialogue went something like this: "Cliff, that was a helluva show we saw last week. Query: We understand you have the rights to it." "Yes." "Hmm. Well, there might be something we can do—are you willing to sell it?" I'd say, "Yes, sure ... but, by the way, *I* go with it." There would be a long pause then, "Yeah, well, okay sweetheart, we'll get back to you." Well, seven years later they had never gotten back to me.

Meanwhile, I went on doing other things, including films. But they were obviously of less historical importance. I had a contract back in those days with Columbia Pictures, and I was pretty much forced to do what they handed me. But I did have an enviable record at Columbia; I went on suspension more than anyone for the period of time I was under contract. That was to me a very impressive record. The way it worked—they would call you in and hand you this piece of tripe and I'd read it, and say, "No, I really don't think so." They'd say, "Oh, yes." And I'd try to be diplomatic, saying things like, "This really isn't for me"—trying to hold on to a certain sense of integrity. They'd say, "Okay, you're under suspension." That meant I couldn't do another movie—but, thank God, I could do television, so I could at least pay the rent. The television shows kept me alive and in public view, and also helped me maintain some kind of standard as an actor. Slowly but surely the films they offered me got better.

Meanwhile, trying to get *Charly* off the ground became a seven-year crusade. Every time I tried to talk to the great myopic moguls, the dialogue would be, "Listen, kid, we know you'd do a helluva job—but it won't make a nickel at the box office." They'd even get out the files and start reading chapter and verse about other movies that had been done about mental retardation and how much money they'd lost. I argued, of course, that any movie's success depends on the ingredients that go into it. I felt the public needed something like this, to come out of the closet, if you will, as far as recognizing that mental retardation was an illness, it was something that respected no economic, social, or ethnic groups of people; it struck everywhere. So, it was time to confront it and not be ashamed to admit we had a child or a relative who's mentally retarded.

We spent seven years listening to "No . . . no . . . no." Or even worse, "You're crazy . . . you're crazy!" But, thank God, with that old obstinacy of some misplaced gene that came down from one of my revolutionary ancestors, I continued to hang in there. And I finally got a call from the late Selig Seligsman, God rest his soul, who was a big honcho with ABC Paramount—which is not to be confused with ABC Television. He said, "Cliff, I may be crazy and I know you've been getting a lot of turndowns on this for a long time. But you know, my wife, Muriel, has been kind of telling me I really ought to do that film with Cliff Robertson. So I'm going to go on a hunch, but you're going to have to give up a lot." And I said, "Listen, I'll give up anything except my relatives—or maybe even a few of those."

So I made the deal with ABC Paramount—and I was to play Charly. They gave me a list of directors that they would okay, and among them was Ralph Nelson. Now, he had come to me a couple of years before that and said, "If you ever get this picture made, I wish you'd consider me—I'd love to direct it." I remembered that, and Ralph was fine with the studio. Then we talked to some writers, and among them was Sterling Silliphant. We seemed to see eye to eye on where the screenplay should go. So that was how we got started.

Needless to say, I had a lot of ideas that had accumulated during this seven-year research period, and I was able to lay those out on Sterling. He was one of the most ego-less writers. So many writers, especially the younger ones, begin to be so defensive about every "if," "and," and "but"—and it begins to be a bit tiresome sometimes. But Sterling was a delight to work with. I wrote a number of scenes in it and they pretty much listened to me on the basic construction. The actual shooting style was not mine—it was Ralph Nelson's, but he was very generous and gave me a great deal of freedom.

We had two weeks of rehearsal in New York before we started shooting in Boston. We actually started with another actress, Anne Heywood, who turned out to be not quite right. So on thirty-six hours' notice, Claire Bloom came over from London and jumped right into it—and she was perfect. What a delight to work with—as was everybody on this picture. It was a happy experience.

FROM AUDIENCE: You obviously have a mobile, expressive face. But in the first part of the film did you have some special makeup to look more jowly? It was remarkable how the contours of your face changed.

ROBERTSON: No, no special makeup. I worked from the inside—but I'd had seven years of digesting the character. I can't explain it. I still think acting is one of the more mysterious art forms. I'll give you an example: the night before the first day's shooting my wife and I were preparing for bed and she said, "How're you going to play him?" That sort of stopped me. I said, "What do you mean by that?" She said, "*Physically*—how will you play him?" I said, "I don't know." She looked at me and said, "You've had this property for seven years—you've been to all these workshops, and you can't tell me how you see him?" I said, "No, at this minute I can't tell you." I went to work the next morning and Ralph asked me if I wanted a run-through, and I said, "No, crank 'em up." That's what is called "going with the instrument," I guess—I just went with it. But I had had seven years of osmosis—normally an actor doesn't have that privilege. So when you have that kind of background you *can* go with the instrument.

Normally, when I have, say, two months to think about a role, I'll cut it up in eighteen pieces and examine each piece of the character, all sides, look at it, then put it back together and look at it again. Then cut it up again, give the pieces different positions, so that I literally know the character so well that should the director ask me—and as a director I ask this—"Given a certain set of circumstances, what would this character do?" I would expect the actor to say, "Oh, this character would do this and that, but not the other thing." I feel you should know a character that well.

[After *J.W. Coop*]

CRIST: I really think *J.W. Coop* seems even better now—and I saw it a couple of times when it first came out. What about the genesis of this film, Cliff?

ROBERTSON: I have an uncle who has a ranch out in Colorado, and my wife and I and our daughter go out there occasionally. One night, after a couple of bourbons, he said, "Why don't you write a story about a contemporary cowboy who isn't some kind of Marlboro man, but a real, modern-day cowboy?" That planted a seed—so I thought about it for a while and finally decided it was time to do this story.

I wrote the story in what we call a step outline, about sixty pages. Then I got a job writing for money for someone else—and in trying to keep a schedule, I found I was falling behind on my own project. So a friend suggested that I get someone else to write a first draft—usually you have two or three drafts based on your story. I didn't like that idea too much, but my scheduling problems became rather desperate so finally I said okay. I couldn't afford any of these Hollywood writers, and didn't think they were right for it anyway. Someone put me in touch with a guy who'd never written a screenplay before. He said he'd like to try it, but he wouldn't do it without his partner. I said, well, fine. They retreated to wherever they went and ten days later they called me to say they had finished the script. I said, "Gee, I used to be a newspaper reporter and I know how to work fast, but that's really *fast*."

I read their script. They had completely thrown my story away—and they wrote a script about an ex–rodeo rider who was living in Mexico City with a girl and had turned into a dopehead. I don't know what they were using when they wrote it, but it was a pretty wild script. But Hollywood being what it is—and the Writers Guild having the rules it does—although these two guys weren't members of the WGA—that's why you see their names on the screen credits. That's okay. I threw that script away and subsequently wrote this story in about six weeks. If anybody asks you if the Academy Award means anything, aside from making a little more money, I can tell you that whereas it took me seven and a half years to get *Charly* made into a movie, with *J.W. Coop* it took me seven days. I sent it to three people, and all three said they wanted to do it. Columbia, being a studio with all its resources, was where I decided to go. They asked where I was going to shoot it and I said I didn't know exactly, but I knew where it would *not* be shot—and that's in Hollywood. We ended up shooting it in Texas and in central and northern California, and in New York City and Oklahoma. The studio also asked me how much I planned to do the film for. I said less than $800,000. They pointed out that if I could make *J.W. Coop* for under $800,000 I had to be the producer also, because I couldn't afford to pay a producer's fee with that kind of budget. That's where the fourth hat came in—and it's the one hat that really gave me a little bit of a headache, because producing is quite alien to writing, directing, and acting. But we did it.

I did the directing on one condition—that I could have a videotape camera, which I rented for $150 a week, to record every scene that I was in. Afterward, I'd pull up under this little canvas tarp and sit there and play back the tape of my performance just to see if I was doing the right kind of work. This allowed me to keep my director's hat off while I was acting. The problem of acting while you're directing is that when you're in a scene there's always one portion of your mind that's kind of measuring how it's going: you're not entirely objective. But with the videotape I was able to do that. And in the future, I will always use this system.

FROM AUDIENCE: Did you meet your budget?

ROBERTSON: Yes, we came in *under* it. We used a lot of tricks. I mean, everything is real. Whether you like it or not, it's an honest picture. About 80 percent of the people in it never acted before, they're all real people. We completed the film for $776,000.

CRIST: You shot *J.W. Coop* in about thirty-five days, didn't you?

ROBERTSON: Thirty-three days.

CRIST: This is one rodeo movie that shows you the real grit of rodeo. You get a variety of angles on the riders—and there's the one shot through the legs of the horse in pursuit of the bull.

FROM AUDIENCE: Where *was* the camera in that shot?

ROBERTSON: The camera was in front of some vital parts of the horse—I'll tell you that. I wanted that shot, but the cameraman just absolutely refused to try it. So I got together with this stuntman who was also an amateur photographer. I said, "Listen, let's rig up something with an 8mm camera and see if we can do it." So we strapped an 8mm camera to the horse's belly—and it worked okay.

I would never have created the rodeo atmosphere on a movie set—no way. The big reason our picture is so authentic is that I had gone to the Rodeo Cowboys' Association in Denver a long time before and told them I wanted to do this movie. They had never lent their active support to Hollywood on *any* rodeo movie—they're very insular, they go their way and Hollywood can do their thing and they don't want any truck with us. But I had one thing going for me—my uncle who's a rancher in Colorado. They knew that and they also knew I was trying to tell an honest story about rodeo, and then I showed them the script. And they allowed me to film at actual rodeos. On *Junior Bonner* poor Sam Peckinpah had to go to Arizona and rent a rodeo ground and get all those people and then change them around every day so they looked like a different crowd. Then he got a mechanical horse for McQueen to hop up and down on. This is very inhibiting for a director. So I was lucky because of the RCA [Rodeo Cowboys' Association].

We were actually the first to start a rodeo movie, then several others came along shortly after. All these other rodeo pictures cost much more than ours did, and they had lots of money behind them—a lot of money for promotion. I guess the word got out that we had a pretty good picture, because the others were really rushed into release. I had the misfortune to come out in a disastrous year for Columbia. We got, they tell me, the best reviews of any picture Columbia had that year. But we were between two multimillion-dollar disasters, and the result was that the money initially budgeted to promote *J.W. Coop* went to a little beauty called *Lost Horizon* and another picture. So we didn't have much influence; our picture opened and just sat there, and in some cities the other big rodeo pictures came out first. I had no control over that.

CRIST: *J.W. Coop* was certainly a critical success, but it just was not sold, it had no clout. Columbia's other big blockbuster that year was *Young Winston*. And when you have two such films, that's where the publicity money goes—not to a movie that comes in for less than a million dollars. But, Cliff, ultimately, you didn't lose money on this one, did you?

ROBERTSON: No, we were the only one of the rodeo pictures in that period that did end up in the black.

CRIST: If you will, Cliff, please tell everybody the marvelous story you told us earlier about the motorcycle cop in *J.W. Coop*.

ROBERTSON: I was telling Judy that in order to keep my budget down I didn't hire a casting service. I do believe in casting services, but in this case, I couldn't afford it. So I rented a little place in Hollywood and I'd go see people all day and into the night—a tremendous number of people, most of whom hadn't really acted before. On this particular night, it was about one in the morning, this guy came in.

He hadn't been invited to audition and I asked him what he was doing here. He said, "Well, I saw a lot of people ou-ou-out front and I th-th-thought they must be gi-gi-giving something away so I lined up." Now as a director you tend to think that these people are really actors trying to do a number to get a job. But he was real, he had never acted before. The more we talked the more I realized I *had* to put this guy in my movie. And quickly I thought I could rewrite that scene with the cop. So I asked him if he'd like to learn a couple pages of dialogue. He said, "Well, uh, (sniff) I never done no acting b-b-before (sniff)." I said, "That's okay, that's good . . . I'm going to rewrite this scene and if I do, do you think you could learn it?" He said, "I guess I c-c-could (sniff), Mr. Robertson; I'll try."

His real name, by the way, is Son Hooker. So I said "Son," I said, "I'll get this dialogue to you tomorrow; learn it, and on the day you join us, wherever we are, we'll shoot it. You won't have any problem." So I rewrote the scene—obviously stealing *his* character. I wrote what I could see of him. Three weeks later we were shooting at Palmdale—I had sent out word for Son to be there. The crew by now thought I was really going crackers because I was coming up with stranger people every day. Then they saw this guy coming in. Well, I realized he was nervous, and he had the script with him all crumpled up as obviously he had really been studying it. I sent the crew over to the other side of the road and I went over to the car, the old Hudson there, and I said, "Okay, Son, let's rehearse." And he didn't say a word. I said, "Okay, c'mon—let's go." And he just stood there. I said, "Well, did you learn the script. Are you ready?" He said, "Yeah (sniff), yeah." I said, "Okay . . . go."

"Right . . . (sniff, sniff) . . . I'm on the side of the road on my motorcycle and this old 1949 Hudson comes down the street and I start up my motorcycle and I follow that '49 Hudson and I turn on my siren. The '49 Hudson goes off the road and I pull up the motorcycle and I get off it and I walk around the '49 Hudson and I walk up and I say, 'You didn't hear me did ya?' And you say, 'No,' and I say (sniff), 'I guess it's 'cuz of the wind.' And then I say, 'What is this piece of shit here anyway?' And you say 'A Hudson,' and I say, 'A Hudson??' "

He said the *whole* scene—*my* lines, his lines—and when he was through he said, "Is that okay?" And I said, "That's beautiful, Son, that's the way it's going to be." And that was our rehearsal. Then we got to the shooting and he couldn't remember whether to tell me whether to put my right hand on the wheel or my left hand, so he said, "Put the right . . . the left hand . . . as usual . . . the right hand!" That's *all* Son—all his own bit, and the crew was going right up the wall. People in this business come up to me and say, "Gee, what a performance you got out of that guy," and I say, "Are you joking? This guy did it all himself." On my part it was just a matter of having the courage—maybe the foolish courage—to see a guy like that and say we're going to put this person in our movie.

FROM AUDIENCE: We were talking about the scene with the riders in the trailer, and we were wondering what's the story on this woman, was she real?

ROBERTSON: I stole that Big Marge character from another real-life character—who happened to be *that* lady. That lady is not an actress, she's a forty-five-year-old housewife with five kids—she's my wife's niece, okay? She talks just that way and behaves just that way; she's bigger than life. And I thought I'd love to have a woman in this playing a stock contractor, as they call them, and I'd like her big and horsey—and I thought: *Marge.* So I wrote this without her knowing it, and Marge was over at our house after I'd written it and I said, "Hey, Marge, how'd you like to be in a movie?" "Hell— I don't want to be in no goddamn movie! Let Aunt Dina do all that crap, I don't want any of that Hollywood stuff." And I said, "Hey, hold it. This isn't a Hollywood movie, Marge, this is *different*." So I told her about it, although I didn't tell her what I was *really* saying, I just told her it was a rodeo story, and she likes horses and cattle. So she said, "All right, let me look at the damn thing." So I gave her the scene and she went in another room for half an hour. She came out and said, "Damn, this gal talks just like me." I said, "Is *that right?*" and she said, "Yeah, sure is." So I asked her if she thought she could do it; it would be a scene with just me and a bunch of rodeo cowboys. "Rodeo cowboys, eh? I think I can hack that." Boy—she got along with those cowboys, I tell you, they were having a ball all the time—it was just a perfect meld. So that's the story on that. Her name is Marjorie Dye and she's married to a junior high school athletic coach, has five kids, and lives in Santa Monica. And whenever I see her now she says, "Hey, Cliff, when we going to do another movie, baby?"

FROM AUDIENCE: Can you tell us a little bit about the role for Geraldine Page?

ROBERTSON: I had written that as a cameo, obviously, but I wanted to show that when J.W. goes back to his hometown, things have changed. It seemed to me that his mother being who she was—very poor with no education—would have probably slipped into senility. I love that old house and I love that long, long porch. I wanted the sense of a woman living in the past, and as she walks down that walk with J.W.—seeing him for the first time in all these years—I wanted them actually walking into the past. She talks to him like a little boy. And she talks about WPA and FDR.

Now Geraldine is a friend of mine, and although we've never worked together, we knew each other from Actors Studio days. So I sent the script to her thinking that she'd never consider so small a part. But, typical Geraldine, she said she'd love to do it.

I'll tell you a story about the actor's sensibility, as opposed to that of someone like a technician—someone like a first assistant director, he's dealing in logistics. Now Geraldine had flown out from New York, exhausted after being on several short flights to get there. She arrived on the set at eight o'clock while I was on another location, and about nine the first assistant came to me panicked and said, "She's here—but she's just sitting there, she hasn't touched her makeup or anything." I told him to relax. At about nine-thirty I went over to her and she said, "Hi, Cliff honey, how are ya?" And we started talking about Rip—Rip Torn, her husband—and the old days. Now, it's about ten o'clock. And about ten-thirty she started to put a little bit of makeup on—we're talking about the character, but not too much, just easing into it. Finally, she said, "What about lipstick?" I said, "Maybe you could put it on like you hadn't looked in a mirror—sort of smeared around. And why don't you wear some white bobby socks and some curlers in your hair. It would look sort of sad." Very casually, very easily, what we were trying to do was become related. After all, she was playing my mother—and she could be my sister. We were not *saying* "Let's get related," it was just a reflex of an experienced actor, just like an old race horse—you *know* those things. But this director's assistant was climbing the walls. At noon Geraldine and I were still in the dressing room. So I told the assistant to break for lunch and take a good long one. Finally at two-fifteen—after the assistant had made a couple of calls to Columbia telling them he didn't know what was happening, but we didn't have any filming in—at two-fifteen we cranked up the camera, and we finished a two-day shooting with Geraldine half a day early. Once we got started it just *worked*. She's that kind of actress.

FROM AUDIENCE: I didn't get the point of the money that you left on your plate.

ROBERTSON: Senile people do funny things . . . they get cagey and suspicious. And that line of Geraldine's in which she said, "Your dad say anything about envelopes?" That was her way of reminding her boy that when he worked he should bring home some money. She was too proud in that hardshell Baptist way ever to say, "Give me your money." There's a great pride about money, but it's a necessary thing. So in this case, I just put the money on your plate. Maybe that was too subtle. There are other things maybe that only one out of ten people pick up. I've always been accused of going too fast over things. But I'd rather go too fast than give you what I call a rib shot—a rib shot to me is where a director is practically poking you in the ribs saying, "Hey, *get what I'm doing here?*" I *hate* that, I would rather let you miss it.

CRIST: That's one of the hallmarks of *J.W. Coop*, which becomes more obvious on the third or fourth viewing—everything is so totally understated. The visuals are what movies are all about.

FROM AUDIENCE: In how many scenes did you do your own stunt work, and how often did the stunt man fill in?

ROBERTSON: Well, when we were shooting I heard that McQueen was deciding he wanted to do a rodeo picture. Now I knew that McQueen might ride a motorcycle, but I knew he wouldn't ride a bucking horse, or a bull. I didn't think any of the other fellows would. But I thought, well, I'm going to ride these bulls. I spent almost a year going around the rodeo circuit absorbing the life and trying to get into it. And I knew after about three months that sooner or later I was going to do some riding. You do little tricks, you know; our insurance policy wouldn't let me ride during shooting—but afterward, I went to this bull ranch with a bootleg cameraman, set up the camera, and got footage of me riding three of the bulls. After three, I figured, hell, maybe I got into the wrong career. I thought maybe I'd better call my agent, and call my wife—and tell them I'm going on the rodeo circuit. I really enjoyed it. But then I rode a fourth bull, and that experience dispelled all my rodeo ambitions. I was pretty lucky, actually, wasn't hurt too much.

FROM AUDIENCE: When you were working on the script—did you have in mind this more or less bloody ending?

ROBERTSON: My original idea was to show a gradual sinking, if that's the word. To show J.W. off in some two-bit rodeo just hanging on for dear life. But I'm a fast one for changing my script. If an actor is working with me and something comes out that's better than what I've written, I'm going to go with it. To me, what I write is not deathless prose. When I saw the rushes of Johnny's ride I said, "Well, that's our ending right there." It was a very honest ending.

Some of the exhibitors said the picture would have made a lot of money if J.W. had ridden off in the sunset with a girl. But that's just the biggest lie in the world. Hollywood has been pulling that hype on us for years. First of all, with the differences between J.W. and the girl here—the differences in their ages, education, and social background—it would have been a big huge lie. This girl wouldn't have stayed married to him for twenty minutes. This was honest. People keep asking me if J.W. died. And all I say is that in my mind he didn't die, he probably wound up working behind the chutes. I knew guys like that—when their riding days are over they still hang around rodeo.

FROM AUDIENCE: That girl seemed to offer some salvation for him and I really believed something would happen there.

ROBERTSON: That would be another movie, wouldn't it? What that girl represents to me is a characteristic among a lot of young people. Not in spite of, because of their academic education, they have a great appetite for another kind of education—getting out on the road, seeing the country, meeting people who are not from their own backgrounds. It's a very healthy curiosity. And a girl like this would be, for a while, hung up on a guy like J.W.

CRIST: To me, she's one of the film's social props. J.W. Coop was trying, like so many other misfits, to be part of the time in which he has no part. The girl is a symbol of that. Because of the girl he grows the mustache and sideburns and takes her to that zippy hotel—where he looks out to survey the heights he has attained, and sees those acres and acres of cars parked in front of him. That's a marvelous moment.

ROBERTSON: I picked that hotel for that reason. At the time, I wanted freebies—and I got that hotel free. People are always interested to find out how you can make a movie for less money than anybody says you can, so I'll tell you some of the tricks. When we went to that hotel, oh, gosh, you'd be surprised at the people who were staying there or working there who said, "Boy, you sure picked a beautiful hotel." Well, I picked a beautiful hotel for my purposes. I mean, that *red* bed—it's dynamite!

I'll give you an example of how you can run into trouble with unions. When it was announced we were going to do the picture, I got a call from one of the important people with the transportation union out in California. They gave me this big stroke number and said, "Hey, Cliff, dynamite, terrific that you're doing a movie and that it's not going to be a runaway production, you're doing it here in this country." And he ended up saying, "We figure you're going to have about eight drivers on this picture." I said, "Hold the phone—I don't think so. I've scouted all my locations and we're staying within five miles of each location. We all have driver's licenses. Look, I'll go along with you to take on some drivers, but I can't accept eight." And he said, "Aw, c'mon, you big Academy

Award—winning movie actor, you." I said, "Listen, pal, I'll trade my salary on this picture for the salary of any one of those drivers on location." Because for two drivers on location, it would cost me $1500 a week. Multiply that times the number of weeks we had to shoot the picture—and none of that cost would be reflected on screen. Then he asked me what I had against drivers. I said, "Look, pal, I belong to four unions and I don't have anything against union drivers, per se, but I don't like the idea of getting up at five-thirty in the morning, having a sleepy driver open up the car door while my cameraman and I and our assistants pile in, and we go out to the location, and after we step out of the car that driver will close the door, roll up the window, and turn on the air conditioning, pull out the racing form, and then after a while doze off. Then at twelve o'clock he'll be the first one into the lunch line, then go back to the car. We work all afternoon and into the night and then at night he'll drive us that three miles back to the motel and then we stumble in at the wee hours to start preparing work for the next day. He's up there at the bar drinking beer and watching the Johnny Carson show. It's just not right." He said, "Any other reasons?" I said, "Yeah, we can't fit eight drivers into the one truck that I'm using on this picture." The guy from the union finally said, "Well, you're either going to have eight—or none." And I said, "Okay, that's cool, I'm closing up production right now. But I warn you, I'm going to have an interview with *Variety* and the *Holly-wood Reporter,* and it'll make a wonderful page-one story, showing how one craft is choking the lives of all the other crafts." Two days later he called and said, "Will you settle for three drivers?" I said okay. We weren't trying to cheat anybody—we just didn't have that kind of money.

[After *Masquerade*]

CRIST: This is the "whipped cream" of the program—just a fun movie, and maybe Cliff can tell us how it came about.

ROBERTSON: Someone in England had sent me a script of a serious spy story—or *they* thought it was serious. I thought it was hilarious because it was riddled with every cliché in the book. This was years ago. I kept telling my agent to say thanks, but no thanks. I went to Mexico to make a picture and I got a call from this woman saying that her boss was somewhere over the Atlantic with this script and he was coming to talk to me about it. I had to admire his tenacity. He arrived on a Sunday morning about six and I met him at the hotel. He said, "I know you've turned down my script, but what I want to know is if you were me, what would you do?" I said, "Frankly, I'd slash my wrists." He said he didn't think he wanted to do that. He said surely there was something he could do with this. And I said—and this was before they had all these spoofs on spy stories—I said, "You've got so many clichés in this thing, instead of trying to get rid of them and make a straight spy story, why don't you underline all of them and point out that this is a spoof on spy stories." He contacted his people in England and they said fine, so then I felt kind of obligated and I told him that before he signed up some expensive writer in Hollywood, he should look up a friend of mine in New York—he'd never written any movies, but he has a cinematic mind and he's a bright guy and I felt he could do the job. So he went to Hollywood and talked to a couple of expensive writers, then went to New York, met my friend, and fell in love with him. I got a call from my friend asking me what I had done. All of a sudden he was involved in this movie, he'd never done a movie before. We talked out our ideas on the long-distance wires a few times. Dissolve.

I go to Benidorm, Spain, to make *Masquerade* and here's my friend wearing a huge straw hat with his name on the back of the chair, and he looked up at me and said, "Hi, baby." Incidentally, his name is Bill Goldman, William Goldman. And he subsequently wrote a screenplay that earned more than any other original screenplay before it—it was *Butch Cassidy and the Sundance Kid*.

But that's how Bill Goldman got his start—on *Masquerade*. I haven't seen this picture since then, and I must say I have a lot of ambivalence about it.

FROM AUDIENCE: Do you have any new projects you can talk about?

ROBERTSON: I'm really at a happy spot in my life right now, where I just want to write, direct—make movies, quietly. With my record—it took me seven and a half years to get *Charly* off the ground, right?—so the way I go I'm probably good for about three more movies while I'm alive, because it takes me so long. But I've got a thing I haven't gotten around to, a crazy story about a World War I flyer. That's one project, and I've got another project, a book written by one of our best American novelists, now dead. His widow and daughter want me to direct and act in that. There are a couple of others—but nothing on paper right now.

FROM AUDIENCE: Do you have any plans to work with your wife, Dina Merrill?

ROBERTSON: We've worked together about seven times and enjoyed it. I've written a role for her in the World War I story, a role she could do quite well. It is important to work together—for family peace if for no other reason. But by the same token, it can be a delicate balance. It's like a man teaching his wife to drive. Not all women can take direction from their husbands. I've never directed her, but when we work together as actor and actress she relies a great deal on my ideas. My wife needs a director—she's very good and very hardworking, but she needs someone to say here's what we should do with this character. I'll tell you a funny story. I really shouldn't tell you this story, it might get a little touchy here. Well, all right, I will. Years ago I was a bachelor . . . I was married once before—although I knew my present wife before I knew my first wife, we've known each other many, *many* years. She was always trying to get me to go do some summer stock, and I'd say, "Look, Dina, that's a luxury nowadays, I've got responsibilities and I've done all that stuff and it doesn't really prove too much, unless it's something really, really unusual." But she wanted very much for us to do some stock.

Okay. I'd gone on suspension again from Columbia and I got a call from my wife-to-be, Dina, in New York, and she said, "Okay, buster, what's your excuse this time? How about doing some stock?" It was in May. I said, "Look, Dinie, let me give you a little bit of information. Summer stock is now big business, and whereas in the old days they could cook these things up at the last minute, now summer stock operators go out and corral people and properties months ahead of time. This is May, and first of all you've got to get the play that's right for the two of us, you have to get the rights to it, you have to get a director, you've got to get a rehearsal hall, and you've got to get bookings." She said, "If I can do those things, would you be open to it?" I said, "Well, sure." Thirty-six hours later she called, she had a place, *The Voice of the Turtle*, a director, a rehearsal hall—and six bookings. And all of them met my price. I said, "Any time you want to quit acting and be my agent, you're hired." She's one of the most organized people I've ever known in my life, she's really got it all together—and she'd make a brilliant producer.

FROM AUDIENCE: How do you see yourself in, say, five years from now? Which direction would you like to go in?

ROBERTSON: Well, I would never be happy the rest of my life if I thought I'd be confined to acting. I started out as a newspaperman; I thought I'd be a writer when I first came to New York. Then the first job I got was acting—so I took a detour. But we all have fantasies, and my fantasy is living somewhere out of the city where it's kind of quiet, and there are green trees and relatively fresh air, and I have a lot of yellow paper and pencils. I see myself there very quietly writing screenplays and then *very quietly* going out and making them into movies. Then I'd let someone else go out and sell them. Producing is not where my head is; basically it's into writing, directing, and acting.

In 1976 Robertson made a film called Obsession *for Columbia Pictures—an association that led him to alert authorities to the fact that the studio head David Begelman had forged Robertson's endorsement on a $10,000 check. The actor didn't work in Hollywood for a few years afterward, but in 1983 he was seen in* Class, Brainstorm, *and* Star 80, *made his debut as a regular on a prime-time TV series in ABC's* Falcon Crest, *and in 1985 was in* Shaker Run. *He devoted himself to writing and to serving as the AT&T spokesman. His recent film work includes* Wild Hearts Can't Be Broken *(1991) and Francis Coppola's* Wind, *due in 1992.*

Walter Matthau

▼▼▼

After serving with the Army Air Corps in World War II, Walter Matthau returned to his native New York and joined a dramatic workshop at the New School. Three years of study and summer stock led to his Broadway debut as an eighty-three-year-old bishop in Anne of a Thousand Days, *and he subsequently appeared in sixteen Broadway plays, including* Will Success Spoil Rock Hunter?, Once More with Feeling, *and* A Shot in the Dark.

In his first film, The Kentuckian *(1955), Matthau played a villain so convincingly that he was cast as a heavy in his next dozen or so films. But even as a crazed killer—in 1963's* Charade, *for example—Matthau exhibited a certain wry humor. As a result he landed a co-starring role with Jack Lemmon in Billy Wilder's comedy hit* The Fortune Cookie *(1966)—for which he won an Academy Award as Best Supporting Actor. His next films were* A Guide for the Married Man *(1967) and* The Odd Couple *(1968), co-starring Jack Lemmon, in which Matthau re-created his Broadway portrayal as the slovenly Oscar Madison. By the time Matthau came to Tarrytown to preview* Casey's Shadow *on the weekend of March 17–19, 1978, he had also made* Hello, Dolly! *(1969),* A New Leaf *(1971),* Plaza Suite *(1971),* Kotch *(1971),* Pete 'n' Tillie *(1972),* Charley Varick *(1973),* The Sunshine Boys *(1972, and another Oscar nomination),* House Calls *(1978), and* California Suite *(1978).*

[After *Kotch*]

CRIST: I picked *Kotch* because it has been one of my own beloved Matthau movies. And after all these years I find it even more touching. In a way, I would have liked to show *Kotch* back to back with *Sunshine Boys* because there are portraits of old age and there are portraits of old age. These two are quite dissimilar. What really strikes me about *Kotch*—in terms of the portraiture—are the mouth movements and the walk. Walter, even though I know that probably from the age of ten you were eighty years old—how did you really refine the portrait of Kotch? And how did you and Jack [Lemmon] get involved in this project?

MATTHAU: Jack looked unhappy one day. And I said, "What's the matter?" He said, "I've got this wonderful script and I've got Fredric March, who really wants to do this, but I can't raise any money." He said he could have gotten money for Spencer Tracy—but he died. I said, "What kind of part is it? Is it an old guy?" He said, "Yeah." I said, "Why don't you let me play it?" He said, "You wanna play it?" I said, "Let me read it." So I read it, and I said, "Okay, I'll play it." He said, "Can you play an old guy?" I said, "Eh . . . yeah, I've played old guys." He said, "Well . . . great, let's see if we can get the money." So we went around trying to get the money but couldn't. Everybody said, "Matthau playing an old guy? Sure, he can do it on stage—but in the movies?" And they knew it was not the kind of picture that was going to make any money. It didn't have blood and sex. Well, we got ahold of Marty Baum, who used to be my agent and was then president of ABC Pictures. And we said Lemmon directs, Matthau will be in it, and we can do the picture for about $2.5 million. He said, "Okay, fellas, let's go." That's how we did it.

Now, regarding Kotch's walk—what I tried to do was imitate an old judge who is about ninety now, and still sitting on the bench in Brooklyn. Never wears a coat in winter. He's kind of a marvelous old New Yorker, with very flowery speech, stands *very* straight. He doesn't have the facility of sight or hearing but he's a marvelous judge. He talks very rapidly, and is constantly aware of his grammar. I guess I also thought a little bit about Walter Huston in doing that role. For the mouth, I was doing my father-in-law, Carol's daddy, who's ninety-three and goes to work every day; he's a consultant at Hughes Aircraft. He's constantly pursing his lips. I think what he's doing is making sure he has his teeth in.

CRIST: In *Sunshine Boys* you seem to me to portray a very New York old man, whereas Kotch is more a Nebraska-California old man. Did you have a Wasp figure in mind in this portrayal?

MATTHAU: I figure I was not Jewish in this picture. But my son was. The girl who played my daughter-in-law is Jack Lemmon's wife, and she's Jewish. But she looked the most goyish.

CRIST: I was interested to learn you used very little makeup in this.

MATTHAU: Very little. I put on a gray wig. As a matter of fact, there were two wigs—one that was very good. It was too good, too silky—I didn't like it. When I wore it I felt out of character, because there was this expensive wig on my head. The cheap wig gave me the right feel for the character. The rest of the makeup was just taking a pencil and going over my own lines—in my face. And the walk, well, my natural walk is bent-over and slow, laconic. So I stood up straight and walked as fast as I could—and I looked old.

CRIST: *Kotch* didn't make much money, did it?

MATTHAU: It didn't lose money. I think I got $197—last week.

CRIST: Well, over the years—it's a living.

MATTHAU: Every four months—$197?

CRIST: What was your working relationship with Jack Lemmon as director?

MATTHAU: Well, Lemmon would come over to me and I'd say, "You're not going to tell me how to act or anything, are you? I mean, what do you want?" I'd say, "You just go back behind the camera—and shut up." He'd say, "Okay, Slick." Every once in a while I'd let him talk—just to make him feel like a director. I think he did a splendid job. I didn't realize what a splendid job he did until this minute.

FROM AUDIENCE: I'm curious about one of the credits . . . Frugal Filmways. Is that a Lemmon-Matthau joke?

MATTHAU: *Frugal Filmways?* That must have been a Lemmon-Carter joke. Richard Carter, who is a publicist, produced this picture with Jack.

FROM AUDIENCE: Why does a movie like this cost that much? $2.5 million seems awfully high.

MATTHAU: I can answer it by telling you this. One day, when I was doing *The Odd Couple*, we had a scene on Riverside Drive. I was having dinner later with my brother Henry, so I told him to come on over and take a look at the shooting. He came over and he saw about fifteen trucks, and maybe three or four limousines; he saw about ten or fifteen electricians, and he saw about eight men doing stuff with the camera. He saw about thirty-five or forty men—and a lot of trucks. And it was obvious that whatever these people were doing, it was going to cost $40,000 a day—not counting equipment. And not counting the actors. And my brother said, "Oh, it's a big deal, huh?" It is. Let's say you have a five-day week and an eight-week shooting schedule; that's forty days of shooting. And let's say it's $40,000 a day—how much is that? $1,600,000. And you haven't paid the writers, you haven't paid anybody *above the line*. The same picture would be $3.5 million to $4 million today. I don't think it has to cost that much. I think there's a great deal of waste.

I think you could do that picture for half the money. But there are questions of unionism—and all the things we fought for when we didn't have unions.

FROM AUDIENCE: Have you tried directing?

MATTHAU: Yes, in 1958. I was doing a picture called *King Creole* with Elvis Presley, and a friend of mine, who was a cardiovascular surgeon, decided to become a movie producer. He decided that while he was doing surgery. Then his brother quit the textile business in Philadelphia and came to Hollywood. The two of them bought a screenplay and wanted me to direct and to star. And also to do some rewriting. And, if I didn't mind, would I make out the W-2 forms? Well, I did that, and I cast the picture every morning— in Schwab's drugstore. My leading lady was my wife, Carol, who then went under her acting name, Carol Grace. It's also her writing name—she did write a very good book, called *The Secret and the Daisy*. Anyway, she played a gun moll and I was a gangster. And I found it laboriously irritating to direct. I have absolutely no powers of command. If I asked somebody to do something and they'd say, "What did you say?"—I'd say, "Well, don't do it. Don't do it if you don't feel like it. I just thought you should walk over there." And they'd say, "Hey, c'mon . . . why should I walk over there?"

Well. The picture is called *Gangster Story* and you can see it on television, whenever there's a full moon, around four o'clock in the morning. It's a dreadful picture. I wanted to call it *Chopped Herring*. But the producer was afraid people might think it was a Borscht circuit comedy. I've never directed since—and I never will again. Unless somebody puts a machine gun to my head.

FROM AUDIENCE: In *Kotch* the central character seems to be onstage all the time, and the focus of all attention. Was the role particularly demanding?

MATTHAU: No. It's easier to be onstage all the time than come in and out, unless you can do your in-and-outs in one period of time. Movies, you see, are a lot like sitting in the trenches waiting for word—from somebody who doesn't know what the hell he's doing—about when you should move out.

FROM AUDIENCE: How do you feel when you sit in the audience and observe yourself on screen?

MATTHAU: I was thinking about that. I watched it like a fella who didn't know the fella who was acting the part. Swear to God. I was completely—as far as I know—*completely* objective about it. I was enjoying it. This may sound a little schmucky—but I thought the guy who was playing that old man was pretty good.

CRIST: From an evolutionary standpoint, you're one of the very rare actors who has continued to play character roles while developing into a leading man. Is it just luck, or did you decide at certain points in your career, now I'm going to try this and now that?

MATTHAU: No, not the latter. I think I've had a great deal of luck. Also, I was stricken with a heart attack about twelve years ago, and stopped smoking. And I think that not smoking cigars made me feel a little more like a leading man. That's gonna sound dopey. It probably is. But that's my theory—that a man who doesn't smoke is more of a leading man.

CRIST: I'll go along with saying a man who smokes *cigars* is not a leading man.

MATTHAU: But what about the schmucks smoking cigarettes?

CRIST: Ohh, there's Paul Henreid, with *two* cigarettes.

MATTHAU: But today we know that's not romantic. It's idiotic. I saw a bumper sticker the other day in California. It said KISSING A MAN WHO SMOKES IS LIKE SUCKING A DIRTY ASHTRAY.

FROM AUDIENCE: A while back I saw you on television in an old Alfred Hitchcock episode. And I wonder if you did a lot of television in your early career?

MATTHAU: Oh, yeah. I used to be on the *Philco-Goodyear Playhouse* every week. I worked cheap. It's true. I found out $400 for doing a show was very cheap—the other guys were getting $600. My agent would call me. She'd say, "Walter, they want you for Othello." I'd say, "Who?" She'd say, "Goodyear-Philco." And I'd say, "Great! How much?" I was angry about getting cheated before, you see. She'd say, "Walter, it's *Othello*—what do you care how much?" I said, "Well, I care, how much?" She said, "Two-fifty." I said, "*Two fifty?* I get four hundred dollars." "It's summer prices." I said, "Summer prices? It's October." She said, "Walter, what do you care, it's Othello?" I said, "I want $1500 and that's it. If you can't get it for me, that's fine. Please tell them that I want $1500." She called me the next morning. "*Walter*. They've changed it to Iago—and they'll give you $750." I said, "I'll take it."

FROM AUDIENCE: Did you look upon your television days as good experience?

MATTHAU: Oh, yes, good experience. It was like a lot of opening nights. I had about sixteen or twenty plays on Broadway, maybe about sixty or seventy plays in summer stock. And maybe fifty opening nights on television—that's a lot of television. Maybe that's why I had a heart attack at forty-five.

FROM AUDIENCE: Which part most closely fits the Walter Matthau you think you are?

MATTHAU: I don't know—I'm still finding myself.

FROM AUDIENCE: What motivated you to go into show business? Was it money?

MATTHAU: Money was the last thing. That's the last thing in the world *any* actor thinks of. Nobody really thinks they're going to make money being an actor. Wait a minute, I take that back. I was getting $90 a month from the government to go to school—and that was a big motivation to go to school. Now, why I chose dramatic school was because of my whole childhood and background—a lucky combination of sociological and environmental events all tangled up with the genes. It all came out together, and what it told me was, "maybe acting is a good spot for you."

FROM AUDIENCE: Did you enjoy working with Glenda Jackson in your new film [*House Calls*]?

MATTHAU: Very much, very much. A peachy pro. She's a beautiful, professional workman, and a delicious lady.

FROM AUDIENCE: Can you choose the parts you want?

MATTHAU: No.

SAME AUDIENCE: Can't you be more discriminating than most actors?

MATTHAU: No, because a lot of parts I want they give to Robert Redford. But I have a little more choice than I used to have. I can say "no thank you" now—and I do until things start looking a little shaky. Then I get tired of not working and scared of not working—so I work.

FROM AUDIENCE: How come you took the role in *The Laughing Policeman*?

MATTHAU: Yeah, I didn't think very much of that picture either. And I hated doing it because I had to eat lunch in the morgue a lot. It read much better than it came out. Sometimes literary merit becomes an obstacle in the making of a motion picture. Sometimes it doesn't. You also have to have other elements to make it work. *Laughing Policeman* sure did not work. And I'll never speak to you again for mentioning it.

FROM AUDIENCE: What about *Charley Varick*. Do you like roles like that?

MATTHAU: I had been looking for something like that to break away from the Neil Simon comedy syndrome. And Don Siegel came up with *Charley Varick*. I read it and thought it was a pretty poor melodrama. It had about 700 loopholes. I actually threw it away, because I didn't want to bother with it. I remember throwing the script into the fireplace. Then I started talking to Siegel. I kind of liked him. Every time I made a suggestion—I had about 700 questions—he'd say okay, we'll fix it. So we went into it. Besides, my agent said I had to do one of these melodramas, that it was very good for the foreign market. And I guess it was. I enjoyed doing that picture, but it's not a solid piece of dramatic work. Am I right? It's entertaining, because it's got money in it, the Mafia, a whorehouse.

SAME AUDIENCE: Didn't you get the British Oscar for *Charley Varick*?

MATTHAU: I got the British Oscar but it was for two pictures— *Charley Varick* and *Pete 'n' Tillie*. In Great Britain, if they give you an award, it's for whatever body of work you've done that year. So if you've done six pictures, they'll put all six pictures on the figurine.

FROM AUDIENCE: You mention Neil Simon; some critics lately have commented that his work has suffered since he moved to California. I wonder if you could comment on this view, and whether you think his type of humor is suitable for today.

MATTHAU: The man is the most successful playwright on the planet. More so even than William Shakespeare. I'm not saying he's *better* than Shakespeare. Just more successful. And has a marvelous facility for crackling lines and jokes which he uses on the spine of the story. Sometimes they get in the way, but with some good direction and legitimate actors, that can usually be ironed out. I love to read his stuff.

SAME AUDIENCE: Are you suggesting that some of the performances of his more recent stuff have not brought out the best of Neil Simon?

MATTHAU: On the contrary. I think that the performances of some of Neil Simon's stuff make him look even better than he is.

CRIST: I think you're right—because when the performances are below the best, that's when you become aware that Simon's people aren't really talking as people—they're talking *lines*. I had that feeling seeing his newest Broadway play, *Chapter Two,* but maybe it was an off night. However, for the first time I felt I understood what some people feel about his work, that he simply writes an exchange of fast, smart lines. But in *The Goodbye Girl,* I thought the performers were so very appealing and so good in transcending the material.

MATTHAU: My next picture is going to be a Neil Simon picture. And I'm going to try some very outrageous things in it. I have an idea or two, very outrageous. I'll see how it works out. It's *California Suite*. You know, that's four stories like *Plaza Suite*. I'll be in a sequence with Elaine May.

FROM AUDIENCE: Since *Sunshine Boys* was George Burns's first major film role, how did he affect the flow of the picture? Was he able to keep up? I imagine it was a lot of fun working with him.

MATTHAU: Yeah. You see, he had been having a triple-bypass heart surgery, and I was supposed to be doing the picture with Jack Benny. Well, I sent Burns a telegram in order to cheer him up. I said, "Listen, I'll get rid of Jack Benny and you can have the part." It's ironic. Black humor—call it what you will. When Jack Benny died and they asked me what I thought of George Burns for the part, I said, "Excellent." It would have been totally different with Jack Benny.

FROM AUDIENCE: Did you yourself ever see Smith and Dale?

MATTHAU: Yes. Well, half. I only saw Smith. Dale was dead. I never saw them perform. But I heard them on *The Ed Sullivan Show*. I have a cassette of it, and played it often. When I played the doctor sketch I used Charley Dale. When I played the character of the guy, I was doing Smith. Dale had a very high voice, Smith a deep voice. Smith is still around, he's about ninety-five, and he was in the epilogue we did in the Old Actors' Home in New Jersey. But that was cut out of the movie.

[After *A New Leaf* and *Pelham One Two Three*]

CRIST: Let's backtrack to *A New Leaf*. As someone remarked last night, as we left the screening room at about 2:15, it's probably a good thing that Paramount took control of the film away from Elaine May, to cut it, or we'd still be sitting there. This happens to be one of my favorite films. I think it's one of the most exquisite comedies we've seen recently, with brilliant performances. But something just goes wrong about two-thirds of the way through, characters just disappear, plot developments are just incomplete. I never had the nerve to ask Elaine May about it—you don't ask things like "What happened during your last abortion?"—so I sort of wondered if I could ask you.

MATTHAU (SIGHING): It was a very weird project to start with. But Elaine did have *two* murders in the picture. There was a murder of a blackmailer, played by Bill Hickey, and the murder of Jack Weston. And the subsequent activities in getting rid of the bodies were outrageous and unique and funny. When I saw the rushes of that, I couldn't stop laughing. All that was cut out by the brass at Paramount, because, as one wag put it, "What's so funny about murders?" I said, "Yeah, yeah—*Arsenic and Old Lace* was a very sad film, with all those bodies in the cellar." There were many other things. Of course, Elaine at the time was very hesitant about making any final decisions on the film. She called Mike Nichols a lot. And she never really started a scene until 4:30 in the afternoon. She'd have to work herself into it. Elaine is the kind of lady who doesn't really start to live until it gets dark. She doesn't eat until it gets dark, I know that. Once I had a two-quart jar of pickled herring, and I said, "Have some herring." She ate the whole two quarts. She hadn't eaten in a week. She just forgot to eat.

FROM AUDIENCE (MATTHAU'S WIFE, CAROL): You made that up.

MATTHAU: I didn't make it up—I was just exaggerating for purposes of illustration. Anyway, Elaine had a great many weird and unique ways of doing things. Weird in a wonderful sense, you know. She's really an artist, totally insane. She's brilliantly innovative and immaculately perceptive. She's also very beautiful. The fellas at Paramount decided to make a schlock movie out of her picture, just so they could sell it. I guess I didn't tell you enough. Ask me a few questions.

CRIST: I'm curious about the ending. It didn't seem quite sure how it was going to end.

MATTHAU: Yeah. And also I think I changed characters. I was trying out several different characters for future use.

CRIST: There's such a lovely freewheeling feeling about this movie— such an improvisational feeling, particularly the scene with the one-sleeve nightgown. I just think about that and I break up.

MATTHAU: Well, I'll tell you about that scene. I was not speaking to Elaine at that time—I was very angry with her because of something she'd said to [Charles] Bludhorn, who runs that outfit, Schlock and Western. Is that the name of it? Oh, Gulf and Western. Now, we were in Jamaica where Elaine insisted on shooting that scene. We could have shot it in my living room in California, because we have that kind of shrubbery there. But we had to go to Jamaica because we were only $2.3 million over budget. And I said, "Elaine, I heard what you told Bludhorn." She said she didn't, she *swore* she didn't. A couple of hours later, I was in one of the bungalows, taking a shower, and suddenly someone rips open the shower door and it's Elaine. I thought it was going to be like from *Psycho*. But she fell to the floor and said, "I swear by all that's holy that I never said that."

It was a funny scene—my wife helping Elaine out of the shower so I could rinse off. Those things happen, you know.

Well, she started cutting the picture, and two years later they were still looking for her. She got one of those moviolas and was holed up, literally, in a hotel—the Gene Autry Hotel right on Sunset Strip. The Paramount people couldn't get in or out. There were all kinds of threats and lawsuits, the marshals came. And she knew some gangsters from Chicago who were related to a relative who was with the Capone gang—and the whole thing became so melodramatic, and so totally ridiculous. And Paramount, of course, was paying 9.5 percent interest on the money they had in the movie—which was a great deal. So they finally released the film, in that form—which was not nearly so good as Elaine's picture. I think Elaine's picture would have been a classic. Maybe she could still put it together.

CRIST: It would be interesting if someday she could get the footage back and put it all together. I think the only one to have the opportunity to do that was George Roy Hill with *Thoroughly Modern Millie*, after it was clear he had been quite right. The movie was slaughtered, and he was invited back to redo it—but I believe he had the pleasure of saying "Up yours! I'm no longer interested."

Now, how about *Pelham One Two Three*—which seems to be a beautifully constructed film, and it offers a different kind of performance for you because you're an isolated protagonist. And you have no real confrontation with the antagonist until the end.

MATTHAU: My stuff was written during the making of the picture. I bumped into an old pal named Gabriel Katzka, who was going to produce this film, and I asked him what he was doing and he told me about this project, working with Peter Stone. I said, "Oh, Peter Stone, I did two of his pictures, *Charade* and *Mirage*, and I love the way he writes." I said, "Is there anything for me in it?" He said, "Nope." I said, "Well, will you let me read it?" He said, "Sure." So I read it, and I loved it; I love the smell of New York in it. But I didn't like Peter's obligatory use of obscenities. Peter, being a big baby, now has permission to go crazy in the nursery, and so he's going to do every naughty thing that's possible to do. But there was no part for me, except the black Transit Authority patrolman—who was about thirty-two. I said, "Well, I'm a little older than thirty-two, but I think there's a lot of black in my background—although I'm not sure. So why can't I play it?" They said, "You wanna play *that?*" "Sure." They said, "We can't give you your salary." I said, "Okay, give me less." So they gave me the part and then they started adding stuff. That's when it really goes awry, when you start adding stuff. They thought they'd throw in a couple of Matthau lines. It didn't always work out. But that's how I got the part.

FROM AUDIENCE: There's a scene in which you're wrestling with one of your fellow Transit officers at the headquarters. It seemed to me that the scene didn't quite fit your character, or his.

MATTHAU: Yes, but I had to get mad at somebody. Look, I hang around the studio all day, and everyone says, "What a *nice* guy, what a *sweet* guy, he is a peach." I go home and I kick the shit out of my wife. Figuratively, figuratively.

FROM AUDIENCE: Did you really think the obscenities were out of place in this picture?

MATTHAU: Yes, I always think that obligatory . . . no, not obligatory, what's the word?

FROM AUDIENCE: Gratuitous.

MATTHAU: Thank you. Gratuitous—that's close to obligatory. I always object to gratuitous obscenities unless they enhance the character or the story. I don't think they are necessary because essentially, I think, drama is imagination. Dramatically, you know, you vitiate the power of a good obscene word if you use it too much. So you may have to hold back when you're doing something that smacks of real life, you may have to pull back and say "I'm not going to mirror life exactly in order to give this script more dramatic value." There may be more drama in *not* saying the obscenity.

FROM AUDIENCE: But aren't there people who go to movies just to be titillated like that?

MATTHAU: I think the producers think about that a great deal. Most of the scripts I read today have the obligatory—I knew I'd get that word in—exploitation of language. The producers think it's necessary to titillate in that way.

FROM AUDIENCE: Speaking of dialogue, how much leeway do you have in changing lines of a script?

MATTHAU: Depends on who the director is, and who the writer is. I have absolutely no leeway at all with certain directors and writers, a great deal with others. As a matter of fact, I have been discussing this recently. You very rarely change anything that Neil Simon writes, very rarely. I did make some changes, in the beginning. I once asked him to take out a line that Felix said in *The Odd Couple*, and he wouldn't do it. So I sent a letter and signed it Professor Heinrich von Schmutz, and explained in psychological jargon why that line should be out, and he took it out immediately.

FROM AUDIENCE: The character in *Pelham One Two Three* was created for you. Was the one in *Earthquake* created for you also?

MATTHAU: No. Jennings Lang, who purports to be my pal, called me and said I have a cameo for you and I'll give you $5,000 for your favorite charity if you do it. I said, "Okay, Jenn." I figured a cameo meant there would be other people doing the same thing, I'd be on for a second or two—as Matthau. When I saw what he wanted I hesitated. But he said, "Look, we'll cut the scene down." I was supposed to be making toasts to all these people—and he said he would just use one. I'd be making a toast to Golda Meir or something. But he double-crossed me—he used those shots throughout the picture. And he used my stand-in to do all the dancing. So it looked like I had a real part in the picture. I'm rather embarrassed by it.

SAME AUDIENCE: Is that why they used your real name?

MATTHAU: No, that's not my real name. My real name is Matthow—M-A-T-T-H-O-W. That's my real name. What you see in the credits for *Earthquake*—Matuschanskayasky—that was a made-up name.

FROM AUDIENCE: In *Pelham One Two Three* the lines seemed like they came right out of your mouth. I was wondering how much actual input you had on the script.

MATTHAU: About 4 percent. The lines you liked were mine. I drank in that picture, by the way. [Robert] Shaw likes to drink—British actors like to drink. We were working at an abandoned subway station in Brooklyn, and there was a great restaurant across the street named Queen—much better than Gage and Tollner's. Queen is an Italian restaurant. It was about five below zero and we had to keep going back into this abandoned subway, and Shaw was drinking. And I said, "I don't work with an actor who drinks." And he said, "Why not?" I said, "I just don't." He said, "Why don't you have a drink?" I said, "Okay, I will." So I'm not a drinker—but I had twice as much as Shaw did. So tell me, what was that picture about?

[After *Casey's Shadow*]

CRIST: Several people asked about the horse race in slow motion—a metaphor?

MATTHAU: No, most of the horses I bet on run that way. I think the race is unimportant in this film. This is a painting; it's a piece of time that's analogous to our time on the planet, it's a piece of life. If you want to see Mickey Rooney on the horse and the guys in the stands hollering and the gamblers betting—then that's another movie. The only thing I disagree with in this, I would have had Johann Sebastian Bach's "Jesu, Joy of Man's Desiring" playing during that slow-motion race. And then I would have had two orgasms.

CRIST: One of the more fascinating scenes was the birthing of the baby . . .

MATTHAU: Whenever they need somebody to deliver a baby, they say, "See if you can get Matthau."

CRIST: I don't know if everyone noticed in the credits, but there was a real-life veterinarian in the film—his hands were used in the scenes showing the actual delivery of the foal. Martin Ritt, the director, was with me in Dallas earlier this week at the USA Film Festival, where we showed *Casey's Shadow*. And Marty said this birth scene had to be done in South America, in Buenos Aires, because of the time of foaling. The film had to be shot in the wrong season. Then, of course, Walter and the other actors are brought into the scene—and all through the film, which was virtually completed before that scene, the various horses that were used, about six or seven horses at different stages, they all had to have their white socks put on. They were painted on, to play the horse with the four "white socks." Then came the birthing of the foal and, in what was a one-in-a-million shot, according to Marty, who's a gambling man, it was born with four white socks. That makes you believe, doesn't it?

In general, Walter, the validity of the character you played literally astounds me. What are your feelings, for example, about your accent? You pointed out that on your first day of shooting you didn't have the accent yet, and you said "thank you" instead of . . . well, how would you say it in Cajun?

MATTHAU: They're very articulate about their inarticulation. "Thank you" becomes "tank you." It's dis and dat. Which is *not*

Brooklynese. Cajun is actually a bad actor's way of doing a Brooklyn accent. When I first started, I listened for months to the Cajun accent, and did a pretty good imitation of it. Marty Ritt said, "Nobody's going to understand a goddamn word." He said I should just use a general accent of the region—which is Texas, Tennessee, Oklahoma, vaudeville southern. As we got into the picture, as we got into Louisiana, the accent became more and more Cajun, more southern Louisiana. As a matter of fact, a fellow came over to me when I was in Apaloosas County. He said, "Scews me, ma name is Moorgan Goodeau, and Ahm the district attorney here in Apaloosas County, and Ahd like to invite yew over to ma house for some kosher gumbo." He said, "And then, if you care to go over to the synahgogue . . ." I said, "Are you a Jew?" And he said, "Ahm the rabbi, too." He wasn't kidding.

FROM AUDIENCE: Mr. Matthau, you have two movies being released this week—and a made-for-TV movie. How do you juggle your time to work that in? Do you ever take a vacation?

MATTHAU: I take a vacation when I'm working on a movie. It's very relaxing for me. And it's not a case of doing everything at once. *Casey's Shadow* was made about fifteen months before *House Calls*. It was a coincidence that they came out at the same time. Both studios were very hardheaded about it: they wouldn't change the release dates. Once they had contracted for a theater and they thought that was the right move, they would not in any way alter, modify, or rectify the release dates—much to my chagrin. What I'm doing in the publicity tour is talking about both pictures—as you can tell from my laryngitis. See, I wouldn't have laryngitis if I were just talking about one movie.

FROM AUDIENCE: Why was *Casey's Shadow* rated PG instead of G?

MATTHAU: I guess it was because of the birth scene of the foal. The birth of an animal is very dirty. We still follow Neanderthal thinking in things like this.

CRIST: The PG is to warn parents, allegedly, that there's something in a movie they wouldn't want their children to see. But in this scene, of course, there's an eight-year-old boy watching the birth of the foal.

FROM AUDIENCE: What measures are taken to protect and care for the animals in a film such as this?

MATTHAU: Oh, there are very strict rules. The horses that collapsed were given very mild tranquilizers and they were watched over by a lot of people. There are more people taking care of animals on a set than people taking care of actors. If they took care of people the same way we'd have a very highly developed society.

FROM AUDIENCE: Everybody sure drank a lot of Budweiser beer in this movie.

MATTHAU: I don't know what the payola was on that. We didn't know about any deal. But I tried to cover the label with my hands, because I don't do commercials. I probably will in a couple of years, but at the moment I can afford not to do them so I don't do them. I don't think it's a good image for an actor. But if you've got to do them, you've got to do them—I guess it's better than selling sporting goods at Macy's.

FROM AUDIENCE: Did you ever do a real Western?

MATTHAU: Yep, I did about five of them, mostly as the villain. Or a sheriff. Let's see, I did *Ride a Crooked Trail,* with Audie Murphy; *The Indian Fighter,* with Kirk Douglas and Lon Chaney, Jr. I guess *The Kentuckian* was sort of a Western. *Lonely Are the Brave* was sort of a Western, although I didn't ride a horse in that one—I rode a Jeep. *Casey's Shadow.* That's it. Why do you ask? You have a Western you want me to do?

FROM AUDIENCE: In view of the recent trends, would you consider doing a *Casey's Shadow II*?

MATTHAU: I don't think I have ever or will ever do a sequel. Unless I need the money.

FROM AUDIENCE: Don't some actors hesitate to take a role co-starring with some cute, freckle-faced, scene-stealing kid?

MATTHAU: I would hesitate only if the kid were a silly actor. That's a total myth—about not wanting to compete with kid actors. Any actor with one shred of intelligence doesn't think that way. The stronger the picture, the better it is for the actor—whether he's playing opposite a cute kid or not, whether he plays against horses or snakes or whatever. I don't think that way. The stronger the characters, the better I like it. Just in a practical way, it makes sense. The more appealing the other actors are, the better a film does at the box office. The better it does at the box office, the more money I make.

CRIST: Do you have a piece of the action? And if so, do you think you're going to collect? What is all this we hear about actors never getting their percentages?

MATTHAU: It's the same as any other business. There's a little padding here and there, but when a movie company does it, there's more publicity about it. It's like why do so many actors get divorced. Actors don't get divorced any more often than the manufacturers of ladies' bags and belts, or policemen. I don't think the chicanery in the movie business is any more prevalent than in any other business. Do you know the knavery that goes on in the legal profession? Do you know how much lawyers have stolen from me?

FROM AUDIENCE: I heard that you and Barbra Streisand had trouble working together during *Hello, Dolly!*.

MATTHAU: What did you hear? Doesn't it make good copy to have stories like that? Sells tickets, right? *Hello, Dolly!* grossed $48 million, right. Those are *stories*. What else are we going to talk about?

FROM AUDIENCE: In both *Kotch* and in this film, *Casey's Shadow*, there are some very special human relationships established, relationships between an older person and a younger one. This seems like a very special message, a message of love. Do films like this have a lot of meaning to you?

MATTHAU: Oh, a great deal of meaning. I think always—consciously or unconsciously—I tend to gravitate toward anything that has a message of love.

FROM AUDIENCE: What's your next project?

MATTHAU: *California Suite*—from Neil Simon's play, of course. I play the fellow who finds the prostitute in his bed. And my wife is Elaine May. Already I can't keep a straight face.

In the last few years, Matthau has been seen in Little Miss Marker *(1980),* Hopscotch *(1981),* First Monday in October *(1981),* Buddy-Buddy *(1982),* I Ought to Be in Pictures *and* Survivors *(1983),* Movers and Shakers *(1984),* Roman Polanski's *Pirates* *(1985), and* The Couch Trip *(1988).*

Burt Reynolds

▀▀

Burt Reynolds entered the world in Waycross, Georgia, and he entered show business—after an auto accident forced him to abandon plans for a career in professional football—in an acting class at Florida's Palm Beach Junior College. From there he won a scholarship to New York's Hyde Park Playhouse, which eventually led to a Broadway debut in a revival of Mr. Roberts. *That led to a Hollywood contract and numerous TV appearances in such series as* Riverboat, M-Squad, Gunsmoke, *and* Dan August.

Reynolds made his movie debut in 1961 in Angel Baby, *and for the next few years starred in a succession of action features with such titles as* Operation CIA *(1965),* Shark *(1968), and* Skullduggery *(1969).* Deliverance *(1972) was the first of his films to become both a critical and a financial success. Although he says he's not sure exactly how many movies he's made, among those that deserve to be counted are:* The Longest Yard *(1974),* W.W. and the Dixie Dancekings *(1975),* Hustle *(1976),* Nickelodeon *(1976),* Semi-Tough *(1977), and* Smokey and the Bandit *(1977), which ranked second only to* Star Wars *as the year's top grosser. With* Gator *(1976), Reynolds made his bow as a director—directing himself. He did the same thing in* The End, *a black comedy which he previewed for Tarrytown guests on the weekend of April 21–23, 1978.*

[After *Deliverance*]

CRIST: As someone just remarked, this is not a film for the tired businessman. What amazes me about *Deliverance*—and this is the test of a finely *timed* film—each time I see it, it goes so quickly. And initially I didn't realize just how multifaceted it is. Burt, can you start by telling us how you came to do *Deliverance*?

REYNOLDS: I got down on my knees and begged. I'd read the book and because I was born in Georgia I knew the difference between the Atlanta southern speech and northern Georgia's. Which is the difference between us and Yugoslavia. Atlanta southern is a very refined accent, very refined, while northern Georgia's is hard, *real hard*. You can hardly understand it at all if you're from Atlanta. When I read the book the first thing that came into my mind was, gee, I hope they can get guys who can do the accents well—never dreaming I'd ever have a shot at doing the film. Then I heard the same old stories you always hear—that they're going to get unknown actors. *Then* I heard Marlon Brando was going to play Lewis and Henry Fonda was going to play the part Jon Voight played. And I thought, well, they'd never make it down the river.

In the early stage of my career I had to be very careful not to become Phyllis Newman—a talk-show personality. After hosting some talk shows, I can tell you, they're hard to find, people who can come out and make fools of themselves and be interesting and funny. John Boorman, the director of the film, called me and said, "I want to see you about this film." I was terribly excited. I was in New York at the time, hosting the *Tonight* show. I flew back to Los Angeles, went in to see him, and asked what he'd seen me in. He said, "I saw you on the *Tonight* show." And I said, "How could you think of me for this picture because of the *Tonight* show?" He said, "Because there were five people there and you were in control. I want a guy who's in control." I turned around and Jon Voight, whom I'd never met, walked in. Voight, who's always very much into the character he plays, had already been in rehearsal a couple of weeks and he was doing a southern accent. I started talking with him—in a southern accent—and we immediately got into an improvisation together, about going up to this river—which later turned out to be the improvisation over the opening credits. We did it first in that office. I was there maybe a total of an hour; I got up to leave and Voight shook my hand. I liked him immediately. I turned to John Boorman and Boorman said, "You've got the part."

I was stunned. Mind you, this is the guy who'd done *Navajo Joe* and *Operation CIA* and a couple of other biggies, and I thought: This can't be happening, I mean this is a big, *big* film. I was sky-high.

Then we went to Georgia and I realized I had to really look like an expert in a canoe. Strangely enough, the only one of the four of us who had ever been in a canoe was Ned Beatty. There was a lagoon—literally a lagoon like in Central Park, placid, quiet water. I'll never forget this: we walked down with the two canoes, I got in one with Ned Beatty and Jon Voight got in the other with Ronny Cox, and we paddled out in this quiet lagoon. John Boorman was standing on a hill with two propmen. We were out there a total of ten minutes and both canoes tipped over. And I remember as I was swimming to the shore I heard the prop guy say, "We're going to be here a *long* time, a *long* time."

Then I met this incredibly imposing man, James Dickey, who is six-foot-six, wears a cowboy hat all the time, big belt buckles. I don't know how many of you are familiar with his other books, but he is a wonderful poet, a *wonderful* poet. And the kind of man that after he has four martinis you want to drop a grenade down his throat—he becomes a total ass. He only called us by our character names. He always called me Lewis, always called Jon Ed.

One night Dickey and I were walking along in the parking lot and he said, "You know, it actually happened." I said, "What?" He said, "You know it really happened." I said, "You mean the story?" He said, "Yep, but don't tell any of the others. You're the only one that could handle it." I said okay. Fade out. Five years later, Jon Voight and I are talking one night, and I said, "Do you know what Dickey told me one night?" Jon said, "I don't know what he told you but he told me it actually happened." I found out later he told Ronny Cox it had actually happened, he told Ned Beatty. We then met the four men that it was about; one was a banker, one was a lawyer. The guy who was Lewis was really a fascinating guy, I mean a really strange man who was in his middle forties, and every single weekend he went out and did something that could risk his life. Tested himself like that every single weekend. And Dickey wanted to be Lewis—he *desperately* wanted to be Lewis, not the Voight character, which is who he was. And what I think happened . . . I don't think the rape actually happened. Probably that started to happen and nobody did anything about it. And they came back to Atlanta, and Dickey regretted it. Knowing Dickey as I do, I think one of the great thrills of his life would be to kill somebody in the act of saving someone's life. To him, if you don't have a gun rack in your house, you're a homosexual.

Anyway, Dickey said to me, "Have you read a book called *Zen and the Art of Archery?*" I said no, and he said, "You must read that book, boy, otherwise you'll never be Lewis." I said I didn't have the book and he said, "*I* have the book." So he gave it to me and I read it; it's an incredible book. What it says is that *you* don't release the arrow—the *arrow* releases you, and it goes where you want it to go.

We got to rehearsing every day. The four of us became so close. We would rehearse all morning and then go get in the canoes in the afternoon. In the original script there was a scene where we're shooting targets—in fact I talk them into going on this trip while we're shooting targets. And supposedly I never miss. We went out to shoot and I couldn't hit anything—I was hitting my feet or hitting the trees or hitting the mountain. But when I got the character, when Lewis started coming to me, we were rehearsing one day and I knew I had him. We got into this scene with the bows and arrows and I picked up the arrow and I shot seven arrows into the bull's-eye about forty yards away. And *I* didn't release the arrow; *it* released me. Now, nothing like this had ever happened to me before. We went on with the scene and Boorman said, "Okay, fantastic, you've got it." Freddy Baer, the archery expert who was there to help us, said, "I've never seen anything like that in my life." Now, once more out of character, I picked up the bow again and shot—and the arrows went into the trees. We started rehearsing again, and again, in character, I shot seven arrows into the bull's-eye.

We then went down to the river—and we got into the boats *in character.* I was Lewis, totally confident, unafraid of anything. We started down the river and they said, "Okay, you can stop there," and I said, "No, we're not going to stop." We rounded a corner, and ahead it looked like Niagara Falls. To us, it *was* Niagara Falls. Ned Beatty was screaming at me, "Stop, stop the boat," but I was *Lewis.* We went over the rapids, didn't tip over, pulled up to the side, got out, brought the canoes back, and Boorman said, "Why'd you do that?" I said, "I don't know." I was compelled to do it. That was the end of the rehearsal but we got back in the canoes—and *then* I fell over. It was *only,* only when I was within the character of Lewis that I could *not* tip over the canoe, I could *not* miss with the arrows. It's never happened to me before in a character, and never since.

FROM AUDIENCE: Were some of those actors really hillbillies?

REYNOLDS: Really, there were four actors from Hollywood in that picture. And the other guys . . . let me tell you about the guy with no teeth. Before I got into acting I used to do a Wild West show in North Carolina. I used to get shot and fall off a roof every hour, for $100 a week. And in this Wild West show, there was a guy who had no teeth in front; he couldn't read or write and he stuttered. But I loved him and I always thought to myself, God, this guy is such a good actor. Fade out. Fifteen years later we were trying desperately to find a guy who had no teeth in front, because that was a plot point. And I said to Boorman, "I remember this guy from the Wild West show and his name is Cowboy Cower." They sent word out and he showed up for a reading. And when he came Boorman took me aside and said, "Did you tell him what to wear?" I said no, I didn't. He came in bib overalls with no shirt and no shoes. He sat down and Boorman gave him a script. Now, I had forgotten to tell Boorman that he couldn't read. Boorman said, "Do this part right here," and of course there was this *long,* long silence. I didn't know what to do. I wanted to help bail him out. But then he looked up at Boorman and he said, "I f-f-f-forgot my glasses." There was another long moment, then I said, "That's okay, Cowboy, I'll tell you the lines, and you just say 'em any way you want to say 'em." So I said, "The first line is 'Get over there against that tree and take your pants down.' " And Cowboy says, "Get o' . . . get over there agin that sss . . . s-s-saplin, and take yer p-p-p-panties down." Boorman said, "You've got the part." Then Boorman said, "Now I have to tell you some things. First of all, this role pays scale—which is three hundred and some dollars a week." The man had never *seen* that much money. "Secondly, this man you're going to play, he has sex with another man. I mean, he *rapes* another man." There was this long silence again and Cowboy said, "Well, that's all right, I done a lot w-w-w-worse things than that."

FROM AUDIENCE: I want to know how the other actors learned how to run the rapids? I know you've been a stunt man and could do things like that . . .

REYNOLDS: Well, doing stunts and handling rapids, one has nothing to do with the other. We *all* had to learn how to ride the rapids— and the four of us literally did everything in this picture ourselves. Vilmos Sigmond, the cinematographer, who is incredible, had the camera on a long, long lens. You know, when I was in London I was fortunate enough to meet the director Stanley Kubrick. He literally ran up to me at this party and he said, "How'd you shoot that picture, how did you shoot it? It was you in the canoe?" "Yeah," I said, "it was us. We just did it." He said, "But how? Where were the cameras?" They were on rocks, up on the hills. We shot the picture with a crew of about twelve. And I must tell you that at least ten times I—and the other guys on the picture—were almost killed. Without exaggeration. We were lost, didn't have a chance. But we somehow managed to get ashore. We just did it, but I don't know how we did it. I'd never attempt to do it again, I *couldn't* do it again.

FROM AUDIENCE: Why do you think this film was successful?

REYNOLDS: There is a certain genre of film—like *Wages of Fear*— that represents terror, real terror, man against the elements, man testing himself. It's a great French film that unfortunately some guy tried to make again.* And I stole from the film, unashamedly, the idea of the broken bone sticking out of my leg. It was a pork bone that I bought at a butcher shop and broke in half and then tied around my leg. I'm not comparing *Deliverance* to *Wages of Fear*— but it is a classic. Because of the fact that the four actors did everything themselves; because Boorman was an Irishman who came and attacked the difference between Atlanta and northern Georgia, like night and day, and his fascination with it. Sometimes the fascination of someone from Europe about something in our country results in something better than what we can do. Sometimes, of course, it is disastrous, but in this particular case I think it was wonderful.

FROM AUDIENCE: Seems to me that the film is half yours, and half Jon Voight's, and the two pieces don't seem to connect. And also, I think that the film is half an action/adventure film and halfway trying to deliver a heavy message.

REYNOLDS: A good observation. First of all, when we crash at the bottom of the falls and I break my leg and it's all bent out of shape, I did, I think, the best scene I've ever done in my life in a picture. It was about a seven- or eight-minute scene—but it's not in the movie. Now, that scene is where I make him, literally *make* him [Voight]

*William Friedkin's *Sorcerer,* a $20-million failure.

climb the mountain. It was staggering to me that Boorman cut it out of the film; first of all because, to me, Voight so *suddenly* turns into Jungle Jim and starts climbing up this mountain. It never quite came together. When I went to Boorman and said, "Why are you cutting this out, it's my first important film," he took me aside and said, "Because the first half of the film is yours, the second half of the film is Voight's. It has to be that way. With that scene, he never gets it from you. He *has* to take the picture from you." I said, "I'm not fighting for me, I'm fighting for the picture—I think it *needs* that scene." He said, "No, you're wrong." Now, *Deliverance* did make $43 million, but that doesn't mean it couldn't have been a better film, and it could have been clearer. Judy and I were talking about this earlier—when you saw it tonight, Judy, did you miss that scene?

CRIST: I was conscious of it not being there. But for me it works as a transition point. For me, so much of Voight's propulsion up the mountain is the aftermath of terror. And he does carry the theme, far more than Lewis—who is, essentially, the guy who doesn't change. It is Voight who takes over the "game"; as you say to him, "Now it's *your* game." Basically the movie is about survival. What I was very conscious of tonight was the extreme power of the events and action—it's just jet-propelled. And in thinking of that scene and its omission, I felt that it might weight the movie at that transition point, instead of going forward into another theme. I don't think I miss it that much, the dynamics work awfully well for me.

FROM AUDIENCE: I assume that when you first saw the movie you felt you'd done a good job and you were proud of it and so forth. But there are other movies that I go and see and say, "Wow, how could they make this movie, didn't they know what was happening?" How do you feel when you're in a movie like that?

REYNOLDS: You're going to see a picture this weekend that was critically massacred, called *Lucky Lady*. In the middle of the film, I knew we were drowning, knew we were sinking. But what happens to me, what happens to most professionals who care about their work, is that you start to fight harder, you work harder. The ship is sinking, do whatever you can, stick some mud in that hole, grab this, you know—you just work that much harder. But unfortunately, sometimes, that's when I see a lot of actors do what I call the constipated school of acting. It becomes "uuhhh" [straining]—

and that's bad acting. I like acting you can't catch. When you make it look easy, you're doing it right.

What happened in *Lucky Lady* is that we had a director [Stanley Donen] who'd done some films that were wonderful, just *wonderful—Singin' in the Rain, Two for the Road, Bedazzled, Arabesque*—great films. But he was lost when he got out there with those boats. He was wonderful in the bedroom; the opening part of the picture is wonderful and the relationship among the three of us—Liza [Minnelli] and [Gene] Hackman and myself—is terrific. I mean we all three really, really care about each other. But when we got out there on the boats in the ocean—suddenly we had Captain Queeg directing us. You know those things that airline workers wear on their heads so they can't hear the sound of the engines—well, he wore those because the sound of gunshots scared him. Hackman and I got so angry that the next time we played a scene we just mouthed the words, making no sounds at all, and he said, "Cut, print." The sound man ran up to him—unfortunately he was a Mexican who didn't speak English that well—and he said, "There is no . . . no sound." And he screamed at him, "You're fired." Hackman and I had to tell him, "You idiot, you can't hear us because you've got those cockamamie things on your ears."

And you couldn't tell the good guys from the bad guys—you didn't know one boat from another. He didn't know anything about action; he was lost out there. He shouldn't have been doing that kind of picture. He should have been doing a romantic light comedy, which he's brilliant at. So, to answer your question—when you know you're sinking, what you do is you fight, and you try. I fought Donen, Gene fought him. I hung him over the side of the boat one time. Gene turned into Popeye Doyle and tried to drive over him with his car; Liza danced on his head—I mean, we did *everything*. He just didn't know what he was doing in the action sequences—and that's why the picture failed. Other than that, I think *Lucky Lady* is a helluva picture.

FROM AUDIENCE: Is it true that *Lucky Lady* had several endings?

REYNOLDS: Yes, there were three endings. We went to see a screening of the picture and in the ending that Liza and I wanted, Gene and I die. It was an incredible scene, very well shot. There's a fade-out and it comes back fourteen years later, and she marries this guy who has lots and lots of money. She has two children, and nobody knows she was ever a bootlegger or had ever been on a boat in her life. And they go out on this huge three-masted schooner, and they're sailing alone, and it's now 1950 or something, and she says to the captain, "Do you mind if I take the wheel?" He says, "The winds are pretty heavy, think you can handle it?" She says she thinks she can, and she takes the wheel and she turns right into the wind—the sails billow up and guys are running all over the boat—it was an electrifying scene. The tears are running down her face, she's sailing this boat into the wind—as she had done before. You suddenly see in her mind these two guys that she loved and cared about. It gave the movie such texture—and quality, I thought.

So when we were asked to go to this very famous press conference on the *Queen Mary*, Hackman wouldn't go. Liza said, "I'll go, but I'm not going to say anything." And I said, "I'll go on one condition: I'm not going to lie." Those guys figured I was kidding. When I got there, somebody stuck up his hand exactly as you did and said, "Did the movie have three endings?" And I said yes. And he asked which one I liked. I said one that is not in the movie. I was asked if I thought the movie worked, and I said no. I said, for me, I love Jack Lemmon, I'm *crazy* for Jack Lemmon, and this was the closest thing I'd ever done in my career like him. I thought of him constantly when I was doing the part. I loved Hackman in the picture, and I loved Liza in the picture—but for some reason it doesn't quite come together. But, yes, it had three endings—and you will see the *happy* one.

CRIST: We'll continue the conversation tomorrow. Meanwhile, we're going to see *The Longest Yard*. Anything you want to say about it ahead of time?

REYNOLDS: No, not ahead of time . . . well, only that there is an enormous amount of improvisation. Believe it or not, the picture was not a comedy when I was given the script. [Robert] Aldrich and I had a bargain: he'd say, "Okay, you do your schtick version," and I'd do my schtick version for the crew. And the crew would laugh. Well, 99 percent of the schtick version ended up in the movie. And believe it or not, in the original script, Eddie Albert shoots me in the back of the head when I go to get the ball. When we finally got about 75 percent into the movie, Bob Aldrich and I both knew that if you kill this guy, you kill the movie. But we wanted the audience to be afraid that he would be shot.

CRIST: So you're going to get another happy ending.

[After *The Longest Yard* and *W.W. and the Dixie Dancekings*]

CRIST: I meant to point out yesterday that in *Deliverance,* James Dickey played the big sheriff at the end who talks to Voight when he's leaving by car. This comes to mind because the man who played the policeman at the dance in *W.W. and the Dixie Dancekings* is Hal Needham, who then went on—I guess courtesy of you, Burt—to direct *Smokey and the Bandit.* How many of you have seen *Smokey and the Bandit?* [Scattered applause] That's really interesting, because very few people I know saw *W.W. and the Dixie Dancekings.* It's the kind of movie that doesn't play the East Side art theaters in New York. And I think of this not only as a piece of Americana, not only a "feel-good" movie, but also as a deeply satiric one throughout. It has a great deal of wit to it. Unfortunately, not enough people in the so-called movie-conscious community really see this kind of film. Its director, John Avildsen, is one of my favorite directors; I've known him since the days of *Joe* and he almost invariably has trouble making movies. I don't know whether it's because he's an artist, or because he's a different personality at work, or what.

REYNOLDS: A little of both.

FROM AUDIENCE: Did *W.W. and the Dixie Dancekings* make a lot of money?

REYNOLDS: Yes, it did. Not a lot of money: it made around $15 million, something like that. It was considered a box-office hit that year. It's interesting, as Judy said, that certain people don't see pictures like *Smokey and the Bandit.* The "film cinema buff" unfortunately sees the name Burt Reynolds and says, "I know what kind of picture this is going to be." And he doesn't see those films because he's interested in another kind of film. Well, so am I. I'm interested in making different kinds of films. I think I have. When we made *Smokey and the Bandit* we felt, as we did with *W.W.,* that we'd make our money south of the Mason-Dixon line. When the first receipts came in on *Smokey and the Bandit,* we'd made $24 million south of the Mason-Dixon line. I said, well, we're home free. *North* of the Mason-Dixon line it made $42 million. It is now up to $180 million. Now Judy, I don't know what people you're talking about who haven't seen it—but I don't even *care* who they are. . . .

FROM AUDIENCE: The rumor was that you made *Smokey and the Bandit* for a friend and you worked on a percentage. Is that true?

REYNOLDS: It's true. My friend is Hal Needham, who's my room-mate. He's my age and it's time he stopped falling off buildings. [Needham is a stuntman] He brought me this script. I said it was the *worst* script I've ever read in my life; it was a terrible script. He said, "Well, what'll I do?" I said, "Well, you've been in the business so long you must know some writer. Who do you know?" He said he knew James Lee Barrett. Barrett wrote what I consider a really wonderful Western called *Shenandoah*—the Broadway musical was based on it. Needham went to Barrett and he read the story that Hal had written and he said, "This is the worst piece of crap I've ever read in my life." But he agreed to write a screenplay—which he did. It turned out to be kind of a *Mad, Mad World* idea—a chase—but there were no jokes in it. The movie was there structurally, and we did have James Lee Barrett, and I told Needham he could go to a studio with that and I thought he'd get the money. The studio came back and said we had to have a star. I said okay, I'd do it.

At the time I was not feeling very well, and in fact I was sick—very sick. But it was okay because all I had to do was sit in the car. I had never worked with Sally [Field] before, but I wanted her in the picture very badly—so I called her on the phone and she said, "This is a terrible script." I said, "I know, but we can get in the car and improvise and do all kinds of things and make it work." I called [Jackie] Gleason. He thought it was a terrible script and I told him he could say what he wanted to say, I'd say what I wanted to say, and we'll get a crazy guy like Jerry Reed on the other end of the CB—Jerry is a CB freak—and he'll do all that Jerry Reed stuff—and something will happen.

Then they brought in two more writers. And, having done a lot of pictures in cars, I know that you don't want to be alone in a car. So I said we've gotta get somebody with Gleason—just to bounce off of. So I said, "Give him a son. He doesn't have to say anything, he could be an idiot." So we came up with the Mike Henry character. I worked a total of only four weeks in the picture—in the car. I got out of the car for two days. And I've made more money on that picture than on any other in my life. It's been an incredible financial success for me—and now Hal Needham is a very hot director.

FROM AUDIENCE: Do you do all your own stunts?

REYNOLDS: I do a great deal. I used to do everything that I could. There was a period in my life as an actor—I'm being very candid—when I was somewhat ashamed of being an actor. It's a silly way to make a living, you know; you come in and a guy hits you with a powder puff and you go out and somebody hands you a gun and you squat behind rocks and start shooting each other and you say other people's words. It wasn't until I'd been a successful actor and had made a lot of money that I realized how really hard it is to be good. And I wanted to be a good actor, desperately wanted to be good. Up until that time, I used to say, "For this money—*I* should take the car off the cliff, *I* should jump off the building, *I* should fall off the horse." A lot of pictures I did, which were bad pictures, when things got dull, I'd say, "Well, look, I'll just jump out the window here. You throw a punch and I'll go out the window." That's why in all my pictures guys are going out the window, cars are turning over—because I'd say, "It's a little dull here, let's turn the car over." As I got older, I started falling out of windows less.

My acting—well, I've worked really hard for twenty-two years to make it look really easy. When people say to me, "You just play yourself, you just have fun," they don't realize how hard it is to make it look easy, to make it look fun, and make it look like I'm just walking through it. That's what I *want* people to say, I work hard for them to say that. I really don't want them to come up to me and say, "Boy, you really *acted*."

I never caught Spencer Tracy acting. I was under contract to Universal in 1958 and '59, and they were doing a picture called *Inherit the Wind*. I went every single day and sat in the back and watched Tracy and Freddie March act together, and Tracy would change every single take—just a little inflection. Freddie March did *everything* the same; they were equally good as actors, but had different ways of doing things. Because Tracy changed something a little each time it made the other actor better because he would have to react to what he did, and it was moment-to-moment acting.

Eventually, Tracy saw this pudgy-faced kid back there, every day, with this riverboat outfit on, and he said to me one afternoon, "Are you an actor, kid?" and I said, "Yessir, Mr. Tracy." And he said, "It's a great profession—so long as nobody ever catches you at it."

FROM AUDIENCE: Do you find it more difficult, as an actor, to be in a film where the script comes from another medium as opposed to an original screenplay?

REYNOLDS: More difficult? If it's a classic situation—I mean, a book that's a classic, like *Deliverance*—I actually find it easier. Because the words are everything. Despite all the things I've said here about improvising, and I love to improvise, you gotta have the words. Words are the most important things. If I were the head of a studio, the first thing I would do, I would stop paying actors a million dollars and I'd start paying the Neil Simons and the Larry Gelbarts a million dollars. Actors are not worth a million dollars, the words are. With the words, you can get any actor. But they do it backward: they go get the actor, then they get anybody for a writer because they know that with that actor and anybody's words they can do a picture. With me, it's a different situation, because unfortunately—I say "unfortunately" because of Mrs. Crist, not because of the people—I'm considered a personality, a personality and an actor. That's a very difficult situation to be in. You can't please both the people and the critics. If I as an actor attempt to do something that's not the guy on the *Tonight* show, that's really different from that guy, the people who really like the personality—and I love them for liking him, because he's me—well, those people are disappointed. And they tell me so. But I'm an actor. I *want* to act. You see before you a very well-paid movie star . . . and a starving artist.

FROM AUDIENCE: I wonder if you have an interest in live theater, and if so, what kind of play attracts you?

REYNOLDS: I was very near to doing the play version of *Semi-Tough*. I was so crazy about the book; David Merrick owned the rights and I was going to come back to New York to do it, ready to accept the slings and arrows as a Hollywood actor coming to New York, because I knew everyone would forget that this was where I started. But then David decided, for some strange reason, to do it as a musical. My musical track record is not that thrilling, and so I decided not to do it. Then Merrick decided to do it as a film. To answer your question, I wanted very much to do *Chapter Two*. They weren't interested. I would have come back for that—and I'm very interested in doing the film.*

FROM AUDIENCE: What are your feelings about *Nickelodeon?*

REYNOLDS: In order to talk about *Nickelodeon,* you have to talk about Peter Bogdanovich. You're talking about a man who did something quite extraordinary. He was a film critic. He then went

---

*Since made, starring James Caan.

out and made *The Last Picture Show,* which won a few nominations for the Academy Award. He was very *resented* for that. Not openly, but somewhere down deep inside, the critics said . . . kill. He went on to make *What's Up, Doc?,* which made a fortune, another commercial success. Then he made *Paper Moon,* which was an enormous success.

Now, the critics were waiting. They had their knives out. They *wouldn't* have had their knives out, except that Peter has an incredibly unfortunate personality. When he goes on a talk show, he acts like he studied humility with Gene Barry. He becomes the most pompous, arrogant person. Personally, he really isn't that way. When you get him away from the spotlight there's a kind of boyish charm about him. He's not a pseudo-intellectual, he's a true intellectual. And all he ever wanted to be in his life is a movie star. He doesn't want to be a director; he wants to be a movie star. He *loves* movies, loves them. He made a fatal mistake—which a lot of directors make after they've had a string of successes: they think they can make anybody an actor or an actress. So he took a property, *Daisy Miller,* which was a very difficult, almost impossible task to begin with—even if you have Jane Fonda. But with Cybill Shepherd it was truly impossible. It was a disaster, and the critics had their chance—and they *killed* him. But that wasn't enough. He bounced right back and said, "Okay, now I'm really angry. Now I'm going to make a musical, and I'm going to make a Cole Porter musical." That was *At Long Last Love.* The Cole Porter fans are *fanatics* about Cole Porter. There were no words, no script—Peter can't write a script, Peter's a terrible writer. So he had these awful scenes between these wonderful, wonderful songs, and because he loved Ernst Lubitsch—we were going to do it live.*

I said, "Look, I don't mind taking a chance." People are always accusing me of not taking chances, but I said, "I'll take a chance, I'll sing and dance. But why do I have to do it *live?* Howard Keel doesn't do it live, why do I? I mean, there hasn't been a live musical since Ernst Lubitsch." Peter said, "That's why—we'll get great credit for it." I said, "But it won't say up there on the screen, 'He's singing *live.*' " I had a wire stuck in my ear, a wire went down my pant leg. It all had to be done in one take, no cuts, because you had to start the song and end the song while listening to this piano

---

*By "live," Reynolds means the musical numbers were not dubbed, and sound was recorded during the action.

player a block away. And right in the middle of singing "You're the Top," I get all this gibberish in my ear and I've got a Tijuana radio station. I say, "*Wait-a-minute*, stop!"

I was also working with a lady, Cybill Shepherd, who is not a singer or a dancer but who had studied opera for two years. And whom the director was madly in love with. Mind you, one number would have to be done in *one* day. I'd do a song and she, for whatever reason, didn't like it. She'd look at him and say, "I didn't like it," and we'd do it again. We'd do thirty-five takes. I had to look at her and think, "Boy, I gotta be good in this one, this may be the one she likes." There were no subtitles saying anything about that.

So, then, you gotta think why in the world did I ever do another film [*Nickelodeon*] with the man. And it's because he's a wonderful filmmaker, and there's a wonderful film in Peter. It just shouldn't be written by him. Now Ryan O'Neal and I are old friends, since way before he was on *Peyton Place* and I was on *Riverboat*—and we'd always wanted to do a film together. Also, I idolized Orson Welles: he was supposed to play what turned out to be the Brian Keith part. They had a wonderful script called *Starlight Parade*, which I read. And I thought, with Peter's sense of history about cinema—I mean, he's incredible—this could work. With the right people. So I committed, on the basis of *Starlight Parade*. I then went away and came back and there was a picture called *Nickelodeon*, which Peter had written. *Starlight Parade* was thrown out.

Nickelodeon, for me, had just beautiful isolated scenes. But Peter hates sentimentality more than anything in life. I happen to *love* sentimentality. That was what was lacking. None of the characters in the picture were likeable—I thought they were very selfish. We talked before about what you do when you're in the middle of a picture and you realize it isn't working. This wasn't a collaborative effort, really, because Peter doesn't listen too much to actors; so I figured I had to do something to save myself. I said, "Well, I'm going right to instant-humble and charm; I'm going to Gary Cooper, to "gosh, oh golly gee, ma'am, I'm really proud to be here, and how'do." I tried to be *so* likeable, because I knew Ryan's character wasn't likeable, the other people weren't likeable; Peter never gave them a chance to be sweet. It's terribly important, I think.

Nickelodeon never quite came together; the characters didn't come to full circle. And it didn't work—*critically* it didn't work. For

Peter Bogdanovich to have a hit, he has to be four times better than any other director—and he will be. I promise you this.

CRIST: I had a unique experience with Nickelodeon. Those of you who've been here before know that I'm a great Bogdanovich fan. I was so in love with the *pieces* of Nickelodeon, and so taken with the passion he has for the past of movies. I was in the minority: I thoroughly enjoyed Nickelodeon on first viewing. Then I looked at it again a few months later, and I realized that as a pure movie-lover, I'd been too hooked, I'd been deluded by the bits and pieces. The pace of the movie is so wrong, so off. On second viewing it absolutely collapsed. The basic problem—and you put your finger on it, Burt—was the people. I had cared about the history, but I suddenly realized I didn't give a damn about the human beings embodying it. I've known that if I like a film it improves with age—or if I dislike it, it gets worse on second viewing. This is the one experience I've had in recent years where a second viewing showed every flaw. I think Nickelodeon is a movie-lover's delight—but not if you like good movies.

FROM AUDIENCE: How do you feel about going out and promoting your own film?

REYNOLDS: I was the first actor ever to go on a television show and say, "Look, this movie is a turkey." That's now become very much in vogue, but I was the first to do it because I had a lot more turkeys to talk about than most people and I also thought it would be very amusing. But I've never promoted a movie I didn't believe in.

FROM AUDIENCE: Do you have any plans to direct again?

REYNOLDS: I want to direct more than anything. When the opportunity came up to direct The End I was doing Lucky Lady. I was sent a script and I called the person who sent it and I said, "This is a terrible script." They called back and asked if I wanted to direct it. There was this awful silence. And I said, "It does have certain qualities." I worked so hard on Gator.* I wish I'd brought it here—particularly because of a couple of scenes I'm very proud of. In one of the scenes I wanted the leading man, especially me at the time, to say to a woman, "I love you"; then she would say, "That's nice, but look, I'm going to New York, I have a chance to be the next

*His first directorial work, in 1976.

Barbara Walters, and you think a martini is an Italian boxer, and you are nice, physically attractive and we get along great, but we have nothing in common except that you were nice while I was here. But I'm today's woman." In every movie I've ever been in, the guy always leaves the lady crying; she's pregnant and the house is burning and he's driving off down the street. I wanted to play that scene because it does happen to men as well as women. So I wrote the scene and I also wrote the love scene on the beach, which I thought was terribly romantic and chic, right out of a Frank Capra movie. Molly Haskell, who was at that time writing for the *Village Voice,* was the only critic who picked up on it, and she wrote about this so-called male-chauvinist macho pig that everybody had pulled out of the centerfold magazine who had done this picture and done a total reverse with such reverence for women. She took those two particular scenes and wrote about them for three paragraphs. I sent her on an around-the-world tour after that.

CRIST: I like the ermine coat, too.

REYNOLDS: Okay. *The End,* which is a picture that had been sitting in Hollywood for six years, was written for Woody Allen. It's not a how-to picture on how to enjoy death without really trying. It's a story of one man. It's not *your* approach to death—or anybody's you know, it's not *mine.* But my feelings about the picture when I read the script were so strong that I wanted to do this film. I wanted to act in it, but nobody I knew wanted to direct it. They were afraid of it. I said I'll direct it; nobody cared. It got to the point where I had done a couple of pictures that made a *lot of money,* and I could have gone into the studio and said, "I want to do the Dom DeLuise story, and I want to play Dom DeLuise, and I want Dom to play my mother." I could have said *anything.* And they would have said, "Can you bring it in for a million?" At that time they were so hungry for product, and they knew because of the computer that if you had a picture with these actors, for this amount, you could make money. It didn't matter if it was good or bad, it was just a judgment from the computer. I said, "I'll bring this picture in for $2 million and I'll go out and get these people." I named some unbelievable people—and had no idea if I could get them—but I got them. And it was, for me personally, the most wonderful experience I've ever had. Directing is everything—it's the difference between being a chess player and a chess pawn.

When people ask me why we don't do a remake of such-and-such a film, I say it's *crazy* to do a remake of a *successful* film. Nobody realizes how lucky it is to have a successful film. But there are millions of unsuccessful films that had brilliant scripts. Let's do one of them. Maybe the first time they were cast wrong, they had the wrong director, they were distributed at the wrong time, whatever. Let's go back and look at some of those pictures from the forties and fifties, the wonderful scripts that didn't work. Let's do them—but to redo a *Gone With the Wind* or *Mutiny on the Bounty* is insane, it's crazy. They're works of art and should be left alone. You can't do them better, and if you do them brilliantly that means you're just as good as the guy that did it the first time. Besides, you've got that person embedded in your mind anyway. I was offered Gable in *Gable and Lombard*. And I said no—about eleven times. The eleventh time, they offered me such an amount of money it was indecent to turn it down. And I said to them, "I'll play Tom Mix, because Tom Mix is dead. I only play dead people. But at night, when I turn on the television and I see Gable—he's alive."

[After *Lucky Lady*]

CRIST: This, of course, is the movie of the many endings, and I never saw this ending. The one that was shown to the film critics in New York wound up with a scene of the three of them in bed—about twenty years later. They all have gray hair—it really looked like something out of an eighth-grade play. I've never seen such abominable makeup. You could just see the powder in the hair and the cotton-wool eyebrows.

REYNOLDS: I'm glad you liked it, Judy.

CRIST: And that ending had been shot at very great expense in Rome, because Liza at that point was making a far more unfortunate film with her father and Ingrid Bergman, *A Matter of Time*.

REYNOLDS: Liza had exactly half a day to get twenty years older and do the scene with Gene and me. We were in this strange Italian studio, got into this enormous bed, and did the scene. I turned to Gene during one of the rehearsals and I said, "Am I crazy, or do we look like we're in a high-school play?" It was too late to get our own makeup man over there—but I'm not sure it would have worked if we had come off looking like Dustin Hoffman in *Little Big Man*.

CRIST: No, makeup wouldn't have helped that scene.

REYNOLDS: Wish you'd come to the point.

CRIST: I know that actors have an entirely different view of something they've been in—but I much prefer the ending that is now on *Lucky Lady*, where everybody lives happily ever after *à trois*. I just could not swallow that movie if suddenly the two guys are blasted away in the course of a gunfight, which was the original ending, and then, poetically, having Liza in her old age take the wheel of the ship—as Burt described the scene.

REYNOLDS: I thought I described it beautifully.

CRIST: You did—and it almost got to me, and I was perfectly willing to tack it on the movie today, but I just couldn't hack it. I think it would have contradicted the whole movie to have the two of you killed.

REYNOLDS: I was wondering—did anybody except me have a problem telling the good guys from the bad guys in the boats? I mean, I was out there . . . and I didn't know whom to shoot at, didn't know what the hell was going on. And in the audience sense, there was nobody to cheer for. John Ford had this theory, which I totally agree with, that you can take a thousand Indians over the hill and shoot them all, and you can say, well, that's interesting, a thousand people just got shot. But, if you get to know three people, your heavies, if you get to know them just a little bit, and you bring them over the hill and shoot them, you've got an important moment in the film. We didn't know anything about anybody, so when people would get blown out of the water, you'd think, oh, that was an interesting explosion . . . but you didn't really care.

I think, in this picture, it was a brave thing to establish the *ménage à trois*, with us in bed. It was very brave of Stanley to want to do it that way and I thought it was brave of us to do it. We did take a lot of lumps for it. Hackman, I gotta tell you, was not crazy about the idea of getting in bed with the two of us; he thought we'd never get away with it. And I said if we have fun and we do it with class, we can get away with anything—a philosophy that's meant the destruction of my life.

CRIST: I think that is the distinction of the film, that it takes a very 1930s romantic theme and handles it in very seventies fashion, and I for one felt it was extremely palatable. What I really like about the movie is the three people—and the woman being something quite different from just a girl who's chased. She manipulates the situation among the three of them. On the other hand, the more you think about it, they don't change, they're just the same as they were at the start—and that's the film's weak point. This to me is a very important thing in looking at films, because you want it to be something beyond a photograph—there has to be some kind of change somewhere in a situation, in a person.

FROM AUDIENCE: If Liza Minnelli hadn't taken that role, would it have been someone like Madeline Kahn?

REYNOLDS: No. I love Madeline, but she was not considered for this. I'll tell you a story behind the story. George Segal was set to play Hackman's part, and I didn't believe that I could play a kind of schlemiel—that kind of weak, lovable guy—to Segal. Because I thought that on film I'd be too strong for him. I'm not talking about strength in acting ability . . .

CRIST: Yes, because he *is* a schlemiel on film.

REYNOLDS: He's a wonderful schlemiel—and I thought we'd be just *two* schlemiels. So George got out of doing the picture—all kinds of things came up and he was almost sued, but he got out.

Then came the problem—rather a concern from the studio— about whether Liza was pretty enough for these two guys to be killing each other over. I personally feel that has nothing to do with why you'd kill someone over a lady. Jane Fonda would have been sufficient to the role, but I think Jane Fonda can do *anything*. At that time there was not yet a Marsha Mason or Sally Field—in a big way. Liza and Barbra Streisand were the only women who could sell tickets.

FROM AUDIENCE: I'm curious to know how this did financially, and, in general, how you gauge what spells success for a picture?

REYNOLDS: You think this way: if a picture costs $2 million it has to make $6 million to break even. So this picture cost $14 million. Multiply that, three times fourteen, and you realize it isn't into any profits yet, but it's not that far off from being in the black.

You know the majority of reviewers really hated this film, and I think there were a lot of reasons for that that went beyond the film itself. I think there was resentment at that time for films that cost that much money, which really should have nothing to do with whether you like a film or not. If you're going to review a film, you have to put the blinders on and say, "I don't know this actor, don't know how much this film cost." But people were so *incensed* that *Lucky Lady* cost that enormous amount of money that they wanted to kill it.

CRIST: There are things that build up during the making of a movie, the things you hear—so-and-so has left, and so-and-so has come in, and so-and-so is getting millions. It can go on for a very long period and it builds up kind of a bad miasma and unfortunately, I think, a lot of critics are affected by it and they go in with a "show me" approach to the film.

REYNOLDS: I must say that I've been guilty of that, as a filmgoer. And I *love* movies. But when I saw *A Bridge Too Far,* and I'm a fan of Redford's, I heard that he got $3 million and worked two weeks. I went to that film and I saw some *brilliant* English actors eating all the American actors alive. Every one of the Americans was such a cliché. I hated them. And by the time I got to Redford I hated him so much that I wanted to throw stuff at the screen! So I got sucked into the same thing I was just saying that critics shouldn't get sucked into.

CRIST: It's one of the tragedies of business. You can't raise the kind of money that went into *A Bridge Too Far* until you can see that you've got Robert Redford—then someone in Japan is willing to give you the money. But you're so right about the British actors, and Redford, for his two weeks' work, was on screen approximately two and a half minutes. That turned out to be one of those "Hey, there" spectaculars—when you say, "Hey, there's Robert Redford—oops, hey, there's Ryan O'Neal."

FROM AUDIENCE: Mr. Reynolds, you've complained about being stereotyped, so is it possible for you to come up with some of your own ideas for films or characters?

REYNOLDS: That's exactly what I'm doing now. I'm only doing projects now—I've committed myself and will have no excuses—because from this day on, I'm only doing what I want to do. Literally, I used to say things like, "Where's this movie going to be shot?" And they'd say, "Jamaica." I'd say, "I'll take it." Or they'd say, "We've got this movie with Dyan Cannon," and I'd say, "Gee, I've always liked her, I'll take it." I never used to care what the character was about, and as I grew as an actor I found out how difficult it was to find a good script.

FROM AUDIENCE: Would you ever go back into television?

REYNOLDS: If I do it'll be one of two ways, either to produce a special, or do something I think is uniquely a movie-of-the-week. There are certain scripts you get that are wonderful ideas, but they're movies-of-the-week. I think *Sybil* was a good example of that. It could hold up for two nights—or four nights. It was fabulous. But, if it had been a theatrical film and regardless of how brilliant the reviews would have been—and they would have been brilliant for both Sally [Field] and Joanne [Woodward]—it would have been a difficult picture to get people to pay money to see. Yet there was a phenomenal audience for that picture on TV—50 or 60 million saw that on television.

FROM AUDIENCE: You say you have director approval; do you also have decision approval?

REYNOLDS: No. I have such respect for the director—especially now that I've directed, it's even worse. I'm in a terribly precarious position. I just screened *The End* the other night for Alan Pakula—I'm about to do a film with him in October [*Starting Over*]. He said to me after, "I have such mixed emotions about working with you now—because this subject matter you handled in this film, I would be petrified to do. How are we going to get along?" I said, "We'll get along great—I loved the last director I worked with, on *The End*, so I'll love you. I'll give you every bit the respect I gave him." I have enormous contributions to make other than just showing up and being there. If a director doesn't want them, I think that's his loss. But I've never in my life said to a director, "Don't put the camera there; give us a close shot here." He's the director. I come as an actor, a professional, and do what he says—you have to, it's a director's medium.

FROM AUDIENCE: I'd like to know just how you go about directing yourself as an actor. Do you use videotapes?

REYNOLDS: Yes, I used videotape, and I got so objective with this guy. I'd look at the videotape and say, "I've got to talk to him about that," and I literally thought of him—me—as another person. The only problem I had—and it was a big problem—was getting into a two-way scene, a scene that doesn't belong to one actor or the other. I loved this film so much, I felt so unselfish about it—I had a terrible time *not* giving away scenes. A friend on the set would constantly come up and say, "You forgot your closeup, schmuck. You did everybody's closeup but yours." I wasn't protecting myself. Partly, I guess that comes from being worried about the people on the set saying, "Hey, look, he's doing a tight closeup of himself." But I'll get over that. If I'm given the time that Woody [Allen] was given to grow, I'll get over that.

FROM AUDIENCE: Several months ago we spent a fantastic weekend here with Jon Voight and *Coming Home*—who incidentally predicted we'd have a fantastic weekend here with you; he said he loved working with you. One of the things he mentioned that relates to what I want to ask you was that he got the part he played in *Coming Home* by hounding Ashby, constantly telling him why he should have the role—really fighting for it. My question is, what role have you really thought you were good enough to play that they didn't want to give you, that you'd fight that hard for?

REYNOLDS: That part that Jon played in *Coming Home*. . . . I'm not kidding now, I'm not being funny. He did fight for it, but Jon and Jane's relationship goes back a long, long way, during the whole Vietnam situation. And she felt enormous loyalty to Jon, and rightly so, because Jon spoke out when the rest of us were running around trying to make a living. She loved him for that. That would have been a tremendous part for me if I were going to try to convince some people I could go into that kind of heavy, heavy area of dramatic-romantic acting, which I would like to do. That would have been the perfect part to do it. And that was one of those roles I wanted to do very much. But the relationship was too strong there between Jane and Jon. There's also a theory that if you have a Jane Fonda, you don't need me, supposedly. I disagree in one sense, because I think Jane's audience is not my audience—and vice versa. It could have been wonderful for the two of us because I could have gotten a lot of rednecks into seeing *Coming Home* and they would have been thrilled. And it would have been good for them.

FROM AUDIENCE: What about some of the roles Jack Nicholson does? I see a lot of interchangeability between what he does and what you do. I'm thinking of *The Last Detail*. I can really see you in that picture.

REYNOLDS: There are three pictures Jack did that I wanted to do, and one that I would have killed for—that was *Cuckoo's Nest*. When I saw the play the first time Off Broadway I said I *had* to play that part, I *had* to play it. I was down in Nashville doing W.W. *and the Dancekings* and this man named Milos Forman showed up on the set and said, "I want to talk to you about doing this movie *One Flew Over the Cuckoo's Nest*," and I said, "That's my part, I've waited all my life to play that part." He said, "Well, it's between you and one other actor." And I said, "But there's nobody in the business who can play that kind of comedy better than I can. Who's the actor?" He said Jack Nicholson. There was a *long* pause and I said, "Well, the nominations are coming out tomorrow," and Forman said "Yeah." And I said, "I guess Nicholson will be nominated for *The Last Detail.*" And he said, "Yeah." And I said, "See ya." He said, "No, you've got a chance," and I said, "No, I don't. But I love you for thinking of me and taking the trouble to fly down here." As you know, the next day Jack was nominated for an Academy Award. As you may *not* know, they had a terrible time putting that project together, because everybody was afraid of the subject matter. UA didn't want to do it. But when they got Jack to say yes, they got the money and everything went through. But at that time I didn't have anywhere near the power it takes to put a big project together. But thank you for saying that. I'm a big, big fan of Jack's. He's a sensational actor.

FROM AUDIENCE: I'm curious, because in all we've seen so far, you don't get the girl. Really, you don't play many romantic scenes.

REYNOLDS: If you want to come to my room later ... Seriously, in talking about my producing and putting some projects together, I happen to believe that the next big hit—and I'm not talking about *The Other Side of Midnight*, but a step beyond that—the next big commercial hit is going to be when somebody makes a really wonderful love story.

It's anticipation. In my mind, anticipation in a motion picture is the most exciting part of it. The anticipation of a fight is ten times more exciting than the fight itself. When a man walks in a room and another man stands up, and one guy breaks the bottle and the other guy takes a knife and they walk around and circle each other—you can make that moment go on forever. When a man looks across a crowded room and sees a woman—and this was another scene I put in *Gator* that wasn't in the script, because all my life I wanted to play that scene. I want to spot somebody across a crowded room and have her look and me look and me look and her look and me look. We did that for twenty minutes in *Gator*. I think that if somebody does it and does it right, it will be the biggest runaway hit—if it's done with grand style and humor and directed well with very good actors. And I'd like to do that picture, to answer your question. As to why I haven't done it before—when you do something well, or not even well, but when you do something that's very, very successful, as I have in a certain kind of film, then 99 percent of the films I'm offered are in a car talking to a redneck sheriff. There are not a lot of ladies in them, there's not a lot of witty dialogue. Believe me, if you can be funny in a car going 120 miles per hour, then it's easy to be funny with Marsha Mason in Neil Simon dialogue. It's hard to be funny in a car going 120 miles per hour, especially if you have no funny lines to say. If you can be romantic in the back seat of a car with your leg sticking out a window, you can be romantic if you've got a good script and a director like Fred Zinnemann.

I co-produced a picture with Bob Aldrich called *Hustle,* and I thought that Catherine Deneuve and Burt Reynolds, boy, I thought that would really work—because my fans were not her fans and her fans not mine. And when I saw her on television selling whatever it was, I just thought she was the sexiest lady I'd ever seen in my life. But the picture didn't work. It was the story of a prostitute and a cop—and it just didn't work. It wasn't Bob's fault, not Catherine's fault, and I don't think it was mine. We *tried* to do a love story, there was a lot of kissing and a lot of rassling and thrashing around the room. But there wasn't anything romantic about it.

When you look at those great romantic pictures of the forties— again, it was anticipation. Robert Montgomery never got together with a girl until ten minutes before the credits.

CRIST: I think that *The Goodbye Girl* is a step in that direction, and that *Coming Home* is certainly a love story.

REYNOLDS: But, Judy, don't you agree that those pictures weren't *sold* as love stories. They got people into *Annie Hall* by . . .

CRIST: By calling it a "nervous romance."

REYNOLDS: Right. Actually, *Coming Home* was billed as a romance because at the time they were scared to talk about Vietnam.

CRIST: I think it's evolutionary, because *Unmarried Woman* is another step forward; its point is not living happily ever after but that you can live quite happily alone. But you're right, I think we're ready for a red-hot romance. I want one where one partner does not die of a mysterious disease.

REYNOLDS: Right! I would love to do a film where a woman—and this is every woman's dream—a woman is married to this terrifically stable, wonderful, honest guy, and this terrible rogue enters her life. He's awful, but great in the sack. And she has both of them, and in the end she goes off and lives her life, but we think maybe they're going to meet sometime, someplace on down the line. I would of course play the nice husband, the dignified guy.

CRIST: And Gene Hackman would be the rogue.

[After *The End*]

[*Dom DeLuise on the platform with Crist and Reynolds*]

CRIST: As they are wont to say in Hollywood as they walk out of screenings noncommittally, "Well, you certainly have a *picture* there." I must say that I've never quite gotten a reaction to a movie like this before here, and this is the third movie I've shown here without my seeing it beforehand. I had shown them all with trepidation, but felt, what the hell. The first one was *The Sting*; the second was *Paper Moon*. And this is the third one. I like this movie very much, for a variety of reasons—and I'm sure we'll get to them. But Burt, for starters, I was curious when you mentioned earlier that *The End* was intended for Woody Allen. Had it been written at the time by someone who thought Woody would work with someone else's material?

REYNOLDS: Woody had mentioned the idea—I'm not sure how to phrase this—that death could be funny, if filmed the right way. I assume Jerry Belson, who wrote the original screenplay, had contact with Woody and went forward with it; then, of course, Woody got involved with his own projects and didn't want to do anything not under his banner. They went for Dustin Hoffman, who loved it but was afraid of it. It went around, and then Paul Newman, strangely enough, took an option on it for a year. One of the reasons I was able to get Joanne [Woodward] was that she was familiar with the script, and loved it. After Paul had it, it went around a few more years. Always when it got to the studio brass, they said there was no way they were going to do this picture. I mean, it just can't be done commercially. People will not go to see a picture about death and laugh; it's just too frightening.

When I read it the first time it was about three years before I got to do it. I had a meeting with James Brooks, another wonderful writer, who then owned it. Jerry Belson was there and I told him I loved the piece, and he said, "Well, you're not right for it." I said, "I don't want it for me, I just want to direct it, I believe in it." And he said, "Well, you're not a big enough director." "Well," I said to him, "someday I'll be big enough to come back and buy you both out." Which didn't turn out that way. Jim let go of the project, then a guy named Larry Gordon got hold of it, and I was finally in a position to go to UA and say this was the project I wanted to do. They said fine. Some of them had not even read it, and when they did read it, there was such a scream. I got panicky phone calls from Mike Medavoy, who said, "We'll let you do the picture on one condition, that at the end of the picture a guy runs up at the end of the film with a set of X rays and says you've got the wrong set of X rays." I said that would be cheating, the biggest cop-out in the world. If we're going to do it, we'll do it all the way. We argued back and forth, and finally they said, "Well, if you can do it for under $2 million," and I said, "I can do it for under $2 million and I can get Joanne Woodward and Pat O'Brien and Myrna Loy." I didn't have any idea if I could get those people.

Dom DeLuise was down in Miami. I was doing *Semi-Tough*, and we were on the beach and I walked up to him and said, "There's something I want you to read." I gave him the script and he flew back to California. I guess you read it in the plane.

DELUISE: My wife read it to me.

REYNOLDS: I forgot, you can't read. Then I got this call saying he loved it. And then I took all those people with that budget to UA and said I can do it in seven weeks, and we went from there. But it was really, really a tough picture to get off the ground.

DELUISE: But you also rewrote it. There's no screen credit, but he dissected the script word by word, scene by scene, and he improved the picture enormously.

REYNOLDS: Well, there's a lot of me in it. A lot of it had to do with personal experience. I was very, very sick for a year. I'll just tell you one quick story of why I wanted to do this picture. One night I had chest pains really bad, and I thought this was it. Now mind you, when fans want to find my house they buy this little map, and for another dollar they get the combination to the door. There's no problem in finding my house. I called for an ambulance and said I think I'm having a heart attack. The ambulance couldn't find my house. They could have gone and got a movie-star map. I went out and waved at them and they waved and went by. So then I laid down in the street and they finally stopped. We went to the hospital and there was nobody in the hospital that could do anything for me. So finally they shoved me into a room and started giving me intravenous injections. Over in the corner of this room were three wonderful old Jewish men playing cards. I was lying there thinking this was it, I was going, and I'd never made a really good picture other than *Deliverance*. I heard this knock—literally a knock—on the IV bottle. I looked up and there was this wonderful old face and he said, "You play cards?" And I said, "I'm dying." The old man said, "We're all dying. Come play cards." So I went over and I played cards. And I thought this is the way I'm going out . . .

The things that happened to me during that year when I was very, very sick were so funny and so real. And it would be nice to get to a point where we can laugh about dying. You know, Howard Hughes died, and there's no way you can buy yourself out of it. We're going to have to deal with it, and if we can deal with it making jokes about it then I think it makes life better. That's why the picture was very important for me to make.

In looking at the picture now, I see a lot of things wrong, a lot of things I wish weren't in it. But all in all, from the time Mr. DeLuise arrives in the picture, it sails along.

CRIST: Did you very purposely and consciously surrender your "good ole boy" character?

REYNOLDS: Yes, it was very calculated to try to find a new audience, an audience I've never had before. And I hope, really hope, that I don't lose the ones I already have. There will be an interesting thing, when those people in Tuscaloosa, Alabama, come into the theater to see *Smokey and the Bandit,* and the only thing they see is a guy who's gonna die. It's a long, long time before a truck comes over a ramp.

CRIST: I wondered if that scene was an homage to your past.

REYNOLDS: That's exactly what it was. I said at the beginning that if this picture doesn't make it, and it is going to be my little contribution to try to show somebody I can do something else—then let me put one tiny little car jump in there, one tiny little crash.

As you can see, there are lots of places in this movie where you can get trapped, but there was one pivotal scene to me that was very important. Fortunately, I had a little actress that you fall in love with, that's Kristy McNichol; it was terribly important; it had to be real. She's his daughter and so important to him, and he's so important to her. I had an eight-minute scene to make the audience fall in love with her—it was a pivotal scene, because at the end, in the drowning scene, he's out there and he knows he has nothing to live for—and he thinks of her. We had elaborate setups for the drowning scenes—different voice-overs, a whole funeral scene at one point. But we took all that out, because I realized that the only thing important to him in life was her.

Another thing I realized in making this movie is that it's a two-part love story. One part is a love story between Dom's character and me. We fall in love with each other out of depression because he's the only person who understands that I want to kill myself. The picture had three endings. One of them was that when I started to swim back in to the beach I wouldn't make it. I'm sure that some of you, if you've ever been in a hairy situation on an airplane or somewhere, where you started to pray—you make a lot of promises. Then, the minute you land, you forget them all. I've done it a lot; I've made a lot of bargains with God. Some of them I've kept—I don't drink. I said, I want to start this dialogue with God. The second ending is that Dom finally shoots me—shoots me in the head and kills me, then celebrates the fact that he's finally accomplished something and did something right. We realized that it was a terrible idea.

Then we came up with the idea, as we were shooting, of the *From Here to Eternity* shot of the lovers rolling around in the surf. And I thought, if we can pull this off people will scream. And I thought, that's the end of the picture, you can't follow that. Then we came up with the knife. And we came up with the end as a freeze frame of the knife coming right at me. And it looked like he was going to kill me. But I didn't want to go out that way. I wanted the picture to end, whether he lives for another six months or a year or whatever—with this guy chasing him. He's still gonna be chasing him, and he still loves him—but he says, "Stop, I don't want to die anymore!" To me this is the only real ending.

FROM AUDIENCE: I was just wondering how you felt about us as an audience. Did we laugh when you wanted us to laugh?

REYNOLDS: You were wonderful. This is a strange picture, because having seen it a couple of other times with other audiences, I know what's going to play—whether the audience is a sophisticated one or not. The one scene that I feel should come out now is the death-therapist scene—with Carl Reiner playing an optimistic death therapist who has a heart condition. I felt that everybody in this room knew that character was going to die before he died. We spent five minutes or eight minutes setting up a joke that everybody got before it happened. It is a good scene, and Reiner is wonderful in it, but as Bob Aldrich told me one time, you'll start out with a scalpel but you've got to end up with an ax. And sometimes what you cut is your best friend.

FROM AUDIENCE: You've directed two films now, *Gator* and *The End*. How do you feel about them now, and the differences between them?

REYNOLDS: The difference between the two screenplays is of course enormous. It's like comparing the first woman you fell in love with and the woman you married. You can't compare. I love them both—like they are both my children. Except one of them isn't very bright and didn't do very well, but I loved him: he was my child, I did everything I could for him. The next one is pretty bright, and has more of a chance.

FROM AUDIENCE: I'm wondering how this film is going to be sold to the public. How will it be presented in newspaper advertisements?

REYNOLDS: That's a very good question. The campaign is very important to me, for obvious reasons. So I got Gahan Wilson—who does the Charles Addams–type cartoons in *Playboy*. The ads are bizarre, macabre. For example, one is a drawing of a figure representing death, with the scythe, sitting in a theater eating popcorn with a corpse next to him. And the caption underneath is, "Gee, this is my kind of picture." There are a bunch of those strange Wilson cartoons. Another ad is of Dom hanging me and laughing; in another one he has a gun at my head, and I look very doubtful. The ads are terribly important, because we don't want anyone to think that it's another action-adventure comedy. We have a tremendous television campaign, for which I wrote and directed some scenes that are very macabre, so that there isn't any question about what the picture's like.

FROM AUDIENCE: There seems to be a company of players developing around you, isn't there?

REYNOLDS: Yes, that happens to all directors—because you get comfortable with certain people. You think about John Ford—he had those same people, and there's a reason for that. A director can look around at his cast and he knows the weaknesses and strengths in every one of them, what they can do and can't do. The danger, of course, is that a lot of the pictures start looking like a lot of other pictures. Altman has a company of people he brings along from picture to picture. You know, Gene Wilder said to me, as did Mel Brooks, that once you do a picture with Dom, you'll never be able to do a picture without him. But let me tell you something: he gives as much as he takes. But the time he spent in doing things that make the crew laugh, as wonderful as he is, all that time when the crew was laughing cost a lot of money. If I added up the time I spent saying, "Come on, settle down, cut it out, Dom," I could have taken a week off the budget of that picture. But it is worth it— because the morale of the crew is so wonderful when he is doing crazy things. And when he wasn't doing crazy things, I was. If this picture works commercially I'd love to do another picture with Dom. We're thinking of a script about the Corsican brothers who were born Siamese twins, are cut apart and separated—and every. time one falls in love the other gets a warm feeling.

CRIST: I'm sure there were a number of people who did not like the movie. The subject is bound to turn off a good segment of the population. So if you were one of those, don't hesitate to speak up. We don't need total euphoria.

FROM AUDIENCE: There were a couple of things I found very honest and true, but having a man face death in that way—I found it all just totally unrealistic.

REYNOLDS: I can only tell you this, having been in that position, where I thought I was dying, it was looking back at it that I saw it as slapstick, very funny. This is not a how-to picture, it's about one man and how he faced death. If you're asking me if I could do it that way, my answer is yes. If you tell me you couldn't, I believe you and I respect that. But, you know, if a doctor told me today that I was going to die in a year, well, tomorrow night I'd go on the *Tonight* show and I'd say, "Hey, I'm gonna die in a year, I want everybody to know it, I want as many cards and letters as I can get, I want everybody to love me." I'd do exactly what Hubert Humphrey did. He had about eleven eulogies given to him before he died; he was a very brave and wonderful man; we all loved him and cried for him. Every time I saw him on television I got tears in my eyes. And he *loved* it; he loved every moment of that—I believe it. His wife says that Hubert died the way he wanted to die—he did it publicly. If the doctor told me I had a year to live, maybe while I was in his office I'd be strong and say, "We're not going to let anybody know about this." Then I'd go out to the elevator and ask somebody to push the button fast—because I've only got about fifteen minutes to live. I'd tell everybody, *everybody,* because that's the way I am. Now I find that rather black comedy, maybe, but nevertheless, I find it funny. Sad, but funny.

FROM AUDIENCE: I had one major problem with the film: with the exception of Dom DeLuise, you didn't care about anybody. You were weak and spineless, your wife was snotty, the girl friend couldn't get it together. You can't really like anybody except Dom DeLuise, who happens to be a paranoid schizophrenic.

REYNOLDS: That's exactly what I wanted. Because when he swims out to sea, he has no reason to come back for anybody—that's exactly what I wanted. Thank you.

FROM AUDIENCE: I think nobody really knows how he'd react if he's told he's going to die. The real possibility that you might die is much different from when you just think about it. To joke about cancer, I just can't stand it.

REYNOLDS: I understand that, I understand that. This isn't about cancer, and I purposely never mention the word "cancer."

CRIST: This is what I meant by referring to the people who are not going to like the movie, because in dealing with death, you're dealing with something very personal. And I think you run the same risk as in dealing with a movie about sex. Death and sex—not taxes—are very personal things.

REYNOLDS: I totally agree, and I also think that the younger the audience, the easier it's going to be for them to handle this picture. When I was in my twenties, I never thought about it, or in my thirties. But now, I'm losing friends my age and it's a frightening thing to deal with. But again, this is not meant to be a movie making fun of death or saying this is the way it should be handled. It's irreverent. It's black, it's verboten; it's a terribly challenging, scary, brave thing to do to make a picture like this, because it could very easily die, if you'll pardon the pun.

CRIST: What I really liked about it was the setting up of the people. This is a guy who's been a phone real-estate salesman. It's not as if you are immediately asked to relate to him and therefore make it an empathetic experience.

FROM AUDIENCE: Throughout the whole picture there were interesting symbols, like a shadow of a cross on your forehead when you're sitting in the car. Was it conscious on your part to put in some of those special touches, or am I reading something into the film that really isn't there?

REYNOLDS: Well, I'll tell you, I met Fellini once in Rome and I talked to him about *La Dolce Vita*, which was a film that I wanted to run here this weekend, by the way, because it affected my life so much. I told him everything that the film represented to me, and I went on and on for over an hour. And then I said, "That's what the film is about, isn't it?" He said, "If that's what you saw, that's what it's about."

I worked very, very hard on those particular things you pointed out. The cross was there to be a startling moment.

FROM AUDIENCE: How much research did you do on death and dying? You did seem to follow the psychological pattern that has been studied—denial and bargaining and then depression and final acceptance.

REYNOLDS: There was a scene that was not in the picture—it was such a heavy, heavy scene with Sam Jaffe. Sam and I had a talk about dying: I admitted to him why I was in the hospital. He said, "You came to ask me what it's like." And I said, "Yes, I'm sorry, I'm ashamed, but that's why I'm here." He said, "Dying is embarrassing, it's expensive, it's painful, it's awful." And then, after a long pause, he said, "It's not a nice thing." That scene was so well done, so touching, that you never recovered from it. In terms of research—yes, we did, and I did personally talk with some experts, people who work with the dying, about the different stages of pain and what the character would be going through and how he'd be able to handle it.

CRIST: Now we're going to see *Semi-Tough*, which was Burt's most recent film before *The End*. All the Reynolds characters that you've seen chronologically this weekend come together in the character in *Semi-Tough*, and I'm pleased to find that Burt also thinks this is the best version of that character that he's ever done. *The End* certainly signals that you've gone on to something else. So for that reason, there's added interest in *Semi-Tough*, and I think you'll have a good time.

[After *Semi-Tough*]

FROM AUDIENCE: In *Semi-Tough* you seemed to be enjoying yourself so much. Was it because you were directed that way or was something else happening? Were you improvising, or what?

REYNOLDS: I'll tell you something—because I assume *People* magazine is not here (they're everywhere, and always wrong)—I didn't get along artistically with Kris [Kristofferson]. I found him to be terribly unprofessional and told him so. To his credit, he became very professional with me from that moment on. Unfortunately, I didn't tell him that until the picture was half over. We improvised hardly anything at all in that picture. Michael Ritchie is very tough about that. He's not tough about your bringing something to the character and rehearsing, but he likes to see a scene over and over and over again before he puts it on film. We did a lot of rehearsals. I felt incredibly free within the boundaries of Billy Clyde Puckett because, as we've discussed, I've been doing Billy Clyde Puckett for about ten years, and finally had some good, wonderful dialogue to do—very funny dialogue. I know that character so well—there's a guy I kind of based it on, Don Meredith, who's a good friend of mine, and I think that's who Jenkins based the character on. So I did a lot of things Dandy did—wardrobe-wise—that silly raccoon coat, that flair that Billy Clyde had, I took from Don. Those were all my ideas . . . but as far as writing things, I can't take credit for any of it, that was Jenkins's script. Jill made it look that way. Kris had a very difficult job, because his character never made that circle that we've talked about. He just stayed on one level, and you realize he's a very selfish character. Kris is a very intelligent man and he knew that he had to become the heavy. If the audience didn't want Billy Clyde and Barbara Jane to get together, we had no movie. And quite honestly, when I met him, I thought, Boy, I'm in trouble, this guy is so charming, and so good-looking. As an actor he does have an awful long way to go yet, but as a film persona—there's something about him on screen, he's just so likeable—and there's no acting school that can teach you that.

FROM AUDIENCE: This may be more of a statement than a question. You have said several times during the weekend, Burt, that you're anxious to get into new areas of acting. That's fine, and you've shown us this weekend that you can do that. But there are many of us who enjoy the characters you have played before, and you're very good at that type of acting. There are many other serious actors who couldn't possibly do what you do, so I hope you don't abandon what I think is your unique talent, and I hope you realize we appreciate it.

REYNOLDS: Thank you, I really do appreciate that. I did a Barbara Walters interview last week, which will be on soon. I don't know what's quite left of me after she got through, she's a very probing lady. But I said to her that there's a kind of misconception—from a *Time* magazine article and other things—that because I did want another audience, I didn't want to leave the impression that I never wanted to go back and play W.W. again, or a character like that. I just want to prove something—that I can stretch as far as I can stretch as an actor, to satisfy that yearning inside me. And truly, it's not for the critics, but for me. Once I do that, quite honestly, I'm sure you'll see *Smokey Goes to Paris.*

FROM AUDIENCE: In *The End,* did working as both actor and director present any special problems?

REYNOLDS: The only problems were the mechanical problems of dealing with your own tiredness, and trying to be up for comedy and giving to the person you're acting with. And then being there all the time as a director. I had to be two people, constantly. I'd be numb by the weekend. Every Saturday I'd get all the illnesses I'd staved off during the week. And the last day of the picture they had to carry me away.

FROM AUDIENCE: You've said what you want to do most is direct, but listening to you this weekend as a raconteur, I hear a writer in you. Would you want to add another hyphen and become actor-director-producer-*writer*?

REYNOLDS: Yes, I would. Certain people have been after me—because of certain contributions I've made to screenplays—to do a screenplay. But it is the loneliest and toughest job. *McCall's* wanted a story from me about my childhood, and I tried to write, but it was so painful. I found that the hours seemed to be dragging on, there wasn't the enjoyment. If I were doing a play or movie that would be easier for me, because I know that medium. But writing I found really tough. There are a couple of guys—and Woody [Allen] certainly isn't one of them—who've gone into the writer-producer-director area that I don't think belong in one of those categories. Writer is usually the one that is the weakest.

CRIST: I think Woody is able to function as intensely as he does as writer-director-star because he has very good co-producers. You need somewhere a firm sounding board. It does flabbergast me that you can divide yourself that easily—and it does seem that one of the achievements of *The End* is that you took a character that was different, increasing your own problem as an actor, while directing. This is far more adventurous, for example, than *Gator,* which was far more familiar.

REYNOLDS: Also one of the dangers is that there is no one around to tell you you're wrong—that's the biggest danger of all. They're afraid. You're surrounded by people who just keep telling you how good everything is because they're being swept along with the success of this high roller. I see that happening with Mel Brooks now. I thought *The Producers* and *Twelve Chairs* were just extraordinary films. But I've seen Brooks get progressively—I hate to use the word—crude. I used some pretty crude stuff myself—but I would never go as far as he does. He'll do *anything* for a laugh, anything, at any time. And he's gotten away from caring about the full person—those people in *The Producers* were full people, you cared about them.

FROM AUDIENCE: I must say that what you have accomplished is a most remarkable thing—there are more failed actor-directors than any of us care to name. The fact that you've done this is absolutely remarkable.

REYNOLDS: Thank you. I'd really like to take a minute here to answer some of the things that were brought up last night. I thought about what a gentleman asked: why, if this man is going to die, does he want to commit suicide? This isn't really a story about suicide, it's a story about a man who wants desperately to live, *desperately* to live. He can't kill himself; he proves it time and time again. In the end what he says is, "I want to see another sunset." There's hope. If I have to die, I don't want to die today, dammit, I want to live today.

Maybe if I were dying, my picture would really be accepted. But I have to tell you something, I have a right to make that picture, because I *will* die. We all will. I don't know what it's like to die, but I can tell you that in the middle of the picture I got so close to everyone working together that I kept thinking to myself, Dear God, don't let anything happen to me until I finish this picture. And if anything *does* happen to me—boy, will they be able to *sell* this.

FROM AUDIENCE: I'd just like you to comment, Judy, on what you feel about this new direction for Burt Reynolds?

CRIST: I've been letting it gestate, and the thing I like best about *The End,* as a project, was that it was adventurous. I thought he would play it a lot safer. And I think everybody needs an adventure, and too few people take it. This was a very high-risk venture, and although Burt has been associated with comedy, this is another kind of comedy. Basically it is black. I immediately think of Jack Lemmon comedies—which are Wasp comedies in which there really is no basic self-pity. It is a lot cooler, less pratfall-prone than Mel Brooks's, and far less introspective than anything Woody [Allen] ever dreamed of. It comes from an entirely different experience. And another aspect of his courage is that Burt didn't make himself a "good ole boy" in this situation, which would have been another crutch. For me, this works very well—and it's a fresh path in between the things that are uniquely his; it shows a satiric eye that has been apparent before, but now shows itself expanded into a new dimension. It is a singular path and one brilliantly taken, for starters—and I say for starters because, of course, there are some very rough things. The ending, however, is beautifully structured, taking you from that moment of relief when the two men are rolling around in the surf—in the *From Here to Eternity* embrace—then being brought right back up to hilarity and that Keystone Kop chase right up to the last freeze frame. You walk out laughing, because in your head is the idea of that ongoing chase—a very funny one, utterly classic, reversal to a fat man chasing the nervous thin man. The whole film, for me, built to this marvelous ending— with truths along the way.

But you cannot really make declarative statements about comedy. And the awful thing is that the more a critic says, "Oh, I found it absolutely hilarious," the more you are damaging the film because the next person walks in—and he sits down and says, "Go ahead, be hilarious."

FROM AUDIENCE: Are there any actors that you really want to work with—or to direct?

REYNOLDS: We talked before about my wanting to work with Jane Fonda, because our audiences are so different. I'm always surprised, when I meet someone like Jane, and she says she wants to work with me. She certainly didn't see *Smokey and the Bandit*, so how could she know my work? She's very aware of what's happening with other actors and actresses. She gets tapes of films and she finds out. When I met Jane Fonda and she said I want to work with you, I said, "Wow," and when I met Marsha Mason and I liked her, she said she wanted to work with me someday. So I guess to answer the question, you want to work with people who want to work with you, number one. I've always been a Sophia Loren freak—I'm not sure when it started, it probably goes back to breast feeding: I only know that I met her on a show, and I had the personality of a dart; I couldn't talk, I just sat staring at the floor. It became so embarrassing. She had never seen me on a talk show before, and didn't know I could talk. She just saw this poor man staring at the floor, but she had been told that I was funny, that I had done a lot of movies over here. She kept trying to draw me out, and finally she reached over and kissed me on the cheek, at which point I couldn't talk at all. So, yes, I would *die* to work with Sophia Loren—if I could talk.

In 1979 Burt Reynolds founded the Burt Reynolds Dinner Theatre in Jupiter, Florida. That year he made Starting Over, *followed by* Rough Cut *(1980),* Paternity *(1981),* Best Friends *(1982), and in 1983 Blake Edwards's* The Man Who Loved Women, *co-starring Julie Andrews. His "good ole boy" pictures were* Smokey and the Bandit II *(1980),* The Cannonball Run *(1981),* Stroker Ace *(1983), and* Cannonball Run II *(1983). He directed himself in* Stick *(1984) and his later films include* City Heat *(1984),* Malone *(1984),* Rent-A-Cop *and* Breaking In *(1988), and* Physical Evidence *(1989). In 1990 he undertook a CBS sitcom,* Evening Shade.

Mark Rydell

▀▀

New York–born Mark Rydell entered show business through music. A graduate of the Juilliard School of Music, he spent five years as a jazz pianist in Manhattan nightclubs before deciding to become an actor. He then won a scholarship to the Neighborhood Playhouse and later studied at the Actors Studio. Rydell the actor found work on television, appearing in the popular soap opera As the World Turns, *on Broadway in* Seagulls over Sorrento, *and in John Cassavetes's film* Crime in the Streets *(1956).*

It was in television that Rydell got his first opportunity to direct; he turned out more than 650 one-hour TV shows, including prizewinning episodes of I Spy *and* Gunsmoke. *Beginning in 1968, Rydell directed* The Fox, The Reivers, The Cowboys, Cinderella Liberty, Harry and Walter Go to New York, *and* The Rose. *The last was previewed when Mark Rydell was a guest at Tarrytown October 26–28, 1979.*

[After *The Fox*]

CRIST: *The Fox,* I believe, was your first film, in 1968. Maybe you'd like to tell us how it came about.

RYDELL: I had been enjoying a reasonable success as a television director, having spent many years as an actor, working on Broadway and doing a lot of television. Then I went to Hollywood and became a television director. I directed a lot of *Ben Casey*s and *Gunsmoke*s, and so on. Now the screenplay for this picture had been knocking around for quite a while because it was a sort of sexually audacious theme for that period, although I'm sure it seems somewhat mild now in relation to where movies have gone. It was very hard to get this picture off the ground, but the producer, Raymond Stross, a man with an eye for the buck, knew that as a new director looking for a career move I could invest this picture with the kind of passion it needed. I had been turning down offers for pictures because it's very important that a director's first picture be successful, or you can really be set back and wind up spending the rest of your life in television.

So I read the screenplay, which was not very good. The story, as you know, is based on a novella by D. H. Lawrence, and the original story contained the personal elements that I enjoy as a director. I like to find the drama in interpersonal relationships. There are many other directors who are very successful making pictures I could never make—George Lucas, for example, and *Star Wars*—that's a picture I would just not know how to do. I don't have any compassion for characters like that; I don't understand them. If I understand anything, it's human relationships, and I felt this picture offered me the opportunity to function in a way that could serve the material well.

I also felt—daring. I like to lead, as opposed to follow; that's always been a problem of mine. This picture offered the opportunity for being a pioneering kind of movie in the sense it was the first American movie, I think, that dealt with certain issues of eroticism and sexuality in a way that could be thought of as dignified. So when Stross brought me the picture I agreed to do it, and I got a writer, Lew [Lewis John] Carlino, and we locked ourselves in a hotel for two months and wrote this screenplay.

CRIST: What about the casting?

RYDELL: Well, Stross's wife is Anne Heywood, so they came as a package. One has to be realistic in life and accept the way things are. It worked fine with her. Then I knew Sandy Dennis very well, having worked with her at the Actors Studio, and I knew Keir Dullea. Very little was spent on this picture. Today, a low-budget film costs a minimum of $5 million. *The Fox* cost $1 million and grossed somewhere in the neighborhood of $25 million at the box office. It was a very big critical and commercial success.

CRIST: Two things stand out for me, seeing this film again for the first time in eleven years: first of all, I'm struck by how much a *director's* film it is. It is so much a film of silences. And doesn't it come as a shock at the end that you have seen only three characters throughout—and then that fourth character suddenly enters. Also, I was knocked out by Anne Heywood, who comes across here as a commercially beautiful version of Glenda Jackson—without, unfortunately, Miss Jackson's gifts. When I commented on this to Mark, he had an interesting reply.

RYDELL: Well, Anne Heywood's performance is really a trick. When we started rehearsing the first day with Anne Heywood and Sandy Dennis—Sandy is an extraordinary actress, and Keir is terrific and both are very experienced—it became immediately clear that Anne Heywood was not a very gifted actress. But the problem was solved, I'm sure most of you feel that from watching this film, which gave her a very big boost as an actress. But the enigmatic nature of her performance was achieved by omission. That is, I pulled away most of her dialogue and lit her in shadow—and made her a mystery. It's an example of how, as a director, one has to adjust to what you have, take the best out of what you have. This was a girl who did not have a lot of acting talent, but who did have a very interesting look. And if photographed properly and edited properly, she could seem to give a very competent performance.

FROM AUDIENCE: I *adore* what you did with Anne Heywood, but I must say I don't like Sandy Dennis because she's *always* Sandy Dennis.

RYDELL: This was Sandy Dennis's second important film role—her first was in *Who's Afraid of Virginia Woolf,* which was not yet released when I cast her in *The Fox.* So this was her first starring role, and the Sandy Dennis you saw afterward was a variation on what you saw tonight.

FROM AUDIENCE: Who's responsible for the music?

RYDELL: The score was an Academy Award score by Lalo Schiffrin. For those of you who are interested in music, I'm a graduate of the Juilliard School of Music, and I went to Chicago Musical College and my career before I was an actor was that of musician and composer. When it came to the decision about how to score the film, we felt the look was very ... Japanese, and very singular and lonely and cold. We felt the film looked like a Japanese print, and Schiffrin really did a wonderful thing musically with that idea.

FROM AUDIENCE: Will you elaborate a little bit on the symbolism of the fox?

RYDELL: Oh, yes. Lawrence was a man of deep sexuality and great mystery. And the fox in this picture, in the very primitive sense, is the representation of the male spirit, his concept and the girl's concept of the male spirit. The way that Anne Heywood related to the fox was clearly as a sexual object. The fox was the marauder, the one who came in and stole the chickens and ate them. He was an invader of sorts. In some sense we tried to make Dullea's character look very foxlike, and we lit him in a certain way that made him seem very animal. That's the Lawrence idea—it's full of mystery. Keir Dullea's killing of the fox is his replacement of the fantasy and his insistence that he is there and a *real* male.

FROM AUDIENCE: I'd like to comment on the beautiful sepia tones this was photographed in—was that an extension of the coloration of the fox?

RYDELL: This was the first film of a rather famous American film photographer—William Fraker. He had been a television-commercial photographer. We did consciously look for very pastel tones to convey a certain lyricism; we wanted nothing harsh.

FROM AUDIENCE: How did you manage to work so well with the fox, and are the animals really killed in the film?

RYDELL: No, no, no. I wouldn't do that. Although I must tell you, we did kill a chicken. Only one. But we did not kill the fox. Now, the fox was persuaded to go along that path because we used a very simple trick of placing cans of sardines in the snow. The fox was sniffing along, following a trail that was laid out for him. After all, you can't say to a fox "Go there, run across that."

FROM AUDIENCE: Do you think this film would be successful if you made it today—and what changes would you make in it?

RYDELL: Well, as I said earlier, I think this was really a pioneering film—ten or eleven years ago there was no sexuality of this nature in American films. Judith mentioned that the silences in this film are important, and oddly enough, there's an Ingmar Bergman film called *The Silence,* which had a great deal of influence on me. This is as Bergmanesque as I've ever been. I think this film could easily play on television now. In those days it was absolutely unheard of to see a scene where a woman masturbates, or see a love scene between women. The problem was how to do it tastefully and with affection, so that you sensed the commitment of feeling between two people. I think the film might enjoy success today. Seeing it now, if you want me really to confess the truth, I think I'd be more subtle, I wouldn't underline things as much as I did then. I feel now that it's a bit heavy-handed.

RYDELL: Why would a producer take a chance on a director like you—knowing you'd done only TV things like *I Spy* and *Ben Casey?*

RYDELL: Well, he was a very perceptive guy. And also he may have been motivated by the fact I'd work very cheaply in those days. No, actually we had a number of long talks, and in a sense I auditioned for him. I think he sensed that I understood the kind of personal relationships that were necessary for the film. Also, in those days I was very hungry, *desperate* to make my first film.

FROM AUDIENCE: How do you go about explaining to an actress that you're cutting half of her lines because you don't think she's very talented?

RYDELL: You never tell that to an actress. You always have to do something positive—with anyone you work with. A director is a kind of leader whose job it is to lubricate all the talents of the people around him, and aim them all in a common direction, which he decides. In order to do that you have to affirm people, you have to support them, you have to make them feel they can give you their best. When I removed Anne's dialogue, I convinced her—because I was convinced—that the moments would be better if they were silent. A director, in a sense, has to . . . lie. You have to do what's necessary to get the actress to achieve what it is you want. And of course you can never, never attack any actor's courage or sense of spirit. You always have to buoy them up. An actor is a very delicate object, and also a very courageous artist, because the actor has only himself for his instrument. A violinist has his violin, and so on in the other forms of art. But an actor—from his toes to the top of his head—is an instrument. And in order to play on that instrument, he has to feel confident. So it's necessary to nurture and be affectionate and loving and respectful. Anne Heywood could not know at the time, of course, what we were doing—but it was necessary to point her in a positive direction, to give her something else instead of the dialogue—something she could do.

CRIST: One thing that I became conscious of, Mark, looking at the film again, is the inner glow, the warmth you feel in that house between those two women. I'm aware of the inner heat and the cold that's outside.

RYDELL: It's lovely to hear that, because the truth of the matter is that every object in the house, every color, was chosen in warm tones to support the erotic tension in the house and everything in the exterior was in the blue tones to emphasize the cold. Those are the kinds of things that are done that have an unconscious impact on people. You'll be seeing in some of the films we'll be watching in the next day or so that I'm very careful to select things like that. I think color has real impact. The choice of colors is seemingly inadvertent—but it's not. Every garment is selected for a particular kind of emotional tone.

FROM AUDIENCE: Was it intentional, then, that they all had red hair—like the fox?

RYDELL: Yes, right.

FROM AUDIENCE: I saw the film when it was first released . . . but I don't remember all those erotic scenes. Did they cut them the first time and save them up for now?

RYDELL: This is the film as it was released—exactly. It's very interesting, though, if you ask somebody who saw the film ten years ago—as I've had occasion to do—to describe the sexual scenes: they would describe them in much, much greater detail than they were presented. They are presented in this film by omission. The love scene between the girls is really quite mild, it's just close-ups of lips—you don't really see anything. But in describing what they remember, most people will tell you a lot more than they ever saw.

[After *The Reivers*]

CRIST: *The Reivers* was Mark Rydell's second film, and this is an entirely different film as well as a marvelous example of growth and confidence. It is also one of only two truly successful film adaptations that I know of of works by Faulkner. The other one is a very small film called *Tomorrow* with Robert Duvall, a black-and-white film that I've shown here a couple of times. Like your film *The Reivers,* it captures the very essence of Faulkner. Would you tell us, Mark, how you developed this property?

RYDELL: *The Reivers* came to me by default. It was originally scheduled to have been directed by William Wyler, but Wyler became ill. This was quite a difficult picture to make, because you had to move around the country a lot; there was very little studio work in it. It was a physically demanding film, so Wyler felt he was unable to do it. Then they hired John Huston—and he became ill. And I was just then enjoying some success with *The Fox.* Also, I went to school with Steve McQueen, and I must tell you that he was part of the effort to get me to do the picture. So I got the picture by default, but it had already been very well articulated by Irving and Harriet Ravetch, the deans of our screenwriting world. They are really lovely people, very brilliant, and they have a great feeling for a certain kind of Americana.

You know, it's very, very difficult to turn a novel into a movie. Sometimes I think it's impossible, because, in effect, you're taking something that's 400 or 500 pages and somehow reducing it to a 110-page screenplay, which if typed like a novel would be about 30 pages long. A screenplay, you know, is mostly dialogue—with lots of spaces on the page. It's almost a Herculean job to distill the essence of a novel and still capture it. I think *The Reivers* is an example that it can be done by people who do love the book.

CRIST: *The Reivers* was responsible for making—or at least renewing—the careers of two actors. One was Will Geer, who had been on the Hollywood blacklist and had not acted for twenty years. It was *after* this film that he went on to work on TV in *The Waltons.* And the other actor is Clifton James, who has probably become a multimillionaire by playing redneck sheriffs. This was his debut. Also, of course, another fine actress in this, who died not long after, is Ruth White, who has the very brief part as the madam in the whorehouse.

RYDELL: And the old man, Juano Hernandez, another great actor, also passed away. And Rupert Crosse, the black actor, who had, I think, the potential to be one of the great American actors. He died about seven months after the film was released—of lung cancer. He was nominated for an Academy Award for this—it was his first real part. Rupert was a great loss, all six feet, six inches of him. He had great spirit, great humor, and was really a great talent. He was the man who played Steve McQueen's partner, a young man.* It may be interesting for you to know a story about Rupert. He was one of the very young, militant, feisty, black fighters. He was an actor who was usually broke, didn't have a job—although he was around Hollywood for years. First of all, he looked like a string bean, and any actor he tried out with was always at least a head shorter. Rupert was a member of the Actors Studio, where I teach, and I told Steve McQueen I wanted him to meet Rupert. Now Steve doesn't like actors or actresses who are bigger than he is. He's a wonderful actor, but he likes to be the boss—and very much a part of the relationship between these two in the film was that neither one would back down. But Steve didn't realize quite how courageous Rupert Crosse was. Steve finally acceded to my wishes to cast Rupert, because I was insistent. And I told Steve, "Look, Rupert's never had a job like this, and I think it's important that we do something to make him feel really a part of this unit. So why don't we have a little party at your home, a little cocktail party, and we can invite Rupert and make him feel like a part of the important cast." So Steve, of course gave a party.

Now, Steve has quite a fabulous house. I prepared Rupert for this, but he really was quite awestruck by it all. He had a few drinks and talked to everyone, then Steve took Rupert to his gymnasium, and started talking about his abilities at karate. Steve's a big martial arts enthusiast. Rupert just sat and listened, being quite cordial. We were all about to go into the dining room when Steve started showing Rupert this particular move. Rupert said, "You could get knocked down if you did that." Steve said ". . . What?" And the room froze. And Rupert said, "I said you could get knocked down if you did that, you're very vulnerable in that position." Steve said, "Show me." And I was thinking, Oh boy, here goes the picture. Well Steve made his move and Rupert, in a flash, flipped him over and threw him down three or four stairs into the library—and he landed under a pool table. Everybody in the place was stunned—and I was horrified. But Rupert just walked over and reached down and picked Steve up. Steve, to his eternal credit, laughed—and they

*Will Geer died in 1978, and Steve McQueen in 1980.

grabbed each other, and that episode was the nucleus of their equal—separate but equal—relationship. And that's how that handshake thing between the two of them developed for the film. That night, that's the way they shook hands.

FROM AUDIENCE: My recollection is that *The Reivers* was not that successful. A couple of years later 20th Century–Fox came out with *Sounder,* which had some similarities, and *Sounder* was extremely successful. Do you have any explanation for this?

RYDELL: This picture did enjoy some real success; it made a lot of money and it was critically reviewed well. It wasn't a smash, I guess, but it has become a kind of cult film. Colleges ask for it, film festivals ask for it all the time. *Sounder,* I think, dealt more directly with a black problem at a time when that was a major issue, whereas this is a film that more directly approaches the concept of morality during the period it depicts.

I must tell you, we shot this picture in Mississippi, and I had no idea of the nature of the racist cruelty that existed so strongly in 1969. I mean, Rupert could not go to certain restaurants. We were in difficult company there. I found it very shocking. You know, Hollywood has this kind of bad reputation, but our company did have some impact on those little towns, I'll tell you. I just wouldn't allow some things to happen. Things have changed a great deal since then.

FROM AUDIENCE: In light of what you say about race relations in Mississippi when you made the movie, if the story in the film is an accurate one, the white man and black man seem very close.

RYDELL: Oddly enough, this is a real kind of relationship, although the lines were clearly drawn during that period, it's true. However, there are people—including Marlon Brando, who's a friend of mine—who thought this was a racist picture. I was deeply offended, and we had a big fight about it. Brando thought it was not fair to depict that kind of close relationship between a white man and black man during the height of the struggle that the blacks were having in the South to reach equality. But I don't feel it's a racist film. I think Rupert plays a tough, honorable character who stands quite tall and has great dignity throughout the film— although he's kind of a foot-shuffling black. That was part of his character. He found a way to do an Uncle Tom with dignity.

[After *The Cowboys*]

CRIST: This weekend provides an interesting exercise in the timing of films. *The Cowboys,* in its time, which was 1972, was an extremely controversial film. When I saw it, I could not for a moment imagine what was controversial about it—but it caused a major brouhaha. Tell us how you came to *The Cowboys.*

RYDELL: *The Cowboys* came across my desk as an unpublished novel by William Dale Jennings. It was submitted by a literary agent in a batch of unpublished manuscripts. I read the first thirty or forty pages of this one and I saw that it was a story about John Wayne taking a bunch of kids across the West—and I knew it was something for me. Of course, it wasn't *John Wayne* in the book—just a character named Will Anderson. But I really was dying to make something new, something tough and rough, and at the same time I'd be able to exercise my feelings about fathers and sons, and succession, and so on. The material moved me, so I optioned the book and brought it to Warner Brothers and gave Ted Ashley and John Calley copies of the manuscript. I felt so confident about this I told them they had twenty-four hours to make their offer. I went home terrified, because I'd put a great deal of money into optioning the material, and if they didn't buy it, I was in trouble. The next morning they called me, and they were desperate to make the picture.

CRIST: This film is probably one of the most powerful uses of the Western that I know. The furor, naturally, was over the violence—particularly the involvement of children with violence. Did you anticipate any controversy about that?

RYDELL: I tell you, I *didn't at all.* I felt—and do feel—that it's an intensely moral film: it's about responsibility. It is, after all, about the Old West, and violence was very much part of the life of that period. There were no police around to turn to in the situation those boys faced. And one of the things that attracted me to the material was that it was *un*violent. The father figure was a tough man, a hard man—but nonviolent, and an honorable man whose job was to train those boys to be men. He was very reluctant to engage in violence—I like that aspect of the film. And I must tell you I did not anticipate the furor—that's the right word—that it created. The picture opened third in a week which started with *Straw Dogs,* a really violent film by Sam Peckinpah—and *Clockwork Orange.*

I remember lunching with Judith after she had seen *The Cowboys* in a screening room with other critics. If my memory is accurate, Judith told me that some people were enjoying the film very much until the moment when the boys break out the guns. Judith suggested that some critics might feel that John Wayne was training children to kill. I thought that was the furthest thing from the truth, but Pauline Kael did write a rather scathing review and attacked me personally.

CRIST: In subsequent discussions of *The Cowboys*—and movies like *Walking Tall*, which I didn't like, and *Death Wish*, which I did—one question keeps coming up: Do you really believe in vigilantism? My reply is always no, but I believe in good old revenge. Actually, *The Cowboys*—which I've just seen now for the fourth time—really performs a basic Aristotelian function for me—purgation. Every time one of those kids gets the bad guys, I'm with him. And, of course, the final punishment of the Bruce Dern character is what I'm waiting for. I think it was very courageous of Wayne to take the part, by the way. It was a real switch for him—to be killed off halfway through the movie.

RYDELL: This is the way it was in the original novel, but there was a lot of pressure put on me by the studio to have Wayne just wounded, and to have him perform the Roscoe Lee Brown function in the rest of the film—to guide the kids to the recapture of the herd. But Wayne was tenacious: he said, "Nonsense, the whole picture functions on this ... those kids have to do what they have to do because of that father figure. It's not so much revenge but the completion of a responsible task to which they've committed themselves." He was tenacious about it.

FROM AUDIENCE: How was it directing John Wayne—considering the fact that he was such a big star and you were a relatively young director?

RYDELL: Let me tell you a story about it. Of course I was anxious; you know, he's a man of enormous experience and knows more about the West than I will ever know. I'd done a lot of episodes of *Gunsmoke* for TV, that was my exposure to the West. I'd never been in this kind of country—it just took my breath away. In Santa Fe and Colorado you can see for fifty miles and there's not a television antenna. I just couldn't believe it.

Wayne and I had our first altercation very early on in the film.

We were filming the beginning of the trail drive, where the 1500 cattle leave the ranch. There were many cameras in operation—about five cameras. We had the cattle, eleven boys, Wayne, Roscoe Lee Brown—eleven "double" boys who were out of camera range, plus all the wranglers, also out of camera range, who were controlling the herd of steers. It was a very complicated shot. I was up on a big crane, facing all the cattle. Wayne was there and Roscoe here, and the boys behind. Now we had to start the cattle. You don't just say "go" to cattle—you kind of start them in the back and they begin to ripple forward; and when they were all moving I could roll the camera. Because it took some minutes before the cattle got moving and the cameras could start, I was waiting there for the cattle to move, waiting to roll the cameras—and Wayne, thinking we were ready, when in fact I was not, yelled to Roscoe, "Move out, Roscoe." And I blew my cork! I jumped up and shouted, "Don't you *ever* do that—you're an *actor* here, I'll tell them when to move." And as I was yelling at him, I thought, Oh God, I'm fired. I was screaming at him. I was right and he knew I was right, but I really let him have it—in front of many, many people. He said, "All right." And they moved back and waited, and waited. We did the shot, which took another hour—and my heart was beating like crazy the entire hour.

Finally the shooting was over, and Wayne got in his car and went home. The crew came over to me one by one, to shake hands—almost as if they were saying good-bye. I was very worried and the Ravetches [the screenwriters] were too. They said, "Oh my God, Mark, what did you do?" It was in front of so many people. If I'd had any sense I would have come down off the crane and talked to him privately. But I was enraged. And I was safe up on that crane. When I got back to our offices in Santa Fe that night, there were five messages from Wayne—he'd been calling every fifteen minutes. I took the bit in my teeth and called him and he said he wanted to have dinner with me. I figured that was it; he was going to call Warner Brothers and send for Andy McLaglen or one of the directors with whom he had worked before. And they would pay me off and that would be the end of it. Even though it was my picture, and I was producing and directing, I was easily expendable. They could do without me but not without him. Well, we had dinner; we finished a bottle of tequila together, and he never once mentioned my scene earlier. And from that day on, he called me "sir." He was a remarkable man, I tell you. He respected what I had done, he knew I was right—even though I had been brash—so my relationship with him was wonderful, and I treasure it.

FROM AUDIENCE: What if John Wayne hadn't been available or said no?

RYDELL: Sure, I had backups in mind. But in all of my pictures, and I mean this without exception, I've always gotten my first choice. I've always been very fortunate—I'm also very tenacious, and I pursue them. It took me a long time to get Alan Bates to do the film you'll see tonight, *The Rose*. I had to convince him, and I flew to London and convinced him. I camped on his doorstep.

FROM AUDIENCE: Was *The Cowboys* a financial success?

RYDELL: Yes, it was. It would have been a bigger success had it not faced the furor that it faced as the result of people associating Wayne's politics with the training of children to kill. It came out at the height of the anti-Vietnam violence, and it received a great deal of injury by reviewers who told parents not to bring their children to it. It's interesting . . . you can be hoisted on a kind of artistic petard; the better you do it, the worse it is. Somehow, the violence—the brutal fight between Wayne and Bruce Dern and the brutal killing, the murder of Wayne in front of those children—all of this had to be executed with savagery, or the rest of the picture wouldn't have worked. You had to feel revulsion for the Bruce Dern character; you had to see the brutality. And somehow, the more real you make it, the more dangerous it is. I feel if you're going to show something violent or brutal—then show it: let's look at it as it is, and let people judge. That fight was meant to be a brutal fight; the killings of all the men are quite savage and brutal. So in a strange way, the better you make it, the more dangerous it is to an audience.

FROM AUDIENCE: Since you were at one time an actor, can you ever see directing yourself in a film?

RYDELL: I've been tempted, I must tell you—but I've always withstood the temptation. Because in order to be an actor, a really good actor, you must surrender to the environment, to the situation, to the fantasy. You cannot watch yourself or manipulate yourself, you just have to surrender to the situation and trust in a surge of craft and talent and all that. And the nature of directing is judging— you're always judging. So whenever I think of directing myself, I think, well, how would I do it? When I stand in front of that camera to surrender myself as an actor, I have to give up my judgmental faculties—in order to perform properly. There are some people who've done it—in particular Woody Allen. But I think he has a lot of help—particularly a good cameraman, who's also a director now, named Gordon Willis, who also photographed many other wonderful films—*Godfather I* and *II* among them. He has a very good directorial eye. So Woody, in effect, has a director present—a man with a director's eye. But personally, I can't surrender the reins.

CRIST: I think with Woody there is the added factor that he is the writer, he is his own creation. He is not bound by someone else's character.

RYDELL: Also it depends upon the kind of acting and the kind of directing you do. I'm very much inclined toward very emotional behaviorial work, like the Dern role. But in order to do that kind of part, you really have to surrender. It's not an intellectual part, not verbal, as Woody Allen's usually are. The action is usually going on around Woody Allen—he's usually quite witty and clever, a good actor, although a modest actor. But Woody Allen could never play Bruce Dern's part.

FROM AUDIENCE: I seem to remember a remark that John Wayne made about *The Cowboys*—that Bruce Dern would never be forgiven for killing him. Do you think that role had anything to do with the fact that Dern has played a lot of psychotic types—and killers—and never really has become a big star?

RYDELL: I don't think that's the reason. He did enjoy the role—and I use the word "enjoy" because that's what it was, he loved it, the role of being Wayne's assassin. I don't think audiences blamed him for it. I think they do recognize his skills. He's a wonderful actor. But Dern does have a very interesting, very complicated and complex personality which, I think, keeps him from a certain kind of stardom. He's just not a romantic leading man.

FROM AUDIENCE: How did you go about finding stunt men for the boys? Did you use midgets? [Laughter]

RYDELL: Well, that's not so funny! The stunt people who performed some of the more dangerous riding and bucking sequences were just very, very small stunt men—jockeys and others, who had very frail bodies. And then there were kids who are in the professional stunt world—people who look young—they may be eighteen but look fourteen. So there are a number of people you could use—and we used them all in *The Cowboys*.

CRIST: I'm surprised no one has commented on the John Williams score—some of it has become quite famous, has it not?

RYDELL: Yes, the opening music during the credits has become a quite famous piece of modern music—John Williams has been asked to play it on a number of occasions. He has played it at the Albert Hall in London, for example.

[After *The Rose*]

CRIST: It's obvious that we do not have unanimous opinion about *The Rose*—which is as it should be. I happen to like this movie very much. Like most people who love movies, I love movies about the glamour of show business, about "stars." The superstar of the sixties, of course, was the rock star—and this movie captures for me not the birth of a star—which is an old story—but the death of a creative artist. It's a very complex film and even seeing it this second time I feel a need to try to sort out my feelings about it. But before we get into that, Mark, please tell us how you came to *The Rose*.

RYDELL: The movie had been in gestation for about ten years. It was originally designed to be the story of Janis Joplin. About seven years ago they came to me to direct it. I felt at that time that the only person in the world who could play the part as I viewed it was Bette Midler. The studio at that time didn't recognize that as the truth, and they were reluctant to have me offer it to her. They wanted to use an actress and then dub in the voice of a singer. But being an ex-musician and having certain feelings about artificiality, I refused to do that. So I left the project.

It then went through many permutations, and many different drafts—it began to become fictionalized. Then it was decided to depart from the life of Janis Joplin and create a new character. The film then went through many other directors before it finally came back to me—this time with Bette Midler. So I'd like to put to rest once and for all the idea that this character is Janis Joplin. It's not Janis Joplin—but it is, I hope, faithful to her spirit and faithful to the spirit of those artists who are driven—as is The Rose—to venture into areas of great danger and who pay an ultimate price for venturing into those areas. And I hope it is respectful of such people.

I've been sitting here thinking to myself, look, this is a very special audience, and do I really want to give you permission to be unkind? In a sense I learn much more if you are honest with me. It may be a little painful, but it would be helpful to me. I'm not asking you to be cruel—but, let me just say this quickly, this has been a very, very stimulating time for me. I feel it has been a good interchange and I have learned a great deal from it. And in a sense, we've all become very quick friends. Don't let that condition you. I know that this is an audience of a generation who suffered, whose children suffered during the sixties, and who had feelings about rock and about what happened at this time. I know that some of you may not be rock 'n' roll fans, and may not have moved with your children into the seventies and eighties as easily as you might have. What I'm asking—in a very clumsy and awkward way, I guess—is for you to tell me really how you feel. Because it will help me to understand.

FROM AUDIENCE: This is a tour de force performance by Bette Midler, of course, and I was completely engrossed by it. But as soon as the movie begins, she is immediately doomed in my eyes.

RYDELL: And in mine.

SAME AUDIENCE: Okay, and there's no way out for her and her unhappiness, and it takes a long time for her demise. Meanwhile, the show is great.

RYDELL: Interesting.

FROM AUDIENCE: I couldn't understand a word Alan Bates said.

RYDELL: Well, you're not alone. I'll try to explain the Bates role. There are men, managers, promoters whom I know, who choose that role because of a certain impotence in their own life. They attach themselves to something very powerful and very strong, as a borrowed strength, and they are motivated beyond all things to keep that strength alive—because it is *their* strength. I believe they are ambivalently sexual people, often asexual, and this is their sexuality—the attachment to great power justifies their existence. They'll do anything to preserve that power. That is the heart of this character—he's like a chameleon; he's able to provide at any moment what is needed in order to keep her moving. He will lie, he will cheat, he will push, he will cajole, he will romance—there's nothing he won't do. He's like the William Morris agent. By the way, William Morris is my agency, so I say this with some pride.

SAME AUDIENCE: I understand what you're saying about him, and I got that in the film. What I object to was not being able to understand his speech.

CRIST: It was the heavy Liverpool accent. It's a very hard accent, and he speaks quite rapidly and you have to be able to tune in. This added a dimension for me—because so many guys like this are of the Beatles school, from that generation, and they are British, and real toughies.

RYDELL: He's a common, street-born type, from humble origins—as many of those rock managers were from England who came over here and dealt with both American and English stars. They are street hustlers—tough, mean, and, unfortunately sometimes, their accents are difficult to understand. It was a choice I made—some think it's right, some think it's wrong. But it's accurate. I could have had him speak more clearly, but I think it would have been at the sacrifice of a certain kind of authenticity.

FROM AUDIENCE: One thing that did puzzle me about his character. He's a sharp guy, and it seems obvious to me—and I would think obvious to him—that he's pushing her, the Rose, to the point of destruction. If she dies, destroying herself, he too is destroyed. So therefore, is he purposely trying to destroy her?

RYDELL: Well, you must remember that he doesn't witness everything you witness in the film.

CRIST: And he does think the big thing he has accomplished with her was getting her off drugs.

RYDELL: And she has "been there" many times before. Drugs were part of her life—she was a heroin addict and he picked her up out of the gutter and straightened her out. She's been boozing and straight and clean and on a high many, many times in their lives. And this is the time when he makes an error. I think it's part of the picture that he's a destructive guy—although those guys themselves don't die. Only the artists are destroyed. This was the thing I was hoping, you see, for *our* generation—I include myself in "our" generation, because although a lot of people think I look young, I'm fifty, so I share some of your feelings. But what I wanted to accomplish was the realization that this star, the spirit that this star contains, the self-destruction, the fact that this star is eaten up by her life . . . this is not just a rock star, and this is not just about the sixties, although it was set in the sixties. I think she reflects Marilyn Monroe, she reflects Jimmy Dean, she reflects Montgomery Clift, she reflects Judy Garland, Lenny Bruce—people of our time and prior to our time. I wanted this picture to exist on its own, away from the particular time setting, so that you could understand the agony of this kind of human being in any period. It could happen in the twenties, in the sixties, and it could happen again in the eighties.

FROM AUDIENCE: Mr. Rydell, in the way you describe your view of this film as having a universal meaning—that didn't come across to me at all. I think one reason for this is that nowhere in the film does she show any real respect for her craft, for her art. I didn't get any feeling of here's someone with a deep understanding of what she's doing, in terms of being an artist.

RYDELL: This is a question that's rather critical for me. I have to ask the rest of you, do you share this gentleman's view?

[RESPONSES OF "NO" AND "NOT AT ALL" FROM AUDIENCE]

RYDELL: Oh, thank God. You know, the first thing she says in the film is, "I'm not singing what I like . . . I've got to sing better, I don't like it." I think there's no way you can perform as an artist and not be a craftswoman. I think we see in this picture the expression of—and I say this unashamedly—the expression of true genius. When Bette Midler sings a song like "A Man Loves a Woman," which was in one of the early concerts—the kind of surrender she is able to deliver, that's the work of a major artist and craftswoman, in my view.

SAME AUDIENCE: I'm not talking about Bette Midler, because I think she was marvelous. I'm talking about the character.

RYDELL: Even so. You can't get where she is without respect for your craft. That doesn't happen by accident.

FROM AUDIENCE: Two things: first, I wouldn't be surprised if Bette Midler got nominated and/or won an Oscar for this.* Secondly, at

*She was nominated for Best Actress. Sally Field won that year for *Norma Rae*.

the end of the picture I was totally exhausted. I was *in* that film. It was hard for me *not* to become part of that film.

RYDELL: Listen, I want to repeat those words for anyone who didn't hear. . . . [Laughter from audience] I very much appreciate that.

FROM AUDIENCE: How much did *The Rose* cost?

RYDELL: Nine million dollars. But, you know, we see on television what they advertise as "the million-dollar movie." Well, you can't make a *trailer* for a million now. A low-budget film—what's considered a low-budget film—is now about $5 million. That's how costs have escalated. Twenty-million-dollar films are not unusual. From twelve- to fifteen-million budgets are average.

FROM AUDIENCE: I have the feeling this is going to be an extremely popular film—but not with our generation. It was echoing the agony of the sixties, what caused *our* agony.

RYDELL: I think you're absolutely correct about the fact that people of our generation will resist this material because it's very painful and sensitive to us. The drug world, the rock world affected our children and caused us much agony—and after all, 1969 was a time of enormous polarity in our nation, and we were all very pained by that, because the country was torn asunder at that time. It's my sincere hope that the quality and the depth of the work by Bette Midler and others in the film will overcome prejudices. I was very disturbed during the first concert, and I didn't know whether or not to cut out the chant "Drugs, Sex and Rock 'n' Roll," because I knew it was like pushing a button for our generation, reminding us of all the things that caused us pain. But I felt that we had to be honorable to the film and to the truth of the time, and that was the truth of it then, certainly the truth of the character.

[After *Harry and Walter Go to New York*]

CRIST: We sometimes have a major problem showing old films, as we did last night. I thought this was an ordinary print of *Harry and Walter Go to New York* until I realized with horror it's one of those versions you see on television—with all the titles squeezed together. Anyway—let's start the discussion of *Harry and Walter*.

RYDELL: And let's make it as short as possible. I must tell you, I hate this film. It's one of those terrible mistakes one makes in life.

The picture was a failure. It deserved to be a failure. It was an attempt at certain things that didn't work. But what you saw didn't give that failure the opportunity it might have deserved. I stayed for about an hour, and I saw that at least twenty-five minutes of the first hour of the film had just been cut out. Not only was it cut out—you were watching in essence what we call a scan print.

Panavision is two and one-third times wider than it is high. So for the screen to be one foot high, it would have to be two and one-third feet wide. The screen on your television set is one and a fourth the height to width. So television can't show you all of a Panavision film. Somebody in the television studios decides where to focus on the screen, on your two and one-third feet of film; they decide what one foot of it to focus on. That's what you're seeing. So that all the care that's put into the composition of a frame, like a painting—and I can tell you there are great artists involved in this—all that care is destroyed. Then, also, because people in television seem to think that television demands closeups—the focus will zoom into a particular closeup, a medium closeup, say. You're often at the mercy of technicians who are not even good technicians. So you were seeing, literally, about one-third of what was shot, in actual size, and about half of what was shot in footage in the original film. All the character relationships are removed—along with the major story points.

Actually, the real aim here was to make a modern Laurel and Hardy movie—with a certain social undertone. A *modern* Laurel and Hardy—that's what the effort was, but it didn't work. And it's unfortunate, but in the motion picture industry, where things are so expensive, there's no tolerance for failure. When you fail, you fail *loud*. And *Harry and Walter* was a failure—for which I apologize. May I never make another one—although I'm sure I will.

FROM AUDIENCE: Didn't you get some sense of that while you were making the picture?

RYDELL: Nobody sets out to make a bad movie. There's a characteristic of innocence that happens on a picture. I had high hopes. I thought it was going to be an interesting period piece, kind of clownish, a kind of burlesque. I didn't know. The audience told us. The critics were very loud when they told us. Nobody went.

On reflection, I can see that I was captivated by an idea that was not a commercial idea. I loved the idea of trying to make Laurel and Hardy, with those guys—[James] Caan and [Elliott]

Gould. I loved Michael Caine; he's a charming and gracious man. And when everything was put together I really thought it was all there. But it just didn't work. I have no excuses.

FROM AUDIENCE: How long are you involved with each film you make?

RYDELL: I've never been able to make a movie from start to finish in less than two years. The relationships are intense; they are, in effect, like a marriage—they are that intimate. That is to say, the people you're working with have to trust you, they have to reveal their deepest secrets to you. One of the things I admire most about artists is that they're willing to reveal very painful, private moments. I suspect somewhere in my soul of souls that artists are able to reveal so much because it's temporary. It's like people who cannot have long-term relationships—they can have affairs, passionate affairs, as long as they know that in a year or whatever, they can go to somebody else. I don't mean to denigrate the relationships—because they are genuine and loving and good and honorable. But at the end of two years, people leave and go on to another project, a new lover, a new director, a new leading man. I don't mean lover in the literal sense . . .

CRIST: Not in all cases . . .

RYDELL: Well, never in mine, I must tell you—never in mine. I can't mix business with pleasure. Not in that respect. But in making a film there is a sense of love that goes on that is not unlike an affair. The danger is, it cannot be an infatuation. You cannot be infatuated with a project or a role, because two years is too long to sustain an infatuation; you have to find something that's genuine and real between you and the project that connects on a deep level, so you can explore it fully. Then the parting is sad, although, of course, we see each other. I see Bette Midler; she's been asking to work with me again. But when we see each other now, of course, it's not with the same intensity.

FROM AUDIENCE: Have you ever had bad experiences with actors?

RYDELL: Yes, there are a couple I had a very tough time with. But even those, when I reflect upon it, came out of the intensity of the relationship. Steve McQueen is a very difficult man. He's not very bright, but he's very shrewd and very talented, he's a very gifted guy, but he's very strong willed. Working with him on *The Reivers* was difficult because he wanted to be the boss, and I wouldn't let him. He was a very strong influence, and I had to fight very hard to retain control because he was testing me at every turn. He was difficult. I outlasted him—because I'm very tenacious. But to this day, Steve and I are friends—I like him a lot, and I'm eager to work with him again, even though I know we'll have the same battles, because that's his nature.

But, for the most part, I do love actors—I love them because they are like children, in the best sense. They really are. And I mean the oldest of them and the best of them. I used to go to the gym with Laurence Olivier, and when we finally got around to talking about acting he was drawing me out—he wanted my approval. Like a child, actors reach out for a certain kind of affirmation from you, they want you to say "*very gooood.*" They want your applause.

FROM AUDIENCE: Can you tell us literally how you worked on *The Rose?*

RYDELL: Well, I'll try. It took eight years for *The Rose* to go through its various stages of development, through various versions of the screenplay. It was almost produced, then a company would pull out, or the stars weren't available, and so on. It took eight years to get to me. Then the script had to go through a final rewrite, which took about four months of working intensively with the writer. Then there is a four- to six-month period during which I prepare the film. That is, I organize all the necessary people involved for the final preparation in shooting it. Which is, by the way, the shortest period in the making of the film. During the six months, cameramen are hired, production crews are hired, costumes are designed, the people in the cast are brought together, locations are found and decided upon. Budgets are prepared and schedules are devised—showing that you have to be in this place at this time; transportation has to be arranged—there's endless minutiae. Then comes the shooting part, which is generally, I'd say, a four-month period—involving about eighteen hours a day. Sometimes it's three and a half months, sometimes five—and with certain directors, it's eight.

After the shooting phase, the editing phase begins, and you can have somewhere between 300,000 and a million feet of film to examine and compile. Every foot of film has to be gone over, and putting it all together in the way you want may take from six months to a year. You then have to move on to a dubbing stage, where all the sounds in the film are put together. Every door slam, every voice in the background has to be blended until you can hear exactly what it is you want. That can take four to five months.

CRIST: I recall talking to Fred Zinnemann, who had just returned from Europe making *The Day of the Jackal.* I asked him what he was going to do next, and he said, "Well, you know, I'm over seventy—and it takes me almost two years to decide what to do with the next two years of my life." Now, for you, way under seventy, what are you going to do next?

RYDELL: Well, it's a difficult problem. A writer who has written many films that you would respect—among them *Bridge on the River Kwai, Doctor Zhivago,* a great English writer named Robert Bolt who works very often with David Lean—has written a screenplay based on an incident that takes place in the eighteenth century in South America. It's really quite brilliant. A very noble effort, about a certain kind of heroic martyrdom. The material is *worth* two years of effort—not all scripts are. This is something you can be proud to stand behind. But what has to be considered is that to do this film properly, you have to go down to the Amazon jungle and spend a year there, and maybe get malaria and whatever other diseases lurk. I mean, that's the *real* jungle—not Central Park. This kind of location has an effect on many things—your relationship with your children. Do you take your children to such a place? Do you separate yourself from those who are near and dear to you for a year? There are a lot of responsibilities involved. So I've been weighing this decision for three months. If it were not for the fact that I derive so much pleasure from my children and the relationships in my life, I would go. But I'm reluctant. And I'm ashamed of being reluctant because the picture is worth our attention.

That's one project I'm trying to work out. There's one other—a picture based on a novel by Robert Penn Warren called *A Place to Come To,* which is a rather beautiful love story. I wouldn't have to go to the Amazon—only to the American South. It takes place in a rather aristocratic southern area, the Carolinas; it spans fifty years and it's an important work by a major American poet and novelist. So it also attracts my attention. Those two projects are prominent right now for me. But who knows? I'll probably wind up making another *Harry and Walter.*

*Rydell wound up making *On Golden Pond,* which won three Oscars.

FROM AUDIENCE: I noticed on the credits for *Harry and Walter* that there are two other Rydells listed in the cast. Are they any relation to you?

RYDELL: One is my son. It was just my son and myself.

SAME AUDIENCE: No—there was another.

RYDELL: Oh! *My mother!* Let me tell you who she was. If you remember a scene in the theater, Charles Durning is sitting next to Diane Keaton and there's a woman next to him who gets mad at him and slaps him. And I thought, my mother slaps better than anybody!

SAME AUDIENCE: What about all the new young directors?

RYDELL: Well, I don't think they're getting the kind of money we're talking about now. There was a time, a few years ago, when there was a plethora of films by young filmmakers. The studios were giving them a chance, because they'd let them make $2 million or $3 million films, and they figured they'd give the kids a shot because the studios could always make their money back in television. But the major projects rarely go to inexperienced people.

CRIST: Some directors manage to hit it big when they're young, of course. There's Steven Spielberg and George Lucas—but they're not wunderkinder anymore. They have to *produce.*

RYDELL: Look at George Lucas, whose first picture was *American Graffiti*. The studio, in its blindness, did not even want to release *American Graffiti*. It had no stars in it; it was about a bunch of kids running up and down the street in cars. They didn't think it was worth the money to distribute the picture. Francis Coppola threatened them: he said he would buy the film and distribute it himself. Then the studio got scared and thought they'd see what was going on. So they released the picture and it make $60 million; it cost somewhere in the area of $2 million. As a testimonial to that same studio's blind stupidity, when Lucas later came to them asking for $5,000 to develop an idea he had, they looked at the idea and said, "Nah, this is silly—you've gone too far." Well, he took it to another studio—it was *Star Wars*. Which made over $200 million. He wanted $5,000 and they thought he was out of line.

FROM AUDIENCE: Are studios obligated to keep a director on once he's started a film?

RYDELL: No. A director can always be fired, but his salary has to be paid. It depends on what the situation is, if a director is directing *and* producing, if it's his property, and so on. With *The Cowboys*, for example, I stuck my neck out and bought the material, so when the studio wanted to make it, they had to come to me. I'm then in a much better bargaining position—to bargain for the fee for the picture and the percentage of profits I'll receive. If the picture is a hit. If the studio comes to you with a picture, you can still get a big salary and a percentage, but you don't have quite as much leverage if it's their material. So in a sense, a director is always looking for material to option—at risk. If I find a book or something I like, I may have to go out and borrow $50,000 to get an option on it for three months, against a $500,000 sale price. Now, if I go to a studio and they look at it and say no—I'm in trouble. I'm rolling the dice, too. But in order to avoid those situations, studios have their tendrils out to every publishing house, every literary agent. They try to find those books that have movie potential long before we directors or producers get a chance. We're in a kind of battle with them because they're hungry to make pictures, too.

FROM AUDIENCE: Why aren't there more women directors?

RYDELL: There are a number of very good young women directors now—Joan Micklin Silver, Claudia Weill, who did *Girlfriends*.

CRIST: Joan Silver has a movie coming out now, *Head Over Heels*, and this is her third movie. She did *Hester Street* and *Between the Lines*. I know that we sometimes think there really ought to be at least two hundred women directors, but they're moving in there and getting more and more opportunities, although still not enough of them.

RYDELL: It's a very selective profession, you know. There are lists, "A" lists and "B" lists. In other words, a studio will have a list of what certain actors are worth in order to have banks invest in a certain motion picture. It's all very carefully charted—what an actor's been known to draw in Germany, for example; what successes he's had in each country and in each region of this country. It's a highly documented profession; banks do not risk their money unless there is evidence to justify it. Now the list of "A" directors is very, very small. There are not many directors functioning in our business in comparison with other businesses. I would bet there are fewer than fifty directors who are really bankable. In fact I would bet it's a lot less.

FROM AUDIENCE: Do you think now that you could ever go back and make a low-budget picture like *The Fox*?

RYDELL: *The Fox* would now cost $5 million. I have no resistance to doing a picture of merit—at whatever budget. I don't judge a picture by its budget. I judge it generally by how it touches me. Does it reach me? Does it matter enough to me to give myself to it for two years? But as I move through my career, my salary has increased. And now I get the full budget of *The Fox* just for myself. Right?

SAME AUDIENCE: But I'm asking if you wanted to make a small, low-budget picture—could you?

RYDELL: Sure I could.

CRIST: Just in very simple terms ... once you've driven a Rolls-Royce, would you want to go back to driving a VW bug?

RYDELL: Unless it has a great engine ...

In 1980, Rydell directed Henry Fonda and Katharine Hepburn in their Oscar-winning performances in On Golden Pond. *In 1983, he made* The River, *co-starring Mel Gibson and Sissy Spacek, and he returned to acting in* Punchline, *in 1988, with Tom Hanks and Sally Field.*

Sydney Pollack

▲▲

Indiana-born Sydney Pollack came to New York in the 1950s and got a job as an acting teacher at Sanford Meisner's Neighborhood Playhouse. He then became an actor himself, taking roles on Broadway and in many of the major television shows originating from New York at the time. Migrating to Hollywood, he broke into directing through series television—more than eighty episodes of major shows over a period of five years during the early 1960s. His first feature film was The Slender Thread *(1965), and his first Academy Award nomination was for* They Shoot Horses, Don't They? *(1969). He has directed fifteen films and produced his own and others' since 1975 and gained a reputation for working with high-powered stars such as Robert Redford, Jane Fonda, Barbra Streisand, Robert Mitchum, and Burt Lancaster in such films as* The Scalphunters *(1968),* Jeremiah Johnson *(1972),* The Way We Were *(1973),* The Yakuza *(1975), and* The Electric Horseman *(1979). He came to Tarrytown for the weekend of November 23–25, 1979.*

[After *They Shoot Horses, Don't They?*]

CRIST: This is an unforgettable film if only for the ballroom sequences. For starters, Sydney, would you tell us how you and *They Shoot Horses* got together?

POLLACK: It was a novel by a kind of Hollywood-hack screenwriter, Horace McCoy. It was written in 1930 and sold almost no copies at all—but immediately became a cult classic in Europe. It's a much better known novel in France than it ever was here. Some fourteen people owned the novel at various times and tried to make it into a film—starting with Chaplin, the first man to buy the rights to it.

Because of the nature of the story, rather down and depressing, it was always considered a very risky financial venture and no studios would back it. This was my second try at it. I had originally come to it in 1966 and began to work on the screenplay but couldn't get the money to do the picture at that time. I then inherited it as a picture in 1969. It was originally going to be directed by a very talented screenwriter named James Poe; it was going to be his first film. He had done the screenplay. Some two months prior to the start of principal photography, the company let James Poe go and I got the shot at doing it.

We shot the film all on one set as you can see—stage four at Warner Brothers. We shot it beginning in January 1969, and opened Christmas 1969. It did okay commercially but hardly what you'd call a hit. It did well critically and in terms of awards. It was the first serious dramatic role that Jane Fonda had played. She was married to Roger Vadim at the time and she had done a series of films à la *Barbarella*. She was going through a lot of turmoil in her own life and really, for the first, becoming the politically committed lady we know now. So she was in a transition period emotionally, and really dug her way into this role—as you can see.

It was an interesting film for me to shoot because of the challenges of trying to sustain the film for some two hours essentially in one set. And on top of that, depicting one single activity over and over fights against certain obvious pacing mechanisms. The combination of their getting more and more exhausted as the picture goes on, and your not being able to go to a new place for variety or relief—from that point of view, technically, it was a very challenging picture. But the cast—particularly the principals—had a real esprit during the making of it, and they worked like hell. Half of them never went home. They lived in those clothes, and they all got to know each other very well. It was an odd sort of overlapping between life and work.

CRIST: The cast itself is so remarkable—even beyond Jane Fonda. It was such a change of type for Gig Young, who'd always played the playboy roles. This is such a gritty, sodden, lower-depths character.

POLLACK: The man who actually produced the picture—Chartoff and Winkler are credited as producers—was a man named Marty Baum, an agent for years both in New York and Hollywood, who represented Gig Young. One of the clients he most wanted to have in this picture was Gig, who I initially felt was all wrong for the role. I had seen Gig play these charming rogues, and that was not needed for this film. Marty was insistent: he asked me to meet Gig and talk to him. We were about six weeks from starting the picture, so we had to do it right away. Well, I got a call that he couldn't come in to see me because he was very sick with the flu, and I said, "I don't know what to do, I can't wait the week out because I'll have to get somebody else."

I then got the word that although he was very, very sick he was going to come in and see me. He came in, and he'd been very feverish and was now in a cold sweat and very shaky. He started talking to me about the picture and I began looking at this shaky guy who had a stubble because he hadn't shaved, with the sweat all over him. It was a whole other Gig Young—and it became clear he could play this part, if I could get him to be the way I saw him in the office, which wasn't that difficult to do.

CRIST: Am I right in remembering the scene showing the marathon race—that that was shot on roller skates?

POLLACK: I directed it on roller skates—and shot it, too. There's a camera that's made for skydiving, it has a fifty-foot load. It doesn't ordinarily take anamorphic lenses—this wide-screen process you see is called an "anamorphic" process. But the people at Panavision took a lightweight 50mm lens and designed it so it would fit on this little hand-held camera. So on lunch hours I used to take roller-skating lessons. We had to have a roller-skating coach there because, as you may have noticed, the two referees for the marathon are on roller skates, which was the case in those days. So I practiced roller skating every day. Now the whole sequence wasn't shot that way, but there are a number of shots that make you feel like you're in the group and those are the ones I shot myself holding that little camera.

CRIST: Memory plays tricks, but it seems to me that one of the things that disturbed people at the time of this film's release were those flash-forwards to the trial, and so forth. Had there been more of them originally?

POLLACK: I'm sure that most of you do not know the book, but on the first page of the book there is a blank page with just one sentence in very bold type: "The prisoner will please rise." The narrative starts on the next page and it's narrated by the boy played by Michael Sarrazin. It starts, "I first met Gloria in a park one day . . ." You go on a chapter or two, then there's another blank page with a single sentence: "Do you have anything to say in your defense?" So you start out reading the book with this ominous sense that something terrible is going to happen. Which means that time present is the trial, since that's the way the book starts, and the story itself is a flashback.

When I first came to the project, for reasons I can't explain, I felt awkward dealing with the marathon itself as time past, because that meant it had already had an absolute conclusion—and that eliminated a certain degree of suspense for me. I wanted the marathon to be taking place now. Which meant that the only way I could keep the sense of the ominous was to make this trial in the future, which was a rather awkward thing to try to do.

We saved those sequences for last, and both Marty Baum and the producers said to me, "You don't need them, Sydney, they're just going to intrude." I didn't know whether I needed them or not, but I wanted to have them. I had torn those pages out of the book and read the book without them—and I felt it didn't work. I felt there was something campy about it, a kind of campy reminiscence of the 1930s. However, in those days I wasn't in a position to overrule anybody, so I was given one day to shoot the flash-forwards. I stylized them in that very awkward style, in blue and white. We put the picture together with the flash-forwards in, and the first person to object was Jane. The producers also objected to them. And I said—and it's one of the few times in my life I've been right—I said, people are going to laugh if you take them out. Everybody thought I was crazy.

We took the picture up to San Francisco, played it on a Friday night—Jane was in the audience. The flash-forwards were out, and the audience was having a wonderful time laughing at the inside jokes about old movies. And when Michael Sarrazin takes the gun at the end, and says, "Are you ready?" the audience just roared. They no more bought the fact that he was going to kill her than the man in the moon. Everybody was ashen afterward, Jane in particular; she just kept saying she didn't believe it. But I think that what happened was the people got caught up in the memories of the thirties, a time that seemed so distant from where we were now, and they were totally unprepared. I think McCoy sensed this when he had written the book, that there is some necessity to root the reader—or the audience—with this ominous sense that you were headed for disaster right from the beginning. So we put the flash-forwards back in, tried it with another audience, and it worked. It was the most criticized aspect of the film.

So, after ten years of thinking about this, the only thing I would do differently, if I were doing it again, is to film the flash-forwards stylistically so that they were as close to the reality of the ballroom as possible—even to keeping the sound of the ballroom going behind them. But I would not have given them up.

CRIST: At the time I first saw it, I was absolutely shocked by the ending. I thought that Jane Fonda had portrayed a survivor; I believed in her from the very beginning as a person who could take anything to survive and to win. Watching it now, of course, I can see the seeds of the loser in Jane's character, and the fascination with death, which I gather was much stronger in the book. But in the film I felt there was no warning as to what was coming, so I just hated that last scene—and wanted to ignore it.

FROM AUDIENCE: I'd like to know more about the film's connection to the book. Was the title the same?

POLLACK: Yes, and the last lines were, "Why'd you do it, kid?" "Because she asked me to." "You're an obliging bastard." "They shoot horses, don't they?" We took the liberty here of continuing the marathon—in the book it's closed down. But just purely from an existential point of view, I wanted the indication to be that the marathon would continue, that there wasn't any winner or loser, it just went on and on.

You know, this often happens with filmmakers. I don't know how to get around it, but you do tend to lose objectivity when you work for two years on something; you tend to want to overclarify. You get worried that people won't get it. I guess I was terribly worried that nobody knew the book and that the meaning of this odd answer—"They shoot horses, don't they?"—as the total reason for killing somebody would not be accepted unless I somehow made it very circular, with the allusion to the horse falling in the field. That's in the book. In the end when they go out on the pier and she takes out the gun, Robert remembers a scene running in a field with his grandfather and the horse falling, and his grandfather killing the horse. So we pulled that up front and used it as a prologue, and put the main titles over it. It bothered me tonight, seeing that image of Jane falling in the field, that's where it gets very, very heavy to me. I wouldn't do that if I were doing it all over again.

FROM AUDIENCE: Were the marathon sequences shot in continuity? Did they really build to that exhausted state?

POLLACK: Because we were in one set, this is one of these rare instances in moviemaking that we could shoot the picture in continuity. What we did, essentially, is start *with* makeup and gradually get rid of it—to where we were using almost no makeup. The derby races themselves—those ten-minute runs around the floor—they were shot in continuity, and with multiple cameras. We had doctors there as a safety precaution, because some of the cast members were not so young. And I had to run them for a while before I turned the cameras on. We only rolled the camera about three times a day; we'd rehearse, place the cameras, and then roll them for these good long takes, then everybody would rest for an hour and a half or so. It got very exhausting. Some of the people were carrying others. Like Jane literally carried Red Buttons around for two days.

FROM AUDIENCE: What motivated Jane Fonda to do this film, what was in the character that appealed to her?

POLLACK: I can only give you my opinion, but from my observation, I knew she was in an emotional transition for herself. As I said, she had played these sex comedies where she was always the sex kitten, and I think this film represented a strong political statement for her—in this case, capitalism having run amok, if you will, with this kind of degradation that came out of the Depression. A couple of other things: this was a really meaty role, a woman with a brain who was not a sex object. Number two, the fact that she had lived in France—while married to Vadim—meant that she knew this book very well; she was aware of the esteem with which it was held. In France it was a classic, a very beloved book—because you must remember that in the late thirties and early forties, Sartre and de Beauvoir were beginning to form existentialism. All of a sudden a guy comes along writing about real people in a real setting, and gives them a kind of metaphor for their philosophical concept of the basic hopelessness of man's existence. So they leapt on this book. And Jane, while living in France, was in that whole crowd, so there were many reasons why she liked it.

FROM AUDIENCE: How did you get that scene where Jane Fonda was shot in the head?

POLLACK: Well, that's a very interesting technical question—I can answer it if you really want to hear it. It was a combination of many factors having to work at exactly the same time. First, here's a two-sentence lesson in optics. We have wide-angle lenses and long-focus lenses. The long-focus lens has a narrower field of view than the wide-angle lens and tends to change perspective. You and I see things as if through a 50mm lens, so distances look exactly as they really are. If I use a long lens, this room will look two-dimensional and not three-dimensional—that is, the rows of people I see here will look stacked up on top of each other, not behind each other. If I use a wide-angle lens, the heads of the people in the front row would look like pinpoints, and would look two miles away from the next row. This is very valuable in fight sequences and the like, where you want to exaggerate.

Now normally, in shooting a blank shot, you put a half-load of blank powder into the shell of a bullet in a gun. And it makes a big ball of flame shoot out the front of a gun when you pull the trigger. But you would burn somebody to death if you stuck a gun at point-blank range to their head and did it. So I had the technical problem to solve of how do I get the flame without hurting Jane. We used a gun next to her head that had no blank in it. Now if you can imagine that she's over there, and the gun's over there, if we use a very long lens—just remember that it will compress everything and make it look very flat—I can then take a man and bring him halfway between me and Jane and line his gun up exactly with the other gun. And this guy halfway between us has a gun that's going to shoot a flame. When I print the picture that flame is going to go right in front of her eyes.

Now that shot had to be very steady. So we propped the guy's hand up on a stand and lined it up with the camera. Then, to the gun that was in the hand of the guy who was standing next to Jane we attached a little syringe with a ball full of black powder, so that when he pulled the trigger, somebody else squeezed the ball so the black powder burn hit the side of her head, while the flame from the other gun went across her face. Now at the same time her head was up against a white pole. So we took a wad of cotton and soaked it in artificial blood and put it in a slingshot and hit the wad of cotton against the white of the pole at the exact same time we fired the gun and squeezed the black powder . . . I'm not done yet. Then there was a little electric fan for her hair. When a woman with long hair moves to the side very fast, her hair flies in the opposite direction. So we had a guy with an electric fan which had to be kept running because otherwise you couldn't get up to speed fast enough. So this guy held the fan tipped down, so at the instant the gunshot happened he whipped the fan up and blew her hair one way which made her head look like it was moving the other way. So all of those things had to happen at the same time. And when you do something like this you just have to keep doing it over and over and hope you're getting it right. We did it about six times, just guessing. We were shooting at four times normal speed, turning ninety-six frames a second instead of twenty-four frames, so it's in slow motion when you look at it, and there's no way to tell if you've got it right while you're doing it. I would go "one-two-three-go," and everybody would do everything. The hardest part of all this, by the way, was having Jane keep her eyes open. Just psychologically, when you say to someone, one-two-three-go, the reaction is to blink. But in slow motion the blink would look like an eternity. So with the gun going off and everything, she had to try to keep her eyes open.

[After *Jeremiah Johnson*]

CRIST: As Sydney just put it, *Jeremiah Johnson* is more of a movie of mood and character than of story line. To me it's the quintessential ballad. My usual cliché: now, Sydney—could you tell us about the genesis of this movie?

POLLACK: This movie was the first film I did after *They Shoot Horses*. Redford and I had been friends for quite a number of years. I had worked with him once before on a film called *This Property Is Condemned*, but I had met Bob as an actor in a small picture we did together in 1960 called *Warhunt*. We had remained friends and our families remained friends, and I had a home up in the area where we did the snow sequences in the picture—in the resort area called Sundance that Bob owns. We used to spend a lot of time in the mountains and had always looked for a film to do in that setting. In early

1971 a friend who had been an agent, Joe Wizan, sent me a screen-play by John Milius called "The Saga of Liver-Eating Johnson," based on a real character, John Johnson, who was buried at the veterans' cemetery in Los Angeles. He had become quite an early-American legend through his prowess as an Indian fighter.

Milius, if you know his films, is a little bit bloodthirsty, to say the least, and wrote a rather literal treatment of a very macho guy who killed all these Indians and ate their livers raw. It was a dis-gusting screenplay, actually, but it had this heroic character—and it had the mountains. It was based loosely on a textbook, published by Indiana University Press, called *The Crow Killer*. It was a schol-arly book, used in history classes, and was merely a factual report of Johnson's life, which we followed closely and accurately in terms of events only. That is, it was a fact that he married a Flathead Indian wife, that the Crows did in fact kill her while he was out on a spring hunting trip, and when he returned he found the bones of her skeleton, plus a small skull—which is the first he knew of her pregnancy. He then embarked on a vendetta that lasted some fifteen years against the Crow nation. He was extremely feared and re-spected by the Crow nation and they did, in fact, begin to send one warrior at a time after him. This "war" existed until Johnson dis-covered a monument to himself that had been built by the Indians. At that point, he made peace with the chief and went to Cheyenne, Wyoming, where he became sheriff and lived out his days. And because he was in the cavalry during the Spanish-American War, he was buried at the veterans' cemetery.

When the picture was over the children of Cheyenne, Wyo-ming, took up a collection to have his body exhumed from the veterans' cemetery and Redford and I went to this new funeral in Cheyenne, where Johnson was reburied with all these mountain men there. There are actually a bunch of guys who run around with those muzzle-loaded muskets and wear buckskin clothes and camp out at night—and still call themselves mountain men. And they were the pallbearers—quite an interesting funeral.

To get back to the original question. I took the screenplay and went to work with another writer friend, David Rafael, who has worked with me on almost every film I've done. We then invented this whole family life. There was a woman called Crazy Woman, whom these mountain men did take care of; her family had been massacred by Indians and she was traumatized by the attack and could not feed herself or take care of herself. The mountain men would drop off deer carcasses for her. Many of the other characters were real characters—such as Bear Claw Chris Lapp, played here by the late Will Geer, who was also a very famous mountain man.

So we went to work on a story about this guy who'd kill Indians and eat their livers, or eat the bark off trees, and would go around and beat people up with poles—it was a bloody mess when we first got it, and we worked very hard to come up with a kind of ode or ballad to that early time in America. It was a difficult picture because there's no strong narrative line to provide some discipline. It took me a long, long time to edit the film—eight months, actually. The film sustains itself on character and moods, and therefore rhythms. It's not nearly as easy to put together as a film where you go from "And then what happened?" to "And then what happened?"—and you have a discipline telling you how to pace a film and cut it with narrative events.

This was also a very difficult film to shoot, as you might have guessed, because of the snow. That snow was twelve to fifteen feet deep, tough just to try to walk in. But if you can imagine carrying cameras and arc lights around in that kind of snow—it was extremely difficult. Plus the fact that there is no such thing as "take two" without moving to another location, because if you have virgin snow and track it up, you can't go back and do the scene again. In addition, horses and mules will not walk in snow that's deeper than five or six inches. They'll panic and try to get up on you; they want something solid. So we had to use miles and miles of chain-link fence, which we got in six-foot widths maybe a hundred yards long. Then we'd lay it down in the snow and go away and let it snow five or six inches on top of that, and then do our scenes with the horses on the chain-link fence—which acted like giant snowshoes—to keep us all from sinking way down.

From that point of view, it was a difficult film to make, and the texture of it came out in the doing. I went to David Rafael, for example, and said, "Write me a short story." You couldn't write a *screenplay* about the family life. Because the woman spoke Indian, the boy was mute—what the hell were you going to write? Who's going to say what to whom? So I said write me a short story about a guy who marries this squaw. He wrote about a ten-page story and then Bob [Redford] and I would sit up late at night and talk about it. It was a question of literally trying to improvise the centerpiece of the picture as we went along, trying to get some sense of a family life. We had some very accurate technical advisers. One, Larry Dean

Olson, who teaches wilderness survival at Brigham Young University, advised us on the lore of the mountains; then we had a Crow Indian teaching dialect to the girl, and keeping us as accurate as possible. Actually, a lot of the early missionaries who had settled that area were French, so the Indians in northwestern Wyoming, Utah, and Montana began speaking pidgin French.

If I had to say in words what *Jeremiah Johnson* was about, for me it was about a man who wanted to find some place in the world where he and only he was in total control of his own destiny, and found that no such place exists. There are rules of civilization no matter where one goes, even into uncivilized areas. Nature has a code of ethics you cannot violate. Everything that lives creates some morality, if you will, some code or standard within which beings must behave and submit themselves to. This was a man who thought he could escape the need for any structure or ordered civilization and found he couldn't. And when he violated the Indians' set of rules or morality, he sowed the seeds of his own destruction. He could wander as high as he wanted to on that mountain; as a matter of fact, the original ending of the picture showed him at the top of the mountain, totally frozen in ice—where he had become, in a sense, a monument to himself. He had just climbed, and kept climbing until he began to freeze. That was why, originally, we had a scene in which he saw that frozen man. That was meant as a premonition of what was going to happen to him, and in fact, the frozen man was played by his double—so he had some similarity to him. It got very arty, and pretentious . . . when I saw it, it was just too much; you expected to hear bells or something.

CRIST: . . . I've noticed that you work with sort of a repertory company of actors—why is that?

POLLACK: There's something marvelously efficient about working with actors that you know. There's less time wasted with diplomacy and more time used in getting the performance.

CRIST: I'm sure that one of the major questions that will come out of this weekend is based on the fact that, out of your eleven movies, Bob Redford has been in five. Over the years he has zoomed to star-power. Beyond the terms of your personal friendship, has working with him changed?

POLLACK: Well, it has and it hasn't. I mean, it changed in the sense that we've both gotten older and in a curious way somewhat more confident, so that in the films I've done with him most recently—particularly *Electric Horseman,* let's say—we've taken on more responsibility for the writing ourselves, and have had less dependence on writers. In *Electric Horseman* as well as *Three Days of the Condor* we took a germ of an idea and went off and developed it ourselves, continuing even after shooting had started. In that sense, it has changed.

In terms of what you would think might change—that is, does he behave differently as a person—not in ways that I can see. I'm sure he does. If someone knew him fifteen years ago and hadn't seen him since, they would see changes now. But I don't see them myself.

FROM AUDIENCE: Did Redford do the fight scenes in *Jeremiah Johnson?*

POLLACK: Fight sequences, like all stunt sequences, are really broken down into hundreds of little mosaic shots which you cut together to create the illusion of a stunt. And in that mosaic as it's broken down, there are sections of it that are more dangerous than others, and in both sections you usually use a double, then do what we call "cover it" with the real actor. There's as much stunt work in accepting the punch and creating the illusion of really being hit as there is in swinging the punch—and there are guys who are expert at that, and usually, in a full shot, they can make it look better than the real actor. So these scenes are a combination of Bob and stunt people—depending on how acrobatic or how dangerous the stunt itself is. He didn't do any of the work with the wolves, for example, because they were real wolves, and dangerous, and the stunt man had to be heavily armored. We weren't about to use Redford's arm for that.

FROM AUDIENCE: Were there any live animals killed in the making of *Jeremiah Johnson?* It would seem incongruous, since Redford claims he'd never kill anything.

POLLACK: There was one live animal killed. We called the state game department and asked them if they'd bring us a sick animal—they pick up and isolate sick animals and eventually kill them—and there was one elk, which was actually shot by two state game officials who were off-camera. We did not want to take the chance of having anyone miss the shot and wound the animal. So the state sent two sharpshooters, and they dropped the animal instantly.

FROM AUDIENCE: How much do you get into changing the words people say, actually changing the script?

POLLACK: We make enormous changes. Film scripts are not like theater scripts—and that's been the cause of much consternation by screenwriters, who are very, very offended by what we terrible directors do. And I'm very sympathetic to them. But you see, it's not the primary means of communication in film. The words are really supportive—and it's only because of our own lack of imagination that we rely so strongly on the words anyway—because we're all very influenced by plays and other forms of entertainment of which movies are derivative. And it's something that you change all the time, not only the lines but whole scenes, whole concepts of scenes. When a picture begins to emerge and you begin to see two people together on screen—let's say Redford and Fonda in *Electric Horseman*—it becomes immediately apparent, let's say, that you've written a scene that is totally unnecessary in order to explain, for example, their attraction to each other. Fonda walks into a room and Redford walks into a room and they look at each other and you take two closeups and then you say, "Why the hell did they write that scene where she tries to figure out why she finds him attractive?" You don't *need* it. Sometimes actors change lines without consulting you, and sometimes they do it very well—better than what's in the script. Sometimes if you try to be very careful in the script, which I do try to be in the last draft, if you try to be very precise with the choice of each single word, then you get uptight with the actor who won't say the line right.

FROM AUDIENCE: One of the things that strikes me is that in your films we've seen so far, the people end up almost suicidally trapped in an unavoidable fate, that the ending is inevitable.

POLLACK: That's an interesting observation. As I've gotten older and done more films, it's something I read more and more often about my own work. I would constantly read articles—at first they were only from Europe, but now they tend to be written in America, too—that would say, for instances, all my films are "circular." And I kept saying, what the hell is "circular"? Then I started looking at my films, and, by God, they are circular. But what does that mean? I don't know what it means. Then the articles began to say Pollack's films are all concerned with culture clashes, or they're all concerned with destiny, or so and so. And I think all those things are true, and that's fair to say and I'm fascinated to hear about this. But this is not something I set out consciously to do.

When you direct a picture you may be concentrating on a particular task at hand, which taps all sorts of areas in your unconscious that you're not aware of. Those areas seep into the work itself. If I took a love scene from any one of my pictures, or anybody else's, and set it up as a hypothetical experiment and had, let's say, Frankenheimer direct it, myself, Coppola, Mark Rydell—five or six or ten directors—you would get that many different love scenes. The same scene, same actors. You'd get a lyrical love scene, an erotic love scene, a tender love scene, a cynical love scene, a sophisticated love scene. Not in what they say, but in the actual handling of the actors—how do you place them, are they standing or seated, what's the lighting? Is it all in one shot and does the camera keep moving around them? Is it staccato and in cuts? Is the camera focusing only on eyes, or is it details of hands and skin? Now, in the doing of that, you take a kind of lie-detector test; you can't lie, something of who you are and what you believe in gets in there. Just as it's not untrue what actors make you feel about the characters they play. Robert Redford is not Jeremiah Johnson, but it would be impossible for him to play Jeremiah Johnson without certain of those elements in his own persona. He can't do it otherwise. He's calling on things that exist in him. While it's a terrible lie to say that Redford *is* the Sundance Kid, or Hubbell Gardner in *The Way We Were*, or Bob Woodward in *All the President's Men*—he *is* all of those people. There are parts of him. In that sense, there are major parts of me in all of my films, some of which I'm not aware of. It's not something I've gone into too much, because, to tell you the truth, I don't want to know too much about that. I'm very aware now, in making a picture, thinking, "Oh, Jesus, what are those people going to say now? Are they going to write that this is one of those x-y-z pictures?" The minute I start to think about it I get paralyzed, so I can't think about it.

Just to take a simple example, and a clear one. In *They Shoot Horses, Don't They?* there was a lot written about the philosophical meanings, the moral lesson about man's inhumanity to man, and survival, and so on. I can't direct a picture thinking about any of that because it won't help. It does not have anything to do with the craft of directing. It's something else. The only thing I can think about is what makes me want to go to work every day. Aside from the technical challenge, what *They Shoot Horses* was about for me, what moved me and made me passionate about it, was a kind of heroism. I was so moved by the fact that in the marathon, when that horrible siren went off to start the dance again, they all came back every time. That said something very positive to me about human nature. That with *all* this punishment, these are the rules, you play the game—the game is you rest for ten minutes and when the siren goes you come back and do it again. It's like Tom Wolfe's book *The Right Stuff,* about astronauts getting in these rockets. *That's* the rule—if you sign up to be an astronaut you have to get into that six-thousand-pound rocket and it lights up behind you and you don't know whether you're going to live or die. What makes a guy get into one of those things? Well, there's something very thrilling to me about that. But again, I don't say that anybody else gets that out of *They Shoot Horses.* Everybody else sees the picture as something so grim and horrible and depressing, and look how awful we are to each other.

But if I went into the film thinking that, I could never direct it. What I have to isolate is what's exciting to me, what's positive to me, what makes me want to do it, what can it illustrate that is a good thing? In the case of *They Shoot Horses*—as in the case of all my films, for me only, not for everybody else—I have to find the positive. I don't mean this to sound like a sophomoric lesson in morality, but it has to be something that turns me on. It may not be related to what you see, but it gave birth to what you see. I think my films have been changing—as anyone's would be—and I suspect they're becoming more positive.

FROM AUDIENCE: In listening to you talk about how you find scripts and how you redesign them, I'm wondering—what is the function of the producer? Doesn't he often find the script and hunt for a director and make many of these decisions that we've been discussing that you make?

POLLACK: Not so much any more. The function of the producer has changed radically over the last twenty years. There was a time when the producer was essentially the shaping force in films. I can contradict that, too, because if you look at the films of Wyler and Capra, say, who worked under the producer system—they all gave their own stamps to the films. But what you have today are two major media—television, which is a producer's medium. That is, the producer is the constant on television and the director comes in for a single episode of a given series. The look of the program is designed by the producer; he does the post-production work in putting it together, editing the material. So that all of the programs you see on television owe their look or their style to the producer.

There's a completely different system operating in films. The producer today can be anybody—and often is anybody—anybody who gets an idea and puts a package together. Depending upon the relative degree of artistic strength of the parties involved, the producer either will or will not dictate the artistic terms on a picture. It's very rare—*very rare* and almost nonexistent—that a producer dictates the artistic standards of a film. Ninety percent of the producers functioning today are ex-agents. As agents they get a flow of material, they handle artistic clients. Let's say that in a given agency you have a guy who handles Jane Fonda and two writers. Now he might get a piece of material that he's supposed to sell to a studio, but at this stage of his life he's been an agent for twelve years, and says the hell with it, I'm not going to sell it to a studio, I'm going to quit the agency, and I'll go see Jane and go see Sydney and I'll put this package together. In fact, that's how *Jeremiah Johnson* happened. The producer on *Jeremiah Johnson* was my agent and Redford's agent and found this script—and quit the agency business. He's a producer now, he puts the elements together—and from that point on, his position gets less and less significant. It emerges again at the time of selling the picture—if he's that kind of producer. Take a producer like Ray Stark, let's say, one of the most famous and successful producers—I've done three films for him—*This Property Is Condemned, The Way We Were,* and *Electric Horseman.* Now Ray's expertise is in seeing the potential in selling a project like *Electric Horseman.* He'll send it to me and to Redford, he'll help us get Jane—and then he disappears until the picture's finished. Then he'll come back in and help find the logo for the picture, and make sure it opens in such-and-such a theater, and he'll figure out a way to do a party where everybody comes in cowboy clothes—all that stuff that I don't really care about. Once the movie is made I *care* about the way it goes, but I don't have the head or the time for getting involved. I don't care if the film is shown in a theater that seats three hundred or six hundred, or whether it's on the West Side or East Side. There are people who have to think about all those things. And that's usually what a producer does now. Maybe there are exceptions, but rarely.

CRIST: Does the producer put up the money? You skipped over that part of it.

POLLACK: I skipped over that because no, the producer does not provide the money. The only people who provide money today are the major studios and anything else you hear is a myth. I mean, there are fly-by-night tax-shelter deals where you can do a single picture. But, finally, when you say "put up the money"—you can pay for a picture with private money, but you cannot get it seen without a studio. There's no such thing as distributing a picture by yourself. You can't do it, it's impossible. And in that sense the major studios still exercise an octopus hold on this industry. It's quite possible to go off and go to German tax-shelter money, or Houston oil people, and raise five to ten million. You can get the actual hard dollars it costs to make a movie. But then what do you do when it's racking up interest at the rate of 15 percent—how do you get this movie into the theaters? Are you going to the theaters and make a deal with them? Do you know how long it would take you to go to eight hundred cities and eight hundred theaters and make a deal with them? You can't do it. At that point you go back to the studios. A lot of people prefer to shortcut that process and go to the studio to begin with. Get your $10 million from the studio. *That's* what the producer does.

In Europe the producer does raise money, because films there have a much narrower distribution and cost a lot less. European producers do have the responsibility of physically going out and raising money—as producers do on Broadway. But there's a hold-over myth from Broadway that extends to films. Producers in films, per se, do *not* raise money, not in American films. What they do is take a meeting with Ted Ashley at Warner's or Alan Ladd when he was at Fox, or whatever might be the current head of the studio, and say, "Here's the package—will you do the picture?" They say either yes or no, and the money is raised or not. Producers can't go around getting $500,000 here and $200,000 there because films today in America just cost too much. A really cheap Hollywood film would be $8 to $9 million; that's about as cheap as you can do it. And you don't raise that kind of money privately.

FROM AUDIENCE: Mr. Pollack, what is your reputation for coming in under budget or at budget or above budget?

POLLACK: I have a lousy reputation for coming in on budget, really. I've done it on several occasions, but the pictures of mine that have been the most successful, therefore the best known, are always the ones that have disastrous budget consequences. I don't think there's any correlation—but the pictures I've done on budget or below have all been flops. I'm sorry—there's a glaring exception: *Jeremiah Johnson* came in half a million under budget, and was one of the most successful films I've ever done. The picture cost $3 million at that time, which was very cheap, and it has *netted*, in film rentals, an excess of $36 million. Now, that means its box-office gross has been close to $90 million.

But *Jeremiah Johnson* was a unique picture in that sense. There were no lines around the block, ever. It made its money slowly over a long period of time, by doing half-filled houses. It opened Christmas week along with *The Getaway* and a lot of big blockbuster pictures and didn't do well at all. But at the end of six weeks when those other pictures began to taper off, the distributers said there's something funny going on here, *Jeremiah Johnson* wasn't falling off; we did the same business in week seven as we had the first week. So they let it run and it ran solidly.

[After *The Way We Were*]

CRIST: We were just reacting to how this film improves with age. Its major stock in trade is nostalgia, and now even the 1973 ending seems nostalgic, especially the politics of that last scene. Sydney was just telling me about the future he saw for those characters. Tell us all.

POLLACK: I was half joking, half serious. In the making of the film I really fell in love with those two characters in a curious way, because I think they're parts of all of us. I think of them both as being half of a whole person—there's the committed person, and the other one. So, falling in love with the characters, I felt, gee, this is left very open-ended, here's this daughter who's going to grow up in the sixties; the film ends in 1952 or 1953, and it's now the seventies, and I started to wonder what would have happened to all of those characters. And I know the daughter, Rachel, probably would have gone to Berkeley in the sixties, and probably would have been a political radical, probably heavy into drugs—which would have pained Barbra enormously—but she would have been very proud of the political activism. And I would imagine that at some point or another she would have needed to call on Redford to help her handle the daughter.

So I have always imagined beginning a film with a dinner scene, where Redford had to come to dinner with David X. Cohen and her. I could see Barbra running around the kitchen trying to get this meal ready—a pot roast. And then I figured that Redford would go up to Berkeley to see the daughter he'd never seen. And he'd have an affair with the daughter's roommate. I knew that at some point the character of J.J., his friend, would have committed suicide, because he was a guy who was *dangerously* lost in the past, to such an extent he would never have been able to deal with today. And Lois Childs, the very pretty "beige" girl, I would assume would have written a wonderful, best-selling book on feminism, would have become a Gloria Steinem kind of lady. Then I know that Redford and Barbra should end up together somehow, I don't know how.

CRIST: The vogue is for geriatric love stories, so maybe we could see them in a retirement home together.

POLLACK: I joke with Barbra about it all the time and she keeps saying, "So when are we going to make this sequel? When I'm sixty-five?"

FROM AUDIENCE: Watching this a second time now, it seems in a sense an American *Scenes from a Marriage,* in that it's about people loving or not loving each other in and out of marriage and continuing the relationship.

POLLACK: Originally there was a completely different ending—not the ultimate ending, but the penultimate ending was much more political than what's there now. It's why there's a disjointed feeling in the third act of the picture—where you can see the surgery. This film has been successful from a commercial point of view, extremely successful—but it never has been an ultimately satisfying picture in terms of what it set out to do. The audiences were just plain bored when we got into politics. They wanted to know what was happening with Bob and Barbra. And so I had to weed out most of the rest of it.

CRIST: I want to pursue this, because at the time a number of us felt that the film was a sellout. Do you think the emphasis got switched, and the audience shunned the political aspect *because* you were dealing with superstars?

POLLACK: I think that's part of it. There's no question about the fact that what hooks you immediately into the picture are those two characters; there's something so improbable about this match and therefore something so right about it. They're absolutely as opposite as you can get, and you can't help but become interested in what's going to happen with them. And in a sense there's a great lesson in it, because I always had this argument with Arthur Laurents, that the book was ill-conceived. I'm going to make a terrible exaggeration here, but I said it's like dealing with Dachau through two people who are neighbors of Dachau. They live next door and see people coming in and they jabber at each other at the terrible things—or the good things, depending on how they see it—that are going on at Dachau. Because the two leading characters seemed to be observers and nonparticipants, it seemed to me to be a terrible cheat. Which is why the first act works so much better than the rest of it. Because she's in the *throes* of it in the first act, she's in the Young Communist League, she's hawking the leaflets, she's on the barricades. He's observing all this and wondering what the hell it is that makes some lady run around putting in all this time into cranking out little leaflets and standing under the trees bothering everybody to hand them out.

It gets less and less believable and less organic to the picture as the picture goes on and as their direct involvement in the conflict gets more distant. It becomes meretricious, if you will, more token, to drag in the politics because neither one of them is caught up in the politics.

Originally, I had said to Arthur Laurents and to Columbia Pictures, the only way you can do this properly is to begin this picture not in college but at the House Un-American Activities Committee hearings, where the man on the stand being questioned is Hubbell Gardner, and in the hearing room is Katie Morosky. And you make the time-present structure his testimony—and make the entire picture a series of flashbacks in the same way that act one is a flashback anyway. You don't have to alter anything, you tell the same story, except that what's triggering her memories is watching him slowly knuckle under to this pressure and weigh his instinct for survival as a writer against his own morality. Then at least you have put the protagonist in the center of the fire, in a way, and what is otherwise political talk becomes organic drama. My objection to the other way was that it was *yenta*-ism carried to the extreme, it was two neighbors gossiping about the blacklist. And it drove me crazy, I kept saying this is baloney—these people were jabbering on the sidelines. It's very easy to talk about the morality of someone who's not caught up in the throes of it; it's another thing to be in the throes of it. Essentially, it was like violating the first simple rules of drama—that you have someone just observing a situation and then passing judgment on it.

FROM AUDIENCE: It seems to me that the relationship between Hubbell and Katie starts to fall apart before the scenes you mentioned—when she comes back to L.A. from the Washington demonstration and he meets her at the railroad station, for example.

POLLACK: That's right, it was disintegrating for some time. Actually, for Hubbell and his pals, the best time for them was when they were in the Army—or the Navy or whatever—during the war. Since then it's been downhill for them. Hubbell goes downhill very quickly, in a curious way. He never was really able to deal with the complexities of growing up. But I think of Hubbell as a guy who'd be a late starter. I think this man will be a helluva man in his late forties and early fifties. He'll go in that cycle that people go in, where he'll come back to something that's very solid. Which is what interests me about the possibility of a sequel. I would see the sequel ending with him becoming very active politically.

FROM AUDIENCE: How do you feel about the picture now?

POLLACK: My feelings are quite ambivalent. My strongest feelings in favor of it are the two performances, which I think are wonderful. But the picture is very unfinished in many areas. First, in the political area. The single most difficult problem we had with the picture, was also the reason it took me so long to get Redford into the picture. It took me six months of doing *everything,* literally, except beating up on him, to get him in the picture. He did *not* want to play that character. The character as written was just a male sex object. He was a man with no convictions, no point of view, a glamorous golden boy with nothing inside—which is everything that Redford did *not* want to be associated with.

What I saw there was a potential. I wanted to find some sort of defense for his position, not because I admire or agree with people who don't do anything, but because I feel there is an honest, opposing argument to those people who commit themselves at the drop of a hat. I think there's a danger in both directions. There's a knee-jerk reaction to causes in this country that drives me just as crazy as the people who don't do anything. And I wanted to try to find some way for Hubbell not to be so passive. In that book, all Hubbell does is go around saying, "Oh, Katie, don't do that." That's all he does. That scene in Union Station that someone referred to is not in the book at all; that's the scene we created for the picture to at least make him angry, at least make him come out and say, "Look, this is grown-up politics and it's stupid and dangerous. And this is all going to blow over, and all you guys who think you know right from wrong today are going to be damned embarrassed ten years from now." Now, he's not right—but at least it's a point of view.

If I could do it again I'd love to find more articulation for that character, because I think there are the seeds of a marvelously interesting character in a person who has, let's say, a *long* view of life. Katie sees as far as her nose. She's wonderful and committed, but it's this cause today, and tomorrow another one. Hubbell takes the more existential view of things. There's bad and good in both. But it was easier to articulate what's good in her point of view than to articulate what's good in his point of view.

Among the many failures of the picture, the two that stand out the strongest are its failure to deal satisfactorily with the political issues it raises, and perhaps its failure to present a fair, honest contest between these two opposing philosophic approaches to life.

FROM AUDIENCE: Despite the negative things you say about it, the movie worked and we loved it.

POLLACK: Well, it worked to the tune of $250 million. It's the kind of picture a lot of people know, and they hum the music.

FROM AUDIENCE: Have you ever been totally satisfied with anything you've done?

POLLACK: Not totally, no. The whole point is to keep doing it till you get it right.

FROM AUDIENCE: Didn't you *like* Katie?

POLLACK: I *love* Katie. And I say again that I think of these two characters as components of a single person. What I feel is that if Katie had a little more of Hubbell she'd be better and if he had a little more of her, he'd be better. They're invaluable to each other.

There's no way you can measure these things, actually, but the more difficult acting role in the picture is Redford's. It is the most demanding, the most challenging, and the most internalized. There are not the arias that she has to help carry it—his is all internalized in a presence, an attitude, an understanding of being imbued with the character. I happen to think the character is quite close to Redford.

FROM AUDIENCE: Is that how you got him to change his mind, by showing him that?

POLLACK: I got him to change his mind by pure persistence.

FROM AUDIENCE: How would you assess the talents of Barbra Streisand, and do you want to work with her again?

POLLACK: She's brilliantly talented, breathtakingly talented—but she's a special girl to cast; you can't put her in everything. I couldn't have her playing the Indian girl in *Jeremiah Johnson*. She's just not right for everything. But she's brilliant, and I spend some time with her now talking about new projects. I want to do a musical with her.

CRIST: No question that she was magnificent in this. It's certainly one of her most controlled performances. She's still, however, probably the only Communist activist of the thirties who worked as a waitress and had red fingernails to *here*. But that's something I'd never fault the director for.

POLLACK: It's like the length of Redford's hair. You can go only so far with these things.

CRIST: Yes, from what I know of the World War II Navy, he would have been in the brig half the time for not having a haircut.

FROM AUDIENCE: It seems to me—in this film and in the others we've seen—that you have a way of sustaining a romantic relationship, which I think is admirable and even courageous as a director.

POLLACK: As I said earlier, you can't do anything that you don't in some way believe strongly in or are fascinated with or love. I couldn't do a picture that didn't have a love story in it; I just couldn't. It would bore me. That doesn't mean it has to be a huge love story, that it's the whole picture, but somewhere in it ... otherwise, what's the point? You're just watching eight guys attacking a castle or something and I don't know, that's just boring to me. Everybody does what interests him most. Roman Polanski can scare the living hell out of you—because he likes that. And Hitchcock has been doing that kind of thing for years. Everybody has his own area in which he functions best.

[After *The Electric Horseman*]

CRIST: It seems to me you lean toward the "reluctant hero." I see the same Redford character in your most recent movies together— the Chaplinesque reluctant hero.

POLLACK: The reluctant hero—if you want to take that as a statement, you're right; it is the same guy in *Three Days of the Condor* as in *The Electric Horseman*. That is, the little guy who takes on a whole organization and beats it. In the case of *Condor* it's the CIA. In this one, it's the corporation, a bureaucracy. That exact theme perhaps isn't present in the other pictures, but there are other similarities. I can't help it. They're not necessarily things I would think about, but they're there. Chaplinesque? I'm not a film student, per se, and never was, so I'm not an authority on Chaplin's films. But that reluctant hero I do like as a character. The individual who takes on a large, harmful, impersonal bureaucracy is appealing.

FROM AUDIENCE: I had the feeling at least for the first third of the picture that Redford's character didn't have any direction. He was an aging cowboy, not happy, drunk most of the time—and then, all of a sudden, he becomes concerned with this horse. Doesn't that disturb you that in the first third of the film, you don't have any direction for your main character?

POLLACK: Well, in fact, what I was trying to do was show you a man who had once been himself a champion—in the prologue of the picture. He'd had the blood, if you will, that that horse had. He was a champion. And they're hanging lights all over the horse— which is what they're doing to him. Now, Redford's too old and too busted up to keep doing rodeo and he makes a lot of money for promoting this breakfast cereal, and he tries to talk himself into the fact that he's living the good life when, in fact, he's humiliated by what he's doing, going out to roller derbies and high school football games lit up like Liberace, with a cereal box. It's a humiliating way for a champion to end his life. Now, when he sees the horse, who's also a champion, who's having the same things done to him— substitute the drugs for the horse for the cowboy's booze, put the lights around the horse's neck and bring him to a cereal convention—all of a sudden the cowboy is able to identify with the horse and is able to do for the horse what he's not able to do for himself.

He's not, after all, as perceptive as you are at this point, having seen the picture. He's *in* it—not observing it. He's caught in the middle of it. When you're in the throes of something like that, you're not always observing yourself. He's not aware that he's pathetic; he's only aware that he's struggling in some way to overcome this bad feeling. All of a sudden, when he looks at the lights on the horse, at that exact moment he gets the idea to take the horse. He's even a little shocked the next morning when he wakes up with the horse in the desert. It was a very impulsive thing. I was never confused about his lack of direction; he was lost and had to be lost. Otherwise I don't think you would have accepted an act that outrageous as a way of getting out of the shape he was in.

[After *The Yakuza*]

CRIST: I am going to be the first vice-president of the Yakuza cult. It is a totally non–Sydney Pollack movie, in that it's a complete departure. It's that rare American film that gets beyond the surface of another culture—and does it powerfully. Sydney, how did you come to do this film?

POLLACK: Right after *The Way We Were* I was looking for another picture, and Paul Schrader—who has since done several films, both as writer and director—was just beginning to be hot in Hollywood. Warner Brothers had paid an awful lot of money for the screenplay and Robert Mitchum was already cast in the picture. It was sent to me by John Calley, the head of Warner's, and while I liked the theatricality of it, I was really put off by the violence, number one. And number two, I had evaluated it, in the form it was in at the time, as a very clever commercial ploy to mix a gangster film with a kung fu film, which really didn't interest me. But I saw something worthwhile in it, if it could be rewritten. So I agreed to do it and went to Robert Towne, a man whose work I respect enormously. He agreed with the potential of it.

We started work on it, and I began to steep myself in these Yakuzaiga, as they call them. They're a sort of Japanese version of the AIP low-budget motorcycle pictures. It's not a form respected by the Japanese intelligentsia; on the other hand, it's a popular form. They make them in about two weeks. And the biggest star of all of them is the gentleman you saw in this picture—Takakura Ken, who is very unusual in style. Japanese theater is very exaggerated in style, coming out of the Kabuki theater, and the acting style is bravura—externalized and exaggerated. There's a sense of conscious theatricality in most Japanese pictures. But in watching the work of Takakura Ken, I felt he'd been influenced by American films, and as it turned out he had—particularly by Henry Fonda, who was his idol. He's also larger in stature than most Japanese. Mitchum is quite a big man, so Takakura Ken was a good match.

The only catch was that in order to get Takakura Ken we had to do the film through a certain film studio in Japan. Some of these Japanese studios are mostly gangster-run operations—run by these Yakuzas—some of the people there don't have any finger on *any* hand. This is a true story: one of the Japanese transportation captains messed up on picking up a star at the airport. Afterward, he came into the production office with the first joint of his little finger wrapped up in a handkerchief—and he presented it to the production manager as an apology. Now you laugh, and I do too. But you see, they find the idea of a gun twice as barbaric and twice as cruel and think it horrifically humorous that a human being would have to go around with these things that make explosions and hurl inert pieces of metal right through vital organs. They find that absolutely barbaric. To them, there is the responsibility of doing it yourself— which is a great part of Zen. There is no concept in that culture of "I'm sorry." Being sorry comes from Christian myth, which has to do with the fact that it is possible for someone else to take care of your sins. The phrase "I'm sorry" means one is absolved of all guilt. They find that absolutely ludicrous. They believe that the only clear, fair way to atone is to harm *oneself,* which is why in that culture there is hara-kiri, where someone does away with himself. Now the twentieth-century derivative of that is to maim oneself in some small way, as a method of expressing honest regret over the person wronged. If you think about it for a while, it makes every bit as much sense as a bunch of grown-up people going around committing a bunch of sins and making mistakes and saying, "I'm awfully sorry." It doesn't do any good.

All that got fascinating to me as I began to work on the picture, and screen more and more Japanese films and go to Zen monasteries and speak with the Zen masters and deal with the Japanese in as honest and deep a way as possible—which was minimal in the time I spent there. It takes five or six years of living in Japan to understand that you can't *ever* understand the Japanese. That's not an exaggerated statement. It's impossible for the Western mind to comprehend that in totality. There's the unbelievable contrast there—the people who will spend forty-five hours in quiet contemplation carefully arranging every rock in a garden that is nothing but pebbles . . . and then there's the way they'll scream *"Banzai!"* as they're killing you. It's a strange set of contrasts, very hard to reconcile. They've become very understanding about Western ways, but in truth we were always offending them, no matter what we did.

The Yakuza was probably the most enriching learning experience I've ever had in making a picture. Each picture is a challenge in terms of research and in becoming an expert on a subject. You're always amazed at how little you know when you do a picture—even on a film like *They Shoot Horses, Don't They?* I didn't realize I didn't know a damned thing about the history of this country in the early part of this century. But here, in Japan, there was really a whole new world opening up to me. The combination of working in Japan with an all-Japanese crew proved to be a very enriching experience. As for the film—there's bad news and good news. Being as objective as I can be, I feel I was able to achieve a certain degree of authentic style that belonged in that country and in this genre. I think there's some real sentiment without sentimentality and real emotion in the picture. It's saddled with the necessity to communicate so much fact for the Western audience that it becomes, for me, a very talky film, and gets bogged down in explaining the bare minimum of knowledge our audiences here must have to appreciate the drama that's going on. If you don't understand that code of honor, then it's impossible to understand all the shenanigans these people have to go through to atone.

All in all, it's a film I'm proud of, but it is not one of the most successful films I ever did—for various reasons. I see its virtues, and a great many of its weaknesses, too. But it nevertheless remains the most exotic experience I've ever had in filmmaking, and I wouldn't be surprised if its influences continue in my own work in other pictures—just a sense of structure and organization which is inherent in all Japanese art, the design sense, if you will, the preoccupation with simplicity, the elimination of excessive decor is a very valuable lesson to learn.

CRIST: Also, as you said to me earlier, this has its romantic love story between two people from completely opposite cultures. And there is a true love story—in a completely asexual way, of course—between the two men. Very Pollackian.

FROM AUDIENCE: I'd like to know how much you literally contributed to the screenplay—that is, are you the "auteur" of this film?

POLLACK: I've never known how to deal with the whole auteur business. I'd be much more comfortable thinking of myself as an auteur if I actually wrote screenplays. You know, if you hire a decorator for your home and then go away for six months and come back, the job is all done—then, you really can't take any pride in it; it's not yours, in a way. But if you're there to pick every swatch of cloth, and pick a picture of a couch, then have the decorator go out and make a couch with the cloth you picked out—you may not be physically decorating the house yourself, but you are dictating the look it's going to have. That's about as close an analogy as I know how to make of the way a director who's a nonwriter works with a screenplay. The scenes are collaborative in concept, and once they're executed on a scene-by-scene basis, we go over them line by line, concept by concept, moment by moment. And the same is true with the order of scenes, until you get to the end. I do not sit down with a blank piece of paper and put down dialogue, but I did work hand in hand with Schrader, who did two rewrites before I hired Towne. I finally felt Schrader could not work deeply enough in terms of the people's emotions, that he had a great theatricality and a great bravura sense of the visually stunning, but he could not really write a scene between people. So I went to Bob Towne.

FROM AUDIENCE: The fact is, you are drawn, however unconsciously, to certain types of material.

POLLACK: Absolutely. As I said before, what you see in certain material does not always come through to others. Essentially, almost any creative act is free-associative—it has to be. It's the same process that psychoanalysis is based on. You can have tremendous tension when you're working—which you do, and tension can be an enemy of creativity, in an odd way. But you train a part of your unconscious to be as relaxed as possible and to *associate*. It's just like dreaming: you begin with one thought, and where your own creativity comes in is that you would associate differently from someone else. You have to find something to concentrate on to start the associative process. For me, the something to concentrate on is always what I would call the armature of the piece. It's not necessarily what other people will see. In this case it was a poem called "Stopping by Woods on a Snowy Evening," which has those lines, "The woods are lovely, dark and deep./But I have promises to keep,/And miles to go before I sleep." The phrase that was most suggestive or evocative to me all through the picture, and what I wrote down in the margin of the script all the time, was "promises to keep." Now it's not literally translated in my mind as "promises to keep"; there's a music to it that dictates to me even a style in an odd way. I saw this as a picture about antiques—antique people, outmoded people, the people whose values did not change to meet the current vogue; they were people who had an absolute set of values and lived by them, no matter what the consequences were. And since it was so much a question of obligation and duty, and those values, which are essentially old-fashioned values, this concept of keeping promises, of promises to keep, was the most generative phrase I could find to keep charging myself creatively during the work on this film.

FROM AUDIENCE: There were a few times in this film when you brought the viewer up to a point where you felt, well, the movie is over. . . .

POLLACK: I have that problem. I don't know what it means—I have it with every damn picture I've ever done. I have too many endings. I mean, I have it in *every* film I've ever done. I keep saying, "I'm gonna fix it this time"; then I get into the picture and it's got fifty endings. That's why the business with the letter is so screwed up in *Electric Horseman*; one of the endings was paying off that letter. As it is I've got four endings—they let the horse go, then they say good-bye by the bus, then she says good-bye at the television station, then he's walking along the road. Well, I had another one in there—I had this bus scene where you ended with the two of them.

In my early films I just used to slash them out. Boy, going all the way back to *This Property Is Condemned*, my favorite scene is not in the picture—a beautiful scene at an old train station, with Natalie Wood and a traveling salesman. Ray Stark came to the preview and quite rightly said, "Jesus, Sydney, you've got seventeen endings—get rid of some of them." I don't know why I do it, but I just can't seem to come to an end with something.

FROM AUDIENCE: How fast can you see the film that you've shot?

POLLACK: If you're working in the U.S. you look at the film you've shot the next day, but it's not in any order, of course, and doesn't make any sense. There's a great misconception about editing film—most people think it's a question of figuring out which scenes stay in and which don't stay in. That's not really the editing process. The editing process essentially is putting the *scene* together. If we were shooting the scene we're in now, I'd have the camera, say, on you all the time, reacting to what I'm saying. I'd have a camera holding both Mrs. Crist and myself, then I'd have a single camera on her, a single camera on myself, probably a big group shot of everybody, and then clusters of people in the audience. Let's say this scene we're shooting lasts five minutes. I would see maybe fifty minutes of the scene played through completely from each one of these angles. Now what do I start with? Should I first establish where we are by an overall shot, or should I start with a woman's head nodding and not know quite where we are, then go to a larger shot and then reveal the setting? So the editing process is much more complicated than saying this scene is in and this scene goes.

The day after the shooting I see all of this rough film, maybe it hasn't been fixed for sound—you might not be able to understand half of what's said. What I see the next day is just the raw material, and usually the editor is with me. I'll give the editor some general instruction, like I want to begin on the lady who asks the question, and go on to get reactions. He'll put the scene together in the most general way—and it'll usually be too long and it won't work for some reason. The editor will do that through the whole picture. When I finish with the picture he's usually about ten days to two weeks behind me. So I have that much time to relax a little bit and get unkinked. Then I go back and look at what we call a rough assembly, because that's all it is—it's loosely and roughly assembled. That is for me always the most depressing and the most disastrous thing in the world—because the picture just looks awful. It doesn't look like it will ever be a film. The first assembly of *They Shoot Horses* was four and a half hours, *Electric Horseman* was three hours and twenty minutes and nothing made any sense—the chase sequence was the most boring thing in the world.

Everybody works differently. At this point I usually like to sneak up on the picture a little bit. I'll go into the projection room, which has a forward and back control—called a rock-and-roll room. I'll take a sequence at a time and begin to analyze it without cutting any major sequence yet. First I want to see if every sequence is as good as it could be—as if the whole picture was just that sequence. Then I put them all together. At that point I'll start to drop sequences out, then the final work is done in the editing room itself—I have to go into the editing room.

We have a machine now that has three separate viewing heads, which look like three small TV screens. And let's say I do five takes of me talking to you—and let's say each take is different. The take that's been selected I'll put up on one head and two of the others go on the other heads and I'll run them down. Then I'll say to the editor, "Take this line from this take and that line from that take." Now you have to use a bridge shot each time because you can't slice two takes together—they won't match. I'll be in this position at one point, and shifted around in another. But I can go from me here to a shot of you nodding your head—even if I have to steal it from somewhere else—then come back to me sitting here and most people won't remember that the last time you saw me I was sitting another way.

Or I may take certain off-stage lines and synch them into my mouth. For instance, when I take your closeup, I'd have to be standing here doing the dialogue over again so you could respond by nodding your head. And although I'd be off-camera I'd still have the sound man picking up my voice. And it's possible when I'm watching your closeup I'll hear a line reading in my voice that I like better than the line reading when the camera was on my face. So I'll take that sound track and try to fit the line reading I prefer into the movements of the mouth on the take.

FROM AUDIENCE: We've heard you be quite critical of some of your films. How long does it usually take you, after you've made a film, for you to see it objectively?

POLLACK: It varies, but it usually takes me quite awhile. I'm not in any sense objective about *Electric Horseman* yet, but I think I'm fairly objective about *They Shoot Horses, Don't They?* or *Jeremiah Johnson*. I probably could be fairly objective about *Three Days of the Condor*. To really be objective I think I have to do at least one more film, and get totally immersed in a new film—it's like a cleansing process. Once you get a new project in your system you can clean out the other one and probably be as objective as you're capable of being. I don't know that anyone's ever totally objective. And just because I say certain things are wrong, by the way, doesn't mean I'm totally objective. You just get to a point where you can see some of the mistakes, but maybe you don't see all of them the way someone else would.

FROM AUDIENCE: What are you going to be working on next?

POLLACK: Right now I'm working on several things in development stages. I am doing something right now, an experiment I've never done before. I'm producing a picture that I'm not directing, which stars Willie Nelson, the popular singer who's in *Electric Horseman*. That's a film called *Honeysuckle Rose* with Willie Nelson, Dyan Cannon, and Amy Irving, which is being directed by Jerry Schatzberg. And yes, I'm finding the producer's job a boring one.

FROM AUDIENCE: How is it that *Electric Horseman* is being released by two companies—Universal and Columbia?

POLLACK: That's becoming more and more common now, when a picture goes over $10 million in cost. You may have to spend $6 million to $8 million opening the picture—in publicity. You then have interest to pay on that $18 million, say 15 percent or 16 percent. You're now up to $21 million. Then you have to buy a thousand prints at $1500 a print, so you're at $22.5 or $23 million with some additional overhead expenses. It winds up $25 million for a $10 million picture. So companies like to spread the risk a little bit, and when a film goes over $10 million, you quite often will see co-productions between two studios. That's not true on a picture that the studio is fairly convinced will be a blockbuster; studios will stick with a $20-million or $30-million picture sometimes, as we've seen. But as a rule, you'll see co-productions quite often—going all the way back to *Towering Inferno*, which was Fox and Universal.

FROM AUDIENCE: How can an unknown writer approach a producer or a director with a script?

POLLACK: It's very difficult, it really is. For anyone who's in the position I'm in, you get flooded with unsolicited material. And you can't read them all. Number one, there's *too much* of it, and number two, you're legally prohibited from reading it by your attorneys. Because if you, for example, wrote something about a cowboy and a horse, and you happened to send that script to my office and the envelope was ripped open, you could sue me and *Electric Horseman* and claim that I plagiarized your idea. So I'm really forbidden from reading any unsolicited material. If a script arrives on my desk and I haven't asked that it be sent there—I just automatically send it back to whoever sent it. I don't know *how* young writers break into the business, but they *do;* if they are enterprising enough and talented enough they find a way. It's the same with breaking into being a director. I don't know exactly how it's done, but it is.

CRIST: Sydney, I've been meaning to ask you this: how is television as a training ground for feature films?

POLLACK: For me it was wonderful. I'm eternally grateful to television, which is an easier medium to break into, by the way, because there's such a great turnover. I had five years of television experience, which was absolutely invaluable. The stakes are not as high. As a matter of fact, so many of us expect television films to be lousy, that if somebody does a good one, we think it's terrific. And if you did a bad one, that was normal. We'd do one every other week; we'd prepare one week and shoot the next and be on the air two weeks later. It was like cooking a meal—you got the results right away. You didn't have to wait two years to see if you messed up.

So from that point of view it was wonderful; you could experiment and you weren't dealing with millions and millions of dollars. From 1960 to 1965, when I was in television, there were still a few anthology shows left, where they'd do an original drama each week rather than series television, where you have the same characters. I did a lot of serial television too, but I also got the chance to do a lot of anthology work, which is like a miniature picture. It's an original, one-hour drama that you do. The construction is different, it's usually five acts instead of three—so you can accommodate the commercial breaks—so you have to create some artificial climaxes every nine minutes.

FROM AUDIENCE: Is there anything you have not yet done in films that you feel you must do? And in general, how would you evaluate yourself and your career?

POLLACK: There isn't any one unexecuted project, per se. There's a lot I haven't done yet that I hope to be able to do, but it's not specific in my mind. I'm sure it will define itself in terms of other work. I don't think one ever gets to the point where one feels, okay, there it is, my definitive film; now I should go do something else. I'm the worst person to try to evaluate myself—as any of us are. If I had to label myself in some way, I would describe myself as a kind of traditionalist, I suppose, in terms of cinema. Clearly, I'm a victim of the films I saw as a child—which were not so much art films as pop entertainment. I've never been a chic director in the sense of art movies, if you will, or an auteur type of director—an innovative director like an Altman, or someone who's more responsive to the totality, like Francis Coppola. My work is generally in the middle area of popular entertainment—large-budget commercial Hollywood films with stars, which were essentially the kinds of films I saw when I was a kid.

I have occasionally made sort of hybrid mixtures—and sometimes that's pleasing, but mostly it's very distracting. I'm *chastised* for odd mixtures, rather than praised for them. Take a film like *Jeremiah Johnson*—those people who didn't care for it didn't care for it because it was not a *pure* Western. What fascinates me the most as I get older—aside from the fact that as we all get older we get more and more fascinated with what's autobiographical, though I don't mean it literally—I'm fascinated by those feelings and emotions with which I'm most closely connected and therefore more qualified to speak on.

The other thing that interests me is taking the forms that I grew up with—which are classical forms—and, without violating the form, experimenting with the *content* of it. *Jeremiah Johnson* is very classically structured as a Western—but the content of it is not typically Western. Any more than the content of *Three Days of the Condor* is typically thriller—it's a thriller in form, but it deals with other things. It deals with ideas that are more interesting to me than, say, heroin smuggling, which was what the novel was based on. *The Yakuza* is a perfect example of what you could call a gangster picture—and some people expected it to be a kung fu picture, a martial arts picture, which is usually based on very simplistic moral issues with good guys and bad guys and righting certain wrongs. One doesn't usually get as complex as *The Yakuza* gets. Whether that's a weakness or a strength I really believe will only be decided by time.

It's very hard for any of us to be objective during the heat of the moment about a film. Films that we consider to be classics today were not at all considered classics at the time they were made. It takes a number of years to put them in perspective. Some of the films we feel are serious pieces of art were at the time they were made essentially popular entertainments. They were pieces of entertainment that were done as contract-fulfillment obligations. In the course of a lifetime you do your work, and if you have something to say it'll get said despite what you may do. And in a body of work you'll have a certain number of good pictures, a certain number of fair pictures, and a certain number of not-so-successful pictures. There isn't a hell of a lot you can do about that, except work hard.

FROM AUDIENCE: If you ever give up directing movies, would you consider being a teacher? You are really a magnificent teacher.

POLLACK: I was a teacher originally. I mean I was an acting teacher—I wasn't an academic. When I originally went to New York to the Neighborhood Playhouse in the early fifties to study acting, I finished school in 1954 and the following fall I came back on a fellowship as assistant to the head of the department and taught acting. That same year I opened a studio of my own on Fifty-sixth Street, and spent the years between 1954 and 1960 teaching acting—to augment my own work as an actor.

FROM AUDIENCE: Do you come from a theatrical family?

POLLACK: No, my father was a druggist, my mother a housewife. And I saw too many movies . . . which is what a nice Jewish boy from South Bend does.

Following The Electric Horseman, *Pollack directed Paul Newman and Sally Field in* Absence of Malice *(1981) and produced* Honeysuckle Rose. *In 1982 he directed and made his screen-acting debut as Dustin Hoffman's agent in* Tootsie. *This wildly successful comedy won an Oscar for Jessica Lange as Best Supporting Actress, and Academy Award nominations for both Pollack (as Best Director) and Hoffman (as Best Actor) and as Best Picture.*

In 1985 Pollack directed Meryl Streep and Robert Redford in Out of Africa, *which won seven Academy Awards, including Best Picture and Best Director. In recent years he has served as producer of many acclaimed films, including 1989's* The Fabulous Baker Boys *and 1990's* Presumed Innocent. *In 1990 he directed* Havana, *his seventh film starring Robert Redford and his fifteenth as a director.*

Gena Rowlands

▼▼

Gena Rowlands was still a teenager when she left her native Wisconsin to go to New York and fulfill her ambition to be an actress. She enrolled in the American Academy of Dramatic Arts and while performing in a student play was spotted by John Cassavetes. They were married shortly thereafter.

Joshua Logan "discovered" Rowlands while watching her on television and decided to give her the lead opposite Edward G. Robinson in Paddy Chayefsky's The Middle of the Night, *which ran on Broadway for eighteen months. She was then brought to Hollywood to make her first film,* The High Cost of Loving *(1958). Her second,* A Child Is Waiting *(1962), marked the first time Rowlands was directed by her husband.*

Although Rowlands has worked in films by other directors— Lonely Are the Brave *(1962) and* The Brink's Job *(1978), for example—and has appeared frequently in television features, she is best known for her performances in films written and directed by Cassavetes. In addition to* Faces *(1968), these include* Minnie and Moskowitz *(1971),* A Woman Under the Influence *(for which she received an Academy Award nomination in 1975),* Opening Night *(1977), and* Gloria *(1980, and another Oscar nomination). She was in Tarrytown for the weekend of September 26–28, 1980.*

[After *Minnie and Moskowitz*]

CRIST: Like Gena, I had not seen *Minnie and Moskowitz* for nine years. When I was talking with John [Cassavetes] about the program this weekend he said, "Of course you'll want *Minnie and Moskowitz*." I got the message that this was among his favorites. So I looked back at the review I had written on this film nine years ago. I said then that it was a very uneven film, but "what is good about it, however, is so very good, one must overlook its flaws." And while I was watching tonight I was thinking, *What flaws?* This was truly an avant-garde film. What I had regarded as a flaw was an advanced entrance into ellipses-style concepts that we now totally accept. The approach to the single woman, the focus on the feminine psyche, were so deeply perceptive that they were jolting then. Now you can appreciate what's being said here. For starters, Gena, please tell us how *Minnie and Moskowitz* came about. You'd already done *Faces,* with which John really stunned everyone.

ROWLANDS: You know, it was nine years ago and to tell you the truth I can't remember how we got started on this film. I remember that I wanted to do a comedy, though John never makes a film that is totally a comedy. He always builds it on a dramatic form.

When your husband is the director, and you're discussing his film with someone else, you're always at a disadvantage. If you say something nice it sounds as if you're bragging, and if you don't, it sound as if you're putting him down. So I'm going to brag a little bit. I think one of John's unique qualities is that he has a way of being able to find comedy in a tragic situation without losing the tragedy. We don't care *where* people laugh; we don't care if they laugh out of embarrassment or recognition or just think it's funny or whatever, because we have noticed that people laugh under very unusual circumstances. I've always thought that John has been able to find comedy in situations that other people would be afraid to find comedy in. They would be afraid it would be misinterpreted. I think *Minnie and Moskowitz* is a good example of this in his writing and directing.

When this picture first came out, there hadn't been a long tradition of "single women"—it was just beginning to present itself as an idea and a life-style. As I came out of the first screening of this for the public, a young woman, marriageable age, said to me, "Oh, I loved the picture." I said, "Great, I'm glad you did." Then she said, "But you should never have left the first guy." I said, "You mean the married guy that beat me up and betrayed me, and brought his son to the place where I worked and humiliated him and me and his wife— and everybody else in sight?" And she said, "Oh, yeah, but I mean he was so *attractive.*" And my blood ran cold. Now that *was* an unusual reaction, though it was not the only time I'd heard it said. Another thing I heard said many times concerns the scene with Val Avery, the blind date with whom I had lunch. People said, "Oh, that's so over-done! My God, he's a madman—it's so overplayed." Many critics singled out that scene and said, "So overdone—an example of John Cassavetes's overindulgence." Now, tonight, I heard laughs of recog-nition from women in the audience. There were many women here who *exactly* understood that situation and have been in situations like it and perhaps worse. It is not that unusual a thing, as an unpro-tected woman, to run into this total madness. I see how the years can change a piece of film.

CRIST: I totally agree. Now, there's something that came up at dinner that I'd like you to talk about, which is how *Minnie and Moskowitz* is really a *family* picture, in a real sense. The minister at the end is played by your brother. And then we have the mothers— Lady Rowlands plays Gena's mother and Katherine Cassavetes plays Seymour Cassel's mother. How did they get into the act?

ROWLANDS: Actually, there were many more Cassaveteses and Rowlandses in this picture than that. The baby at the end was our daughter, the little girl in the ballet tutu was our other daughter. I don't know—this was just something John wanted. When he creates a character, he often writes for certain people—and of course he knows my mother's strengths, and his mother's strengths. The Shirley Temple story was my mother's. I think any woman with a daughter my age has seen her daughter as Shirley Temple, with the golden curls and dimples. Then all of a sudden she is grown and marrying this totally unsuitable person that she is not supposed to marry. I was really nervous about having our mothers in it, but John had supreme confidence in them. And sure enough, they took off like the Lone Ranger. Part of the marriage scene, you know, part of it was taken from our actual marriage.

CRIST: Someone suggested earlier that there may be a kind of woman who almost invites violence.

ROWLANDS: Yes, I think that's true, and I definitely think Minnie is that type of woman. And I think much of that comes from inexperience, and much of it comes from a protected background where everyone loves you. You really can't conceive of the fact that someone doesn't love you, doesn't value you for what you are. It's a trap that women can fall into—women who don't have a grasp of who they are.

FROM AUDIENCE: Did you think that your character was desperate enough to take her own life?

ROWLANDS: Yes, I thought of her as just this side of suicide.

CRIST: That came across very clearly, the quiet desperation in the conversation she had with the other woman, her fellow employee. The other woman, by the way, was beautifully cast.

ROWLANDS: That was Seymour's mother! I forgot about that.

FROM AUDIENCE: In the scene where John hits you, did you have to rehearse that often?

ROWLANDS: Actually, no. Again, one of the things that John is very adept at is shooting a fight scene, or a violent scene without any violence. It even looked violent on the set. The secret is that the person who's doing the hitting is in the foreground, and he pulls his hand *back* to the camera; it's not the forward motion of the slap you see. Then, as the person hits you—and all this has to be timed rather well—his hand doesn't touch you but as it *looks* like he's hitting you, you have to snap your head back—like this. At the same time, what I did was the old stage trick of clapping my hands loudly. Now you don't need that on film because you can always put the sound in. But, I don't know, it's just fun to do. So, we did it ... but the crew threw down the lights and anything else they were holding and rushed and grabbed John by both arms. That's how realistic it looked to them. We had to do it over, of course. You know, the only injury we had on that film was during the love scene when Seymour laid me down gently on the bed and he leaned over too far and hit himself on the head on the corner of a table. That's why he's wearing that Indian mask at the end of that scene.

CRIST: I'm wondering about your own participation in the writing and preparation of the films you're going to star in.

ROWLANDS: To be perfectly honest about it, very little. There has been a growing rumor that I do quite a bit—and I've tried to take some advantage of that rumor. But I believe it's only a product of the women's movement that people hope I actually am a co-writer with John. I cannot say that that is true. We talk about scripts all of the time. I'd say maybe 80 percent of our life together—the other 20 percent we talk about the children—but about 80 percent of the time we talk about scripts and ideas and why people do things, and what we saw, and the irony of how much more dramatic people are in real life than they are on film. You wouldn't dare put in a movie some of what you see in real life. Nobody would believe. We talk about the scripts we haven't done—John's written many scripts we have not done. Many ideas we started to talk about never came to fruition. Some of them we hope to do in the future. But I have very little input in the script. In fact, we don't even talk about the script while he's actually writing it.

My personal feeling is that all creative writers need a certain amount of time when they're creating something where nobody should criticize them at all—*at all*. Even if the criticism is valid or good, they should just shut up, and let that person create. Because at a certain point you have to make it your own—not the world's, but your own. Later on you can share it. It's true of the other creative arts, too. I know that as an actress there's a certain place in rehearsal when I'm just feeling out the part—I don't want to *hear* from John. Or anybody else. Then, once I feel I have it, I don't mind any amount of criticism. And that's true with our scripts. Once the script is finished and John walks in and says, "Here, take a look at this and see what you think," then I know he's ready. I'll say anything then, and he doesn't mind. We'll change things if something doesn't seem real. Or sometimes I'll say I can't do something and he'll convince me that I can.

CRIST: Then do you get a shock when you read something such as your own wedding scene?

ROWLANDS: Well, in the beginning, when you're young, you feel guilty about something like that. You say, well, goodness, am I going to expose my own life? Is that right? As an actress—or an actor too—you find that you feel guilt, because no matter what situation you're in, there's always that third eye watching what's happening. I mean, you can be at a funeral of someone you love and you can be in very profound grief—and yet there's something inside your head that cannot help noticing what everyone is doing. It's a very hard thing to come to terms with when you're young. But you do come to terms with it, and you either quit it—or don't. And

I think this is true of writers also . . . they're all so very exposed and vulnerable in that sense. I'm not going to admit to any more.

CRIST: Okay. Is there anything you want to tell us about our next movie, *Strangers*, which was made for television?

ROWLANDS: *Strangers* is the story of a mother and daughter who don't get along. They're bitterly estranged, but the daughter comes back after twenty years, and for some reason she's trying to make it up with her mother. The mother is played by Bette Davis, who, when I was a young girl, was almost a sacred person to me. I didn't realize then why she meant so much to me, as a performer. But I've realized since that she showed an independence in her character and her personal life that was not common at that time. I adored her so much as a performer that when they offered me that part to play opposite her, I didn't want to do it. I thought, She means so much to me, what if I get in there and find out she's an old poke who talks about how good the old days were and how lousy the new days are? What if all my illusions were broken? But I couldn't resist the temptation and at the end, I'm very happy to say, she's everything you ever wanted her to be. She's no pussycat—she's just a great and independent artist and I loved every minute of working with her.

CRIST: It was another weekend here, with Bette Davis as our guest, that *inspired* this movie—because the producers, Bob Christiansen and Rick Rosenberg, were here and they met Bette Davis for the first time. It was right here that they turned to Bette and said, "Would you do a movie with us?" And she said, "Boy, just find one for me."

[After *Strangers* and *A Question of Love*]

CRIST: Since we have now seen two of the films you've made for television, perhaps this is the point to ask you what the difference is in working for television or theatrical movies?

ROWLANDS: Television movies vary a lot in the attitudes toward them. *A Question of Love,* I would say, was shot with such care and seriousness—everyone was very concerned, not just the actors and the producers, but also the research people and, God knows, the lawyers, who were worried all the time. There was an unusual amount of care and of feeling given to this piece. It was based, you know, on a true case,* so everyone was concerned that it not be an embarrassment or humiliation to the people involved, though there was a lot of controversy anyway. Generally speaking, most TV movies are slapped out—I mean by that that they are shot fast. Now I don't object to shooting fast, I like to shoot fast, but very often the people are not prepared because they haven't gotten the script they need; new pages don't come out until that day's shooting, so the actors don't have a proper chance to study. It's a difference in attitude and speed—not that the same thing sometimes doesn't happen in making theatrical movies, too. It does, but it seems more than normal on TV movies.

CRIST: When you were asked to play this role, did you have any hesitation? There's sometimes the feeling that playing a homosexual or a lesbian could be the end of your career—especially when you are indeed established as a star. How did you feel about it?

ROWLANDS: Well, when they first sent the script, my agent told me it was about two lesbians who wanted to adopt a child. He obviously had not read the script. I thought it was an interesting concept—from a human point of view. So I read it, and it was so much more than had been presented, and I was immediately caught by the character. The only thing that held me back was that I had never played a real person before. Usually the character, a fictional character, is something you have created—it's like giving birth. You're responsible for it. But when it's somebody real, and you know that their son is watching, and their mother is watching, and the schoolmates are watching—suddenly, in the middle of it, I began to feel that I actually might hurt something in one of their lives. I never heard that we did; I never got any bad reaction from the people involved.

CRIST: You never met the real woman?

ROWLANDS: No, I didn't want to. I just didn't want to—it was confusing to me as an actress. And I'm not sure I'd like to play another real person—unless she were dead and couldn't defend herself.

CRIST: How did the casting of Jane Alexander come about?

ROWLANDS: It was important to me who the other actress would be—because I didn't know the producer or director, I wasn't sure

---

*The story is of a divorcée who loses custody of her child when she moves in with her lover, also a divorcée with a child.

how they were going to approach this story. I didn't see that they could vulgarize it too much. The last part of the script, all the action in the courtroom, is the actual material. We didn't change a word of it—as incredible as it seems. But I held out. I wanted to know who the other actress was and they said the other actress wanted to know who her co-star would be before she would commit. Then, when they said it was Jane, I had no hesitation—she's a wonderful actress and I really respect her.

FROM AUDIENCE: In the two television movies we've seen, I haven't noticed that much less quality than in many theatrical movies. Why does a theatrical feature have to cost so much?

ROWLANDS: I agree with you. I think it's preposterous the amounts of money that are being spent unnecessarily. Some pictures just really cost a certain amount of money, but there is enormous waste and an enormous snob factor in theatrical pictures—and it's a question of showing how much power you have. In California that's an extremely important question with directors and producers. And if they can spend $30 million they'll spend $30 million. I do think it works to the intense detriment of the industry. These two films you've seen are extremely high quality technically for television pictures and they were abnormally expensive. The four weeks to make A Question of Love was a long, long time. We had a rehearsal period, which is unknown on television generally.

CRIST: Are there salary differentials in TV and theatrical film work?

ROWLANDS: Yes, you get less money on television. And I do believe that salaries are also out of line at a certain point. But on the other hand, are actors going to turn it down? Their agents are going to go for it; it's business to them—and 10 percent of $10 million is much more than 10 percent of $500,000. The agents think you're crazy if you consider what you're doing an art.

FROM AUDIENCE: I'd like to know how you prepared for the scene in which you have to testify in court; the emotional intensity of the scene is just incredible. How did you get ready for that?

ROWLANDS: I had a director, Jerry Thorpe, who was very easy to work with. He's a director who leaves you alone—which is high in my book. What's hard about making pictures is that, when you're trying to prepare for a scene like that which is highly emotional, you'll be sitting there and people all around you are talking—"bring that light a little closer," or "let me check your makeup." They're doing their job—nothing wrong with that—but they're constantly talking. So anyway, Thorpe says, "How do you want to do this scene? Do you want to come in and get used to the courtroom, or would you rather stay in your dressing room and I'll set up everything and talk to the other actors and the crew, so you don't have to be part of any of it." I said, "I can't tell you how grateful I'd be if we could do it that way." So I just went to my dressing room and sat a couple of hours while they prepared, so when I came in it was quiet, no one was talking—it was just as if it were a real courtroom. I sat down and we shot the scene. It was Thorpe's sensitivity that made it so easy, in the end.

FROM AUDIENCE: If you had had to reshoot it—would you have been able to keep the emotional intensity of it?

ROWLANDS: Well, you have to have cover shots of everyone's close-ups—so we did shoot it maybe twelve or fifteen times. And that is the big breaking point with actors—whether you can repeat something. Actually, if they don't wear you out with the first two or three takes, if a light doesn't blow, if you get lucky—you get in on your first take when you're really strong. Every actor has problems and my problem is energy—I have constantly to conserve my energy, because I get so emotional I just fall over. That's a lack of technique, it's not good—I don't say this as praise of myself, it's a criticism. I work on it all the time—to try to shape it up. If I can get my takes early, then I don't get aggravated in doing it over and over.

FROM AUDIENCE: Did you do any special research with the problem of lesbian mothers?

ROWLANDS: No, I didn't do any research with lesbian mothers, because I feel a mother is a mother, to tell you the truth. As far as lesbianism is concerned, I do have friends who are lesbians, but I don't go into it much with them. I did look at some court cases, some lesbian custody cases, to see what behavior I could see.

CRIST: Gena told me a story earlier today about the ending of *Strangers.* But before she repeats it, I'd like to ask those of you who saw it, do you remember, early on, when they planted the tomatoes together? How many of you thought that at the end, there would be a big red tomato? Or that her last supper would involve tomatoes?

Let's have a show of hands. Well, *we* know movies the way Bette Davis knows movies, as Gena is going to explain.

ROWLANDS: Well, Judith had mentioned how strange it had seemed to just drift off at the end. I said yes, but that's what we had tried for, although, originally, Bette was supposed to come up with that red tomato, saying, "We did it, we did it." We shot that scene. I remember that it was a terrible day, very stormy—although it was supposed to be bright and sunny. It was up in Mendocino in northern California, an area that looks like the East Coast. They keep it that way in order to shoot there. Anyway, it was a dark day and I've always wondered if that made the shot too lousy to use. Or did the producers just say no, we're not going to use that tomato? All I know is that Bette was really angry, because she thought the tomato symbolized the whole point of the story. I said, "I don't know, Bette, the tomato does wrap it up a little too much." Judith and I were just talking about the difference in structure in the pictures of the 1930s and '40s. I mean, we can say, "Oh, they were so obvious." But none of us were really offended at the end of *Dark Victory*, with the dogs and everything—it *worked*, like gangbusters. There always had to be a wrap-up; but now, certain subjects are just different; they just don't wrap up neatly.

CRIST: I find nowadays, in watching television, I'm so frustrated by the freeze-frame fade-out, I want to shout back at the screen, "Come on, *you* put on the ending, I'm not going to write it for you!" One thing I want to ask you about working with Bette. Did you see any difference in the way she prepares or goes through an emotionally charged scene from the way you do?

ROWLANDS: I couldn't see any difference in the preparation. In fact, we work in a similar way, in that we've both said a lot before we come to the set. Many actors like to work spontaneously, without saying the right lines, for instance, so they're not confined or immediately boxed in—until they've gotten their bearings. I like to work the other way; I like to know my lines so well that I don't even have to think about them—and I trust that they'll come to my lips when they're supposed to. They usually do. The big difference between us, on the set, was that I always played loud music in my dressing room each morning and Bette would come by and say, "How *can* you do that?" And I'd say because I just can't wake up unless I have some sort of stimulation in the morning. She likes total silence to concentrate in the morning—so they put her dressing room over there, and mine over here. Outside of that we really enjoyed acting together, we really liked each other—after the first few days. We were feeling each other out those first days. But I got along with her very well, and became very fond of her. She's a tough lady—but in a nice sense.

[After *Opening Night*]

CRIST: This movie could serve as a lesson—if that's what we intended, and we didn't—about the difference between the television movie and the theatrical movie. Accessibility. The theatrical film is not as readily accessible—or acceptable—to a wide audience. It is a far more personal statement. This is a very dense two-hour-and-twenty-minute movie, which has great personal complexity to it, and it's very difficult to say immediately, oh yes, I like it or didn't like it. All of John Cassavetes's movies are difficult, in a sense, because they're extremely subjective. But before we even get to what it means to each of us—why don't we ask you, Gena, to tell us about the genesis of the movie?

ROWLANDS: Over the years people have asked us many, many questions about our work, so we began to think that it would be interesting to make a movie showing what goes on in the theater. We didn't want to do a scholastic treatise on it; we wanted to do a story not just showing what happens, but showing *emotionally* what happens—and showing how the performers themselves separate what happens in their lives and in the characters they play, and the things that are threatening them in their lives as well as onstage. Basically, we thought it might be of interest to do something about performing artists who had worked together for many years, who are used to being successful, but who suddenly find themselves working in a *flop*. And they're working just as hard as they ever did in their successes. This picture does demand a lot from the audience, a certain knowledge about what's going on.

CRIST: I wonder if in your minds there is a comparison with *All About Eve*. Both films are concerned with an actress in crisis, albeit for totally different reasons. The two films bear very strong comparison—the thesis really is the generational changes, but the young girl you're confronted with here really represents you. You told me earlier that when you filmed the last scenes of the play—

which is a sex–drawing-room comedy, the audience to which you played *was* a regular theater audience. How did you film it?

ROWLANDS: We took it to a theater in Pasadena, California, that looks much like some of the Broadway houses—we didn't have enough money to shoot it here. And we invited an audience in a newspaper ad—it created quite a lot of excitement in the Screen Extras Guild. I mean we were doing this with our own money; we couldn't afford to hire screen extras, so we put an announcement in the paper that said, "Anyone who would find it interesting to watch some actors work, and stay quite a good deal of the day . . . and if you have some nice clothes, please wear them." Well, the theater was filled—to show you how nice people can be, they came in black tie and beautiful gowns, and they sat there all day. Oh, we did lose a few here and there. We told them we were going to play a couple of scenes, because we just could not film the whole play. But we briefly explained what the play was about and said it didn't make any difference how they reacted, if they laughed or didn't laugh, if they wanted to walk out, whatever. So we ran through it—and I was very much surprised that it went so well.

FROM AUDIENCE: How do you interpret the way that these actors behave in this story?

ROWLANDS: What we wanted to show is how actors—if pushed too hard by things in their own lives, their own personal relationships—how they could destroy an author's work without any mean intention, really. By the end, they were just after each other. The play was obviously a disaster. The audience might have been kind—but they knew it wouldn't run. I'm not sure how successful we were really, in showing how things get blown out of proportion when they're not supposed to. It's because of the human pressures artists feel—just as other people do.

FROM AUDIENCE: The actress you play is going through a frightening crisis about her age and the younger woman coming up to replace her. Isn't this a problem unique to American actresses because of this country's youth consciousness?

ROWLANDS: I used to think it was American, but after talking to European actresses, I'm not sure. In the first place, in Italy, you're terribly old as an actress when you're thirty. But I do think that in France there are a certain number of aging actresses who can still sustain a career, but not many, really. We try to keep up youthful appearances in Hollywood, and the European actresses do the same thing. Some of them don't—like Signoret. She just goes for it, and I admire that. Everyone's always saying she should lose twenty-five pounds—but what other woman do you know of that age who consistently plays great parts? Everybody adores her; she's a great talent—and all people can say is why doesn't she lose weight. Look at Barbara Stanwyck—she looks about eighteen, she is frighteningly young on those commercials, beautifully slim—and she doesn't play any parts at all. I bet she hasn't been on film in five years, and I know she would like to be. So perhaps there's a greater advantage—a greater commercial advantage—in accepting your age and playing roles depicting the problems of your age and your time, as Simone Signoret has done. But the ego dies hard, you know.

FROM AUDIENCE: Did *Opening Night* have any commercial success at all?

ROWLANDS: We did show the picture in Los Angeles. We opened, we got terrific reviews, and did terrific business—we played fourteen weeks there. Then we had *no* distribution offers whatever from any American distribution company. Now there were people who said they'd take the picture, but you have to realize that this is an extremely costly effort, to sell a picture. In any of the pictures we have made, we've never had a television commercial—except for films like *Gloria,* which is playing now, which is being released by Columbia. *They* are paying for those TV commercials, which is an enormous advantage. When the distributors take on a picture, they have to pay for a certain amount of advertising. I mean, people have to *know* your picture is opening and at what theater. That's the minimum they have to know—and we figure, with ticket prices being what they are today, they should also know some little something about what to expect. In the case of this film, a filmgoer should at least know he's going to a rather complicated movie about actors and their professional and personal relationships. But we had no distribution offers that would include the cost of promotion. And that is not an uncommon position for the independent filmmaker to find himself in. So we distributed it in Europe—and did wonderfully with it. We're very happy with it.

CRIST: You know, in New York City alone, just to open a picture, you need a minimum of $50,000—that's just for the opening, not even enough to keep it going for a week. I understand that John has now held back the distribution rights for this country, in effect saying "up yours"—and has given it to museums. He hasn't even let it be distributed to colleges.

[After *Gloria*]

CRIST: Now we've seen yet another facet of Gena Rowlands, actress—here she is as girl gangster. This is my second viewing of the film. The first time around I saw it as a marvelous extension of women's lib. One of my favorite scenes comes when Gena mows down those gangsters in the car—which goes into a spectacular crash. And then she turns around, very coolly, and says, "Taxi." I guess all my life I'd wanted that kind of thing to be done by a woman. Joan Blondell and Glenda Farrell played gun molls, but they were still pretty passive. And if they'd tried anything like Gloria did, they'd also have to be killed off by the end of the movie. With *Gloria,* this second time something clicked for me in a different way. I find it a funny send-up of, say, a Charles Bronson movie, except here Charles Bronson is a woman, and the blond doxy in trouble is instead a small Puerto Rican boy. Once again, all this proves that we each see what we want to see in a movie. Gena, perhaps you can tell us what you see in *Gloria*—starting with how it all came about.

ROWLANDS: Once again, it was as big a surprise to me as it was to you. John had said, "What would you like me to write for you?" This has almost become a game with us, in a way. As a writer he'll toss out an idea—just "that much." And I'll make a comment hinting of something. And then we don't talk about it anymore. In this case, when he asked what I'd like him to write for me, what role I'd like to play, I said, "Well, I'd like to work with a child." But I never dreamt I would be working with a child in this manner. The reason I wanted to work with a child is that they're so fiercely independent and you just have no idea what they're going to do. So they keep you honest, on your toes. I've always benefited as an actress every time I've had the opportunity to work with a child. So John says, "Okay, I have something in mind."

And then one of those strange things happened, because the next day a head of a studio called John and said, "You don't have a script for a child, do you? Because we need a script for Ricky Schroeder." John says, "Funny you asked. I *am* working on a script for a child, but it wouldn't be suitable for Ricky Schroeder, because this is a Puerto Rican child."

FROM AUDIENCE: Did you set out to play *Gloria* as farce?

ROWLANDS: No—I never play anything except for reality, to the best that I can do it. It may come out farce, but that wasn't my intention. I don't know how to describe what this is ... it's not farce. It is satirical, but I thought it was necessary to play very realistically *against* the actual written style of it. Much of it has a fairy-tale quality, and as Judy was saying, it's like an old Bogart movie or Cagney movie or something. It was meant to have that quality. *Gloria* was meant as entertainment—except that, right now, John is very interested in the relationship between women and children.

FROM AUDIENCE: Would a character like Gloria have worn sunglasses all the time? And was that your idea to make her such a heavy smoker?

ROWLANDS: The sunglasses are partly because of my own personal sensitivity to sunlight. If you want a lot of shots with me squinting, you can have them—if I'm not wearing sunglasses. So if there's any legitimate place to wear them, I do—and in general people do wear them a lot now. As for smoking—I only gave up smoking a few months ago. Well, as you can see, I haven't entirely given it up, but I have cut down to a pack a day from three and a half. It's true, I am *always* smoking. As a matter of fact, Bette Davis, you know, is *always* smoking. So during rehearsal for *Strangers* I said, "This is going to look kind of funny on film if both of us are standing there blowing smoke at each other." She said, "Oh well, I'm getting sick of everyone seeing me smoke, anyway, so you smoke and I won't smoke." So she didn't. And I think it's the only picture she's ever made in which she never had a cigarette in her hand.

CRIST: That's noteworthy, at least to me. She was the one who turned us all on to cigarettes—wasn't she?

FROM AUDIENCE: Miss Rowlands, how was Buck Henry cast in *Gloria*?

ROWLANDS: It was just one of those things that happen—John's agent is Buck's agent, and Buck said to his agent, "I'd love to be in Cassavetes's new film—I'd love to see how he works." Both John and Buck, of course, are directors and actors and writers. John said, though, that he didn't have anything for him—he said he had a part that Buck would be wonderful in, but that it was just a small part and he couldn't ask him to do it. But Buck read the script and thought this role was not like anything he'd ever done before, and that it would be a good acting experience for him. So he played the husband, the father of the child, in the beginning of the picture.

CRIST: Well, it is sort of odd—the child is so very Puerto Rican and his mother is very Puerto Rican, and then there's Buck Henry—for no good reason whatsoever.

ROWLANDS: Actually, a Puerto Rican man probably would not have been an accountant for this particular gang.

FROM AUDIENCE: When Gloria and the kid wind up at that apartment it's sort of mystifying. We don't know where they are.

ROWLANDS: That's just one of the things John likes to do in pictures. There was originally a line in the taxi, where I said, "Now get in there, we're going to my sister's apartment." Then John cut that line. And I said, "But then they're not going to know whose apartment that is." He said, "Who cares? It's an *apartment*—an apartment of a friend, or a sister." That's very much in John's way of thinking. He doesn't believe in everything being laid out, especially if it's not some essential quality. Just to help the audience know where they are, that's not something that John considers enormously important.

FROM AUDIENCE: How do you explain who and what Gloria was supposed to be?

ROWLANDS: Well, I tried very hard not to make her appear to be a hooker, even though from what we've seen of tough women like that all of our lives, we've been conditioned to think they are prostitutes. My own background for her was something like Virginia Hill, if you know who that is. She was what used to be called a bag woman, someone who carries illegal money from Las Vegas; someone who'll go to prison and won't talk when she's caught. She's a working part of the mob. And maybe she was a chorus girl when she was young, and because nightclubs are a hangout for gangsters, the chorus girls can make these alliances with the mobsters; they may fall in love with one of them, and suddenly find themselves in a new line of work.

FROM AUDIENCE: Did your husband write the part just for that child?

ROWLANDS: No, John held an open call—and ten trillion kids came. I said, "How are you possibly going to pick one?" John never reads any actor for a part, by the way, no matter what age—he just talks to people. So he said he'd talk to these kids and the ones he remembered would mean something. And he picked this one out in about three days—John Adames. He was only six, and he was so macho. Now, you must realize that every leading man is a special problem. In this case we had a leading man who doesn't lead, so you have to learn your lines a little differently. When we were rehearsing, I said, "How are we going to get this kid to know his lines?" John said, "You'll just go over and over them with him—until he's comfortable." I said okay, but rather reluctantly, because that's not my favorite way of learning lines. So we were in rehearsal. Remember that this child had been acting for four days. We were going through our lines, and, I must admit, my mind was wandering, and I got to a line that said, "Don't be stupid." And he said, "Wait a minute, you're not going to say that like that, are you?" I said, "What did you say?" He said, "You're not going to just say, 'Don't be stupid' like that, are you? I mean, you've got to say it like 'Don't be stupid!' " I said, "Hey, let's get this straight right from the beginning—you learn your lines, I'll learn mine, and we'll work with each other from that point on." I didn't want it to get out of hand on the fourth day of rehearsal. He was really strong—very strong about offering his opinions. I kept my eye on him every single minute. When John gave him the part, he said, "Look, Johnny, do you really want to do this part?" He said "Yeah, I want to do it." Then John said, "Think about it a minute . . . it's summertime, there will be lots of things you won't be able to do. You won't be able to go swimming or play with your friends. Making a movie can be boring. It can get hot. If you're doing it because someone else thinks you should, but you don't really think it's such a great idea—it's not worth it. So take a couple days and think it over." So Johnny took a few seconds and he said, "Let me ask you this—how many words will I learn on this movie?" John said, "Oh, three hundred." The kid said, "Three hundred words . . . I go back to school and I know three hundred words more than everybody in my class." Now, in a million years, would you think a child of six or seven would even consider such a thing? He was a unique little thinker.

FROM AUDIENCE: Aren't there strict regulations about the working conditions and the hours put in by a child that age?

ROWLANDS: California has much more strict laws on that than New York. And it *was* summer vacation. Johnny did have to have an adult member of his family with him at all times, and John is very solicitous of kids anyway; he never overworks them. They have beds around to take naps; they can have just about anything they want. But it is true that the laws in California are much more protective of child actors.

[After *A Woman Under the Influence*]

CRIST: As I've said before, seeing a film again can give you peripheral vision about it, and last night I was absolutely astounded at reliving *A Woman Under the Influence*. I could well understand, Gena, why you did not want to see it under any circumstances—let alone at a midnight showing. This film was made in 1974. Do you remember how it developed?

ROWLANDS: John and I had been talking, as usual, about stories and ideas—and just life, generally. I started out on the stage, you know, and part of me wants to go back, and part of me doesn't, but at that time I thought that I'd like to do a play. And John was interested in writing a play—which he had never done at that time. He asked what I was thinking of, what kind of play. I said I didn't know, I would like to do something that relates to women right now, some modern problem that people are struggling with—and at the same time, I'd hope it would be a problem that women have always struggled with, but that we could see it in a contemporary way. It was some time before he wrote the play; it was quite a complicated idea. But he finally brought it to me and said, "See what you think." So I read this play . . . and I just couldn't believe it. I couldn't believe John wrote it. I don't mean to be sexist, because I don't really believe that women can't write for men and vice versa—but I really couldn't believe that a man would understand this particular problem. I was astounded and moved by it—and at the same time I realized I couldn't play that on *stage*. I couldn't last two nights playing that—and in a week I'd have to be hospitalized. Then I felt like the basest ingrate in the world. I told John I didn't know exactly how to put it, but I couldn't possibly do this on stage. We talked about it and he said he understood, and then he said, "I think I have another idea."

He went away, mysteriously—and actually I would have stopped him if I'd known what he was doing. He wrote *two* other plays with the same characters—and if you saw all three plays on successive nights it made a whole, or you could see each play individually of itself. In the two new plays the other characters had more to do, but my role would still have been quite substantial. Well, if you think I felt like an ingrate the first time—I said, "I don't think you really understood what I meant. Doing three plays is not going to be easier than doing one play." We talked seriously about it for awhile, trying to see if there would be any way to do it. Finally he said, "Well, then, I'll make it a screenplay."

So he wrote it as a screenplay and we took it to the studios and their reactions were the same—it's an impossible script. It was an art film and nobody wanted to see art films—and "Nobody wants to see a crazy middle-aged dame, anyway," as one studio executive put it so charmingly. So we decided we'd do it ourselves, in Los Angeles. We didn't have the money to do it, but we had a lot of friends, all actors, and interested in the project. So they all helped us. And we just did it.

CRIST: Of all your films together, I think that this is the most fully realized. But *A Woman Under the Influence* could be cut. It is John's strength that he is willing to give every moment its due—but it's a virtue that does work against him, because this film is too long for popular consumption.

FROM AUDIENCE: I'd like to know how you arrived at some of the facial expressions you used and the gestures with your body that really did indicate madness.

ROWLANDS: I don't know how or why I do anything like that. All I know is that this woman couldn't speak, she could not express herself. And when you can't speak—when you're playing that kind of part and becoming involved in it—then things will start happening with your body. The human spirit will not take it silently. If you cannot express something verbally, it will come out in some way— and in her it came out in bizarre physical gestures. But I didn't plan it, I didn't plan anything physically for this picture. I seldom do. For *Gloria* I did plan her walk before we started the picture—but that's one of the few times ever that I've planned something physically.

FROM AUDIENCE: Do you have any plans now to go back to the theater?

ROWLANDS: Well, I have been thinking about it recently quite constantly—for some reason I've been dreaming about it. I've always had dreams that I'm on stage, at different periods in my life—usually I'm doing *Anastasia*. But now I've been thinking about it a lot. My children are old enough not to need me so much—our boy is twenty-one and on his own, and our girls are fifteen and ten. So it would be conceivable now to take on a play, whereas it wouldn't have been a few years ago. As usual, I do and I don't want to go back. The "don't" part is that I have never been able to develop the necessary discipline *not* to think about my character till it's time—like seven o'clock at night. I think about it all the time, the first moment I wake up; I dream about it, I think about it during the day and during the performance. There's only a few hours *after* a performance that I can get the character out of my mind—so that I'm so exhausted with it at the end of a few months. So, it's overwhelming, the idea of taking a play on for a long run. If I could do a limited engagement of six weeks or something, I think I could handle that. *Middle of the Night* played two years, and I was emotionally exhausted from it. And I thought then that I'd never do that again. But now limited engagements are being done more than they used to be—so I *am* thinking about it.

CRIST: Your son is, in fact, active in the theater, isn't he?

ROWLANDS: Yes, our boy graduated from the American Academy this last April—and he has a part in a TV movie being shown in October called *Reunion*, should you be watching.

CRIST: And by a strange coincidence, as I was preparing my *TV Guide* reviews this week, I put on a cassette of one of the TV movies I had to review, and there in the credits was "Introducing Nick Cassavetes." And I was so pleased to report to his mother that he comes off terrifically. Gena has not yet seen the movie.

FROM AUDIENCE: Miss Rowlands, what is your favorite picture that you've made with your husband?

ROWLANDS: For me, the favorite is *Woman Under the Influence*.

FROM AUDIENCE: To what extent now are your films improvised . . . and weren't some of the earlier ones complete improvisations?

ROWLANDS: On the first picture we made, *Shadows,* that was all improvised—they did it all in workshops and filmed it, and no one expected to release that film. It was done as a classroom exercise, but it turned out well, and created some interest, so it was released. Then John used a bit of improvisation in *Husbands.* We *do* use improvisation, but not as widely as people think. We start with a very complete script. John's theory is that if there's something wrong, it's wrong in the writing. If you take actors who can act in other things and they get to a scene they've honestly tried to do— and if they still can't get it, then there's something wrong with the writing. Then you stop, you improvise, you talk about it. Then he'll go and rewrite it—it's not just straight improvisation. I'm asked a lot about this, and it's true, when I look at the films and I *see* that they look improvised in a lot of different places where I know they weren't. But I think it's because it's the way John shoots, and the lighting. It's not in the script at all. John uses a general lighting so that you are freer to move than in most pictures. In most pictures, honestly, there are marks on the floor that you have to hit or you'll be out of focus. And that's very hard for an actor—to be thinking about your part and about hitting your marks—and you can't look at them either. But John doesn't believe in that—being an actor himself, John realized how hard that is. So instead of lighting in spots, he lights the whole thing. Then he gets a very good camera-man and a very good focus. And if, in a scene, you feel like going across the room—then go. Usually the cameramen will stop you; you have to fit into their way. With John, the actor is first, so that all the rest of the crew has to follow the actor. We wear battery microphones a lot—which are pretty well perfected now; a few years ago they were awful. So, sometimes, I think it's not the actual dialogue that makes John's pictures look improvised—it's the fact that people are moving freely on the film. We all do *like* to do improvisation to a degree. I'm not as adept at it as Ben [Gazzara] or Peter [Falk]. They are awfully good at it.

CRIST: Certainly in *Husbands* the feeling was that it was almost total improvisation among three friends.

ROWLANDS: Not as much as you'd think. I know that's one of the pictures that people point to as being an improvised picture, but those three guys worked awfully hard to make it look that way. There were a couple of scenes that were improvised—in the bar, I think. But most of the scenes were in a script.

FROM AUDIENCE: How did you meet John Cassavetes?

ROWLANDS: Well, I was going to the American Academy of Dramatic Arts. I had just come from Wisconsin, and John had gone there a few years before. And we were doing our examination plays. At the end of the year you do a play with an audience, and you hope maybe an agent is going to walk in. We were doing *Dangerous Corner* and I was playing Frieda. John came in, as many students did who had gone there before. He saw the play and he came backstage. And we were married a few months later.

FROM AUDIENCE: How do you feel about working with other directors?

ROWLANDS: I don't have any prejudices against other directors— although I do think John is number one, I must admit. But I just look for the part—I don't look for the director. If the part's right, I figure I'll work it out with the director later. But until the last few years, there was really *nothing*; no parts. Now there are. So if I run into a good part with another director—sure I'll do it.

FROM AUDIENCE: Why is it that so many of the same actors keep showing up in your films? Does John just prefer using New York actors?

ROWLANDS: In the beginning, whoever was working with us was doing it for the love of doing it. You get very attached to people like that, you know. And you all go through a lot of hard times, financially and other ways. So you get close. Actually, because you see certain people, you do forget that you see a lot of new ones in each movie. But you do see Val Avery, for instance, as often as possible. Val was the guy in the taxi cab in *Gloria,* and the crazy blind date in *Minnie and Moskowitz.* And also once you've played together it's like repertory, you get to know each other, you get a rhythm, you don't have to start at square one. Nothing was really planned. I can't say that John had a master plan behind this. It was all natural.

FROM AUDIENCE: How many films has John directed without you?

ROWLANDS: Well, he did *Shadows* that I wasn't in, and I had a small part in *Faces*—and what was that first one with Bobby Darin? *Too Late Blues.* Actually, he wrote *Too Late Blues* for Monty Clift and me, but the studio didn't want either one of us, so he did it with another cast and it turned out fine. Then I did a very small part in *A Child Is Waiting* that he did with Judy Garland and Burt Lancaster.

And he did *Chinese Bookie* that I wasn't in at all. So he's done quite a few without me. But in the last few years we've done quite a few things together.

FROM AUDIENCE: Do you have some preference for playing these neurotic women?

ROWLANDS: I don't know—maybe there is a basic flaw in my character. I am very attracted to this kind of part. It's a real commitment to make a movie—and if you're going to make a movie you should make it *about* something. John and I both believe there's a deep level of craziness in the normal person that most people won't acknowledge. So we don't consider these people as neurotic as perhaps others would consider them. I just like dealing with a woman who is in the middle of some real crisis, rather than a romantic comedy or something that other people do better than I do. If I'm going to spend three or four months doing a movie I'd like to do something about people who fascinate me, although they do upset me, too. *Woman Under the Influence* upset me terribly; for a long time after the shooting I was very emotional about that character. She was the hardest for me.

You know, I get so very fond of these characters. I *don't* mean I can't tell the difference between them and real life, but I do think of them as friends. Sometimes I'll wake up thinking things like, "Oh, I hope Gloria worked it out." Now, I know that's not quite sane, but it has been harmless enough so far.

FROM AUDIENCE: You've talked about the length of John's films, and many people have commented that most of his films could be cut. Is there a particular reason why he refuses to shorten most of his films?

ROWLANDS: Well, not to go for the easy answer—but we like them that way. I'm not being smart-ass about it; I understand what the studio people think . . . but we simply like our pictures the way they are. We always feel that those who think our pictures are too long can leave the theater. In the first place, everyone's concept of time is different. Ninety minutes was *it* for movies for years and years, not because a ninety-minute movie was purer or better in any way—it has nothing to do with anything, except that exhibitors can show more movies in a day. They can show double features—and get people to come. When we made *Faces* the ninety-minute rule was still sacred; and *Faces* ran two hours and forty minutes, and you would have thought we had gone into a church and thrown rotten tomatoes around. The comments were so out of proportion: "How *dare* anyone have the ego, the self-indulgence, et cetera." We said, "Wait a minute, fellows, we don't want you to show a double feature with it anyway; nobody could possibly see this movie and another movie."

The length of a film has nothing to do with anything but economics. Every sacred cow in the business has to do with economics. But after *Faces,* all movies started getting longer, because they just did. We just like long movies. We think people are mature enough and emotionally stable enough that they can go through a long, emotional movie—it's not good to cut off an emotion. Most people like to avoid pain, and I can understand their point of view. But this is our view—to show it all. And if people want to walk out, as I said, that's okay. Actually, it was in *Woman Under the Influence,* at a certain point there would be this mass exodus from the theater. I wasn't watching the movie because I can't, but at an opening I hang around to watch people watching the movie. That's the hard thing about movies. You make a movie, then you wait a year before anybody sees it. When you're onstage you can tell what an audience thinks, you can feel them and hear them, and they'll tell you, too, if they don't like what you're doing. But in movies you have to wait and wait. And you think, was I wrong? Am I out of touch? You have this terrible curiosity, and you lurk about the theaters seeing who goes in, are they young, or old, men, women, black, white— whatever? So with *Woman Under the Influence,* at some point there would be this huge exodus . . . and the first night I was thinking, "Oh, my God, we haven't even gotten to the hard part." But what we found was that these people were going out in the lobby to have a cigarette or get something to eat and hang around the lobby a few minutes, and then would go back in. So we try to leave enough minutes in our movies for those who want to visit the lobby.

In 1982 Gena Rowlands and John Cassavetes made one of their rare appearances together in Paul Mazursky's Tempest. *And in 1983 he was repeating his triple-threat role as writer-director-actor in the film* Love Streams, *in which Rowlands co-stars (they play brother and sister). She appeared in* Light of Day *(1987) and Woody Allen's* Another Woman *(1988). John Cassavetes died in 1989. Rowlands's most recent film was* Once Around *(1991).*

Guy Hamilton

▼▼

A truly international filmmaker, Englishman Guy Hamilton was born in Paris and began his career in movies as a "clapper boy" in a French studio. After World War II he returned to Britain, where he was an assistant director to both Carol Reed and John Huston (working on the legendary African Queen) *before directing his first film,* The Ringer, *in 1952. Since then, Hamilton seems to have specialized in films with an espionage and/or wartime theme:* The Intruder *(1953),* The Colditz Story *(1954),* The Best of Enemies *(1962),* Funeral in Berlin *(1966),* The Battle of Britain *(1969), and* Force 10 from Navarone *(1978).*

Hamilton is probably best known for directing four of the series of super-hits based on the adventures of James Bond, beginning with Goldfinger *(1964) and including* Diamonds Are Forever *(1971)—both starring Sean Connery—and* Live and Let Die *(1973) and* The Man With the Golden Gun *(1974), with Roger Moore as Bond. Hamilton handled a much milder form of adventure in* The Mirror Crack'd, *the 1980 Agatha Christie mystery he screened during the weekend of November 28–30, 1980.*

[After *A Touch of Larceny*]

CRIST: Before we get into a discussion of this film—which reminds me once again what a crush I had on James Mason, when he and I were young—I'd like to ask you, Guy, what was it that turned you to film?

HAMILTON: When I was a very small boy I wanted to be a deep-sea diver. That was pre-Cousteau. That didn't work out. But when I was a kid I saw hundreds and hundreds of movies and I just decided to be a movie director. Very simple. I'd done a bit of acting, I'd tried a bit of writing, and I wasn't good at either of those. But any profession in which you told stories fascinated me. I suffered intensely because in the thirties, to be a film director in London—when I was destined to go into the diplomatic corps—was like wanting to run a brothel. But I persisted, and a few things fell lucky for me. When the war broke out in 1939 I was in Paris and I managed to get into a French film studio and said I want to be a director; they said fine, you don't get paid. I was seventeen at the time. Such *chutzpah*. I got shoved into the accounting department, which is the greatest way to learn about the movie business. I licked the wage packets for a whole studio for a whole week—and I wasn't being paid for this.

At the end of the week, the guy who gave me the job asked me what I knew about the film business. I said, "All I've done is lick wage packets." He said, "Aha! But you have discovered that apart from film stars, directors, and cameramen, there are powerhouse operators, gardeners, sweepers, et cetera." And in one week, I had, of course, learned the composition of what a major film studio looked like—and I bless that man to this day. He then said I could join a camera crew as a clapper boy. I said to the cameraman, "I want to be a director," and he said, "Ah, but it's a visual medium so this is where you should start." I was then totally convinced I'd be a cameraman and then a director. Halfway through the picture the boom operator got sick, and I became an assistant sound man. Booms in those days were bamboo poles, and you hung onto them for a long time—it was very painful and very boring. But the sound man said that pictures were only nickelodeons until sound came in, and it was through sound that you heard the actors, their timing, their feelings. He convinced me. I was going to become a sound operator and then a director.

But amongst the other things I had to do at that French studio—all this for about five dollars a week—was to empty the cutting-room bins at night. And there they said, this is where all the magic of motion pictures is made; it's all in the cutting room. We thought it all out. At the end of that movie, this wonderful, wonderful man said, "Now, Guy, you've been with us X number of weeks—what have you learned?" I said, "Well, I'm a little confused because, you see, it's a visual art but movies were only nickelodeons until sound came in and then the whole magic is done in the cutting room—and I don't quite know where to go." He says, "Right. You've learned the first thing. If you want to be a director, you must remember all technicians talk shit, and your job as a director is to get all these wonderful people to work together to help you make a story." And, after that, I went into the Navy for a little bang-bang time. That's about the start.

CRIST: And when you came out of the Navy, you became an assistant director.

HAMILTON: Yes, being an assistant director is a wonderful opportunity to watch some great work. However, I learned much more from working with bad directors, watching them get into and out of problems. I think the younger generation of filmmakers today haven't got enough depth, really, they haven't had enough time seeing how actors are handled, or how directors behave themselves or cope with situations—how they cope with the front office and the problems that go on daily. Because to be a director, all you need is a hide like a rhinoceros—and strong legs, and the ability to think on your feet. Those are the three basic requirements. Talent is something else.

CRIST: I notice that on this film, *Touch of Larceny*, the assistant director is Peter Yates, who of course came to our consciousness as the director of *Bullitt* and several other films, and of course made it in a big way with *Breaking Away* last year. And now he has a new and extremely interesting movie called *Eyewitness* coming out in the spring. Were you the first to hire Peter Yates?

HAMILTON: No, I was the first to make him a first assistant. I think Peter does have great depth because he has worked on many sorts of pictures and he's worked on good pictures, bad pictures—which you do as an assistant. I'm delighted with and proud of Peter's success because, as Carol Reed taught me a great deal, I hope I've handed down something. You hand down a bit of your tradition, which one can choose to reject or use, as the case may be. But there's a great continuity in our business.

CRIST: To bring us up to *Touch of Larceny*—do you remember the genesis of this 1960 film?

HAMILTON: I do remember some of it. Ivan Foxwell was a young man—he's about the same age I am—who wanted to be a producer, and I wanted to be a director. So we teamed up and made a movie called *The Intruder,* which had a fair amount of success. Then we made a picture I was longing to do, called *The Colditz Story,* which was about POWs and was remade as *The Great Escape* over here many years later. We then said, "We are really the hottest thing on two legs," we'd gone from success to success. So we decided to make a drama and we made the sexiest, most avant-garde picture that's ever been, called *Manuella,* and it was quite revolutionary. And it bombed—it really bombed. That did us some good. It wasn't a bad picture, but we had ignored the public a little bit—don't give them what they want, that's too obvious; let's give them what we think they should have. We both learned a salutary lesson from that. I have always been a huge admirer of Ernst Lubitsch and that type of comedy, and I said I wanted to make a comedy. Foxwell came up with a book called *The Megstone Plot,* a rather hard-nosed thriller, and he said, "Keep the comedy for the next one." I thought the plot was tremendously funny—and I just couldn't take it seriously, it was so outrageous. I said yes, we can do this, but it's really the comedy I've always wanted to do. I said there's one problem—we have to find a reason for James Mason to do this. It has to be for love. So once we were over that hump, I felt we could go on and have fun with it. Now, since it is Thanksgiving weekend, *Touch of Larceny* is the first turkey I have to offer you this evening . . .

CRIST: I was raving about the dancing scene, which I thought was so marvelously done, very erotic. But you shattered my illusions about that scene . . .

HAMILTON: I'm rather proud of it, actually. In those days, and still today, there's a problem in working very, very close to artists. The zoom lens has changed a little bit of that. But in those days, particularly in black and white, lenses were very rigid, and if you used a very close shot, you focused with a tape and, by goodness, no one could move. So obviously, if people are dancing it's nigh impossible to focus on them—they go in and out of focus all the time and you never know what you've got. It's agony. It so happened that a few years before, I was working on a film as an assistant director, and there was a big Viennese ballroom scene. The prince and the leading lady were waltzing in the imperial palace—everything was lit, the crowd waltzed divinely, and it was perfect. Except for the leading man, who had leaden feet and couldn't count to three, let alone dance. So here was the ballroom scene, and the leading man couldn't do it at all. Problem time. We came up with a solution that was rather clever; we got a camera dolly on which we mounted a turntable, and we hooked that on to another camera dolly carrying the camera, so the whole thing could be dragged along. The leading man and leading lady were positioned on this turntable, along with myself and another assistant—we were sitting just out of camera range—holding on to their bottoms. And to the beat of the music we went *one*-two-three, *one*-two-three—helping them move back and forth. The audience didn't really notice that they were about six inches higher than the rest of the dancers.

Now, it seemed to me we could do a more sophisticated version of that trick for the picture you've just seen, and that consisted of putting the camera on brackets on a platform equipped with roller-skate wheels and a little bar going out of it which was tied around James Mason's middle. James is a good dancer, by the way, and wherever he went, the camera went with him. So we were able to use the most enormous lenses, and they were really *fixed*. The cameraman was also delighted because he was able to put lights just to catch their lips, for example. And everything was perfectly in focus as they floated around the dance floor.

CRIST: Could you tell us a little bit about *The Best of Enemies*?

HAMILTON: This came along a little later, and was actually my introduction to international filmmaking. I was minding my own business, and Dino De Laurentiis—who was a strange, unknown Italian producer at that time—had this idea for a story. I went to Rome to talk it over with him. It was a fascinating discussion because he didn't speak a word of English and I didn't speak a word of Italian. But off we went. I worked for about six months in Rome on the script. It was very difficult because Dino had lots of Italians in cupboards writing. I had *my* writer and we were working on *our* script. By this time I was speaking a little bit of Italian; Dino's English did not improve that much. It was a rough picture, because I had an Italian crew. But I had that wonderful man, David Niven—who said, "Guy, what have we got ourselves into?"—and

Alberto Sordi, who was a very very big star in Italy and, above all, a De Laurentiis star.

The picture for me is satisfactory in some places, but not in other places. It got quite fun toward the end—Dino used to go into the cutting room at night and put in a lot of closeups of Alberto Sordi, and I used to come in in the morning and take them all out again. Dino then fired me, which he couldn't quite do, and a wonderful man who was then head of Columbia Pictures, Mike Frankovich, came over to straighten it all out. The thing that saved my neck was that Dino had made a mistake. He had signed a contract giving Niven top billing, but his contract with Sordi was that Sordi had top billing.

This is the most unattractive part of our business—having to fight for what you believe in for your baby. In general, this picture is my view of war. I know that things have happened since, but this, which was made in 1962, almost twenty years after the war, was my feeling, my statement at the time. Again, it's in terms of comedy—because I think you can say the most important things entertainingly and amusingly.

[After *Funeral in Berlin* and *Diamonds Are Forever*]

FROM AUDIENCE: Since these James Bond movies are not noted for great dramatic performances, and there are so many special effects, do you ever feel as if you're directing traffic when you're doing these? They must be terribly complicated.

HAMILTON: They're not complicated, although there's diligent pre-planning. One of the rules with the Bond pictures is that you're not allowed to have a leading lady who can act—because we can't afford them. This is very serious, for if ever we were to have a real leading lady, the next time around we'd have to have another one. And in no time at all we'd have to have Jane Fonda for $2 million and up. People go to see the hardware and James Bond—and if you've got that going, the rest of the cast will pay us to be in them. Those are the ground rules. Do I have the feeling that I'm directing traffic? You do have little interest in the actors apart from Bond, there's no question about that. And when you're on location it's very hard work to get all that hardware working together.

FROM AUDIENCE: What part of your total output goes to the special effects and stunt situations?

HAMILTON: I never believe that anything is going to work. There's no reason why it should. Murphy's Law reigns supreme in the picture business more than any other business. Therefore, the greatest waste of time and money is to be on location and to be all geared up and a stunt doesn't work. So I never let myself get into that situation. I insist that it's all rehearsed beforehand *and* I've seen it visually. There is something in the car chase you may not have noticed. The car going up on two wheels was an act I saw in France. And when I came over here I was convinced there would be somebody in an auto stunt show who could do the same thing. And sure enough there was—a Canadian stunt driver. So I flew him in and we talked about the two-wheel and he said no problem at all. He said, "I do it driving-side up." I said, "I don't get you—please explain that." He said, "The French do it with the guy driving on the low side, I do it where I'm sitting on the high side and it's much more difficult." I said, "I'm sure it is, but all that matters to me is the car running on two wheels."

Then there were a bunch of Hollywood stunt drivers who said the Canadian couldn't do it, they could, and because of the unions they weren't going to let him in. I had four of those red Mustangs—and, to make a long story short, I failed to complete the stunt shot while we were on location in Las Vegas. We had a shot of the Mustang coming out of the alley on two wheels. So the shot going into the alley had to be done on the lot at Universal on that last night before we went back to the U.K. Car after car we failed to get up on two wheels—and I really blew my top. I had to leave the next day to start shooting in London, so I left the second assistant director to shoot it. So then they got the Canadian stunt guy. The shooting took two nights. It was all a very expensive operation.

So, when I'm looking at the rushes in London what do I see but that the car goes into the alley with the driver's side up—and comes out the other way around. Do we reshoot it? What do we do? What we did was—there is one shot in the middle of the scene that shows Sean [Connery] and Jill [St. John] in the car—and one instant they're on one side, then quite suddenly, they're on the other side. Somewhere in that alley, magically, the car flipped over.

FROM AUDIENCE: After being involved in a movie so much, preparing it, filming it, going over the rushes, and editing it . . . how do you feel sitting here like this watching them now?

HAMILTON: Making movies is a bit like having babies. It lasts nine months, and you go through morning sickness. The only difference I can figure out between having a baby and making a movie is that when the movie is delivered, you have no love for it at all. If people like the picture, terrific; if they hate the picture, I'm sorry. I hope to be pregnant again. I have no love whatsoever. It's very difficult for me to sit and watch some of these pictures because I *know* their weaknesses. There comes a moment in time where you have to lock the picture; people are putting on special effects, and music. So you lock the picture and can't fiddle with it anymore. That's it. Then comes that horrible moment when you're dubbing—which is an incredibly boring process—where you do about one reel a day, and that reel is run about twenty times... and you're sitting there, stunned with boredom, and for the first time you say: "You know what we should have done?" And it becomes absolutely clear to you what you should have done to make that point better. But it's too late. So in the particular reel you will have a *hate*. In the case of *Goldfinger* I have to walk out for one reel. We were booked to open at the Radio City Music Hall—or somewhere—on December 15, and we were still shooting in Fort Knox on about November 9. And the producers were completely indifferent to the fact the picture wasn't cut. What we did, the editor took the front end and I took the tail end—and I'm not a bad editor—and we *met* halfway. That was the idea. We never did meet so there's this reel of rough cut in the middle. We were so convinced that when we showed it to the producers they'd say, "Fellows, we'll give you one more week." But they said, "It's great, what's wrong?" I'm convinced that every time the picture is shown the audience is going to stand up and start yelling at that point—but they don't. In every picture I've ever made, there's always something shameful, blush-making, that I can't bear to look at.

CRIST: And the critics all write, "That stunning scene is his absolute apogee as a director...." Right? The Bond films are now considered a genre of their own—how did that come about?

HAMILTON: We actually got the whole thing going in *Goldfinger*. The two producers were historically very important to Bond—because one of them was only interested in tits, and the other one was only interested in gizmos, machinery and the like. So you could talk to one, and if the subject wasn't about sex and women—not interested. And then Harry Saltzman would say, "I found this fantastic place in southern California where this thing is three miles long and seven miles high, and God, can you do something in there?" Those were the contributing factors of these two producers [Albert R. Broccoli and Saltzman], who fought like cat and dog as they got richer and richer. They got so rich, in fact, they began to take turns producing each picture. That's when I stepped out for a few years until they sorted that situation out.

Bond is a family thing; we all knew each other—we had a total vocabulary. It would take me the rest of the evening to explain to you what we meant by "It's not Bondian." You could find a tremendous setting, but it wouldn't be Bondian. Bond could not just come into a bar and sit down and order a drink; you had to do something different to make it Bondian. Whatever other people do is not Bondian. We would have only the vaguest idea of the scripts, because we couldn't use the Fleming books. The reason for that is that when Fleming wrote them the locales he used were new and interesting places to go to. The first few pages were always fine, full of violence, then you'd go to someplace like Saratoga where there's horse racing. Maybe it was the *in* place in the thirties, but no longer. And the highlight might be that the climax takes place on someone's private train. But not in this day and time—you couldn't make an ordinary chase scene on a train the highlight of a James Bond picture.

Usually the first thirty pages of the script were fine, but then what do we do, because we've got no story whatsoever? Cubby Broccoli was an old friend of Howard Hughes, and he told me about a nightmare that he had, in which he went to see Howard Hughes and it *wasn't* Howard Hughes, it was somebody else in his penthouse in Vegas. I said, "That's a wonderful story—let's use it." I mean, Howard Hughes is the only guy in the world you could kidnap and nobody would know he's missing.

So, with that, we went to Vegas. We thought we'd have ourselves a ball in Vegas. But once there, we began to look around—what can we do with James Bond in Vegas? In no time at all, we had the cooperation of the Las Vegas officials, and we had set up a car chase for around the town. Then, whilst I was preparing the picture in L.A., I left my car in a car park in Los Angeles and there was some kind of smashup in the car park, and I've never seen so many cars ruined. So I said, "That's it, we'll carry on the chase in a carpark, smashing up cars." So we go on looking for things of this ilk.

Bond, of course, never goes down back alleys. It's not Bondian to take James Bond to Marseilles. You cannot take him to dirty places; there has to be luxury. We take audiences on holiday, to all those places you'll never go. You may have noticed that there's a fundamental trick in these things. We never go back to the same place twice, which is part of the expense in making these films. We have James Bond check into his hotel, and someone says, "I'll meet you in your suite." But we've already seen him walk around his suite, haven't we? So Bond will say, "No, no, I'll meet you in the Starlight Room." So they meet in the Starlight Room, and you have a scene there. And he meets a girl and there's no "Is it your place or mine?" It's *definitely* hers, because we haven't seen it. Now, she can't just have a room, and we have to decide where her pad is, how to get there—like up a ladder, or by dinghy or something. Anything to keep moving.

CRIST: Was there much difference between working with Sean Connery and Roger Moore?

HAMILTON: Yes, Roger Moore is a pussy cat compared to Sean. It's tremendous fun rehearsing a fight with Sean—you know, he's not very interested in the rehearsal and wants to get on with it; meanwhile he's punching the stuntman who's spitting out his teeth. He'll say, "Oh, sorry, I hope I didn't hurt you." A director's function is to use an actor's strength and cover up his weaknesses. The thing is to be aware of the weaknesses and how to cover them up. You get some actors who are clumsy with props. Sean is very smooth with props. He moves beautifully so you always try to get him in situations where he can move.

Roger, however, is extraordinary in that he cannot run. He literally cannot run—it looks as if he's got a broomstick up his backside. When he told me that he couldn't run I said, "It's easy, just one foot in front of the other." I didn't know what he meant until our first shot with Roger in New Orleans running away from something—and the whole unit burst out laughing. I nearly cried, and he said, "I told you—I told you you should have brought my stunt double with you." We had to do the shot, so I got all these lorries, trucks, and everything around to hide his bottom.

CRIST: That's one of his weaknesses . . . what are his strengths?

HAMILTON: He's got charm. Roger has grown into the part. It's not the way I think Bond should be, and it's not the old Bond that we all loved. But it's a Bond that's going down very well with the public, there's no question about that.

CRIST: Yes, I rather like him—he's more suave. It's kind of "The Saint Goes Wild."

FROM AUDIENCE: I have a two-part question. First, your use of cranes to lift people up. We saw one I think in *Funeral in Berlin* and three or four times in *Diamonds*. And second, if you were to do *Diamonds* again, would you depict the gay people any differently, other than holding them up to ridicule?

HAMILTON: On the subject of the cranes, the great problem with the Bond films is that you've got a four-hour script to tell in two hours—that's what gives them their pounding drive. It's in my contract that the Bond movies had to come in under two hours and it's hard work piling all that stuff in—which leads me on to the use of cranes. That's one method of getting an actor from the bottom to the top of an oil rig. You waste thirty seconds of screen time getting him up ladders, so isn't it lovely when you can go *whish* and there he is on the deck. We do anything that can cut back on what we call dead footage—people walking toward the door and anything like that. On the subject of the gay characters, we were always looking for new sorts of villains; why shouldn't they be gay? That was my argument at the time. Gays could be as frightening and spooky as anyone else. It's always a difficulty finding a new villain for Bond to meet. I think if I made it now I might have some very different thoughts. I made the villains black in *Live and Let Die,* and I got plenty of flack from the black community. I said, "Do you want to be taken seriously? Do you want to have parts for black actors? You can't all be Hamlet." If the villain is Chinese, you're going to get flack from our Oriental brotherhood. Whoever is the villain is going to be knocked.

CRIST: Well, I felt that the women in the Bond films had no personality at all, initially. But they were allowed to develop and achieve almost equal status in *The Spy Who Loved Me,* for example.

FROM AUDIENCE: But all of it is bigger than life, it's a spoof and a fantasy, and you have to take it in that context.

HAMILTON: I think it's hysterical that an audience of intelligent people will discuss Bond seriously.

CRIST: Well . . . that's where it's *at,* and if you're going to be a movie fan you're going to be a movie fan—and you take Bond as seriously as you do the grand auteurism of Bergman.

HAMILTON: Well, for me, Bond is part of the history of motion pictures. Bond is *Perils of Pauline,* laughs, excitement, thrills. The trick of Bond is all of those things—it's all basic, it's all of that, except that it's packaged 1980. And it's the packaging that fools people into thinking it's new. But it's basic.

FROM AUDIENCE: In addition to the hard work in making the Bond movies, did you actually have any fun?

HAMILTON: Some of it was fun because you were working from strength. In other words, nobody breathed down your neck about money. I mean, you *knew* you were going to make money. So you'd say, let's throw another ten cars over the cliff. Help yourself, have twenty. And there were moments when I felt a bit guilty about it. My real pleasure with Bond is that it gives you an insane sense of power. I mean, for a director to do a James Bond is the most high ego trip. The pre-credit title sequences are always very important, because what do they say? They say, "Children, sit down, leave your brains under the seat and come for a great big marvelous ride!" That sets the tone. You get an insane sense of power because you can say look at my left hand, and while everybody's looking at my left hand, I bang them with the right. And a few minutes later when you say look at my left hand again and they say, "No, we're going to watch the wicked right one," then you pop them with the left. You play with the audience. And to *know* that they're going to be there, ready to be played with again by those rules—it's a joyous, really joyous feeling.

[After *The Mirror Crack'd*]

CRIST: I guess I read *The Mirror Crack'd* about 1962, and just recently I was reading Gene Tierney's autobiography. She had a mentally retarded child, you know, and the child was institutionalized. This was the major tragedy of Tierney's life and led to her own nervous breakdown. Then, about ten years later Tierney ran into a woman who told her this curious story of how, when she was a WAC during the war, her barracks had been quarantined with German measles, but by George, that hadn't kept her from going to the Hollywood canteen when Gene Tierney was appearing there. Gene Tierney just stood there and heard this perfect stranger tell her how she had given her the German measles when she was pregnant with her child. Apparently Agatha Christie had heard this story many years before Gene Tierney made it public in her autobiography, and she based the plot of *The Mirror Crack'd* on the actuality of the case. Which is art imitating life.

FROM AUDIENCE: I'm a little unclear about the logistics of the last few minutes of the film. My impression is that Elizabeth Taylor poisoned herself even before her husband gave her the chocolate with the poison in it.

HAMILTON: If I fail to get across what I mean up there—mea culpa. What I meant was that Rock Hudson is totally unaware of his wife's guilt until the inspector starts talking about the notes. Hudson rushes up to the bedroom and says, "Why didn't you tell me about the notes?" Elizabeth gives him a vacuous excuse. It's from that point on that Hudson is aware there could only be one person responsible for the murders—and that is his wife. He brings in the hot chocolate in order to put her out of her misery. She is sensitive enough to know, or to suspect, that almost certainly that chocolate is poisoned. She knows her husband is saying good-bye to her. She decides she really can't let him be accused of murder, and that after all the awful things she's done, she's going to take her own life and put an end to this nonsense. That scene to me is quite moving, when they are saying good-bye to each other on different levels—and he believes he's killed her—and she knows that by not touching the chocolate there will be no blame for her husband.

FROM AUDIENCE: Who put the poison in her coffee that day?

HAMILTON: Miss Marple covers that—she says she even had to pretend to be her own victim, and put poison in her coffee. I *hate* Agatha Christie because, you see, these are the things I don't care about. There is no explanation about how Elizabeth Taylor managed to put the poison in her coffee at the studio. Give me twenty minutes with the writer and we'll work out some schleppy routine—and it would take ten minutes on the screen to do. If you sit down to watch an Agatha Christie you have to take those things as she wrote them because otherwise it could be intensely boring. Any Agatha Christie scene out of her books is just questions and answers. "Now on the night of the sixteenth, you were wearing yellow socks. . . ." If you're not careful, that's the sort of drivel you can get involved in. Please don't ask me these awkward questions, because I don't care. And you shouldn't be caring, you should be watching the picture—and be carried with the characters and the emotion, and not the boring mechanics—which you can read in a book, but can't do on the screen without getting very pedantic and pedestrian.

I found great sections of *Murder on the Nile* intensely boring because I honestly didn't care who did it. That's the terrible danger to me—of not caring, out of these twenty suspects who sit there with egg on their faces, and you ask them questions, and they answer. The only way it can work for me is if the suspects have lives and characters of their own, so we have something to bounce off.

FROM AUDIENCE: There was such a sense of time and place in this for me—that English town, and how it was invaded by this Hollywood movie company. I found all that interesting enough—I could have done without a murder.

HAMILTON: That was what most attracted me to the story—to try to contrast the Hollywood exotics with life in a little English village—where each side thinks the other is extraordinarily strange.

FROM AUDIENCE: How did you get Kim Novak to make a movie again after all those years?

HAMILTON: Well, I think she's just marvelous. And I went up to Carmel and got her away from her llamas. I said, "Come and be the Hollywood queen of 1953." I wanted, you know, the greats of the 1950s. It wouldn't work so well with modern faces.

FROM AUDIENCE: How did you come to choose Angela Lansbury for Miss Marple—was she the original choice?

HAMILTON: We have two or three wonderful actresses in England who could play Miss Marple—I'm thinking of Celia Johnson, for example—who were of the age. But they would be totally meaningless as box office. Angela is both a name and a magnificent actress—so you don't look any further.

We took a long time trying to get her character. What was interesting was that Angela wore no makeup. There are few actresses who would go that far. We did a full-day test in England before we started. Angela wore corsets and I made her just sit. You know, she's a big athletic girl, but sitting there, she began to feel those corsets, and how to sit, and how to move around. Once she began to *feel* the character, we were away to the races.

FROM AUDIENCE: What about Elizabeth Taylor? It took tremendous courage for her to play that role—she had been torn down by the press about her weight, and about aging. And this picture, with the badgering back and forth between Taylor and Kim Novak, especially the digs about Miss Taylor's weight, that must have touched a nerve.

HAMILTON: Elizabeth is a very gutsy lady, very gutsy. When I gave the script to Taylor and Novak I knew that Novak would really love it and wonder, "Can I really *say* this?" Miss Taylor, when I saw her in Washington, was about ten tons on the hoof—but she promised to go to a fat farm and look great. Unfortunately, she genuinely had a sickness and was in a hospital. But she didn't lose a great deal of weight. And I thought, oh, Elizabeth is going to give me a hard time—and now Novak *cannot* say those lines. But Elizabeth hooted with laughter and said, "Don't worry, I can look after myself." And I loved her from that moment on. I said, "Why do you keep eating sausages and drinking beer, Elizabeth?" And she said, "Because I love English sausages, and you have to have beer with them." She eats, eats, and eats—and says, love me as I am. And I love her dearly. I think she's a remarkable lady.

FROM AUDIENCE: When Elizabeth Taylor first appears on the screen in this film—wearing the flowered hat—she looked quite slim. Were those scenes shot when she had lost a little weight?

HAMILTON: She did go on a very strict diet before the film and, I must say, turned up looking tremendous. Also, I have a wonderful cameraman, Chris Challis. If the actress doesn't move, it's possible to set the lights just so and do what we call a "Rembrandt." The problem comes when the actress moves because, of course, you can't light for every position of the head and body.

Now I have a firm belief that the entrance of your leading lady is vital—because it's your first impact. You say, "Oh, my God, she's put on weight." Or, "Oh, doesn't she look gorgeous?" That's where you are looking—particularly you ladies, you can be very bitchy. So it's important how you see them the first time. Then, having come to whatever conclusion you come to, you can then be harsher with the lighting, and take a little less care. So we took a lot of time creating the first impact, that first entrance in the flowered hat—she looks gorgeous. I then hide her behind flower pots and things as she's walking. But whenever I can, I sit her down and do another Rembrandt job just to let you know she is a gorgeous-looking lady.

CRIST: Also, I think this may be the first time that Taylor became a comedienne. I'd never seen her being funny.

HAMILTON: Yes. She had a shyness about it. We had to say, "Go, go, go ... don't be afraid." And we did a lot of off-screen rehearsing; she really worked very hard.

FROM AUDIENCE: I'd like to know the significance of saying in the credits that the picture was "a Guy Hamilton production."

HAMILTON: You get more money. I don't want to be a producer—it's incredibly boring—but it does give me a little bit of control over the casting, over the scripting. We are very lucky in Europe—the director is taken more seriously. Well, not more seriously. In the United States, the top banana is the producer. In Europe, the producer is there to serve the director. So when we get into these internationally made pictures you have to try to defend your position. If you're the producer, you go find the money, you tell me how much to spend—I will consult with you. But there are certain areas, such as the designing of the sets, finding the locations, and so on—I concede that. You will give me a hard time over the casting. I will say, "Here's a perfect actor for the part." And you'll say, "But when I sell that to ABC Television, they would rather have someone who's currently a hotshot because of some little TV series." One has to negotiate all those things as best one can. That is the significance of a "so-and-so production."

CRIST: Well, now we're going to see an action-drama of a few years ago. Is there anything you want to say about *Force 10 from Navarone* before we see it?

HAMILTON: It's not my favorite movie because it was a very unhappy movie to make—a miserable movie to make. Also, it was largely misunderstood in that it was meant to be a farce, but people take it too seriously. They think they're looking at *The Guns of Navarone,* which was all about brave men. This is about idiots—*nice* idiots, they have all my sympathy. One thing is that I'd worked with Edward Fox and he's an actor I love dearly—and he's the only thing I enjoyed in the picture.

FROM AUDIENCE: What connection does this have to the original *Guns of Navarone?*

HAMILTON: It's a sort of sequel, using a certain kickoff point relating to the first movie. Then it becomes a new story. A fifteen-year gap had gone by, you know, and David Niven couldn't climb into an airplane—let alone get out. He wasn't too young in the original version. I would have loved to have had him—but it wouldn't make sense. The other star in the original was Gregory Peck.

CRIST: So instead of Gregory Peck and David Niven, you have Robert Shaw and Edward Fox playing the two survivors of the original guerrilla force.

[After *Force 10 from Navarone*]

CRIST: I know that Guy did not speak fondly of *Force 10 from Navarone*, but I think it's a terrific, gung-ho adventure. Guy, you mentioned earlier that Carl Foreman owned the *Navarone* title—how did that work?

HAMILTON: After the success of *Guns of Navarone* in 1961, Foreman had been asked by Columbia to do a sequel and he wrote one. But for reasons that I really don't know, they couldn't get Niven and Peck together again. So the script lay on a shelf for twelve years. Another producer found this lying around and he and Carl got together to start the thing up again—and that's how it was resurrected. The script had its weaknesses and I asked to rewrite, and Carl said, "Help yourself." I was looking for a method whereby four idiots could blow up a dam. You have to get some surprises in that situation, because you know from the moment the picture opens that the climax is going to be blowing up the dam.

FROM AUDIENCE: How did you film all that rushing water?

HAMILTON: That was done in Malta, where there is a tank which goes on the sea. The great problem about water is getting rid of it. So the advantage of the Malta tank is that you suck the water in from the sea, and it goes back into the sea. Obviously, there was a real dam, and in the Malta tank, I built a twenty-foot model. We were cross-cutting between the real dam and the model, and every time you think it's a phony shot we go quickly back to the real thing.

FROM AUDIENCE: Wasn't any of that shot in Yugoslavia?

HAMILTON: Yes, all the rest of the picture was shot in Yugoslavia. I asked them if we could blow the dam up, but they weren't keen. They wouldn't let us take out the bridge, either.

CRIST: Do you want to elaborate on something you said earlier about your feelings after you've completed a movie?

HAMILTON: I think one remembers the fun that one had on a picture—or the disasters. You really live a life for about nine months which is very closely involved with your crew and the actors, and together you fight your way through the hurricane, or whatever. I remember with affection incidents and people that the pictures remind me of, but some of the actual pictures I still find difficult to look at. A lot of pictures I see I can't even remember what's going to happen next, and I don't even remember shooting that shot. I was surprised at the sort of technical facility in *Touch of Larceny*, and the more complicated camera movements that I tend not to do now, because when you get older, you simplify things. And there are still moments in every picture when I think, "Oh, God!"—and they give me no pleasure to watch.

I remember when I was assistant director to Carol Reed I used to get a lift back to the studio in his car, and I used to try to get him to talk about *Odd Man Out* or *The Way Ahead*—which was wonderful, I thought—and I wanted to hear him talk about it. How did he do that, or this? And he said, "Oh yes, I remember that picture— that was the one where the leading lady had the curse twice a month." And that was all he remembered of some masterpieces! I found that difficult to accept, but now I know what he meant.

CRIST: To backtrack a minute, when you were talking about when you're working on a movie you finally have to say "That's it," and commit yourself to what you have. From your point of view, how does it happen that we get a $38-million disaster like *Heaven's Gate*?

HAMILTON: There's another one lying around like that, you know. Warren Beatty has been shooting a picture in England called *Reds*, and if the film were stretched end to end, I think it would reach the moon. He hasn't seen any rushes, he hasn't selected any takes. It's all going to be done in *due course*. I believe there are two ways you can operate as a director. You can either shoot the film, see the rushes—or not see them, then go away, and in three weeks or so return and your editor has put an assembly together. There are quite a few directors who work that way on the basis that they can then step back and see the woods *and* the trees. I don't believe in that. I insist that the scene I shot yesterday be assembled by six o'clock tonight—and I have to look at it.

What happens occasionally is that this little baby—your picture—will sometimes grow two heads. You must spot that early, and one head must be chopped off immediately. Or you may find that that one is rather good, that new direction, and you begin to see in your mind that it takes on a life of its own. It's only by running what you have once a week that you can see it. You begin to realize things. In the darkness of the screening room I can hear my voice saying, "We now cut to the getting-to-know-you scene." But then, you begin to think, "That sounds like a really dull scene. These two actors have just taken one look at each other and you expect to see them next in bed. Who needs a getting-to-know-you scene?" So I think you must be on top of your picture.

Now as to length of your picture—this is a perpetual problem. You should have your continuity lady—preferably one who has worked with you and knows your style—to time your script. I find that they're never off by more than four or five minutes. If the script times out to a three-hour picture, that's what you're going to get. But if you want a two-hour picture, then you've got to go back to your script. I ask my script coordinator in the morning, "How long do I have for this scene?" And she says, "Two minutes, fifty seconds." So off I go. Then I find I like a certain facet of the way the character looks. And I decide to set up a rather complicated track shot. Then I start with a shot of the doorway and decide to move everybody in through that. It's all very moody, very nice, and I'm very pleased with myself. Then the script lady will ask, "Do you know how long that runs? Fifty seconds." Then I must go commune with myself—because it means I've got only two minutes to do the rest of the scene. I have to get on with it. I must discipline myself if I'm going to end up with a two-hour picture. You do this each scene, every day.

CRIST: Going back to your early days, what, for instance, can you tell us of your experiences as assistant director on *The African Queen?*

HAMILTON: Oh, that was a marvelous time. [John] Huston and Sam Spiegel, whom I have great love for, were running to the end of a three-picture contract they had together and, both being very strong characters, they were beginning to get a little touchy with each other. I first met John in Claridge's Hotel, where his room looked like an armory. There were people who were selling him crocodile guns and elephant guns. John wanted to shoot an elephant—that was really what the whole picture was about as far as he was concerned. And he went off with Peter Viertel, the writer, and all three of us landed in Nairobi with this armory of stuff, which was promptly confiscated, as you are not allowed to shoot defenseless animals in Kenya. I didn't see John for several days thereafter because he was off in a little light plane and discovered the Belgian Congo, where you *could* shoot defenseless animals, and he also discovered a location for the film. John literally dropped a white handkerchief out of the plane and said, "I've found the location—I've spotted it over there." The art director and I wandered around the Belgian Congo and actually *found* this handkerchief. You could not make *African Queen* today because artists have in their contracts that the location can't be more than twenty minutes from a five-star hotel. There we built a camp out of bamboo, and everybody piled into the camp and it was a wonderful experience. We all roughed it out there.

John never got his elephant, I'm glad to say. He disappeared occasionally, and Katie and Bogie were really anxious to get out of the jungle as were we all—and we worked very hard. The joke was that there we were running up and down these rivers with the *African Queen* and we could have been here on the Hudson. The African scenery is not glamorous, it's got no feeling of jungle at all, and there we were, miles from everywhere. And I remember one day we were all moaning, "What are we doing out here, sweating, with all these mosquitoes. We could shoot this on the Thames." And it began to get through to John and he said, "C'mon, let's make it African." So we all went off with boxes of Kleenex into the bushes—and we were making flowers out of Kleenex. We found that by using some blood we could make red flowers—so John was quite interested in this. And he'd look through the camera and say, "Make some more flowers over there." So the whole unit would pop over with their Kleenexes and make marvelous orchids.

FROM AUDIENCE: In casting, are you at all influenced by personal friendships and wanting to do favors for people?

HAMILTON: I've always made it a rule never to have a friend in a picture. What I do have is a sort of repertory company which over the years grows up. You had a small-part player, who did something maybe very unflashy, but he did it beautifully. Maybe it was his timing in opening a door—you were pleased with that, the way he expressed something. So you say I'll use him again when I need that sort of character. To me actors have certain personalities and I see them in a certain light. I like to take actors who've always played heavies and make them nice people—or the other way around.

FROM AUDIENCE: I'd like to ask you about the originality of the actor's performance. When an actor does a piece of business, for example, where he has to light a cigarette and something distracts his attention. In looking away, he accidentally burns his finger. . . . Now, whose choice is it for that piece of business that happens to turn out well. Will a director automatically say, "Let's leave that in?" Or will he make the actor do it over again?

HAMILTON: Ahh . . . you arrive on the set in the morning and you have a very clear idea of how this scene should be played. The actors come on, they also have some idea about *themselves*. An actor, rightly, is only thinking of himself—he has never read any of the script that doesn't concern him. He may be amazed to be told, for example, that there's a funeral scene. And he'll ask, "Whose funeral is it?" I don't knock that attitude—because that's what an actor should be, totally involved in himself. But once you have three characters on screen—the director has to make them play together. So you sketch the scene out. It's essential that the actors are comfortable. I move rather well and can do things . . . while Rock Hudson has very long legs and what I do may be awkward for him. We have to try what makes him comfortable. When they're all comfortable, someone may say, "I have a wonderful idea—suppose I smoke a pipe?" That's usually an insecurity bit because he has a long passage with nothing to do. So you try it in rehearsal. And by the time he's got his tobacco pouch out, filled the pipe—it's his time to speak again. And he still doesn't have his matches out. So the pipe idea goes out the window. But don't discourage the actor from contributing something. Sometimes they come up with lovely ideas, and you can elaborate on them. The thing is, the actors should feel at ease.

CRIST: Can you think of any actors you've worked with who are exceptionally creative?

HAMILTON: I think they all are—in varying degrees. I'm a rather hard director in that I don't like the pattern I have in mind being broken up. So I tend to be rather firm. My joy is that when we're working that way an actor will say, "Hey, it all plays—there's no problem." Because if you allow actors to take off they can be bouncing on the table in no time at all. Which might be rather good—for some other picture.

FROM AUDIENCE: Do you think actors are now trying to gain more control not only of their own roles, but of the pictures themselves?

HAMILTON: Yes, since the studios have lost their authority, so to speak, there is a new generation of actors who are highly intelligent and who can read a script well. They know whether it's suitable for them or not, and they take a great interest in the production. Sometimes it comes off very well, and other times it can do damage to the whole texture, because it becomes too personalized from their viewpoint, and they're ignoring that there are many other characters in this story.

CRIST: One of the things that fascinates me is the luck of casting. You were telling me last night how you thought you had discovered a new James Bond.

HAMILTON: After I had done *Goldfinger* a long time went by. I was called back and asked if I'd be interested in doing *Diamonds Are Forever* because they had a problem—Connery was out, so would I launch the new James Bond. We did a lot of tests in London of suave young men—total failure. We started again in California and tested some boys there. And I was watching a chat show one afternoon when I saw James Bond—I mean, he was *sensational*. He had a twinkle in his eye, he moved with grace—I just flipped my lid. I called the producer and said, "I've found James Bond—no further worries. Sure, he's American, which means everybody in this country will love him. In England there will be a bit of a flap, but remember, in the rest of the world James Bond talks Chinese or Japanese or Italian." So Cubby Broccoli met this fellow and was reasonably impressed. He took it up with UA, and they said, "Oh no, c'mon, he's a stunt guy. He just got lucky in a TV series, but it's mostly stunt stuff—he's going nowhere at all. No way will we let you have that guy." I'm talking, of course, about Burt Reynolds.

Guy Hamilton's recent films include Evil Under the Sun *(1982), his second film based on an Agatha Christie novel, starring Peter Ustinov and* Remo Williams . . . the Adventure Begins *(1985).*

Jay Presson Allen

▀▀

After an apprenticeship writing television dramas during the 1950s, Jay Presson Allen first won international acclaim with her stage adaptation of Muriel Spark's novella, The Prime of Miss Jean Brodie, *a hit in both London and New York. In 1969 it was made into a movie with Maggie Smith playing Jean Brodie, for which she won a Best Actress Oscar.*

Following another Broadway success, Forty Carats, *Allen went on during the 1970s to write screenplays for* Cabaret *(1972), earning an Academy Award nomination,* Travels with My Aunt *(1972), and* Funny Lady *(1975)—and to create the popular, long-running television series,* Family. *Allen's 1980 script for* Just Tell Me What You Want *was adapted from her own 1975 novel of the same title, and marked the beginning of her collaboration with director Sidney Lumet. She was both screen writer and executive producer for Lumet's* Prince of the City *(1981) and* Deathtrap, *released in March 1982, which Allen previewed for Tarrytown guests during the weekend of October 23–25, 1981.*

[After *The Prime of Miss Jean Brodie*]

CRIST: In the biography we were given, we were led to believe you started writing for television, then got into theater, then into film— is that the right chronology?

ALLEN: I guess so, yes. I did some TV stuff first, then I wrote *The Prime of Miss Jean Brodie* as a play. Alfred Hitchcock got a copy of the play, he would never tell me how, and then asked me if I would do a screenplay for him. I did *Marnie*.

CRIST: And how did you turn back to *Brodie?*

ALLEN: Because it had not been produced at the time. The producer's wife became ill, so we postponed production. We did not take it to London for production there until after *Marnie* was made.

CRIST: What was it like to rewrite yourself?

ALLEN: It's very difficult. You get locked into a certain approach. I was not totally happy with the film of *Brodie*. The book is an extraordinary piece of work which I thought had the makings of a real movie, a movie-movie, not an adaptation of a play. But when people *buy* a play—and that one was a very expensive property— they want to see what they bought on the screen. And that's what they got. I find the film a little plodding, a little slow, not as filmic as I thought it might have been.

CRIST: For myself, I've felt your movies have become more and more filmic. And perhaps it's looking back now that you see that.

ALLEN: No, I felt that way from day one, but I had no powers to convince the studio otherwise. I just got through working on another screenplay for Fox [20th Century–Fox].* This time they took it away from a very talented young writer because he had deviated so much from the book. And they came to me. I said I thought it was a wonderful screenplay. They said well, it wasn't what they wanted, and would I do what they wanted. So I did. The producers were happy with what I did for them, and then Robert Redford read the script and he wanted to do it. Redford is *brilliant* about what's right for him; by the same token, he'll read a script he thinks is good and if it's not right for him he'll think he can fix it. Some things are not fixable. I had been in that position with him before. I knew it wasn't going to work—he was not right for it, was never going to make it right. But he fooled around with it and finally he made the producers so angry they took the project away from him.

*The script Allen refers to is *The Verdict* (1982); David Mamet wrote the screenplay and Paul Newman starred.

So they called me and asked if I thought Sidney Lumet would direct it and I said I thought he would be very interested. In the meantime, the young man who'd done the script in the first place—his name is David Mamet—had an Off-Broadway revival of his play *American Buffalo*. Lumet had gone to see Al Pacino in the play and he had been very impressed with David Mamet. He took him out to dinner and he asked him if he'd done a screenplay and Mamet said yes, but the studio didn't like it. He gave it to Sidney as a sample of what he wrote and Sidney loved it. So when I went to Sidney and said "Are you interested in this?" he said, "Yes, but I'd rather do David Mamet's script." So in the meantime these poor guys, the producers, had paid me and Redford's people all this money—then wound up with the original script.

CRIST: One thing about which I've speculated—when you are a playwright, you are the cock-of-the-walk, are you not?

ALLEN: You can be—if you're prepared to close the show. Legally, you *can* shut the show down. In point of fact, very few people do that. In a play you do have a lot of leverage—which you do not have in films.

CRIST: But at the time of *Miss Jean Brodie* in 1966, screenwriters somehow were the low men—and maybe still are.

ALLEN: They still are.

CRIST: I was wondering how much the playwright has to do with casting, as compared with the screenwriter?

ALLEN: In a play, the playwright has everything to do with the casting. I mean, you have complete veto or say-so. In film, you generally don't; most writers do not. In *Brodie*, of course, I did. I wanted Maggie [Smith], I thought she would be wonderful. And she did, in fact, win an Academy Award. Actually, I didn't think she was as wonderful as you might have. I didn't like her in the beginning of the film. I found her very mannered. I thought she was marvelous after about a third of the way in. She was working with a director who is a fine technician, but not great with actors. And she has a tendency to be very mannered if she's not pulled back.

FROM AUDIENCE: In the TV series *Family*—which is my all-time favorite, incidentally—did you use some of *Brodie* in creating the character of the mother?

ALLEN: No, not at all. I think of Brodie as an inordinately silly, romantic, very foolish creature. Lovable, but not a grain of common sense. The mother in *Family* is polar from that.

FROM AUDIENCE: You remarked that you were displeased with the beginning of *Jean Brodie*—you thought it was sluggish. Do you ever have any input, is your opinion ever sought regarding the editing of a film?

ALLEN: Sometimes. But not then. It wouldn't have made any difference; it was *written* sluggishly. It had a sluggish progression.

FROM AUDIENCE: Why did they take *Family* off the air?

ALLEN: It just ran out of steam, that's all. That was an interesting project—it purported to be about the 1970s, but the sensibility of it was the 1950s. That was the trick of it.

FROM AUDIENCE: I'm interested, Mrs. Allen, that you're not as impressed with *The Prime of Miss Jean Brodie* as most of the people here are. I wonder, if you made it today, what would you change?

ALLEN: That first third—which was very heavy with exposition—that could have been *levitated*. I think it could have been a lot more filmic—and I know that's a jargony word. But everything didn't have to move so linearly. It could have taken a bit more to the air. There were other things. I thought Bob Stevens, who played the painter, the art teacher, was desperately miscast. Something was just not right. Although Stevens is a *glorious* actor, I just did not like him in this film. I loved the music master, Gordon Jackson. And, actually, I liked Celia Johnson almost better than anything in the film. She was a great star on the English stage, and in English film. She's a wonderful actress—but when she was first cast, I disagreed with the choice. I thought, "Oh God, she's gorgeous, she's a great, great beauty, so what's going to happen when she and Brodie lock horns? There will be the feeling that there's a sexual contest going on." I was afraid that something extremely misleading would come into the script. That's why I disagreed about Celia Johnson. I was very, very wrong. She was superb.

CRIST: Do you want to talk a little bit about *Funny Lady*—which we are about to see?

ALLEN: We were talking about this earlier. That it's not uncommon with writers generally, and certainly not uncommon with writers in films, to look at the finished work, and all you can see in it is what you hate. The things that work, that are good, they don't seem to belong to you, they seem to have been written by someone else. And you think, "Why, that's wonderful! Who wrote *that*?" All the stuff that sounds so rubbishy, *that's* the stuff *you* wrote.

There was a very major problem with this film which was that Barbra Streisand did not want to do it. She did not want to do it in a very strenuous way. And she gave the director, Herbert Ross, a bad time. She did not want to play a thirty-five-year-old . . . and eventually an older . . . woman. Herbie had to spend an unconscionable amount of rehearsal time with her on the scenes. I felt that, unlike most musicals, it was the book that got the attention and the numbers that suffered. Because finally she delivered on the scenes. I thought she was great. But the musical numbers were terribly uneven. I felt that she threw away two lovely comedy numbers that Kander and Ebb did for her. The movie is called *Funny Lady,* and, while she's funny in the scenes, she is not effective in the two big set-comedy routines, one of which was almost totally cut. The other wound up under titles.

Herbie took the rap, but in my opinion the lady bore considerable responsibility. When she's good, she's very, very good and the rest is also applicable.

I don't know. How can you force an artiste to deliver what they don't feel like delivering? Right or wrong, she did not *want* to do a sequel to *Funny Girl.* My impression is that [Ray] Stark had her cross-collateralized on three films and that she was, figuratively speaking, escorted to the set every day by a team of lawyers.

FROM AUDIENCE: Do you think James Caan was properly cast in this?

ALLEN: I'll tell you—we had looked and looked and looked and had read *everybody.* Robert Blake was a contender. Young unknowns like Robert De Niro and Richard Dreyfuss—guys well under six feet, like Billy Rose. But Ray [Stark] didn't want to go with any of those people and finally settled on Jimmy Caan. And I thought, Well, that's it. You cast that gorgeous young man, then you make her utterly contemptuous of him and still in love with that old phony—and there goes the movie. Once again, I was wrong. I think Jimmy is wonderful. And I was very grateful for him. No, he doesn't look like Billy Rose—but he acts the ears off of a scruffy, cheapo manipulator and somehow manages to make him irresistible.

CRIST: My own experience with *Funny Lady* was that it was the first sequel I had come across that was, I thought, better than the original.

ALLEN: I wish I felt that. Actually, many of the scenes come as close to satisfying me as anything I've ever worked on. The scenes I remember best—and don't remember writing, because they just seem to have come out of nowhere and consequently they work—those scenes are still wonderful to me.

[After *Prince of the City*]

CRIST: Can you tell us, Jay, about the genesis of this project?

ALLEN: I read a review of the book in *The New York Times,* ran out and bought it, read it, put it down, picked up the phone, and tried to buy it. It was already bought and assigned to a writer-director team. I was very upset because I had just finished making a picture with Sidney [Lumet] and I thought *Prince of the City* was absolutely definitive Lumet material. But I didn't see any point in showing it to Sidney if we couldn't have it—so I didn't. And then I began to smell that maybe the other arrangement wasn't going to work out. So I got the book to Sidney, and he read it and flipped and wanted instantly to do it. We sat around and waited with our fingers crossed and finally the other deal did fall through and we got it.

CRIST: Until this moment I thought that it was Sidney who would have gone to it instantly at the beginning—simply as a counterpoint to *Serpico.*

ALLEN: Well, directors aren't necessarily great readers, you know. They have a tendency to read *scripts.* Generally, the material does not begin with directors. Sidney and I had just finished a project [*Just Tell Me What You Want*] and had another one set to go, but Sidney got so excited about *Prince* that we postponed *Deathtrap* and did this first.

CRIST: This was your first venture into production?

ALLEN: No, I'd produced *Just Tell Me What You Want* and an earlier movie in Hollywood.

CRIST: And you were involved in casting *Prince of the City?*

ALLEN: The casting is what I'm proudest of in the whole film. As I was waiting, Sidney began seeing actors I would consider at the outer limits because we wanted as many unknown faces as we could possibly get. Thanks to Sidney, who has made most of his movies in and around New York, there is now a pool of acting talent—thanks to *Serpico* and *Dog Day Afternoon,* for example—comprised of ex-cops and ex-hoods. And they're *smashing.* I mean, if they're forty years old and still alive, by definition they have to be pretty good actors. We've got seven convicted felons in the film—I defy you to pick them out, I don't think you can.

We have one guy who's a chief of detectives in New Jersey. He plays the big bail bondsman, the villain. He'd never acted, of course. Sidney narrowed the choices down for me. I saw, I'd say, maybe a thousand actors. I think Sidney saw well over 5,000. There are 120 or 130 speaking parts—I don't know. But we never had one single disagreement in the casting—it was bang, bang, bang!

CRIST: How did you hit on Treat Williams, who had been the hippie in *Hair,* and the wonderful private detective in *The Ritz?*

ALLEN: I didn't hit on him, Sidney did. I didn't like *Hair*—I thought Milos Foreman's work was wonderful, it was a well-done movie, but I do not respond to the material. It isn't interesting to me—and Treat wasn't interesting to me for *Prince.* Sidney thought he was wonderful, and really, really wanted to go with him from the beginning. He had tremendous opposition from the studio, because there were a couple of very big stars who wanted to do it. But after we read Williams a couple of times and read him with some other actors, I felt I had to back Sidney up. If we'd made it with Hoffman, for instance, he would have been wonderful but it would have been a different movie. You have to believe the character is only thirty years old. Both Hoffman and De Niro are too mature. Travolta was also one that other people were talking about, but his quality seemed very wrong to us.

CRIST: My own feeling was that you did have to get a relatively unknown actor because of the ambivalence of the character.

ALLEN: I think the thing about not knowing those people added tremendously to the film's effect. I think it was a brave decision, and it was difficult to hold the line with the studio. Everyone was very fretful—I mean, fretful like *rivers of blood.*

CRIST: About the only familiar face in it is Jerry Orbach's.

ALLEN: We were in the office and talking about who would play the four partners, and Sidney said, "Well, you know, Levy is pivotal."

And we named three actors—among whom was Jerry. And we both said instantly, "Let's just go with Jerry. If he's got the time, let's not even talk about anybody else." So that was an instant piece of casting.

FROM AUDIENCE: Why is it that the movie industry has made such tremendous technical strides, and as far as I'm concerned cannot create realism on the screen without muffling the language? Where is the enunciation and diction? We go halfway through before I'm sure I hear what I'm hearing.

ALLEN: Well, if you think you are in trouble, think about the people in Dallas. Think about audiences across the country. I must say I agree with you. I've just seen *True Confessions,* which is a very difficult film, but a *brilliant* one, and I heard one word out of every six. You've got to understand that the movies are in the hands of technicians. *They* hear it. Sidney hears every word, he knows exactly what everybody is saying. And I keep saying what difference does *that* make?

FROM AUDIENCE: The movie business is in *our* hands, not their hands. Besides the difficulty in understanding the dialogue, this film is a little complicated to begin with.

ALLEN: Yes, this film is very complicated. It's complicated on levels you're probably not even aware of. You've got what, in effect, is a foreign language to people outside of the Eastern urban area. Then on top of that you have a sound track that is brilliant but very difficult. Then you have music *over* the sound track. I didn't enjoy *Star Wars* because I couldn't understand what anyone was *saying.* That doesn't seem to bother young people. But I want to hear the *words.*

FROM AUDIENCE: I thoroughly enjoyed the film—which is, I think, a universal response here. But I thought the whole business was going to concern undercover work related to narcotics. Then suddenly, somewhere along the line, there was a transition and the central character was involved with other things. It was hard for me to make that transition.

ALLEN: He was involved in *corruption*—and it didn't make any difference what it was about. I think it's astonishing that audiences follow this film as well as they do. This was written and designed and directed to be a three-hour movie. There was never a time when we didn't think it would take us three hours to do this story. Sidney spent almost a year cutting this film. It was a *killer* to cut. And so many nuances *had* to go, so much connective tissue. The subplot was cut out entirely. Two scenes that I thought were the best in the film are no longer with us—because they were part of the subplot. And the fact that you are able to follow this story, to a large degree, is remarkable to me. I think people follow it emotionally rather than literally.

FROM AUDIENCE: I'd like to know about how the film is connected to the real story. Were there a lot of changes?

ALLEN: We've had a lot of fuss in the press about this, because it is based on real people and some of them are still out there screaming. Look. A case explodes in the headlines. It is read by a journalist who gets excited about it. He does his research and writes a book. The book attracts the attention of a studio; the studio buys the book. They hire a screenwriter. That's me. A dramatist, if you will. A dramatist *dramatizes*. A dramatist attempts to boil details down to an essence, tries to fit it all into a movie time frame. He tries to clarify certain characters. He makes up dialogue, invents scenes— fills out characters, condenses five characters into one. That kind of thing. That's what one does.

Bertrand Russell said if he had one word to take to a desert island, the word would be "but." So I did all of those things, *but* in *essence*. This is as truthful a film as I knew how to make. And I had, as Bob Daley [author of the book] before me had—I had endless hours of Bob Leuci's tapes—Leuci was the real-life Danny Ciello, a very shrewd cookie; every tape he made for the authorities he copied for himself. So I had all of that. I had access to Leuci. I had the district attorneys. I had virtually everybody on tap. I had the book, but I also interviewed the real people and occasionally I came to totally different conclusions from the book. But, in *essence,* it is the same story. And it is a true story. There has been screaming and hollering that it isn't—but it is. And it's certifiable—I've got the tapes.

Of course, it's very thrilling to Sidney and me when this film is praised for its great realism. However, *stylistically,* it is *not* realistic. Because of the way the film is shot. In the first hour it's almost all long shots, very few closeups. Then you move in closer, and closer and closer—until the end, all you're getting is a screen with just one face in it. It's a very, very stylishly shot film. When the reviewers commend us for the sense of realism, we giggle a little. We're very pleased with ourselves.

FROM AUDIENCE: In regard to this, one thing that really appealed to me was the sets. There was such a wonderful contrast between the very lavish federal offices.

ALLEN: Another decision to go for style rather than realism ... more lavish than any federal office there ever was in the history of this country. But the point is that we thought this movie was going to run three hours. And somehow, one needed to feed the eye. One didn't want the audience to sit through three hours of *Mean Streets*. Sidney did something brave—he saw the work of a young Polish cinematographer on a television show. He was twenty-eight years old, had never done a feature film, and Sidney said, "I want him." My heart *just stopped*. I thought, There goes the ball game. Well, Andrzej Bartkowiak is enormously talented ... and actually this film is very beautiful.

FROM AUDIENCE: During the showing here there was occasional applause. Did you have the same heroes as the audience?

ALLEN: I think Ciello's *survival* is heroic; that is what is heroic to me. The most applause comes, as far as I can remember, when Jerry turns over the D.A. who harasses him. The audience applauds then because they're set up to applaud. They've had no relief from tension until that moment. I did not find Levy a heroic character—but I did find him a very understandable character. I don't think anybody should find him heroic. But they do, and I must say, that bothers me.

FROM AUDIENCE: Does the original author ever have anything to say about how the book is treated?

ALLEN (laughing): Not if I can help it. You cannot open that can of worms. You sell your book, you go to the bank, you shut up.

FROM AUDIENCE: Please don't think this is a criticism ...

ALLEN: Oh, I can take a *little* criticism.

SAME AUDIENCE: ... but how can you tell us that *all* the film industry is aware of the bad enunciation and speech of the actors ...

ALLEN: I didn't say that at all. I said *I* was—I'm not the film industry, for Chrissake.

SAME AUDIENCE: But then you do tell us we should stand up and make ourselves heard ...

ALLEN: But you do. I don't think audiences are going to this movie across the middle of the country. I do feel that audiences miss at least one-quarter of this film. It's not just the sound but the fact that it moves so fast—you can't really identify most of the characters till you're two-thirds of the way through. And let's be honest, it is an elitist film. You have to know how to listen. And evaluate. And emotionally it's a difficult film—you're given no guidelines.

[After *Just Tell Me What You Want*]

CRIST: I remember that even on *The New York Times* there had been a split reaction about this film. The second-string critic didn't like it because it was not about nice people. And I think three-quarters of my joy in it, and I believe Vincent Canby felt that way, too, was that it was *not* about nice people. Which made it a rare and special thing.

ALLEN: Comedy is generally not very "nice."

CRIST: Not only that, but comedy is a terribly *personal* thing. I find, as a critic, that I can kill a film I like when I say it's funny. Because not all of us are going to think the same thing is funny. We all know what's tragic—but we can't agree on what's funny. And, of course, you can *murder* a film by calling it hilarious because then all your readers go into the theaters and sit there with a grim look on their faces and say to the screen: "Go ahead ... *be hilarious.*" Comedy, I think, is the most difficult thing to achieve—and I wonder, Jay, how you as a writer approach comedy. First of all, you began this as a novel—and both the novel and the movie have been acclaimed as a roman à clef. I'm sure you had *somebody* in mind—although we will not ask you to name who it is.

ALLEN: Actually, in my life I've known about six men like that. There's one Hollywood guy who claims it is himself—and it isn't. It's three very specific men and a little bit of three others. The guy who claims it's about him—well, there are only two lines from him. They were funny lines and I asked if I could use them. He said yes, then went around telling everybody I'd written a book about him. When I heard he was doing this I called and said, "Listen, you don't want to do this. You may not like this book and you'll wind up very embarrassed." Which he did.

CRIST: What are the lines?

ALLEN: One was "I'm a dead Jew," which he would come out with, you know, if his oatmeal wasn't warm. The other was a line that was used in the book but not the screenplay.

Max represents a kind of man that, as a dramatist, I am naturally attracted to—because the energy level is so high. Which makes for drama and comedy. It also makes a lot of Max forgivable. Many of his assaults are committed under a kind of frenzy of energy—and thinking he can take care of everybody. Guys like that aren't *necessarily* baneful. You want to be alert around them, you know ... but most of them aren't really out to kill you. Maybe they're out to kill somebody, but not necessarily you.

CRIST: This was your first producing venture. How did this change your participation in the film?

ALLEN: Well, you can whine more. You can make them listen to you whimper and whine. That's about it. Unless you're Dino De Laurentiis producing in Italy ... producing today is advise and consent. You're in at the beginning. You have some input into casting and, of course, as producer-writer I had a great deal of input. But both the writer and the producer are generally going to take a back seat to the director. Sometimes "producer" is just a vanity title to shut somebody up, or give him less money. But if you really are fulfilling both functions—as writer and producer—you have a lot of input. Whining rights.

CRIST: I think that Alan King and, unexpectedly, Ali McGraw are what make this movie work.

ALLEN: You're absolutely right, they're what make it work once you're *in the theater*—but they didn't pull anybody in. In the middle of the country you couldn't whip people into the theater, they just wouldn't go. Alan was a particularly risky piece of casting. But Sidney and I wanted him very badly. Actually, we got together to do the film largely on the basis that both of us wanted Alan in that part. The studio went along with great trepidation—and it turned out they were right. When we didn't get overwhelmingly good reviews, *nobody* came to see it. Alan should have at least had an Academy Award nomination; he was totally ignored.

I thought Ali was better than she's been since her first movie. She's a wonderful, lively, vibrant human being—funny and intelligent. And although Ali's been around a long time, she'd never been worked by a real actor's director—she was very humble, she put herself completely in Sidney's hands. Of course, she was nervous starting off, and the first part of the movie shows that—the film doesn't "catch" early on.

There are a lot of problems in the first part of the movie . . . the first ten minutes can be fatal when you're doing comedy—because you've got to tell the audience *fast* that they're *safe*. We had shaky times there. I think the first twenty minutes of the film are very dicey. For a lot of reasons. However, as the story established itself, Ali got better and better. The film was shot as close to sequentially as possible and, by the time Ali got to those really difficult scenes toward the end, she was ready for them. I don't know anybody who could have played that long, difficult hospital scene any better than Ali did. I thought she was wonderful. We screened the dailies—no one was allowed to come to them but Alan, and when he saw the first rushes of Ali in the hospital scene, he said, "I'm in love."

CRIST: She was superb. Especially in that fight scene . . . which I consider the greatest fight scene ever filmed. I mean, you can take *Body and Soul* and shove it, you can take *Rocky* and shove it . . .

ALLEN: That *was* wonderful, wasn't it? That was a very hard scene for Ali—it was hard for her to *pound* Alan like that. She's a very gentle person. Of course it was rehearsed and choreographed, as if it were Kabuki. The big thing for Ali was to try to get some real heft behind her swings. To *mean* them.

FROM AUDIENCE: Before you commit yourself to a project, what do you look for?

ALLEN: I'm usually attracted by a character, a strong dramatic character—I'm excited by personality. Much more than by plot or situation. *Prince of the City* was a combination of the two. *Tell Me What You Want* was mostly character. *Funny Lady* had a good strong character, very powerful—and *Jean Brodie* the same thing, not much story but a powerful character. So clearly, that's what generally appeals to me. We'll be seeing *Deathtrap* tonight, and those of you who saw the play will remember what the wife was like in the play. Well, for that role we cast Dyan Cannon—the object being that she be very much *alive* before she's dead, you know.

CRIST: Actually, in two of these films you were coping with real people, not just characters.

ALLEN: Well, Fanny Brice, of course, didn't have to be treated so realistically. Although the producer's wife is Fanny Brice's daughter ... she's Ray Stark's wife. But one was only obliged to treat Fanny realistically within the framework of her theatrical myth.

CRIST: I was hoping that even though *Just Tell Me What You Want* was not a success, it would really do something for Ali McGraw's career.

ALLEN: We did too. Except for her very first movie—*Goodbye Columbus*—Ali has never been allowed to show her *wit*. And she's funny, she's full of beans, she's kind of sweet-tough—but somehow she's always playing those sad-sack, head-tilted, lip-trembling boring women—and she's not technically a skillful enough actress to pull that off. But then who is? Ali has a wonderful personality and it's maddening not to have it used.

FROM AUDIENCE: Alan King is known for his comedy takeoffs on big business—the telephone company, the airlines, and all. How did he feel about playing a big businessman?

ALLEN: I listened to the most remarkable thing. Alan was producing a couple of films himself during the time he was filming this one. And he came in one day just filled with stories about the negotiations he'd been through. I heard him telling about it ... and what he was doing, in the negotiation, was using some of Max's lines—I mean verbatim. It was so funny. My goddaughter was there and she was indignant; she said, "He thinks *he* wrote those lines." And I said, "He'd *better* think he wrote those lines."

FROM AUDIENCE: I'm interested in why you chose Myrna Loy to play Max's secretary. I don't know if anyone else felt this way, but every time I saw her I said to myself, "I can't believe that's Myrna Loy."

ALLEN: That's one of those things where you're damned if you don't and damned if you do. You want somebody wonderful in the part. You're not going to get anybody wonderful in that part at that age who's not familiar to an audience. Now, if you go for somebody as famous as Myrna you have a lot going for you. You know you will get good value, plus her name looks wonderful on the marquee.

You get a good deal of publicity. At the same time you have the problem of everybody saying, "Oh, look, that's Myrna Loy."

CRIST: What I liked about her role is that she seemed to be the character she had always played, grown older. Still the smart, efficient, cynical woman. I like to think that if Fredric March died after *The Best Years of Our Lives,* she might have become a secretary for the next thirty years of her life.

FROM AUDIENCE: How much did it cost to do *Prince of the City?*

ALLEN: It came in at under $10 million—which is on the low end of the scale for today. I doubt any other major director would have brought it in at that price. It was scheduled for thirteen weeks and came in at twelve. *Prince of the City* was kind of a miracle of logistics. Sidney knows *exactly* what he's going to do when he comes to the set. There's no wasted motion. You say a director will do six-for-one—that is, six takes for one print. Some do thirty-to-one. If Sidney prints three takes it's a big deal. The only other director I've ever worked with like that was Hitchcock.

FROM AUDIENCE: Every career has its highs and lows—what were yours?

ALLEN: That's really very hard to say. I have efficient glands. I'm not easily depressed. I don't think the world comes to an end if a movie fails. I don't really have very bad lows. My work has been a fairly steady progression. I've been lucky.

FROM AUDIENCE: Of the movies we've seen, which was the most difficult to write—and how long does it take you to write?

ALLEN: Oh, I'm very, very, very fast. That is, the *typing* is fast. But the gestation period, who knows how long that takes? Nobody knows; no writer in the world can honestly tell you that, because it's an unconscious thing that happens. *Funny Lady* took longer to write because there was so much research. And it was fun; I was having a good time doing it and I was not under any hard deadline with it. *Prince of the City* was a weird experience; it was the only time I've ever collaborated on a script [with Sidney Lumet]. It was a true collaboration. I wanted Sidney to direct it, I wanted to produce it, and I did *not* want to write it. But Sidney wants everything done yesterday—so that meant getting it written "overnight."

It was a very difficult piece of material. I don't know how

many of you have read the book: it goes back and forward in time, there are a zillion characters, it's very fragmented, very hard to bring into a sequential focus. I said I was tired, didn't feel like doing it. Sidney said, well, he didn't want to direct it if I wouldn't write it. And he said, would I do it under *these* circumstances . . . ? Now, I've always worked with good directors, but Sidney is the best structuralist I've ever dealt with. He really does know what should come before, what after. He said, "Suppose I tackle the book, break it down chronologically. We get together to choose what we want to put in the movie, what we want to take out, the characters we want to deal with, et cetera. Then I will structure the thing." And he said, "What the hell, I can really write the action scenes." It was a very sweet, generous offer because structure is a tedious, difficult, hateful thing to me. Still, although it was a very generous offer for Sidney to make, it was also unnerving. Suppose he got to *writing?* Suppose while he had a pencil in his hand he'd start turning out scenes—then he'd bring them to me and I'd have to say, "garbage!" Then there goes the ball game. But Sidney is persuasive and persistent. Which is what directors must be, by definition.

So that's what happened. I couldn't go to work on *Prince* for about two weeks, and he came to the office every day—we share an office—with his legal pad and his sharpened pencils and he would sit in the office for eight hours like Mr. Gibbon's "Scribble, scribble, scribble . . . " And, you know, my heart just sank. It seemed that the results *had* to be fatal. Sidney's and my tastes vary a great deal; we're very often far apart on what one or the other of us considers tasteful. Finally, he came and handed me almost a hundred pages. It was a tense moment. But I read it—and it was just wonderful. He had, in effect, written a kind of first draft. He hadn't attempted too much in the way of scenes and characterization, but he had done what is, for me, anyway, the donkey work.

In the writers' union, when there's an arbitration about who did what . . . and that happens very often in films . . . when scripts are taken away and given to other writers—whoever got there first with the structure is always going to get credit. Always. Even if not one line of that writer's dialogue remains in the final version. The first guy, the structuralist, gets credit. And quite rightly.

So I took Sidney's hundred pages—I mean, I was just in hog heaven—and in nine days I turned out a 365-page script. I know that sounds extraordinary and in a way it is, but in another way it's not. Because it was also the first time I'd ever done anything having to do with living people. So if ever I came to a spot where I was stuck, I'd pick up the phone and call the guy, and say, "What happened here? Give me another line . . ." It was very loose . . . *Prince* was written in a hot heat and it was produced the same way, directed the same way. And I think that when a film happens like that, sometimes you get the artists' best work—certainly their most excited work.

FROM AUDIENCE: Ms. Crist, you mentioned that half the critics liked *Just Tell Me What You Want* and half didn't. I wonder what those who didn't like it said?

CRIST: I said the two critics on *The New York Times* had been divided. Jay would know about other reviews better than I.

ALLEN: Most of the reviews were good—but the reviews that really counted were not. The most important ones were not. The critic's *age* seemed to be germane. Younger critics seemed to be profoundly shocked by it. I don't mean sexually shocked, I mean shocked by the morality. You can do anything if it's drama—but not if it's comedy. We felt we'd fallen among the Red Guard. I mean these stern young people sermonizing at us—young people who apparently had never seen or heard of Restoration comedy. Everybody over the age of forty knew the difference. I found it rather alarming. The movie is just a lark—a light, larky movie, that's all it is. But the younger critics seemed to regard it as some sort of sociological statement.

FROM AUDIENCE: Are you going to make money on it—or do you care?

ALLEN: Of course I care . . . it was a total loss, a wipeout. It cost $10 million to produce, the advertising distribution fees would have come close to $3.5 million—putting it about $13.5 million. It sold to television for $4 million. Fini.

FROM AUDIENCE: Is this why you wear black?

ALLEN (laughing): In a roundabout way. When I'm anxious I over-eat. Then I *have* to wear black.

[After *Deathtrap*]

CRIST: Now it can be told that this is kind of "let everybody play critic" time, because you are the very first people to have seen the film in this form. *Deathtrap* is not in its finished form; therefore we'd be extremely interested in getting your reactions—pro and con. Don't feel you *have* to find fault with it, but if you have something constructive to offer, don't be shy.

FROM AUDIENCE: I enjoyed the film very, very much ... but for some reason I was uncomfortable in the very beginning, up until the point Dyan Cannon was murdered. I can't explain why, but it just didn't seem all together yet.

ALLEN: Where I have a problem with the film—and I do not believe this is going to be fixed the way I wish it to be—is the part in the very beginning before he comes into the house. Comedically, it's very unsteady. There has been a major cut in there that takes out the reason for the Michael Caine character being so distraught when he comes home. The fact that he's hung over and that he's had a terrible night is all very well—but he's almost in a state of hysteria when he first comes into the house and has that fit. As it was written and as it was shot there is an encounter, a harrowing, unspeakable encounter, with a terrible female cabdriver. There is a storm, there is an encounter with the psychic that happens on the road, lightning strikes, a tree falls. He has a harrowing morning. So there is good cause when he goes into that frenzy. As it is now—with the morning *cut*, he has to go into that high-anxiety aria without anything to back it up. I don't believe there's really any margin for error in the first ten minutes of a comedy. When that's shaky, the spillover of unease that you give your audience can pollute the whole work.

CRIST: We had been talking earlier in the day about being too regional in movies, and one thing in *Deathtrap* that probably won't travel well out of New York is that nobody knows that Montauk is the end of the line after East Hampton, and that it does cost fifty-two bucks to get back there by cab.

ALLEN: When the script was first written it was written for the terminal at Hartford—which is a city terminal. It's a desolate looking place, with all those tracks, quite ugly. Then when we found the windmill—we all thought, oh yeah! Let's have the windmill house, that's more important than doing it in Connecticut. So we changed the locale to Long Island—and the terminal at the end of Long Island is just a lovely little place, so instantly you lose the horror of arriving at that station. And we lost all the other stuff too.

FROM AUDIENCE: There's a bad technical mistake in all this—because you can't just get on the train in New York and fall asleep and ride all the way to Montauk. You have to change trains in Babylon.

ALLEN (laughing): But we wanted that windmill house, you see.

FROM AUDIENCE: Besides, by the time this picture comes out the Long Island Railroad will have changed its schedule.

FROM AUDIENCE: It confused me at the ending, when the action accelerates. It's so dark, you can't see exactly what is happening, who's doing what to whom . . .

ALLEN: That's right, that's our other big problem. The end is extremely confusing—and for that, I think there *will* be retakes and it will be fixed. I think it will work when it's properly done. I hope it will.

FROM AUDIENCE: There are some of us here who think everybody was killed at the end—and some who believe nobody was killed. So you sort of lose the whole point of the story.

ALLEN: Well, Chris Reeve kills Michael Caine and then dies, and Irene Worth takes the play and claims it as her own—and it's a big hit. The ending is as simple as that. But it's very unclear the way it's shot.

CRIST: Having the psychic take the play is the big deviation from the stage play, and one which I rather like.

FROM AUDIENCE: In the very beginning, when Christopher Reeve came in I thought his acting was terrible and I was very glad he was killed off. Then when he came back in I thought his acting had improved tremendously. Was that intentional—was he supposed to be awkward in the beginning, or what?

ALLEN: I thought he was wonderful all the way through.

CRIST: Remember that the character he is playing is an awkward student playwright. I thought he was tremendous, but I'm not surprised—because I thought in *Superman* his transitions from Clark Kent to Superman and vice versa were simply superb, and they were done without makeup.

ALLEN: I think very few people even in the business understood what a brilliant thing he did in *Superman,* and how difficult it was.

CRIST: When he became Clark Kent he suddenly shrank in size—he did it by relaxing muscles, and he went through internal changes—I think he's a tremendous actor. And I thought he and Caine played very well together. I'm also a great Caine admirer.

ALLEN: I agree. The chemistry between them was wonderful.

FROM AUDIENCE: I'd like to know what you as a screenwriter had to do to a play to put it on film?

ALLEN: Well, of course the tradition is that you do what they call "open it up"—that is, take it outside the original set or sets, make it bigger. You can't do this to this play—not really. Putting in scenes at the New York theater in the beginning and again at the end was just about it. Most plays are wordy, very verbal—and the best movies most frequently are not. In this you can't get away from the wordiness, really, because it's only through the talk that you can cope with the plot. The plotting was so very tight—I mean, that's what they paid their million dollars for, and that's what they wanted. So it was a question of first cutting away the underbrush—simplifying, simplifying—simplifying the rhetoric as much as anything. I tried to make the people a *little* more real. I'll give you an example: in the play right after he kills the boy, or appears to kill the boy, he says "Points for neatness—right on the rug." This brings a *big* laugh in the theater. I knew it wouldn't get a laugh on the screen—because you've just seen a very realistic death, and you're not going to laugh right after that. On the stage, an actor can even force a laugh out of a line. So you have to exercise certain judgment about what's going to play—especially as the thing becomes more realistic on film, which it inevitably must. I tried to make it a little more real. I inserted all the stuff about the psychopath business in an attempt to explain the boy, and the thing about Caine's not wanting to wind up on a talk show babbling about his misspent life.

The main problem for me in this story is that I could never believe that the wife would believe so instantaneously in the husband's intention to kill. That if she'd lived with this man for eleven years, she won't instantaneously say, "Ah, yes, he's going to kill this boy and he's going to do it tonight." That drove me crazy—and I tried in a million small ways to make that more credible.

CRIST: You did for me. I haven't seen the play *Deathtrap* since it opened, but it seems to me you made the wife nutsier, frothier.

ALLEN: It's a totally different character. At the same time that you make her a little ditzy, you also must give her some rationale for her emotions. At least you try. It's still hard—there's still a tremendous burden left to the actress. I was most grateful for Dyan Cannon's skill.

FROM AUDIENCE: Can you tell me something about Michael Caine as a person?

ALLEN: He's an absolutely smashing fellow. He's also wonderfully professional—he makes the set an easy, pleasant place to be. He makes performers who aren't necessarily just wonderful to work with—wonderful to work with. He's very clever . . . but he's also a prodigal actor, who is careless of his talent. He takes lousy parts, he takes the money and runs. He should have been back in the theater a dozen times. He's an extraordinary actor—and he has thrown away a lot of it. He's also an adorable man.

FROM AUDIENCE: What was the ending of the play—and how was it different?

ALLEN: The only weak point in the play was the ending—it was a terribly unresolved thing where the lawyer and Helga chase each other around—each claiming the play. I found it extremely unsatisfactory.

FROM AUDIENCE: I loved Irene Worth as the psychic—and especially that wonderful hat.

ALLEN: There's another scene after the wife's funeral—where Caine walks to the psychic's home. It's a very good scene and I hope it will go back in. Because now you see her in the beginning and you see her in the end and there's nothing in between. In fact, to make you care at all what happens in the end, you need something in the middle with her. You find out in that scene that she's got five daughters and no money and she's having to work very hard to scrape up a buck, and she doesn't get the psychic messages the way she did when she was younger. Irene Worth is a splendid actress, and makes it a very lovely scene. I think we might put it back in, it would be helpful. Now, you have no reason to know why she wants the play for her own at the end, or why you should be pleased that she has it. More than that, after you see that scene in which Irene is so wonderful, you *want* her to have it.

[After *Cabaret*]

CRIST: How do you feel about *Cabaret*? To me, this is just an extraordinary work. You know you can't trust writers, you can't trust directors, you can't trust actors—they don't know what they've done. It takes the rest of us to let them know. And our previous experience had been the stage production—which had knockout musical numbers in it, a wonderful score. But no book.

ALLEN: But it had a great concept.

CRIST: Yes, and before the stage musical there were the stage play and the "traditional movie," *I Am a Camera*—and at the heart of it all were the 1939 Berlin stories of Christopher Isherwood. But it seems to me the film *Cabaret* is an extraordinary achievement. The way had been paved by a film like *Oh, What a Lovely War* and a few edgings toward changing the film-musical form. But I think this became the epitome of its genre. Please tell us how it came about.

ALLEN: Well, basically we knew what we did *not* want to do. There were three people involved in the creation of the film—myself, Bob Fosse, and the producer Cy Feuer, who played a very active and positive part in the making of the film. All of us were in awe of the production values of the play, the concept of the stage and the Kit Kat Club and the Joel Grey character—all truly remarkable. We loved the score—thought it was Kander and Ebb's best work. But we really didn't like the rest of the show. It seemed like a show that was ten years past the point. The idea of not playing the boy honestly and directly as a homosexual—as is the character in the book from which it all came—seemed antediluvian, dishonest. So we knew what we didn't want to do. What we did want was to go back to the source material, the Isherwood stories, which were remarkable in their time and are still remarkable. That's what we worked from.

CRIST: What were your concepts in casting?

ALLEN: It was always for Liza [Minnelli]. It was to be *for Liza*. Nothing else was set. The rest of it was up for grabs. It was made on an extremely low budget, really on the cheap. It was a split production—Allied Artists and ABC Pictures. ABC was okay, they just put up the money and let us roll. But this outfit called Allied Artists . . . We got this gentleman who got into the production for $300,000—that is a minuscule amount for a film. This film cost $3 million. It was made in Germany—and it was really a shoestring production. Anyway, when we had a draft of the screenplay that we felt was a good draft, I got a call from Cy and he said, "They're holding back and we're going to have to go up there and have a story conference." He said, "I just want to tell you now, because he's a professional Jew—and he's going to give us a hard time." He said, "I don't want anybody blowing up in the meeting." Cy said, "Bobby [Fosse] promised me he'd be quiet, I want you to promise me you'll be quiet." I said okay; it's easy to be okay if you're warned. So we went to the meeting, and this man and his *secretary* presented us with I don't even know how many single-spaced typed notes on their *collective* objections to the script.

Out of all those pages, which I still have on file, I'd say that about seven-tenths of them had to do with any mention of Jewishness in the script. So we sat there very calmly looking at all this nonsense. I was okay. Cy was okay. But I looked at Fosse and he was just bright red. I thought, "Here we go," so I jumped in and started yattering at the gentleman from Allied. "I can certainly understand your feelings and I appreciate your sensibilities, but look, I'm half Jewish myself, and I must tell you that I'd be profoundly offended if someone made a film about Berlin in the 1930s—and there was no mention of a Jew. And I can't think of any of my friends who wouldn't take to the barricades if that's the way this film was attacked. It's not a subject you can back out of." He kind of listened and we went over all his points, which we knew we weren't going to change anyway. And nobody exploded and the meeting went along okay; we were assured of the money and *got out*. We were *drained*. We didn't speak to each other in the elevator. We got out on the street. Still no one spoke. Fosse, Cy, or me. I started to get into a taxi and Cy said, "Jay, I've been working with you for a year—and I didn't know you were Jewish." I said, "Well, I'm not, Cy, but if you think I'm going into a meeting like that with an ethnic liability, you're crazy."

CRIST: The blending of plot and performance numbers was so absolutely remarkable in *Cabaret*, and that had to be written, did it not?

ALLEN: Yes, that was all in the script. I worked more with Cy Feuer, who never got any credit, than I did with Bobby—who was on another project during most of the writing of the film. He would come in at odd moments when he was able, but I worked largely with Cy.

CRIST: Do you remember how Michael York was chosen?

ALLEN: I just never thought anybody would be better for the part than Michael. That was pretty much the consensus. It was always Michael York—once we had the script.

CRIST: Joel Grey seemed to peak in that role—he's never gotten anything to compare with it since.

ALLEN: I think Joel is an extraordinary performer. But there are not many film parts for what Joel does so brilliantly.

FROM AUDIENCE: Mrs. Allen, you told us yesterday that you hated to do the structuring of a screenplay. It seems to me that among the things you brought to *Cabaret* was structure.

ALLEN: Sure. When I say I don't like doing it, that doesn't mean I don't do it. It's hard to say at this late date who did exactly what. Everyone contributed to *Cabaret*'s structure. But I know I certainly did my share. I worked on that script for ten months—which is a very long time for me.

FROM AUDIENCE: The progression of the decadence was so wonderfully done. It was almost imperceptible, but the country disintegrated before our eyes.

ALLEN: Yes, that was diagrammed. Things like that don't just happen. The Berlin stories weren't structured at all, really—except for Sally's progress. Pulling it all together was awfully hard work.

FROM AUDIENCE: Didn't *Cabaret* win an Academy Award?

ALLEN: Many. Best picture, and Bobby was best director. Liza for best actress. Joel won for supporting actor.

CRIST: Did you get a screenwriting Oscar?

ALLEN: No, I did not, and I didn't expect one. I had reservations about this film because I thought it could have been a *great* film. I don't think it's great, but I do think it's a very *good* film. But the dramatic scenes lacked dimension. And the way Fosse chose to shoot them was so humorless. And he didn't really like Sally. He seems to see women as either Madonnas or whores—nothing in between. He never liked Sally. I think he was contemptuous of her. And it shows; it's up there for me.

FROM AUDIENCE: Mrs. Allen, you seem so self-effacing. Do you think any of your films are great?

ALLEN: No. I'm not self-effacing, I just don't think there are many great films. I think *Cabaret could* have been great, and I think *Prince of the City* comes damn close.

CRIST: Next question. Mrs. Allen, are you going to direct?

ALLEN: Never. Basically, it's a man's job. [Groans from audience] You don't know what directing is. You can't conceive of what it is. It is *dominating,* in the most militaristic terms, an unstable, potentially explosive situation over a period of a year. A director can have little else in his life during the term of the film. You can't be a mother and direct a film—certainly not a young mother. And I don't know how you can do it physically past a certain age. It's like leading troops into battle. It's a horrible job. I wouldn't consider it—ever.

FROM AUDIENCE: Did you write the book *Just Tell Me What You Want* with the screen in mind?

ALLEN: I assumed that I would have a screenplay in it, yes.

FROM AUDIENCE: Would you rather do screenplays without being involved in production?

ALLEN: What I *really* like to do is a very swift rewrite for a great deal of money. Then I'm out of it. There's no emotional commitment at all—your name's not on it, you're home free.

FROM AUDIENCE: Who chooses where the film is to be photographed on location?

ALLEN: Well, generally the film itself dictates. If you've got *Prince of the City,* you make it in New York City. *Just Tell Me What You Want* was a film that would normally have been made, because of costs, in California, in a studio, had it not been for a director who prefers to work out of New York—Sidney Lumet. And I'm more likely to involve myself in a film that's going to be made in New York—because I live in New York, and this is where I want to be.

FROM AUDIENCE: Have you ever been angry enough to want to take your name off the credits?

ALLEN: Yes, and I've done it.

FROM AUDIENCE: Which films?

ALLEN: I won't tell you ... that's why you take your name off. [Laughter]

FROM AUDIENCE: What is the favorite of the movies you've done?

ALLEN: *Prince of the City.* I enjoyed the making of it. It was a new experience for me to work from a real situation with real people. It was an exciting movie to make, an exciting movie to publicize. And I like the results. Also it's very seldom that someone will give you the money to make that kind of movie. It's difficult to get that privilege.

FROM AUDIENCE: You know what surprised me about *Prince of the City*? There's almost no violence in it at all.

ALLEN: There's almost no *physical* violence. The violence is psychic—emotional, mental violence.

FROM AUDIENCE: With cable television coming into the marketplace and the great demand for films and stories and so forth—where are we going to get all the scriptwriters and storytellers?

ALLEN: Well, I don't know where you're going to get them—because we don't have a good training ground for dramatists in this country. The standards are very low. When we started *Family* I was told that I was not to be shocked at the very low caliber of the writing. I had to understand that by the time I read the scripts that got to me—hundreds of others, the worst of them, would have been culled out—that what I got would be the cream. Well, the cream was largely sour.

FROM AUDIENCE: Are you saying that for the mass market you won't really have to be too sharp?

ALLEN: No, what I'm telling you is that we paid just as well as any other show and anyone who wanted to write for us and was an acknowledged union writer, and some who weren't, could have a try. Out of five years of scripts, this was the way it worked—two came in that were filmed *as they were*. Every other script that came in, either assigned or submitted, was rewritten to a lesser or greater degree—largely a greater degree—by Carol McKeand, who was the story editor. She was, of dire necessity, very skillful. Then I usually polished her scripts. Even then, I would say that one script out of maybe five was a script you'd really be pleased to have your name associated with. Look, there are never more than a dozen good anything at any time—including dentists. Excellence is just not there for the picking. It's there only when it's demanded, and there certainly is no demand on network television.

FROM AUDIENCE: I notice that in the films we've seen, a lot of the same names keep showing up—the editors, et cetera. Do you choose to work as a team with certain people?

ALLEN: Sidney and I have worked as a team on three films. We didn't meet each other and say let's make three films—we met each other on one film and said, okay, we'll do this other one. Then another one came up. We made three in a row together—which was a first for him, and a first for me. A director *must* work with a team—in the way that nobody else in this business works with a team. And there is this great pool of technical talent in New York that has, in the main, been trained by Sidney. They are his people. Sure, you get a great prop man, you use him every time you can get him. One reason why you can make that movie for $10 million instead of $22 million. It's saving time, knowing the quality of the people doing the work for you. Sidney has worked with Tony Walton, the set designer, many times. Burtt Harris, who was a production manager and is now a line producer, has made, I think, eleven films with Sidney. On the really creative side, with a writer—it's very unusual for a director and writer to work together so often. Not in Europe—but in this country it's unusual.

FROM AUDIENCE: Does Mr. Lumet keep his editor on the set every day?

ALLEN: What an editor does is get the dailies together every day to look at. The editor is in charge of those dailies. So the editor is there every single day. That does not mean he's there on the set looking at every shot. He doesn't do that. He's in an editing room.

FROM AUDIENCE: Does an actor or actress ever verbalize that he's uncomfortable with a line of dialogue?

ALLEN: Oh, all the time. But that's done in rehearsal, generally—if you have the privilege of a rehearsal. Some films don't.

FROM AUDIENCE: Is it really necessary in this day and age to have such extensive use of rough language in movies, and semi-nudity and things like that?

ALLEN: The way I feel is, if the reality of the situation *demands* it, then do it. If it doesn't, don't. In *Prince of the City*—that's the way they really talk. I think many people are uneasy when they first hear that language, but generally they settle down because the feeling comes that you're not really dealing with obscenity—you're dealing with a paucity of vocabulary. And the nudity . . . well, I'm an old puritan: I hate it. I won't go see *Body Heat*. I just can't stand to see sex that's that explicit on screen—it just embarrasses me. I'd love to pick up on *Body Heat* in the second half, when I know it's going to be a good old James M. Cain kind of thriller.

FROM AUDIENCE: After *Deathtrap*, are we to assume that if you don't write something good in the next year or two, you might have to kill somebody?

ALLEN (laughing): No.

CRIST: However, we don't know about Ira Levin.

FROM AUDIENCE: Mrs. Allen, this is a small point, but you always see on movie credits someone called a Best Boy . . .

ALLEN: I don't know what a Best Boy is. Do you, Judy?

CRIST: He's the electrician's helper.

ALLEN: I've been meaning to find out for thirty years. You know, everybody gets credit now. You look at the old movies and you have a director and the cast and a screenwriter or two and a producer—that was about it. Now, you've got the producer's secretary's gofer—it goes on and on.

FROM AUDIENCE: As a screenwriter, do you try to construct your writing in such a way that your audience becomes a participant in some of the violence?

ALLEN: Well, sure—because it's scarier that way. If it's just gratuitous violence, then you can just turn your head away and come back again. If the violence invades your head, there's no escape. The expectation is what's really terrifying. I think one of the most frightening movies ever made was *The Thing* . . . the original one with James Arness. And what was frightening wasn't the Thing itself—which was just that great big carrot—it was the fact that the set had so many windows, and so many doors. You couldn't watch them all at the same time.

FROM AUDIENCE: Yesterday you mentioned working with Hitchcock—could you tell us any anecdotes about him?

ALLEN: He was wonderful to me, and there's no way I could ever repay his generosity. He was a great teacher—he *loved* to teach. And Hitch didn't really like men. He just liked females ... he was really an old Turk, he just wanted to be surrounded by women all the time. And he wanted to fence them in. I had to go to California for his film. It was to be made at Universal Studios in the San Fernando Valley. I wanted to live close to the studio so I could bicycle to work, which upset Hitch. I didn't understand his objection—it was really that he felt "de-classed" by my bicycling to work. Hitch was very class-conscious. He was always after "them." And the fact that I was living a a modest hotel in the Valley and wanted to bicycle to the studio was losing face for Hitch. He loathed it, so he told me that he couldn't get insurance on me if I bicycled. And I bought that—of course when I knew him better I understood what the problem was.

Anyway, he said we just couldn't have any bicycling, and I said, "Okay, I'll just get a little Volkswagen." But he couldn't stand that either. So he began to send a limo for me. Hitch was very, very possessive. He would just envelop you. And it was lovely having the limo, nothing wrong with that, but finally I realized that I had been out there for over two and a half months and I had not put my foot on cement. I'm a New Yorker, so I'm used to a great deal of *indifference*. Nobody cares whether you ride or walk or *crawl*. I'd never worked for a studio, I'd never worked *for* anybody, that was my first time. And I began to get claustrophobic. So I got up one morning and I thought, "The hell with this—I'm walking to the studio." It was only about four miles, and I thought I'd take my time, stop for a bit on the way—it was a beautiful day. So I called in and said, "Tell Hitch I'm going to walk to the studio this morning," and the secretary said, "Oh, Mrs. Allen, you can't do that ..." I said, "It's okay. Just tell Hitch that I'm walking," and I hung up. So I started out on old Ventura Boulevard, which is pretty cheesy but filled with all kinds of crazy shops to look into. So there I was, walking along, feeling *good*. This went on for about half an hour, forty minutes, before I began to get an uneasy feeling. Finally I turned, and there was the limo creeping along behind me. I went back and asked the driver what he was doing. He said, "I have to follow you, Mrs. Allen ... because you might get tired." And I said,

"No, I won't get tired, honest." But he said he had to do this. I said, "Okay, I'll get in the car and you drive me to a filling station—because I've got to go to the ladies'." So he drove me to a filling station, I got the key and went in—and I went out the window on the other side. Then I called Hitch and said, "*I'm loose.*" [Laughter]

Blake Edwards and
Julie Andrews

▰▰▰▰▰▰▰▰▰▰▰▰▰▰▰▰▰▰▰▰▰▰▰▰▰▰▰▰▰▰▰▰▰▰▰▰▰▰

Blake Edwards began his career as an actor (appearing in twenty-six films) before becoming a screenwriter, director, and producer—three jobs he frequently handles simultaneously. From the mid-fifties through the sixties, Edwards worked on more than twenty films—including such dramas as Experiment in Terror *(1962) and* Days of Wine and Roses *(1962)—and created several television series, notably* Peter Gunn. *Edwards is most known, however, for his film comedies; he has, for example, written and directed all six of the* Pink Panther *movies starring Peter Sellers. In 1969 he wrote, produced, and directed* Darling Lili, *and that year married the picture's leading lady, Julie Andrews. She has starred in three of his most successful recent films:* 10, S.O.B. *and* Victor/Victoria.

Born to a British show-business family, Julie Andrews made her London stage debut at twelve and her Broadway debut at nineteen in The Boyfriend. *In 1956 she created the role of Eliza Doolittle in* My Fair Lady, *playing it on Broadway and in London for nearly four years, and in 1961 she starred in another Broadway hit,* Camelot. *Her first film role was in* Mary Poppins *(1964) for which she won an Oscar as Best Actress. That same year she played a dramatic role in* The Americanization of Emily, *but returned to musicals with* The Sound of Music. *Among her other credits are*

Hawaii *(1966)*, Thoroughly Modern Millie *(1967)*, Star *(1968)*, *and* Darling Lili—*which led to her marriage and collaboration with Blake Edwards.*

The two guests were at Tarrytown for the weekend of November 27–29, 1981.

[After *Experiment in Terror*]

CRIST: I had not seen *Experiment in Terror* for a very long time, and what really strikes me now is how very innovative that film was in its time. Could you tell us a little bit of the development of this concept?

EDWARDS: I can't remember precisely how we got the property, but Lee Remick and I decided we wanted to make another film together, and at the time I was having some success with a television series called *Peter Gunn,* so I was working in that genre—and kind of naturally headed in that direction. The book itself wasn't particularly innovative or exciting, but I felt the bones of it were good and I had used San Francisco and knew its photographic possibilities, so the screenplay was structured for San Francisco. We just tried to be as original with it as we knew how. I apologize to the writers of the novel—I think they knew I didn't think it was any great shakes—but I just tried to make something a little more out of it. If I succeeded—terrific.

CRIST: Would you change anything in that film today?

EDWARDS: Oh, God, yeah. I don't know what it would be at this point, but everything I do I want to change. That's why I didn't come in and look at this one tonight. I usually want to change a lot of things.

CRIST: In the last ten years or so you've gone into a completely different kind of genre. Would you ever go back to making a thriller?

EDWARDS: Oh, I'd love to. If I could find a thriller, I'd love to do it. I keep looking . . . one doesn't come to me—not an original, and not yet anyway. The difficult thing today is that there're so many people doing this; it has become a science now—how to scare you out of your wits. I'd like to find a different way of doing that. I mean, Hitch did it for us, as brilliantly as anyone can do it. It's hard to top that.

FROM AUDIENCE: I wonder about your decision to make the film in black-and-white, instead of color.

EDWARDS: In those days [1962] black-and-white was more acceptable than it is now. I think it was a combination of things . . . partly the budget, partly the fact I was shooting *Peter Gunn* in black-and-white, in a non–wide-screen process. I was used to that. And I guess also because it made the world interesting and shadowy. I like black-and-white. You can't shoot black-and-white well anymore because they don't have the labs to do it. They just don't have the people to process it correctly anymore.

CRIST: The black-and-white photography in this is quite powerful, really—because otherwise things might have been "pretty" and distracting.

EDWARDS: Unfortunately, if you control color you could be just as effective, probably, in that respect, as black-and-white. You could desaturate and make it almost black-and-white, and when you wanted a color, you could use it to stimulate whatever emotion you want to stimulate. The unfortunate thing is that the first print of a film may have all of that, but by the time it gets into eight hundred or a thousand prints, certain color effects just don't hold up. So the whole thing is lost. It's unfortunate that you can't have better control, but you just can't. We just finished a film *[Victor/Victoria]* in which we planned from beginning to end a kind of color progress. The film starts in the thirties, in the Depression, in Paris and Julie is like the poor little match girl. Everything is bleak and gray and there isn't much color in it. As the story progresses and things get better, she becomes more successful and falls in love and everything gets brighter. It's not just brighter colors, but different colors—it's the use of color to stimulate a particular emotion. If you see the first run in maybe the first three theaters in which it'll open—then it will all work. From then on, you're lost.

CRIST: I was looking back at reviews of *Experiment in Terror*—I was not then reviewing—and everyone thought it was an art film. It was rather adventurously arty, although there are some unintentionally funny moments . . . when the FBI agent walks in and says, "There's a fog rolling in." I have a feeling that there are also some structural things that would not exist if the film were redone today. What dates this film more than anything is the attitude regarding the FBI. Nowadays there's instant cynicism about the FBI's operations.

EDWARDS: Actually, I'd like to comment on that line. It wasn't in the original at all—what happened was we got up there on Twin Peaks to shoot, and *the fog rolled in.* So it had to be noted, somebody had to say something about the fog to explain what the hell was happening up there. It was terrible. In fact, the studio wrote a memo back telling us to stop sending the fog through so fast. They thought it was special effects.

CRIST: Most of your movies, Blake, involve an interesting behind-the-scenes story. Tell us about *10.*

EDWARDS: Well, *10* was a picture I wrote six years before I finally got it made. I was having a bit of trouble with MGM at the time: I made two films for them that were disasters, not so much in terms of box office but in terms of my relationship with the studio.

CRIST: Which films were they?

EDWARDS: One called *The Wild Rovers,* which was simply destroyed by the gentleman who ran the studio. And another one called *The Carey Treatment*—which I've never seen. It didn't do badly. But it was at that time I wrote *10* and delivered it to them. MGM owed me a paltry sum—you wouldn't believe it if I went into it—and I said don't pay me, just give me the script. Which they were delighted to do. Six years later I finally got the chance to do it.

ANDREWS: Tell them why it sat around for six years—because nobody wanted to do it.

EDWARDS: Yes, they'd say, "Who's interested in a rich songwriter who sees a pretty girl and makes an ass of himself? Who cares?" And I kept saying, "Yeah, but don't you think it's funny?" I'd get kind of blank stares. Actually, I knew better than to ask that, because not an awful lot of people in the industry have a great sense of humor. Particularly when it comes to reading scripts. Then, suddenly, in Hollywood terms I was "marketable"—I had made a number of films that made staggering amounts of money and they wanted me to make more of those. I said, "Okay, I'll make more of those provided you do this one." I really kind of blackmailed them into it. And, grudgingly, they said yes.

Suddenly, at the last minute I lost my leading man—George Segal quit on me. I thought I'd never get this stuff off the ground but, luckily, sweet Dudley came along and you know the rest. Regarding Segal—on the Friday before the Monday we were to start shooting, he said he wasn't going to do it. It finally boiled down to script reasons. Well, I went to his house and begged him and told him a lot of people would be out of jobs because of this, that he wasn't being professional. But he just refused to do it. So we shut down at that point. It looked as if the picture wasn't going to be made. I begged Orion to give us some time to recast—and I found Dudley. It worked out great. This has happened to me twice, I might add. My career could best be described as "serendipity." I've been very lucky. It happened with the original *Pink Panther*. Peter Sellers was not the original Inspector Clouseau. That was Peter Ustinov—who also quit the Friday before the Monday we were to start shooting. It's true.

CRIST: That's absolutely amazing—because in both instances it was creating stardom for the two replacements. Speaking of star-making, how did you come to cast Bo Derek as the perfect *10*?

EDWARDS: With her it wasn't tough, I must say. I walked into the office and took one look . . .

ANDREWS (laughing): Now that's not what you told me. Blake had run some film on maybe six or eight ladies, and he wasn't really a hundred percent happy with any of them, although a couple came very, very close. I remember that I received a telephone call from him the morning he interviewed Bo, and he said he came around the corner and came to a skidding stop—because there she was! She was dressed in just a sort of sack with a belt at the waist and little mukluk boots on—and nothing else, I would guess. And Blake said he just *knew*, he didn't need to audition her or test on film or anything. He just phoned and said he'd found her. At least that's the way I remember it.

EDWARDS: There's a saying in my house—"My wife . . ."

ANDREWS: No! [She breaks into laughter.]

CRIST: You can't stop there. What *is* the saying in your house?

ANDREWS: Well, I think *his* saying is, "*I* have something *my wife* wants to tell you."

CRIST: I wonder, Julie, if you would talk about playing opposite Dudley Moore—who's so totally different from George Segal.

ANDREWS: When Blake cast Dudley, I said, "Well, surely you don't want *me* now, because it's going to look so ridiculous—I do tower over him."

EDWARDS: By about eight inches.

ANDREWS: I was thinking, foolishly, that I would be terribly embarrassed and that Dudley would be terribly embarrassed. But Blake said, "No, no, no. I think it would be great—it would make the relationship more unusual." So I said, "Well, give me something to relate to. Why would she fall in love with this pipsqueak—who is adorable, admittedly—but why?" And he said, "Okay. If he were just a butcher down the street you probably wouldn't be interested in him; but if he were a very, very talented man . . ." First of all he cited Frank Sinatra and Ava Gardner; he was quite small and she was quite tall and, for a while, they connected very well. Also, a great friend of ours is André Previn, who is not very tall, but he's the most dynamic man to meet and talk to, and so bright and intelligent and *very* attractive. When Blake mentioned André and said to relate to *him,* I said, "Ah, now I see what you mean. If I think of Dudley in that light I can do it." And it worked.

FROM AUDIENCE: Was *10* as much fun to make as it was to watch?

EDWARDS: Yes, it was, as a matter of fact. Dudley is a joy to work with, just terrific.

FROM AUDIENCE: Miss Andrews, *10* seemed to indicate a change in direction for you—a new, more sophisticated image. Can you tell us what motivated the change?

ANDREWS: Well, first of all, *thank God* it happened, because if I was stuck with *Mary Poppins* now, I'd look absolutely ridiculous. Hopefully, one does grow and mature.

EDWARDS: We had tried to change the image for some time, not in a conscious way of saying, "Okay, let's break the mold and change it." We knew that she was stuck with it, and it wasn't all that bad— but I've always seen Julie as a terribly talented actress, and when I started working with her, I thought in those terms. I didn't say, "Well, if she plays a German spy—in *Darling Lili*—we're going to break the mold." That was a by-product of my thinking, but I knew she'd simply be terrific in *10*. She did me a favor doing that role. Fortunately, we try to do as much as we can together, not only because we appreciate each other's work but because that's our life-style—we prefer to be together rather than apart. So it was easier to talk her into it than for her to say no, because it allowed us to be together and work together and that's fun. It's *hell,* sometimes . . . no, it isn't really.

ANDREWS: Actually, I think the best answer to your question is that I have done slightly different roles, such as *Hawaii* and *Tamarind Seed*—but the things one is best remembered for are the popular musicals—*Sound of Music* and *Mary Poppins*—and they're that other image. You get bracketed after a while. People say, "Oh, *that's* what she does." Even though you may be able to do different things, and unless somebody has the insight to say maybe you could do something fresh and different—then people see you for what they've already seen you do. Thank God Blake feels I can do something else.

FROM AUDIENCE: Miss Andrews, would you be interested in returning to the Broadway stage again?

ANDREWS: Yes, I am, except when you're happily married and have a large family—between us we have five children—I just don't know many people who can manage all that. When you think about the people on Broadway, they are either just making it big in their lives and aren't yet committed to home and family—or they are people like Betty Bacall and Lena Horne, whose children have grown up. It's very, very hard. I wouldn't want to uproot my children from their schooling and ask Blake, who's a very busy man also, to wait on me for the better part of a year—if the show is successful. If a show is successful, you have to guarantee the producers they can get some money out of your performances. I think maybe somewhere down the line I'd *love* to come back to Broadway. Oh, God, if Stephen Sondheim asked me to do a musical I'd probably do it tomorrow. But I'd prefer to wait.

[After *Days of Wine and Roses*]

CRIST: As we all know, *Days of Wine and Roses* was done remarkably well on television. Considering that, I wonder how you felt about approaching this one, Blake, which was in a sense a "remake."

EDWARDS: Yes, I was apprehensive about *Days of Wine and Roses* but my apprehension quickly faded when I found out whom I'd be working with. It was an exciting prospect to work with Jack [Lemmon], and actually he requested me, because he wanted to bring to it a sense of humor. He felt it was essential that Joe have a sense of humor—Jack was perfectly capable of giving the character a sense of humor, but he wanted a director who understood that, along with all the terrible things that happen to each of us in our lifetimes, there are funny things in the midst of tragedy. I was so flattered to be wanted on those terms, I really didn't allow that good television show to intimidate me too much.

FROM AUDIENCE: Cliff Robertson was so great in the original television play. I just wonder why Jack Lemmon was chosen over Robertson.

EDWARDS: Actually, the property was obtained by Jack Lemmon, so it wasn't the studio this time saying, "Let's not use the right person in it." The lady in the original, Piper Laurie, was wonderful, just wonderful. And I know for a fact that Jack didn't cast Lee [Remick] to spite Piper. There were a lot of reasons: Jack and Lee were with the same agency, the agency was putting a package together—all of those things came into play.

CRIST: I think that one of the essential differences between the Cliff Robertson version and the Jack Lemmon version is that Jack's character is fuller, larger for the large screen. The other was drearier, basically. I think Piper did a far better job. Lee Remick's problem is that she's just too beautiful, and when she's falling apart, when she's supposed to look awful, she's still so exquisite.

FROM AUDIENCE: I would think making this movie would be a strain.

EDWARDS: Of course. It was a very emotional movie. I used to go home with migraines and throw up because I'd see these two people so involved with what they were doing—and we all got very much involved in the subject of alcoholism, and spent a lot of time going down to drunk tanks and AA meetings. I'd had some personal experience with it in my family, and when we were shooting it—for example, the scene where Jack was in the straitjacket—I'd find we'd have to shoot it about four times, different angles of it. The last time I yelled "Cut, Jack," and I finally had to send some guys in to calm him. He'd really gotten out of control, he had lost it, he couldn't bring himself back. I went home that night with a splitting headache. He was terrific, he'd gotten it all out and he went home and had a drink.

FROM AUDIENCE: The woman in this story, does it work out in the end that she can't get into AA?

EDWARDS: Sure, she could get in it—if she wanted to make the commitment. But she didn't want to make the commitment, she couldn't do it. There's a very interesting story I love to tell about the end of this film. Because when we started to make it, the man who was head of Warner Brothers, J. L. Warner, said, "I don't like the ending: we should have a happy ending." Our producer, who had not produced a film before that and was really unfamiliar with the infighting that can go on, asked what he could do. I said, "Just go on and make the movie—there's nothing you can do now, and if you start trying to do something now you're going to lose. So let's try to get it done and then we'll fight the battle when we have to."

So it came time when J. L. wanted to see the movie, and we went up into his private projection room—myself and the producer, Lemmon, Lee. And Mr. Warner came in with a rather attractive looking lady, kinda brassy, a little bit loud, but interesting. I thought, gee, I know her from somewhere, but I couldn't place the face. So we saw the film—and I knew what was going to happen and it happened. When it was over Warner stood up and said, "Well, you've got to change it, you've got to reshoot it—you've got to put a happy ending on it." And this lady who hadn't said anything and was obviously very moved by the picture turned to Warner and in wonderful street language told him he was out of his mind. He said, "Who asked you?" and she said, "You did, you invited me here to see this movie and I've got a right to talk about it." And again, she used some wonderful street language.

He was stuck, and I didn't know why. I couldn't figure it out, because people like J. L. Warner, I don't care who you are, it's just not easy to change their minds. I found out later she was a lady about town who was strictly his lady—and I'm sure if he hadn't agreed with her she would have walked out on him. So I owe the ending of that movie to a lady of the night—bless her!

FROM AUDIENCE: Has anyone other than Henry Mancini scored any of your films?

EDWARDS: Yes. Not many other people: I did a film called *Wild Rovers* with a wonderful score by Jerry Goldsmith, but I keep going back to Hank. Listen, when you've got a good tailor, you keep buying the suits.

[After *S.O.B.*]

CRIST: *S.O.B.* looked like such enjoyment for all. Could you tell us something about that film's long and—I understand—tortuous history.

EDWARDS: It all started about ten or eleven years ago when I was having a lot of serious trouble with several major studios. The trouble got worse and worse to the point that my wife and I left Hollywood and dug a hole in Europe and decided we would make films and be creative over there for a while—to kind of lick my wounds. It took a year at least until I was able to get some objectivity on it and, as is my way quite often, to have a sense of humor about it. I decided the best therapy would be to write about it. So I wrote it. And from that point to the point we were allowed to make it—which was about nine years—it was turned down by every studio. Finally, because I was sort of in vogue again, I was allowed to do it. It was that simple, and that complicated.

CRIST (to Andrews): And you were part of it from the beginning?

ANDREWS: Yes, I was. I had to soothe his troubled brow and be tactful for a number of years—because he was so mad. It was kind of wonderful to hear him writing it. We live in Switzerland and Blake works in an attic studio there, which is just above our bedroom. And I would hear him giggling away—he'd be writing, for instance, scenes like the idiotic credits of Felix Farmer's films that the guru recites at the end, "The Invasion of the Pickle People," and things like that. He'd let me read the pages every day. It was a much bigger script in those days, and I think the length of time it took to get the film made actually created a much more tight, cohesive piece, eventually.

CRIST: And I think it probably made it a lot funnier, because instead of looking back in anger, it is looking back with satire. I have found that *S.O.B.* is a movie you either hate or adore. It's very difficult to be in the middle about it—and that's proof to me that it is a good movie.

FROM AUDIENCE: I'd like to ask—is Hollywood *that* decadent? Are people there *that* callous? *Why* have you done this film?

EDWARDS: It's very hard for me to answer you without defending the piece—and I can't defend something like this. It's there, and you either like it or you don't like it. If it assaults you in some way that you resent—I cannot help that. You see, I see the community in which I live, the film community, in a particular way. Now, as to whether Hollywood is like that—first of all, it's hard to say "Hollywood." We lived there for a long time, we still have a house there—even though we do live in Switzerland—and there are a lot of wonderful people in Hollywood. But it's an expedient town, and people deal with expediency only. For me to sit now and tell you what the town is like would take hours, and I wouldn't be articulate enough to do it. The town is like what you saw—but again, I have to qualify. *Part* of the town is like that. This is in a sense an allegory, but in a much greater sense it is absolutely true. I can tell you stories that happened to me and happened to friends that make S.O.B. look like a sweet fairy tale.

Hollywood is a crazy place because you're dealing on the one hand with terribly talented people and on the other hand with people who govern those talented people and who have no talent themselves. You see, what I felt in the film, all of that was a tapestry—all the abrasive elements, all the sexuality, all of the selfishness and all that—that was a tapestry against which some wonderful things were happening too. I mean, there's the relationship between the men—they were not perfect, of course. Our heroes were antiheroes, to be sure.

It is all based on a lot of truth. There's practically nothing in the movie that hasn't happened; it may be exaggerated a bit, to make it entertaining, I hope. If you're asking, "Is the town really like that?" I have to qualify, again, and say, no, the town is not—but a certain section of the industry is very definitely like that, in spades. If I told what it was *really* like it would be unacceptable. And not funny at all. And that's why I wrote S.O.B. I felt it was necessary to say, "Hey, this is what goes on." And it goes on in big business, too, I know it does.

FROM AUDIENCE: I like S.O.B. and saw it twice before tonight; I find it a very moral film.

EDWARDS: That was what it was intended to be. And if that came across—then I've reached you. It is a morality tale, to be sure.

FROM AUDIENCE: Would you say that a certain chaos is part of the way you work?

EDWARDS: Chaos is part of my life.

ANDREWS: Thank you, dear . . .

EDWARDS (to Andrews): You're the one thing that keeps it in perspective.

SAME AUDIENCE: What I mean is all your pictures seem to be dealing with chaos, about things coming apart.

EDWARDS: Well, I'm slightly preoccupied with that—either directly or indirectly I get involved in projects where I try to put things together and make sense out of insanity, and solve those chaotic problems. That's just part of me.

ANDREWS: I think that *S.O.B.* is probably the most chaos that Blake has ever controlled; I mean, it's *brilliant* control of chaos. And I don't know where you're going to go from there, Blake.

FROM AUDIENCE: I'd just like to ask Miss Andrews if you yourself had any problems with the semi-nudity in the film—and what was your children's reaction? [Laughter from audience]

ANDREWS: Well, the babies haven't seen it yet, and heaven knows when they will. I asked our son whether he minded—or would mind—before we did it. He said, "I think it's *great*—go ahead, Mom." Which was lovely. I guess when I first saw the script I did have some qualms, but when you've lived with something for eleven years, by the time we did get around to it, it wasn't so bad. I had some thoughts—I guess I wondered if I should, whether I had any kind of debt to the public or anything like that. But I finally said, for God's sake, I ought to be allowed to grow up. And it's a wonderful role—and these scenes weren't gratuitous. They were done—excuse the pun—to make a point. [Laughter] And they did.

FROM AUDIENCE: Mr. Edwards, how honest and straightforward can you be in your dealings in Hollywood?

EDWARDS: It depends. As I said, Hollywood's an expedient place, but it's no more expedient than Madison Avenue. The stakes may be higher, but that's all relative, really. Hollywood's unique in that, as I said before, people who don't really have the credentials are telling people who do what they should and should not do. And that's a little crazy. You could compare it to deciding to take some of your hard-earned money and investing it in oil. Then you decide you're going to sink a well yourself—so you go out and hire a geologist to find out where to drill your well. Then comes the day when the geologist says, "Okay, I've done all the research, you've paid me all this money because I'm the expert and I say this is where the well should be drilled." Then you capriciously say, "No, I think it would be more fun if we put it over here." That's what the Hollywood studios do. They'll hire experts, let the experts start a project—then they'll try to control them. It's like, "Don't let the really creative children play in the mud." They want to control them. I don't know any studio head at this point who's really ever *made* a film, who could go into the cutting room and sit down and know what to do, or go into a dubbing session or walk onto a stage and talk to an actor. And yet—they tell you how to make movies.

It's phenomenal, really, that the business has gone on this long. It's like a wonderful, beautiful beast that people keep shooting arrows into, but somehow it struggles up and still makes it, still glitters. We keep calling it a business—but I don't think that in the *first* place it is a business. In the *second* place it's a business. I think first it's a creative enterprise. That's where it starts.

FROM AUDIENCE: Are you concerned at all about any negative effect *S.O.B.* might have on your own career?

EDWARDS: If I was concerned at all, I wouldn't have made the film. I got over that a long time ago. I've been successful; I've been that fellow who was as good as his last movie and couldn't get a job and I found my way back to being successful again. I don't worry about those things anymore. I really don't. That's a little bit a lie in that I like to work, it's important that I work, and I hope that eventually I'll be able to start a company wherein I'm totally financed and don't have to deal with the establishment.

What you see up there in *S.O.B.* is true, albeit exaggerated, and it exemplifies one of the things I think J. L. Warner said—he said, "I don't want to ever see that man on this lot again—until I need him." And it happened that way. The head of a major studio, when he saw *this* picture, said, "He's a son-of-a-bitch, but I want him for his next film." I mean, he *hated* it, but because I now have a reputation for making a succession of films that made hundreds of millions of dollars, I'm a commodity. They're not all that way—don't misunderstand me—but an awful lot of them are. If you're successful in films, if your films make money, then chances are you'll get hot again—you'll get a job.

CRIST: And *Victor/Victoria* is completed, and the next *Pink Panther* is on its way.

EDWARDS: Yes, I can always do a Pink Panther, you see. That keeps me going.

CRIST: Can you tell us a little bit about *Victor/Victoria?*

EDWARDS: I'm really very proud of this one. I haven't bragged about a film—I didn't brag about *S.O.B.*—but I will brag a little bit about this one because I think it's the best thing I've ever done. It was a joy, just great. It's a very complicated film because it's about roles people play. Which is something I've always been interested in. You know, we change according to the people we're talking to. The film deals very strongly with homosexuality, it deals with a very strong heterosexual love affair that is having problems because neither one is being honest within the relationship. Julie plays a woman pretending to be a man pretending to be a woman. Very complicated, and it goes on from there.

CRIST (to Andrews): Did you love every minute of it?

ANDREWS: Yes, I did. It turned my head around a little bit because I play a lady who's down-and-out in Paris, having absolutely no money, and I'm persuaded by Bob Preston to become a female impersonator. As Blake said, I pretend to be a man—dressing up as a lady in performance. At the end of my act I take off my wig and reveal that I am a man. But in reality, I'm a woman underneath that. So I'm playing on two different levels. It was one of the points of the film, that we all have problems with our identities and we all should be what we can be. It doesn't matter what we are; just be honest about it. And when I began playing a man, getting into the role, my head just turned completely around. I began wearing men's clothes, and had my hair cut short . . .

EDWARDS: I have to say that not only was Julie pretending to be a man, she was pretending to be a man who was gay . . .

ANDREWS: . . . while knowing I was a woman. When I'm doing the love scenes with James Garner I know I'm a woman feeling a woman's feelings. So it was very confusing and terribly interesting to do, really stimulating.

Following the success of Victor/Victoria—*for which Julie Andrews, Robert Preston, and Lesley Ann Warren received Academy Award nominations*—Blake Edwards began production on The Man Who Loved Women, *starring Julie Andrews with Burt Reynolds, released in December 1983. Since then he has made* Mickey & Maude *(1984),* Blind Date *(1986),* That's Life *(1986),* Skin Deep *(1989), and* Switch *(1991), starring Ellen Barkin and Jimmy Smits.*

Julie Andrews appeared in 1986 in That's Life *and* Duet For One.

Richard Brooks

▰▰

As a newspaper and radio news writer, Richard Brooks moved from his native Philadelphia to New York City and then, in 1941, to Los Angeles. He began writing screenplays the next year, working with John Huston, John Sturges, and other directors on such films as Key Largo *(1948) and* Mystery Street *(1950). During these years he also published three novels. The first one,* The Brick Foxhole, *was the basis of the 1947 film* Crossfire.

Brooks credits Cary Grant for making it possible for him to direct his first film, Crisis *(1950), which he also wrote. The twenty-three movies he has directed and/or written since then include* Blackboard Jungle *(1955);* Cat on a Hot Tin Roof *(1958);* Elmer Gantry *(1960), for which Brooks's screenplay won an Oscar;* Sweet Bird of Youth *(1962);* The Professionals *(1966);* In Cold Blood *(1967);* Looking for Mr. Goodbar *(1977). Richard Brooks visited Tarrytown April 16–18, 1982.*

[After *Blackboard Jungle*]

CRIST: I was just saying to Richard that for *Blackboard Jungle* he assembled the most talented classroom ever—on or off screen. How was this movie put together?

BROOKS: Someone just asked me if we had difficulty getting the money to make a movie on this particular subject. Well! I didn't really have that much to do with it, because I was under contract and they just said, "Here, do it." In fact, the way it came to me was that I had been working on the script of *Ben Hur* for a producer friend of mine named Sam Zimbalist. I was to write a new script and direct it. Well, after about four or five months I went to Sam and said, "Sam, I gotta get out of this movie." Sam said, "What are you talking about, are you crazy? We've got people scouting locations." I said, "I can't help it, I can't stand this little bastard." Sam said, "What are you talking about? Didn't you see the silent version?" I said, "Yes, yes, it was marvelous—and this will be a tremendous success if I don't make it. I don't like it. I think you should get someone else." He said, "Who?" I said, "You should get the best—like Wyler." He said William Wyler wouldn't do it; I said maybe he would.

So I saw Willie, and I said, "Willie, I've got a tremendous project for you—*Ben Hur*." He said, "It's already been made once, why the hell would I want to remake it?" I said, "It needs someone like you, Willie. Anybody can do the action, but for the rest of it— they need someone with a little class. Besides, you might want to get out of the country for a year or two." But he said, "I'm stuck with a piece of shit—this book they gave me. I'll tell you what, why don't you read this thing, and I'll read your goddamn script." So the book he gave me was *Blackboard Jungle,* and Wyler did *Ben Hur.*

CRIST: And that's how movies get made . . .

BROOKS: That's right. *Blackboard Jungle* cost $360,000 to make— and that includes the music, because they wouldn't give me a composer. See, I heard this piece of music on a radio station driving home from a disastrous poker game—and I remembered it. When I finally wrote the script it was to this record. When we shot the picture we played the record every day—the kids rocked to it, danced to it. When it came time to do the score the studio said, "Hey, you've got a B picture here, forget it." So I said, "Well, let's buy this record then." They said, "Do you mean that piece of crap?" I said, "It seems to be right for the movie—I wonder how much it costs?" So they said they'd give us unlimited use of "Rock Around the Clock" for $4,000—and we could *own* it for $5,000. We said, "You must be nuts," so we bought the rights on the music *only for the picture.* That's how it was made.

You know, when this picture was finished they didn't want to release it. As a matter of fact, Clare Boothe Luce made it famous. There was a film festival in Venice, Italy, then, and someone saw it there and said they were going to give it a prize. Now at that time Clare Boothe Luce was ambassadress to Italy from the United States, and she was the honored guest at the Venice Film Festival. And she said she would not appear at all if this picture played. It turned out that she had not seen the picture, but a congressman had, and said that it must have been made in Russia and that it was really a terrible, terrible movie, and un-American. So she said she wouldn't have anything to do with it. The moment she said she would not appear and the picture was withdrawn from the Venice festival—well, immediately France allowed it in, then Germany did, then England. So Mrs. Luce really helped the picture—and I never had the chance to thank her.

CRIST: It's fascinating to look at *Blackboard Jungle* today, because what was going on at that school seems so mild compared to what we know happens today. But at the time, everyone wanted to deny that this had any accuracy whatever. And I must say, I myself resented this film deeply. That was long before I became a critic. At the time I was an education reporter: I had taught in city schools and felt that this was all a gross exaggeration. But life immediately caught up with Evan Hunter's book and Richard Brooks's film. Did you have any problems casting the film?

BROOKS: It was very interesting that Glenn Ford was in this movie at all. Everybody else turned it down. When Ford was suggested to me I said, "Gee, I don't know, in his last few movies he's the guy wearing the long hair, standing in the wings waiting for the crippled soldier to finish his song on stage. I don't remember the names of the movies, but he's always playing those parts." They said, "Yeah, but he really wants to do this." And I said, "*Of course.* He needs the job." Finally, we had nobody else and we had to start; so we said okay, Ford should do it. But I said to Pandro Berman, the producer, that he had to cut his hair a little. Do you know that he sat there in the barber's chair and every time the barber cut a little hair off, Glenn wept. *Literally.* He said, "Please stop, nobody will know who I am." I said, "That's good." It took six or seven hours to cut his hair, because he was weeping. But do you know? He's never changed his hairdo since—he loves it.

CRIST: How did you get Sidney Poitier?

BROOKS: I just asked him if he wanted to go to work. As simple as that. He was getting more money than anybody else in the class, so they wouldn't allow me to rehearse with him. Then I *couldn't* rehearse for about four days, because without Sidney I didn't know how the scenes would work as far as the composition for the camera. As a matter of fact, we shot the picture in something like twenty-eight or twenty-nine days.

FROM AUDIENCE: In watching you watch the movie, I was wondering if you'd do anything different with it today?

BROOKS: I'd treat it differently today, because I think the conditions are a little different, and we have more latitude in telling a story. But I am a different person today than I was then, a different person than I was yesterday. I think I haven't seen this movie since it was released, and I almost wept because I remember how gorgeous I was then, I had so much energy—and oh, God, it was great to be young. I like the movie, it has *very* pleasant memories for me. I really believed in things then. I hope I still do.

FROM AUDIENCE: Would you change the upbeat ending of the film?

BROOKS: I think I'd make the same ending. The reason is something that occurred to me tonight. We had decided quite early on that the movie was *not* about a kid with a knife, it was not about recalcitrant students, it was not about the bad guys in the class. It was about a teacher who really wanted to teach. The opposition to him was one thing, because without a good and bad guy you don't really have a good story. But the conclusion was that he would not stop teaching. That's the real interest for me. I *want* him to continue teaching—*there* in that dirty hole, that school where no other teacher wanted to teach. And I wanted the students to say okay, I'll keep coming back to school. I would retain that trust.

Let me tell you something, there are three examples of what a good drama ought to be—in my opinion. You take the story of Socrates, the story of Joan of Arc, and the story of Jesus. Now at one time his students come to Socrates and tell him, "Don't teach here, you're really in trouble . . . they really want to kill you, let's all go somewhere else, you don't have to die." But Socrates said, "That would be a negation of everything that I have taught and want to believe in." And so in the second act you have him getting the chance to make a decision, that important decision.

Same with the story of Joan of Arc, which is a great story because when she says she hears voices, they throw her in the cooler. Finally, they say to her, "Maybe you didn't hear voices—because if you did, you're going to have to burn." In the second act she says, "But I *did* hear voices." She makes the *decision*. The same with the Jesus story. "Are you the King of the Jews?" they asked him. He could have said no. Why is that story remembered? Because he had a decision to make. That's good story writing. Here, you have someone who has to make a decision—and that's why I like this story. The teacher has a choice and he makes his own decision—for good or for bad. I think that's important in thinking about story structure. You can have a script with forty fine scenes and not have a good story told—because the structure is not right. Structure, to me, is the most important single element in making a worthwhile movie—aside from the initial idea.

FROM AUDIENCE: As a writer, do you feel an obligation when you adapt someone else's work to be faithful to that original work? Or do you feel you have the latitude to do what you want to do to make it a good movie?

BROOKS: I knew somebody would ask that question. A writer is the most important element in making a movie. And when I'm directing, although I resent myself as a writer, I still realize that what I'm doing when I'm directing is writing the film. And the editing room is the final rewrite. But to me it's important—if I'm going to film a book, or a play, or a short story—that I at least am faithful to the intention of the book. That was true of *Elmer Gantry*—and I learned a big lesson from Mr. [Sinclair] Lewis on that. I met him because he had written a review for *Esquire* magazine about the first novel I had written. It was a complimentary review so I wrote and thanked him—and he sent back my letter (he didn't waste a page) and wrote on the back that if I ever came to New York to call him. At that time I was in the Marine Corps, at Quantico, and I got a thirty-six-hour pass and went up to see him. I called him and he said, "Meet me at the Astor Bar." It was on Broadway at 45th or 46th Street. We met there, had a few drinks, and he asked me what I'd like to do if I got out of the Marines alive; and I said, "Well, one of the things I'd like to do is maybe do a movie about Elmer Gantry." He said something quite interesting. He said, "If you ever do, read all the critics and what they had to say about the book. H. L. Mencken didn't like it very much and he was quite acerbic—

but he was right about some of the things he said about it. Maybe you'll find out something about the book by reading the criticism because they had some pretty good critics writing about novels in those days." Finally he said, "When you find out all you can about the book, when you make the movie—make a movie, don't make the book. I wrote the book, you make the movie. Just make it a good movie." That helped me very much. He made me less fearful.

CRIST: I think that was such an enlightened view for a writer.

BROOKS: Oh, it was. There are some writers who ask how you can leave out that scene or chapter or confrontation. Well, sometimes it just doesn't work because you're dealing with two different media. When you read a book, your first reaction to the printed word is intellectual, your brain has to digest the words. Your first reaction to the words on stage is intellectual, although the secondary reaction—if the words are put together well—may be emotional. Movies are almost exactly the opposite. When you see movies you will have an emotional reaction—very much like music. How many lines do you really remember from any movie that you ever saw? Very few, I venture. But you remember how Bette Davis looked when she walked up the stairs to go to her bed and die in *Dark Victory*. You remember how Bogart was reading that letter and the ink ran, while he was waiting for Ingrid Bergman in *Casablanca*. You remember how the fog looked as he walked off with Claude Rains and said, "This is the beginning of a beautiful friendship." But the final result of a movie is that you remember images—and feelings that you have. Well, when all the images are put together, you may have an intellectual response as well.

FROM AUDIENCE: Considering the subject of *Blackboard Jungle* and the time it was released, did you have any trouble with United Artists? Did they complain about the subject matter?

BROOKS: That's a good question. They didn't even want to release it. I remember that first preview was in Encino, a suburb of Los Angeles. Clifford Odets went with me, and I remember he was quite shaken by the movie. The next day I heard about the cards that had been passed out to the audience—those things where they ask all these questions. "Do you like the movie?" "What are the best scenes?" All that crap. And they had the usual forty-seven cards that said "it stinks," or "drop dead" and so on. But a number of people said they'd recommend the picture. So then they decided to send the picture to New York—without the director, just the film editor—to a theater on Lexington Avenue somewhere. And they had the same reaction they had in Encino. So they decided to release it, sometime in February, I think, in 1955. And I got a call from Mr. [Joseph] Schenck to come up to the Loew's building, overlooking Times Square. He said, "My boy, look down there at the theater— it's eleven o'clock in the morning, it's raining, and people are standing in line to see your movie. Why are they standing in line? Why do they like this movie?" I said, "I don't know—I don't know why they stay away, I don't know why they go in." He said, "You won't tell me. But, you know, it shows that you *know something*—because they're buying tickets." That's the answer to your question.

FROM AUDIENCE: Was the movie a financial success?

BROOKS: I wish we all made that kind of money. As I said, it cost about $360,000 to make, and that picture, the last I heard, made over $16 million—I'm talking about studio gross. That's when they charged maybe twenty-five cents or thirty-five cents admission. Yes, it was very successful. I'd like to have a piece of that. My salary for writer and director was something like $18,000. Before taxes. Which was a lot of money to me at the time—don't misunderstand.

FROM AUDIENCE: Why don't we see *Blackboard Jungle* on television?

CRIST: You do. It was on recently, in fact—on one of the independent stations.

BROOKS: I wouldn't know, actually—I'm afraid to take a look at it to see how much they've cut out. I had no rights about that at the time.

CRIST: When I saw it recently it was practically whole. I mean, they should be so lucky to get a youth movie like that today. You don't have to bleep a thing in that movie, they were such sweet-spoken kids.

FROM AUDIENCE: I thought I noticed something. In the scene in the garage Sidney Poitier said, I think, "I don't give a damn." But before, I think I heard him say, "I don't give a hoot."

BROOKS: Yes, there were several things. For example, when the teacher who uses racial slurs was asked where he was from—as he started to answer the Elevated went by and his answer was lost. I said, "Why do we have to do that?" They said, "Well, if he says he's from Indiana—somebody in Indiana may sue." There was another thing: there was a light switch at the door of the classroom, and everybody touched it when they went in or out of the room, so it had fingerprints all over it. But every morning we'd come in and someone had washed the light switch. I said, "What the hell are we doing? There are supposed to be fingerprints there—these kids use the light switch, don't wash it off." The next morning, it was all washed clean. I said, "What is this, some nut who just likes to wash off fingerprints? Or is this the policy of the studio?" Finally I get a call from Mr. Mayer, who said, "Don't you understand? We don't have fingerprints in an *MGM movie*." So in those days, you couldn't say damn . . . you couldn't have fingerprints around the light switch.

[After *Sweet Bird of Youth*]

CRIST: Someone remarked on the utter realism of [Tennessee] Williams's eccentric characters—and I think that's evident in this case in the play's translation to the screen. Did you consult Williams?

BROOKS: I never met Williams. We talked on the phone—he was in Key West—and we talked about the movie. His main concern was that the play was set in summertime, so you cover the furniture with bedsheets—"Make sure you do that," he said, and "Make sure you shoot it on the Gulf, because you can't find these locations anywhere else." So I went down to location hunt and drove from New Orleans to Pensacola, all along the Gulf, looking for the various locations. We had very little money to make the movie. Then I came back to California, got a car in San Diego, and drove to Los Angeles. Of course it *looked* like the same road, the same houses— the same hotel. We rebuilt the front of the Hotel Coronado. Well, when the picture was shown to Tennessee in New York, he said, "It just shows you, when you have the *real thing*—how it looks."

FROM AUDIENCE: Did Geraldine Page win an Oscar for this performance?

BROOKS: No, she didn't. But there was an Oscar. The first day that Ed Begley came to work—we'd already been shooting over two weeks—he did the first scene, and afterward I said, "Ed, let's have a talk." He said, "You didn't like what I did." I said, "No, it's not that, you're fine. There's only one problem: you're playing him like he's the worst villain in the world." He said, "Well, I'm a real son-of-a-bitch in this thing." I said, "But, Ed, *you* don't think so." And, I said, "As a matter of fact, you weren't the first choice for this part." His mouth fell open, and he said, "Wh-who ... was going to play it?" And I said, "Ed, the perfect man for the part is Randolph Scott." [Laughter] He said—as they used to say "*Sonny Tufts???*"—he said, "*Randolph Scott??*" I said, "He's gorgeous, he's absolutely perfect for the part." So Ed said, "So you want me to play Randolph Scott?" I said, "Yes, as well as you can." And he got the Oscar—for supporting actor.

CRIST: Regarding your marvelous casting in this—it was not easy to get Miss Page for that role, was it?

BROOKS: No, no. The studio wanted everybody except Geraldine Page. They would have settled for Ava Gardner. They had a whole list—Susan Hayward ... they even considered Debbie Reynolds. They wanted *anybody*—except this woman who had done it on stage. Well! I said I didn't think the others were quite right. I didn't have the final say, but I was troublesome. I said, "Would you take Garbo? I can understand Garbo playing this part." And they said, "Yes! If you can get Garbo, okay." But of course, Miss Garbo wouldn't do it. Anyway, I finally said, "We really ought to use this woman." They said, "She's a dog, she doesn't look like a movie star." I asked that we make a test on her. I had not seen the play— and to this day I haven't seen the play. But I told Geraldine to pick a scene and to come out to California. She did, and we photographed the scene—and the bosses at MGM looked at the test. They said, "She will never be in this picture as long as there's an MGM. Out. Finito. Don't talk about her anymore."

I looked at the test again. I thought it was pretty good, but then I realized they were talking about her appearance. So I said let's make another test—just a silent test. I said to her, "Why do you wear your hair that way? It's not that you're not a movie star, but that you just don't look the way a movie star is supposed to look." She said, "I played this role for over two years on Broadway, what the hell are you talking about?" I said, "Well, sometimes, you know, you look like a truck driver. So you have to worry about that. Also I want to get you a wig, and we'll do something with the makeup." Now, that wig, that hairpiece she's wearing in the picture cost at that time close to $3,000—that was *real* hair. Then I told her, "Why do you always smile like *that*?" She said, "Well, I have a very ugly smile." "Who told you so?" "My husband," she said—

her husband, Rip Torn. I told her she didn't have an ugly smile, that she was a beautiful woman, and we were going to put this wig on her—and she'd see.

So we put the wig on her, we made her up, and we did the test. Then I took it to the largest theater, with the largest screen, at MGM. And she looked at this large image up there and she said, "Oh my God, she's beautiful." And she always referred, from that moment on, to herself in the role as "that woman—*she.*" She was never herself. Then, when the MGM people saw the test, they said, "Well, get *her.*" [Laughter] But Paul [Newman] certainly helped. He said he'd walk out of the movie if she didn't have a shot at it, and that helped a great deal. He gave me more muscle than I had. And wasn't he gorgeous in this? My God, he made me cry.

FROM AUDIENCE: I was very impressed with the way you handled the flashbacks and the dreams, using mirrors and all that big space.

BROOKS: Well, I'm very conscious of composition—and studied it with a master painter. There are some painters who use the space allotted to them on canvas exceptionally well. I'm conscious of every frame of a movie. CinemaScope is an unnatural form to begin with—unnatural to the eye. What we did there was written into the screenplay, then as director I followed through on it—and fought all the way to keep it. All this was worked out from the beginning, though they were never sure they were going to use those scenes. I just always liked the idea of this gorgeous creature, Chance, standing there, and being in both the past and the present at the same time. I thought that was important.

FROM AUDIENCE: I was fascinated by the fact that the sex in this movie is very erotic in some ways, but very inexplicit. But the violence is not—you let the violence flow very freely. At least that's my impression.

BROOKS: We couldn't show the raw sex, we weren't allowed to. In fact, in *Cat on a Hot Tin Roof,* which preceded this by a few years, we weren't allowed to use the word "homosexual," let alone *do* anything about it. So far as sex was concerned, it had to be implied rather than shown. As far as the violence is concerned, it was mostly offstage—or *begun* onstage or *finished* onstage. Violence can be treated in many different ways—and the violence in this was treated just in dialogue alone.

CRIST: Yes—the literal violence was the overturning of the car. It's only in your head that you see the stroke of that cane come down across the beautiful Newman face. You see the cane raised, then you hear a thud—you do not see it strike. Throughout this movie you are constantly filled with terror from the threats of violence—but the violence is not literalized, nor is the sex.

SAME AUDIENCE: But in that hotel scene when he comes back and threatens Lucy . . .

BROOKS: You don't *see* her fingers smashed.

CRIST: No, he just clamps down on the top of the box.

SAME AUDIENCE: Well, it takes *very little* imagination . . .

BROOKS (laughing): That's right.

CRIST: That's what movies are all about.

FROM AUDIENCE: You had a lot of violence in *The Professionals,* which I thought was a terrific picture.

BROOKS: There was some violence in *The Professionals,* yes, but you never saw the blood. There was one drop of blood on [Robert] Ryan's shirt—throughout the entire movie. There was no other blood. Now, if you see the next picture, *In Cold Blood*—there are people who have told me, "I cannot watch that picture, because I cannot stand all the blood in that movie." *There is no blood in that movie.* This picture is in black-and-white . . . the color of blood is just too much for me. Seeing the blood is just something that the viewer establishes in his mind—and, as Judy said, that's what movies are all about, this illusion. The violence in *The Professionals* was in the action—it was choreographed almost like a dance.

CRIST: I must explain why we're not showing *The Professionals* this weekend. Because, although this is Richard Brooks's first time at Tarrytown, I've shown *The Professionals* eight times. I am in *love* with that movie, but I thought I just had to skip it this time.

BROOKS: I'd like to take a moment to answer a question from a woman whose daughter is a writer—and it seems the daughter has been suffering through writer's block. The lady asked me what she could do about it. That's a very difficult question. And I think it may interest all of you—whether you are writers or not—because in one way or another, aside from the fact you are here because you're interested in movies, you're interested in life because this is the *live* art now. Some of my dear friends, great artists and people such as

Alan Lerner—his list of plays as a writer and lyricist is unchal-
lenged, almost—he hasn't written anything in a few years, and I
don't know why. Except, I know what it is to put a blank piece of
paper in the typewriter, and look at it for hours. The last few years
of his life Clifford Odets didn't write anything. We talked about it,
he said he was working on two or three plays—but he couldn't
seem to get it on a piece of paper. It's something you're afraid of all
the time. Every time you start with another piece of paper on
another day, there's that thought—what if it doesn't come?

I don't know how to answer this question except in this way.
Dealing with my own craft, the movies, if you're interested in
movies, in making them—in the creative end of it, in front of or in
back of the camera—you'd better like it a lot. You better like
movies *so much* that nothing is going to stop you—nothing at all,
including failure, including the inability to complete something.
You have to stay with it. Because only then do you have a chance.
Those people back there in those offices, they're watching, and if
you just slip one time, they'll kill you. I don't mean kill you dead—I
mean they'll kill you as an artist. They'll kill every dream you ever
had. So you've got to run it—and you've got to be prepared to *eat
shit*, all your life—otherwise you're not going to make it.

FROM AUDIENCE: Along that line, could you tell us why it took
thirteen years to make *Elmer Gantry?*

BROOKS: Well, nine of those years the studio simply said no. They
wanted to do stories about the preacher who got baseball uniforms
for the team of neighborhood kids. Or they wanted a priest who
sang songs. Or they said it was okay to do a movie about the
Protestants who had to raise money for a new church roof. Terrific!
But this story—about everyday life, about someone abusing a form
of religion, a form in which people meet and face their problems—
they weren't interested in that. That went on for nine years. Then it
took two years to write the screenplay. Of course, all that time the
studio said, "Well, go someplace else and make it." Which is what I
finally had to do. Then [Burt] Lancaster said, "Okay, let's do it."
This is a money business, of course—and once a picture is successful, they'll make nine more like that. Every studio in town turned
down *Star Wars* twice. That's a fact. Now they're all trying to make
pictures like it—which, of course, they won't do.

FROM AUDIENCE: When a book or play is sold to the movies, does the author know what kind of changes will be made, or does that come as a complete surprise?

BROOKS: In most cases it's a surprise, yes. They are very often right—but sometimes wrong. I wrote a book called *The Brick Foxhole*, which was made into a movie—by other people, not myself—called *Crossfire*. It was the first movie made, in this country at least, dealing with anti-Semitism. Now the principal character in the story was a homosexual who was driving in his car one day, and some of the boys picked him up and beat him up. The producer came to me one day and said, "This leading character, we can't mention that he's a homosexual, it's against the code, so do you mind if we change him into a Jew?" I said, "Hell, that's the same problem—they're outsiders, nobody likes 'em." There was also a young Jewish boy in the story I'd written. So they changed it—and I think they did a marvelous job. They had to change the story in order to make the movie.

Some authors and playwrights have a legitimate complaint that the intention of the piece, the thrust of it, has changed their meaning. It's difficult for me to collaborate with another writer, because I don't have the temerity to say to another writer, no matter who, "I think you're wrong—that's not the way the story ought to go." Because that writer may be right. There may be five, ten, or a hundred different ways to do a story—*my* way is not the only way, it may not be the best way. But I can't tell that to anyone else, I cannot rewrite someone else's work *with* him, or her, because it's too painful for them and therefore it's too painful for me. I have enough pain. I'm a victim of the weak. I don't care if you're strong, I can deal with you. But if you're weak—I'm a sucker, I'm a goner. I'm gonna cry . . .

CRIST: As a prelude to seeing *In Cold Blood*—would you tell us why it was filmed in black and white and not in color, and why it does not star Paul Newman and Steve McQueen?

BROOKS: I wanted to do it in black and white, first of all, because of the subject and material. Color would have "prettified" it, made the film look pretty—color has a way of doing that—whereas fear and this kind of terror, this comes in black and white. The second thing is that the head of the studio came down a day or so before we started shooting and said, "We'd like you to do this in color." He brought a small reel of a film that John Huston had been shooting in Italy, a picture called *Reflections in a Golden Eye*. They had washed the color film, they had treated it in some way so that it was almost lacking in color. They said it would be very easy to make a black-and-white film from the color. I said, "What the hell is important about the *color*? It's wrong for the movie." They said, "Well, when it comes time to sell it to television—they won't play it unless it has color." I said I just couldn't see that. So they said, "Well, in that case—how about Paul Newman and Steve McQueen to play the two boys? We'll trade off—you can use black and white if you use Paul and Steve." I said, "You must be crazy." They said, "Don't you like Newman? You've worked with him twice." I said, "I *love* him—he's one of the best actors in America. And I like Steve McQueen—and of course they can play the roles. But they're not right for the movie. Why do you want them, tell me *why*? Look, if you lived in a farmhouse and your nearest neighbor was two hundred yards away, and the doorbell rings about one in the morning, and you go to the door and Paul Newman is there, you'd say, 'Paul, come in and have a drink.' But if it's a guy you don't know, your heart will skip a beat, and you'll wish you'd never opened the door. And that's exactly what happened in the story." So the studio guy said, "Well, either use McQueen and Newman, or make the picture in color, one or the other." I said, "Look, go home. Leave us alone. We're starting shooting tomorrow—we're making it in black and white, we've got two guys nobody knows." He said, "But we're talking about $5 million more at the box office. At least $5 million." But we made it in black and white, without Steve and without Paul.

[After *In Cold Blood*]

CRIST: One of the questions that always comes in reaction to this film, is whether it's for or against capital punishment. The first time I saw *In Cold Blood*, I thought it was a powerful statement against capital punishment, particularly that stunning end. Maybe that was because of my own feelings—and I think you will see what you want to see in the ending. What did you feel, Richard?

BROOKS: One of the reasons I wanted to make this is that I thought the book was a special sort of documentary on Americana at the time. I also felt I had something I wanted to say in the movie, anyway, which has to do with capital punishment. This movie represents the way I feel about it—but that doesn't mean you should agree.

Now all of these locations are the real locations—from the bus station in the beginning through the hotel, all through the wheat fields of Kansas, including the Clutter farm—and the penitentiary at the end. We must have made six or eight trips across Kansas. The people of Kansas didn't want us there. They were very disturbed by the book—not because it wasn't a good book, but because it was about them. They felt a little naked about it. They're very private people, too, and they thought, oh boy, Hollywood—they'll come here and "do it" to our daughters and all that. It was like a circus come to town. Then, when they realized that I got up at five o'clock in the morning and started looking for locations—they realized that we were working people, also. The Kansas Bureau of Investigation wouldn't even talk to me the first four months until they found out I wanted to portray *all* the men who worked on the case. Then they let me into their files. Finally we were in the prison—and this comes to the question you raised, Judith—there were two chaplains at the prison, one was Catholic and one Protestant. We had many discussions—every time I'd go through that part of the state I'd drop off and we'd have a little talk. As a matter of fact, the priest gave me that little book that Perry had given him—at the end. I said to the chaplain, "Why are you here, why do you do this?" And he said, "Because it's hard for them—and if I can help them in any way, I try to do it." I said, "But are you sure you're not perpetuating the death penalty? If you don't believe in it? Let me ask you a question—if Jesus Christ had your job, would he go up there and do that, be with a condemned man at the last?" The question seemed to disturb him very much. He said, "I don't really know." We corresponded for several months and I told him, "I don't feel qualified to take someone else's life—I might do it in the heat of passion, in a moment of anger or in defense of myself. But for the impersonality of the state to take a position of eliminating a life—I wouldn't know how to go along with that." That doesn't mean I'm right, or I wouldn't be capable of it. But I think it's terrible to take anyone's life, whether we do it legally or illegally. That's my feeling, that's one of the reasons I made the movie.

I talked to the executioner, the hangman. He was quite a fellow. He said, "I try to make them as comfortable as possible, and do it as quickly as I can." I said, "Do you know whether they choke—or strangle?" He said, "No, I do the rope so I break their neck—I don't want to hurt them." It's a crazy world we live in. I saw an execution once, covering it as a reporter, and I'll never forget it. I'll never forget the smell—it was an electrocution, not a hanging. This is not an appeal for you to change your mind—or anything of the sort. This is just a piece of life. But I think we should look in the mirror once in a while, to see who we really are, what we really believe—what we'd really do.

FROM AUDIENCE: I'd like to hear you talk about your directorial skills—in directing these two young and inexperienced young men—[Robert] Blake and [Scott] Wilson—and getting such terrific performances out of them.

BROOKS: I just started to infuse as much of myself into them as I could. There's a very effective sequence toward the end, when Perry Smith [Robert Blake] is talking about his father and he's standing by the window. The reason it was raining in that scene is that it was raining the night they were executed, and I promised Truman [Capote] we would have it raining. Truman was there during the execution—and he was very affected by Perry Smith and their relationship. Now, when the scene was shot it was in one take . . . and on the very first take Robert began to cry, he couldn't contain himself. When he came to the point about how happy he was he had a real home . . . the chaplain asked him, "Then you don't need your father anymore." And he said, "But I do—I hate him. . . ." And then he'd always break and say, "and I *love* him." Then I'd say, "Robert, we have to do it again. You cannot weep in this scene—let the outside world weep for you. But if you cry, they do not have to cry for you—and I want them to weep for a life that's going to go away. Even a life of this man who's committed this monstrous act." It took four or five takes before Robert could stop weeping. But the element of weeping is still there in the rain—outside it's weeping.

One of the other things that occurred was in the Clutter house. We were there shooting one night, it was November and very cold and blustery. The cast had a very difficult time. I said to the man who played Mr. Clutter, "Do you know how terrifying it is to wake up and a flashlight is shining in your eyes—and you cannot see who is behind that flashlight? That's terrifying." He said, "But I'd be able to see the other lights." I said, "No, we're shooting this entire sequence with flashlights." Now Connie [Conrad] Hall, our cameraman, said, "How the hell do you expect me to shoot this with just flashlights?

We won't get an image." So we had two special flashlights created—with several batteries—that gave us enough light and that was used as bounce light, but that was all; those flashlights lit the sequence.

We had lots of discussions about what induces fear. And for some people—it's just darkness. They learn that as children. But we'd discuss this—to generate for ourselves as well as for the picture an atmosphere of fear. Fear of what happens to a group of innocent people when their home is invaded—it's terrifying to be helpless. All of those feelings we tried to expose in this picture. Whether we failed or succeeded—I don't know. You'll have to ask yourselves.

I'd like to say something about this *kind* of movie. I don't think I could have gotten this movie made today, because we're now in a phase of moviemaking in which most of the major studios are looking for movies that will make them $100 million or $200 million in profits. Like *Star Wars* or *Empire Strikes Back* or *Raiders of the Lost Ark*. I don't know where it is written that every picture has to make $100 million. There aren't that many dollars in this country to begin with, and if you're going to make twenty pictures a year and each one of them is going to make $100 million—then you could take over the government. If every picture has to be that popular—we might miss many fine pieces of work. If you have the patience, you go to see some of these interesting pictures—they won't be the most popular pictures in the world. But maybe they have a thought or a seed that might be helpful—might open up your life a little bit. You might even get another look at yourself.

FROM AUDIENCE: What was Capote's reaction to the film?

BROOKS: Well, he didn't see a script and he knew he wasn't going to see one. He didn't see any parts of the picture at all until it was over. There was one time that we were shooting in the wheat fields of the Clutter farm, and Capote arrived from San Francisco with a planeload of people—there was an Italian television crew and a French television crew; *Look* magazine was there, and *Life* magazine was there. It was quite a group. I didn't know they were coming—I just got word from my assistant that there was a plane coming in with Mr. Capote and he had about twenty-five people with him. They had more cameras on the plane than we had on location. So he arrived, and he took over the town. Finally, he said, "Aren't you going to be shooting in the house? I told these people they could come over and make some shots there." I said, "Well, go in the house and make some shots." He said, "But *you*'re not going to shoot there while we're here?" I said, "No, Truman. You're a big, big star. You're bigger than the two boys and anything in the movie, you're bigger than all of us put together. You're a superstar. Your presence here right now is messing up the whole movie." He said, "Brooksie—you want me to go home? These people have come from all over the world—they want to write about the movie and take pictures." I said, "Yes, I know—take your pictures, but please go. Like tonight." And he said, "You don't like me?" I said, "I love you, Truman, but stop fucking up the movie—and go home." He said, "Okay, Brooksie." So they all got on the plane and took off. He was of great help in that respect. [Laughter]

FROM AUDIENCE: There does seem to be an imbalance in the presentation of the two men. I'm a lot more aware of what's going on with Perry [Robert Blake] than I am with Dick [Scott Wilson], especially in the childhood sequences. Was that a choice on your part?

BROOKS: No, that's the way the book was written. Mr. Capote's relationship with Perry was much closer than it was with Dick. They corresponded at great length. Anyway, Dick was not one to expose himself—he had many faces, many attitudes about life, but never his own. He assumed the coloration of wherever he was at the time. I never met either boy, I didn't come to Death Row there until after they were executed. But I think if you read the information in the book, there's much more information about Perry than about Dick. Dick had a sort of macho attitude, somewhat cavalier. When Wilson played it he gave it sort of a high-school simplicity, when he looked at the four detectives and said, "Glad to see ya." They were shocked; if he'd gone into some kind of diatribe they would have felt better. They felt guilty. I want all of us to feel a little guilty. Not only Jews should feel guilty—*everybody* has a right to feel guilty.

FROM AUDIENCE: You were talking about how the black-and-white film set a mood—and I think the musical score certainly did that too. It worked so magnificently.

BROOKS: You bet your life. It's a terrific score. And Quincy [Jones] is one of the most talented men I've ever worked with in my life. He's special, he really is. And he's an original—he's a classicist as well as a contemporary musician. And his score here has been copied many times by many people. It's amazing how much this music, especially the bass, plays as a complement to what's happening.

FROM AUDIENCE: You talk about wearing two hats—as a writer and director. When you write, do you think of what you're going to be doing as a director? Do you envision the closeups, for example?

BROOKS: Never, never. When writing—that's *it,* I don't see any people who are actors, I only see the characters in my mind as generally how they ought to look, how they ought to walk—how they feel. I'll think about whether they're going to be cracking their knuckles or whether their palms get wet or whether they just sweat on the upper lip. It's just visualization—but never dealing with shots. When I see a script that has *all* of the shots in the script—and I've begun to get them more and more—things like: "Fade in . . . we dolly in closer along the pavement to get the actor's pair of shoes— pan up to the man's trousers and up to his head, behind the right lens of his eyeglasses . . . looking through to see that he's near-sighted . . . then pulling back into a long zoom shot . . ." Well! *Where's the story?* Is this writer crazy? What are all these crazy mechanics? He doesn't even know what system we'll be shooting in. Is it going to be CinemaScope, where you have certain problems with lenses, and problems with composition? Is it going to be in color, in black and white? Forget about that stuff. That stuff comes when you get actors on a stage and you begin to walk through it— and suddenly it begins to have a life of its own, through these people. Then you begin to know—at least I do—where the camera should be, what size it should be. If you have a certain structure, you may be able to take a 28mm lens, but some others might not. That becomes very important. If I use a long lens—I won't see the person behind you in focus at all. So the lenses and the angles can be decided on only when you see a particular scene, where it's going to take place.

[After *Wrong Is Right*]

CRIST: Small doubt that we offered you a change of pace—both figuratively and literally. I find this movie very much in the *Dr. Strangelove* tradition—the heart of the matter is exactly the same— what has changed in eighteen years is the technology. There is the Swiftian notion that when a thinking man looks around at this world, he either screams or laughs. And perhaps this kind of laughter—which does fade as you get into the film—is the only reply to the world today. How did you come to *Wrong Is Right,* Richard?

BROOKS: This movie is an expression of the fact that the whole world is going crazy. And I'm right there with 'em, going crazy too. I don't know what to do about it. About three years ago, I had just finished a movie, and I looked around and thought, What would happen if the ultimate weapon fell into the hands of someone who was irresponsible, or insane—or who just wanted to go out of this world in a big splash? In front of the cameras, of course. Because the big countries just might not start an atomic war—though, right now, who knows? But if they don't, if they all want to be the good guys, they might very well hire a surrogate—such as a terrorist group—to do the job for them. And they would not be blamed. That's how the idea began.

To try to get the information—because I didn't know much about international terrorism at the time—I went to the Rand Corporation, which is a think tank, and talked to a man who was head of their department on international terrorism about what world conditions might be like a year or two in the future, because it was going to take that long to get the picture ready. I mean, I knew that terrorists were hijacking planes and shooting kneecaps in Milan. And the Baader-Meinhof gang is functioning together with a Red group from Japan, and so on. So I said, "What will it be like two years from now?" "Well," he said, "according to our estimates there will be a big change. Right now they're frightening everyone but not telling why they're doing it. In order to sell what they want to get across, they're going to begin to use the media." He wasn't talking about newspapers, which go into happenings with a cool, intellectual depth. What the terrorists want is an emotional response—that fear. They need a stage—and that would be television. I said, "Do you mean they're going to buy time?" He said, "No, they'll find out where events are taking place, and stage their protests where the television cameras are." And, of course, that's what began happening. An example of it was just recently—remember those fellows who jumped out of a truck in Cairo to assassinate President Sadat of Egypt? Afterward, they just stood there, waiting to die. So since I started writing this a few years ago, events have rapidly caught up to it. This movie is really saying, "Yes, we ought to be able to laugh at ourselves . . . *but,* we've got to look around before it's too late." And, God, I'm only thirty-nine, and I *love* this place. I love this world and want to enjoy it—I don't·want it blown up. That's one of the reasons I wanted to make the movie.

FROM AUDIENCE: When you killed off Katharine Ross—wow, I couldn't believe it. She was billed above the title and I thought she was the major star, but very quickly she disappears.

BROOKS: Yes, there's a reason for that, and I might as well tell you the reason. If you have someone such as Katharine Ross, who's the second famous name in the billing, and if she's gone from the movie in almost thirty minutes, then *everyone becomes vulnerable*. That was a very important factor in this dramatic structure—you should think it can happen to anyone. *As it can.*

FROM AUDIENCE: It seemed to me that the tone of the film hovered between Dr. Strangelovian satire and James Bond cartoon adventure, and I was never sure what way to respond to it. Secondly, the pace was fast, and I like that, but about one-third the way through the film I found the pace was *so* fast, I found myself not being able to understand the characters, or care very much about them.

BROOKS: Yes, as a matter of fact, Judith and I were discussing that at dinner just before the movie was run. I was concerned that there are certain audiences who will be "caught behind," because of the pace. The fact is that I tried to do this in this contemporary form of today—and tomorrow—where the eighteen-year-olds to the twenty-five-year-olds have become accustomed to watching prime-time television and have been battered by these consistent flashes that go through their mind, the volume of sound, all of that. I hope you have the patience to go back and see it a second time. I think it will be a lot more fun for you.

SAME AUDIENCE: Is this film then aimed at that younger audience?

BROOKS: No, it is aimed at everybody—I hope. It was done in this style because that's the style I feel is coming now.

FROM AUDIENCE: I just want to say that your satire as far as the networks are concerned is *not* satire. Inside, it's cuckoo land. And when you get into the power of these TV personalities . . . how can you satirize that?

BROOKS: I wasn't trying to satirize it at all. I was simply trying to state it. What I'm trying to do is say this is the way it is. When Dan Rather—who's a very fine reporter—climbs up a hill in Afghanistan and meets the rebel chief and says, "Hi, I'm Dan," and he's wearing a costume like Lawrence of Arabia—what the hell do you think that is? That's cuckoo land.

FROM AUDIENCE: Mr. Brooks, have you ever acted in a movie—or done an Alfred Hitchcock type walk-on?

BROOKS: No, I don't have that talent. I'm perhaps one of the few directors never to appear in a movie, although I was invited to act in one by Steven Spielberg. He said he wanted me to play General Joe Stillwell. I didn't know what movie he was talking about—it turned out to be *1941*. So, you see . . . Anyway, I can't act.

FROM AUDIENCE: Did you do the voice-over at the beginning of *Wrong Is Right?*

BROOKS: No, no, no . . . That was Sean Connery. All I did in *Wrong Is Right* is just say, "Special Report by Patrick Hale." But in *Sweet Bird of Youth* there was a newsreel that I narrated.

FROM AUDIENCE: In *Elmer Gantry* Burt Lancaster was more wonderful than usual. I wonder if you got that Academy Award–winning performance out of him by letting him do his own thing—or by telling him Randolph Scott was meant to have that role?

BROOKS: No . . . Burt is a very inventive actor, extremely facile. And he was at the top of his form at that time. He understood the part very well, and what I did with him was show him as much material as I could find, aside from the script itself, on the man after whom he was modeled—much more than the character in the book. I'm talking about Billy Sunday. There are some old newsreels on Billy Sunday. So Burt watched the old films, and he put together a combination of thoughts and ideas and energies. That's how it came about.

You know, in all the pictures I've made, I've never had trouble with a star or top player—or with extras. It's sometimes the people in the middle, and it all has to do with vanity, which is a very destructive element in the making of any movie. But no, I'm not responsible for Burt's great performance—he is.

FROM AUDIENCE: Mr. Brooks, I understand you started out as a screenwriter—writing *Key Largo* and some other of my all-time favorites. I was just wondering if it was difficult for you to become a director—and why did you want to do it?

BROOKS: Yes, it was difficult. In those days a screenwriter wasn't even allowed around the set. Of all the scripts I'd written, I'd never *seen* any being made. The first one I was allowed to see was *Key Largo,* and that's because John [Huston] had been a writer himself—and he taught me the need for rewriting. Which is of course the essence of making a movie anyway . . . rewriting and rewriting and rewriting and rewriting, until the picture's released. John said, "You can come on the set—they won't pay you, of course, but you can see how it's done—and we need some rewrites." That's how I first came on a set.

And here's a story: I said, "John, what will I do if I don't have John Huston to direct a script I've worked on?" He said, "Well, kid, you'll do it yourself." And I said, "Suppose they don't let me do it myself?" And he said, "Well, don't give them the script." The next thing I know, the cameraman comes over—he was a great cameraman, Karl Freund—and he says, in his heavy German accent, "My boy, you are going to be a director." I laughed and said, "I'd like to be . . . but?" He said, "I have for you your first lesson in directing." The next day he came in with a brown paper bag and inside were two small cans of 16mm film. He says, "You got projector? You run these pictures." So I took these two reels home and I put them on my 16mm projector—and here was a pornographic movie—the kind they made then where the men wore black socks and disguised themselves with painted mustaches. They were terrific! I ran them twice. Then I brought them back the next day and I said, "Karl, they're terrific." He said, "*I* make. I am *producer.* I am *director,* I am *writer.* I am *not* actor." I said, "That's fine. But what is the lesson in directing you want me to get?" He said, "Well, when you are directing, there will come times when you will say to yourself—should I put the camera maybe up there, and shoot down? Maybe I should put the camera under the table—and see the legs. Maybe I should be far, maybe I should be close. Where do I put the camera—to be different, to be exciting, to be entertaining? You'll think of this many times when you're directing." I said, "Yes?" He said, "You watched my film very closely?" I said, "Yes, yes." He said, "Well, when you make pictures and you run into this kind of problem of where to put the camera . . . remember one thing: *Get to the fucking point!*" [Laughter and applause]

If it hadn't been for Cary Grant I wouldn't have even become a director. I had written my first script at MGM and Mr. Mayer kept saying, "My boy, you're a writer. Do you know how great it is to be a writer? Why do you want to be a director?" But I had a contract with MGM that the first script I wrote for them I was to direct. I was told by the producer, Arthur Freed, that they had gotten Clark Gable to play the part. "So how could you expect to direct Clark Gable on your first movie? First of all, he wouldn't do what you told him." I said, "How do you *know?*" Freed said, "Don't make trouble—the next picture, you'll direct it." So Mervyn Le Roy directed that one—*Any Number Can Play*—and I started writing another script.

About seventy pages into it, I'm a little depressed so, as would sometimes happen, I decided to go out to the track. I was out there at the track and somebody introduced me to someone—I look around and there's Cary Grant. You know, *that's* how a director should look—like Cary Grant or Howard Hawks, but not like a monkey like me. Anyway, Grant seemed to recognize my name. He said, "Are you a writer?" I said yes. He said, "I just read something you wrote called *Crisis,* I think." I said, "Yes, but there's a problem with that, Mr. Grant, I want to direct it—and I just don't know what they're going to say." He said, "If the rest of the script is like this . . . hey, if you can write it, why can't you direct it? What you don't know—*I* know." Right there he said, "Let's do it." And *that day* I became a director.

FROM AUDIENCE: When you look for actors and actresses for particular roles, are you looking for a certain chemistry between people—or do you just select them and hope the chemistry happens? Sometimes it doesn't.

BROOKS: Oh yes, I've run into that. No, what I do is try to see their other work, then we'll talk. I try to find out what they feel about this sort of role, whether their understanding of it is similar to my own. It takes a lot of talking. Making tests to me means nothing. I may have a stupid cousin I could make a test with, and in three days I could make him look terrific. But I don't have three days to make every scene. I have maybe eighteen minutes to make one. If I ever do make a test I may put a thousand feet of film in the camera and just say, "Go ahead, do whatever you want to do—what I want to know is about you, the actor, and what your personality is. What makes you laugh or weep—or put the sparkle in the eye? How do you move?"

In the case of Geraldine Page, she didn't move well, I thought, as the movie star she was playing. So I asked her to go watch a movie for me—I had it run for her. It was *A Stolen Life*, where Bette Davis played two parts. Well, Geraldine could have been highly insulted that I asked her to see this. But she came back to the set and she said, "Don't say *anything*. That bitch can walk *away* from the camera and look like a star. I know what you mean. Don't worry." She was marvelous. She came down the stairs—like a movie star.

So, it's a combination of those factors and the pliability, the malleability within a person that permits that person to release themselves, to fulfill a character. Here's something I was talking to Judy about. Do you realize that the actors who play the *bad* guys on screen are usually *terrific* people—and they're unafraid to release whatever they have to release to play the bad-guy role? But the actors who play the *good* guys—they never could play a bad guy, because there's something inside of them they never want to reveal. I think maybe Gregory Peck is the exception—he's a terrific guy who's played a couple of bad guys.

FROM AUDIENCE: Are most directors paid on a straight salary, or commission or percentage—or a combination?

BROOKS: That depends. Most directors like to be paid immediately, because they don't trust the studios. I have a different deal—I don't take any money, just a piece of the picture, so that they'll let me alone. I invest *me*. The studio tries to get the money—then we'll see each other when the movie's over. But in that case they have to pay the minimum director's fee and the minimum writer's fee—which I think runs about $18,000 each for a feature film. That is deducted from the money I will get—if anybody ever buys a ticket. That's my way of working. But many kinds of deals are made.

FROM AUDIENCE: How involved are you in the editing of your films?

BROOKS: I am quite involved. I will work with the editor, we'll discuss a scene—work it over, find out what the intention was when I shot it, and so on. We don't begin to edit until I finish shooting. Not even an assembly of a film. I can't do both—it's impossible for me to do both at the same time. I'm usually rewriting every day. But editing is the final form of writing—after the filming. And the editing is vital. But to edit—just to put pieces of film together—is not enough. You should also have a story sense. If you don't, you are a mechanic. Editing is *vital*.

CRIST: As is the musical score. You've worked quite a bit with Quincy Jones—he did *In Cold Blood* and *$*. You told me how you work in adding the score to your films—can you go through that again?

BROOKS: I hear music all the time I'm writing and shooting. By the time we begin to assemble the movie the first time—we're putting sound in. We score the entire movie from records. We cannot use that score, of course. But I don't want the executives to see the assembly of the movie without music—a good dubbing job—no matter how many times they tell you, "Listen, I've been in the business for thirty years, for God's sake, I know how to look at a movie." Well, my father drove a car for thirty-five years and he was a lousy driver until the day he died. That doesn't mean anything. The executives are used to seeing completed movies—and that's the way they should see them, with sound—with music. So I score the whole movie—with all the cues.

Quincy, who's a remarkable composer, will then spend *hours* making tapes and asking me why I put this type of music in this scene, detailed questions, to find out exactly what I had in mind. And the music I picked for the first assembly—naturally I couldn't use that as a score—that would guide Quincy as to what I intended. He based his entire score for *In Cold Blood* on the bass, the instrument, which was quite marvelous.

Michel Legrand also has this marvelous capacity to find out what a scene's intention is. I worked with him on one movie—which was ignored throughout the world—but the score had a hit song that made the composers as much money, I guess, as any song they've ever done. The song was "What Are You Doing for the Rest of Your Life?" The movie was *The Happy Ending*, which was about the fact that maybe, for some people, marriage doesn't work.

CRIST: But like practically all of your movies, it was a little ahead of its time.

FROM AUDIENCE: I notice there's a tremendous advertising campaign now for *Wrong Is Right*.

BROOKS: There is? I'm glad to hear it.

SAME AUDIENCE: Yes, there are TV spots, and [Sean] Connery is on a lot of talk shows. When you make a percentage deal, do you make a commitment about how much they're going to put into advertising?

BROOKS: No, I don't have that much to do with that. They claim they know much more—and they probably do. I've no control. Sometimes they have the decency to consult or ask me about it, but never about how much advertising or where or whether it will be TV or radio or newspapers. No, I don't have the rights, and I don't really have the knowledge about marketing and public relations. That's what Ray Stark is supposed to be doing. He's a partner in this picture. He should know what to do with the picture, know what the markets are for it. Today, I hear they bring an audience in to see a picture and ask them to push a little button if they like certain scenes. How the hell are they going to get involved in a movie and push buttons at the same time? And preview cards— Columbus would still be in Spain if they waited for preview cards.

FROM AUDIENCE: How far down the list do you go in selecting your actors—I mean you choose the stars and supporting players, but do you get involved in casting the really small parts?

BROOKS: All the way. Even to the extras—we pay the extras an extra five dollars just to come in to be interviewed, because I believe actors are very important to a picture. I get along very well with extras, because I really believe they are actors. I caught an assistant director once saying, "Okay, we need some more bodies over here. . . ." When they took me off the ceiling, I couldn't wait to throw that guy off the stage. They're not *bodies,* they're people. Officers and titles and logos *do not* make movies. People make them. People in front of the camera, people behind the camera. *People make movies.* Not buildings, not slogans, not big limousines. People are important—and if we don't care about each other on the set, what the hell's the use of my making a movie where the [premise] is that I care about people? *And* . . . a movie doesn't exist until there are people out there watching it. Until an audience responds to a movie, there is no movie. I want to say that this weekend has been terrific, because I've received an education here from all of you. There's been as much input—well, *more* input from you to me than the other way. Because looking at your faces—I rarely see faces anymore. When I go to a movie I stand at the back and see backs of heads, I can't see how people react. But here, I can see the reaction in your faces. Especially when you're upset with me.

Richard Brooks's recent films are Wrong Is Right *(1982) and* Fever Pitch *(1985).*

Steven Spielberg

▼▼

Steven Spielberg has been making movies since he was a teenager in Arizona, and he was all of twenty-five when he directed his first theatrical feature, Sugarland Express, *in 1973. That was followed the next year by his first blockbuster,* Jaws, *and then in 1977 by* Close Encounters of the Third Kind. *In 1979 Spielberg encountered his first and, to date, only critical and box-office failure with the comedy* 1941.

Raiders of the Lost Ark, *directed by Spielberg from a story idea by his friend and fellow movie mogul George Lucas, became the box-office champion of 1981, and by the time Spielberg appeared at the Tarrytown weekend in September 24–26, 1982, it was clear that* E.T., *released three months earlier, would be the box-office champ of 1982 and, in fact, of all time.*

Spielberg also produced E.T., *and he has been a producer on several films directed by others, notably 1982's* Poltergeist *(directed by Tobe Hooper), on which he also served as co-screenwriter.*

[After *Amblin'* and *Duel*]

CRIST: I was thrilled by *Duel* when I saw it in 1971 on television, but seeing it now without commercial interruptions on a large screen is an entirely new experience. Tell us what you did in editing this for the theatrical print.

SPIELBERG: Well, with a television show, before each commercial there's a musical crescendo that's supposed to leave you hanging—and that introduces the commercial. All I did, very simply, was cut out all the commercials and take out the musical crescendos and put the pieces tightly together, that's it. But I also added about fifteen minutes of footage for the European release. In American television you have a seventy-four-minute film for a ninety-minute show, but in Europe they won't accept a theatrical film under ninety minutes, so I had to add about fifteen minutes.

CRIST: What were the scenes you added?

SPIELBERG: One of them I shot mildly under protest—where the driver calls his wife from a Laundromat. I didn't really want to show the wife, but I conceded to my producer, who thought it was very important to see some of the driver's home life, his wife, his kids playing with toys on the floor.

CRIST: Did you select the toys? I noticed there was a robot there.

SPIELBERG (laughing): Yes, toys are me.

CRIST: Can we go back a bit to talk about *Amblin'*?

SPIELBERG: Must we?

CRIST: Don't you want to? I think it was an absolutely charming film, and I wonder what inspired it.

SPIELBERG: Commerciality and the motion-picture business in Los Angeles. I wanted to be a movie director. [Laughing]

CRIST: You picked a lovely story that could be absolutely wordless.

SPIELBERG: That's because I couldn't afford sound. [Laughing]

CRIST: Now we know where all art comes from.

SPIELBERG: Right. The movie was made when I was a student at Long Beach, I was about eighteen and a half at the time. I wanted to shoot this in 35mm, because nobody was giving me the time of the day with my 16mm stuff. I had half a dozen of them, but producers would not sit down and look at that gauge. But they will take a 35mm home with them to watch in their fancy screening rooms. So I made this in 35mm; I wanted to tell the story of two kids who fall in love while hitchhiking—without exchanging anything verbal. We made the film for about $10,000 in ten days—in the worst time of the year: August, in Palm Desert, California. It was about hundred degrees plus out there. We had a big screening and the producer got his money out of it. He was a young guy, Denis Hoffman, who was hoping to become a professional producer; he had money and believed the short-form cinema was the best approach to busting into the movie business—as I did. We had a screening before a lot of industry people, but it was mostly casting directors who came. I didn't need casting directors. As a result, one of the actors in the film won an immediate contract. And by word of mouth, the guy who was head of Universal television, Sidney Sheinberg, saw the film and called me up to his office. He said he was very impressed with it, and asked if I wanted to come work there. I said, "Well, I haven't graduated yet." He said, "What do you want? Do you want to be a film director or do you want to get through college?" And I said, "College? What college?" [Laughing] So I signed a seven-year contract with Universal in 1969.

CRIST: Was *Duel* the next film you made?

SPIELBERG: No, I made *Night Gallery,* the first thing I did professionally. I went from Cal State at Long Beach to Stage 15 at Universal—where Joan Crawford met me at the door. She was in *Night Gallery.* After that came some episodic television shows—*Marcus Welby, M.D., Owen Marshall,* then *Name of the Game,* with Gene Barry. I also did the first *Columbo,* with Peter Falk and Jack Cassidy, the pilot. And that *Columbo* episode was what landed me *Duel.* It's a stepladder process—you're only as good as your last rung.

CRIST: I gather that *Duel* is based on an actual experience.

SPIELBERG: Yes, Richard Matheson wrote a short story for *Playboy* magazine called "Duel"—and I recall it was inspired by a real-life episode that happened to Richard in Colorado. A marauding truck driver who might have had too many No-Doz tablets just chased Matheson for twenty miles. Richard was forced to go from forty to sixty to eighty miles an hour—as fast as his car could go—in order to escape from the truck driver. Then he wrote the story for *Playboy.* My first secretary read the story, put it in front of me, and said, "You have got to make this movie, it would be a wonderful thing." That's how I got involved.

FROM AUDIENCE: If you could do anything differently now to re-make that movie—what would you do?

SPIELBERG: Well, I'd like to have about twenty-five more shooting days so I could plane the edges of the entire movie—which are full of splinters. I shot the movie in fourteen days, which is not a lot of time, considering all the coverage of the truck, of the car. We probably shot the film on a fifteen-mile stretch of highway, and what took the time was we had to turn the car and truck around, then turn them around again for take two. There were very few take twos. If I had to do it over again, I would do it for the motion-picture screen, not the television screen. This is to say, I'd make it a little tougher, I'd take all the narration out, all of Dennis Weaver's inner monologues and probably most of the dialogue and try to make it one of the first silent movies since . . . Gance's *Napoleon.* I objected to the amount of dialogue the network imposed on the show. They forced the pro-ducer, George Eckstein, and the writer, Richard Matheson, to keep adding narration internalizing Dennis Weaver so the audience would understand his deepest fears. I don't believe you need that.

CRIST: I would think that on television you do need it, because of the distraction of the interruptions, but certainly not theatrically. Weaver always struck me as a very good choice for this—I find him an extremely interesting actor, very versatile—and I thought he could have done all this silently.

SPIELBERG: Yes, because he's so expressive. I remember him best from *Touch of Evil,* where he played the insomniac day manager of that motel out in the desert. He has a wonderful, almost a Japanese attitude toward acting—out of the Kabuki school, if you really let him go. He's a wonderful guy to work with and he was so *into* the driving of the car he'd rarely let a stunt man get behind the wheel; he wanted to do it all himself.

CRIST: How much of the truck driver did you want to let us see? Would you have been happier if we had not seen him at all?

SPIELBERG: You barely see a hand signaling Dennis Weaver to pass. Or when you see a shadow in the cockpit of the truck, this is a kind of esoteric reality. But *never* to identify whether the driver is human or nonhuman—that would, I think, push the film into a type of science fantasy.

CRIST: It's such a remarkably ugly truck.

SPIELBERG: There's an interesting story behind that truck. We had a casting call for trucks. Absolutely true. On the back lot the production manager lined up about ten trucks for me to choose from. I felt so powerful walking along, kind of like Field Marshal Rommel reviewing his panzer corps. This was the smallest truck of all the semis on the back lot—the smallest one, but the only one that had a great snout. I thought that with some remodeling we could really get it to look human. I had the art director add two tanks to both sides of the doors—they're hydraulic tanks, but you ordinarily wouldn't have two. They were like the ears of the truck. Then I put dead bugs all over the windshield so you'd have a tougher time seeing the driver. Dead grasshoppers in the grill. And I gave the truck a bubble bath of motor oil and chunky-black and crud-brown paint. It layered, bubbled, and pocked in the sun and eventually hardened. That was its makeup for the rest of the movie. Then we added a half dozen license plates so you would perhaps assume that this truck had dueled with many cars across six to eight states.

FROM AUDIENCE: Did you have to re-create the truck to film the additional scenes?

SPIELBERG: Yes, because we destroyed the truck in the first twelve days. Then I had two days to shoot fifteen minutes—to make a length acceptable to Europe—so once again we went back to cast the truck. And we were so lucky. We found the *same* truck, the only difference was there was more space between the cab and the trailer—almost three feet—it's very noticeable. Also, we were told we couldn't wreck this truck, because it had a good engine and was a relatively new vehicle that had just been overhauled.

FROM AUDIENCE: Roads seem to play a very important part in some of your films. Is this happenstance or on purpose?

SPIELBERG: That's an interesting question, because I've always thought that good stories always take place on a highway—a written and structured highway that transports you somewhere. You have a suspicion of where it's going to take you and you can't wait to find out, but there's so much fun along the way you almost hate to get to the end of the road. I really like that whole concept, that linear, straight-arrow approach to telling a story on film.

FROM AUDIENCE: Who did the *Psycho*-like music for the truck scenes in *Duel*?

SPIELBERG: Billy Goldenberg. It's a compelling score because it was all performed with African instruments. The whole orchestra consisted of eight players, and most of them had been raised on these instruments. Billy was putting together a group and he got these artists in to play, and a lot of the music was *not* written—a lot of it was improvised right there to the movie screen.

FROM AUDIENCE: Were they actually driving that fast in the picture, or is the camera undercranking?

SPIELBERG: For about half the picture the camera undercranks twenty frames, occasionally eighteen frames. A couple of those shots look kind of phony, because the speed ran away. Sometimes your crystal synch motor doesn't keep synch and the motor slows to twelve or maybe ten frames. There're a few shots I had to use because I had only so many days for the initial version, I couldn't really cover myself, even though some of the shots of the cars were almost too fast. In the other half of the film the cars are moving at normal speed. We had a camera car that was an amazing device, first used in the film *Bullitt*. It was a made-over Corvette with the fiberglass body removed and the cameras mounted very, very low, three to four inches off the ground. Just by being low to the ground you get an amazing sense of speed and velocity—you can't get that sense from up high looking down, only from low gazing up. And more important, that angle gave the truck some Godzilla proportions. We also had a camera mounted on the top of the truck, with the widest distortion lens—I think about a 9.5 fish-eye lens.

FROM AUDIENCE: In *Amblin'* they seem to fall in love in a drainage ditch, which looks a lot like the drainage ditch in which E.T. almost dies. Was there a reason for that?

SPIELBERG: There are just . . . thousands of drainage ditches around the country. They're hard to avoid sometimes. You're seeing things I never noticed—that's also very interesting, I knew there was a drainage ditch there but I hadn't made a connection. Listen, I'll be very honest, I'll not bullshit any of you about the symbolism I intended. If I intended it, I'll tell you.

CRIST: When you watch a number of films by the same director, some very odd things come out. When John Schlesinger was here, someone asked him why his movies always had funeral scenes. And it had never occurred to him, but there was a funeral in every one of his films. It happens, but he really didn't have a fix on funerals.

FROM AUDIENCE: Did you have a good sense of the structure in *Duel* before you shot it, or did you build it, and build the tension, in the editing?

SPIELBERG: Well, it's a combination of both, because for one thing, the short story in eighteen pages in *Playboy* was fraught with tension. I was very lucky to find a good piece of material that already had that suspense. But of course you can blow the suspense. A lot of the movie was story-boarded, but not like I usually story-board in the conventional sense, with drawings of little squares representing shots. This was story-boarded from an overview. I had an artist paint an entire map, as if a helicopter camera had photographed the entire road where the chase was taking place. And then that entire map had little sentences—like, "This is where the car passes the truck," or "This is where the truck passes the car and then the car passes the truck." And I was able to wrap this map around the motel room, and I just crossed things off. When we were shooting, I'd try to progress eight or ten inches on the map—sometimes two feet if we had an exceptionally good day—until the entire map was shot. That overview gave *me* a geographical sense, a lot of help in knowing where to spend the time, where to do the most coverage, where to make a scene really sing out.

FROM AUDIENCE: Was any thought given to another ending?

SPIELBERG: Yeah, there were a lot of ideas—especially from ABC. In the script, the truck explodes. I thought that was too easy. We've all seen things explode—it's almost symbolic to the climax of an exciting chase. I thought it would be much more interesting to show the truck expiring, slowly ticking away—the truck's a nasty guy, you want to see him twisting slowly, a cruel death. I just took it upon myself. I thought, I'm the director so I can change the script. I just won't blow the truck up. Well, when the network saw the film, all they kept saying was, "It's in your contract to blow the truck up, *read* your contract." George Eckstein, our producer, had to stay in the shark tank a long time with these folk. I waited outside. In television I took a not very active part in producing my own shows. But he was very strong and he talked them out of forcing Universal to force me back out to blow the truck up.

FROM AUDIENCE: Is it more difficult to make a movie like *Duel*— and even *Amblin'*—without dialogue? Isn't that more of a challenge to the director?

SPIELBERG: No, for me it's a lot more fun. I really prefer to make movies that tell a story by what you visualize and what you feel and what you *sense*. Having characters sit across the table from each other and talk . . . I mean, I loved *My Dinner with André*, but you'd probably never catch me making a movie like that.

CRIST: At the time you did *Duel*, you didn't have much freedom of choice, did you?

SPIELBERG: I think that I probably had more freedom than other directors who first get started in episodic television, because I "camera-cut" most of my films, so film editors have no idea how to put together my stuff without my being there. It would be really hard to turn over the unedited pieces of one of my movies to a stranger and ask him to make some sense out of it. That's what William Wellman did on *Wings* to save his job. When the investors wanted to fire him for being so far over schedule, he just quit—and they went to put the film together and couldn't do it, so they had to hire him back a couple of days later. They came to his house and begged him. Wellman told me that story himself a few years before he died.

CRIST: To each his job security.

SPIELBERG: Right. But in television I think there's not that much concern about what the director is doing as long as he comes in on budget and on schedule. If you're a good boy and deliver a movie— economically—well, then, visually, you can probably do anything you'd like.

CRIST: How did you come to *Sugarland Express*?

SPIELBERG: Well, I wrote the story for *Sugarland,* based on a story from the newspapers. It was about a husband and wife attempting to recapture their little boy from the child welfare bureau and foster parents in Texas. I began to research it and thought this would be a marvelous human interest story on which to base a first feature film.

CRIST: We're all going to see *Sugarland Express* tomorrow morning, but tonight, of course, we'll see—again—*Close Encounters*. Are there any questions any of you want to ask Steven before you see it?

FROM AUDIENCE: In the Special Edition of *Close Encounters,* you made lots of scene changes. I'm curious about why you cut a couple of scenes—one in the electric company. And why did you cut the scene at the press conference, in which the Air Force was denying that UFO's exist?

SPIELBERG: I also cut part of Richard Dreyfuss's crazy "gardening" in the backyard—these were excised because I always felt the second act was the weakest area of my movie, and I tried very, very hard to fix the second act after the first sneak preview—but I simply didn't have the time, because my sneak was very late and the movie was already committed to hundreds of theaters across the nation. There was just no time—it was a work-in-progress that I literally had to abandon. And, despite the phenomenal success of the film, I had no satisfaction, as a filmmaker; that was not the movie I had set out to make. So when the film was a big hit, I went back to Columbia and said, "Now I want to make the movie the way I would have if I'd had those few extra months. I need another million dollars to shoot some added footage." Those added scenes were in the original script, by the way, not just scenes I concocted for the Special Edition, but they were scenes that became expendable when the budget became inordinate. The scenes you mention that were deleted were compromises that I believe thoroughly balance the second act, creating more of a rhythmic parallel between the François Truffaut story and the Richard Dreyfuss story. Almost every other scene is a juxtaposition between the domestic suburban story and the government cover-up story.

FROM AUDIENCE: The final scenes in the Mothership—were they in the original script as well?

SPIELBERG: No. That was something I wanted to do. I was really curious about what the inside of the Mothership was like, myself—I wanted to see it. So . . . I built it.

FROM AUDIENCE: Do you think it worked?

SPIELBERG: No. If I had a *Special* Special Edition, I think I'd cut it out.

FROM AUDIENCE: How did those five musical notes in *Close Encounters* evolve?

SPIELBERG: Out of about four thousand notes that John Williams played with one finger. He was sitting there for six hours saying, "You like this? How about this?" He wrote down five-note combinations almost the entire day. We kept finding combinations we liked—we narrowed them down to a hundred, then to fifty, then down to twenty-five. He had guests come over and he played the themes for his guests. We finally narrowed it down to two or three—I like the combination we selected. Because the notes [he whistles the *Close Encounters* theme] do not make a complete statement, you expect the music to continue. We needed some kind of combination that solicited a response.

[After *Night Gallery* and *Sugarland Express*]

CRIST: I might remind you that Steven was only twenty-five years old when he made *Sugarland Express*. It was my feeling that this movie was a critical but not a popular success, and you were telling me earlier about some of the reactions to it at the time.

SPIELBERG: When I first sneaked the move in San Jose, the audience loved it, and they were really with it. But in the last fifteen or twenty minutes, of course, you can hear a pin drop. All the preview cards came back and we sat in the corner and read them. Almost everyone commented at how devastated they were when the boy was shot and killed. And then, of course, the audience really turned on the Goldie Hawn character. Some people were actually offended that Goldie Hawn was in this sort of movie, because they'd rather see her in a light comedy. I disagree, but that's how most of the preview audience in San Jose felt. Of course the picture opened and closed in about three weeks. There are ten thousand screens in the U.S., and this movie played on only three hundred—which was sort of a shame.

CRIST: It really is a shame, because I certainly feel it is an extraordinarily true statement about ourselves and our values, and it also has the courage, from the filmmaker's standpoint, not to have everybody live happily ever after. To me, Goldie Hawn had been just a *Laugh-In* performer—but this movie gave me an inkling of her true potential.

FROM AUDIENCE: How did you know she'd be capable of doing this role?

SPIELBERG: I didn't know. What happened was, this was my first feature and the executives at Universal said, "We'll let you make this movie, but first you have to get a producer who knows how to

produce—we don't want to trust you with the producing chores."
So we got the script to Dick Zanuck and David Brown, who liked
it. Now I had my strong producing team. Next, they expressed
anxiety about my directing my first feature—without a movie star.
They said get a movie star. I had about seven or eight really pointless lunches with movie stars, who were very happy to read the
script and sit down and talk with me. But they all said no, this
wasn't their cup of anything. Then I got the idea of Goldie for the
girl—I always thought she *was* a dramatic actress, for she took her
comedy very seriously. So I met with her—we had a great afternoon—and you could tell she was thousands of kilowatts smarter
than the people of *Laugh-In* had ever allowed her to demonstrate.
She understood the script, she understood the role. Most of her
relatives came from Texas, so she could do the accent without much
effort. Well, the studio was ecstatic! She had just won an Academy
Award for Best Supporting Actress [in *Cactus Flower,* 1968]. Of
course, she cost more than all the police cars and a lot of the other
production values. I made the picture for about $2 million, and out
of that $300,000 was Goldie's salary. Today that's a low figure for
a star. In 1973 that was plenty!

FROM AUDIENCE: The music is phenomenal. How did you come up
with it?

SPIELBERG: Well, I've been collecting sound tracks since I was about
nine years old. My first sound track album was something called
Destination Moon. I've been collecting sound tracks ever since I can
remember—I've traded with people all over the world. I love doing
that—and I used to make my 8mm home movies when I was a kid
by taking the sound track from some score like *The Great Escape*
or *Spellbound* and inventing a movie *to the music.* The music always came first—the music always inspired me to tell a story and I
could use the sound track as like a post-synch. What happened was
that I became very familiar with John Williams when I heard two
scores—one called *The Reivers* and another score he did, which
was unfortunately never published but I have a tape, also from a
Mark Rydell film, *The Cowboys.* Two wonderful Americana scores.
When I heard both scores I had to meet this modern relic from a
lost era of film symphonies. John viewed my rough cut and decided
to score the picture. I wanted a real Aaron Copland sound for my

first movie. I wanted eighty instruments, a colossal string section. But John politely said no, this was for the harmonica—and a very small string ensemble. He was right on.

FROM AUDIENCE: Do you enjoy writing as much as directing?

SPIELBERG: No, I can't stand writing. I have to do it, but I have a real hard time with it. I do it in order to communicate what I really feel personally. I've had such a happy experience working with Melissa Mathison on *E.T.* and communicating through her all my ideas about *E.T.* In most cases, when I sit down with a writer and say, "I have an idea," it never turns out quite right. It has happened every time I've had an original idea and sat with a writer, and eventually I have had to return to the electric keyboard and just do a whole new movie—usually from scratch. I do this because I find some of my ideas are not so easily expressed on liquid paper.

FROM AUDIENCE: Your short scenes with that baby captured the real essence of a two-year-old. All performances you get from children are so natural—what's it like to work with kids? How do you do it—how many takes did it take to get that scene with the dog in *Sugarland*?

SPIELBERG: Well, first of all, that baby was the producer's son, Harrison Zanuck. Dick was with me one day when I was looking at kids, and he said, "Why don't you give my son a try?" So, I said, "Sure, Dick, anything you want." Harrison had a great laugh, just a wonderful laugh. And what I did with Harrison—I had seen him play with the dog between setups—I gave him a piece of cake, and I just let him play with the dog and let the film roll. That's when you burn film—the kid does nothing but play in the grass, and off-camera there are hundreds of technicians throwing the dog into the picture to give Harrison a chance to feed it. Well, the dog got close to Harrison and he gave him a little piece of cake and he began to say, "Doggie, doggie," as he was feeding the dog. For some reason Harrison Zanuck was terrified of Louise Latham, who played his foster mother—although he loved Merrill Connelly, who played the foster father.

CRIST: I wondered why the father kept carrying the baby around.

SPIELBERG: Exactly! So I had Louise come and take Harrison away from the dog—which doubled his anguish. He burst into tears and kept screaming all the way into the house. The second time she took him from Merrill—when the reporters are talking to them at the doorway—she says, "He's our baby now," taking the baby away from Merrill. And, of course, Harrison, on cue, bursts into tears. That's not me being a good director, that's me being a bad baby-sitter.

FROM AUDIENCE: Referring back to your feelings about scripting, you've been involved in two projects with Larry Kasdan—were you attracted to those two projects because of the strengths of the script? I don't believe you were involved in writing them.

SPIELBERG: I found Larry through his screenplay *Continental Divide*. On *Raiders*, I introduced Larry to George [Lucas]—we both hired Larry—and he worked very, very closely with an outline George had written on his own. Then George and Larry and I essentially made up the rest of the movie. There was a very good structure going in and some good characters that George had told me about that first got me interested in the project. At this point in Larry's career he was shy, reserved, maybe even a bit intimidated. He sat there making notes for about five days. Then he went away and one day returned with a marvelous first-draft screenplay.

FROM AUDIENCE: Getting back to *Sugarland Express,* which I think is such a good film, is there a chance for a rerun in the theaters?

SPIELBERG: Actually, no. The film has already been on free TV. Probably more people have seen *Sugarland Express* than many profit movies—because on TV we got a very good rating—because of Goldie, I assume. We earned something like a twenty-five or thirty share. I think that represents almost 30 million viewers. So, with the average ticket price $3.50 times 30 million . . . [Laughter] More people saw *Sugarland* on TV than probably saw *Close Encounters* in theaters.

CRIST: After *Sugarland* you then continued with Zanuck and Brown to do *Jaws.* Which brings up the writing question. If I were teaching film courses on how to write adaptations, to me *Jaws* is one of the most stunning examples of a film based on the right *filmic* pieces of a book. I thought the selections made from the book were superb. Can you tell us a little bit about the development of this script? Was it true, as we heard at the time, that this was being done page by page?

SPIELBERG: Yes, that's true—page by page. When I came on the project I asked Dick and David if they would grant me two wishes, as actual conditions for my doing the film. One was that I didn't want to show the shark until much later in the movie. The book introduces the shark in the first few pages—he's described in detail. And then the shark becomes a major character. I thought Jaws would be more menacing as an invisible idea. Second, I wanted to lose the love triangle between the ichthyologist and the then-cuckolded husband and his wife. And Peter Benchley was very happy to make these changes; he didn't feel we were collapsing the dynamics of his novel. Peter was great. However, he just didn't like writing in Los Angeles. He would go to his home in the East and write. Also, Peter had contracted another novel to write, *The Deep.*

So when Peter finished second drafts he departed and I was holding a script that I was not quite ready to shoot. David Brown suggested a writer, a guy named Howard Sackler, who had written *The Great White Hope,* and David said jokingly this movie is about a Great White Shark—so why don't we hire Sackler?

So Howard came for a meeting and he was great: we analyzed the book and we picked out the four or five elements that made the book so enthralling—especially the last hundred pages. And then we wrote an original screenplay to fit the last one hundred pages of the novel, but I still wasn't satisfied because, like Peter, Howard had another commitment. So about four weeks before we began shooting, I went to New York City and checked into a hotel and wrote my own version, a one-hundred-and-twenty-page rewrite of Howard's rewrite of Peter Benchley's. It made it a tiny bit better, but I still wasn't enthusiastic about *Jaws*; there were great gaping holes. No character development; you didn't like the people very much. I knew what I needed to do was cast the movie and do something that is very frightening to me—which I understand Bob Altman does quite a lot—you subjugate absolute control to meaningful collaboration; everybody gets into a room to determine jointly what kind of movie we are going to make here. Is it going to be a picture about the shark—or about the heroes who kill the shark? I hired a man named Carl Gottlieb, who was an old friend of mine, and he came with me to Martha's Vineyard essentially to polish the script as the actors sat with me every night—often only twenty-four hours before the shot—and *improvise.*

[After *Jaws*]

CRIST: It's really amazing . . . the most horrifying shot in the entire movie, to me, is seeing the corpse in the window of the sunken boat. So I see this for the third time; I've set myself for it, I know it's going to happen—but it's still scream time. Is that kind of terror produced only in the editing? How does one get the right psychological moment—and just hit the right nerve?

SPIELBERG: Well, the shot you're talking about, when Ben Gardner's head appears out of the hole, this *wasn't* an accident, it *wasn't* in the editing. What happened was this: I previewed the picture in Dallas without that sequence, but instead another shot in which Dreyfuss goes under the ravaged boat with his flashlight, shines the light into a gaping hole, and there is this face staring back at him. The flashlight catches the face. In Dallas this sequence received no reaction—none at all. It was telegraphed by the duration of the shot itself—you knew something was going to happen because Richard was going into a black hole. I expected a scream there, too, but it didn't happen in Dallas. So when I got back from the preview I went into my film editor's swimming pool and I set up the whole shot again, with the same head, a section of the boat—with Carnation milk and bits of aluminum foil to pollute the chlorinated water so that it would look more like silt in the ocean. And I did this sequence about twenty times—twenty shots with different timings, with Richard arriving at an empty hole and then unexpectedly the head races out at him, sometimes with the head coming out and then Richard arriving, sometimes a dual arrival, other times about half a second apart, other times just a fraction of a second apart. Sometimes I had Richard arriving at the hole and looking over his shoulder and suddenly hearing a noise, then out comes the head . . . I did it so many different ways.

Maybe thirty takes later I selected five that I imagined might be pretty scary for an audience, and I invited about thirty people to a screening of just that single scene. They had no idea what *Jaws* was, just that it was a best-selling novel and I had been a hundred days behind schedule filming it. These were unsuspecting sound men and music cutters, people in editorial—a bunch of postproduction folk from Universal. They all came into the screening room, and I put my secret choice at the head of the reel—followed by four other choices. They reacted differently every time. First time they screamed and jumped out of their seats. The second time, no reaction at all, and I figured that was because now they knew what was coming. But the third time—just because of the sheer timing of the face appearing in the hole of the boat—that third choice got a better reaction. I wound up previewing the movie again in Los Angeles and that single moment produced the loudest scream. What it is . . . it's the tension of knowing there's something in the water, and you know we're not going to take you underwater and show you yet another red herring—not at this point in the picture. Somehow, psychologically, everybody knows that now and finally something is going to happen—but what it is and precisely when it is, that's up to me. That's what makes it fun to make movies: *I* know and you don't.

FROM AUDIENCE: Did you plan to have that loud chord of John Williams's music as part of the scare?

SPIELBERG: That's part of the scare. The chord, of course, comes after the face comes out. First you react to the face, then the chord comes a fraction of a second later. It's very easy to scare people with noise, to lift you from your chair with a loud sound. John Carpenter does it with his films all the time. Billy Friedkin did it in *The Exorcist,* with the bureau drawers opening—it wasn't so scary to hear the drawers opening, but he had the volume turned up all the way, and you jumped out of your seats when you heard it in Dolby Stereo. That's one way of doing it, but I think another interesting way is to let the assault come for your eyes.

FROM AUDIENCE: I love what you did with color—the way everyone on the beach was bathed in pink—right after you first see blood in the water.

SPIELBERG: You know, to get the ocean to run red with blood takes approximately a hundred times more blood than the human body contains, because the ocean dissipates it so quickly. We were putting in a kind of tempera solution with an oil base—just so it would create a slick. But even though it was oil-based phony blood, it still was swallowed by the ocean. We could *not* get the deep red that I wanted, that was impossible, because you only get a kind of pink quality. Actually, if I had to do this movie over again, I'd probably spend more time with the lighting. We had so much trouble making this movie, we never waited for the right photographic moment. Sometimes the scene would be backlit, the sun behind you; just as often the sun would flat-light everybody, from the front; there was no continuity to the color of the water. The water goes from gray to black to yellow only because the sky kept changing. I was ready to shoot only when the special effects were ready for us—whether the sea was choppy or slack when special effects said the shark was ready, I'd go for it.

As you probably read in the newspapers, the shark rarely worked on cue. We all knew it, the people who built the shark knew it, the shark himself knew it. Walter Cronkite became a good friend—he lived on the Vineyard and he'd taken a month off just to go boating, and he'd come on the set all the time. One day he saw a shark test; the shark was supposed to leap out of the water and jump onto the boat, but something happened underwater with the hydraulic platform and the shark got twisted around on its cable and came up tail first—it was pure humiliation! Walter turned to me and said, "Have you ever considered a career in broadcasting?"

CRIST: I think that some of the crudities of this film help make it more effective. There's not an arty moment in it. What I really like about *Jaws* is that it's so linear; it doesn't stop for anything. When I read the book, which was just before the movie opened, I was really struck with admiration because Benchley managed to make something hefty out of something very slim—with all the romance, the political complications with the town board, and so on—which made it a very good read for on the beach. To me, really good horror is always done in bright sunlight. The beach people in the movie are so colorful, and so beachy—when terrible things are happening a hundred yards away—that it intensifies the horror. Maybe if you did it over you might inject a note of artiness or portent or something—which could be totally irrelevant to this movie.

SPIELBERG: You're right, I would really ruin this movie on the second try. You should never really overcook—when people taste it and say it's pretty good, simply ask them if they want seconds.

CRIST: I've been meaning to tell you that I think you did improve *Close Encounters* with some of the added scenes. But, if you do it for a third time, please don't let us into that damned mother ship. What we imagine in there is so much better.

SPIELBERG: Well, what you saw was sort of like the Hyatt Regency. I've stayed there so many times, I know what it looks like inside.

CRIST: It's one of the perennial questions—what would you do if you could do something over again?

SPIELBERG: With *Jaws* I'd work more on the shark, so that, even by the end of the movie, you still wouldn't view him as clearly. Because even if that was a real shark twenty-five feet long, you wouldn't believe a shark could get that big. I remember I asked my art director to paint three sharks—full size to scale on three pieces of drafting paper. I said, "Make an eighteen-foot shark, make a twenty-six-foot shark, and do a thirty-six-foot shark." Now, the eighteen-foot shark looked like a normal shark that would have been in a real Jacques Cousteau documentary. And the thirty-six-foot shark looked like a Japanese horror film—it really did. We stood there and said, "Oh, God, would anybody believe this?" Of course they wouldn't. The difference of ten feet is the difference between a movie that is semiplausible and a movie that is science fiction. The twenty-six-foot size is just right, but I would have preferred to keep it under water a few more inches—for a few minutes longer.

FROM AUDIENCE: At the time you did *Jaws,* both Richard Dreyfuss and Roy Scheider were relatively unknown. Is there some reason you went with them rather than a box-office star?

SPIELBERG: Yes, it's the same reason I don't go with box-office stars for most of my movies—with the exception, perhaps, of *Sugarland.* I had an original cast in mind for *Jaws,* and most of them were movie stars. I did try for Lee Marvin; he was my first choice for Quint, but he wanted to go fishing for real; I didn't pursue that idea of getting stars, because I think it's really important when you're watching a movie that you don't sit there and say, "Oh, look who's in this picture. What was his last picture, wasn't that a good one? Didn't you just love her in such and such . . . ?" I'm not saying I'll never work with a Robert Redford or a Paul Newman or a Burt Reynolds—I would certainly love to. I'm saying that for certain special types of movies, where half the struggle is verisimilitude, if Burt Reynolds had played Richard Dreyfuss's part, there would have been too much imagery of Burt in other movies, with fast cars, attractive women, and blazing action. In my opinion it takes ten to fifteen minutes for the memory to overcome the record of one's past. I had two producers who really gave me my head. Anything I wanted to do was fine with them. They agreed that we should not go after the half-million-dollar players, but should get good people who would be good actors in the right part and would be semianonymous.

FROM AUDIENCE: You're really a great spinner of yarns. I'm wondering where you got that quality, that interest in telling a story as best as you can.

SPIELBERG: I don't know if that is something you grow up with when your parents teach you to read—by having stories read to you. My father was a great storyteller, and my grandfather was amazing. I remember hearing stories from him when I was four or five and I'd be breathless, sitting on the edge of his knee. My grandfather was from Russia, and most of the stories were very indigenous of the old country. I've always enjoyed telling stories—I was a great storyteller in Boy Scouts; I used to sit around the camp fire and scare forty Scouts to death with ghost stories. I don't know if that's missing today: do parents sit down and tell their kids the stories they remember or imagined? If I had kids I would, I'd fill their minds with fictitious nonsense—I think that's healthy for young people.

FROM AUDIENCE: Going back to *Close Encounters,* how did you choose Truffaut?

SPIELBERG: Well, I *wrote* the movie for François Truffaut—never having met him, and never believing he would say yes. When I was at the typewriter I used him as a role model—he's angelic, he's benevolent, he's benign, he's good with kids—he *is* a kid, that's always who the Lacombe character was for me. I never imagined he would say yes. I went to everybody else—I had meetings with Lino Ventura, Trintignant, and we had contact with Yves Montand, a lot of different people—a lot of whom, surprisingly enough, wanted more money than Richard Dreyfuss was asking. Then I finally said to heck with it, I'll call Truffaut—maybe he knows who I am. I had no idea how much he knew about American filmmakers—I knew he knew Hitchcock. Anyway, I got his phone number from a friend in Paris and called him, timing it so it was breakfast time for him. His secretary said he'd love to talk to me, so he got on an extension phone and his secretary, who spoke English, interpreted for us. I introduced myself, in French, and his secretary said to me, in English, "Yes, yes, he knows you from *Duel.*" I was really knocked out by that—and there we were talking about *Duel* over the telephone.

We talked about ten minutes before I got around to saying, "Listen, this is a strange request, but I'd love for you to consider performing a major part in my new film; I'd like to send you the script." He said, "Send it immediately, I can't wait to read it." I sent it to him, and it was the fastest response I've ever had from an actor—he got back to me by telex about forty-eight hours after receiving the screenplay, saying, "I'd love to play the part of Monsieur Lacombe; here's the number of my manager to make the agreement." I couldn't believe it. We had *François Truffaut*. A month later he came to L.A. for costume fittings and we met for the first time. I asked him, "Did you understand the script, the French translation, and do you understand the story I want to tell?" He said, "Yes, the French translation was very, very good, but I do not know what this movie is—or what it's about." He said, "You must tell me someday, when you have time. . . . I am only concerned with Mr. Lacombe. I want to be a good Lacombe for you—I don't care to know the story, or what you're trying to say, what the meaning is—I just want to be a good actor for you." Months later we were in the middle of shooting in Mobile, Alabama, where our base of operations was, and he was then editing, I believe, *Small Change,* and he was also writing his next movie—he was doing ten things at the same time. I went over to him and said, "Why are you really in this picture?" He said, "I'll tell you—I'm writing a book called *The Actor* and I'd be a hypocrite if I had never been an actor for another director."

FROM AUDIENCE: I was fascinated by your use of music as a means of communication in *Close Encounters,* between the aliens and the earth people. Did you have in mind what they were trying to say?

SPIELBERG: First I had a mathematical equation—I had some help on this and even I can't explain it now. But it was a kind of Morse code. I felt this should be expressed musically, not in beeps or squeaks, so I rearranged the story so it would be more of an emotional communication, between the species of man and the aliens. These scientists were going to go over those tapes someday and realize they have nothing on them but music, and it's not going to mean anything more than what you heard and what you interpreted from your vantage point. After billions of years in the solitude between the stars, two planets meet and sing hello. I've always been fond of the idea of opera, and I've always felt if you have something to say you should sing it with great bravura. I wanted both *Close Encounters* and *E.T.* to be a little bit operatic—I wanted them to gush, so to speak. Sometimes I think that to make a point in film you have to make your point stronger than you would in real life; I feel I can reach more people by being a little more over-the-top with the music and the feelings—especially in *Close Encounters*. There are so many reactions at the ending of *Close Encounters*. I wanted to hold on the faces of the technicians. What are they thinking? Do they want to go on the ship with Dreyfuss? Are they relieved they're not going? What's going on inside them right now? It could have been half again as short—the end of *E.T.* could easily have been trimmed by two minutes. But I just felt I wanted faces to say it all. I like World War II train-station good-byes—remember how long those good-byes were in railroad stations in all those World War II melodramas?

FROM AUDIENCE: In *Close Encounters*, why did the aliens take those people away for such a long time, then return them, only to exchange them for other people?

SPIELBERG: You understand that the returnees were all people who were abducted against their will, and the people who were going aboard the ship were a group of NASA-trained scientists, men and women. Then the other group who had the implanted thought were really the people the UFO-nauts wanted. They were the intended ones, the chosen few, to go aboard Mothership. The aliens didn't want the astronauts, that wasn't part of the plan. They had gone around sprinkling their little fairy dust on people to implant the image of the mountain so someday they'd see it on television and wander to that place in Wyoming and be accepted on board. *Their* choice; it was not supposed to be ours. Richard was maybe one of hundreds of people who were marked by a close encounter of the second kind, to take that journey. Of course during the making of the movie we joked around a lot about having people like Judge Crater or Amelia Earhart come off Mothership. And Glenn Miller.

FROM AUDIENCE: Can you describe your creative process? What goes on in your head?

SPIELBERG: Ohhh—you're asking me a *question*. Gee, I don't know . . . I don't know how many of you in the audience are in occupations where you are paid for creating something that didn't exist before you put your mind to it, not before you put a lot of money into technology to help you create it. It can be as simple as writing a story—where once there was a void, and now there is an idea. Everybody has experienced that wonderful feeling of finishing a story and saying, "Gee, this is terrible, but I did it and it's done."

The struggle you have in the process, to get the words on paper, that's a universal struggle. Ideas come when you least expect them. My ideas come when I'm not forcing them. My subconscious often governs me much more than my conscious.

SAME AUDIENCE: Do you look through the eye of the camera in your mind's eye?

SPIELBERG: I usually see the whole movie on the ceiling of my bedroom at night. I look up and see it, and say, "If I can only remember that—and put that on film just that way!" That's what makes perfectionists dangerous people, because that mind's-eye view is something you don't want to lose, you don't want to compromise in the real three-dimensional world. I don't live in that three-dimensional world, I create in a real Looney-Tune world. But when you get on the floor with a movie, and you've got a hundred people working for you and you're responsible for millions of dollars, all of a sudden those little daydreams become a source of anxiety because now you have to realize them. The factory whistle has sounded. Now you must deliver. That's why making *Jaws* was so hard; it was a much better picture in my head than it ever was on the screen.

FROM AUDIENCE: One of Hollywood's great stock-in-trades used to be madcap comedy. You've done that with *Raiders*. How come more people don't try it?

SPIELBERG: Well, I also tried *1941*. That was my idea of *Mad World* meets *The Russians Are Coming*, and it turned into the most expensive movie in Hollywood that year. That was sort of my '41-gate. That didn't spoil me for making a madcap *Hellzapoppin* type of comedy again, but it does tend to cramp your style when everybody gangs up on ya. Ya know what I mean?

SAME AUDIENCE: Are you happy with the way *1941* turned out?

SPIELBERG: I'm not unhappy at the way the film turned out. I think the film was somewhat misrepresented in the sales approach to the public. The film was really a spectacle, not a spectacular. It was really a cross between comedy and nonsense, yet it was sold as one of the funniest pictures in the world. People went into it expecting to laugh for two hours and they wound up kind of plugging up their ears for the last hour and a half. If I had it to do over again,

I'd do a lot differently—a *lot*—but the first thing I'd do would be turn the sound down about 50 percent.

CRIST: I think that comedy is probably the very hardest thing to do, because we are all ready to agree on what is tragic, relatively ready to agree on what is deeply touching. But, what is funny? You'd get a hundred different views on that in this room. I deeply respect people who undertake comedy because it's such a mad gamble. There's one gentleman here who absolutely adored *1941*, and was very disappointed we weren't showing it. I told him I really didn't like *1941*, and that's why I didn't press for it being here.

SPIELBERG: I *know*, I read your review. I always read Judy's reviews. Let me say one thing about that. When I'm working with drama—and anything that isn't comedy is essentially drama—I get very brave, and then the humor comes easily to me. But with *1941*, when I was faced with "being funny" and I couldn't come up with the sight gags or the one-line jokes, I began falling back on drama. And I brought to that movie a real bedrock foundation of logic. Rather than going crazy like *Airplane* or *Kentucky Fried Movie* or *Animal House,* instead of doing that—I fell back on what I knew best how to do, which is how to dramatize and intensify a story. I think there was an improper balance between the two.

CRIST: And yet in *Raiders* there are so many, if you'll excuse the expression, hilarious moments, so many wonderful gags.

SPIELBERG: That's because I was working in the adventure genre, in which bad people were going to be killed. It wasn't a *Road Runner* cartoon. If you fell off a cliff, you stayed on the ground. I felt courageous and said, "Gee, while we're at it, let's throw in some jokes." The original Kasdan script had very little humor, maybe one or two funny lines. One of the funniest was when Indy's asked how he's going to get a horse, and he says, "I don't know, I'm making this up as I go along." That was maybe the only funny line from the original script. Everything else was invented during the shooting. It's always fun to add the funny touches. So much in *Jaws* was added—the whole sequence where Robert Shaw finishes an entire beer, then squeezes the beer can in a very macho way, and Richard, who's drinking from a Styrofoam cup, looks at him and crinkles his Styrofoam cup—that was just something I threw in that day. That was fun. In all the movies I've made, if a day goes by when I don't think of something that wasn't in the script I feel I've let that day down, I haven't contributed as a director.

FROM AUDIENCE: You seem to have a special gift for directing actors into revealing body language.

SPIELBERG: Sometimes the best thing I can do is cast the movie well. If you cast well then half the battle is already won, because even if the actor doesn't listen to anything you say, you're at least responsible for half of his performance. You reached into a crowded world and pulled a man, a woman, or a child from thin air and plugged them into your vision. That's a contribution. Beyond that, I really believe in letting actors contribute ideas of their own to the character they are playing; also when I direct, it's not really a dictatorship. I don't walk around saying, "Stand here, say it this way, don't use your hands."

FROM AUDIENCE: Do you do things in two takes?

SPIELBERG: With the kids in E.T. I did things in one or two takes. But with adults, I'll do things in seven, eight, or nine takes, depending. In Sugarland I had a very strange situation; Goldie Hawn was spontaneous like a child from takes one to three. After three she became a little tired. Bill Atherton, who's a stage actor and used to rehearsals, would take at least five or six takes, and by take seven, he was terrific. Just because Goldie was the star, I wasn't willing to give up on Bill because Goldie was perfect on take three. So there's a lot more coverage in Sugarland than in most of my movies, where Goldie has a single or an over-the-shoulder shot, or where Goldie stands in and I'm looking over her shoulder at Bill. He's on take six or seven. But I was not that lucky with Goldie and Bill in a two-shot sustained master, because they were always good at different times. That's a problem you always run into.

FROM AUDIENCE: Apropos of what you were saying about casting, and about working with children—how do you find such extraordinary children, especially the young ones, like Cary Guffey in Close Encounters and Drew Barrymore in E.T.? They were wonderful.

SPIELBERG: Thank you. It took a long time to find those kids. I looked at five hundred kids for E.T., and about two hundred fifty of those were from the California area, and most of them had their 8 × 10 composites, they had been up for hundreds of commercials; and the early meaning of life to them was saying things like, "Gee, I went up for a Quaker State commercial last week, I didn't get it." I kind of gave up after a while and went for unknowns—which is riskier. Henry Thomas had very little experience in film. He made only one film before this. He was just a regular kid who knew more about real life the way you all know it. Cary Guffey had never acted before; Drew Barrymore had never done anything before—except she was the offspring of the great Barrymore tradition. It's also a matter of luck and knowing what you want, and waiting with the patience to find the right kid.

[After *Raiders of the Lost Ark*]

CRIST: Steven said at the beginning of the film that he was just going to stay about five or ten minutes, because there was something he wanted to see. But he really proved himself true blue and stuck it out to the end. Someone asked me to ask you which of your films you enjoyed making most, so I'm asking you. But I figure it was *Raiders,* because it's somehow the most carefree, lighthearted, and *movie*-movie of your movies.

SPIELBERG: I sometimes think that hard work and pleasure do *not* go hand in hand. The most enjoyable experience I ever had on a sound set was *E.T.*—because of the children, and it was just a love relationship all around. This was the second most enjoyable experience. It was one of the most enjoyable films for me because we knew we were making a movie-movie. The first day of shooting was the day in the submarine pen where the German's coat didn't fit Indiana—which you were mentioning to me.

CRIST: Yes, I told Steven that all my moviegoing life I've wanted somebody to knock somebody out and take his clothes—and *not* have the clothes fit. He did it. It was the sweetest movie revenge moment I've seen.

SPIELBERG: Revenge, revenge . . . *revenge is mine.* It's fun to do something like that when you're making a movie. The first day of shooting I saw that all of the extras were tall, yet there was this one short guy. This was not in the script and he looked totally out of place and I was going to remove him, because he didn't look like a big, strapping Nazi soldier. Then I thought, maybe *that's* the guy Harrison tackles and brings down behind the sandbags—takes his clothes and the clothes don't fit. And when I did that—that inspired the crew, and nothing surprised them from that day on.

FROM AUDIENCE: In your use of special effects, do you think up all these exotic things, or does someone else do that?

SPIELBERG: I guess I thought up the ghosts, the electricity from the ark, the wall of fire, and the clouds opening up and all that. Then I make my crude little sketches. There's an artist, a brilliant man named Joe Johnson, who works over at Lucasfilm, and he would take these ideas and put them on paper. Then, for this particular sequence, Joe Johnson and his special effects group sat down and came up with some extra thoughts that complemented my own, and we mixed up all our ideas. He made the drawings, which turned into something that could be photographed. That's pretty much the process.

FROM AUDIENCE: What about the snakes?

SPIELBERG: The snakes were real; there were no opticals there at all. That was my contribution. This is really George Lucas's story, but my two main contributions to this movie were the rolling ball and the snakes. I said to George, after that, whatever else you want to do, I'll be happy just being the director.

FROM AUDIENCE: Could you explain your collaboration with Lucas on *Raiders*?

SPIELBERG: Well, George, of course, conceived *Raiders* about ten years ago and developed it with a director named Philip Kaufman—who's doing a movie called *The Right Stuff* now. Then Phil pulled out, and George told me the story in Hawaii before *Star Wars* opened, and I thought it was a great story because—and this prompted his telling the story to me—I told him that someday I wanted to do a James Bond-esque movie. George said, "I've got something better than James Bond," and he told me the Indiana Jones story. It was about an archeologist-playboy who goes around the world looking for antiquities, and in this particular story he's looking for the ark of the covenant, and it's a slam-bam, shoot-'em-up cliff-hanger. That was it, the whole story.

Then we got together, along with Larry Kasdan, and designed the individual scenes. George wanted a scene in Nepal. I never questioned that. I mean, nobody ever questioned why, in *Close Encounters*, I wanted to have the Mothership look the way it did. So I didn't question George when he said, "I want a scene in Nepal, and I want a really neat scene where she slugs him—the girl's got to slug the guy." It's as crude-sounding as that, that's what a story meeting is like. Now we had to figure out *why* she hits him. Well, gee, when she was about thirteen years old she lost her virginity, then he never spoke to her again, he walked out. We worked backward. We thought of about seven or eight or nine key set pieces— really exciting scenes. We all wanted a truck chase—but we didn't know where it would go in the movie. I wanted an opening scene that gave the impression that we were witnessing the third act of a previous *Raiders* movie. We were just at the tail end of that movie; you get to miss all the boring parts, but you get to see the exciting climax before the movie you actually paid to see begins. And George was very particular about having a submarine in the film— somewhere, somehow. Also, George wanted the monkey to go *"Heil Hitler!"*—that was his idea. So it's kind of like a Johnny Carson doing that Karnak character . . . you have all the answers but you must make up the questions. That's how we developed *Raiders,* we all had our favorite thing to do in a movie like this, and somehow it amalgamated and became a movie.

FROM AUDIENCE: Who conceived the action where Harrison meets the swordsman who's flipping around the scimitar and Harrison pulls out his gun and shoots him? That was terribly funny.

SPIELBERG: There's a story behind that, too. *Every cheap gag in this movie has a story behind it!* This is one of the better stories. We had devised a sequence—and this was something Larry Kasdan wanted—it would be the definitive duel between a swordsman and a man with a whip. How does a man with a whip overcome a giant with a scimitar? We'd worked out a scene that was very exciting—it had Harrison backed up against the wall, and the guy was chopping at Harrison and just missing him, and Harrison was snapping the whip and the scimitar was blocking each snap of the whip. It was all very exciting and I couldn't wait to shoot the scene. I also couldn't wait to get the hell out of Tunisia. I mean it's the summer playground of the PLO. We wanted out of there so bad we could taste Hawaii—we could taste the Mai-tais. It was just around the corner—to get out of Tunisia early.

Then Harrison came to work that day—the first day of a scheduled two-day, very complicated, totally action-fraught, whip-and-sword duel. Harrison came to the set a little bit like George Burns when he walks out on stage sort of scrunched down, a little bit hunched over. Harrison had once again eaten "out." The worst *turistas* he'd ever experienced. I was really worried that we wouldn't get *any* of this fight finished, because Harrison was in such agony. Then I thought, well, I really want to film this fight, but I also really want to get out of Tunisia, so I said, "Why don't you just pull out your gun and shoot the swordsman and we'll get on with the next scene." He said, "Great!" And it was that fast. We did a couple of cover shots of the guy flashing his sword around. Harrison wipes his brow, pulls out his gun, and shoots the man dead. It was the old John Ford story—we rip out two or three pages of script, we're another day ahead of schedule! [Laughter and applause] The thing is, you never realize what you have until you show it to a large number of people. I just thought this was a clever way of getting out of Tunisia early—I had no idea what the reaction would be.

CRIST: Steven, you seem to put a lot of faith in previews.

SPIELBERG: I put a lot of faith in previews because that's one thing that tells you if your movie works. If nobody laughs, you're in trouble; if it needs screams and nobody screams, you're in trouble; if people start getting up and going out to the bathroom or for a cigarette and start to walk back slowly, you're in trouble. There are so many signposts. I use screenings often to reconstitute scenes, to use other scenes I never thought about using, or cut the movie down. In *Close Encounters* there was the big question of whether I should actually use Jiminy Cricket singing "When You Wish Upon a Star" at the end. I previewed the picture twice in Dallas, one night with the song and one night without it, and the preview cards almost convinced me that the song was too much an infraction of the truth people felt we were telling about visitation from other worlds, so I lost the song.

FROM AUDIENCE: Are you stuck in a release date by the time you have a preview—is there a problem with a deadline that prevents reshooting?

SPIELBERG: Yes, we're usually on a deadline—and there's certainly a problem with reshooting. On *Raiders* we did some shooting after the preview, but not much at all. I preview answer prints, I preview the corrected color—nobody comes out and says, "The color hasn't been corrected, folks, please forgive us." We don't do that, because it's a final film; I preview in 70mm, six-track—so you get the full impact of what the film will be like in a good theater.

FROM AUDIENCE: There's a scene in South America where Indiana's running out of the cave temple and the door is coming down and he has to make that quick roll under the door. I was curious to know, one, how long that took to shoot and, two, was the timing a little bit off there, because one shot has the door about three-quarters of the way down, then it's only about halfway down.

SPIELBERG: You're not supposed to see those things. You're supposed to be watching Harrison—not the door. Give me a break. That's true, there was a slight continuity problem that was impossible to fix in the editing. You found me out.

FROM AUDIENCE: What's the secret of directing a crowd scene? When you have about five hundred people in a single take—and most of them don't speak English?

SPIELBERG: It takes a good assistant director. Plus a good local assistant director, who can talk to the people in their own language. I'll tell you one interesting story: I wanted a lot of extras for one particular sequence to be in certain places, so we put markers down on the ground for them, about two hundred little crosses on the ground so they'd know where to stand. But we didn't get the shot before lunch. When we broke for half an hour all the extras picked up their little crosses and went to lunch with them. When they came back, they were saying, "Where do I stand, what do I do with these?" Crowd control is really tough. It is not easy in any country.

FROM AUDIENCE: What did *Raiders* cost?

SPIELBERG: About $20 million. For me, that's cheap.

FROM AUDIENCE: I really admired the gutsiness of the Karen Allen character. Where did that characterization come from?

SPIELBERG: I think from old Howard Hawks movies, with special inspiration from Joanne Dru, and maybe from Patricia Neal. I screened a lot of movies for Karen before we went to London. I showed her *Hud*, and I showed her *Red River*—I showed her movies in which women were really perky, like spitfires, and I said, "This is the way I hope you'll be."

CRIST: I loved our introduction to her, in a drinking contest in Nepal.

SPIELBERG: I wish you could have seen the original shot, it was so great—it ran six minutes—but there was just no place in the movie for it. A six-minute drinking contest all in one shot. It took you from complete sobriety to total inebriation. But in a film paced like this one, that was one of the first things to go.

FROM AUDIENCE: How do you time the releases of these movies which have sequels?

SPIELBERG: There are a couple of factors: *when* I'm available to direct it, and how long it takes to make a movie this size.

[After *E.T.—The Extra-Terrestrial*]

FROM AUDIENCE: At the very end, E.T. points at Elliott's forehead and says, "I'll be right *here*." Did he point there because you were trying to signify that as the location of the third eye?

SPIELBERG: I've always thought this was where everything took place, right here—the mind, the center of your own universe. That was in the script from the beginning. I couldn't wait to get to that scene.

CRIST: Did you have to resist doing more tricks in *E.T.*?

SPIELBERG: No, I didn't want to do *any* tricks in *E.T.*; that was one reason I made the movie. With the exception of *Sugarland Express,* I haven't made another movie so free of technological tricks. And because of that, every time I had the opportunity to do another special effect, I resisted it because, as Elliott says, "This is *reality.*"

FROM AUDIENCE: Is there any impact on the children in a movie like *E.T.*, or is everything so technical that they don't really fall in love with E.T.?

SPIELBERG: No. Everybody on the set fell in love with E.T. He was so real. I mean, when I'd yell cut, like every actor E.T. would relax, exhale with nervous exhaustion, make faces at his work in the last take, that kind of thing. We all knew he was real—especially the younger kids, and most especially Henry Thomas, who played Elliott. He was really simpatico with E.T., in a way that went beyond the movie. After his original videotaped test—which won him the part, because he did a wonderful improvisation—we gave him a screen test with E.T. It was E.T.'s first test, to see how he looked in color. Henry is not a boy who smiles a great deal; I was worried when I cast him because he did everything beautifully, he was wonderful in the test, but he never smiled. But in that first film test, when he looked at E.T., he couldn't keep the smile off his face—he laughed, and I think he felt like crying.

FROM AUDIENCE: What was the significance of the jangling keys?

SPIELBERG: Well, it's a pretty scary sound—jangling keys. I thought that would be a nice abrasive sound to warn when danger is around. E.T. could hear it, Elliott could hear it. The keys were also symbolic of officialdom. I got the idea of the keys from a producer, Gary Kurtz, who produced *Star Wars.* When Gary was a film student, he always carried a set of keys on his belt—and you could always hear Gary coming a mile away.

FROM AUDIENCE: Was *E.T.* the original title?

SPIELBERG: There was another title—*E.T. and Me.* Melissa wanted it, and so did most of the people who worked with me. The studio loved *E.T.* too—so it was one of those little struggles. I liked *E.T. the Extra-Terrestrial,* and I knew people would abbreviate it anyway. Actually, our working title, for secrecy, was simply, *A Boy's Life,* so no one would know what we were up to.

FROM AUDIENCE: Would you describe the technical humanization of E.T.?

SPIELBERG: No, not so soon after you've seen it. This is the first group I've discussed *E.T.* with. And, with all the interviews I've given, I've never gotten too deeply into the actualization of E.T., simply because I think that we're all still kids—and some of us want to know, but those who don't want to know *really* don't want to know. I could just see hands going up to ears when I start talking about it—so, I won't.

CRIST: I agree. It was only about fifteen years ago that I learned about the tornado in *Wizard of Oz.* Mervyn Le Roy was talking about how, finally, they got the tornado in the movie by having somebody swirl a black silk stocking in front of the camera. I've never forgiven him for telling me that—and when I watch *The Wizard of Oz,* I know that it's *not* a silk stocking.

FROM AUDIENCE: Why didn't you show any adult faces—until the end—except for the mother?

SPIELBERG: Well, this was the legend of a child's world, and I felt that violation into that world was going to be a breach of faith. I didn't consider the mother an adult—she was just one of the kids as far as I was concerned. I wanted to save the first adult face for the man who wears the keys for the sad instant when E.T. falls into the grasp of the real world. I wanted to wait until then, to bring in that world of tall shadows. Also, I was kind of influenced by the old MGM cartoons of Tom & Jerry—you'd never see any people, you'd see therapeutic shoes, and skirts, and a hand would reach down and grab the cat. Or someone would come into the shop and swat the cat—and a foot would kick the cat out the door into the snow. That's something I grew up with, adults being taken seriously from the waist down.

FROM AUDIENCE: Did you cut out any scenes with E.T.?

SPIELBERG: A couple. One scene where E.T. wanders into the mother's room when he's getting sick. She's lying on the bed asleep, she's actually half naked, *G-rated* half nakedness. He's standing there in his bathrobe and he looks at her and he's breathing kind of heavy. It's because he's sick, because he's sick! That's one of the reasons it came out of the movie—he looked simply lecherous. But there was one touching thing in that scene—his hand reaches out toward her cheek and you're not sure what he's going to do, but he just wants to leave one Reese's Piece on her pillow.

FROM AUDIENCE: Could you tell us how you get involved in the editing process? Do you yourself sit at the machine—do you tell an editor what you want?

SPIELBERG: I myself don't physically cut—George Lucas physically cuts. It's something I can't do—you know, I'd cut my hand off with a splice. To physically cut is something I don't have the patience for. I do spend an inordinate amount of time in the editing room with the film editor. In most cases I like to sit with the editor and look at the dailies and outline where everything goes—then let the editor put everything into a first assembly, which takes about two or three days per scene. Then I look at it with the editor on the weekend, usually—because I cut while I shoot. Then we'll do a second cut, I'll make changes. This is great, because by the time we're through shooting, usually two weeks later I can see my entire movie assembled. Then, for two to three months or however long it takes, I spend time experimenting changing scenes around—trimming, extending. I love editing—I love editing more than I love shooting the movie. It's the most fun I have making the picture. But I also have very good editors, who have remarkable ideas and can really make major contributions to the picture.

FROM AUDIENCE: Did you make any editing changes in *E.T.* after your preview?

SPIELBERG: Just a couple of small things—a couple of places where I thought the audience wanted to respond and I had to cut too quickly. One scene was when the boys make their escape from the van and yank that tube down the driveway—the preview audience started to applaud but before you knew it, the van had stopped and Elliott was telling the bicycle boys to meet him at the top of the hill. So I extended that shot as long as I could, as long as I had film— just so people would be satisfied they were executing a great escape. And I added a couple of things, in the Halloween scene when E.T. sees Yoda—in the preview he just turned and ran after Yoda. But after the preview I added the thing with E.T. saying, "Home, home-home, home." We found that the audience loved E.T.'s voice so much, we added a few voice bits with Ben Burtt—who created E.T.'s voice. I may have added a few other minor things after the *E.T.* preview, but they've slipped my mind. Next to *Jaws,* it was the best preview I've ever had. Then I got really worried—I get nervous *after* the preview. Because good previews don't necessarily forecast a successful movie.

CRIST: I'm sure you've read the articles, Steve, that say *E.T.* has a mythic quality, with echoes of the Christ story? Did you have in mind creating a film that would be a metaphor for a spiritual experience?

SPIELBERG: No, I didn't. It's interesting, the only time Melissa and I sort of looked at each other and said, "Gee, are we getting into a possibly sticky area here?" was when E.T. is revealed to the boys on the bicycles and he's wearing a white hospital robe and his "immaculate heart" is glowing. We looked at each other at that point and said, "This might trigger a lot of speculation." We already knew that his coming back to life was a form of resurrection. But I'm a nice Jewish boy from Phoenix, Arizona. If I ever went to my mother and said, "Mom, I've made this movie that's a Christian parable," what do you think she'd say? She has a kosher restaurant on Pico and Doheney in Los Angeles.

FROM AUDIENCE: How does the development of the musical score parallel the development of the film? Is it put together while you're doing the film—or afterward?

SPIELBERG: Usually what happens is when I finish a movie I put temporary music into the picture. When I first assembled *E.T.* I cut certain classical passages. I use classical music in that way, and what that does is give the composer some idea of what I have in mind. In *Close Encounters,* I wanted to hear discordant sounds, musical warbles that were a little unsettling... a little unearthly. John [Williams] is just a genius at this. John doesn't need much cueing. As a matter of fact, *E.T.* is the only film of mine John ever saw that had the temporary music in it. Usually he just looks at a naked cut with bad sound, dialogue you can hardly hear, and just scratchy noises in the background, and he gets an overall impression, musically, of what the film is about. I wanted a much more gentle score for *Jaws,* something kind of like what John did for Robert Altman's *Images,* a kind of haunting piano. John looked at me and said, "Hey, this is a scary pirate movie." And he came up with that bump-bum-bum-bum-bum . . . you know. A really primal, scary, Stravinsky-type of noise.

FROM AUDIENCE: The little girl in *E.T.* calls her mother Mary—is there any reason for that?

SPIELBERG: Well, yeah. Because my younger sisters never called my mother Mom. I called my mom, Mom. My three younger sisters call her Lee. Her name is Leah. I grew up with my sisters always hollering "Lee." It's nice, sometimes, to address your mother by her first name.

FROM AUDIENCE: Do you read a lot of science fiction?

SPIELBERG: No, I don't read much science fiction at all. My father used to read all the dime novels—they were always in the bathroom, piled high. But I never read them. I did read a few of the classics, but that's it.

FROM AUDIENCE: How did you choose Reese's Pieces candy?

SPIELBERG: We had M&M's in the script, originally, but the M&M company said no to us, they were just not interested in getting involved in movies. They wouldn't give us permission. They finally said, "It's more trouble than it's worth."

CRIST: If you hear of a mass suicide somewhere, you'll find out it's the Columbia Pictures executives [who had rejected the film] and the M&M executives, and who else?

SPIELBERG: A lot of people turned us down. Some of the people, like Kenner, really in good faith wanted to do the movie, but I think what happened was they came on the set a couple of times and they looked at E.T. and found him *inanimate,* so grotesque they just couldn't relate. They hadn't read the script, they just didn't see how that kind of creature would have any human appeal. I couldn't blame them. E.T. did look a little bit like a troll somewhere in a foggy forest. He did have that effect on people who didn't understand the movie, or who didn't give themselves a chance to know E.T.

FROM AUDIENCE: This is a little thing—but why is E.T.'s neck so skinny?

SPIELBERG: E.T.'s neck was skinny because I didn't want anyone to think there was someone inside. There was never anyone inside . . . except in certain walking scenes. When the neck goes up and down—that *is* E.T., he is the performer, there's nobody inside making the head move or the face move. It's real.

SAME AUDIENCE: One more question—how did you shoot that scene with the bicycles flying in front of the sun?

SPIELBERG: Well, we waited for the sun to get very low, then we told the kids to go fly their bicycles across the sun. We said, "Ride like the wind, ride like the wind." And wow—they flew right across. . . .

SAME AUDIENCE: I brought that on myself.

SPIELBERG: No, no, no . . . I didn't mean to embarrass you. There's all sorts of little tricks that I'd love to talk about on every movie *but* E.T. It's the strangest thing. I have the toughest time being candid about how E.T. was done. I'll tell you all about the shark in *Jaws,* I'll tell you about the Mothership in *Close Encounters*—but right now while the movie's fresh I find it impossible to show you E.T.'s birth certificate.

FROM AUDIENCE: I notice that when E.T. points through the window there appear to be rainbow colors—then, at the very end, there was a rainbow. Was that intentional?

SPIELBERG: Not really. Jim Bissel, who did the sets, made a really neat little boy's room. I wish I'd had a room like that when I was growing up. He decorated it based on research of what kids have in their rooms—not the clichés, but something fitting to Henry Thomas's character. He showed me those rainbow shades—and I just loved the colors, so that's what I picked. The rainbow at the end was an afterthought. I had that idea long after the movie was essentially complete. It was one of the last-minute opticals in the picture. I wanted the ship to say good-bye and leave a gift in the sky.

FROM AUDIENCE: Did the rainbow have any reference to *The Wizard of Oz*?

SPIELBERG: Well, you know, *The Wizard of Oz* occurred to me a lot, in my life and in my films. No, the rainbow at the end of *E.T.* is really just sort of a salute—not to say that "Life is better where we come from, over the rainbow." But essentially to say that "I'm leaving you something—but I will be back, someday."

FROM AUDIENCE: Why do you think you're so successful?

SPIELBERG (laughing): You mean—why me? I'd love to answer that question but I don't have an answer for that.

CRIST: From my standpoint, Steven succeeds because when he wants to tell you about the American fiber, or wants to tell you about a basic childhood dream . . . to put it in the very crassest terms—he tells you a damn good story. Instead of trying to tell you mythic truths about civilization, he just tells you a damn good story and you can see it through your own eyes. It works every time.

SPIELBERG: Thank you very much. You see, I didn't want to answer your question—because I wanted to hear it from Judy.

In the latter part of 1982, Spielberg co-produced the four-part Twilight Zone, *of which he directed one segment. He directed two* Raiders *sequels—1984's* Indiana Jones and the Temple of Doom *and 1989's* Indiana Jones and the Last Crusade—*and 1990's* Always. *The three* Indiana Jones *films,* Jaws, *and* E.T. *are five of the eleven all-time highest grossing films. Add* Close Encounters of the Third Kind *and his producing 1984's* Gremlins, *1985's* Back to the Future, *and 1988's* Who Framed Roger Rabbit? *and he has, as producer or director, a third of the top twenty-seven all-time money makers.*

Anne Jackson and
Eli Wallach

▼▼

Anne Jackson and Eli Wallach were established Broadway actors by the time they married in 1948. It was that same year that Jackson was nominated for a Tony for her role in Summer and Smoke, *and Wallach began acting in the long-running hit* Mr. Roberts. *Their joint appearances on Broadway include* Rhinoceros *(1961),* Luv *(1964), and* Twice Around the Park *(1982). They each won an Obie in the production of two one-act plays by Murray Schisgal,* The Typist *and* The Tiger *(1962)—and* The Tiger *was adapted for the first film Jackson and Wallach made together,* The Tiger Makes Out *(1967).*

In her Broadway career Jackson also won Tony nominations for Oh Men! Oh Women! *(1953) and* Middle of the Night *(1956). She has appeared in sixteen movies—among them* The Journey *(1959),* The Secret Life of an American Wife *(1968),* Lovers and Other Strangers *(1970),* The Bell Jar *(1979), and* The Shining *(1980)—and a number of TV specials, such as* A Woman Called Golda.

In addition to the plays in which Wallach has co-starred with his wife, his major Broadway credits include Antony and Cleopatra *(1947),* Mr. Roberts *(1948),* Teahouse of the August Moon *(1954), and* The Rose Tattoo *(1951), for which he won the Tony, Donald-*

son, and Theater World Awards. Wallach was given a British Academy Award for his first movie, Baby Doll *(1956), and among the nearly forty other features he has made are* The Magnificent Seven *(1960),* The Misfits *(1961),* How the West Was Won *(1962),* Lord Jim *(1965),* The Good, The Bad and The Ugly *(1967),* Movie Movie *(1978), and* Girlfriends *(1978)*

Besides The Tiger Makes Out *and* Nasty Habits, *the two stars have appeared together in* How to Save a Marriage (and Ruin Your Life) *(1968) and* Zig Zag *(1970). They came to Tarrytown for the weekend of April 15–17, 1983.*

[After *The Tiger Makes Out*]

CRIST: How do you two feel about this film seeing it now? This was the first time one of the stage plays that you had done together was made into a film.

WALLACH: This was made about fifteen years ago and seeing it now, you *know* there's nothing you can correct or amend in it. It's finished. It's still lovely to see, to see all those faces. You saw Dustin Hoffman in the movie. We produced the film, Annie and I, for Columbia, and Dustin was hired for two hundred dollars for the one day. He got $4.5 million for *Tootsie*! But right after that, Mike Nichols was looking for an actor for *The Graduate* and asked if we could show him some of the footage of this film—which we did, and he hired Dustin. So Dustin's second movie was *The Graduate*. There are other faces in this you recognize—Charles Nelson Reilly, Bibi Osterwald, Bob Dishy, Elizabeth Wilson, Frances Sternhagen . . .

JACKSON: You know what I thought when watching the film? I obviously got over the self-consciousness of watching myself on the screen, and what I was paying particular attention to was the extraordinary modernity, if you will, of this film. Those first shots, for example, of people walking and the music playing—that's the kind of thing you see in commercials today. A lot of what Woody Allen did later is reminiscent of the comic philosophy and the invention of *this* writer [Murray Schisgal] in *this* film. For example, that scene when the character goes to the post office and goes up to the clerk and says, "I want attention." And the postal clerk says, "Don't tell *me* about *attention*. Let me tell *you* about *attention*!" We see this kind of thing done in a lot of Woody's things. I find it tremendously interesting and complimentary that artists grow with each other's work.

When we first started this film I thought, It is a play, and how do you extend it into a movie? I don't like to see plays extended into movies because they are written for you to listen to—and a film is a *moving* picture. But I have to admit that I saw this tonight and I laughed at the freshness and the spontaneity of Murray Schisgal's humor and his philosophy. I found it very, very modern—and timeless. So I'm proud of it; I'm proud I was a participant.

CRIST: Was this your first producing venture?

WALLACH: And our last. This movie cost $750,000 and it was shot in eight weeks—downtown in Greenwich Village. As producers we kept getting statements from Columbia Pictures. I wound up owing them $1,800,000.38. I asked my lawyer, "Do I have to pay it?" He said, "No, no—they put *all* the expenses on those pictures." So we got a minimum salary on the movie, the Screen Actors Guild minimum. We never made any money on it. Oh, we get checks occasionally, when it's shown on television, for eighteen dollars.

CRIST: How do you think the film version compares with the original stage production?

WALLACH: When I saw the first rough cut of the movie, I wanted to kill the director [Arthur Hiller], because after playing it for a year Off Broadway and four to six months in London and in Los Angeles we knew where the treasure was buried, we knew where the laughs were. Some of those things were lost in the film version. However, I found compensations for that because there were inventive and funny things in the movie—some of those things were very, very funny. You know, one of those kids seen picking at the crabgrass is our daughter Katherine, who was then seven. She's going to start a movie in Rome next month.

JACKSON: She's eight now.

CRIST: These Wallach women never age! Hasn't *The Tiger Makes Out* become something of a cult film?

JACKSON: Yes, it's become quite a popular film with young people who see it—it has its real aficionados. People will call up at three o'clock in the morning to tell us they're showing it on television.

CRIST: What about the difference between acting a role on stage and in the movies?

WALLACH: There's one important point: in movies, you're doing little pieces of the play, and you put a piece here, a piece there, and another piece there. The advantage of having done it as a play is that we have had a run on it, we had the continuity of the characters. I knew when the character would explode—I remember the carryover from the scene before. Good movie acting is the most difficult thing in the world. It's like trying to do a crossword puzzle in your head. Because four days after doing a little piece you think, "Hey, I shouldn't have done that. *Now* I realize what I should have done. But it's too late." Movie acting for the actor, the real actor, is terribly difficult.

JACKSON: But, Eli, that's not true for the director. Film is a director's medium. The stage is for the writer and the actors, I believe.

WALLACH: The first movie I made was by Tennessee Williams and directed by [Elia] Kazan.* I had heard that when you're on the screen your head is about sixteen feet high—and if you open your mouth too wide they can see your tonsils, your inlays and everything. So the first time I appeared on the screen Carroll Baker said to me, "Hi-oh, Silver." And I said [with mouth closed] "Iii-ooo." Kazan said, "Cut. What are you doing? We don't want the Japanese version." He said, "Say it." So I did. The point is, the stage actor comes with a set of prejudices about movies. It's very difficult for the stage actor. When a scene is finished he'll say, "Can I do it again?" Because, on the stage, he *can* do it again—the next night you can correct something that didn't work. That's the joy of acting on the stage. In the movies you can't quite make those corrections; therefore, I feel it's even more difficult. Maintaining that performance and making it work is a remarkable accomplishment.

JACKSON: The point is, my sweetheart, that's the director's responsibility. You really have to trust the director; you have to surrender your vanity to the director.

FROM AUDIENCE: Given your personal relationship, do you find it works for you in making each other your own best critics?

WALLACH: I don't know about being our own best critics. We have a mutual mediator in a play, you know. When we're in a play together we don't carp with one another. We do it through a third person. I say, "You tell her . . ." She says, "You tell him . . ." It

*Baby Doll, 1956.

works better that way. I'll tell you, early in our career we worked in a play together called *Rhinoceros*. I said to Anne at one point, "Are you going to do *that*?" She said, "Mind your own business, that's *exactly* what I'm going to do." She did it—and every reviewer picked that thing out as one of the most innovative and inventive things of the evening. So from then on, I shut up.

JACKSON: I think that the advantage that we have is that I admire Eli as an actor, enormously, and I don't have to go through the process of worrying whether if I do something I'm going to be stepping into his territory. I don't have to do the "getting-to-know-you, getting-you-to-trust-me—I-won't-steal-your-scene-and-I-won't-upstage-you" routine. We protect each other; we both know where the values are in the play once a director has pointed that out to us, and we just protect each other on the stage. But you don't have to go through the getting-to-know-you process and therefore you can go further faster. And I always related to Eli as the character in the play—not as my husband, or as Eli. When I begin to see him come through with a character, it's very exciting to me to see what that character is because it's always somebody I don't know.

FROM AUDIENCE: Do you consider yourselves stage actors who do an occasional film? How do you see yourselves?

JACKSON: I feel I'm lucky to get a job, whatever it is. We think of ourselves as actors, and we're living in an age now where you do television and you do film and you do stage—you learn how to do it all.

FROM AUDIENCE: Since you're both such good actors, in your personal relationship—can you tell when the other is acting?

WALLACH: In a fight sometimes you go beyond where a fight should end because you think, "No, I can't give in because it's too *delicious* now." That happens.

CRIST: Anne, is there anything you specifically remember about the making of *The Secret Life of an American Wife*, with Walter Matthau?

JACKSON: I remember that Walter Matthau had had his heart attack earlier that year and he was then recuperating. There were some scenes I had in bed with Walter—and he was so devilish. He'd say,

"Remember, you're dealing with a man who has a cardiac condition." I loved him, loved working with him; he's a very, very fine actor. But he did make me self-conscious and broke me up a lot. And I'm a very, very easy person to break up—I've been reported to Equity a number of times because I laugh when I'm not supposed to.

[After *The Secret Life of an American Wife* and *Baby Doll*]

CRIST: Eli, how did you get the part in *Baby Doll*, your first picture?

WALLACH: I was in a play on Broadway called *Teahouse of the August Moon*. I had done it about a year in London and nine months in New York when Kazan came to me with the movie offer. I thought it would be wonderful but I was still under contract to the play. Maurice Evans was the producer and he said he'd let me do the movie if I added two weeks to my contract for each week I worked on the movie. The movie was supposed to last eight weeks, but it lasted thirteen, so I had to do twenty-six more weeks on the play. But I was happy to do this. Anne had just had a baby and was in a play with Edward G. Robinson called *Middle of the Night*.

Baby Doll was all shot in Mississippi except for one scene, in the attic, which was shot at a studio in Brooklyn. Everything else was done in Benoit, Mississippi. Those were very tense times in America in 1955. We had to be very careful in Mississippi.

CRIST: It's amazing to think of the climate of thirty years ago in this country. *Baby Doll* instantly got a condemned—or C rating—from the Legion of Decency and it became a *cause célèbre*.

JACKSON: It's interesting to me to remember that the character of Baby Doll in the one-act play that Tennessee wrote was an enormously heavy woman, and the original play ended with a real act of vengeance. When they did the film it was after Eli had made his Broadway debut in a starring role in *The Rose Tattoo*, in which he played a Sicilian. So it was natural for Kazan to hire Eli as another Italian, the character Vaccaro. Tennessee then changed the concept of *Baby Doll*, after having been through *The Rose Tattoo*, which also ended on a tragic note. He turned *Baby Doll* into a kind of romantic film, and in using Carroll Baker as that young, luscious, innocent girl he made the film into a very different kind of triangle—which, for me, is more emotionally successful than the play.

WALLACH: This film was of course condemned by the Church, and Cardinal Spellman got into the pulpit and said that any Catholic who saw this film was in danger of being excommunicated. When asked if he had seen the film the Cardinal said, "No, but if your water supply is poisoned, there's no reason for you to drink the water." Now when I think of what went on the other night in *The Thorn Birds*, on network television with the priest in bed with a woman, I think, God, we've come quite a way! Actually, Joseph Kennedy had quite a lot to do with the condemnation of this film— it was not allowed to be shown in any theater in New England.

I must say, when I watch the film now, the scenes have a compactness and a tension, regardless of when it was made. The film was lit by Boris Kaufman—the cinematographer who was a genius in black and white. Sometimes it would take him three hours to light something. And Kazan used to whittle and wait and mumble. The actors were rehearsing all the time. And when the lighting was ready Kazan would say to the actors, "Whenever you're ready, just give me a signal." So when we were ready we'd signal and he'd say, "Action," and by then our "motor" was running at the speed of the film. When I saw this today and first looked at myself of nearly thirty years ago, I said, "Who's that?" As a matter of fact, we were in Paris last year and went with a young girl, a friend of ours, to see *Baby Doll*. It has been playing on and off in Paris for about ten years, and it's always sold out. It's a cult film. But this time in Paris, after I had already come on the screen, our young friend said, "When are you coming on?"

JACKSON: She did not! He loves to tell it that way.

WALLACH: I saw *you* last night*—and you were something!

FROM AUDIENCE: Why exactly was the movie condemned by the Church?

WALLACH: Because of the fact of two people being married—and not consummating the marriage.

JACKSON: I also think it was the way in which the South was depicted. And it was almost a biblical story of greed and vengeance. I

*In *The Secret Life of an American Wife*, 1972.

think it was a variety of reasons—because you had seen husbands and wives being unfaithful to each other on the screen before that.

CRIST: But in those days, they all died for their sins. Just sixteen years later, with *The Secret Life of an American Wife,* it was commercially popular to say that if you had a little adultery in the afternoon—that was how to clear your sinuses and save your marriage. There was that big leap from the middle fifties into the late sixties.

JACKSON: Yes, that's right. And in the mid-fifties there was great political tension in the country. It may have hurt the film that Kazan was not a very popular man at the time. Also, anything that came from the Broadway stage was considered suspect.

FROM AUDIENCE: Would you care to give an opinion on Kazan's statements on morality both in this and in *On the Waterfront,* and the other image we have of him testifying to Congress during the Un-American Activities hearings. It just doesn't seem to fit.

JACKSON: He is a complicated man. In spite of what my husband and I feel about our political stand and his reneging, as it were—I mean, he sang, he was a *snitcher.* But he is a great artist, in my opinion. He has always identified himself with the strongest playwrights and artists in the country, so I'm ambivalent about him. I disagree with him politically, but I admire him tremendously as an artist. That's all I can say about it. Did you ever see *America, America?* I think that film expresses a great deal about what Kazan is trying to say about himself as a person and as a thinker. He knows about his own ambition, and where he's coming from in that film. As I say, I'm ambivalent. And what I know of him, in a personal relationship, I trust him. So it's a difficult situation for me.

WALLACH: Kazan will have to carry that monkey on his back for a long, long time. That's his problem. However, at the time we made *Baby Doll,* we were concerned about making a good movie, and I think he was brilliant in guiding that movie through. I think he's brilliant in getting you involved, empathetically, in what's going on on the screen.

FROM AUDIENCE: How did Kazan and Tennessee Williams get along?

WALLACH: Well, you must remember that when Kazan did this movie he had already done *Streetcar Named Desire;* he had done *Camino Real,* he had done *Cat on a Hot Tin Roof.* So there was a strong relationship. But they disagreed a lot. Kazan is ruthless in cutting—he has a marvelous sense of how he wants a scene to work. But they got along.

FROM AUDIENCE: Did the controversy about the film have any repercussions as far as your being able to get a job?

WALLACH: You know, stage actors at that period had a superior attitude about movies. It's only after you work on a few that you get addicted. But, initially, I thought to myself, I don't want to do movies anymore. I want to do plays. I went back and was in *Major Barbara* with Anne and Charles Laughton was the director. We were in the *theater*. Finally, after two or three years had gone by I got a call to do a movie called *The Lineup*. I read the script—and I killed five people in one day. I said, "I don't want to do this, it's terrible." They said, "Well, you get to go to San Francisco, it's an intriguing idea." Finally, as a joke, I said, "Okay, I'll do it for fifty grand; ten grand a killing." They said, "Okay, you got a deal." So in my second movie I was a gangster. It was directed by Don Siegal, who's an extraordinary action director. It was the grandfather of all those chase movies we have now. But there were no career repercussions directly because of *Baby Doll*.

CRIST: How was it, Anne, working with George Axelrod, who was both writer and director for *Secret Life of an American Wife?*

JACKSON: Let me put it this way: I have a very strong directorial sense, and when I see a film I get terribly frustrated because I know what I want to cut. I look at it and I start cutting and trimming. With George Axelrod, who's a very fine man, there were times when I wanted to get up and say, "All right, let's cut the dialogue." Or, "It's got to go faster." I said to him when I first started working on the film, "There's too much talk for the movies." Then I inadvertently cut an entire three pages in the first scene I had with Walter [Matthau]—and Walter, who also has a marvelous ear and is a fabulous actor—said, "I think it will be all right." I didn't do that deliberately, but through the picture I did make little trims. I also once worked in a play that was directed by its author; they love their words, but there are usually *too many* words.

[After *The Misfits*]

CRIST: The reviews on *The Misfits* were decidedly mixed. But it was written by Arthur Miller, directed by John Huston, and had that high-powered cast. How was the film from your point of view, Eli?

WALLACH: It wasn't a happy experience, making this film, because Miller's marriage to Monroe was breaking up while we were filming it. And everything the characters said made Marilyn more upset. She had a rough time doing it. I find the film quite interesting.

People always worry about the horses, but there was an ASPCA man on the set all the time we worked with the horses. It was very dangerous working with wild horses—they don't know about movies. People think that Clark Gable died because of the sequences with the horses. If anything, he was a professional. He'd do a stunt once or twice, but if they needed a retake he'd say, "Get somebody else, I won't do it." So he knew exactly when to stop. At five o'clock each day Gable would climb into his Mercedes with the gull wing and take off across that dry lake at a hundred miles an hour to go home. He had a wife who was pregnant, and he looked forward very much to his first child. He died ten days after the picture. He never saw the child.

And Monty Clift too had problems—similar to Marilyn's. I don't know what their problems were, but both were rather self-destructive at the time. Huston was like one of those cowboys in the movie—as far as being a free spirit goes. It was a hard schedule, three months on a dry lake in the desert. But I find that what comes across in this picture is a human quality that grips you—you get involved in the film, more so than films today. I was in a movie called *The Deep*, which I call *Shallow*. Now, for a five-dollar movie ticket they'll take you underground, in the water, in the air—but, emotionally, they won't take you anywhere.

CRIST: How was it working with John Huston?

WALLACH: Huston doesn't give you directions. He doesn't say, "I want you to do it this way or that way." He allows you to explore, but if you go beyond the bounds of what he has in mind, he'll cut. I'll never forget one scene—Marilyn and I were in the truck, side by side, and Huston had the camera shooting across me to Marilyn. I assumed that when he finished he would put the camera on the other side and shoot me. But he said, "Fine, that's it." Which meant he wasn't going to shoot facing me. I said, "Mr. Huston, ahh . . . I don't understand." He said, "Listen, kid, never tell me where to put my camera or how to shoot. You just act." Well, I was angry and upset and very bitter. Then, a week after he saw the rushes, he said, "Okay, we're reshooting that scene—and I'm putting the camera over there. *And you shut up!*"

But I love John because he's a true adventurer.

FROM AUDIENCE: How do you compare your performances in *Baby Doll* and *The Misfits*?

WALLACH: Well, I feel that the script in *Baby Doll* is better and my performance more contained. I think the work I did under Kazan's guidance was, for me, more of a piece. In *The Misfits* the focus kept shifting, and the inconsistencies in the character disturbed me. I don't know, I see myself now and I think, Gee, *why* did I do that? Or, I wish I had another crack at that. I could fix it, I could do other colors. But the worst thing you can do is get wrapped up in what you've done in the past. I want to go on. Listen, I spent seven years making Italian movies—I could write something called *My Adventures in the Spaghetti Trade*.

FROM AUDIENCE: How did you get the part in *The Misfits*?

WALLACH: Marilyn insisted I play in this movie. We had known her for five years. She'd come to New York in flight from 20th Century–Fox and that contractual disagreement. We became very close buddies, she used to baby-sit for us. She was wonderful, a wonderful lady. She saw *Teahouse of the August Moon* about twenty times because she'd never seen a play. She was fascinated with any actor who could do a scene of more than two minutes. So she insisted I do this movie. Originally the billing was Marilyn Monroe—and me. Then Clark Gable came on the picture, and I moved over. Then it was Clark Gable, Marilyn Monroe, and me. I went below the line. Then Monty Clift came in and I was fourth. Then they said they needed a lady like Thelma Ritter for that role. She was marvelous—and she said she'd do it on condition that she get fourth billing. So I wound up fifth.

FROM AUDIENCE: How did you two meet?

JACKSON: We met doing a one-act play by Tennessee Williams called *This Property Is Condemned*. A friend of ours, a lady who was a director, was supposed to meet Eli as a prospective boyfriend—I mean, it was matchmaking; he didn't come to try out for the play. I was there to be in the play. When Eli arrived she remembered that she had seen him in a play before he had gone into the

Army, so she cast him in *This Property Is Condemned*. There were only two people in it—so there wasn't much choice for us.

FROM AUDIENCE: I wonder if there's been a strain in your marriage from the fact that one of you may have gained more attention than the other.

WALLACH: No, I don't think that was it. The separations were difficult. It used to be "Join the Navy and see the world"—but it became "Join the movies and see the world" because I went off and made films not only in Italy but in Cambodia, in Mexico and Greece, in Canada—everywhere except India and Australia.

JACKSON: Yes, the separations were difficult. And also, if you are an actor and you have a marriage—and it's true for both sexes—there is something you have to give up in order to get something else. As a young actress I began the classic way—with Chekhov, and once you've tasted a Chekhovian play it's very difficult to do other plays, modern plays, although the next really great play I did was by Tennessee Williams. I love language and I love those plays. When the children were quite young I was invited to go with Tyrone Guthrie to join his repertory company in Minneapolis. That was a very tempting offer—something I really longed to do. But it was impossible: it would have meant the whole family would have had to move to Minneapolis. I just couldn't pursue that. It was never a problem for me not to do movies—not from a snobbish point of view; I would love to have done films. But at the time I was a young actress and I was "hot," as they say; it meant seven-year contracts, it meant living in Hollywood. And that was something that Eli and I, as young actors, decided against almost immediately.

So once that was solved, having children and having a family certainly fulfilled for me a creative area of my life. And somebody here said something that was very beautiful and moving to me. She said, "One of your greatest accomplishments is your son." Then she told me a sweet little story about something my son, Peter, had done. One time I was in a taxi and the driver said to me, "Are you Mrs. Wallach?" And I said, "Yes," and I waited for the rest of it—"You're married to Eli and you're Anne Jackson" and all that. But he didn't say that. He said, "Are you Katherine Wallach's mother?" He said, "Would you give Katherine my love?" I thought he seemed a bit old to be sending my daughter his love—as she was all of eight or nine years old. I said, "How do you know Katherine?"—being slightly suspicious that this was a nymphet tale. And he said, "I was in camp last summer, I was a waiter, and it was my birthday and your little girl collected all the cupcakes and gave them to me for my birthday." I've gotten terrific compliments about my daughter Roberta—I've gotten terrific fan letters saying, "When is Roberta's film *Gamma Rays** going to show again on television?" So, instead of going to Minneapolis I do have these three lovely children and this very lovely man, and it's something I'm very proud of.

WALLACH: We were sitting at a Chinese restaurant with Roberta once, and these two kids came up to us with their menus—we thought for our autographs. We straightened up, you know how you get modest all of a sudden. And they leaned across us and said, "Are you Roberta Wallach? Can we have your autograph?" Both of us realize, you see, that we have to pass on the baton.

After their appearance at Tarrytown, Eli Wallach and Anne Jackson made a film, Sam's Son *(1983), written and directed by Michael Landon. Since then, Eli Wallach has appeared in such films as* Tough Guys *(1986) with Burt Lancaster,* Nuts *(1987),* The Two Jakes *and* The Godfather III *(1990), and went on to roles in* Article 99 *and* Mistress. *Anne Jackson was most recently seen in* Funny About Love *(1990) with Gene Wilder.*

**The Effect of Gamma Rays on Man-in-the-Moon Marigolds, in which she played the older of Joanne Woodward's two daughters.*

Richard Dreyfuss and
John Badham

▰▰▰▰▰▰▰▰▰▰▰▰▰▰▰▰▰▰▰▰▰▰▰▰▰▰▰▰▰▰▰▰▰▰▰▰▰▰

*Although born in Brooklyn, Richard Dreyfuss grew up in Los An-
geles and began his acting career there at the Beverly Hills Jewish
Center. After a bit part in* The Valley of the Dolls *(1967) and a
supporting role in* The Young Runaways *(1968), Dreyfuss migrated
back to New York and the stage, appearing in plays both on Broadway and off. Dreyfuss's breakthrough year in movies was 1973; he
was seen in* Dillinger *and* American Graffiti. *After achieving stardom in* The Apprenticeship of Duddy Kravitz *(1974), Dreyfuss
went on to make* Jaws *(1975),* Inserts *(1976),* Close Encounters of
the Third Kind *(1977),* The Goodbye Girl *(1977)—for which he
won an Academy Award as Best Actor—*The Big Fix *(1978),* All
That Jazz *(1978),* The Competition *(1980), and* Whose Life Is It,
Anyway? *(1981). The last film was directed by John Badham, with
whom Dreyfuss shared the Tarrytown weekend of May 13–15,
1983.*

[After *Whose Life Is It, Anyway?*]

CRIST: Richard, tell us how you and *Whose Life* got together.

DREYFUSS: Okay. Well, I was called. David Begelman, head of
MGM at the time, called me on the phone in New York and asked

if I wanted to do it. I said yes on the phone, and that was that. I had known about the project because I had been asked at one time to do the play in New York. I had flown to London to see it, then I said no. The reason I said no to the play and yes to the film is that I felt the play was very polite; it stayed away from a lot of the potentially unpleasant feelings, a lot of the realities—and it was kind of boring. And I felt that the film had the potential to be more exciting—and "impolite."

So it was the fastest negotiation I was ever involved in. I asked one question, which was, "Is there a director?" And Begelman said yes, John Badham. I said yes. I met them in New York a few weeks later to discuss their idea of taking the screenplay, as they were developing it, to a theater. I went along with that idea. What we did was, rather than doing the stage production of the play, take the stage production plus some ideas we were working on to add to the story. For example, there was no girl friend in the play. Also, there was not a moment in the play that was physically uncomfortable, and I know—not only through research, but through friends of mine—that the life of paraplegics and quadriplegics, especially the ones in hospitals, is filled with terrible moments, such as falling out of bed. Those things happen every day. So we added these ideas, and we went to the Williamstown Theater Festival and presented *Whose Life Is It, Anyway?*—and it was basically the screenplay. Certain things were added—by John [Badham] especially, who was working out his approach to the piece before we ever went to Hollywood to shoot it. We did the play in the summer, started shooting in October, so we got a chance to work out a lot of things we might never have had an opportunity to do.

CRIST: What was Reginald Rose's participation?

DREYFUSS: He wrote the original screenplay version, but I was not around during his involvement, really. Basically, I must give credit to the screenplay more to John Badham—and the producer, Larry Bachmann, who shepherded [it] through.

CRIST: Why were you attracted by the fact that Badham was going to be the director?

DREYFUSS: John did a film on television called *The Law*; he also did a film called *Bingo Long* [*Traveling All-Stars and Motor Kings*]— and both those films are major favorites of mine, and I wanted to work with him because of that. Also, I knew John, however slightly, because I used to hang out at Universal and try to get work, and he was one of the guys I used to try to get work from. I liked the idea of working for him.

CRIST: This film was a great change of pace for him.

DREYFUSS: It's true. I think John is surprising everyone—and it turns out, he is always changing his pace. *Blue Thunder* and *War-Games* are 180 degrees away from what you just saw. He's becoming what they call a ubiquitous director. I hope that's good.

FROM AUDIENCE: I'd like to know what your personal feelings were in that role—playing a quadriplegic. How did it affect you?

DREYFUSS: Ask me an easy question. There is a film called *A Double Life,* with Ronald Colman, made in 1947—remember that? It's about the "actor's syndrome"—when he's in comedy, he's a happy guy, when he's in *Othello,* he kills the girl. I *have* this syndrome—not that I've ever killed anyone. But I do, to a certain extent, take on the characteristics of the character I am playing. One of the problems I had in doing this film was that, to a certain extent, I became a patient. I became, in many ways, immobile. But there was what I call an "impolite nobility" about this character. I admire his stand, I admire his strength under pressure. I admire that the stand that he takes is such a difficult one to swallow, hard to bear. I was very proud to play that.

You know, when you're a kid, you pretend a lot. You pretend you're stronger, that you're smarter, you're kinder, you're more secure. Obviously, we do this kind of thing when we grow up. As an actor, you have an opportunity to pretend on a more real level— and in this, I got an opportunity to be heroic, for *myself.* Ken Harrison is not heroic for anyone else. His is a very selfish, graceful, desolate nobility. I could play that until the cows come home.

Harrison really did have a lot to contribute—and he had *been,* and *might have been*—but that's not what he wanted. He says, "As long as what I want doesn't hurt anyone else, I have a *right* to what I want."

FROM AUDIENCE: I saw the original British TV version of *Whose Life,* but not the play. I'd like to know about the sculpture of the hand of God at the end—was that something new for the film? Who thought up that last shot?

DREYFUSS: I'll tell you why that was in. Anyone seeing the play was told that this man was an artist—and everyone kept referring to him as so vital, so intelligent, creative, and talented. But in the play, you never saw his lover, you never saw his family, you never saw his work. So we added his lover and his work—which I think was terribly valid. It was John's idea to add the hand of God. I must remove myself from the decision to use it in the last scene—and I plead stupidity here. I did not pay attention to what he was aiming for when he used that composition. I didn't quite see the relationship between the hand and the figure in the bed. So I'm not quite sure what John was getting at.

I'll tell you what I personally object to in the film. That is, that Ken Harrison's work—to me—does not express Ken Harrison. Now, I know nothing about sculpture, but I thought that his work as seen in the movie was too cold, it wasn't warm—it had no humanity. That outdoor sculpture you see in the beginning—in Boston, I thought it was—who cares? I wanted it to be different. But I do absolutely agree that we had to see his work and see how he felt about it.

CRIST: I have to disagree with you—I thought there was a warmth to his work because it was dominated by the girl. There were all those dance figures in the studio—and it was so perceptive to give him a girl who danced. The personal expression of their art—on both their parts—completely transformed the play, which to me was a "talking head" piece. I can see why, as an actor, you may not want to do the part—because you just lie there. But you do have a lot of funny lines.

DREYFUSS: One of the things that my friends said to me—after it was announced I was going to do this—was, "How are *you* going to sit still?" Because everyone has always perceived me as a twitchy actor. That was one of the reasons I wanted to do this. Now, of course, the film is much easier to do than the play because as you know, you shoot a thirty-second scene and when they say "Cut," you know you don't have to lie there for the next ten weeks. That's one of the reasons I wanted to do this on stage—to see if I could just lie down and not move a single muscle in my body. One of the proudest things in my career was the night there were three flies on my face and I didn't do anything about it. *That* was real acting.

FROM AUDIENCE: Did your performance of this character differ greatly when you did it on stage—as opposed to the film?

DREYFUSS: No, I would not say that I did it any differently. I would say this: I'd do it differently *now*. This is one of the two or three performances I've given in my life where I can absolutely say I'd like to do it again. I'd just do it better. I don't know the language for this, really, but there is to me a certain note of commitment in my throat. I would like to approach this character with a different throat. This is private vocabulary for me—when I work. I don't really intend to be understood at this moment. [Laughter] So there! There are some performances of mine I can watch—and some that I cannot.

CRIST: For instance? What's your favorite movie?

DREYFUSS: *Goodbye Girl*. I can watch *Goodbye Girl* and I'm totally satisfied with that performance. I can watch *Jaws*. I can't watch, all the way through, *Duddy Kravitz*. You know this was the first Canadian film that was trying to get *out* of Canada. There was a lot riding on it, and there was a lot of tenseness and pressure—none of which I knew about until I got up there. And we didn't have any rehearsal—not one day, not an hour. We had been told we'd have a week or two rehearsal. So I was scared out of my brains. A lot of that performance is based on fear. I could do it better. The moment it was over I knew that. So I find that one awkward because I don't see what I *do*—I see what I *didn't* do.

FROM AUDIENCE: How do you feel about *Close Encounters*?

DREYFUSS: I'm not only *thrilled* that I did *Close Encounters*—I believe that *Close Encounters* will outlive all of us. I believe it's the only project that I've ever involved myself in, thus far in my life, that carries beyond just making a movie. For that reason, in a sense, I'm sorry I made it: I want to experience it as an audience, and I never have—except when Steven [Spielberg] told it to me, and I read it. I can watch the movie because it's a spectacle—but I just wish I could come to it for the first time.

FROM AUDIENCE: I was very impressed with a film of yours called *The Competition*, which I've seen three times, but it was apparently not a commercial success. I have a question: the synchronization of the music with all of you who looked like you were playing the piano was just remarkable. I believed that all of you were actually playing. What's the true story?

DREYFUSS: The true story is . . . out of the five or six contestants, *one* of them was a professional piano player.

FROM AUDIENCE: The tall thin guy with glasses.

DREYFUSS: Yes, the tall thin guy with glasses. So, the tall thin guy with glasses knew what he was doing. Myself leading the pack—we didn't know nothin'. Through the teaching of a brillant, brilliant teacher named Jean Evanson Shaw, we learned how to mimic and fake selected passages of these pieces. Amy Irving got, pretty much, dead-on finger perfect in her playing. Amy had been able to play the piano a little before—but nothing like that. And I had no experience on the piano or any other instrument—I neither play music nor read music nor have any relationship to music other than listening. I worked with Jean to mimic those pieces. If any of us had been on a sounded keyboard—it would have sounded like the trampling to the elephant graveyard.

FROM AUDIENCE: You were great.

DREYFUSS: Thank you. One thing about *The Competition*—it gave me a very important love affair with Beethoven.

FROM AUDIENCE: What's your next project?

DREYFUSS: I don't have the slightest idea. Can I ask you a question: Do any of you remember when the film *Whose Life* came out? Do you remember how you felt about seeing it or not seeing it? Didn't want to see it, eh?

CRIST: Yes, several people remarked to me that they had seen the play and didn't care to see the movie. I don't know where you're heading—but this is the kind of film that when people learn of the subject matter, they're likely to choose something else for a wild Saturday night at the movies. It lost a lot of money, I believe.

DREYFUSS: It lost a *huge* amount of money. You know, it's very chic and easy right now in Hollywood—myself included—to bitch, moan, complain, and attack film studios for all kinds of reasons—most of which they're totally deserving of. But I was always very impressed with the fact that MGM made this film. It was a dead loss from the word go—and they spent $10 million making it. This film you just saw cost $10 million! And the chances of its making ten cents were slim, or none, and it was made because David Begelman liked it. David Begelman is many, many things, but he had the courage to make this film. It was an enormous gamble, and I've always had a lot of respect for him because of it.

Nothing that anyone could do could make an audience go see it. They did a lot of research on this movie. They found that once you're in the theater, you liked it. But you could not get anyone in—not with baseball bats.

CRIST: Although I found the play depressing, I do not find the movie depressing. The movie seems so much to me an affirmation of living in the fullest sense.

DREYFUSS: You know, for three years I've been hearing the same words—and using them myself: depressing, life-affirming, *not* depressing. I think these are the wrong words to be using here. I think certainly it *is* depressing, but at the same time it's not. There has to be another vocabulary to describe this. We were thinking of saying it was a film with just a bunch of yuks. Everyone worked pretty damn hard to try to get around showing what this movie is showing—but they couldn't figure it out.

There are often occasions, as I think we all know, where we are totally misled by the marketing people. And I have yelled at them about films that I've been in. But in this case I couldn't because I couldn't figure out the right way to market it either. No one could. Because however you try to gloss it over, after saying, "He's interesting and exciting and he's funny and witty and he's this and he's that"—sooner or later you have to say, "He doesn't want to live." *What?* He doesn't want to live? I don't want to see it.

FROM AUDIENCE: Did anyone ever consider that some people may have been persuaded not to see the film because of *you*—that you're someone very robust, vibrant, and you've portrayed very different roles prior to *Whose Life*. I remember when this came out I was turned off by the theme and also because I didn't want to see *you* in this type of role.

DREYFUSS: It's interesting. First of all, there is no machinery for anyone in my business, as far as I know, to really find out what the audiences of America think of or expect of him. You know what the people who hired you think and expect—the studio heads, the guys who write scripts, people like that. But I wouldn't know about what anyone else in the world expects of me. That's number one. Number two: if I did—I wouldn't care. I mean, obviously, what I do for a living I love more than I can possibly express to you, and I want to do it for my own reasons. And if you told me that the only thing you wanted to see me do was *The Goodbye Girl*—for the rest of my life—sooner or later I'm going to want to do something else.

Number three: I don't believe there really is any such expectation. I don't believe that audiences always expect Clint Eastwood to be Clint Eastwood—they'll accept him in a lot of things. They'll accept Dustin Hoffman in a lot of things. Number four: This character—aside from the fact he is immobile—is right up my alley. When I chose the role, I thought, well, this would be a challenge—just lying there. I thought, Can I really do that? Can I totally do that and make my body look dead? That was a challenge. But the other part of it wasn't. The other part was verbal, urban, sarcastic, intelligent.

I can play smarter than me. I mean, I as an actor can play smarter than myself. I know actors who can play dumber than themselves—Robert De Niro can, it's a brilliant thing he does. I can't do it. I didn't go to college, but you think I did. So, in that way, this character was right up my alley.

FROM AUDIENCE: I usually think it's wrong when the star of a stage play does not get to do the movie. It seems unfair. This is nothing personal against you.

DREYFUSS: I agree with you, but those are commercial decisions. The star system, in my opinion, doesn't often hold a lot of water. This is one of those occasions. They thought that by putting someone whom they thought of as a commodity in this film it would help get people to pay money to see it. It didn't work; it probably got as big an audience as it would have if Tom Conti* had played it.

FROM AUDIENCE: What was the critical reaction?

DREYFUSS: Fabulous. Well, there are lots of people who don't like anything, and there are lots of people who didn't like this film. A lot of critics that I read got "into" the film—in the sense that they argued with him. There's a guy in Chicago—Roger Ebert, whose work as a critic I respect—who got into an *argument* about the movie; he ultimately said no to it because he just felt that Ken Harrison should live. I remember meeting him in Chicago and saying, "Don't you understand?" He said, "No, no." That was his position; he became the John Cassavetes character.

CRIST: That's a great critical danger. You start reviewing the movie as you want it to be instead of the movie that is there. That's one of the pitfalls of my profession.

*Conti starred on stage in London and New York.

FROM AUDIENCE: I think most of us who've followed your career look upon you as a sort of cuddly-bear guy. But sharp-witted. The kind of guy you'd like your sister to marry. But in this case you were somehow sharper, deeper—and I think this is your best performance for that reason. It's a big change in your character and personality.

DREYFUSS: Well, thank you. It's so strange. I think in a way I'm not ready to watch this film. I felt I was going through a lot of changes when I did it. I don't quite understand where I was or where I am. Perhaps that has a lot to do with it. When I was about thirty, thirty-one, I stopped saying "I know." This is something you're all familiar with. I used to know *everything,* but now—I *don't know.* I have no basic answers about the cosmos or love and life or whatever. I have felt since then I've been going through a change that has yet to be defined. I would be a fool to say that those kinds of feelings and thoughts are not reflected in my work. So, on one side I'm unwilling or unable to define my work and myself, and on the other hand, much more blithe, much more willing to take chances. But I can't yet define just how it is.

FROM AUDIENCE: Are there any parts you would like to do that you haven't done? You were a great Richard III.

DREYFUSS: Thank you. There are certain historical characters I'd like to play. I'd like to play Napoleon. I'd love to play Disraeli. I'd like to play Huey Long, Aaron Burr . . . I once had a conversation with Christopher Reeve, who said he was thinking about doing Fletcher Christian. I said, "What do you mean, you're *thinking* about doing Fletcher Christian?" I said, "Christopher, give me *your body* for ten weeks and *I'll* do Fletcher Christian."

FROM AUDIENCE: In *Whose Life*—who's really responsible for the dialogue? All those wonderful lines—who wrote them?

DREYFUSS: It's such a conglomeration. There isn't a smidgen of the character of the girl in the original play. All of that dialogue came from John Badham. And I think Reginald Rose, and the producer Larry Bachmann.

SAME AUDIENCE: A producer will really get involved in the screenplay?

DREYFUSS: Absolutely. A good producer will get involved with everything. A *bad* producer will get involved with everything. In this case, in terms of writing the script, he was fabulous. And my-self—I also wrote a lot.

FROM AUDIENCE: I've heard this film is on HBO and wonder how it's being received.

DREYFUSS: It's an enormous hit on HBO. It's a testament to the power of film. You know, people are terrified of seeing this movie in a theater. But people aren't so terrified about seeing it on television. Because television simply doesn't have the impact. Film is a religious experience—it's hard to put it that way, but it is. You commune in a darkened, open room with mythologically huge symbolic figures. There is—on an unconscious and primal level—a religious experience going on that hits you in a way no other artistic form can. Television is a minor convenience. It has no primal impact.

There's a book—can't remember who wrote it—called *The Magic and the Myth of Movies*. It was written in the thirties. It's a book I recommend to you all. Because what you are *here* for—if I may be so pompous—is really to discuss *that* experience. The reason why people can watch, on cable, *Whose Life Is It, Anyway?* or *All That Jazz* or whatever—and not see the movie—is that it's too tough in film. It's why theater never has the audience motion pictures have because theater is even tougher. As an actor I find this a little difficult to speak about, but . . . the actor does in public what you—what we—are afraid to do in private. It is an awesome power that an actor wields, an embarrassing power. When you put that power on screen, and give that actor a forty-foot face, then that person gets to you in a way that is mythological.

Let me take you back a bit: we are all, however religious, *not* very religious. Not in this century. We haven't been religious as a culture since the Industrial Revolution—which is now two hundred years ago. Before that, we had a very real relationship between God, man, work, and the earth. That went away completely with the Industrial Revolution. And not until Lillian Gish, Douglas Fairbanks, and all those people were perceived on film did we have an image of a god on earth. Not for two hundred years. During the nineteenth century we *heard* there was an Abraham Lincoln, but we never saw him. We *heard* there was Queen Victoria, but we didn't see her. Then there was this mysterious thing that Nigerian natives and cowboys in Arizona all saw—for the first time in the history of man there was this image. We were raised for 6,000 years to believe that this kind of larger-than-life image was a god. We are now seeing these images.

I'm not saying that I, as an actor, am a god. I'm saying that this is why film has a power over us. When we sit in a darkened room and symbolically hold hands with one another and say, "Give me this experience"—we are investing religiosity to that experience. So, of course, if there's a painful one or a powerful one—we will be swept up with it. If it's painful, we're not going to deal with it. But if it's on TV, who cares? Because TV has no impact, it is simply part of the furniture sitting next to the potted palm or the refrigerator. It has no impact on a primal level. Am I making sense here?

CRIST: It's a theory I share. My version is that because of the size of the movie screen—and being in the dark—the image just reaches out and encompasses you, whereas with television you're totally in control—it's smaller than you are and at any minute you can turn it off.

FROM AUDIENCE: I take it from your comments that your next starring role is *not* going to be on a TV series.

DREYFUSS: When hell freezes . . . well, no, you never know what's going to happen, but that's not going to happen right away.

FROM AUDIENCE: When you read a play or a movie what do you look for? Do you see your part or the story?

CRIST: You count the lines.

DREYFUSS: Absolutely. I count the lines. An honest answer to that—before a script gets handed to me, I ask, "What's it about?" Then, I'll read my part first. Then, I'll go back and read it again.

FROM AUDIENCE: Is it possible to like your own part—but not the story?

DREYFUSS: Often. Of course it's possible. Al Pacino became a star in a play like that; *Does the Tiger Wear a Necktie?* is an unwatchable play—with a great role. Everything else stinks.

FROM AUDIENCE: Do you ever see yourself as a director or taking some other role in filmmaking?

DREYFUSS: I am producing and developing projects. I have produced one film, *The Big Fix.* I don't have the metabolic system to be a director. Directing is an enormous job, it is a *series* of enormous jobs, behind which—unless you're willing to be a Philistine—is a visual, artistic viewpoint. You have to have the patience of Job, the courage to make decisions on a daily basis, the physical stamina that carries you through a project from pre-production, shooting, post-production, and distribution. That's two or three years of keeping it all together. I don't have it. I never really wanted it. I would just pop a gasket. And I don't have a visual sense. I know what I like—but I can't design it. I would think about directing in the theater, but not in film.

English-born and Alabama-bred, John Badham majored in philosophy at Yale University, then earned his master's degree at the Yale Drama School. He broke into movies the hard way, through a job in the mailroom at Universal Studios. Soon, however, Badham became an assistant producer and then a television director, working on episodes for such series as The Senator, The Bold Ones, Night Gallery, Kung Fu, *and* Streets of San Francisco. *After directing a couple of well-received made-for-TV movies, Badham had his first theatrical release in* The Bingo Long Traveling All-Stars and Motor Kings (1976). *His second feature,* Saturday Night Fever (1977), *hit the box-office big time. Next, Badham directed* Dracula (1979) *and* Whose Life Is It, Anyway? *and then two films that would be counted among the major critical and commercial successes of 1983:* WarGames *and* Blue Thunder. *He shared the weekend of May 13–15, 1983, at Tarrytown with Richard Dreyfuss.*

[After *The Bingo Long Traveling All-Stars, Dracula, WarGames,* and *Saturday Night Fever*]

CRIST: How did your first film, *The Bingo Long Traveling All-Stars and Motor Kings,* come about?

BADHAM: I started with *Bingo Long* in early 1975 and it was filmed during the summer of '75. It came to me as a script from Matthew Robbins and Hal Barwood, two young screenwriters who had adapted a novel of the same name.

What can I tell you about this film, except that we were all terrified to go with an all-black baseball team to Georgia to film it? Actually, we found a wonderful kind of cooperation there. I was raised in Alabama and was amazed to see that in ten or fifteen years since I had left the South attitudes had changed—albeit slowly. I found a very cooperative, helpful spirit—even in a town as small as Macon, where all the restaurants are closed at eight o'clock at night and they roll up the sidewalks.

CRIST: Were there certain things you learned about filmmaking in the course of *Bingo Long* that have stuck with you particularly?

BADHAM: That was my first feature motion picture—as opposed to television—and, as such, I found I was dealing much more with action than with dialogue. In television you become a master at the art of shooting people talking—lots of closeups and variations on closeups, over-the-shoulder shots and things like that—which gets fairly boring to the director after a while. There's a whole different feeling to composing material and shooting things for a bigger screen, where a much wider shot might be just as good as a giant closeup. You can get back a lot farther. A picture like Kubrick's *2001* is almost all long shots; there are very few even medium closeups in that film. Consequently, when you put *2001* on television, it's very hard to get any of the dynamics of it. The technique with actors is identical for feature films and TV—and the requirements of the story are very similar, though, as I said, you may be able to do more action in a movie than in a television show. The good dramatic rules apply in both places.

I was on the phone a lot to George Roy Hill, who was at Universal and one of my advisers during this time. You may not have noticed on the *Bingo Long* credits something called Pan Arts Enterprises—which is George Roy Hill's company. His job, according to Universal, was to kind of supervise everything I was doing. He took a very laid-back position, but was always available to me to consult with. We went over the script in great detail. When you're trying to solve problems, it's always nice to have somebody like that to help out. Even little problems—which now seem to be silly.

For example, we had been looking and looking for someone to play the Jackie Robinson character. Suddenly in came Stan Shaw, this young man with muscles out to here and a face like Bill Cosby. He had this great big smile, the most charming man. He read the script and was just wonderful. So I picked up the baseball and bat that I kept beside my desk, and we walked out of my office across the street to a little park—the casting director, Stan Shaw, and I. We were going to toss the ball around and see what he did. I said,

"Here, Stan, catch." Stan puts the glove up—and the ball hits his chest. "Okay . . . we're going to try that again, Stan. You have played baseball?" "Oh, yes, I got through high school on a baseball scholarship." I forget which high schools give scholarships. But asking an actor if he can play baseball is like asking him—if he's up for a Western—if he can ride a horse. "Oh, yeah—I was raised on a horse." Next thing you know they're out taking weekend crash courses in riding.

So here was Stan trying to fake his way through baseball—and I think he thought you could use the bat like something to kill crabgrass with. I was just in despair over this because we had looked and looked and looked for a good actor. And I finally asked George Roy Hill, "God, what are we going to do?" He looked at me in total disgust, and he said, "You idiot, you double him." I said, "Are you serious? Get a double for this guy?" He said, "Absolutely, just do it." So okay, we get down to Georgia—and for the first stunt we had to do, I got the double dressed in the baseball suit, and I put the camera far back—*way far back*. Actually, the camera was in New Jersey. You had to have a telescope to see Stan Shaw's double. I looked at the dailies the next day, and thought maybe I could get a little closer. One thing I learned is that in the bright sunlight the features of almost anybody will disappear, especially those of black people. It was very interesting to me to see. In the blazing noonday sun, the cameraman would bring out these hot arc lights to light the actors' faces. The darker the skin tone, the more light you have to put on them. So Richard Pryor, who's very light skinned, hardly needed any light at all. But a couple of the ballplayers were very, very black—and one of them was almost blue-black. That poor guy really had to take it—they just had to pour light in to get some kind of reading on his face. So, I found that in using the double—you could get virtually on top of the double, and as long as you didn't put much light on his face, it didn't matter. Stan, I'll say in his defense, worked very hard to get caught up. We sent him not only to batting practice every morning, I also had him enrolled in a ballet class because he was so muscle-bound he couldn't raise his arms.

FROM AUDIENCE: Were the screenwriters black?

BADHAM: No, they were about my color. The original writer [of the book] was also white. I think all of us were somewhat intimidated by the fact that we were white—and felt an obligation to invite participation by our actors and crew; we had a fairly good-sized black crew. So I went to them and said, "You're going to have to help me out, you'll have to save me from being patronizing or condescending in the script—or just doing stupid things."

One thing I believe with a crew and with actors, is that I want them to participate—not feel that I am the dictator. I invite their help and assistance and creative ideas—and I'll sort them out and throw out the ideas that don't work for me. But I try to do it in the nicest way—so they feel they can come back tomorrow with another idea. I think they sensed we wanted to make as good a statement as we could about the black experience at that time—the late 1930s and 1940s—without trying to lay a guilt trip on the audience.

FROM AUDIENCE: Was James Earl Jones your first choice for that part? Somehow he seems miscast.

BADHAM: Did he work for you in the film?

SAME AUDIENCE: Oh, yes—he's a good actor.

BADHAM: Then, let's not say miscast—let's say a little unusual, a little bit of fresh casting. It's nice to say that I know this fellow plays Othello all the time, but maybe we can get something light from him.

FROM AUDIENCE: It's clear that your films have a certain pace and flow—do you get involved in the editing?

BADHAM: If you want to keep control of the film you started out to direct, you should be as close to it as possible. My particular feeling about editing is that it's a very creative art—and a poor editor can kill you as quickly as a good one can save you. What I like to do is employ someone I trust and sit and run the dailies with him as we're shooting it. But unless there's something extremely important I think he might miss, I tend *not* to say anything to him. I let him comment to me. I will not let an editor come on a set—not because I don't like his company, but because I don't want him to see how long it took me to do a certain shot, how difficult it was to get this particular stunt. I don't want him to see any of that. All I want him to look at is the screen and to say "That shot works" or "That shot is terrible" or "It's okay, but I can fix it with such-and-such." So he stays very objective. In that way I have a free, skilled, and very objective kind of opinion coming to me from the editor. I would like him to put the scene together all by himself without my standing over his shoulder, and then, when he's got a whole sequence of five or ten minutes, I will come in and look at what he's done and start to participate with him in the shaping of it. Invariably it will be long and very full, and a little bit overdone. But that's just the nature of it—as in any kind of writing, where you'll put your ideas down on paper, then go back and revise it, rephrase it, and so on.

I had employed an editor on *Bingo Long* at the very last minute. I had wanted to have Verna Fields editing it, but she was just finishing *Jaws* at that time, and all of a sudden Universal decided it would like to have a woman vice-president who would be in charge of the completion of all of Universal's films. They asked Verna to become an executive. She wanted to do that very much, so she couldn't edit my film. I came up with a man who had won an Academy Award about seven or eight years previously, for editing. He was a lovely man and the reports on him were very good. I took him to Georgia with me and I'd see sequences he was putting together and they were—not funny. Now, when you take scenes of Richard Pryor and cut them together and they're not funny—something is wrong somewhere. I immediately blamed myself—that I was shooting it badly, that I didn't know what I was doing with comedy. I felt great waves of self-accusation and guilt at that point. Then, after seeing a few more scenes that weren't working, I decided that I'd probably made the wrong choice of editor in my haste. So I called an old friend of mine who later wound up cutting *Saturday Night Fever* for me. I let the first man go and David Rawlins literally took apart everything that had been done to that point. He took it all apart, to the original form of the dailies, and started all over again. He has a terrific sense of timing, a good comedic sense and slightly bizarre turn of mind. There are some wonderful montages in *Bingo Long*. We looked at some montages in old movies of the forties, so we'd have an idea of the spirit of them and what we wanted while we were shooting.

To me there is no point in sitting in the editing room over the man's shoulder and saying, "Cut here and cut here and here." If you're going to do that you merely need an assistant editor, not someone who costs you several thousand dollars a week. As with everything I do, I try to take advantage of what other people have to offer creatively. And if I'm not going to take advantage of a good editor, I could save a lot of money by doing it myself.

FROM AUDIENCE: How much of the ball-playing in *Bingo Long* was actually done by the actors—Billy Dee Williams or Pryor or Jones?

BADHAM: Just about all of it. Billy Dee did a lot of pitching and he worked really hard on his pitching. In the nature of filming a movie, you could be pitching all day long—but as you know, no real pitcher is going to work more than a couple of times a week and still hope to have an arm left for a regular baseball season. So if we didn't have to photograph him pitching, or James Earl catching, we didn't, just because of the possibility of injury. As it was, by the end of the movie Billy Dee would leave the set and go right to the hospital for physical therapy. I remember that the last pitch he threw was right at the end of the movie—he throws the ball right at the camera and it vanishes; that was a bit of a calculated risk because his arm gave him terrible pain at that point. But we had to get that shot. He said he could throw two or three balls but no more—and not very far. But we got it, and he scooted right off to physical therapy.

Out of that team of nine players, I'd say that five or six were professional actors. The second baseman and the shortstop were from a team called The Clowns—a trick baseball team very much like the Harlem Globe Trotters. They were the ones who knew all the old routines used by black baseball players. This one guy—who has the ball roll down his arm and bounces it on the road at forty mph and catches it again—that guy could pitch two balls to different catchers at different places—at the same time. You saw the one-armed first baseman we had? We found him in a bank in Tennessee working as a teller. He could catch a ball and get rid of it faster than most of us could with two hands.

FROM AUDIENCE: In the crowd scenes—did you use real extras or were those local people?

BADHAM: They were all local people. Macon is a very small, very poor town and a lot of people wanted to be in the movie because it was a good chance to earn a little bit of money. In the cakewalk scene we just lined people up along the street and told them to watch. The actors in the ball team had been rehearsing this dance down the street. So we started the music, and along about the second take or so everybody there joined in the dancing. They were supposed to come walking down the street with the players, but they started clapping, then they started dancing, and they got to know the dance as well as the ball players. I have to tell you, I never had a more moving experience in shooting a film—by the end of the day I was in tears from the joy and spirit of these people. It was a very exciting experience.

Then I got some of the dailies back and realized that, in some of the key shots for the very end, the camera's batteries had run low by the end of the day—so the film was running through the camera a little bit slower than it should have been, which means it runs through the projector a little bit faster than it should. So everybody was way out of tempo to the music—it was like Charlie Chaplin or the Keystone Kops. I didn't behave very well in the projection room that night—I threw a few things around and screamed and hollered. We had to go back and pick up some shots, and at the end it all worked out just fine. But you'll notice that the music at the end actually picks up tempo—it starts going faster and faster, which is what we had to do in order to use some of the shots that were terrific. We had to speed up the music to go along with the action on the screen.

CRIST: Since you mention music—how do you use music while you're filming? Do you have music in your head—on the set, or is it always a post-scoring? Music is so important in your films.

BADHAM: In *Saturday Night Fever,* for example, in the opening we took a tape recorder out with us in the street—we already had a demo made by the BeeGees of "Staying Alive," which was their initial version. But they had promised us they'd always stick to the same tempo in any future versions they did. The tempo was really all I had to have. But I had the rest of the song, too. Every time we shot a shot, that music would be playing, so all the movie that is on screen is in exact tempo to that.

This is not a technique that's peculiar to me; that's the way musicals have been shot for years. In a wonderful picture made by King Vidor, called *Our Daily Bread,* there's about a ten-minute sequence at the end of the film of a community digging an irrigation ditch. Everybody in the town is digging this ditch—and Vidor had music on the set for tempo, so that people with picks, for example, would swing them on counts of one and three—it was a 4/4 tempo. And the people with the shovels were going on the count of two and four. So there was an orchestration of the movement with the music. Consequently the cuts are very rhythmic. It doesn't look as if the music was just plastered over the film, it really blends in, and the two support each other.

In *Saturday Night Fever* the paint can is swinging in the right tempo with the music. Of course, Travolta's feet are going right on the beat. And that makes a big difference for unifying and getting a synergistic action between the sound and the music.

FROM AUDIENCE: It seems to me that the whole point of *WarGames* is that you have these computers going out of control—then you wind up with a benevolent computer deciding it doesn't make sense to fight a thermonuclear war.

BADHAM: Well, you know, it does get into—I won't say a fairy tale—but trying for absolutely 100 percent strict credibility at the end is not possible. What we tried to do was to say that at the moment the computer starts going through all its war scenarios at the end, that it has the ability to launch the missiles—it has the launch codes in hand—and it has removed all control from the people in the war room. So that it is now trying to sort out which of its possible scenarios are the best ones. Then it's going to send off the missiles. Having sorted through every single one of the scenarios it had, it didn't find a good solution to anything. So, as you say, it benevolently returned control to the people because the computer saw no way to win that situation.

I don't know that we wanted to get into launching the missiles at that point. As you notice, we didn't even cut back to closing the doors on the pad. I did have that shot in at one point—but it got to be more irritating than helpful. I think we would have missed the point to have launched the missiles.

FROM AUDIENCE: Why did you decide to have the kid play the game instead of the guy who created the game—now that he was back, and he was there?

BADHAM: Just out of a dramatic sensibility. We had started with the kid. The young boy had gotten us into trouble, and if we could make it so he could pull us out of trouble, it made good dramatic sense—rather than having him turn it over to an adult who seemed to be perfectly comfortable to let him do it. You were always aware that the older man was watching and was there to jump in if there was something he could contribute. But I think we'd have a lot of people angry with us if we had made a switch at that point.

FROM AUDIENCE: It seems obvious that *WarGames* may become to the younger generation what *Dr. Strangelove* was to ours. I wonder if you had done a lot of testing of the film with a younger audience who may not have seen *Strangelove*.

BADHAM: Absolutely. I have no interest in testing it with anyone over twenty-five. Aside from this group—and you guys have probably seen more movies in one day here than most people your age see in one year. The median age of the movie audience today is nineteen. Generally, by the time you get to be thirty or so, you're going very infrequently and have the attitude of "Let's wait until it gets on HBO." So of course I try to test with a proper audience—and young people respond extremely well to it.

What I was able to learn from the preview cards we had was that people in the audience from about twenty-five to about forty—and there was almost no one over forty in those audiences—they described the movie as exciting but also very moving and very emotional. That was the more mature audience. *Under* twenty-five, the phrases "moving" and "emotional" were almost never used. They saw it as exciting, suspenseful, great adventure. Now, I read probably the same things you've been reading, about how kids today are very worried about nuclear war, worried about being blown up. But in the three samples I've taken—one in Houston, one in Phoenix, and one in Los Angeles—we don't get that as much as we get it from adults. The kids are just not as concerned about it, but they get very excited about the movie and there's a kind of electric feeling in the audience throughout most of the film. You get totally spoiled; you never want to run it with adults again.

FROM AUDIENCE: Did you have any problems working with the kid, Matthew Broderick? Did you have some special approach with him?

BADHAM: He's actually twenty. His father, who just passed away a few months ago, James Broderick, was a wonderful actor who was on TV's *Family* for the last few years. So Matthew has grown up in a theatrical family and he has wonderful sensibilities; he has a great sense of good humor. And he's so charming on stage right now in *Brighton Beach Memoirs*, on Broadway. And *Brighton Beach Memoirs* compared to *WarGames* proves to me that he's a wonderful character actor, which is quite unusual for a young man. These are two distinctly different characters. He has a wonderful sort of body language on stage. There's not much body language in *WarGames*—I methodically cut it out and wouldn't let him do it because it looked "schticky" on film whereas it doesn't on stage.

FROM AUDIENCE: I don't understand computers—how did that computer get the boy's phone number and call him?

BADHAM: This is me trying to justify a bit of a leap—because all computer engineers will tell you that computers don't call people—not yet. But we do see Matthew put a program into his computer early on where it methodically dials through all of several exchanges in Sunnyvale, California. That's very easy to conceive. And we are positing in this film, I suppose, a very, very smart computer that has learned how to learn. It's a bit dodgy there in the credibility area. I think Mr. Hitchcock used to talk about kitchen logic, and what he meant by kitchen logic was that you'd go see one of his films and be excited by it, caught up in the action. Then you drive home, park the car in the garage, go into the kitchen, open the refrigerator, and say, "*Wait a minute!*"

CRIST: Wait until you all see *Blue Thunder*—that's very susceptible to kitchen logic, but it doesn't let go of you for a minute.

BADHAM: Yes, you may get half of the night in the kitchen on that one.

FROM AUDIENCE: How does the computer's frustration at the game of tic-tac-toe really relate to the war game that the computer was playing—and its eventual decision to give up.

BADHAM: There was a direct link in our minds—the screenwriter's and mine—between the two events. John Wood, as Falken, says in an earlier scene, "There was one thing I could never get the computer to do: I could never get it to learn the lesson of futility, that there's a time when you ought to just give up." And he uses the example of tic-tac-toe in that particular scene—that it's a silly game and boring and you can never win it. Then Matthew later on takes that game and gives it to the computer as a problem—which I am now going to have to assume Falken never did before. And in allowing the machine to play itself it sorts through millions of permutations of the game in a few seconds and decides there is no way to win—and it learns a kind of futility. At the same time, however, it has also gotten all the launch codes in its hands so another program starts running along with it—and it sorts through all the possibilities. And in having done that with the tic-tac-toe and learned it was hopeless, the computer announces that this is a silly, pointless game.

FROM AUDIENCE: I was struck by the fact that in *WarGames* there really is no bad guy—unlike other films of this genre.

BADHAM: Certainly not in the clear-cut sense—that's for sure. There are a lot more shades of gray in this, but there's no horrible bad guy. This was in our effort to make it as believable a situation as possible—and not as melodramatic. You would not want to dismiss this as some hokey melodrama. There's some good sense to it.

CRIST: To go back, Richard Dreyfuss was telling us how much input you had in the development of *Whose Life Is It, Anyway?* And I wonder how much of such input you had on your other films. I understand you came into *WarGames* after it had been started.

BADHAM: Each film is different unto itself, and when I come into a project I cannot resist the urge to go over a script and start to meddle with it—not necessarily to put my name on it, because my name [as a writer] isn't on any of these pictures and I don't particularly want it to be. But when a script doesn't quite work for me I will either work with the writer to make whatever is bothering me go away, or sometimes I have funny ideas or character ideas. A lot of the humor in *WarGames* I take the blame for—or credit for—because it was fairly flat and serious when I got it. The "famous" general was about as stodgy and deadly and pompous as you could ask. So, I am involved in the script—with the writer, if possible, for it's nice to have somebody to work with. But I'll fix things myself if I have to.

   WarGames was kind of funny because I did not know that the original writers had been removed from the project. All I was presented with was the script, which I had a lot of problems with. But the idea was great. But then I found their earlier scripts and I liked them much better than the later scripts, so I began to put their original work back in. Then it occurred to me in one bright moment that I should just call them up and get them involved again. They were thrilled to come in and help out under kind of bad circumstances.

   Whose Life Is It, Anyway? is something that was, as a play, fairly good—but for the film it needed a lot of director input. So I undertook to do a lot of the adaptation myself. Because the original writer in this case, having worked on the play for many years, was so close to it, he could see it only in terms of these immensely long speeches and staid sort of things. I was trying to get a dramatic flow so that we weren't always in the same room looking at the same bed.

In the play, the character Ken Harrison is always on stage, always center stage, and although the light may not be on him, you're always conscious of him there. That's an excellent device on stage, and I was trying to say, how can we do that on film? That's when I started bringing in video monitors to various other sets, so that Harrison was always there—he was there at the doctor's office, in the nurses' station, he was always in the background. That's a pure director's imput.

The play *Whose Life* was written by an Englishman, and you would think, if you were going to adapt it to an American situation, it would be fairly simple to go through and cross out the English idioms, where they are saying "boot" instead of "trunk," and "windscreen" instead of "windshield" and "lift" instead of "elevator," all of that. You'd think you could go through the script in a matter of hours and make a simple adaptation. It turned out to be more difficult than that because there's really a cultural difference between American and English people. English people behave toward each other in a very polite manner; they're very solicitous of each other's opinions. Underneath there may be great annoyance and anger and hatred, but they just do not want to offend another person. So in the play the characters are constantly apologizing to one another. I mean, you could throw up for all of this politeness. The play was a little long and I think I lost twenty minutes just by crossing out all the apologies. Once you see a problem like that, it becomes comparatively easy to go through the script and make adaptations—make a screenplay that is true to the original. We feel we captured the core of what the play was about, what the author wanted.

CRIST: Someone wanted to know the other night why you didn't use the stage star, Tom Conti. Was that also because he was British?

BADHAM: That was part of it. We felt we needed an American and we felt we needed a major star. We had our choice of just about every major male star—and also Mary Tyler Moore, who was interested in doing the film. So it was one of those committee decisions between myself, the head of MGM, the producer—and the original writer. We all sat in a room and went over these names and all agreed that Richard had the kind of verbal facility and the kind of comedy that was necessary to play someone who could not move. Many actors may have a physical ability but may be verbally slightly inept. If you're going to have someone who can only talk—and that's the extent of his movement—you better have someone who's real good with words, who's bright—as the character of Ken Harrison is. And, with all of Richard's sort of hyperkinetic behavior, I thought it would be fascinating to see what would happen if you locked him in a bed and told him he could not move. Suddenly all of that energy would have to go somewhere—and it would all come out of his mouth, like a toothpaste tube being squeezed.

It was an easy decision to make—it took us about ten minutes or so—as we went over all the possibilities. And Richard knew the play, liked it very much—so it took him a very short time to decide.

FROM AUDIENCE: In watching your films I feel there is a focus on hands—in *Whose Life,* particularly, also in *Dracula* and a little bit in *Saturday Night Fever.*

BADHAM: I'm also waiting for someone to get me on the subject of feet. There are feet for introducing the Travolta character, also feet for the James Earl Jones character; and in another picture, *Reflections of Murder,* there are feet too.

CRIST: And in *WarGames,* when the boy is hiding behind the screen and all the feet come down the stairs. But how about hands?

BADHAM: I know we got on the subject of hands in *Dracula* because Frank [Langella] has the most wonderful pair of hands and he uses them beautifully. He was thrilled that I noticed that because he's very vain about his hands. It's not very often you find fingers that long, hands that beautifully shaped. So it was easy to make a "moment" out of his hands, instead of always going to the same kind of closeup.

I think that Bob Fosse in choreographing a lot of his dances does a wonderful thing with hands, so you don't have to see the dancer's whole figure from top to bottom in order to get a dance movement on screen. A dance movement can be as simple as a closeup of a hand that just does a turn. The hand-of-God statue at the end of *Whose Life* is an aesthetic conceit, but also Ken Harrison's hands were paralyzed and knotted up, which is a very upsetting image. Richard and I found in talking to various quadriplegics that they are very self-conscious about the way they look, and they'd get the nurse to try to straighten out the hand to lie on the bed and look nice. But the damn thing would just kind of curl up on them in a few hours and have this awful look to it. That's very upsetting to them. You can see Richard early in the film getting the nurse to straighten his hands so they look nice, for him, because it drives him crazy to see them so twisted.

FROM AUDIENCE: What was behind the decision to make Ken Harrison's girlfriend a dancer?

BADHAM: I suppose I have a great fondness for dancing. The choice to make the girlfriend a dancer was one that presented a solution to the following problem: What kind of symbiotic relationship can we create between a sculptor and his girlfriend? Does she just live there, is she a teacher, a decorator, a housewife—what does she do? It was a lovely idea to say that she does a kind of physical sculpture, and if he was in love with her he'd certainly be interested in doing pieces that involve her. And, realizing afterward that he could no longer do that—a lot of his creative impulses were through his fingers—and that he had no physical ability to have contact with her, either, was very distressing to him. Those thoughts kept insinuating themselves in his mind to the point he decided he'd have to do something—rather than just sit there and be made crazy twenty-four hours a day.

CRIST: You had mentioned to me earlier that there was a moment when you suddenly realized that *Saturday Night Fever* was a musical. Do you want to talk about that?

BADHAM: When I took the film I read a very nice script by Norman Wexler about a young man growing up in Brooklyn who was really too big for Brooklyn: he had possibilities to go way beyond it, to outgrow that environment. It took him the whole course of the screenplay to realize that himself—and only through a terrible personal tragedy. I accepted the film on that basis, and on the airplane coming to New York to work on it I was trying to cut down the script, to find ways to make it tighter and shorter. And I suddenly realized I had a major musical on my hands. There would be only one line on a page that would say something like, "And they went into the disco and they danced." In my normal reading of the script I had not stopped to think that that meant three minutes of screen time—that one tiny line. In Westerns they used to call it "The Indians take the fort." Just one line on a page and the director is out there a week later—still trying to take the fort. That was a bit of a shock for me, to suddenly find I had all that to contend with—choreography and music and so on. It seems quite self-evident now, but at the time it was a bit upsetting and made the film even more complicated.

But I was delighted because at that point I had been working on another musical for some months—this was a musical called *The Wiz*. I had seen it in New York and fallen in love with it on Broadway. I persuaded Universal to buy the rights to it, and the producer and I worked on the screenplay adaptation for about six months. And one morning I got this cheery phone call from the head of Universal telling me he has found my star for me—that it's going to be Diana Ross. I said, "No, you don't understand, this is a seven- or eight-year-old little girl." We know that Judy Garland did it at fifteen and they had to strap her up and give her pigtails and try to make her look young because in the old Frank Baum book she's five years old. In fact, the whole thing about *Wizard of Oz* is that it's written from a child's point of view. We had conceived of it as something that started in the islands off South Carolina, where there are a lot of almost primitive groups of people living—foot-washing Baptists and people who are just not really caught up to the twentieth century. We were going to start there—and I said, "You just can't do that with a mature woman. There's just no way that the behavior of a little child who's cute and charming can also be neurotic." So we went back and forth and I said finally, "Well, she does sing beautifully and it would be nice to have her voice there. So, I'll tell you what: How about if I just shoot the movie from her point of view?"—meaning I would never photograph her. That was regarded as a smartass remark and totally uncalled for. I finally said, "Honestly, fellas, I gotta tell you, I don't know what I'm going to say to her on the set. I really have no idea how I'm going to explain scenes to her, because it seems so wrong to me." So we parted company, and the product that emerged from that . . .

CRIST: . . . is a testament to your insight and wisdom.

BADHAM: I suppose. I don't know that I would have done any better.* But if there's any virtue in standing up for what you believe in, if there's any reward for that—then *Saturday Night Fever* was the reward, which came about two months later.

---

* Sidney Lumet directed *The Wiz*.

FROM AUDIENCE: In *Whose Life,* some of us disagreed about the meaning of the ending—whether or not he would change his mind. Yet I thought the symbol of the hand of God meant that Ken Harrison would now be in the hands of God. What did you intend in that ending?

BADHAM: I felt there was tremendous ambiguity there. The film is really about freedom of choice and not about the right to die. It's about a man's ability to decide what he wants to do. So you could see it as, "He has the right to make his decision—and it's up to him." On the other hand, you could look at him—cradled in the hand of God—and say, "It's up to God." That probably, in my mind, is the wrong interpretation—if you're going to say the film is about freedom of choice. If that visual image causes you to misinterpret it, then it's probably my fault, for getting so carried away with that hand and misleading the audience in my allowing a particular image to skew the interpretation in a particular way.

I love ambiguity at the end of films—and I think you've seen that in several cases. Audiences, on the other hand, really dislike it. I have had more rocks thrown at me over the ending of *Saturday Night Fever.* And what were they really doing at the ending of *Dracula?* Would you like to know some of the interpretations of *Dracula?* You can't ask me mine—I like it to be up to the audience. I had people tell me that she [Kate Nelligan] smiled because she was carrying Dracula's baby—and there were going to be little Draculas all over the place, with little capes on, those wonderful hands, and their eyes lit up. And they all do ads for Taylor California Champagne. There were interpretations that Dracula got away, that he didn't get away, and [accusations] that I was a rotten so-and-so for not being more definitive at the end. But there is something in me that likes having people walk out of a movie with something to talk about afterward—even with something as fluffy and entertaining as *Dracula* really is. It's easy with *WarGames* because you have plenty to think about there. The *Saturday Night Fever* ending was very ambiguous—we were not trying to say he's going to stay here forever; he may turn around in thirty minutes and get on the train and go back to Brooklyn. He may lose his courage; to stay in New York with the girl is a tough decision. Are they going to get in bed or not? I don't know. At the moment they're kind of hanging on to each other in sadness, but she is saying they're going to relate to each other as friends now. Anyway, in July you'll get a chance to see what happened because there's a sequel coming out,* directed by Sylvester Stallone. They had asked me to do it, but I said, "No, I did that already." And I really don't want to be trying to go home again. I thought it was a smart idea to get Stallone involved—they do make a cute couple.

FROM AUDIENCE: How would you evaluate Travolta as an actor?

BADHAM: He's a terrific actor—very sensitive and very bright. He has not got a Ph.D. but he has tremendous street sense. It may be difficult for him to articulate a particular idea occasionally but you know he's getting at something very penetrating. A lot of his sensibilities are quite remarkable for that particular character, which is my only experience with Travolta. He understood that character in tremendous depth. Plus he has a wickedly bizarre sense of humor, and a lot of the funniest lines in the picture are ones that he improvised on the spot, lines that to me made no sense at all, but he was very funny. For example, when he's first rehearsing the dancing with Karen Gurney, he shows her a combination step that's kind of fun and says, "Follow me through this one." They do it, and she comes up laughing and says, "That's great—did you make that up yourself?" He says, "Yeah . . . aahh, well . . . I saw it on TV—and then I made it up." That makes no sense at all, but it's so charming and funny.

FROM AUDIENCE: I've seen the PG version of *Saturday Night Fever* for TV and found some of the cuts quite abrupt. Did you have anything to do with that re-editing?

BADHAM: Yes, I'm afraid I'm pretty much guilty of it. I knew that somebody would have to do it, and the editor and I said, "Let us do it, at least we'll make it as painless as possible." Sometimes things get horribly butchered in trying to cut it and get it to the point it can be shown on airplanes and on TV. If there were abrupt things in there, I apologize, but we probably had no better way out of the situation. You can't have a gang rape in the back of a car in a PG movie, and getting around that was kind of difficult. And yet Dave Rawlins, the editor, who is so clever, came up with hundreds of solutions along the way that the ordinary TV editor would not have done. By the time we got all of the bad language out, we had lost

Staying Alive, again starring John Travolta.

twelve minutes out of the movie. At least I can take the blame on this, and don't have to say, "Well, it was those dummies out there."

FROM AUDIENCE: How did you decide to become a director? What did you do before this in the industry?

BADHAM: In college I had always wanted to be an actor. But I don't think I'm good as an actor and I could never get cast. Then I'd see this guy out front surrounded by all these women and I said, "Gee, how do you get to meet all these girls?" He said, "Well, you have to be the director."

CRIST: As simple as that.

John Badham, whose kid sister, Mary, won acclaim as the enchanting little girl in 1963's To Kill a Mocking Bird, *has continued an active career with such films as* American Flyers *(1984),* Short Circuit *(1985),* Stakeout *(1987),* Bird on a Wire *(1990), and* The Hard Way *(1991).*

Richard Dreyfuss went on to star in such films as Down and Out in Beverly Hills *(1986) and, in 1987,* Stakeout, Tin Men, *and* Nuts. *In 1990 he appeared in* Postcards from the Edge *and starred in* Once Around, *with Gena Rowlands. In 1991 he won rave reviews as* The Player *in* Rosencrantz and Guildenstern Are Dead.

Michael Caine

▼▼

Michael Caine, born Maurice Joseph Micklewhite, grew up in the Cockney neighborhoods of south London. After serving with the British Army in Korea, he worked briefly in a factory, then broke into the theater—"touring the provinces" for over ten years before gaining recognition on the London stage.

While still working in the theater in the late fifties and early sixties, Caine made frequent television appearances and took small movie roles. His first major film was Zulu *(1964), which led to what Caine considers his breakthrough movie,* The Ipcress File *(1965). The following year four Michael Caine movies were relased in the United States:* Alfie, *which brought him an Academy Award nomination,* The Wrong Box, Gambit, *and* Funeral in Berlin.

Caine's films also include Hurry Sundown *(1967),* Too Late the Hero *(1970),* Get Carter *(1971),* Sleuth *(1972, for which he received his second Oscar nomination),* The Man Who Would Be King *(1975),* The Eagle Has Landed *(1976),* Silver Bears *(1977),* California Suite *(1978, for which he received his third Oscar nomination),* Dressed to Kill *(1980),* Victory *(1981), and* Deathtrap *(1982).*

Michael Caine visited Tarrytown on the weekend of September 30–October 2, 1983, to preview Educating Rita *and discuss his upcoming 1984 release,* Blame It on Rio.

[After *The Ipcress File* and *Alfie*]

CRIST: You first captivated American moviegoers with *The Ipcress File*. Tell us how you made it.

CAINE: That was the sixties in London and there were a lot of fashionable places where everybody went, and I was sitting in this restaurant when I met Harry Saltzman, a producer who was part of the Saltzman/Broccoli combine responsible for all the James Bond movies. He was going off to produce a film on his own. I got a message from a waiter that Mr. Saltzman would like me to have a drink with him. I went over to his table and before I ordered the drink—I never got the drink, as a matter of fact—he said, "Do you know a book called *The Ipcress File*?" I said, "Yes, I'm reading it." I was, just for my own entertainment, nothing more. Saltzman said, "Would you like to play the leading part in it?" I said, "Yes." He said, "Would you like a five-year contract?" And I said, "Yes. Why are you so interested in me?" He said, "I've just seen a picture called *Zulu*, and I think you could play this part very well." So he gave me a five-year contract.

When *Ipcress* was a success, obviously I was worth more money than Saltzman was paying me. And my birthday present for the five years I was with Saltzman—which is *very* unusual, quite incredible in this business—was that he gave me my contract to tear up so I could write my new terms. My birthday is on March 14, in case anybody wants to give me my contract back.

CRIST: How did the *Ipcress* character develop—or did it come to you complete as we see it?

CAINE: No, it developed. It developed first of all from the name. The book was written in the first person, and there was no name—and no dialogue. What we did was make up the dialogue as we went along. But we first sat around and said, "What are we going to call him? He's a very ordinary guy—he wears glasses, he shops in supermarkets for button mushrooms." He was a very ineffectual-looking man. We said, "Let's find a name that doesn't convey anything." So we said, "Palmer—that's a wonderful surname for him." Now you have to remember that I'm sitting with a guy called Harry Saltzman, and he said to me, "What's a first name that doesn't mean anything?" And without thinking, I said, "Harry." He said, "Thanks very much. But in any case, my first name is Herschel—not Harry."

You must remember that this was during the height of the Bond thing, with beautiful ladies and massive machinery. But we've all found out that, in actual fact, spies are very ordinary guys in extraordinary situations. Which is one of the things that made the movie a success to me. I wore glasses—I was immediately *not* a film star. Film stars to me were always six feet four, had perfect teeth, and could do handstands on Malibu beach. They didn't have pimples and didn't need glasses. I think this was the first time anybody appeared as a spy who was just an ordinary guy.

One of the executives at Universal—which put up half the money for this picture—asked me if I really thought Harry Palmer should *cook* for the girl. He said, "Isn't that going to make him look a little gay or something?" But that was a very attractive scene for a lot of women. And, you know, I was at that time a broke actor—I was prepared to cook it *and* eat it. Len Deighton [author of *The Ipcress File*] was an extremely good cook, and in the scene where you saw me cracking the two eggs—those were Len Deighton's hands. I'm blond, of course, and he has black hairs on the back of his hands.

The director, Sidney Furie, really did a wonderful job on the film, I think. Maybe his *Lady Sings the Blues* is a better picture than this, but he hasn't done *many* pictures better than this. But, to give you a rough idea of how people who make pictures—which includes all of us, actors, directors, cameramen, anybody—to show you how we whistle in the dark . . . on the first day of shooting, Sidney Furie took the script and put it in the middle of the ground and set fire to it and said, "That's what I think of *that*." Now that's how he started to make one of the best pictures he will probably ever make. I remember we were all standing around coughing from the smoke of this rather damp script—it was raining—and then he looked at me. I said, "Well, we've got to shoot the first scene." And he said, "Can I borrow your script?"

CRIST: What really makes this movie unique in that era of thrillers is that it has a point of view. Is that something on which Furie decided?

CAINE: That is completely Furie's. I don't think that even to this day Sidney realizes how clever he was in figuring out that if you see spy activities, you never see them clearly; you see *through* something—a window, a lattice. The shots of me outside of Albert Hall were seen through a parking meter. The fight scene in the telephone box was shot from a distance—you don't *expect* to see spies doing anything like that up closely. That was Sidney's view of it, and I thought it was very clever. We've never made another picture together, but if I ever wanted to give any advice to Sidney—which I can, because in Los Angeles I live about five hundred yards from him—I'd want to say, "The next time you make a movie, take a point of view. You may be wrong—but at least do it." Hitchcock always took a point of view; sometimes he was wrong, but not very often. He took a risk. And you know what happens when you take risks—you either come up great or you fall on your face.

FROM AUDIENCE: After you made *Ipcress File,* did you think it would be a breakthrough?

CAINE: I hadn't the foggiest idea. I had made *Alfie,* which hadn't been released, and *Zulu,* which had—and which was moderately successful for me. And I'd made *The Wrong Box,* which hadn't been released. So I had been working all the time—but I still didn't know whether I had a chance in this business. I had *never* had any success in the theater except from the point of view of reviews. I had gotten good reviews and some awards, but no one had ever come to see a play *because* I was in it. The same goes for television. So I never really knew where I was at with any of these things.

Then, suddenly, the reviews came out on *Ipcress File.* I lived in a little mews flat just behind Marble Arch, and I read the reviews, and after all these years—and I'm not soliciting sympathy or anything, but it was eleven years of really hard struggle—I read those reviews and I thought, Today I am an entity. I *knew* when I· read the reviews—even the first one I read, which wasn't so hot. Bond, as you know, is 007; that first review called Harry Palmer 003½. But then the other reviews started to say I was good, and I said, "Ah, these are the really intelligent guys who know what they're talking about." Quite frankly, I just stood in the middle of the flat and tears started to roll down my face. I thought, "My God! Something has *happened* out of what I've done. Maybe I *have* some sort of future." That happens to everyone in any walk of life—there comes a day when you can say, "All of this effort was really worth it!" That's what happened to me on *Ipcress File*—which is why it's so important to me.

FROM AUDIENCE: I see a lot of similarities between you and Harry Palmer.

CAINE: First of all, I wore my own glasses. And, as there was no dialogue for the character in the original book, I made up most of my own dialogue. So you are probably hearing similarities. And I spoke with the same accent and voice I'm using now. Plus the fact that, like Harry Palmer, I have a complete abhorrence of and negative attitude toward authority. Harry treated the bosses of MI-5 and -6 in exactly the same manner I treat the bosses at Fox, Columbia, and MGM.

FROM AUDIENCE: What about the sequels to *Ipcress File?*

CAINE: There were two sequels, but it was a series of diminishing returns. There was a sequel directed by Guy Hamilton called *Funeral in Berlin,* and another directed by Ken Russell called *Billion Dollar Brain.* Ken was a television director who had done documentaries on the lives of the composers. I was such an admirer of his I had commentated some of these documentaries—and I got him the job to direct *Billion Dollar Brain.* But what I didn't realize was that Ken was a lunatic.

And I also hadn't realized that in order to direct a thriller movie, the first thing you have to be—as with all good painters—is a draftsman. Because you've got to know where the suspect was at half past twelve on July fourth. Now Ken Russell, he didn't know where *he* was on July fourth. It's true. He was wonderful for some sorts of things—and in *Billion Dollar Brain* there are wonderful pictorial scenes. But they don't mean anything. You'll see six horses galloping through the snow and in the next shot there are seven, in the next five.

As an actor, you rely on the director to tell you where you are. With Ken you'd suddenly be standing in six feet of snow and you'd say, "Where're we at?" And he'd say, "Standing in six feet of snow." Then you're in trouble. As a movie actor, you concentrate on what you're doing *that* day. At least *I* concentrate on what I'm doing that day. I never see rushes, I never see rough cuts or anything. I only concentrate on *exactly* what I'm doing—because that's 100 percent concentration. I always say to the director, "How is 'he' feeling today?" *He* should tell *me* whether I'm sad or happy—because I cannot tell, as the director can change the schedule. The schedule may change for practical reasons; it may be raining so you're suddenly inside instead of out. The director's first practical job is to tell you where you are—and if you ever want to know from Ken Russell . . .

FROM AUDIENCE: Do you find any differences in working with British and American actors?

CAINE: There's very little difference in actors. First and foremost, before you become an actor, anywhere, you become an out-of-work actor, which means you are an outcast in the society to which you belong. So wherever you go, all actors are basically the same. The only rider I'd put on that is that American actors are apt to live their roles in the evenings—much to the discomfort, I imagine, of their families. British actors, the minute the director says "cut" at the end of the day, they're straight into the pub and can't remember a single line they said all day. That's the basic difference. American actors, I would say, are much more *intense*. Whether that's in the performance or not, I dunno. From my own point of view—what you saw [in *Ipcress File*] was take one or take two. When we get to take three I start getting worried; by take four I'm bored by the whole thing. But a lot of American actors, as a matter of fact most of them, won't get going till about take fifteen. That's why they get paid so much: they work harder than we do.

CRIST: In making *Beyond the Limit,* for example . . . which is such a dumb title, incidentally. I can't figure out what it means.

CAINE: What Mrs. Crist is speaking about is a film I made with Richard Gere, which opens even as we speak. This is a story based on a novel called *The Honorary Consul,* by Graham Greene. What happened on that was that Paramount Pictures, in their wisdom, did market research and found out that half of the Americans didn't know what "consul" meant and the other half didn't know what "honorary" meant. So therefore they called it *Beyond the Limit,* which guarantees nobody knows what it means.

In it, as you were about to say, Judith, I worked with an actor called Richard Gere, who is *very* intense but an extremely good actor. As a matter of fact, Richard has become a big star based on his attraction for women. He's got a pinup image—which he *hates,* and I understand that. The only trouble is, whenever they ask him to take his trousers off, he does. He does it in *Beyond the Limit.* Perhaps that's why it's called *Beyond the Limit.*

Speaking seriously about Richard, I think one day he'll be a wonderful actor. It's just that he strikes me as having some demons of his own which he's fighting all day long—rather than dealing with the demons of the character. Someone like myself, who's much older than he is and much more settled—I'm a happily married man and extremely dull, I do gardening and cooking and all that sort of stuff—when I go to the set I'm completely relaxed about what's behind me; I'm only interested in what's going on in my work. I come sailing through, have a cup of coffee, a couple of jokes, and the guy says "Go" and I go, that's it.

I remember a story about Olivier, who was working with Dustin Hoffman—in *Marathon Man*—and Dustin was going through his *thing* and Larry—Olivier—said to him, "Why don't you try *acting*? It's much easier." I don't know whether that story is true or not, but it does sum up the differences, you know? Basically, with a British actor it's a job, with an American actor it's a vocation. With an American actor, becoming an actor is rather like a lady becoming a nun. Whereas with an English actor, it's like becoming a plumber. Sometimes, no matter how good a plumber you are, if the taps that were installed there in the first place are no good, no matter how many washers you put on, it's still going to leak.

CRIST: On the subject of your being a journeyman actor—during the year you made *Ipcress*, you had already done *Alfie* and *The Wrong Box*. I can't imagine three more dissimilar roles. *The Wrong Box* is an enchanting comedy in which you played . . .

CAINE: I think in American terms you'd call him a Caspar Milquetoast. My two cousins were played by two actors who had never appeared in a movie before, Peter Cook and Dudley Moore. And Nanette Newman, the wife of the director, Bryan Forbes, played the love interest. We were supposed to live nearly next door to each other, my lady love and I, and by coincidence, the houses we used—they were in the Royal Crescent in Bath, in England—had belonged to Lord Nelson and Lady Hamilton. Mine was Nelson's and Nanette had Lady Hamilton's. An historical footnote in case you ever see the movie on television some night.

CRIST: The cast was incredible—John Mills, Sir Ralph Richardson, Peter Sellers . . .

CAINE: Oh, God, yes—I mean, it was a *cast*! There are a couple of people you don't know in America—two that are dead, an incredible English character actor called Wilfrid Lawson, and Tony Hancock. Saying that a man was a genius in radio is a contradiction in terms—like saying "military intelligence." But if there ever was a genius at radio, it was Tony Hancock.

CRIST: And in contrast to that Victorian Milquetoast, you also did *Alfie* that year. Can you tell us a little bit about that?

CAINE: Sure. Lewis Gilbert, who directed *Alfie*, was looking for someone to do the lead, and he was a good friend of the editor on *Ipcress File*—which he had secretly managed to see. That's how I got *Alfie*. The first thing I remember about *Alfie* is that it was all done on take one and printed on take one, because I was an unknown, and they didn't have any money. The whole picture was made for $750,000, so we could never get to take two. Eventually we did get to do a few take twos, but that was later in the picture when we were more comfortable about it. I think they found another $10,000 from somewhere.

Actually we did have to scratch the first two days of shooting. Throughout the film, as you know, I talk to the camera a lot. Larry Olivier talked to the camera in *Richard III* and Albert [Finney] did it in *Tom Jones*. But what we'd done at first was put the camera too far away—and in the first two days we kept bringing it closer. I said, "Why isn't this invisible person, which is the camera, standing right next to me, so I can actually talk to it?" In one scene I have Shelley Winters in my arms—which is quite a trick in the first place—and he [Alfie] just looks over her shoulder, right into the lens, and says, "She's in beautiful condition." But he says it in a soft voice, *intimate*. If the camera is at middle distance and I'm talking to it, I'm talking to *all* of you. But if the camera is *here*, close to me, and I suddenly turn and say softly, "She's in beautiful condition," then I am talking to each one of you singly.

CRIST: It's amazing that the direct approach in *Alfie* does work throughout the film.

CAINE: And it is carried an extremely long way—Bill Naughton carried it right through to the point that when the doctor is examining my chest for tuberculosis, I'm having the main conversation with the camera—and the asides are to the person in the scene. In the beginning we weren't shrewd enough to know that it would work—because, you know, people in movies are really dumb. We don't know what the hell is going on half the time. That's the thing in movies—you can do things and think they work and they don't. Another time you don't know what the hell you're doing and the camera picks up on it and loves it. That's the most dangerous thing—the camera, because it has a personality all of its own.

CRIST: Terence Stamp had done *Alfie* on Broadway. Did you have any feelings about getting the film role?

CAINE: I woke up having nightmares about that. I shared a flat with Terry at that time, because we were both sort of on our uppers. Lewis offered the film role to him before me. I mean, Lewis offered it to *everybody* before me—because I wasn't known. I remember spending three hours trying to talk Terence Stamp, my best friend, into doing it. He finally said he wouldn't do it under any circumstances. Which is why I got the part.

FROM AUDIENCE: I'm very glad *you* took the part because of one particular scene you handled with such sympathy—when Alfie was faced with getting an abortion for his lady friend [Vivien Merchant].

CAINE: Thank you very much. That was one of the reasons everybody else turned it down, because at that time, you see—and I know it's very difficult for us to think back, because we've seen actors do *everything* now. But in those days, only eighteen years ago, there were *movie stars*—and movie stars did *not* procure abortions for young ladies. The picture was turned down on that basis, I know, by Anthony Newley, Laurence Harvey, and a mass of other British actors—based on the fact that they were film stars and could not do that sort of thing.

[After *Get Carter*]

CRIST: Tell us about the background of *Get Carter*.

CAINE: That was produced by Michael Klinger and myself—I didn't take producer credit but we produced it together. We were watching television one evening, each in our own homes, and we saw the first television project that director Mike Hodges had done. We started calling each other and couldn't get through—because we were cross-ringing each other. We both said we wanted to get Hodges to direct *Get Carter*—which we did.

The general idea of doing this one was that there really had never been a sort of definitive British gangster movie, though there had been a lot of American ones. British gangsters in the movies always seemed to be charming, amusing, or inefficient. I grew up in the area from which these gangsters come, and, if anything, they are more vicious than the most vicious gangsters you ever had in America. Some of them put the Gestapo to shame. I have a detestation of all gangsters—I hate people who group together to commit violence. Having grown up around it, I've seen the results of it. So this was sort of my revenge against them, that's all.

FROM AUDIENCE: In the scene in *Get Carter* in which you're watching the film of your niece being sexually abused—how did you conjure up the emotions there, were the tears genuine?

CRIST: His mother told him the dog was dead.

CAINE: Yes. Actually, I have daughters of my own, so it's very easy to conjure up emotions in a case like that. And I can do that anyway, I can burst into tears at the drop of a hat. The one thing I can't do in acting is laugh. And I spend most of my time laughing, I love to have a great time. I'm very amused by life. But when a director says "Laugh," this artificial sort of choking sound comes out. But I can burst into tears at the drop of a hat, I suppose, because—well, I can't remember the last time I literally cried.

FROM AUDIENCE: How successful was *Get Carter* in England and in the United States?

CAINE: It was extremely successful in England, and completely unsuccessful here. MGM took one look at it and sent it out as a second feature with a Frank Sinatra picture called *Dirty Dingus McGee*. Which meant that by the time they got around to showing our film in the theater, there wasn't anybody in there. The distributors here were especially afraid of the picture because of the accents. I had fights on the film with some of the actors who were from Newcastle—because even I didn't know what they were talking about.

Actually, the Americans thought the picture was extremely violent—very, very violent. That was deliberate on our part, because these people *are* violent. The other thing was the picture's kind of strange morality. You have these gangsters who are making and selling pornographic movies—and the gangster I play, because he's got a young niece who's been forced into appearing in one of these movies—he's against the whole idea and tries to *get* these other gangsters for that. I think this morality would go over today more than it did in 1971.

FROM AUDIENCE: Do you really maintain that you have no input into the directing of your films?

CAINE: Let's put it this way: it's a very hidden input. What happens is when you start to rehearse a scene, you start to move about the way the character would, and go to the places he goes, and therefore the director's got to follow you with the camera anyway. You very rarely get the director who comes in with a plan with footsteps all over it, saying, "This is where you've got to go." Really, I don't think I could define what direction is if I tried. Sometimes directors will tell you where to go, sometimes they tell you the performance is not right. Sometimes they tell you nothing at all. Most directors say, "Well, you're a professional actor, you're getting all this money, *you* give *me* a performance. Am I supposed to be standing here telling you what to do?" They usually say, "Do you know your lines?" They say that a lot, directors; you say "Yes," and they say "Right." Then they go away.

FROM AUDIENCE: Did you ever go to acting school?

CAINE: No, I didn't. I didn't know there were such things. Where I came from, you didn't know about things like that—that was part of being educated. That's really being dumb, when you don't know there's a school. I wanted to be an actor. I was an amateur actor while I was working in a factory. I was telling this man I worked with I wanted to be an actor, and he said his daughter got a paper where they advertise for actors, and I didn't believe him. So he brought in this paper called *The Stage* and I answered an advertisement for an assistant stage manager. That's how I started. They gave me one line, then they gave me two, then three. Gradually, I started doubling up on them—until I wound up here today. I never had any formal training. I learned in the most terrifying way—in front of the public. Which means that if ever there's a laugh in the wrong place in a script—I always know it. And no one ever listens to me; I say, "You know, the audience is going to laugh at this, when they shouldn't." They say, "No, they won't." But I'm never wrong about that—because my entire theatrical education consisted of getting laughs in the wrong place. It's the most hurtful way to learn something.

FROM AUDIENCE: At what point did you take the name Michael Caine?

CAINE: I started out using the name Michael Scott, when I was in repertory. But when I got to London I got my first job in television and I had to join the Equity, and my agent told me there was another Michael Scott already. I had just come out of seeing *The Caine Mutiny*, and after I talked to my agent I had a cup of coffee in Leicester Square. And through the trees I could see the marquee—I could just see *Caine*, which was part of *Caine Mutiny*. It's a good job the trees were in the right place, otherwise I would have been called Michael Mutiny. But I saw the Caine and I thought, that's it, I'll be Michael Caine.

[After *Sleuth*]

CRIST: In *Sleuth*, of course, we spend nearly two hours and twenty minutes with just two men who do a helluva lot of talking, so it's amazing to me just how much movement and involvement there is in that movie.

CAINE: The thing is, you'd think that in a movie with only the two of us, you could shoot it in six weeks. In actual fact, *Sleuth* took longer to shoot than any movie I've ever done. It took sixteen weeks because of the special effects, the gadgets and everything. Also, there was the fact that Joe Mankiewicz had to cut away from us all the time—to try to keep it moving. In a film like that, there is no time off. Even if the closeup was on Larry, you had to be behind the camera saying the lines. Plus all the little bits and pieces of special effects that it took forever to do.

Plus the fact that Larry had spent something in the region of sixteen years trying to establish the National Theatre of England, which is now this magnificent edifice on the banks of the Thames, run by Peter Hall. It was something like within four weeks of the new theater's opening—and the same day we started shooting on *Sleuth*—that Larry got fired by the committee—having spent sixteen years establishing the National Theatre. Then it was given to Sir Peter Hall—who, I imagine, is not the closest friend of Lord Olivier. Anyway, the first couple of weeks, Larry was on Valium sandwiches, I'm telling you. It was very, very difficult for this great man, who was suddenly fired by these theatrical bureaucrats.

Let me explain something about *Lord* Olivier, that many Americans don't know. There are lots of actors with the title "Sir." There's Sir Alec Guinness, Sir Cedric Hardwicke, Sir John Gielgud, Sir Ralph Richardson, Sir Michael Redgrave. But *no* actor in the history of England—which is quite long—has ever been made a Lord. He's the first and will probably be the *only* actor to be made a Lord. A Lord is like—the only difference I can think of in an American context is that being a Lord is like being a Rockefeller and being a Sir is just rich.

When I got the part in *Sleuth* I had never met Lord Olivier, and I didn't know what I was going to call him. There were only two of us. I'm very much a working-class actor in a very much class society—which is England. I thought, what the hell will I call him? We were to start rehearsals on Monday and the Friday before I got a note from him which said, "Dear Mr. Caine, when we are introduced upon meeting, I will be Lord Olivier and you will be Mister Caine. After that, I hope you will be 'Mike' and I assure you I will be 'Larry.' " That solved that problem.

CRIST: How did you get the part in *Sleuth*?

CAINE: Do you know I haven't the foggiest idea? I suddenly got a call from my agent who said, "Joe Mankiewicz and Laurence Olivier decided they want you." I had a feeling it was because [Peter] O'Toole couldn't do it. If you think back about fifteen years— O'Toole and I looked very similar. So much so that when O'Toole became famous in a play called *The Long and the Short and the Tall*—from which he got *Lawrence of Arabia*—his understudy, the guy who took over the role, was me. I was sort of following O'Toole's footsteps all the time until we got into movies. And then it didn't matter anymore.

FROM AUDIENCE: You were nominated for an Academy Award for *Sleuth*, and I'm curious to know who could have won the Oscar over you?

CAINE: Both Laurence Olivier and I were nominated for *Sleuth* but the Academy Award that year [1972] was won by Marlon Brando in *The Godfather*.

FROM AUDIENCE: Do you think you'd want to play Shakespeare?

CAINE: I have played Shakespeare. The only time you would have seen me in America, possibly, was many years ago; I did Horatio to Christopher Plummer's *Hamlet* on television. I've never really been interested in Shakespeare from the point of view that I deal in a very naturalistic style of acting. I've tried to make movie acting not acting—but just being a person, even though it isn't me. Shakespeare is basically a declamatory style, and usually you play kings and princes. Kings and princes are pictures that you hold up and show to people—here, this is what a king is like. What I do—or like to think I do, put it that way—is hold up a mirror and say, not "Here is *me*," but "Here is *you*." I try to play human beings. So Shakespeare to me is not as important as it is to a lot of other actors—especially British actors—who always have to go back to Shakespeare and "renew" themselves at the font or whatever. I don't. I am basically a movie actor. Shakespeare *works* in movies now and then, but not often.

[After *Educating Rita*]

CRIST: We know that *Educating Rita* had been a very successful stage comedy in London. How did you get involved in the movie?

CAINE: I went to London and Lewis Gilbert—who had directed me in *Alfie* eighteen years ago—said, "Would you like to do the part of Frank Bryant in the filming of this play?" I had already seen the play about two years before, and I'd seen the performance of Julie Walters as Rita and thought that was a helluva performance. I thought I'd like to be associated with this, and I thought I could make something of Frank Bryant. On the stage in London the part was played by an excellent actor, Mark Kingston, but on stage you don't really notice the guy. When you watch a stage play you watch whoever is talking and whoever is moving, which in *Educating Rita* means that you're watching Rita the entire time. And I remember saying to an actor friend, "I'm going to play the professor, Frank Bryant." And he said, "Whatever for? He's not in the play." I said, "I'll tell you—on the stage you're only looking at Rita because she never stops talking or moving, but in the movie you'll have to cut away to the reactions of the man she's playing with." In other words, in a movie, you cannot get away with just doing a star performance—moving and talking all the time. People become bored with you. You have to show reactions. On stage a cardboard tree is a cardboard tree, and you suspend reaction. In a movie a tree is a real tree, it loses its leaves and gets covered with snow. And that applies to everybody in a movie. Nothing is in isolation as it is in a theater—and you have to play according to the reactions of someone else to what you're doing. One of the things I'm known for in movies is not acting but *reacting*.

The part of the professor was built up and then it became a two-hander. You know, Julie [Walters] had never made a movie before and on the first take—you can imagine what it's like, your first movie and your first take, your stomach is like a knot—I leaned over and gave her a little kiss, and I said, "Good luck, darling." I said, "You make 'em laugh"—which, of course, she could do—"and I'll make 'em cry"—which is what I'd figured out I could do with this role.

I said before that in my acting I've tried to be a person. At movies, you should not sit there and say this is a poor performance by a poor actor, or that it's a wonderful performance by a wonderful actor. If I'm really doing my job correctly you should sit there and say, "I'm *involved* with this person, and have no idea there's an actor there." So, really, I'm trying to defeat myself the entire time. You should never see the *actor,* never see the wheels going.

CRIST: This was the first role in which you physically changed yourself, was it not?

CAINE: Yes, in the sense that I gained thirty-five pounds to do it— and I can assure you, gaining it was much easier than losing it. I grew a beard and left it scraggly. The most extraordinary thing about this movie to me was that it was the first time I had ever played a character with whom I had *nothing* in common. He was middle class and educated—which I am not. It was the first time I played a male lead in a film in which I had everything in common with the female lead. She was a working-class British person trying to move upward in society—which is all that I had ever done. I identified more with the part I wasn't playing. So if I were a critic criticizing myself, it is to me the best performance I ever gave because it was the most difficult for me to do—it was the most removed from what I am basically.*

CRIST: One's first reaction to this story is that it's a reworking of *Pygmalion.* Yet it isn't. Was there a very conscious effort to stay away from that idea?

CAINE: I've read some comments about the similarity to *Pygmalion,* but I don't see that at all. Since some of you are movie buffs you might have seen the performance of Emil Jannings in *The Blue Angel*—the unrequited love of the ugly old professor for the beautiful young cabaret dancer played by Marlene Dietrich. My performance was not based on Rex Harrison in *My Fair Lady,* or on

*Caine won his fourth Oscar nomination for this role.

Leslie Howard in *Pygmalion*. My performance in *Educating Rita* was based on man's unrequited love for a woman out of his class—and that was Emil Jannings in *The Blue Angel*. I gained the weight, chose a deliberately unattractive wardrobe, and grew that beard—which was very uncomfortable, I must say. That's the way I saw the role; I never saw her falling in love with him—I saw him as a tragic figure, a disaster, really, and that's why I liked him. But I had nothing in common with him, because I am not a tragic figure, I assure you.

My character of Frank Bryant was based on two people, both extremely close friends of mine. One is a man who has been a professor of English history who became a famous writer. His name is Robert Bolt—he wrote *A Man for All Seasons* and the screenplays for *Dr. Zhivago, Lawrence of Arabia,* and so forth. He is one of my closest friends, and the professor part was based on him. The alcoholic part was based on my partner in a restaurant in London called Langan's Brasserie. My partner is Peter Langan, an Irishman who is bombed twenty-four hours a day. The role was so truthfully based on him that when he saw the movie he knew it.

FROM AUDIENCE: How do you go about memorizing a script—do you find it easy or difficult?

CAINE: I find that extremely easy if the script is good. The thing is, whenever I dry—which means forget a line on take—I don't say, "I have forgotten a line." I say, "There is something wrong with this line, otherwise I would not have forgotten it." That's not ego, that's to say that if the line is phony I'll forget it—if it's true, I won't. I never forgot any lines in *Educating Rita,* and certainly Julie didn't—because she'd done the play for two years.

CRIST: Someone remarked to me that you certainly choose fine roles. But you said earlier, off the platform, that you really didn't choose—that parts were brought to you.

CAINE: Yeah. My great hero in life is Clint Eastwood—who sits there and does exactly what he wants to, when he wants to, and he doesn't say very much. Which means he doesn't have to get up early and learn a lot of lines. Like John Wayne, he just says "Yep" and "Nope." But unfortunately, I've never got into that sort of box-office position, so I sit and wait for roles to come to me. First of all I choose the great ones, and if none of those come I choose the mediocre ones, and if they don't come—I choose the ones that are going to pay the rent.

Although I live in the United States, obviously I'm an Englishman, and I can't play essentially American characters the way a Newman or Redford or Reynolds could. I can't play a "good ole southern boy"—without which Burt would be penniless. I cannot play the sheriff that Clint does or the wide-open American boy that Redford does, or the blue-eyed American boy, which is what Newman does. So I wind up as a foreigner playing, usually, homosexual killers, transvestite lunatics—all sorts of those strange characters which none of those other people would play. When they want someone to be rotten and dastardly, the first thing they say is, "We've got to get someone who's a foreigner." So that's the way I have survived in Hollywood as an actor—playing things that the indigenous American actor wouldn't play. Plus the fact that I know that somewhere out there beyond New Jersey, there is a place called The Midwest, where the minute I open my mouth on screen everybody's gonna yell "Goddamn liberal Commie fag!" And that's the way it is—I talk different than they do.

FROM AUDIENCE: But couldn't you be a Cary Grant type?

CAINE: Cary Grant is an Englishman from Bristol called Archie Leach, but the great thing about Cary Grant was that he happened to speak with a Gloucester accent. The reason Americans understand him is that the normal accent that you speak is seventeenth-century Gloucestershire. Cary Grant always does this thing that's very slow—and you can understand every word he says [imitating]—the way he rolls his r's and everything, because you speak exactly the same as he does, but you're three hundred years earlier. It's true. The Australians, you know, speak seventeenth-century cockney—from my neighborhood in London. And you Americans find it very difficult to understand 'em when they talk like that— except when they say, "We've just taken away the America's Cup." For the first time in your lives you understood what they said. They speak with sixteenth- and seventeenth-century cockney because they're descended from the prisoners of Newgate prison who were sent to Australia. We always exported the people we didn't want to the colonies—including Cary Grant and Bob Hope and me.

FROM AUDIENCE: Are you interested in directing?

CAINE: No, I'm interested in producing. Because directors have to be on the set all the time, and the one thing I've noticed as an actor in fifty-two pictures is that every time it starts to rain the producer goes back to the hotel and you all sit there and get soaked. And he also has more Monets and Picassos on his wall; and he always has a bigger house than everybody. In Hollywood, anyway. I noticed that very early on, and I thought, *that's* what I want to be. I want all the paintings; I want to be back in the hotel when it's raining.

FROM AUDIENCE: Are you working on anything now?

CAINE: Do you realize this is my holiday? I've been working on four pictures for twenty months, and suddenly I'm going to be on a holiday for about six months—during which time I hope to find another comedy, because I'm very enamored of comedy. Also, I'm setting up a picture of my own, which is based in Hong Kong, about the Hong Kong police department. This is not just another police story; what enthralls me about it is that you have an Englishman and a Chinese working together, so you've got a cross-racial thing. Usually you find that the Anglo-Saxon is the big guy and everybody else is an idiot, or you get the racial backlash where everybody who isn't Anglo-Saxon is great and the Anglo-Saxon is an idiot. I detest prejudice from any angle. So, although the picture would be ostensibly a cops-and-robbers thriller—it will actually be quite different. What I'm trying to do is make an *a*-racial film, if you see what I mean. It's something very dear to my heart.

FROM AUDIENCE: Do you move around the world rather freely—or do you need special security?

CAINE: On no, I don't need any security whatsoever. I have two very close friends, however, Roger Moore and Sean Connery, who have played Bond—they get into trouble sometimes going into a pub or a bar where people have had a few drinks. There are some sorts of kudos in going home telling your wife—or your boyfriend or whatever the hell you are—that you've smashed James Bond in the face. But there's absolutely no point in saying, "Did you see Frank Bryant in *Educating Rita?*" And the wife says, "Yes." And he says, "Well, I just punched him out." Well, Jesus, Bryant's the kind of guy who would have collapsed if you'd spoken to him. So I don't really need a bodyguard—I've played too many dummies.

[After *The Man Who Would Be King*]

CRIST: I have a feeling, Michael, that *The Man Who Would Be King* is one of your favorite movies. Did having Sean Connery as your co-star and John Huston your director override any difficulties you had—because obviously, this was not an easy movie to make?

CAINE: Physically, it was one of the hardest movies I ever had to make, but because of Sean Connery and John Huston, who were wonderful to work with, the whole thing was a very happy time. I can't remember laughing like that on a movie, even though the conditions around us in Morocco were really dreadful. I was sick most of the time. It starts off with the trots, of course, which you get immediately on arriving at the airport. Then I got a sinus thing, then a mild dose of typhoid. And we never stopped shooting all the way through. The typhoid is particularly unpleasant because you go dizzy and can't stand up. But apart from that, it was a big laugh.

The film was shot just outside of Marrakesh in the Atlas Mountains in Morocco, and to go over the Atlas Mountains is quite a shattering journey. You go over a road about as wide as this platform in a truck, with no barriers or anything and literally a 6,000-foot drop. And when you get there you find yourself on the edge of the Sahara, which is dreadful. Some of the tribesmen we brought in were people from the mountains that the Moroccans themselves had never seen. These people had never seen a car or a bicycle or anything, and when they did—and when they got a bit of money—they wouldn't go back to their own tribal lands. At the end of the picture, the Moroccan government had to bring out the Army to send them back where they came from.

FROM AUDIENCE: When you're working on location, what kind of work day do you put in?

CAINE: You usually work six days a week about twelve hours a day. You basically go out around seven in the morning and get home about seven in the evening. If you're in the studio it's a five-day week. Usually when you're on location you're so miserable anyway you want to work six days and get home. Every six weeks you cut another week off the schedule. *The Man Who Would Be King* took only twelve weeks to shoot, despite the difficulties. There were language problems. Some of the other things were silly problems— like the camels, which really are the most dreadful animals. I managed to get a really rotten camel. Sean had a good one but mine was rotten. I'm sure he pulled a switch on me, because I remember starting out the film with a good camel. It was just the sort of thing he would do.

FROM AUDIENCE: Did you meet and marry Shakira in this movie?

CAINE: No, we've been married thirteen years. Shakira married *me*—not Sean, as in the movie. The way she got that part in *The Man Who Would Be King* was that Tessa Dahl—the daughter of Patricia Neal—didn't want to do it for some reason, so she went home. There we were in the middle of nowhere, and everyone was saying, "Now, where are we going to get an Indian princess?" My wife was eating her dinner one night when she looked up and everyone was staring at her. It took me three days to talk her into playing it. Considering she had never acted before and had no interest in it, I think Huston got a wonderful performance out of her.

FROM AUDIENCE: I understand you have another film coming out soon. Something about Rio.

CAINE: Yes, and there's another film I made with Laurence Olivier called *Jigsaw Man,* which is a fictionalized account of a British traitor called Kim Philby who was head of the British Secret Service and who was, in actual fact, a colonel in the KGB for thirty years. That's the *head* of our Secret Service, so you can imagine what kind of state we're in over there. Philby defected to Moscow, and the film is a fictionalized account of how he would come back to England, and why. The picture was made with a tremendous amount of difficulty over a period of a year, because they kept running out of money. I'm slightly worried what that's going to be like when it comes out.

The picture you asked about is a comedy I made set in Rio, with a script by Larry Gelbart, directed by Stanley Donen. My co-star in that is an American actor called Joseph Bologna. It's the story of two middle-aged men who take their two teenage daughters on holiday to Rio. And his daughter seduces me. He finds out that *someone* has seduced his daughter and comes to *me* to help him find the guy who did it. I haven't seen it because I don't see any film until it's absolutely finished, but it's allegedly very funny. I hope it is, because I'd like to do more comedy films. And you know what Hollywood's like, if you make a success at one kind of movie they send you loads of the same kind. This one's been called *Only in Rio, Blame It on Rio,* and *Love Rio.* We're trying to push now to get it called just *Rio.** Anyway, if you see anything with Rio in it . . .

*The final title: *Blame It on Rio.*

FROM AUDIENCE: What's the reason you won't look at the rushes?

CAINE: Because the only thing you can tell from the dailies is whether it's in focus or not. Then you've got two people you can blame—it's either the focus puller or the projectionist. More people have bought their yachts on rushes and gone bankrupt on the premiere. *Everything* looks good in rushes; it looks wonderful. The reason I don't go see a film in rough cut is that I don't want to hear any excuses; I don't want to hear, "Well, look, I know it stinks now but we're going to pull it together and then we'll put the music on and the titles. By the time we've cut this and done that, it'll be fine—don't worry about it." I just want to see exactly what the paying customer is going to see, with no excuses, no recutting, no regrading the color—they've always got some story.

FROM AUDIENCE: Many of us here can't get over what a nice human being you are and how regular you've been. What helps you keep your equilibrium?

CAINE: Thank you very much for saying that. Maybe, for a start, I was flat broke and never had any success until I was thirty years old, by which time my character and personality were completely formed. And I come from a very poor part of London, and so there was no way success was going to turn my head or anything. Also, I have an extremely happy marriage, and I'm an extreme advocate of family life. And, if you're like that, maybe you don't have the chance to be . . . a sort of "movie star," the ones who really think they're something special.

FROM AUDIENCE: You seem so responsive to questions. Do you ever do seminars with young students to help them get into your profession?

CAINE: No. I talk to young actors sometimes on the set, but I never go out and face an audience. Doing this kind of thing actually scares me. It probably doesn't look like it now because I've gotten used to it, but I was scared when I came here. The only time I've had any experience helping actors is when I'm working with an actor who gets into difficulties. In *Blame It on Rio,* I was working with a seventeen-year-old girl who had never even been in a play at school or in an amateur dramatic society. She had never acted at all—and she had a very long, difficult scene to do with me, in a café, and I said, "I'm going to teach you basic film acting in two hours." She said, "Okay, what do we do?" I said, "You sit there and I'll sit here, and we will rehearse this scene." It was a long scene, about six pages—which is long in a movie. So we started to rehearse, and she said, "So what am I supposed to be learning?" I said, "You wait and see." Now, people kept coming by and they'd say, "Oh, sorry, I see you're rehearsing." So I told her, "Okay, bring it down, bring it down." Until, finally, someone came along and sat down and started to talk to us. I said, "We're rehearsing." And he said, "Oh, I didn't realize, I thought you two were talking to each other." And I said to the girl, "*That's* acting, that's what you've got to do in a movie. If he can see you're rehearsing, the camera can see you're rehearsing."

FROM AUDIENCE: Why would they pick an inexperienced young woman when so many other actresses could fill the bill?

CAINE (chuckling): I'll tell you how she was found. She was found by Stanley Donen in a photograph in *Women's Wear Daily*—and the photograph wasn't even a picture of her. She was standing in the background of the picture. Although she has no experience as an actress, she's five feet eleven, seventeen years old, and a cross between Brooke Shields and Marilyn Monroe. So we figured we'd go with *that* and try to teach her how to act. Her name, by the way, is Michelle Johnson.

FROM AUDIENCE: We loved your film *Victory,* but we hadn't seen it till it came on cable television. Was that a film that needed more publicity?

CAINE: *Victory* wasn't given a lot of publicity, no. They test a film, and if audiences don't like it they junk it very fast, because marketing a film costs a massive amount of money. They'll take a loss on it and sell it to television, to cable, to Inflight—I think they'll eventually sell it as guitar picks—to recoup some of their money. *Blame It on Rio* will have twelve hundred prints—which costs a lot—and the advertising budget is between $3.5 million and $4 million just to open it. Then you think about *Educating Rita,* which cost just under $4 million to make.

FROM AUDIENCE: I usually think that if a studio puts a lot of money into advertising a film, something must be wrong with it.

CAINE: That's not usually the case. Usually if they put a great deal of money into it, that means they actually think something of it. Nowadays, they'll dump a film very quickly. I mean, they can be wrong. But the initial publicity is based on the fact that the studio had confidence in a film.

CRIST: Let's also point out that in many campaigns, a movie is sold in absolutely the wrong way, so you find you have no interest in seeing it. A case in point is *Beyond the Limit,* which is being sold as a sex story they tell you in three lines of advertising. So why bother to see it?

CAINE: You're right. It's all in the advert. It says, "When he met her she was a prostitute, then she was his friend's wife, and then she was his." Why go see it?

FROM AUDIENCE: I was astounded to hear you say you've made fifty-two films. What happened to the ones I'm not aware of?

CAINE: Before cable they used to disappear completely; now they keep coming back on television to haunt me. There were a lot of English films, though, which never got a release in America. A film like *Pulp* springs to mind. The worst film I ever made was called *Ashanti,* which was unreleasable. I've seen it on cable, and even for free it seems like a cheat. There were also things like *A Bridge Too Far* and *Battle of Britain,* where you'll have a three-day stint in it.

FROM AUDIENCE: Can actors keep copies of the films they make?

CAINE: I find that you really don't want to look at your films anymore. You don't have a desire to sit down and look at yourself after all of those years. As a matter of fact, after a while, you get sick of the sound of your own voice. I think that's why I do so much gardening and cooking. It's rather like weaving rugs in a lunatic asylum—you don't have to talk and you don't have to think. I always see myself in that house in Los Angeles as a lunatic weaving rugs—but happily.

FROM AUDIENCE: Were there any roles that you almost got that you wish you had?

CAINE: Yes, the Albert Finney role with Audrey Hepburn in *Two for the Road.* I couldn't do it when Stanley Donen asked me to, so he said, "We'll do something one day." Which turned out to be *Blame It on Rio*—eighteen years later.

FROM AUDIENCE: Do you think you'll ever do a Broadway play?

CAINE: It has occurred to me to do it, but the only way I would is, one, if I thought it would be successful as a play; two, if I thought it would be successful as a film; and three, if I owned the rights to both. A lot of actors will say they need to go back to the fountain of their talent. I don't *need* the theater. I had eleven of the toughest years of my life in it. Also, I always found I got bored after about three months doing the same thing over and over again. And I don't see any reason to take a 1,000 percent cut in wages.

FROM AUDIENCE: What do you think of when you see yourself in films made fifteen or eighteen years ago?

CAINE: The first thing I think about when I see an old picture is whether it holds up still. The other thing . . . my wife always says, "You are a much better actor now than you were then." And I agree with her. Sometimes you'd think you'd look back on yourself and say, "God, I wish I were young again." But I look back at myself young and I don't wish I was any different from the way I am now. I'm quite happy the way I am.

Michael Caine's prodigious output has continued unabated since his visit to Tarrytown. In 1984 he made The Holcroft Covenant *followed by Woody Allen's* Hannah and Her Sisters *in 1985. 1986 saw Caine in* Sweet Liberty, Half Moon Street, The Whistle Blower, Water, Mona Lisa, *and* The Fourth Protocol. *The following year he appeared in* Jaws: The Revenge. *His recent work includes* Without A Clue *(1988),* Dirty Rotten Scoundrels *(1988) with Steve Martin, and* A Shock To The System *(1990).*

Movies Shown and Discussed

ALFIE (Paramount Pictures, 1966). Produced and directed by Lewis Gilbert. Screenplay by Bill Naughton, based on his own play. Photography by Otto Heller. Music by Sonny Rollins. Edited by Thelma Connell.

MICHAEL CAINE *Alfie*	SHIRLEY ANNE FIELD *Carla*
SHELLEY WINTERS *Ruby*	VIVIEN MERCHANT *Lisy*
MILLICENT MARTIN *Siddie*	ELEANOR BRON *Woman Doctor*
JULIA FOSTER *Gilda*	DENHOLM ELLIOTT *Mr. Smith*
JANE ASHER *Annie*	

ALL ABOUT EVE (20th Century–Fox, 1950). Written and directed by Joseph L. Mankiewicz, based on a story by Mary Orr. Produced by Darryl F. Zanuck. Photography by Milton Krasner. Music by Alfred Newman. Edited by Barbara McLean.

BETTE DAVIS *Margo Channing*	GARY MERRILL *Bill Sampson*
ANNE BAXTER *Eve Harrington*	HUGH MARLOWE *Lloyd Richards*
GEORGE SANDERS *Addison De Witt*	THELMA RITTER *Birdie*
CELESTE HOLM *Karen Richards*	MARILYN MONROE *Miss Caswell*

THE APPRENTICESHIP OF DUDDY KRAVITZ (Paramount Pictures, 1974). Directed by Ted Kotcheff. Produced by John Kemeny. Executive producer Gerald Schneider. Screenplay by Mordecai Richler, based on his novel. Photography by Brian West. Edited by Thom Noble. Music by Stanley Myers.

RICHARD DREYFUSS *Duddy*	JOSEPH WISEMAN *Uncle Benjy*
MICHELINE LANCTOT *Yvette*	DENHOLM ELLIOTT *Friar*
JACK WARDEN *Max*	HENRY RAMER *Dingleman*
RANDY QUAID *Virgil*	

BABY DOLL (Warner Brothers, 1956). Directed and produced by Elia Kazan. Screenplay by Tennessee Williams, based on his story. Photography by Boris Kaufman. Edited by Gene Milford. Music by Kenyon Hopkins.

CAROLL BAKER	LONNY CHAPMAN
Baby Doll	*Rock*
ELI WALLACH	EADES HOGUE
Silva Vacarro	*Town Marshall*
KARL MALDEN	NOAH WILLIAMSON
Archie	*Deputy*
MILDRED DUNNOCK	
Aunt Rose Comfort	

THE BINGO LONG TRAVELING ALL-STARS AND MOTOR KINGS (Universal Pictures, 1976). Directed by John Badham. Produced by Rob Cohen. Executive producer Berry Gordy. Screenplay by Hal Barwood and Matthew Robbins, based on the novel by William Brashler. Photography by Bill Butler. Edited by David Rawlins. Music by William Goldstein; "Steal on Home" by Berry Gordy and Ron Miller; "Razzle Dazzle" by Ron Miller (lyrics) and William Goldstein (music); songs performed by Thelma Houston.

BILLY DEE WILLIAMS	LEON WAGNER
Bingo	*Fat Sam*
JAMES EARL JONES	TONY BURTON
Leon	*Isaac*
RICHARD PRYOR	JOHN McCURRY
Charlie Snow	*Walter Murchman*
RICO DAWSON	STAN SHAW
Willie Lee	*Esquire Joe Calloway*
SAM "BIRMINGHAM" BRISON	DeWAYNE JESSIE
Louis	*Rainbow*
JOPHERY BROWN	
Champ Chambers	

BIRDMAN OF ALCATRAZ (United Artists, 1962). Directed by John Frankenheimer. Produced by Stuart Miller and Guy Trosper. Screenplay by Guy Trosper, based on the book by Thomas F. Gaddis. Photographed by Burnett Guffey. Music by Elmer Bernstein.

BURT LANCASTER	NEVILLE BRAND
Robert Stroud	*Bull Ransom*
KARL MALDEN	EDMOND O'BRIEN
Harvey Shoemaker	*Tom Gaddis*
THELMA RITTER	TELLY SAVALAS
Elizabeth Stroud	*Feto Gomez*
BETTY FIELD	
Stella Johnson	

BLACKBOARD JUNGLE (MGM/United Artists, 1955). Written and directed by Richard Brooks, based on the novel by Evan Hunter. Produced by Pandro S. Berman. Photography by Russell Harlan. Edited by Ferris Webster. Music by Bill Haley and the Comets; includes "Rock Around the Clock."

GLENN FORD *Richard Dadier*	EMILE MEYER *Mr. Halloran*
ANNE FRANCIS *Anne Dadier*	WARNER ANDERSON *Dr. Bradley*
LOUIS CALHERN *Jim Murdock*	BASIL RUYSDAEL *Professor A. R. Kraall*
MARGARET HAYES *Lois Judby Hammond*	SIDNEY POITIER *Gregory W. Miller*
JOHN HOYT *Mr. Warneke*	VIC MORROW *Artie West*
RICHARD KILEY *Joshua Y. Edwards*	

CABARET (Allied Artists, 1972). Directed and choreographed by Bob Fosse. Produced by Cy Feuer. Screenplay by Jay Presson Allen, based on the musical play by Joe Masteroff, the play *I Am a Camera* by John Van Druten, and the book *Goodbye to Berlin* by Christopher Isherwood. Photography by Geoffrey Unsworth. Edited by David Bretherton. Music by John Kander; lyrics by Fred Ebb.

LIZA MINNELLI *Sally Bowles*	FRITZ WEPPER *Fritz Wendel*
MICHAEL YORK *Brian Roberts*	MARISA BERENSON *Natalie Landauer*
HELMUT GRIEM *Maximilian von Heune*	ELISABETH NEUMANN-VIERTEL *Fraulein Schneider*
JOEL GREY *Master of Ceremonies*	

CASEY'S SHADOW (Columbia Pictures, 1978). Directed by Martin Ritt. Produced by Ray Stark. Screenplay by Carol Sobieski. Photography by John Alonzo. Edited by Sidney Levin.

WALTER MATTHAU *Bourdelle*	SUSAN MYERS *Kelly Marsh*
ALEXIS SMITH *Sarah Blue*	ROBERT WEBBER *Mike Marsh*
ANDREW A. RUBIN *Buddy*	MURRAY HAMILTON *Tom Patterson*
STEVEN BURNS *Randy*	HARRY CAESAR *Calvin LeBec*
MICHAEL HERSHEWE *Casey*	

CHARLY (A Selmur Picture/Robertson Associates, 1968). Produced and directed by Ralph Nelson. Screenplay by Sterling Silliphant, based on the short story and novel *Flowers for Algernon,* by Daniel Keyes. Photography by Arthur J. Ornitz. Edited by Fredrick Steinkamp. Music by Ravi Shankar.

CLIFF ROBERTSON *Charly Gordon*	DICK VAN PATTEN *Bert*
CLAIRE BLOOM *Alice Kinian*	WILLIAM DWYER *Joey*
LILIA SKALA *Dr. Anna Staus*	ED MCNALLY *Gimpy*
LEON JANNEY *Dr. Richard Nemur*	DAN MORGAN *Paddy*

CLOSE ENCOUNTERS OF THE THIRD KIND, THE SPECIAL EDITION (Columbia Pictures, 1980). Written and directed by Steven Spielberg. Produced by Julia Phillips and Michael Phillips. Photography by Vilmos Zsigmond. Special visual effects by Douglas Trumbull. Edited by Michael Kahn. Music by John Williams.

RICHARD DREYFUSS *Roy Neary*	CARY GUFFEY *Barry Guiler*
FRANÇOIS TRUFFAUT *Claude Lacombe*	BOB BALABAN *David Laughlin*
TERI GARR *Ronnie Neary*	WARREN KEMMERLING *Wild Bill*
MELINDA DILLON *Jillian Guiler*	

COUNT THREE AND PRAY (Columbia Pictures, 1955). Directed by George Sherman. Produced by Ted Richmond. Screenplay by Herb Meadow. Photography by Burnett Guffey. Edited by William A. Lyon. Music by George Duning.

VAN HEFLIN *Luke Fargo*	ALLISON HAYES *Georgina Decrais*
JOANNE WOODWARD *Lissy*	PHIL CAREY *Albert Loomis*
RAYMOND BURR *Yancy Huggins*	MYRON HEALEY *Floyd Miller*
NANCY KULP *Matty*	

THE COWBOYS (Warner Brothers, 1972). Produced and directed by Mark Rydell. Screenplay by Irving Ravetch, Harriet Frank, Jr., and William Dale Jennings, based on the novel by William Dale Jennings. Photography by John Surtees. Music by John Williams.

JOHN WAYNE *Will Anderson*	LONNY CHAPMAN *Preacher*
ROSCOE LEE BROWN *Jedediah Nightlinger*	CHARLES TYNER *Mr. Jenkins*
BRUCE DERN *Long Hair*	A. MARTINEZ *Cimarron*
COLLEEN DEWHURST *Kate*	ALFRED BARKER, JR. *Singing Fats*
SLIM PICKENS *Anse*	NICOLAS BEAUFY *Four Eyes*

DARK VICTORY (Warner Brothers, 1939). Directed by Edmund Goulding. Produced by Hal B. Wallis, in association with David Lewis. Screenplay by Casey Robinson, based on the play by George Emerson Brewer, Jr., and Bertram Bloch. Photography by Ernest Haller. Music by Max Steiner.

BETTE DAVIS
Judith Traherne
GEORGE BRENT
Dr. Frederick Steele
GERALDINE FITZGERALD
Ann King
HUMPHREY BOGART
Michael O'Leary

RONALD REAGAN
Alec Hamin
HENRY TRAVERS
Dr. Parsons
CORA WITHERSPOON
Carrie Spottswood
DOROTHY PETERSON
Miss Wainwright

THE DAYS OF WINE AND ROSES (CBS-TV, 1958). Directed by John Frankenheimer. Written by J. P. Miller.

CLIFF ROBERTSON
Joe Clay
PIPER LAURIE
Kirsten Arnesen
CHARLES BICKFORD
Ellis Arnesen

DAYS OF WINE AND ROSES (Warner Bros., 1962). Directed by Blake Edwards. Produced by Martin Manulis. Screenplay by J. P. Miller, based on his television play for *Playhouse 90*. Photography by Philip Lathrop. Edited by Patrick McCormack. Music by Henry Mancini. Lyrics to title song by Johnny Mercer.

JACK LEMMON
Joe Clay
LEE REMICK
Kirsten Arnesen
CHARLES BICKFORD
Ellis Arnesen
JACK KLUGMAN
Jim Hungerford
ALAN HEWITT
Leland

DEBBIE MEGOWAN
Debbie Clay
MAXINE STUART
Dottie
JACK ALBERTSON
Trayner
KEN LYNCH
Proprietor
TOM PALMER
Ballefooy

DEATHTRAP (Warner Brothers, 1982). Directed by Sidney Lumet. Executive producer Jay Presson Allen; associate producer Alfred de Liagre, Jr.; producer Burtt Harris. Screenplay by Jay Presson Allen, based on the play by Ira Levin. Photography by Andrzej Bartkowiak. Edited by John J. Fitzstephens. Music by Johnny Mandel.

MICHAEL CAINE
Sidney Bruhl
CHRISTOPHER REEVE
Clifford Anderson
DYAN CANNON
Myra Bruhl

IRENE WORTH
Helga Ten Dorp
HENRY JONES
Porter Milgrim

DELIVERANCE (Warner Brothers, 1972). Produced and directed by John Boorman. Screenplay by James Dickey, based on his novel. Photography by Vilmos Zsigmond; second unit photography, Bill Butler. Edited by Tom Priestley. Music, "Dueling Banjos," arranged and played by Eric Weissberg, with Steve Mandel.

BURT REYNOLDS	HERBERT "COWBOY" COWARD
Lewis	*Toothless Man*
JON VOIGHT	JAMES DICKEY
Ed	*Sheriff Bullard*
NED BEATTY	ED RAMEY
Bobby	*Old Man*
RONNY COX	BILLY REDDEN
Drew	*Lonny*
BILLY McKINNEY	
Mountain Man	

DIAMONDS ARE FOREVER (United Artists, 1971). Directed by Guy Hamilton. Produced by Albert R. Broccoli and Harry Saltzman. Screenplay by Richard Maibaum and Tom Mankiewicz, based on the novel by Ian Fleming. Photography by Ted Moore; second-unit photography, Harold Wellman; special photographic effects, Albert Whitlock and Wally Veevers. Edited by Bert Bates and John W. Holmes. Music composed and conducted by John Barry.

SEAN CONNERY	BRUCE CABOT
James Bond	*Saxby*
JILL ST. JOHN	BRUCE GLOVER
Tiffany Case	*Wint*
CHARLES GRAY	BERNARD LEE
Ernst Stavros Blofeld	*"M"*
LANA WOOD	LOIS MAXWELL
Plenty O'Toole	*Moneypenny*
JIMMY DEAN	
Willard Whyte	

DIRECTED BY JOHN FORD (1971). Produced and directed by Peter Bogdanovich for the American Film Institute.

$ (DOLLARS) (Columbia Pictures, 1971). Written and directed by Richard Brooks. Produced by M. J. Frankovich. Photography by Petrus Schloep. Edited by George Grenville. Music by Quincy Jones.

WARREN BEATTY	ARTHUR BRAUSS
Joe Collins	*Candy Man*
GOLDIE HAWN	ROBERT STILES
Dawn Divine	*Major*
GERT FROBE	WOLFGANG KIELING
Mr. Kessel	*Granich*
ROBERT WEBBER	ROBERT HERRON
Attorney	*Bodyguard*
SCOTT BRADY	CHRISTIANE MAYBACK
Sarge	*Helga*

DRACULA (Universal Pictures, 1979). Directed by John Badham. Produced by Walter Mirisch; executive producer Marvin E. Mirisch. Screenplay by W. D. Richter, based on the play by Hamilton Deane and John L. Balderston from the novel by Bram Stoker. Photography by Gilbert Taylor. Edited by John Bloom. Music by John Williams.

FRANK LANGELLA
  Dracula
LAURENCE OLIVIER
  Van Helsing
DONALD PLEASANCE
  Seward
KATE NELLIGAN
  Lucy
TREVOR EVE
  Harker

JAN FRANCIS
  Mina
JANINE DUVITSKI
  Annie
TONY HAYGARTH
  Renfield
TEDDY TURNER
  Swales

DUEL (Universal Television, 1971). Directed by Steven Spielberg. Produced by George Eckstein. Screenplay by Richard Matheson from his own story. Photography, Jack A. Marta. Edited by Frank Morriss. Music by Billy Goldenberg.

DENNIS WEAVER
  David Mann
TIM HERBERT
  Gas-Station Attendant
CHARLES SEEL
  Old Man
EDDIE FIRESTONE
  Café Owner
SHIRLEY O'HARA
  Waitress
GENE DYNARSKI
  Man in Café

LUCILLE BENSON
  Lady at Snakerama
ALEXANDER LOCKWOOD
  Old Man in Car
AMY DOUGLASS
  Old Woman in Car
CARY LOFTIN
  Truck Driver
DALE VAN SICKLE
  Car Driver

EDUCATING RITA (Columbia, 1983). Produced and directed by Lewis Gilbert; executive producer, Herbert L. Oakes. Screenplay by Willy Russell, based on his play. Photography by Frank Watts. Edited by Gart Craven. Music by David Hentschel.

MICHAEL CAINE
  Dr. Frank Bryant
JULIE WALTERS
  Rita
MICHAEL WILLIAMS
  Brian
MAUREEN LIPMAN
  Trish

JEANANNE CROWLEY
  Julia
MALCOLM DOUGLAS
  Denny
GODFREY QUIGLEY
  Rita's father

THE EFFECT OF GAMMA RAYS ON MAN-IN-THE-MOON MARIGOLDS (20th Century–Fox, 1972). Directed and produced by Paul Newman; executive producer, John Foreman. Screenplay by Alvin Sargent, based on the Pulitzer Prize–winning play by Paul Zindel. Photography by Adam Holender. Edited by Evan Lottman. Music by Maurice Jarre.

JOANNE WOODWARD
  Beatrice Hunsdorfer
NELL POTTS
  Matilda Hunsdorfer

ROBERTA WALLACH
  Ruth Hunsdorfer
JUDITH LOWRY
  Nanny Annie

THE ELECTRIC HORSEMAN (Columbia Pictures and Universal Pictures, 1982). Directed by Sydney Pollack. Produced by Ray Stark. Screenplay by Robert Garland; screen story by Paul Gaer and Robert Garland, based on a story by Shelly Burton. Director of photography, Owen Roizman. Edited by Sheldon Kahn.

ROBERT REDFORD
Sonny
JANE FONDA
Hallie
VALERIE PERRINE
Charlotta
WILLIE NELSON
Wendell

JOHN SAXON
Hunt Sears
NICOLAS COSTER
Fitzgerald
ALLAN ARBUS
Danny

ELMER GANTRY (United Artists, 1960). Directed and written by Richard Brooks, based on the novel by Sinclair Lewis. Produced by Bernard Smith. Photography by John Alton. Music by André Previn. Edited by Marge Fowler.

BURT LANCASTER
Elmer Gantry
JEAN SIMMONS
Sister Sharon Falconer
DEAN JAGGER
William L. Morgan
ARTHUR KENNEDY
Jim Lefferts

SHIRLEY JONES
Lulu Bains
PATTI PAGE
Sister Rachel
EDWARDS ANDREWS
George Babbitt
JOHN McINTIRE
The Rev. Pengilly

THE END (United Artists, 1978). Directed by Burt Reynolds. Produced by Lawrence Gordon. Screenplay by Jerry Belson. Photography by Bobby Byrne. Edited by Donn Cambern. Music by Paul Williams.

BURT REYNOLDS
Wendell Sonny Lawson
JOANNE WOODWARD
Jessica
DOM DELUISE
Marion Borunkl
SALLY FIELD
Mary Ellen
STROTHER MARTIN
Doctor Waldo Kling
DAVID STEINBERG
Marty Lieberman

ROBBY BENSON
The priest
CARL REINER
Doctor Maneet
NORMAN FELL
Doctor Samuel Krugman
MYRNA LOY
Maureen Lawson
KRISTY McNICHOL
Julie Lawson
PAT O'BRIEN
Ben Lawson

E.T.—THE EXTRA-TERRESTRIAL (Universal Pictures, 1982). Directed by Steven Spielberg. Produced by Steven Spielberg and Kathleen Kennedy. Screenplay by Melissa Mathison. Photography by Allen Daviau. Edited by Carol Littleton. Music by John Williams.

DEE WALLACE
Mary
HENRY THOMAS
Elliott
PETER COYOTE
Keys
ROBERT MacNAUGHTON
Michael

DREW BARRYMORE
Gertie
K. C. MARTEL
Greg
SEAN FREYE
Steve
TOM HOWELL
Tyler

EXPERIMENT IN TERROR (Columbia Pictures, 1962). Directed and produced by Blake Edwards. Screenplay by Mildred Gordon and Gordon Gordon, based on their novel, *Operation Terror*. Photography by Philip Lathrop. Edited by Patrick McCormack. Music by Henry Mancini.

GLENN FORD	ROSS MARTIN
John Ripley	*Red Lynch*
LEE REMICK	ROY POOLE
Kelly Sherwood	*Brad*
STEPHANIE POWERS	NED GLASS
Toby Sherwood	*Popcorn*

FORCE 10 FROM NAVARONE (American International, 1978). Directed by Guy Hamilton. Produced by Oliver A. Unger. Screenplay by Robin Chapman; screen story by Carl Foreman, based on the novel by Alistair MacLean. Photography by Chris Challis. Edited by Ray Poulton. Music composed and conducted by Ron Goodwin.

ROBERT SHAW	FRANCO NERO
Mallory	*Lescovar*
HARRISON FORD	CARL WEATHERS
Barnsby	*Weaver*
EDWARD FOX	RICHARD KIEL
Miller	*Drazac*
BARBARA BACH	ALAN BADEL
Maritza	*Petrovich*

THE FOX (Warner Brothers, 1968). Directed by Mark Rydell. Produced by Raymond Stross. Screenplay by Lewis John Carlino and Howard Koch, based on the novella by D. H. Lawrence. Photography by William Fraker. Music composed and conducted by Lalo Schifrin.

SANDY DENNIS	ANNE HEYWOOD
Jill Banford	*Ellen March*
KEIR DULLEA	GLYN MORRIS
Paul Grenfel	*Overseer*

FROM THE TERRACE (20th Century–Fox, 1960). Directed and produced by Mark Robson. Screenplay by Ernest Lehman, based on the novel by John O'Hara. Photography by Leo Tover. Music by Elmer Bernstein.

PAUL NEWMAN	LEON AMES
Alfred Eaton	*Samuel Eaton*
JOANNE WOODWARD	ELIZABETH ALLEN
Mary St. John	*Sage Rimmington*
MYRNA LOY	BARBARA EDEN
Martha Eaton	*Clemmie*
INA BALIN	GEORGE GRIZZARD
Natàlie Benziger	*Lex Porter*

FUNERAL IN BERLIN (Paramount Pictures, 1966). Directed by Guy Hamilton. Produced by Charles Kasher. Screenplay by Evan Jones, based on the novel by Len Deighton. Photography by Otto Heller. Edited by John Bloom. Music by Conrad Elfers.

MICHAEL CAINE *Harry Palmer*	GUY DOLEMAN *Ross*
EVA RENZI *Samantha Steel*	RACHEL GURNEY *Mrs. Ross*
OSCAR HOMOLKA *Colonel Stok*	HUGH BURDEN *Hallman*
PAUL HUBSCHMID *Johnny Vulkan*	HEINZ SCHUBERT *Aaron Levine*

FUNNY LADY (Columbia Pictures, 1975). Directed by Herbert Ross. Produced by Ray Stark. Screenplay by Jay Presson Allen and Arnold Schulman, from a story by Schulman. Photography by James Wong Howe. Original songs by John Kander and Fred Ebb; music arranged and conducted by Peter Matz.

BARBRA STREISAND *Fanny Brice*	BEN VEREEN *Bert Robbins*
JAMES CAAN *Billy Rose*	CAROLE WELLS *Norma Butler*
OMAR SHARIF *Nick Arnstein*	LARRY GATES *Bernard Baruch*
RODDY McDOWALL *Bobby Moore*	

GET CARTER (MGM, 1971). Directed and written by Mike Hodges, based on the novel *Jack's Return Home*, by Ted Lewis. Produced by Michael Klinger. Photography by Wolfgang Suschitzky. Edited by John Trumper. Music by Roy Budd, lyrics by Jack Fishman.

MICHAEL CAINE *Jack Carter*	GEORGE SEWELL *Con McCarty*
IAN HENRY *Eric Paice*	GERALDINE MOFFATT *Glenda*
BRITT EKLAND *Anna Fletcher*	DOROTHY WHITE *Margaret*
JOHN OSBORNE *Cyril Kinnear*	ROSEMARIE DUNHAM *Edna (landlady)*
TONY BECKLEY *Peter*	PETRA MARKHAM *Doreen Carter*

GLORIA (Columbia Pictures, 1980). Written and directed by John Cassavetes. Produced by Sam Shaw. Photography by Fred Schuler. Edited by George C. Villasenor. Music by Bill Conti.

GENA ROWLANDS *Gloria Swenson*	JULIE CARMEN *Jeri Dawn*
BUCK HENRY *Jack Dawn*	LUPE GUARNICA *Margarita Vargas*
JOHN ADAMES *Phil Dawn*	

A GUIDE FOR THE MARRIED MAN (20th Century–Fox, 1967). Directed by Gene Kelly. Produced by Frank McCarthy. Screenplay by Frank Tarloff, based on his book. Photography by Joe McDonald. Edited by Dorothy Spencer. Music by Johnny Williams.

WALTER MATTHAU
Paul Manning
ROBERT MORSE
Ed Stander
INGER STEVENS
Ruth Manning
SUE ANE LANGDON
Irma Johnson

CLAIRE KELLY
Harriet Stander
LINDA HARRISON
Miss Stardust
ELAINE DEVRY
Jocelyn Montgomery

HARPER (Warner Brothers, 1966). Directed by Jack Smight. Produced by Jerry Gershwin and Elliott Kastner. Screenplay by William Goldman, based on Ross MacDonald's *The Moving Target*. Photography by Conrad Hall. Edited by Stefan Arnsten. Music by Johnny Mandel; song, "Living Alone," by Dory Previn and André Previn.

PAUL NEWMAN
Lew Harper
LAUREN BACALL
Mrs. Simpson
JULIE HARRIS
Betty Fraley
ARTHUR HILL
Albert Graves
JANET LEIGH
Susan Harper

PAMELA TIFFIN
Miranda Sampson
ROBERT WAGNER
Alan Traggert
ROBERT WEBBER
Dwight Troy
SHELLEY WINTERS
Fay Estebrook

HARRY AND WALTER GO TO NEW YORK (Columbia Pictures, 1976). Directed by Mark Rydell. Executive Producer, Tony Bill; produced by Don Devlin and Harry Gittes. Screenplay by John Byrum, Robert Kaufman; story by Don Devlin and John Byrum. Photography by Laszlo Kovacs. Music by David Shire; lyrics by Alan and Marilyn Bergman.

JAMES CAAN
Harry Dighby
ELLIOTT GOULD
Walter Hill
MICHAEL CAINE
Adam Worth
DIANE KEATON
Lissa Chestnut
CHARLES DURNING
Rufus T. Crisp
LESLEY ANN WARREN
Gloria Fontaine

VAL AVERY
Chatsworth
JACK GILFORD
Mischa
DENNIS DUGAN
Lewis
CAROL KANE
Florence
KATHRYN GRODY
Barbara

IN COLD BLOOD (Columbia Pictures, 1967). Written and directed by Richard Brooks, based on the book by Truman Capote. Photography by Conrad Hall. Edited by Peter Zinner. Music by Quincy Jones.

ROBERT BLAKE
Perry Smith
SCOTT WILSON
Dick Hickock
JOHN FORSYTHE
Alvin Dewey
PAUL STEWART
Reporter
GERALD S. O'LOUGHLIN
Harold Nye

JEFF COREY
Dick's father
JOHN GALLAUDET
Roy Church
JAMES FLAVIN
Clarence Duntz
CHARLES MCGRAW
Perry's father
JAMES LANTS
Officer Rohleder

THE IPCRESS FILE (Universal, 1965). Directed by Sidney Furie. Produced by Harry Saltzman. Screenplay by Bill Canaway and James Doran from the novel by Len Deighton. Photography by Otto Heller. Music by John Barry. Edited by Peter Hunt.

MICHAEL CAINE
Harry Palmer
NIGEL GREEN
Dalby
GUY DOLEMAN
Ross
SUE LLOYD
Jean
GORDON JACKSON
Carswell
AUBREY RICHARDS
Radcliffe

FRANK GATLIFF
Bluejay
THOMAS BAPTISTE
Barney
OLIVER MACGREEVY
Housemartin
FREDA BAMFORD
Alice
PAULINE WINTER
Charlady
ANTHONY BLACKSHAW
Edwards

JAWS (Universal Pictures, 1975). Directed by Steven Spielberg. Produced by Richard D. Zanuck and David Brown. Screenplay by Peter Benchley and Carl Gottlieb, based on Benchley's novel. Photography by Bill Butler, Rexford Metz, Ron Taylor, and Valerie Taylor. Special effects by Robert A. Mattey. Edited by Verna Fields. Music by John Williams.

ROY SCHEIDER
Martin Brody
ROBERT SHAW
Quint
RICHARD DREYFUSS
Matt Hooper
LORRAINE GARY
Ellen Brody

MURRAY HAMILTON
Vaughn
CARL GOTTLIEB
Meadows
JEFFREY C. KRAMER
Hendricks
SUSAN BACKLINIE
Chrissie

JEREMIAH JOHNSON (Warner Brothers, 1972). Directed by Sydney Pollack. Produced by Joe Wizan. Screenplay by John Milius and Edward Anhalt, based on the novel *Mountain Man,* by Vardis Fisher, and the story "Crow Killer," by Raymond W. Thorp and Robert Bunker. Photography by Andrew (Duke) Callaghan. Music by John Rubinstein and Tim McIntire.

ROBERT REDFORD	ALLYN ANN MCLERIE
Jeremiah Johnson	*Crazy Woman*
WILL GEER	CHARLES TYNER
Bear Claw	*Robidoux*
STEFAN GIERASCH	
Del Gue	

JEZEBEL (Warner Brothers, 1938). Directed by William Wyler. Executive producer, Hal B. Wallis; associate producer, Henry Blanke. Screenplay by Clement Ripley, Abem Finkel, and John Huston, based on the play by Owen Davis, Sr. Photography by Ernest Haller. Musical score by Max Steiner. Edited by Warren Low.

BETTE DAVIS	FAY BAINTER
Julie Marston	*Aunt Belle Massey*
HENRY FONDA	MARGARET LINDSAY
Pres Dillard	*Amy Dillard*
GEORGE BRENT	HENRY O'NEILL
Buck Cantrell	*General Bogardus*
DONALD CRISP	SPRING BYINGTON
Dr. Livingstone	*Mrs. Kenrick*

JUST TELL ME WHAT YOU WANT (Warner Brothers, 1980). Directed by Sidney Lumet. Produced by Jay Presson Allen and Sidney Lumet; executive producer, Burtt Harris. Screenplay by Jay Presson Allen from her novel. Photography by Oswald Morris. Edited by John J. Fitzstephens. Music by Charles Strouse.

ALI MCGRAW	KEENAN WYNN
Bones Burton	*Seymour Berger*
ALAN KING	TONY ROBERTS
Max Herschel	*Mike Berger*
MYRNA LOY	PETER WELLER
Stella Liberti	*Steve Routledge*

J. W. COOP (Robertson & Associates/Columbia Pictures, 1972). Produced and directed by Cliff Robertson. Written by Cliff Robertson, Gary Cartwright, and Bud Sharke. Photography by Frank Stanley, Adam Hollander, Ross Lowell, and Fred Waugh. Music by Don Randi, Louie Shelton, and the Nashville Marimba Band. Edited by Alex Beaton.

CLIFF ROBERTSON	WADE CROSBY
J. W. Coop	*Billy Sole Gibbs*
GERALDINE PAGE	MARJORIE DURANT DYE
Mama	*Big Marge*
CRISTINA FERRARE	PAUL HARPER
Bean	*Warden Morgan*
R. G. ARMSTRONG	SON HOOKER
Jim Sawyer	*Motorcycle cop*
R. L. ARMSTRONG	RICHARD KENNEDY
Tooter Watson	*Sheriff*
JOHN CRAWFORD	
Rancher	

THE KILLERS (Universal Pictures, 1946). Directed by Robert Siodmak. Produced by Mark Hellinger. Screenplay by Anthony Veiller, based on a story by Ernest Hemingway. Photography by Woody Bredell. Music by Miklos Rozsa.

BURT LANCASTER	SAM LEVENE
Swede (Pete Lunn/Ole Anderson)	*Sam Lubinsky*
AVA GARDNER	JACK LAMBERT
Kitty Collins	*Dum Dum*
EDMOND O'BRIEN	JEFF COREY
Jim Reardon	*Blinky*
ALBERT DECKER	DONALD MCBRIDE
Big Jim Colfax	*Kenyon*

KOTCH (Cinerama Releasing Corp., 1971). Directed by Jack Lemmon. Produced by Richard Carter. Screenplay by John Paxton, based on the novel by Katharine Tompkins. Photography by Richard Kline. Edited by Ralph E. Winters. Music by Marvin Hamlisch.

WALTER MATTHAU	ELLEN GEER
Joseph P. Kotcher	*Vera Kotcher*
DEBORAH WINTERS	DARRELL LARSON
Erica Herzenstiel	*Vincent Perrin*
FELICIA FARR	PAUL PICERNI
Wilma Kotcher	*Dr. Gaudillo*
CHARLES AIDMAN	LUCY SAROYAN
Gerald Kotcher	*Sissy*

THE LAST PICTURE SHOW (Columbia Pictures, 1971). Directed by Peter Bogdanovich. Producer, Stephen J. Friedman; executive producer, Bert Schneider. Screenplay by Larry McMurtry and Peter Bogdanovich, based on the novel by Larry McMurtry. Photography by Robert Surtees. Edited by Donn Cambern.

TIMOTHY BOTTOMS	ELLEN BURSTYN
Sonny Crawford	*Lois Farrow*
JEFF BRIDGES	EILEEN BRENNAN
Duane Jackson	*Genevieve*
CYBILL SHEPHERD	CLU GULAGER
Jacy Farrow	*Abilene*
BEN JOHNSON	SAM BOTTOMS
Sam the Lion	*Billy*
CLORIS LEACHMAN	SHARON TAGGART
Ruth Popper	*Charlene Duggs*

THE LONGEST YARD (Paramount, 1974). Directed by Robert Aldrich. Produced by Albert S. Ruddy. Screenplay by Tracy Keenan Wynn, based on the story by Albert S. Ruddy. Photography by Joseph Biroc. Edited by Michael Luciano. Music by Frank DeVol.

BURT REYNOLDS	HARRY CAESAR
Paul Crewe	*Granville*
EDDIE ALBERT	JOHN STEADMAN
Warden Hazen	*Pop*
ED LAUTER	CHARLES TYNER
Captain Knauer	*Unger*
MICHAEL CONRAD	MIKE HENRY
Nate Scarboro	*Rassmeusen*
JIM HAMPTON	BERNADETTE PETERS
Caretaker	*Warden's secretary*

LOVERS AND OTHER STRANGERS (Cinerama Releasing Corporation, 1970). Directed by Cy Howard. Produced by David Susskind. Screenplay by Renee Taylor, Joseph Bologna, and David Z. Goodman. Photography by Andrew Laszlo. Edited by Sid Katz. Music by Fred Karlin.

BEA ARTHUR
Bea
BONNIE BEDELIA
Susan
MICHAEL BRANDON
Mike
RICHARD CASTELLANO
Frank
BOB DISHY
Jerry
HARRY GUARDINO
Johnny
ANNE JACKSON
Cathy
MARIAN HAILEY
Brenda

JOSEPH HINDY
Richie
ANTHONY HOLLAND
Donaldson
DIANE KEATON
Joan
CLORIS LEACHMAN
Bernice
MORT MARSHALL
Father Gregory
ANNE MEARA
Wilma
GIG YOUNG
Hal

LUCKY LADY (20th Century–Fox, 1975). Directed by Stanley Donen. Produced by Michael Gruskoff. Screenplay by Willard Huyck and Gloria Katz. Photography by Geoffrey Unsworth. Edited by Peter Boita and George Hively. Music by Ralph Burns; songs by Fred Ebb and John Kander.

BURT REYNOLDS
Walker
LIZA MINNELLI
Claire
GENE HACKMAN
Kibby
GEOFFREY LEWIS
Captain Aaron Mosely
JOHN HILLERMAN
Christy McTeague

ROBBY BENSON
Billy Webber
MICHAEL HORDERN
Captain Rockwell
ANTHONY HOLLAND
Mr. Tully
JOHN MCLIAM
Ross Huggins

THE MAN WHO WOULD BE KING (Columbia, 1975). Directed and co-screenwritten by John Huston, based on a Rudyard Kipling story; co-screenwriter and assistant to John Huston, Gladys Hill. Produced by John Foreman. Photography by Oswald Morris. Edited by Russell Lloyd. Music by Maurice Jarre.

MICHAEL CAINE
Peachy Carnehan
SEAN CONNERY
Daniel Dravot
CHRISTOPHER PLUMMER
Rudyard Kipling
SAEED JAFFREY
Billy Fish
KARROUM BEN BOUIH
Kafu-Selim
JACK MAY
District Commissioner

DOGHMI LARBI
Ootah
SHAKIRA CAINE
Roxanne
MOHAMMED SHAMSI
Babu
PAUL ANTRIM
Mulvaney
ALBERT MOSES
Ghulam

MASQUERADE (United Artists, 1965). Directed by Basil Dearden. Produced by Michael Relph. Screenplay by Michael Relph and William Goldman, based on the novel *Castle Minerva,* by Victor Canning. Photography by Otto Heller. Edited by John D. Guthridge. Music by Philip Green.

CLIFF ROBERTSON
David Fraser
JACK HAWKINS
Colonel Drexel
MARISA MELL
Sophie
MICHEL PICCOLI
Sarrassin
BILL FRASER
Dunwoody

CHRISTOPHER WITTY
Prince Jamil
TUTTE LEMKOW
Paviot
KEITH PYOTT
Gustave
JOSÉ BURGOS
El Mono
CHARLES GRAY
Benson

MINNIE AND MOSKOWITZ (Universal Films, 1971). Written and directed by John Cassavetes. Photography by Arthur J. Ornitz, Alric Edens, and Michael Margulies. Edited by Fred Knudtson. Music by Bo Harwood.

GENA ROWLANDS
Minnie Moore
SEYMOUR CASSEL
Seymour Moskowitz
VAL AVERY
Zelmo Swift

TIM CAREY
Morgan Morgan
KATHERINE CASSAVETES
Sheba Moskowitz
ELSIE AIMES
Florence

THE MIRROR CRACK'D (Associated Film Distribution, 1980). Directed by Guy Hamilton. Produced by John Brabourne and Richard Goodwin. Screenplay by Jonathan Hales and Barry Sandler, based on the novel by Agatha Christie. Photography by Chris Challis. Music by John Cameron.

ELIZABETH TAYLOR
Marina Gregg
ROCK HUDSON
Jason Rudd
KIM NOVAK
Lola Brewster
ANGELA LANSBURY
Miss Jane Marple

TONY CURTIS
Marty N. Fenn
GERALDINE CHAPLIN
Ella Zielinsky
EDWARD FOX
Chief Inspector Craddock

THE MISFITS (United Artists, 1961). Directed by John Huston. Produced by Frank E. Taylor. Screenplay by Arthur Miller. Photography by Russell Metty. Edited by George Tomasini. Music by Alex North.

CLARK GABLE
Gay Langland
MARILYN MONROE
Roslyn Tabor
MONTGOMERY CLIFT
Perce Howland
ELI WALLACH
Guido

THELMA RITTER
Isabelle Steers
JAMES BARTON
Old man in bar
ESTELLE WINWOOD
Church lady
KEVIN MCCARTHY
Raymond Tabor

A NEW LEAF (Paramount Pictures, 1971). Directed by Elaine May. Produced by Joe Manduke. Screenplay by Elaine May, based on the short story "The Green Heart," by Jack Ritchie. Photography by Gay Rescher. Edited by Frederick Steinkamp and Donald Guidice.

WALTER MATTHAU	JAMES COCO
Henry Graham	*Uncle Harry*
ELAINE MAY	GRAHAM JARVIS
Henrietta Lowell	*Bo*
JACK WETSON	DORIS ROBERTS
Andrew McPherson	*Mrs. Traggert*
GEORGE ROSE	RENEE TAYLOR
Harold	*Sally Hart*
WILLIAM REDFIELD	
Beckett	

NIGHT GALLERY (Universal Television, 1969), Part II. Directed by Steven Spielberg. Produced by William Sackheim; associate producer, John Badham. Screenplay by Rod Serling. Photography by R. Batcheler and W. Margulies. Edited by Edward M. Abroms.

JOAN CRAWFORD
Miss Menio
TOM BOSLEY
Resnick
BARRY SULLIVAN
Dr. Heatherton

NOW VOYAGER (Warner Brothers, 1942). Directed by Irving Rapper. Produced by Hal B. Wallis. Screenplay by Casey Robinson, based on the novel by Olive Higgins Prouty. Photography by Sol Polito. Edited by Warren Low. Musical score by Max Steiner.

BETTE DAVIS	BONITA GRANVILLE
Charlotte Vale	*June Vale*
PAUL HENREID	ILKA CHASE
Jerry Durrence	*Lisa Vale*
CLAUDE RAINS	JOHN LODER
Dr. Jaquith	*Elliott Livingston*
GLADYS COOPER	
Mrs. Vale	

OPENING NIGHT (Faces Distribution Corp., MGM, 1978). Written and directed by John Cassavetes. Photography by Al Ruban. Music by Booker T. Jones.

GENA ROWLANDS	JOAN BLONDELL
Myrtle Gordon	*Sarah Goode*
JOHN CASSAVETES	PAUL STEWART
Maurice Aarons	*David Samuels*
BEN GAZZARA	ZOHRA LAMPERT
Manny Victor	*Dorothy Victor*

PAPER MOON (Paramount Pictures, 1973). Directed and produced by Peter Bogdanovich. Screenplay by Alvin Sargent, based on the novel *Addie Pray*, by Joe David Brown. Photography by Laszlo Kovacs. Edited by Verna Fields.

RYAN O'NEAL	JOHN HILLERMAN
Moses Pray	*Deputy Hardin and Jess Hardin*
TATUM O'NEAL	P. J. JOHNSON
Addie Loggins	*Imogene*
MADELINE KAHN	
Trixie Delight	

PAYMENT ON DEMAND (RKO-Radio Pictures, 1951). Directed by Curtis Bernhardt. Produced by Jack H. Skirball. Screenplay by Bruce Manning and Curtis Bernhardt. Photography by Leo Tover. Edited by Harry Marker.

BETTE DAVIS	JOHN SUTTON
Joyce Ramsey	*Tunliffe*
BARRY SULLIVAN	FRANCES DEE
David Ramsey	*Eileen Benson*
JANE COWL	PEGGIE CASTLE
Mrs. Hedges	*Diana*
KENT TAYLOR	OTTO KRUGER
Robert Townsend	*Prescott*
BETTY LYNN	
Martha	

THE PRIME OF MISS JEAN BRODIE (20th Century–Fox, 1969). Directed by Ronald Neame. Produced by Robert Fryer and James Cresson. Screenplay by Jay Presson Allen, based on her 1966 play and adapted from the novel by Muriel Spark. Photography by Ted Moore. Edited by Norman Savage. Music by Rod McKuen.

MAGGIE SMITH	GORDON JACKSON
Jean Brodie	*Gordon Lowther*
ROBERT STEVENS	CELIA JOHNSON
Teddy Lloyd	*Miss MacKay*
PAMELA FRANKLIN	DIANE GRAYSON
Sandy	*Jenny*

PRINCE OF THE CITY (Orion Pictures/Warner Brothers, 1981). Directed by Sidney Lumet. Produced by Burtt Harris, executive producer, Jay Presson Allen. Screenplay by Jay Presson Allen and Sidney Lumet, based on the book by Robert Daley. Photography by Andrzej Bartkowiak. Edited by John J. Fitzstephens. Music by Paul Chihara.

TREAT WILLIAMS	DON BILLETT
Daniel Ciello	*Bill May*
JERRY ORBACH	KENNY MARINO
Gus Levy	*Dom Bando*
RICHARD FORONJY	CARMINE CARIDI
Joe Marinaro	*Gino Mascone*

A QUESTION OF LOVE (ABC Sunday Night Movie, 1978). Directed by Jerry Thorpe. Produced by Jerry Thorpe and William Blinn. Screenplay by William Blinn. Photography by Chuck Arnold. Music by Billy Goldenberg.

GENA ROWLANDS
Linda Ray Guettner
JANE ALEXANDER
Barbara Moreland
NED BEATTY
Dwayne Seabler

CLU GULAGER
Mike Guettner
BONNIE BEDELIA
Joan Saltzman
JAMES SUTORIOUS
Richard Freeman

RACHEL, RACHEL (Warner Brothers, 1968). Directed and produced by Paul Newman. Screenplay by Stewart Stern, based on the novel *A Jest of God*, by Margaret Laurence. Photography by Gayne Rescher. Music by Jerome Moross.

JOANNE WOODWARD
Rachel Cameron
JAMES OLSON
Nick Kazlik
KATE HARRINGTON
Mrs. Cameron

ESTELLE PARSONS
Callie Mackie
DONALD MOFFAT
Niall Cameron
GERALDINE FITZGERALD
Reverend Wood

RAIDERS OF THE LOST ARK (Paramount Pictures, 1981). Directed by Steven Spielberg. Produced by Frank Marshall; executive producers, George Lucas and Howard Kazanjian. Screenplay by Lawrence Kasdan; story by George Lucas and Philip Kaufman. Photography by Douglas Slocombe. Edited by Michael Kahn. Music by John Williams.

HARRISON FORD
Indiana Jones
KAREN ALLEN
Marion Ravenwood
PAUL FREEMAN
Belloq
RONALD LACEY
Toht

JOHN RHYS-DAVIES
Sallah
DENHOLM ELLIOTT
Brody
WOLF KAHLER
Dietrich
ANTHONY HIGGINS
Gobler

THE REIVERS (National General Pictures, 1969). Directed by Mark Rydell. Produced by Irving Ravetch; executive producer, Robert E. Relyea. Screenplay by Irving Ravetch and Harriet Frank, Jr. Photography by Richard Moore. Edited by Tom Stanford. Music composed by John Williams.

STEVE MCQUEEN
Boon Hogganbeck
SHARON FARRELL
Corrie
WILL GEER
Boss McCaslin
MICHAEL CONSTANTINE
Mr. Binford
RUPERT CROSSE
Ned McCaslin
MITCH VOGEL
Lucius McCaslin

LONNY CHAPMAN
Maury McCaslin
JUANO HERNANDEZ
Uncle Possum
CLIFTON JAMES
Butch Lovemaiden
RUTH WHITE
Miss Reba
DIANE LADD
Phoebe
ELLEN GEER
Sally

RETURN OF THE PINK PANTHER (United Artists, 1975). Directed and produced by Blake Edwards; associate producer, Tony Adams. Screenplay by Blake Edwards and Frank Walman. Photography by Geoffrey Unsworth. Animation by Richard Williams Studio. Edited by Tom Priestly. Music by Henry Mancini; lyrics by Hal David.

PETER SELLERS *Inspector Jacques Clouseau*	PETER ARNE *Colonel Sharki*
CHRISTOPHER PLUMMER *Sir Charles Litton*	GREGOIRE ASLAN *Chief of Police*
CATHARINE SCHELL *Claudine Litton*	PETER JEFFREY *General Wadafi*
HERBERT LOM *Chief Inspector Dreyfus*	BURT KWOUK *Cato*

THE ROSE (20th Century–Fox, 1979). Directed by Mark Rydell. Produced by Marvin Worth and Aaron Russo. Screenplay by Bill Kerby and Bo Goldman, from a story by Bill Kerby. Photography by Vilmos Zsigmond. Music arranged and supervised by Paul A. Rothchild.

BETTE MIDLER *Rose*	HARRY DEAN STANTON *Billy Ray*
ALAN BATES *Rudge*	BARRY PRIMUS *Dennis*
FREDERIC FORREST *Dyer*	DAVID KEITH *Mal*

SATURDAY NIGHT FEVER (Paramount Pictures, 1977). Directed by John Badham. Produced by Robert Stigwood; executive producer, Keven McCormick. Screenplay by Norman Wexler, based on a story by Nik Cohn. Photography by Ralf D. Bode. Edited by David Rawlins. Musical numbers staged and choreographed by Lester Wilson; additional music and adaptation by David Shire; original music by Barry, Robin, and Maurice Gibb, performed by the Bee Gees.

JOHN TRAVOLTA *Tony Manero*	PAUL PAPE *Double J*
KAREN GORNEY *Stephanie*	DONNA PESCOW *Annette*
BARRY MILLER *Bobby C.*	BRUCE ORNSTEIN *Gus*
JOSEPH CALI *Joey*	JULIE BOVASSO *Flo*

THE SCALPHUNTERS (United Artists, 1968). Directed by Sydney Pollack. Produced by Jules Levy, Arthur Gardner, and Arnold Laven. Screenplay by William Norton. Photography by Duke Callaghan and Richard Moore. Music by Elmer Bernstein.

BURT LANCASTER *Joe Bass*	DAN VADIS *Yuma*
SHELLEY WINTERS *Kate*	DABNEY COLEMAN *Jed*
TELLY SAVALAS *Jim Howie*	PAUL PICERNI *Frank*
OSSIE DAVIS *Joseph Winfield Lee*	NICK CRAVAT *Ramon*
ARMANDO SILVESTRE *Two Crows*	

THE SECRET LIFE OF AN AMERICAN WIFE (20th Century–Fox Pictures, 1968). Directed, produced, and written by George Axelrod. Photography by Leon Shamroy. Edited by Harry Gerstad. Music by Billy May.

WALTER MATTHAU *The Movie Star (Charlie)*	RICHARD BULL *Howard*
ANNE JACKSON *Victoria Layton*	PAUL NAPIER *Herb Steinberg*
PATRICK O'NEAL *Tom Layton*	GARY BROWN *Jimmy*
EDY WILLIAMS *Suzie Steinberg*	ALBERT CARRIER *Jean-Claude*

SEMI-TOUGH (United Artists, 1977). Directed by Michael Ritchie. Produced by David Merrick. Screenplay by Walter Bernstein, based on the novel by Dan Jenkins. Photography by Charles Rosher, Jr. Edited by Richard A. Harris. Music by Jerry Fielding.

BURT REYNOLDS *Billy Clyde Puckett*	LOTTE LENYA *Clara Pelf*
JILL CLAYBURGH *Barbara Jane Bookman*	RICHARD MASUR *Phillip Hooper*
KRIS KRISTOFFERSON *Shake Tiller*	CARL WEATHERS *Dreamer Tatum*
ROBERT PRESTON *Big Ed Bookman*	BRIAN DENNEHY *T. J. Lambert*
BERT CONVY *Friedrich Bismark*	MARY JO CATLETT *Earlene*
ROGER E. MOSLEY *Puddin*	

SLEUTH (20th Century–Fox, 1972). Directed by Joseph L. Mankiewicz. Produced by Morton Gottlieb; executive producer, Edgar J. Scherick. Screenplay by Anthony Shaffer, based on his play. Photography by Oswald Morris. Edited by Richard Marden. Music by John Addison.

LAURENCE OLIVIER
Andrew Wyke
MICHAEL CAINE
Milo Tindle

S.O.B. (Paramount, 1981). Written and directed by Blake Edwards. Produced by Blake Edwards and Tony Adams. Photography by Harry Stradling. Edited by Ralph E. Winters. Music by Henry Mancini.

JULIE ANDREWS *Sally Miles*	ROBERT PRESTON *Dr. Irving Finegarten*
WILLIAM HOLDEN *Tim Culley*	CRAIG STEVENS *Willard*
MARISA BERENSON *Mavis*	LORETTA SWIT *Polly Reed*
LARRY HAGMAN *Dick Benson*	ROBERT VAUGHN *David Blackman*
ROBERT LOGGIA *Herb Maskowitz*	ROBERT WEBBER *Ben Coogan*
STUART MARGOLIN *Gary Murdock*	SHELLEY WINTERS *Eva Brown*
RICHARD MULLIGAN *Felix Farmer*	

STRANGERS (Chris–Rose Productions for CBS-TV, 1981). Directed by Milton Katselas. Produced by Robert W. Christiansen and Rick Rosenberg. Written by Michael de Guzman. Photography by James Crabe. Music by Fred Karlin.

BETTE DAVIS
Lucy Mason
GENA ROWLANDS
Abigail Mason
FORD RAINEY
Mr. Meecham
DONALD MOFFAT
Wally Ball

WHIT BISSELL
Dr. Henry Blodgett
ROYAL DANO
Mr. Willis
KATE RIEHL
Mrs. Brighton

SUGARLAND EXPRESS (Universal Pictures, 1974). Directed by Steven Spielberg. Produced by Richard D. Zanuck and David Brown. Screenplay by Hal Barwood and Matthew Robbins, from a story by Steven Spielberg. Photography by Vilmos Zsigmond. Edited by Verna Fields and Edward M. Abroms. Music by John Williams.

GOLDIE HAWN
Lou Jean
BEN JOHNSON
Captain Tanner
MICHAEL SACKS
Slide

WILLIAM ATHERTON
Clovis
GREGORY WALCOTT
Mashburn
HARRISON ZANUCK
Baby Langston

SWEET BIRD OF YOUTH (MGM, 1962). Written and directed by Richard Brooks, based on the play by Tennessee Williams. Produced by Pandro S. Berman. Photography by Milton Krasner. Edited by Henry Berman.

PAUL NEWMAN
Chance Wayne
GERALDINE PAGE
Alexandra Del Lago
SHIRLEY KNIGHT
Heavenly Finley
ED BEGLEY
"Boss" Finley

RIP TORN
Thomas J. Finley, Jr.
MILDRED DUNNOCK
Aunt Nonnie
MADELEINE SHERWOOD
Miss Lucy

SWEET SMELL OF SUCCESS (United Artists, 1957). Directed by Alexander Mackendrick. Produced by James Hill. Screenplay by Clifford Odets and Ernest Lehman, based on a novelette by Ernest Lehman. Photographed by James Wong Howe. Music by Elmer Bernstein.

BURT LANCASTER
J. J. Hunsecker
TONY CURTIS
Sidney Falco
SUSAN HARRISON
Susan Hunsecker
MARTY MILNER
Steve Dallas

SAM LEVENE
Frank D'Angelo
BARBARA NICHOLS
Rita
JEFF DONNELL
Sally
EMILE MEYER
Harry Kello

THE TAKING OF PELHAM ONE TWO THREE (United Artists, 1974). Directed by Joseph Sargent. Produced by Edgar J. Sherick and Gabriel Katzka. Screenplay by Peter Stone, based on the novel by John Godey. Photography by Owen Roizman. Edited by Gerald Greenberg and Robert Q. Lovett. Music by David Shire.

WALTER MATTHAU *Lieutenant Garber*	EARL HINDMAN *Brown*
ROBERT SHAW *Blue*	JAMES BRODERICK *Denny Doyle*
MARTIN BALSAM *Green*	DICK O'NEILL *Correll*
HECTOR ELIZONDO *Grey*	LEE WALLACE *The Mayor*

TARGETS (Paramount Pictures, 1968). Produced, directed, and written by Peter Bogdanovich, based on a story by Polly Platt and Peter Bogdanovich. Photography by Laszlo Kovacs. Associate producer, Daniel Selznick.

BORIS KARLOFF *Byron Oriok*	ARTHUR PETERSON *Ed Loughlin*
TIM O'KELLY *Bobby Thompson*	MARY JACKSON *Charlotte Thompson*
NANCY HSUEH *Jenny*	TANYA MORGAN *Ilene Thompson*
JAMES BROWN *Robert Thompson, Sr.*	MONTY LANDIS *Marshall Smith*
SANDY BARON *Kip Larkin*	PETER BOGDANOVICH *Sammy Michaels*

THEY SHOOT HORSES, DON'T THEY? (Cinerama, 1969). Directed by Sydney Pollack. Produced by Irwin Winkler and Robert Chartoff. Screenplay by James Poe and Robert E. Thompson, based on the novel by Horace McCoy. Photography by Philip H. Lathrop. Music by John Green. Edited by Fredric Steinkamp.

JANE FONDA *Gloria Beatty*	RED BUTTONS *Sailor*
MICHAEL SARRAZIN *Robert Syverton*	BRUCE DERN *James*
SUSANNAH YORK *Alice*	BONNIE BEDELIA *Ruby*
GIG YOUNG *Rocky*	

THE TIGER MAKES OUT (Columbia Pictures, 1967). Directed by Arthur Hiller. Produced by George Justin. Screenplay by Murray Schisgal, based on his play *The Tiger*. Photography by Arthur J. Ornitz. Edited by Robert C. Jones. Music by Milton Rogers; title song by Diana Hilderbrand and Milton Rogers.

ELI WALLACH *Ben Harris*	ROLAND WOOD *Mr. Kelly*
ANNE JACKSON *Gloria Fiske*	CHARLES NELSON REILLY *Registrar*
BOB DISHY *Jerry Fiske*	FRANCIS STERNHAGEN *Lady on bus*
JOHN HARKINS *Leo*	ELIZABETH WILSON *Receptionist*
RUTH WHITE *Mrs. Kelly*	

A TOUCH OF LARCENY (Paramount, 1960). Directed by Guy Hamilton; assistant director Peter Yates. Produced by Ivan Foxwell. Screenplay by Roger MacDougall in collaboration with Guy Hamilton and Ivan Foxwell, based on the novel *The Megstone Plot*, by Andrew Garve. Photography by John Wilcox. Edited by Alan Osbiston. Music composed and conducted by Philip Green.

JAMES MASON *Commander Max Easton*	HARRY ANDREWS *Captain Graham*
VERA MILES *Virginia Killain*	OLIVER JOHNSTON *Minister*
GEORGE SANDERS *Sir Charles Holland*	ROBERT FLEMYNG *Larkin*

WARGAMES (MGM/UA Entertainment Co., 1983). Directed by John Badham. Produced by Harold Schneider; executive producer Leonard Goldberg. Screenplay by Lawrence Lasker and Walter F. Parkes. Photographed by William A. Fraker. Edited by Tom Rolf. Music by Arthur B. Rubinstein.

MATTHEW BRODERICK *David*	BARRY CORBIN *General Beringer*
DABNEY COLEMAN *McKittrick*	JUANIN CLAY *Pat Healy*
JOHN WOOD *Falken*	KENT WILLIAMS *Cabot*
ALLY SHEEDY *Jennifer*	DENNIS LIPSCOMB *Watson*

THE WAY WE WERE (Columbia, 1973). Directed by Sydney Pollack. Produced by Ray Stark. Screenplay by Arthur Laurents, based on his novel. Photography by Harry Stradling, Jr. Music by Marvin Hamlisch; song "The Way We Were," music by Marvin Hamlisch, lyrics by Marilyn and Alan Bergman.

BARBRA STREISAND *Katie*	LOIS CHILES *Carol Ann*
ROBERT REDFORD *Hubbell*	VIVECA LINDFORS *Paula Reisner*
BRADFORD DILLMAN *J.J.*	PATRICK O'NEAL *George Bissinger*

WHAT'S UP, DOC? (Warner Brothers, 1972). Directed and produced by Peter Bogdanovich; associate producer Paul Lewis. Screenplay by Buck Henry, David Newman, and Robert Benton; story by Peter Bogdanovich. Photography by Laszlo Kovacs. Edited by Verna Fields. Music arranged and conducted by Artie Butler.

BARBRA STREISAND *Judy Maxwell*	STEFAN GIERASCH *Fritz*
RYAN O'NEAL *Howard Bannister*	MABEL ALBERTSON *Mrs. Van Hoskins*
KENNETH MARS *Hugh Simon*	MICHAEL MURPHY *Mr. Smith*
AUSTIN PENDLETON *Frederick Larrabee*	GRAHAM JARVIS *Bailiff*
SORRELL BOOKE *Harry*	MADELINE KAHN *Eunice Burns*

WHOSE LIFE IS IT, ANYWAY? (Metro-Goldwyn-Mayer Film Co., 1981). Directed by John Badham. Produced by Lawrence P. Bachmann; executive producers Martin Schute and Ray Cooney. Screenplay by Brian Clark and Reginald Rose, based on the stage play by Brian Clark. Photography by Mario Tosi. Edited by Frank Morriss. Music by Arthur B. Rubinstein.

RICHARD DREYFUSS *Ken Harrison*	ALBA OMS *Nurse Rodriguez*
JOHN CASSAVETES *Dr. Michael Emerson*	KAKI HUNTER *Mary Jo*
CHRISTINE LAHTI *Dr. Claire Scott*	THOMAS CARTER *John*
BOB BALABAN *Carter Hill*	JANET EIBER *Pat*

A WOMAN UNDER THE INFLUENCE (Faces International Films, 1974). Directed and written by John Cassavetes. Executive producer, Sam Shaw. Photography by Mitch Breit. Music by Bo Harwood.

PETER FALK *Nick Longhetti*	LADY ROWLANDS *Martha Mortensen*
GENA ROWLANDS *Mabel Longhetti*	FRED DRAPER *George Mortensen*
KATHERINE CASSAVETES *Mama Longhetti*	

WRONG IS RIGHT (Columbia Pictures, 1982). Written, directed, and produced by Richard Brooks, based on the novel *The Better Angels*, by Charles McCarry. Executive producer, Andrew Fogelson. Photography by Fred J. Koenekamp. Edited by (and associate producer) George Grenville. Music by Artie Kane.

SEAN CONNERY *Patrick Hale*	HENRY SILVA *Rafeeq*
GEORGE GRIZZARD *President Lockwood*	LESLIE NIELSON *Mallory*
ROBERT CONRAD *General Wombat*	ROBERT WEBBER *Harvey*
KATHARINE ROSS *Sally Blake*	ROSALIND CASH *Mrs. Ford*
G. D. SPRADLIN *Philindros*	HARDY KRUGER *Helmut Unger*
JOHN SAXON *Homer Hubbard*	DEAN STOCKWELL *Hacker*

WUSA (Paramount Pictures, 1970). Directed by Stuart Rosenberg. Produced by Paul Newman and John Foreman. Screenplay by Robert Stone, based on his novel *A Hall of Mirrors*. Music by Lalo Schifrin.

PAUL NEWMAN	PAT HINGLE
Rheinhardt	*Bingamon*
JOANNE WOODWARD	CLORIS LEACHMAN
Geraldine	*Philomene*
ANTHONY PERKINS	DON GORDON
Rainey	*Bogdanovich*
LAURENCE HARVEY	LEIGH FRENCH
Farley	*Girl*

W.W. AND THE DIXIE DANCEKINGS (20th Century–Fox, 1975). Directed by John G. Avildsen. Produced by Stan Canter. Screenplay by Thomas Rickman. Photography by James Crabe. Edited by Richard Halsey and Robbe Roberts. Music by Dave Grusin.

BURT REYNOLDS	JAMES HAMPTON
W.W.	*Junior*
ART CARNEY	DON WILLIAMS
Deacon	*Leroy*
CONNY VAN DYKE	RICHARD D. HURST
Dixie	*Butterball*
JERRY REED	MEL TILLIS
Wayne	*Mel Tillis*
NED BEATTY	SHERMAN LLOYD
Country Bull	*Elton Bird*

THE YAKUZA (Warner Brothers, 1974). Directed and produced by Sydney Pollack. Screenplay by Paul Schrader and Robert Towne, story by Leonard Schrader. Photography by Okazaka Kozo. Music by Dave Grusin.

ROBERT MITCHUM	HERB EDELMAN
Harry Kilmer	*Wheat*
TAKAKURA KEN	JAMES SHIGETA
Tanaka Ken	*Goro*
BRIAN KEITH	KISHI KEIGO
George Tanner	*Eiko*
RICHARD JORDAN	OKADA EIJI
Dusty	*Tono*

Index

• • •